The
Columbia
Retirement
Handbook

●

THE
COLUMBIA
RETIREMENT
HANDBOOK

●

Abraham Monk
General Editor

Associate Editors

W. Andrew Achenbaum
William J. Arnone
Sally Coberly
Nancy Coleman
Jane W. Cooper
Stephen M. Golant
Nancy R. Hooyman
Robert A. Harootyan

COLUMBIA UNIVERSITY PRESS
New York

Columbia University Press
New York   Chichester, West Sussex
Copyright © 1994 Columbia University Press
All rights reserved

Library of Congress Cataloging-in-Publication Data

Columbia handbook on retirement / edited by Abraham Monk : associate
editors, W. Andrew Achenbuam . . . [et. al.].
p.   cm.
Includes index.
ISBN 0-231-07626-6
1. Retirement—United States—Handbooks, manuals, etc. I. Monk,
Abraham.
HQ1064.U5C534   1994
306.3′8′0973—dc20   92-35740
                                                      CIP

Casebound editions of Columbia University Press books are Smyth-sewn
and printed on permanent and durable acid-free paper.

Printed in the United States

Contents

●

PART VI *Health Conditions and Health Care*

PART VII *Housing and Environments*

PART VIII *Individual and Family Life*

Acknowledgments

●

This handbook aims to provide a comprehensive review of what is known about the subject of retirement. Given that the professional activity and scientific inquiry on this subject have evolved in rather diverse and often unrelated disciplines, the task of bringing together a wide spectrum of qualified specialists capable of covering the multiple nuances of the retirement experience proved to be an almost unsurmountable challenge.

I was assisted in this singular enterprise by a committee of associate editors who provided leadership in each of the main areas that constitute the handbook. The associate editors and their corresponding sections are as follows: *Andrew W. Achenbaum:* Part 1, Introduction to Retirement, and Part 10, Future Directions; *Jane W. Cooper:* Part 2, Life Planning; *William J. Arnone:* Part 3, The Economic Conditions of Retirement; *Sally Coberly:* Part 4, Work after Retirement; *Nancy Coleman:* Part 5, Legal Issues; *Abraham Monk:* Part 6, Health Conditions and Health Care; *Stephen M. Golant:* Part 7, Housing and Environments; *Nancy R. Hooyman:* Part 8, Individual and Family Life; *Robert A. Harootyan:* Part 9, Community Involvement, Leisure, and Personal Growth.

The members of this editorial committee were selected in a way that reflects the plurality of constituencies gathering around issues of retirement. As a consequence, the committee is a composite of academicians, researchers, consultants, practitioners rooted in the corporate world and professionals linked to senior membership, volunteer, and service organizations.

The associate editors fulfilled their responsibilities with earnest commitment, patience, and understanding. They initially reviewed the overall outline and design of the book and made recommendations about both the subjects to be included and the potential authors. They subsequently read the drafts of the chapters in their specific sections and suggested revisions, where needed, in order to ensure adequate topical coverage and continuity. The authors undertook their assignments with a similar conviction about the importance of this handbook and invariably came through with requested modifications and updatings.

The completion of this handbook was consequently the result of the active collaboration of many dedicated authors and editors. A special expression of thanks is reserved for Mrs. Linda Chen, at the Institute on Aging of the Columbia University School of Social Work, for attending to the multiple administrative demands of this project. Mr. John D. Moore, Director, Columbia University Press, and Mr. James Raimes, Assistant Director of the Press for Reference Publishing, provided encouragement and expert editorial guidance. Ms. Linda Gregonis assisted with the preparation of the index, and Ms. Marilyn Martin undertook the yeoman job of completing the copy editing of the extensive manuscript.

Abraham Monk
Columbia University

Editors and Contributors

●

W. Andrew Achenbaum, Ph.D.
Deputy Director and Professor of History
University of Michigan
Ann Arbor, Michigan

Nancy J. Altman, J.D.
Consultant
Bethesda, Maryland

William J. Arnone, J.D.
Director, Financial and Retirement Planning
Buck Consultants, Inc.
New York, New York

Dottie Thomas Cebula, M.S.W., M.S.G.
Assistant Director
Senior Care Network
Huntington Memorial Hospital
Pasadena, California

Nancy J. Chapman, Ph.D.
Chair, Department of Urban Studies and Planning
Portland State University
Portland, Oregon

Yung-Ping Chen, Ph.D.
Frank J. Manning Eminent Scholar's Chair in Gerontology and
Deputy Provost
Gerontology Institute
University of Massachusetts at Boston
Boston, Massachusetts

Robert L. Clark, Ph.D.
Professor and Interim Head
Division of Economics and Business
North Carolina State University
Raleigh, North Carolina

Sally Coberly, Ph.D.
Associate Director
Institute on Aging, Work, and Health
Washington Business Group on Health
Washington, District of Columbia

Nancy Coleman, M.S.W., M.A.
Director, ABA Commission on Legal Problems of the Elderly
American Bar Association
Washington, District of Columbia

Jane W. Cooper, M.A.
Senior Training Consultant
The Equitable
New York, New York

Helen Dennis, M.A.
Lecturer
Andrus Gerontology Center
University of Southern California
Los Angeles, California

Stephen M. Golant, Ph.D.
Professor
Department of Geography
University of Florida
Gainesville, Florida

David Haber, Ph.D.
Associate Professor
University of Texas Medical Branch
Galveston, Texas

Robert A. Harootyan, M.S., M.A.
Director, Forecasting and Environmental Scanning Department
American Association of Retired Persons
Washington, District of Columbia

Leonard F. Heumann, Ph.D.
Professor, Department of Urban Regional Planning
Housing Research and Development Program
University of Illinois
Urbana, Illinois

Roger Hiemstra, Ph.D.
Professor, Adult Education
Syracuse University
Syracuse, New York

Nancy R. Hooyman, Ph.D., M.S.W.
Dean and Professor
School of Social Work
University of Washington
Seattle, Washington

Stephen L. Isaacs, J.D.
Professor
School of Public Health
Columbia University
New York, New York

Bruce Jacobs, Ph.D.
Director, Public Policy Analysis Program
University of Rochester
Rochester, New York

Denise D. Jessup, M.S., M.A.
Industrial Gerontologist and
Psychotherapy Resident
Glendale, Arizona

John R. Kelly, Ph.D.
Professor
University of Illinois
Champaign, Illinois

Lawrence J. Kirsch
President
Vice President and
Chief Health Economist
The Segal Company
Boston, Massachusetts

Charles F. Longino, Jr., Ph.D.
Wake Forest Professor of Sociology and
Public Health Sciences
Wake Forest University
Winston-Salem, North Carolina

Richard D. MacNeil, Ph.D.
Professor
Department of Leisure Studies
University of Iowa
Iowa City, Iowa

Lawrence R. McCoombe
Associate Benefit Consultant
Financial and Retirement Planning Services
Buck Consultants, Inc.
New York, New York

Abraham Monk, Ph.D.
Professor
School of Social Work
Columbia University
New York, New York

J. Kenneth L. Morse, J.D.
Supervisory Trial Attorney
Equal Employment Opportunity Commission
Baltimore, Maryland

Joseph F. Quinn, Ph.D.
Professor of Economics
Boston College
Chestnut Hill, Massachusetts

John J. Regan, J.S.D.
Jack & Freda Dicker Distinguished Professor of Health Care Law
Hofstra University School of Law
Hempstead, New York

Sara E. Rix, Ph.D.
Senior Analyst
Public Policy Institute
American Association of Retired Persons
Washington, District of Columbia

Philip L. Rones
Senior Economist
Bureau of Labor Statistics
United States Department of Labor
Washington, District of Columbia

Robert L. Rubinstein, Ph.D.
Associate Director of Research
Philadelphia Geriatric Center
Philadelphia, Pennsylvania

Charles P. Sabatino, J.D.
Assistant Director
Commission on Legal Problems of the Elderly
American Bar Association
Washington, District of Columbia

Dana Shilling, J.D.
Convener
Research Group on Private Sector Funding of Long-Term Care
Jersey City, New Jersey

Michele Spence
Department of Sociology
University of Southern California
Los Angeles, California

Norman P. Stein, J.D.
Douglas Arant Professor of Law
School of Law
University of Alabama
Tuscaloosa, Alabama

Ava C. Swartz, M.P.H., M.U.S.P.
Freelance Journalist and Editor
New York, New York

Patricia S. Taylor, M.S.
Graduate Assistant
University of Illinois at Urbana-Champaign
Urbana, Illinois

Michael L. Teague, Ed.D.
Professor
Department of Leisure Studies
University of Iowa
Iowa City, Iowa

Judith Treas, Ph.D.
Professor and Chair of Sociology
University of California, Irvine
Irvine, California

Monika White, Ph.D.
Associate Director
Senior Care Network
Huntington Memorial Hospital
Pasadena, California

I
INTRODUCTION
TO RETIREMENT

●

1

Retirement and Aging: An Introduction to *The Columbia Retirement Handbook*

●

ABRAHAM MONK

This handbook is being published on the eve of the twenty-first century. In a way it celebrates the provision of retirement benefits for virtually all residents of the United States as one of the greatest and, we can hope, one of the most enduring public policy legacies of the twentieth century. The term *retirement*, however, has a plethora of meanings. Among others, it refers to the termination of and formal withdrawal from a regular job under the provisions of a statutory pension system, a demographic category, an economic condition, a social status, a developmental phase in the human life span, the transition to old age, and a life-style dominated by leisure pursuits or, at least, by economically nonproductive activity.

In this handbook we review what is known about retirement today, in all its multiplicity of meanings, but we also look into where retirement is heading. Of course, a substantial literature covers each of the specific domains subsumed under the term *retirement*, but they have seldom been put together in a single volume that underscores their interconnectedness. That is what we aim to accomplish in this handbook.

WHAT IS RETIREMENT AND WHO BENEFITS FROM IT?

Retirement touches the lives of all Americans. Almost the entire working population contributes to the Social Security funds that ensure retirement benefits, and the overwhelming majority will reach the age at which they can reap those benefits. In fact, Social Security is the most universal public program ever put into effect in the United States. It has been called the "most successful domestic program" in American history and "the foundation of well-being" for people reaching old age (McSteen 1985:44).

Retirement is a novel institution, however. There were no public policies at the beginning of the twentieth century mandating the assurance of economic security for those terminating their regular employment after reaching a mandatory age limit. Neither were there social insurance provisions for the surviving spouses or dependents of deceased, disabled, or retired workers. Even if such policies had been instituted one hundred years ago, they would have been of little direct benefit to most workers. In the year 1900 the average life expectancy barely reached age 46.3. Workers continued toiling until they took their last gasp of air and literally died with their boots on. The few who did make it to age 65 could expect to live an average of 1.2 years, or 3 percent of their life span, beyond that age limit (U.S. Senate Special Committee on Aging 1989).

In contrast, today most Americans reaching the age of 46 would consider themselves "young" or, more accurately, young middle-agers. After all, this is an age at which they are exceeding by a few years—a decade at most—the midpoint in their life spans. Americans do, in effect, live longer at present than ever before, and they can consequently anticipate a protracted period of retirement life. Life expectancy in the year 2000 is anticipated to be 73.5 for males and 80.4 for women. Men who opt to retire at age 62 can look forward to an average of 11.5 years of additional life. Women, in turn, will live an average of 18.4 more years. Therefore retirement does not constitute a fleeting or brief interlude compressed between the end of gainful employment and the inexorable end of life. Instead people may well spend a good quarter of their entire lives, and in some cases even a third, in retirement. So retirement encompasses a substantial portion of an average person's life span.

It must be stressed that these estimates and projections of life expectancy are averages that are valid for all Americans, but they obscure the fact that people of minority groups do not achieve the same averages as whites. In 1989, 8 percent of African Americans, 7 percent of Native Americans, and 5 percent of all Hispanics were age 65 or older, compared to 13 percent of the white population.

These proportions are anticipated to change substantially between 1990 and 2030 because of the higher fertility rates among minority groups. The growth rate of the elderly will be approximately 247 percent for African Americans and Native Americans and an astonishing 395 percent for Hispanics, compared to only 92 percent for whites. The latter will still remain in the numerical lead, given the overall increase of the aged population, but the gap between the number of whites and minorities will narrow. Moreover, African Americans reaching 65 will have a life expectancy much closer to that of whites and will even surpass it by age 80 (U.S. Senate Special Committee on Aging 1991).

WHEN DO PEOPLE RETIRE?

The onset of retirement is not solely determined by the age at which one is entitled to full retirement benefits under the Social Security program. People begin dropping out of the labor force after age 50, and this decline is far more pronounced among men than among women. The rate of work participation for men from age 50 to 64 went down from 86.9 percent in 1950 to 67.2 percent in 1989. At the age of 65 about one in six men—16.6 percent—remain in the work force (U.S. House of Representatives, Committee on Ways and Means 1989). The rate of work force participation by women in the same age bracket actually increased from 27 percent in 1950 to 45 percent in 1989. This is a significant reversal, even if it is still below the rates shown for men in the same age bracket. At age 65, 8.4 percent of the women—or about half the number of men of the same age—still remain fully employed.

It appears then that the overwhelming majority of both men and women have voluntarily or involuntarily left full-time employment before they have even reached age 65. This is the case for 73 and 78 percent of male and female workers, respectively. Many of these women were housewives who never held regular paid jobs in the first place. This trend to early retirement does not constitute a precipitous exodus, but rather a gradual process that accelerates in the last decade preceding age 65. By age 62 the decision to retire early may be particularly influenced by the possibility of drawing Social Security benefits, even if it entails a permanent reduction in the level of those benefits.

The transition to retirement is formally marked by an event, usually the receipt of the first Social Security check. As of January 1992, more than 26 million people had made that transition. These were the beneficiaries of the Old Age, Survivors, and Disability Insurance program (OASDI), more commonly referred to as Social Security. These retired workers constituted almost two-thirds of a grand total of 40 million Social Security beneficiaries, a number that also included 7 million survivors and dependents of deceased retirees and workers enrolled in the Social Security program. More than 2 million new people retire and join the ranks of the Social Security beneficiaries every year.

Social Security is a vast program that covers almost all—95 percent—of the American work force, and the number of beneficiaries is bound to continue expanding because the population of the United States is aging relentlessly. In 1940, 6.7 percent of the American people were 65 years of age or older. By 1980 those 65 or older constituted 11.1 percent, and they will approach 13 percent by the year 2,000. In absolute numbers, there were 9.2 million elderly people in the United States in 1940, and there will be 35.4 million by the year 2,000. That is an almost 400 percent increase in sixty years. The greatest expansion is anticipated, however, during the period from 2020 to 2030, when the "baby boomers" who were born in the 1950s and 1960s will number more than 65 million and will rise to 21.8 percent of the entire population (U.S. Bureau of the Census 1989).

In an economic environment dominated by periodic recessionary and inflationary cycles, Social Security is perceived as the main line of defense against the threats of impoverishment and destitution in old age. It offers a sense of psychological security that probably transcends its actual economic rewards. After all, Social Security alone does not guarantee pulling its beneficiaries out of poverty. It returns, on the average, less than half—about 42 percent—of previous annual earnings, and it constitutes 38 percent, slightly more than a third, of all combined sources of income of the retired population (Grad 1988).

It is obvious then that retirees need other sources of income besides Social Security in order to keep financially afloat. However, Social Security remains the leading source of income for the aged as a whole, and it is the only one that protects them against the risk of inflation because it is tied to the cost-of-living index. As a result of both these cost-of-living adjustments, which went into effect in 1975, and a series of benefit increases that extended from 1968 to 1972, Social Security helped reduce the poverty rate among the aged from 28.5 percent in 1968 to less than half that number, or 12.2 percent, in 1987.

The Social Security program is approaching its seventh decade. It has undergone many revisions aimed, for the most part, at adding new categories of beneficiaries and entitlements and bolstering its reserves. Its basic philosophical premises, however, have remained unchanged: it is a social insurance program, the benefits of which one earns after reaching a certain level of work-related contributions;

benefits are determined—although not proportionally—by those past contributions; benefits are financed entirely through payroll taxes, without a single penny taken from general revenues; participation is compulsory; and the program is intended not to replace previous earnings, but to offer a first tier of income maintenance.

WHAT DOES THIS BOOK CONTAIN?

The Social Security program turned the dream of retirement into a tangible reality. As a consequence, leisure in later life is no longer a luxury exclusively reserved for the privileged few who can afford it. As initially stated, there are many more facets of retirement life than Social Security, and this handbook aims to properly reflect them. Other economic issues must to be addressed, such as the possibility of continuing to work, drawing private pension benefits, and paying taxes. Decisions must be made about where to live and what to do with one's free time. Retirees have changing family responsibilities to attend to, they must watch their health and physical fitness, and many wish to participate in community activities. They must also make legal and financial preparations for many of the changes and some of the losses that occur in old age.

In this book we intend to cover many of these issues associated with retirement. The book is divided into ten parts that deal with related issues. Part 1 describes the historical antecedents of the institution of retirement and reviews its impact on society and modifications made to it over half a century. Part 10 is an epilogue in which two authors separately ponder the new directions retirement is taking, including the impending complexities of financing retirement benefits, the changing demographic profile of Social Security beneficiaries, and the fact that Social Security is evolving into an "age-neutral" program that is no longer antithetical to postretirement employment.

Framed by Part 1, which deals with the past of retirement, and Part 10, which speculates about its future, are eight parts that focus on the present realities of retirement, starting with the transition to retirement and proceeding to review the economic, work-related, legal, health, housing, social, and recreational aspects of retirement.

True, all through their lives people must contend with similar issues—housing, income, health, etc.—and yet retirement is not a mere reenactment of previous developmental stages. The actual event of retirement, coupled with the transition to old age, triggers a unique set of circumstances and creates conditions that bear no resemblance to those of other stages of life. It is the analysis of these distinct features of retirement that constitutes the main rationale for producing this handbook.

Part 2, the first of the eight sections that consider the present realities of retirement, deals with planning and preparing for the transition to retirement. It includes two chapters that examine how people arrive at the decision to leave the labor force. The first attends to the relationship between the accumulation of financial assets and the timing of retirement. It also looks at the incentives for early retirement and the resources needed to maintain one's standard of living.

The second chapter goes beyond economics and health considerations and examines how the decision to retire is affected by feelings and attitudes toward work and retirement. How and at what point do family commitments and obligations influence this decision? How do individuals determine their readiness for this critical transition? The third chapter in this section outlines the informational resources available to assist individuals as they prepare for the transition to retirement.

Part 3 focuses on the economic challenges of retirement, such as juggling a fixed income—which is almost certainly lower than that earned during one's employment years—with the prospects of inflationary pressures and higher expenditures for health care and long-term custodial care. The fourth chapter in this section examines the pervasive phenomenon of early retirement, which was so characteristic of the 1980s, and questions whether it will remain economically feasible. Will the once-popular "window" programs remain in vogue during the 1990s and beyond?

Subsequent chapters address the main tiers of income support— that is, Social Security, private pensions, savings, and investments. These chapters answer questions about the operation of the Social Security program and how it affects the lives of retirees and their spouses, survivors, and other eligible dependents. They also explore the importance of considering earnings limitations in a realistic retirement planning process and the consequences of taxation on Social Security earnings. These chapters also scrutinize the advantages and disadvantages of the different types of pension plans, their "menu" of payment options, and their tax consequences; the rights of employees and their beneficiaries, as defined in federal legislation; and the positive and negative features of different investment pathways and tax-sheltered instruments. One chapter of this section considers the ways in which one can transform home equity assets into supplemental retirement income.

Part 4 tackles the issue of postretirement employment. The very idea of remunerated, and steady work may be inconsistent with the concept of retirement. Only a small percentage of retirees reenters the labor force, but the number of those interested in paid employment, even if on a part-time basis, is steadily increasing. The three chapters that constitute this section examine the characteristics of the job market after retirement, the industries to which retirees tend to gravitate, and the frequency of self-employment. The second chapter discusses alternatives to conventional employment that are emerging as strategies for postponing or extending the transition to full retirement, such as job sharing, phased retirement, job banks, job redesigning, second careers, and volunteerism. The final chapter in this section describes the assortment of placement and referral services that assist active retirees, regardless of their previous level of career attainment, to find appropriate work.

Part 5 of the handbook reviews the legal implications of retirement. To begin with, not all retirements are voluntary; some are forced by subtle age-related exclusionary practices in employment. Consequently, the first chapter of this part assists the reader in identifying age discrimination and tells how to seek redress when it occurs. The next chapter focuses on estate planning, including the strategies available for the transfer of property to heirs and for lifetime and after-death financial planning.

The third chapter describes the legal tools available when individuals can no longer take care of their own affairs because of loss of competence or incapacity. A final chapter inventories the numerous precautionary legal steps consumers should take when considering whether to move to a continuing care retirement community or any of the number of similar forms of assisted living housing options that have sprung up in recent years all over the country.

Part 6, on health, initially calls attention to the health education programs that are aimed at stimulating preventive care and enhancing the functional independence of older citizens. Because older people have, on the average, considerably more health-related expenses than younger people, the second chapter reviews the present range of health insurance benefits and entitlements that help defray those medical bills. However, given that health care costs have reached a crisis level, the third chapter in this section discusses a series of new mechanisms, such as health maintenance organizations, managed care, and preferred provider organizations, that dispense health care at a reduced cost without impairing the quality or the effectiveness of the services in question. The final chapter examines the pros and cons of still another emerging mechanism—private long-term insurance—

which is targeted at financing care to meet the chronic needs of older people, especially institutional nursing home care.

The five chapters in part 7 set forth programmatic responses to particular residential and community needs of retirees. Why do many of them consider moving to sunbelt havens? Is it better to stay in one's familiar surroundings, or should one look for more adaptable housing options? And what about transportation and safety factors? Two chapters focus on the pluses and minuses of age-segregated communities, both those for people who are capable of independent living and those for individuals with physical and functional impairments.

Part 8, on family, addresses the fact that, given recent trends in marriage, divorce, and remarriage and the increasing number of people living alone, retirees can no longer be expected to fit any singular or dominant pattern of family relationships. The initial chapter assesses the importance of the spousal bond and how it affects one's sense of life satisfaction in retirement. The second chapter considers the basic demographic realization that women constitute the majority of the aging population in this country, and it examines the differences by gender in the transition to retirement. The next chapter reviews the retirement experience among individuals who do not fit the normative image of family life characterized in the initial chapter of the section. These are the never married, the childless, the widowed, the divorced, and gays and lesbians. The last chapter in this section focuses on the fast-growing and nearly universal experience of caregiving to older relatives with chronic and disabling illnesses. This is a burden that, as the author puts it, may disrupt the carefully laid plans and high expectations for one's "golden years."

Part 9, the last in the sequence of parts oriented toward present retirement options, deals with leisure and the use of free time. Given that people may anticipate spending up to a third—although a fifth—of their lives in retirement, what do they do with their time when they are no longer working? What kinds of activities do they engage in? Do they find contentment and satisfaction in whatever they do, or do they fall easy prey to boredom and alienation?

The first of the three chapters in this section reviews the activity, leisure, and recreational patterns that are prototypical of retirees but cautions that there are no radical transformations, as people usually remain the same as they were a decade earlier. In a more prescriptive vein, the text suggests building upon a person's lifelong repertoire of skills and interests. The second chapter pursues the same line of thought in more programmatic terms by inventorying specific resources and opportunities in four major leisure areas: education, health, recreational travel, and service activities and volunteer work.

The final chapter describes the opportunities for lifelong education, providing a sample of innovative and trend-setting programs, some of which have become widely replicated models.

This, in a nutshell, is the handbook's design. As noted, it progresses temporally, ranging from past to present to future. Its chapters have thematic continuity, and they include both analytic and practical material. As a consequence, some represent detailed reviews of existing conceptual and research literature, while others are more prescriptive, offering guidance and inventories of resources.

FOR WHOM IS THIS BOOK INTENDED?

This handbook has been written primarily for two potential audiences. The first is made up of the practitioners for whom retirement is part and parcel of their professional responsibilities. This category includes personnel managers, corporate and union officials, guidance counselors, human service providers, preretirement advisers, benefits and entitlements specialists, and so forth. The second group includes researchers, gerontologists, graduate students, writers, journalists, community leaders, policy analysts, policymakers, librarians, etc. To people in both of these potential audiences, the handbook offers the possibility of locating, in a single source, as much up-to-date information as possible on the complex reality subsumed under the term *retirement*.

REFERENCES

Grad, S. 1988. *Income of the Population 55 and Over.* Publication number 13-11871. Washington, D.C. Social Security Administration.

McSteen, M. A. 1985. "Fifty Years of Social Security." *Social Security Bulletin,* 48(8):36–44.

U.S. Bureau of the Census. 1989. Projections of the United States by Age, Sex, and Race, 1988–2080. *Current Population Reports,* Series P-25, N 1018 (January). Washington, D.C.: U.S. Department of Commerce.

U.S. House of Representatives, Committee on Ways and Means. 1990. *Overview of Entitlement Programs, 1990 Green Book.* Washington, D.C.: U.S. Government Printing Office.

U.S. Senate, Special Committee on Aging. 1989. *Aging America: Trends and Projections.* Washington, D.C.: U.S. Government Printing Office.

U.S. Senate, Special Committee on Aging. 1991. *Aging America: Trends and Projections.* Publication #FCoA 91-28001. Washington, D.C.: U.S. Department of Health and Human Services.

2

U.S. Retirement in Historical Context

●

W. ANDREW ACHENBAUM

Definitions of *retirement* in contemporary American society include a range of personal conditions and divergent working and nonworking relationships. According to sociologist Kingsley Davis, the multiplicity of circumstances embodied by the concept of *retirement* confounds efforts to convey all that the term means:

> It can refer to withdrawal from all labor-market activity or only from a particular job. The withdrawal can be voluntary or involuntary; it can be based on age, length of service, health, or disability; it can provide access to a public or private pension; and it may or may not be limited to old age. About the only general meaning of the term is withdrawal from previous employment, but this hardly distinguishes it from resignation or dismissal. The confusion is made worse by the fact that an individual not only retires *from* an activity but also must retire *into* something else, whether paid, volunteer, or leisure activity. (Davis 1988:191)

The clusters of ideas associated with *retirement* in U.S. history have always been diffuse and ambiguous. In this chapter I will trace how definitions changed in America over 365 years, between the settlement of Jamestown in 1607 and the enactment of the 1972 Social Security amendments, which liberalized retirement benefits for senior citizens. Historically, *retirement* was defined in personal terms before it became a major social institution during this century.

Dictionaries record the etymology of *retirement* and related words. In the first edition of *An American Dictionary* (1828), Noah Webster defined *retirement* as "1. The act of withdrawing from company or from public notice or station. 2. The state of being withdrawn. 3.

Private abode; habitation secluded from much society, or from public life. 4. Private way of life." Older people "retired" in any of these senses of the word. Yet none of Webster's definitions applied exclusively to the aged. Indeed, Webster had earlier declared that "the morals of young men, as well as their application to science, depend much on retirement" (Wood 1971:159). Almanacs reported that farmers annually "retired" to their hearths during winter (Thomas 1810).

Occasionally, however, the term did refer to a decision made by an older person. Thus George Washington claimed in 1799 that "retirement is as necessary to me as it will be welcome" (*Webster's New Universal Unabridged Dictionary* 1983:1547). Having retired from the Continental Army in 1783, and the Presidency in 1796, Washington elected to scale back his plantation duties shortly before he died at age sixty-seven.

Retiracy seems to be the only cognate in use before the American Civil War that presupposed a change in employment status during the course of one's life. John Russell Barrett's *Dictionary of Americanisms* (1848) gave the following example: "It is said, in New England, of a person who has retired from business with a fortune, that he has a retiracy; i.e., a sufficient fortune to retire with" (Matthews 1951:1389). Presumably, only a lucky few who had acquired or amassed wealth could afford to enjoy "retiracy" in old age.

Definitions of *retirement* and *retiracy* had changed little by the fourth edition of Barrett's dictionary (1889), but the gloss on *retire* suggests that a shift was underway: "The transitive use of the verb, which had become obsolete, is now reviving in this country and in England. With us, it is used by military men of withdrawing troops. By merchants, of paying their notes; and by banks, to withdraw them from circulation" (p. 525). *Retirement* now embraced military deployments and business transactions, but neither of these expanded meanings captures our present-day notion of the term as a human-resource option. However, the 1907 edition of the *New American Encyclopedic Dictionary* does convey that modern sense in its definition of *retire:* "To make or cause to withdraw from active service; to place on the retired list; as, to retire an officer" (p. 3444). Retirement under certain specific circumstances no longer was simply a matter of individual choice; some other agency sometimes influenced the decision.

That nineteenth-century words and definitions remain in relatively recent U.S. dictionaries reminds us that the English language evolves slowly. For instance, *retiracy* was still listed in the 1971 version of Webster's dictionary. And perhaps this is why "withdrawal from office, active service, or business" was listed after "a falling back [of an army]" and "a withdrawing into seclusion or retreat" as a definition of *retirement*. Nonetheless, words that had gained currency were added. Three new terms were included in the 1971 edition: *retirement annuity, retirement income insurance,* and *retirement plan* (*Webster's Third New International Dictionary* 1971:1939). Terms that refer to institutional retirement arrangements had entered the vocabulary. As we shall see, the process was gradual and uneven, full of structural lags and anomalies.

LATE-LIFE WORK AND "SUPERANNUATION" IN COLONIAL TIMES AND THE EARLY AMERICAN REPUBLIC

Although retirement has become a hallmark of late life, older people throughout most of U.S. history were expected to work as long as they were physically able to do so. In the colonial period and the years of the early American Republic, when the economy was underdeveloped, the elderly were perceived as seasoned veterans of productivity. Their advice and contributions were credited with enhancing prospects for social advance. There were a few instances in which mandatory retirement was prescribed. Some colonial towns exempted those over age sixty from civic chores such as annual road repairs. The aged were excused from paramilitary duty (Demos 1978). Seven states— New York (1777), New Hampshire (1792), Connecticut and Alabama (1819), Missouri and Maine (1820), and Maryland (1851)—imposed upper age limits on judges and justices of the peace (Achenbaum 1978).

No other profession, industry, business, craft, or trade group prior to 1860 required people to stop working at a predetermined chronological age. Older farmers were able to remain engaged in meaningful activities until advanced age. Although the term *old man* has derogatory undertones today, prior to the American Civil War it was a term of respect for a master or foreman (Matthews 1951:1157).

Just because older Americans did not suffer much age discrimination in preindustrial North America does not mean that their employment conditions were as felicitous elsewhere. In Britain in the late seventeenth century, Anglican bishops and reformers such as Daniel Defoe were proposing pensions for workers over 50, the age at which "we go down the hill again and every day grow weaker and weaker" (Phillipson 1990:145). Miners, tailors, and metalworkers seemed particularly vulnerable. Evidence from eighteenth-century France reveals considerable dependency in late life. In the cities the old turned to begging and, in the case of at least one sixty-year-old woman in

Lyon, prostitution (Troyansky 1989:178). Older farmers on the Continent tried desperately to maintain control over their land. They sometimes made contracts with their children in their declining years (Quadagno 1982; Kohli 1987).

Comparable intergenerational negotiations occasionally occurred in rural North America. Most often arrangements were made to provide fuel, shelter, or food for aged widows. By the 1750s some older farmers were converting some of their property into liquid assets. End-of-life retirement contracts between fathers and sons in the colonial period seem to have been rare. Studies of nineteenth-century rural communities in New England, however, indicate that sons who preferred to remain physically if not always emotionally close at home found it advantageous to mortgage farms to their fathers (Smith 1978; Barron 1984; Schweitzer 1987).

The elderly could not always control their fate, as the term *superannuation* suggests. The earliest references to the word in the *Oxford English Dictionary* date from the early seventeenth century. In 1755 Samuel Johnson defined as "the state of being disqualified by years." In 1822, at age seventy-nine, a still-active Thomas Jefferson referred to "two ancient servants, who . . . have a reasonable claim to repose . . . in the sanctuary of invalids and superannuates" (*Oxford English Dictionary* 1971:3158).

Often the vicissitudes of late life merely required a tapering off of activities, not complete withdrawal from the workplace. As Hugh Henry Brackenridge reminded readers in *Modern Chivalry*, "the great secret of preserving respect is the cultivating and showing to the best advantage the powers that we possess, and the not going beyond them" (1804:34). Such an observation echoed Cotton Mather's advice nearly a century earlier to "old folks" that they should "be so wise as to *disappear* of [their] own accord" (Haber 1983:19).

In short, retirement in colonial times and in the early years of the American republic was limited. Since a quarter of all men over sixty-five were penniless at death (Soltow 1975), it is hardly surprising that most had to stay productive in order to survive. And the aged had work to do in a land of yeoman farmers and small businesses. Sooner or later, though, some elderly people became "superannuated" due to debilities. (Around 25 percent of all males over sixty-five fell into this category during the period.) This involuntary cessation of productivity increased the risk of dependency. A few, in conformity with the prevailing principle of "virtue" that was to guide behavior, elected to withdraw partially or fully from political affairs or commerce. Retiracy by choice did not often occur.

RETIREMENT IN INDUSTRIALIZING AMERICA

By the end of the nineteenth century, even those who felt that the elderly could contribute something to society acknowledged that they no longer reflected the majority opinion. New conceptions of "senility" and the labor relations associated with the rising industrial order diminished the worth of the aged as veterans of productivity:

> In the search for increased efficiency, begotten in modern time by the practically universal worship of the dollar . . . gray hair has come to be recognized as an unforgivable witness of industrial imbecility, and experience the invariable companion of advancing years, instead of being valued as common sense would require it to be, has become a handicap so great as to make the employment of its possessor, in the performance of tasks and duties for which his life work has fitted him, practically impossible. ("Independent Opinions" 1913:504)

In response to altered economic structures and priorities, as well as changing ideas about older workers' usefulness, a new trend toward discharging employees after they had reached a certain age gradually emerged in the United States.

The first federal retirement measure became law in December 1861, when Congress required naval officers below the rank of vice admiral to resign their commissions at age sixty-two. Subsequent acts set different retirement ages for different categories of workers. Government clerks, unlike soldiers, did not necessarily have to serve a certain number of years before receiving pensions. In 1920 some uniformity was achieved when the federal government inaugurated a compulsory old-age and disability plan for its half-million civil service employees. (It is worth noting that military personnel, elected officials, and those with preexisting programs were not covered by this provision.) State and municipal governments also established retirement schemes for police officers, firemen, teachers, and certain bureaucrats (Achenbaum 1978; Graebner 1980; Fogelson 1984).

In 1874 the Canadian Great Trunk railroad system established the first corporate retirement plan in North America. A year later the American Express Company permitted workers over sixty who had served at least two decades to receive some compensation upon retirement for life. Variations on the eligibility criteria established by the Baltimore and Ohio Railroad (1884)—a minimum age of sixty-five with at least ten years' service—were adopted by other firms. A few companies designed "voluntary superannuation retirement" plans to encourage long service; most allowed for managerial leeway in administering "compulsory" plans. Some companies made "discretionary" schemes vehicles for handling late-life disability. Others viewed "incapacity retirement" plans as a catch-all category. Employees contributed nothing under most plans, and there were no assurances that they would receive any money upon retirement. Not only were these plans diverse, but they covered only a very small percentage of the labor force. By 1910 only 60 plans were in place (Conyngton 1926; Latimer 1932).

Although such corporate plans protected very few from old-age dependency, toward the end of the nineteenth century workers became quite sensitive to the need to make plans for retirement. Unemployment, disability, illness, and premature death loomed as greater threats, to be sure, but around the turn of the century it was more likely than not that a twenty-year-old would live past fifty-nine (Ransom and Sutch 1986). Aging workers purchased "tontine insurance"; their contributions were put in a fund that was divided among surviving policyholders after twenty years. By 1905 this scheme represented two-thirds of all life insurance in force (Ransom and Sutch 1987). In addition, unions, fraternal groups, and friends in the saloon offered (in) formal modes of retirement support.

The quest for retirement security took shape in all industrializing societies. Like U.S. companies, British companies' interest in retirement was stimulated by their desire for greater efficiency and productivity. However, there was more concern than in the United States to promote old-age savings (through friendly and cooperative societies) and to involve the government in pension affairs (Thane 1982; Johnson 1985; Hannah 1986). Class dynamics were more evident in Europe than in America. Germany's landmark public old-age and incapacity scheme (1885) was aimed at winning working-class support for Bismark's policies. Around 1900 in France, state employees were the group most likely to opt for retirement (Stearns 1976).

The very diversity in plans to effect retirement underscores how little consensus there was about the plans' function in the new industrial order. "The insurance principle is the most prominent contemporary expression of social integration," declared a University of Chicago economist. "And social integration is a chief factor in social progress" (Monroe 1897:503). The author of an article entitled "The Superannuated Man" was not convinced: "The things that most promote the welfare of the wage-earning class militate most against old age employment" (Hendrick 1908:118). Confusion over whether pursuing retirement was in the best interest of employees or employers (or both) affected older workers' decisions and options.

THE EXODUS OF OLDER WORKERS FROM
THE LABOR FORCE

Currently the biggest controversy in the historiography of retirement focuses on when older men began to withdraw from the labor force and the rate at which they did so. (Patterns among women will be treated separately later.) The conventional view (Durand 1948; Long 1958; Achenbaum 1978) holds that there was some decline in the proportion of men over sixty-five who were gainfully employed between 1875, when the first U.S. corporate pension plan was inaugurated, and 1935, when the Social Security Act was passed. The revisionist interpretation (Ransom and Sutch 1986; Haber and Gratton 1993) claims that there was no fall (and, in fact, there was a modest gain among some groups) in employment patterns among older males prior to 1935.

The divergence of opinion reflects methodological disagreements that have philosophical ramifications. Conventional wisdom accepts the published U.S. census reports for some years (i.e., 1900) as representing reasonably accurate counts; it chooses to disregard flawed data (in the 1870 and 1880 censuses) rather than recalculating figures. The revisionists, on the other hand, manipulate the numbers in an effort to reconcile the notion of "gainfully employed," which they believe was probably used in the censuses of the late nineteenth century, with the post-1940 census definition of "labor force participation." Critics, in turn, have challenged Ransom and Sutch's ingenious efforts to distinguish between "productive" and "gainful" employment, questioned their exclusion of individuals who have been unemployed for more than six months, and wondered whether *retirement* is more than merely a synonym for *not in the labor force* (Moen 1987; Streib 1988).

Why does it matter when older male workers began to leave the labor force? The answer determines how the relationship between Social Security and retirement is represented. If there had been little change in labor-force participation rates before 1935, then Social Security should be viewed as an instrument of social control that forced elderly people to take pensions. If there had already been gradual changes in occupational patterns, then to interpret the declining status of aging workers we must assess the interactions of structural barriers (such as personnel rules and recessions) and cultural forces (such as ageism) with Social Security. In either scenario, of course, the enduring (albeit shifting) vagueness of *retirement* was still affected by other influences, such as illness and disability.

The most straightforward reason mandatory retirement plans initially had a minimal effect on older workers' employment behavior is that they covered such a small proportion of the labor pool. And while a devaluation of age was implicit in the rationale for mandatory retirement, it should be noted that other management practices of the late nineteenth century management practices prolonged employees' working lives. Seniority rights, first instituted on the railroads, protected older employees (Licht 1983). Job transfers were made informally, with managers and co-workers enabling aging workers to assume lighter loads and easier responsibilities as guards (Hareven 1983).

Even in the absence of mandatory retirement, moreover, older men would have had difficulty finding gainful employment in industrializing America. The shrinking importance of farming was disadvantageous to the aged (Gratton 1986). Turnover in firms was great: on average, only 41 percent of a given set of employees remained on the job after four years (Alexander 1916; Monroe 1897). This meant that most workers could not meet the service requirements for pensions. Unemployment threatened job security in late life: the aged were not necessarily unemployed more often than younger workers, but they were idle for longer periods of time. In 1890, 26.2 percent of all elderly workers considered themselves permanently unemployable (Rubinow 1913; Keyssar 1986). The natural rhythms of an agrarian work cycle were being transformed by industrialization. According to Abraham Epstein, "Low wages, unemployment, business failures and industrial superannuation are of incomparably greater social danger than idleness or thriftlessness [in producing] misery and dependency in old age" (1928:86–87).

On the eve of the Great Depression, retirement at a fixed age was a discernible, if not yet prominent, element affecting the careers of older people. Of the 550,751 pension beneficiaries in 1929, 10,644 were receiving, on the average, $627 per year from private industrial plans, while 11,306 were getting, on the average, $296 from labor organizations. Policemen and firemen represented the largest class of recipients (20,327) of public retirement benefits. But more than 80 percent of all payments came from military "pensions," which were granted largely to old people and their dependents for war-related injuries and service; not many payments were made to people retiring from civilian occupations (Mills and Montgomery 1938:367), and few got pensions through mandatory retirement.

Ill health remained the primary reason men said they retired. Of the 2,441 retirees surveyed in eleven eastern cities in the 1920s, 28.1 percent gave "old age" as their reason for quitting; another 30 percent mentioned either chronic illness or rheumatism (National Civic Federation 1928:52). Miners, factory workers, and men in steel mills were said to "become prematurely aged." Experts agreed that "as age increases, the hazard from a medical or health standpoint definitely goes up" (*Old Age Security* 1928; Plowman 1930). Industrial accidents caused disabilities and early retirement. Elsewhere, the boundary between disability and old age was also unclear (Kohli 1987).

Given such factors, age per se was not perceived as the paramount factor in making the decision to retire. Only a sixth of those in the survey described above cited "other causes," which included being "pensioned," possessing "affluence," or receiving support from children. A number of personnel managers imposed age limits on hiring, but most experts at the time attributed the preference for younger workers to the hazardous nature of job requirements and the cost of benefits for senior employees, not to age discrimination (Insley 1930; Latimer 1930; "Hiring and Separation" 1932). That nearly 60 percent of all older men worked in 1930 indicates the privileged status of retirement.

The "modern" history of old age began with the enactment of the Social Security Act in 1935. Some scholars argue that the landmark measure was "a piece of retirement legislation, which promised . . . the removal of people from the work force" (Graebner 1980:184; Myles 1984; Quadagno 1988). Others contend that the wording of the original act was deliberately made ambiguous to give employees some choices concerning when to retire (Cohen 1957; Achenbaum 1983). The measure's initial impact on retirement behavior is hard to gauge: During World War II, many older people stayed on the job and others returned to work. After 1945, however, the proportion of the elderly in the labor force dropped dramatically.

RETIREMENT AFTER SOCIAL SECURITY

During the postwar years "retirement triumphed over alternative methods of dealing with the aged" (Graebner 1980:215). Although more than 40 percent of the labor force was unprotected by the 1935 Social Security Act, compulsory coverage during the 1950s and 1960s was extended to farmers, military personnel, and the self-employed so that, by 1974, 93 percent of all people over sixty-five were eligible for benefits. In the process age sixty-five, the system's eligibility baseline, became the benchmark for determining who was "old" in America. Disability insurance, which was added to the program in the mid-1950s, protected people until they could be transferred to the old-age insurance rolls. Early retirement features, which was added in the early 1960s, were actuarially reduced to conform to the cutoff at age sixty-five (Achenbaum 1986; Berkowitz 1987).

Surveys of Social Security beneficiaries indicate that, prior to 1952, the availability of old-age *insurance* (Title II) benefits seldom prompted voluntary retirement. (Gratton and Haber [1993] contend that the elderly poor who were eligible for old-age *assistance* [Title 1] may have stopped working.) With the liberalization of benefits, however, retirement became a more feasible option. Increases in nonwage income alone contributed to a decline of 9.8 percent in the fraction of elderly men in the labor force between 1948 and 1965 (Wentworth 1968; Bowen and Finegan 1969). The growth also stimulated new interest in supplemental retirement benefits.

Most corporate pension plans went bankrupt during the Great Depression. Interest in this retirement vehicle revived in 1948, however, when a National Labor Relations Board ruling, reinforced by several court decisions, made pensions subject to collective bargaining. Arrangements negotiated by the United Steel Workers and the United Auto Workers set the pace. In 1950 only 15 percent of the civilian work force was covered by such programs; two decades later 37.2 percent were so protected. Those who worked for large firms were more likely to retire due to company policy and financial incentives. Paradoxically, men in better-paid positions retired at lower rates than blue-collar workers, even though they were more likely to be eligible for pensions (Slavick 1966; Palmore 1964; Sass 1989). The federal government gradually began to regulate these private plans. The Employee Retirement Income Security Act (1974) established minimum vesting and accounting standards and authorized the creation of individual retirement accounts.

Retirement was becoming a major institution in American society. Most workers could expect to live past age sixty-five, and they considered retirement a right. By the early 1970s funds invested to pay for workers' retirement benefits constituted a quarter of the nation's total equity capital (Drucker 1976). Because supplemental retirement vehicles usually paid benefits only at a fixed age, rules governing retirement became more institutionalized. The stringent earnings tests imposed by Social Security upon retirees' earned income discouraged many from working past retirement. That the 1967 Age Discrimination in Employment Act covered only workers between the ages of forty and sixty-five for ten years correlated with the support given mandatory retirement by labor and management.

Amidst the proliferation of rules governing postwar retirement, many social scientists asserted that "the fundamental social-psychological problem of the retirement role is the lack of clarity and the ambiguity which characterize it" (Donahue, Orbach, and Pollak 1960:334). Retirement had drawbacks. Ernest Burgess deplored the "roleless role" of the "retired older man and his wife" (1960:20). Streib and Schneider urged retirees to pursue "activity within disengagement," by using leisure time creatively or engaging in citizenship/service roles (1971:182–183). Such advice underlined another twist in defining *retirement:* from a "conception of retirement as protection from the hazards of old age in industrial society has grown a positive conception of retirement as a period of potential enjoyment and creative experience which accrued as a social reward for a lifetime of labor" (Donahue et al. 1960:361). A sense of retirement's ambiguity—on the one hand enforcing uselessness while on the other hand giving older people unprecedented freedom—colored the analyses of experts.

Surveys of workers' attitudes indicated a growing desire for a retirement spent in good health with sufficient income. In the 1940s and early 1950s, most people who retired did so because they were in poor health or had been laid off; beneficiaries tended to reenter the labor force only when they needed income. However, a 1954 survey revealed that 72 percent of retirees and 51 percent of those who were retired but working part time were "satisfied" with retirement (Wentworth 1968; Streib and Schneider 1971:148). Twenty-five years later, 90 percent of those asked would report that they had made the right decision to retire when they did. Between 1945 and 1979 the average age of men's retirement fell from seventy to sixty-four. Middle-class retirees desired homes in sunbelt retirement communities and dream vacations (Calhoun 1978; National Council on Aging 1981; Fitzgerald 1986).

Nonetheless, a strong undercurrent of ambivalence that reflects differences in people's circumstances pervaded this seemingly ebullient trend. As late as 1968, 46 percent of those surveyed said that they had not wanted to retire (Social Security Administration 1976:50). Prior to the 1980s, poor health still accounted for more than half of all retirements, particularly among those in low-paying jobs (Steiner and Dorfman 1957; Parnes 1981). Despite efforts to remedy the situation, the first director of the National Institute on Aging claimed that "age discrimination in employment is unrestrained, with arbitrary retirement practices and bias against hiring older people for available jobs" (Butler 1976:4). By the 1970s retirement was rewarding for some, but not all, older Americans.

VARIATIONS ON A THEME

The experiences of older workers who were, for the most part, white male have been used to trace historical patterns of retirement in the United States. The underlying theme of diversity and ambivalence becomes more complex when issues of race, ethnicity, and gender are taken into account. (The influences of class, region, and occupation also merit attention, but there is little solid research yet available.) What follows reinforces a pattern that should already be evident: discrimination in employment opportunities earlier in life affects subsequent retirement options.

Slavery—and the racial discrimination that continued in its wake—made retirement in the black community a rare experience. Since slaves were considered property, they were worked until they were worn out. On some plantations more than half of those blacks engaged as butchers, carpenters, coopers, drivers, hostlers, nurses, seamstresses, and watchmen were over sixty (Joyner 1984:60–63). Many continued to do less and less physically demanding jobs until they died. If the laws did not forbid it, some slave owners emancipated their superannuated blacks, thereby freeing themselves of the responsibilities of elder care. In such circumstances, younger members of the slave community typically cared for their elders, ensuring that they had food and support in their declining years (Genovese 1974; Gutman 1976).

Freedom did not bring great economic opportunities for blacks. Those who remained in the South engaged in mainly agrarian pursuits, often working most of their lives as sharecroppers or tenant farmers. Because it was difficult to acquire many financial assets, most older black men had to work longer than their white male counterparts. That 75 percent of all elderly black men reported occupations in the 1930 census largely explains why labor force participation rates for the aged were higher in the South than in other regions of the country (Gratton 1986). With few exceptions, those who migrated north worked in blue-collar jobs or operated small businesses catering primarily to blacks. Once again, because it was difficult to save much for old age in these positions, a majority of black men over sixty-five could not opt for retirement.

Social Security was not designed to remedy racial economic inequalities. The system may have exacerbated inequities—though historians debate whether this was by design (Quadagno 1988b; Achenbaum 1986). The 1935 Social Security Act did not require farm employers and employees to contribute to old-age insurance. Since a large proportion of blacks were working in agriculture, many were not covered by Social Security. The situation was not remedied until the 1950s. Moreover, political expediency fraught with racist overtones resulted in a set of rules governing eligibility for old-age assistance that prevented many southern blacks from getting help. Social Security amendments that make the benefits structure more progressive do little to compensate for job discrimination.

Yet the economics of old age may not be as important as patterns of morbidity and mortality for those trying to understand racial differences in retirement. Life expectancy at birth has historically been (and remains) lower for blacks than for whites. For a variety of reasons, this race-specific difference holds until about the seventh decade of life, when life expectancy for blacks becomes greater than for whites. Two inferences that may be drawn deserve analysis. On the one hand, black men report a higher incidence of disability than their white peers. This, coupled with relatively high unemployment, has meant that many blacks in middle age might be characterized as "unretired-retired" (Gibson 1986:191). On the other hand, the number of blacks who have to work past age sixty-five proves how hard it is to overcome disadvantages people experience earlier in life.

Gender differences in retirement, like racial ones, reflect variations in employment opportunities over the life course. Historically, most women have worked as hard as men, but they have been paid little, if anything, for many jobs that they have done. As a result, it has been only in recent decades that a growing number of older women have earned on their own a right to a financially secure retirement. Through most of U.S. history the position of women in old age has largely been determined by their status as wives, widows, mothers, sisters, or "dependents," not as "wage-earners." Though usually lacking the institutional force of slave laws, black codes, or quotas, U.S. cultural norms have dictated that men and women operate in separate spheres, the marketplace and the home.

In the past family composition and family income influenced when and for how long women entered the labor force. Around 1900 many families chose to have their children work so that wives and mothers could stay at home. Patterns varied by ethnic and racial group: black and Irish families were less adamant that middle-aged women not seek employment than Italian immigrant families. Girls worked as domestics, in shops, or as teachers before they married. Once widowed, older women often took in boarders, opened saloons, or found part-time jobs (Yans-McLaughlin 1977; Fraundorf 1979; Hareven 1983).

Those women who opted for careers tended to find their opportunities limited to teaching, nursing, or other comparatively low-paying jobs. White women were effectively barred from several professions, such as the ministry, branches of the law, medicine, and some high-risk trade jobs. Black women, both before and after the abolition of slavery, cared for children, cooked, or did washing and ironing, and they did other chores when they became too infirm to perform more physically demanding tasks. Mexican-American widows in the Southwest farmed, sewed, and served as midwives and confectioners (Jones 1985; Reverby 1987; Scadron 1988). Regardless of ethnic/racial background or career path, women found it difficult to save for superannuation; few women's careers ended with a handshake and a pension. Similar patterns in work and retirement obtained elsewhere. British employment contracts made marriage sufficient grounds for dismissal of female employees and their exclusion from pension schemes (Hannah 1986:117).

Social Security has had an impact on women's retirement, but this impact has been filtered through gender-specific employment patterns. The 1935 Social Security Act provided funds to expand mothers' pensions and authorized money for "Grants to States for Maternal and Child Welfare." Old-age assistance surely benefited many elderly women. But women were not accorded special treatment under old-age insurance (Title II); most women qualified for Title H benefits because they were "dependents" or "survivors." Given their sporadic career histories and sex discrimination in pay, wage-earning women typically accrued fewer retirement benefits than their male counterparts. Even though working women made "retirement" decisions according to the same logic as men, differences in work histories mattered as Social Security calculated benefits in its gender-blind manner.

Historically, women have been inclined (and expected) to subordinate work to family. As more and more men leave the labor force in old age, male-female differences in employment past age sixty-five are diminishing. Women tend to be poorer in old age than men because of differences in earnings histories and longer life expectancies. Earnings-sharings schemes and better spousal protection under private pensions have been proposed to remedy inequities, but stagflation and budget woes have impeded reform. Paradoxically, there may come a day in which women and men are more equal socially and possibly economically in retirement than in earlier stages of life. If so, U.S. retirement will have taken a yet another novel twist.

REFERENCES

Achenbaum, W. A. 1978. *Old Age in the New Land*. Baltimore, Md.: Johns Hopkins University Press.

Achenbaum, W. A. 1983. *Shades of Gray*. Boston: Little, Brown.

Achenbaum, W. A. 1986. *Social Security*. New York: Cambridge University Press.

Alexander, M. W. 1916. "Hiring and Firing." *Annals of the American Academy of Political and Social Sciences*, 65:126–144.

Barron, H. S. 1984. *Those Who Stayed Behind*. New York: Cambridge University Press.

Bartlett, J. R. 1848. *Dictionary of Americanisms*. Boston: Little Brown.

Bartlett, J. R. 1889. *Dictionary of Americanisms*, 4th ed. Boston: Little Brown.

Berkowitz, E. D. 1987. *Disabled Policy*. New York: Cambridge University Press.

Bowen, W. G., and T. A. Finegan. 1969. *The Economics of Labor Force Administration*. Princeton: Princeton University Press.

Brackenridge, H. H. 1804. *Modern Chivalry*, vol. 1. Edited by Lewis Leary. New Haven, Conn.: College and University Press.

Burgess, E. W. 1960. "Aging in Western Culture." In E. Burgess, ed., *Aging in Western Societies*, 3–28. Chicago: University of Chicago Press.

Butler, R. N. 1975. *Why Survive?* New York: Harper & Row.

Calhoun, R. B. 1978. *In Search of the New Old*. New York: Elsevier.

Cohen, W. J. 1957. *Retirement under Social Security*. Berkeley, Calif.: University of California Press.

Conyngton, M. 1926. "Industrial Pensions for Old Age and Disability." *Monthly Labor Review*, 22:21–56.

Davis, K. 1988. "Retirement as a Dubious Paradise: Another Point of View." In R. Ricardo-Campbell and E. P. Lazear, eds., *Issues in Contemporary Retirement*, 191–203. Stanford, Calif.: Stanford University Press.

Demos, J. 1978. "Old Age in Early New England." In J. Demos and S. S. Boocock, eds., *Turning Points*, 248–287. Chicago: University of Chicago Press.

Donahue, W., H. L. Orbach, and O. Pollak. 1960. "Retirement." In C. Tibbitts, ed., *Handbook of Social Gerontology*, 330–406. Chicago: University of Chicago.

Drucker, P. F. 1976. *Pension Fund Socialism*. New York: Harper and Row.

Durand, J. D. 1948. *The Labor Force in the United States*. New York: John Wiley.

Epstein, A. 1928. *The Challenges of the Ages*. New York: Vanguard Press.

Fitzgerald, F. 1986. *Cities on the Hill*. Boston: Houghton Mifflin.

Fogelson, R. M. 1984. *Pensions*. New York: Columbia University Press.

Fraundorf, M. N. 1979. "The Labor Force Participation of Turn-of-the-Century Married Women." *Journal of Economic History*, 39:401–417.

Genovese, E. 1974. *Roll, Jordan, Roll*. New York: Vintage Books

Gibson, R. 1986. "Outlook for the Black Family." In A. Pifer and L. Bronte, eds., *Our Aging Society*, 181–197. New York: W. W. Norton.

Graebner, W. 1980. *A History of Retirement*. New Haven: Yale University Press.

Gratton, B. 1986. *Urban Elders*. Philadelphia: Temple University Press.

Gutman, H. 1976. *The Black Family in Slavery and Freedom*. New York: Knopf.

Haber, C. 1983. *Beyond Sixty-Five*. New York: Cambridge University Press.

Haber, C., and B. Gratton. 1993. *Old Age in Times Past*. Bloomington, Ind.: Indiana University Press.

Hannah, L. 1986. *Inventing Retirement*. Cambridge: Cambridge University Press.

Hareven, T. K. 1983. *Family Time and Industrial Time*. New York: Cambridge University Press.

Hendrick, B. 1908. "The Superannuated Man." *McClure*, 32:115–127.

"Independent Opinions." 1913. *Independent*, 75 (August 28).

Insley, J. K. 1930. *The Older Worker in Maryland*. Annapolis, Md.: Commissioner of Labor and Statistics.

Johnson, P. 1985. *Saving and Spending*. Oxford: Clarendon Press.

Jones, J. 1985. *Labor of Love, Labor of Sorrow*. New York: Vintage.

Joyner, C. 1984. *Down by the Riverside*. Urbana, Ill.: University of Illinois Press.

Keyssar, A. 1986. *Out of Work*. New York: Cambridge University Press.

Kohli, M. 1987. "Retirement and Moral Economy: An Historical Interpretation of the German Case." Journal of Aging Studies, 1:125–144.

Latimer, M. W. 1930. "Relation of Maximum Hiring Ages to the Age Distribution of Employees." In D. D. Leschohier, ed., *What Is the Effect and Extent of Technical Changes on Employment Security?* no 3. New York: American Management Association.

Latimer, M. W. 1932. *Industrial Pension Systems*. New York: Industrial Relations Counselors.

Licht, W. 1983. *Working for the Railroad*. Princeton, N.J.: Princeton University Press.

Long, C. D. 1958. *The Labor Force under Changing Conditions of Income and Employment*. Princeton, N.J.: Princeton University Press.

Matthews, M. M. 1951. *A Dictionary of Americanisms*. Chicago: University of Chicago Press.

Mills, H. A., and R. E. Montgomery. 1938. *Labor's Risks and Social Insurance*. New York: McGraw-Hill.

"Hiring and Separation." *1932. Monthly Labor Review*, 35:1005–1018.

Moen, J. 1987. "The Labor of Older Men: A Comment." *Journal of Economic History*, 47:761–767.

Monroe, P. 1897. "An American System of Labor Pensions and Insurance." *American Journal of Sociology*, 2:501–514.

Myles, J. 1984. *Old Age in the Welfare State*. Boston: Little, Brown.

National Civic Federation (NCF). 1928. *Extent of Old Age Dependency*. New York: NCF.

National Council on the Aging (NCOA). 1981. *Aging in the Eighties*. Washington, D.C.: NCOA.

New American Encyclopedic Dictionary. 1907. New York: J. A. Hill.

Old Age Security. 1928. New York: American Association for Old Age Security.

Oxford English Dictionary. 1971. Oxford: Oxford University Press.

Palmore, E. 1964. "Retirement Patterns among Aged Men." *Social Security Bulletin*, 27:3–10.

Parnes, H. S., ed. 1981. *Work and Retirement*. Cambridge, Mass.: MIT Press.

Phillipson, C. 1990. "The Sociology of Retirement." In J. Bond and P. Coleman, eds., *Aging in Society*, 155–160. London: Sage Publications.

Plowman, E. G. 1930. "The Pros and Cons of Hiring Age Limits." In D. D. Leschohier, ed., *What Is the Effect and Extent of Technical Changes on Employment Security?* New York: American Management Association.

Quadagno, J. 1982. *Aging in Early Industrial Society*. New York: Academic Press.

Quadagno, J. 1988a. *The Transformation of Old Age Security*. Chicago: University of Chicago Press.

Quadagno, J. 1988b. "From Old-Age Assistance to Supplemental Security Income." In M. Weir, A. S. Orloff, and T. Skocpol, eds., *The Politics of Social Policy in the United States*. Princeton, N.J.: Princeton University Press.

Ransom, R., and R. Sutch. 1986. "The Labor of Older Americans." *Journal of Economic History*, 46:1–30.

Ransom, R., and R. Sutch, 1987. "Tontine Insurance and the Armstrong Investigation." *Journal of Economic History*, 47:379–390.

Reverby, S. 1987. *Ordered to Care.* New York: Cambridge University Press.

Rubinow, I. M. 1913. *Social Insurance.* New York: Henry Holt.

Sass, S. A. 1989. "Pension Bargains." In P. Johnson, C. Conrad, and D. Thomson, eds., *Workers versus Pensioners,* 91–112. Manchester: Manchester University Press.

Scadron, A. Ed. 1988. *On Their Own.* Urbana, Ill.: University of Illinois Press.

Schweitzer, M. M. 1987. *Custom and Contract.* Ithaca, N.Y.: Cornell University Press.

Slavick, F. 1966. *Compulsory and Flexible Retirement in the American Economy.* Ithaca: New York State School of Industrial and Labor Relations.

Smith, D. S. 1978. "Old Age and the 'Great Transformation.' " In S. F. Spicker, K. M. Woodward, and D. D. Van Tassel. eds., *Aging and the Elderly,* 205–302. Atlantic Highlands, N.J.: Humanities Press.

Social Security Administration. 1976. *Reaching Retirement Age.* Washington, D.C.: Government Printing Office.

Soltow, L. 1975. *Men and Wealth in the United States, 1850–1870.* New Haven, Conn.: Yale University Press.

Stearns, P. N. 1976. *Old Age in European Society.* New York: Holmes and Meier.

Steiner, P. O., and R. Dorfman. 1957. *The Economic Needs of the Aged.* Berkeley, Calif.: University of California Press.

Streib, G. F., and C. J. Schneider. 1971. *Retirement in American Society.* Ithaca, N.Y.: Cornell University Press.

Streib, G. F. 1988. "Discussion." In R. Ricardo-Campbell and E. P. Lazear, eds., *Issues in Contemporary Retirement,* 27–30. Stanford, Calif.: Hoover Institution Press.

Thane, P. 1982. *The Foundations of the Welfare State.* London: Longman.

Thomas, R. 1810. *Farmer's Almanack* December: n.p.

Troyansky, D. G. 1989. *Old Age in the Old Regime.* Ithaca, N.Y.: Cornell University Press.

Webster, N. 1828. *An American Dictionary.* Springfield, Mass.: Merriam-Webster.

Webster's New Universal Unabridged Dictionary. 1983. Springfield, Mass.: Merriam-Webster.

Webster's Third New International Dictionary. 1971. Springfield, Mass.: Merriam-Webster.

Wentworth, E., and D. K. Motley. 1970. *Researches after Retirement.* U.S. Social Security Administration (SSA), Research Report 34. Washington, D.C.: U.S. Government Printing Office.

Wood, G. 1971. *The Rising Glory of America.* New York: George Braziller.

Yans-McLaughlin, V. 1977. *Family and Community.* Ithaca, NY: Cornell University Press.

II
LIFE PLANNING

●

of men (Clark, Johnson, and McDermed 1980; Pozzebon and Mitchell 1989).

Economic Determinants of Retirement

The timing of retirement is influenced by one's total compensation from continued employment, personal wealth, and the availability of other resources in retirement (Fields and Mitchell 1984; Gustman and Steinmeier 1986; and Ruhm 1989). These factors determine the payoff of continued employment and affect the value of leisure time. Considering these factors along with one's consumption needs in retirement allows an individual to determine the feasibility of retirement.

The value of continuing to work depends on cash compensation, the gain in future pension benefits, health insurance coverage, and other benefits of paid employment. Cash compensation after taxes represents the direct value of working. Higher hourly compensation provides a greater incentive for individuals to remain at work. Declines in compensation encourage older people to leave the labor force.

Unemployment and layoffs force people to look for new jobs generally at lower wages and tend to encourage older workers to leave the labor force. A lack of firms that are willing to employ older workers at their previous wage rates causes many people to elect to withdraw from the labor force rather than remaining unemployed and continuing to search for a new job (Hutchens 1988). Firms can encourage workers to remain at work by increasing cash compensation; however, they are prevented by law from reducing wages to encourage retirement. The Age Discrimination in Employment Act (ADEA) prohibits firms from using mandatory retirement to force older workers to retire. Statistical evidence suggests that mandatory retirement was never a major cause of older workers' leaving the labor force (Burkhauser and Quinn 1983).

Most pension participants are covered by defined benefit plans that promise to provide specified levels of benefits based on years of service and earnings. Each of these plans has a normal retirement age and typically an early retirement age (Clark and McDermed 1990). Prior to reaching these retirement ages, an additional year of work increases the value of future pension benefits by increasing the number of years of credited service and generally raising the average earnings used to calculate benefits (Ippolito 1986). The present value of this increase in benefits is a form of compensation for remaining on the job and increases the value of working (Ippolito 1987).

After the worker has reached the required age and put in the years of service necessary to be eligible to begin receiving benefits, the present value of pension benefits tends to decline with continued employment. This occurs despite the fact that future annual benefits may increase. By remaining on the job for another year, the worker forgoes a year's pension benefit (Clark and McDermed 1986).

The decline in the lifetime value of the pension is due to the reduced number of expected years of life expectancy, i.e., fewer years of payments reduce the lifetime value of the pension more 'han this value is increased by higher annual benefits. This decline in the total value of pension benefits can be viewed as a reduction in compensation from continued employment. The reduction in compensation provides workers with a strong incentive to retire (Burkhauser 1979; Kotlikoff and Wise 1989).

The retirement incentives of pensions along with special early retirement programs are a major factor in the timing of retirement for many older people. Recently many companies have offered special early retirement programs that increase pension benefits provided that retirement occurs within a specified time period. These programs are developed by firms to achieve orderly patterns of retirement and to reduce their work forces. The age of eligibility for a pension is a key factor in the decision about when to retire. Changes in pension characteristics have encouraged earlier withdrawal from the labor force (Mitchell and Luzadis 1988).

Health insurance is important to all Americans. The rapid escalation in the cost of health insurance is one of the most significant public policy issues of the 1990s. The value of employer-provided health insurance is an important part of total compensation for older workers. The cost of individual health insurance can be prohibitively expensive to older people. Thus, employer-provided health insurance can be an important determinant in the desire to continue at work.

Beginning in the 1960s, many firms introduced the coverage of retirees into their health plans. Qualified people could retire and continue to be covered by their companies' health plans (Clark and Kreps 1989; Warshawsky 1992). This benefit substantially reduced the cost of retirement, especially to young retirees who are not yet eligible for Medicare. As a result, coverage by retiree health insurance is a strong inducement to retire. Most of these programs link eligibility for retiree health insurance to retirement from the firm and eligibility for the company's pension. These eligibility criteria reinforce the effect of the eligibility for a pension on the timing of retirement.

Greater personal wealth makes retirement more feasible. Greater wealth is associated with earlier retirement, as the wealthier individual can more easily finance his or her consumption needs in retirement. In principle, the form of wealth should not matter; however, the prevalence of one's personal residence as a major component of total wealth may influence retirement decisions.

The availability of other resources will increase the likelihood of retirement. The most important resources to the majority of older households are Social Security benefits and access to Medicare. Social Security benefits can be received as early as age sixty-two; full benefits are paid at age sixty-five, and people also become eligible for Medicare at age sixty-five. Calculating a cash value for Medicare benefits reveals that this imputed value of health insurance represents a significant proportion of total household resources (Moon 1977; Smeeding 1982; and Clark, Maddox, Schrimper, and Sumner 1984).

The largest declines in the proportion of older men in the labor force occur at ages sixty-two and sixty-five (Burtless and Moffit 1985 and 1986; Gustman and Steinmeier 1985). The ages of eligibility for Social Security and Medicare are important factors that determine the timing of retirement for many people. The introduction of Medicare in the late 1960s and the increase in real Social Security benefits in the early 1970s stimulated the decline in the labor force participation rates of older men (Ippolito 1990).

Health and Retirement

The health status of older people influences their decisions to work in several ways. First, poor health may limit the ability of people to perform certain tasks. Declines in productivity make firms less willing to hire or retain workers with such limitations. Therefore, job opportunities and wage offers tend to decline with the onset of health problems.

Second, poor health may make work more onerous and thus reduce the desire to work. Getting to the workplace and completing a full day on the job becomes more difficult. Virtually all studies of retirement conclude that personal health is an important factor governing the retirement decisions of older people (Anderson and Burkhauser 1985; Bazzoli 1985; Sammartino 1987).

The health of one's spouse also tends to influence one's decision about continuing to work. In this case, there are two conflicting forces. First, the decline in the ability of a spouse to work may reduce a family's income and increase health care costs. In response, a person will tend to increase his or her own work effort to generate additional family income. Second, the need to care for a spouse at home may reduce the ability of a person to go to work. Which of these forces dominates depends on the price of home health care, family income, and the earning power of the healthy spouse (Clark, Johnson, and McDermed 1980).

Women and Retirement

One of the most significant labor market statistics of the twentieth century has been the increasing proportion of women who are in the labor force (Golden 1989). By 1980 almost two-thirds of the women aged twenty-five to fifty-four were in the labor force. The labor force participation rate of these women increased further to approximately 75 percent in 1990.

In the first half of the century, relatively few women worked for long periods of time, and female rates of labor force participation were quite low. Personal retirement was not a separate life phase for most women. Instead, the retirement of their husbands tended to mark family transitions in late life. Often the role of the wife as a homemaker was unchanged with advancing age, while retirement from the labor force substantially altered the time allocation of the husband.

Since World War II, the labor force participation rates of women aged twenty to fifty-four have risen rapidly. More women enter the labor force, find career jobs, and spend a significant component of their lives working. As a result, the departure from the labor force in late life is now becoming an important event for women as well as men. As the work histories of women become more like those of men, the same factors influencing retirement become more relevant for women. It has been shown that pensions and Social Security, cash compensation, health insurance, and personal wealth are important determinants of the timing of retirement for career-oriented women (Honig 1985; Pozzebon and Mitchell 1989).

SOURCES OF RETIREMENT INCOME

The cash income of older Americans is primarily from Social Security, employers' pensions, return on assets, and earnings. In addition, most elderly families are covered by Medicare, which provides valuable health insurance. Older people also receive income in kind in the form of retiree health insurance from their previous employers or government benefits in the form of food stamps, housing subsidies, energy assistance, and so on. The value of the in-kind benefits to older households is difficult to determine (Moon 1977; Smeeding 1982).

Over the past three decades, Social Security has expanded to provide benefits to virtually all people over sixty-five. Income from Social Security accounts for almost 40 percent of the income of the average older household. These benefits are more important to low-income households than to households with higher incomes. Social Security provides more than three-quarters of the income of households in the lowest fifth of the income distribution for older households, and Social Security is the only source of income for many of the poorest elderly people. The importance of Social Security declines as income increases, so that only 20 percent of the income of households in the upper fifth of the income distribution is attributable to Social Security (U.S. Social Security Administration 1992).

Coverage by employers' pensions also expanded rapidly during the 1960s and 1970s. As a result, the proportion of older families with income from pensions rose from 15 percent in the early 1960s to almost 50 percent in 1990. Pension income is concentrated among middle- and upper-income older households. Pension income accounts for only 4 percent of the average income of the poorest families, but 21 percent of the average income of families in the top fifth of the income distribution.

Approximately two-thirds of older households have some income from assets, and income from assets accounts for a quarter of the income of all older families. However, this type of income is concentrated among the wealthiest elderly people. Income from personal wealth represents only 4 percent of the income of the poorest households, but a third of the income for people in the top fifth of the income distribution for older households.

The proportion of men sixty-five and older in the labor force has fallen from one out of two in 1950 to one out of six in 1991. The decline in the labor force participation rates of older men means that earnings are a major source of income in fewer elderly households. Fewer than 20 percent of older households continue to have earnings. Among elderly households, earnings are more prevalent among younger and healthier families. Earnings represents less than 5 percent of the total income of households with less than $10,000, but almost a quarter of the income of families with more than $20,000.

The economic well-being of older households is augmented by Medicare and employer-provided retiree health insurance along with in-kind social assistance programs (Clark, Maddox, Schrimper, and Sumner 1984). Medicare is available to virtually all people over age sixty-five and is a major resource to these families. Coverage by company-provided retiree health insurance is primarily limited to middle- and upper-income retirees who also have pension coverage. In general, these programs cover many of the health care expenses that are not paid by Medicare. Social welfare programs provide income only to the poorest of elderly people and generally provide only minimum levels of benefits.

ECONOMIC WELL-BEING IN RETIREMENT

The optimal retirement age is the age at which an older worker decides that he or she has sufficient income from pensions, Social Security, and personal assets to provide the desired level of consumption in retirement. This level of income depends on the amount of income necessary to begin retirement with a lifestyle similar to that enjoyed during the final working years and the ability to maintain this standard of living throughout retirement. This section examines the level of income in retirement relative to the preretirement earnings necessary to maintain a comparable standard of living and the ability to maintain this standard of living in the face of inflation and uncertain life expectancy.

In the past the Bureau of Labor Statistics published budgets for elderly couples indicating their relative consumption needs in retirement. Analysis of the Consumer Expenditure Surveys also shows how consumption patterns change with age. Older households spend a higher proportion of their incomes on health care and food and less on clothing and transportation than do younger households. Understanding changes in consumption needs is important in assessing the feasibility of retirement.

Social Security taxes are paid on earnings, but not on retirement income. Some retirement income is not subject to personal income taxation. Retirees do not have many of the day-to-day expenses associated with going to and from work. Estimates of retirees' expenditures compared to those of workers suggest that in most cases retirement income that is 65 to 80 percent of preretirement income is sufficient to maintain the same standard of living enjoyed before retirement. People with low incomes need a higher replacement ratio than higher-income retirees.

Inflation and the Real Income of the Elderly

A common belief has been that older families live on fixed incomes and are therefore most vulnerable to inflation. This assumption is wrong, as very few if any older people have incomes that are truly fixed and nonresponsive to inflation. To address this issue, in this section all of the major income sources of the elderly are reviewed for their responsiveness to inflation. In addition, the trend in the economic well-being of the elderly during inflationary periods is examined.

The major source of income for most older people is Social Security. Social Security benefits are fully indexed to reflex increases in consumer prices. Benefits are increased each January by a rate equal to the previous year's inflation rate. Since Social Security benefits represent a higher proportion of income for the poorest older people, these are the people most protected against rising prices.

A policy issue is whether the price index used to adjust these benefits is appropriate for older households. In general, studies have found that price fluctuations affect groups differentially during short time periods; however, over longer periods the rate of increase on the goods purchased by the elderly does not appear to have risen much faster than the rate of increase on the goods purchased by the general population (Borzilleri 1978, Grimaldi 1982).

Relatively few private pension benefits are automatically indexed with inflation; however, many plans make regular ad hoc adjustments. These increases are typically less than half the accumulated increase in consumer prices since any previous adjustment (Allen, Clark, and Sumner 1986). Most public pension plans are subject to automatic cost-of-living adjustments; however, many of these adjustments are capped at 3 or 5 percent per year. Thus, retirees with pension benefits are vulnerable to loss of real purchasing power with inflation.

The response of income from assets to price increases depends on the nature of the asset. The price and rate of return for some assets rise with increases in the rate of inflation, while income from other assets may be less responsive to price changes. No general statement can be made concerning the link between asset income and inflation.

Medicare and retiree health insurance provide benefits in kind. As prices rise, so does the value of the health care received under these programs. Thus these plans are indexed to the rate of medical inflation to provide a constant level of purchasing power. A problem arises because the government may alter the benefits from Medicare or individual firms may reduce benefits from retiree health plans. While not directly linked to inflation, these changes may be made in response to rising costs to the public and private providers of health insurance.

If older people continue to work full or part time, their earnings often rise with inflation. In general, the earnings of older workers have the same inflation protection as the earnings of workers of all ages; that is, earnings typically rise to reflect higher prices. But this link is not direct as in the case of automatic cost-of-living adjustments.

This review clearly indicates that most of the income sources of the elderly are not fixed in nominal terms, but instead respond to increases in consumer prices. Examination of the high-inflation period of the 1970s reveals that the incomes of older households rose more rapidly than the income of the population at large (Bridges and Packard 1981; Clark, Maddox, Schrimper, and Sumner 1984). As a result, the relative income of the elderly improved throughout those high-inflation years. This is further evidence that the nominal income of the elderly is not fixed, but instead responds to rising prices.

It is important to recognize the diversity in the economic well-being of older people. Increases in the average economic status of elderly households do not imply that all older families have improved their standards of living, nor do they imply that no older people are poor (Quinn 1987).

Longevity and the Preservation of Assets

Older workers make decisions about when to retire based on current information and expectations for the future. A key factor in this decision-making process is one's life expectancy and health status. The importance of these factors has been reduced somewhat by the almost universal coverage of Social Security and Medicare.

If a person's only sources of income were personal wealth and health declines were ignored, the timing of retirement would depend on the size of wealth holdings, the target level of retirement income, and the number of years of retirement. The longer one expects to live in retirement, the more assets must be accumulated to finance any given level of annual consumption.

Life expectancy at age sixty-five for males increased from just under thirteen years in 1950 to fifteen years in 1990, while life expectancy for women rose from fifteen years to more than nineteen years during the same period. The increases in life expectancy at age sixty-five that have occurred during the second half of the twentieth century implies that individuals must accumulate more savings prior to retirement than before.

Increases in life expectancy may be a "surprise" to older workers; that is, for most of their lives they have planned on fifteen years of retirement, but in their final working years or even after retirement they realize that they can expect to live twenty years after retirement. The increase in the difference between life expectancy for men and women means that the family must plan for a longer period during which the wife will survive alone. Planning for widowhood is an important aspect of retirement planning.

Another form of surprise is that life expectancy is merely an average number of years that people of a particular age can expect to live. Since it is an average, many people will survive for a number of years past the average. People who have been spending down their assets based on a life expectancy of fifteen years will find their ability to maintain their standard of living substantially reduced if they survive for twenty or thirty years.

Lifetime annuities help solve this problem. Social Security pays benefits until a person dies. Most employers' pensions also pay benefits in the form of life annuities. The continuation of Medicare and retiree health insurance until death also gives retirees continued access to health services throughout retirement.

The major threat of outliving one's income comes from the possibility of exhausting private assets prior to death, resulting in a substantial deterioration in one's standard of living. This possibility is increased in the presence of adverse health events that necessitate large private expenditures and limit work opportunities. The probability of spending down one's assets for health-related reasons can be reduced through the purchase of private health insurance, and this possibility is greatly reduced for those with employer-provided retiree health insurance.

CONCLUSIONS

The decision about when to retire is one of the most important choices individuals face. Economic well-being during the final years of life depends on careful planning for retirement and a careful determination of the best age at which to retire from a career job.

Given the complexity and uncertainty of planning for retirement, older workers should devote considerable effort to assessing the feasibility of retirement. Adequate preparation for retirement is a lifetime task. It requires accumulating savings annually, along with careful consideration of the benefits that firms provide, especially pension plans and retiree health insurance. Even with a lifetime of preparation, the timing of retirement will have a considerable effect on one's income in retirement. Therefore, a careful assessment of retirement options is a must for older workers.

REFERENCES

Allen, Steven G., Robert L. Clark, and Daniel A. Sumner. 1986. "Postretirement Adjustments of Pension Benefits." *Journal of Human Resources*, 21(1):118–137.

Anderson, Kathryn H., and Richard V. Burkhauser. 1985. "The Retirement-Health Nexus: A New Measure of an Old Puzzle." *Journal of Human Resources*, 20(3):315–330.

Anderson, Kathryn H., Richard V. Burkhauser, and Joseph F. Quinn. 1986. "Do Retirement Dreams Come True? The Effect of Unanticipated Events on Retirement Plans." *Industrial and Labor Relations Review*, 39(4):518–526.

Bazzoli, Gloria J. 1985. "The Early Retirement Decision: New Evidence on the Influence of Health." *Journal of Human Resources*, 20(2):214–234.

Borzilleri, Thomas. 1978. "The Need for a Separate Consumer Index for Older Persons." *The Gerontologist*, 18(3):230–236.

Bridges, Benjamin, and Michael Packard. 1981. "Price and Income Changes for the Elderly." *Social Security Bulletin*, 44(January):3–15.

Burkhauser, Richard V. 1979. "The Pension Acceptance Decision of Older Workers." *Journal of Human Resources*, 14(1):63–75.

Burkhauser, Richard V., and Joseph F. Quinn. 1983. "Is Mandatory Retirement Overrated? Evidence from the 1970s." *Journal of Human Resources*, 18(3):337–358.

Burtless, Gary, and Robert A. Moffit. 1985. "The Joint Choice of Retirement Age and Postretirement Hours of Work." *Journal of Labor Economics*, 3(2):209–236.

Burtless, Gary, and Robert A. Moffit. 1986. "Social Security, Earnings Tests, and Age at Retirement." *Public Finance Quarterly*, 14(1):3–27.

Butler, J. S., Kathryn H. Anderson, and Richard V. Burkhauser. 1989. "Work and Health After Retirement: A Competing Risks Model with Semiparametric Unobserved Heterogeneity." *Review of Economics and Statistics*, 71(1):46–53.

Clark, Robert L., Thomas Johnson, and Ann A. McDermed. 1980. "Allocation of Time by Married Couples Approaching Retirement." *Social Security Bulletin*, 43(4):3–16.

Clark, Robert L., and Juanita M. Kreps. 1989. "Employer-Provided Health Care Plans for Retiree." *Research on Aging*, 11(2):206–224.

Clark, Robert L., George L. Maddox, Ronald A. Schrimper, and Daniel A. Sumner. 1984. *Inflation and the Economic Well-being of the Elderly*. Baltimore: Johns Hopkins University Press.

Clark, Robert L., and Ann A. McDermed. 1986. "Earnings and Pension Compensation: The Effect of Eligibility." *Quarterly Journal of Economics*, 99:341–361.

Clark, Robert L., and Ann A. McDermed. 1990. *The Choice of Pension Plans in a Changing Regulatory Environment*. Washington: American Enterprise Institute.

Fields, Gary S., and Olivia S. Mitchell. 1984. *Retirement, Pensions, and Social Security*. Cambridge, Mass.: MIT Press.

Golden, Claudia. 1989. "Life-Cycle Labor Force Participation of Married Women: Historical Evidence and Implications." *Journal of Labor Economics*, 7(1):20–47.

Grimaldi, Paul. 1982. "Measured Inflation and the Elderly, 1973–81." *The Gerontologist*, 22(4):347–353.

Gustman, Alan A., and Thomas S. Steinmeier. 1985. "The 1983 Social Security Reforms and Labor Supply Adjustments of Older Individuals in the Long Run." *Journal of Labor Economics*, 3(2):237–253.

Gustman, Alan A., and Thomas S. Steinmeier. 1986. "A Structural Retirement Model." *Econometrica*, 54:555–584.

Honig, Marjorie. 1985. "Partial Retirement Among Women." *Journal of Human Resources*, 20(4):613–621.

Hutchens, Robert M. 1988. "Do Job Opportunities Decline with Age?" *Industrial and Labor Relations Review*, 42(1):89–99.

Ippolito, Richard A. 1986. *Pensions, Economics, and Public Policy*. Homewood, Ill.: Dow Jones-Irwin.

Ippolito, Richard A. 1987. "The Implicit Pension Contract: Developments and New Directions." *Journal of Human Resources*, 22(3):441–467.

Ippolito, Richard A. 1990. "Towards Explaining Earlier Retirement After 1970." *Industrial and Labor Relations Review*, 43(5):556–569.

Kotlikoff, Laurence J., and David A. Wise. 1989. *The Wage Carrot and the Pension Stick*. Kalamazoo, Mich.: Upjohn Institute for Employment Research.

Mitchell, Olivia S., and Rebecca Luzadis. 1988. "Changes in Pension Incentives Through Time." *Industrial and Labor Relations Review*, 42(1):100–108.

Moon, Marilyn. 1977. *The Measuring of Economic Welfare: Its Application to the Aged Poor*. New York: Academic Press.

Pozzebon, Silvana, and Olivia S. Mitchell. 1989. "Married Women's Retirement Behavior." *Journal of Population Economics*, 2(1):39–53.

Quinn, Joseph F. 1987. "Economic Status of the Elderly: Beware of the Mean." *The Review of Income and Wealth*, 33(1):63–82.

Quinn, Joseph F., Richard V. Burkhauser, and Daniel A. Myers. 1990. *Passing the Torch: The Influence of Economic Incentives on Work and Retirement*. Kalamazoo, Mich.: Upjohn Institute for Employment Research.

Ransom, Roger L., and Richard Sutch. 1986. "The Labor of Older Americans: Retirement of Men On and Off the Job, 1870–1937." *The Journal of Economic History*, 46(1):1–30.

Ruhm, Christopher J. 1989. "Why Older Americans Stop Working." *The Gerontologist*, 29(3):294–299.

Sammartino, Frank J. 1987. "The Effect of Health on Retirement." *Social Security Bulletin*, 50 (February):31–47.

Smeeding, Timothy. 1982. *Alternative Methods of Valuing Selected In-Kind Transfer Benefits and Measuring Their Impact on Poverty*. Technical Paper no 50. Washington: U.S. Bureau of the Census.

U.S. Social Security Administration. 1992. *Income of the Population 55 or Older, 1992*. Washington, D.C.: U.S. Government Printing Office.

Warshawsky, Mark. 1992. *The Uncertain Promise of Retiree Health Benefits*. Washington, D.C.: American Enterprise Institute.

4

The Decision to Retire: Individual Considerations and Determinations

●

HELEN DENNIS

The decision to retire is complex. It involves goal setting, strategic planning, environmental scanning, risk analysis, and the weighing of trade-offs, processes similar to ones used in the workplace. Companies make decisions using this process and either succeed or fail. When these are used in making a decision about retirement, it is the individual who is the ultimate winner or loser. Because of the significance of that decision, this chapter examines factors that influence a person's decision to retire, consequences that result from denying the reality of retirement, and some initial steps one can take to make oneself ready for retirement readiness.

FACTORS THAT INFLUENCE THE DECISION TO RETIRE

Most people retire. Usually the question is when rather than if. The timing is most often related to an individual's expected retirement income and health status (Atchley 1991; Karp 1989). However, there are other considerations that influence the decision to retire. Among them are attitudes toward retirement, family commitments and relationships, and the meaning and value of work.

A Positive Attitude

Over thirty years ago, it was found that a positive attitude facilitates good adjustment to retirement (Thompson 1958). Since then, other studies have confirmed this result and also related positive retirement attitudes to retiring "on time"—on a retirement date selected by the employee (Atton 1985; Braithwaite et al. 1988; Ekerdt 1989). A positive view of retirement may be influenced by several realities and perceptions. Four examples are described below: the social acceptability of retirement, one's financial security, whether one acknowledges losses, and the extent of one's fear about the future.

The Social Acceptability of Retirement

A positive attitude toward retirement assumes that individuals perceive retirement as socially acceptable. However, the work ethic, which values being industrious and self-reliant, is not part of the retirement experience for most people. Most retirees do not work, and retirees often choose lives of leisure. Ekerdt (1986) suggests that American society has adapted the "busy ethic," an attempt to justify retirement in a way that is consistent with the work ethic. The busy ethic places a value on leisure if it is sincere and filled with activity and involvement. It acknowledges goals that individuals choose rather than goals that are defined by society's economic system. It allows a retiree to answer the question "What are you doing to keep yourself busy?" with a sense of self-worth. For example, participating in an elder hostel program, playing golf, traveling, gardening, and reading to children in the library suggest sincerity, activity, and involvement—all part of the busy ethic.

Yet for many the term *retirement* is negative, conjuring up images of being a "has-been," useless and of little worth. One solution to this problem is to omit the word *retirement* from the English language (McCluskey 1989). Another is to substitute a word that connotes continued participation in society rather than withdrawal (Friedan and Lazarus 1985). Perhaps what is needed is a word that conveys a sense of renewal to mark not only the end of employment, but the beginning of retirement—a word similar to *commencement*. When individuals graduate from college they participate in a ceremony that is referred to as *commencement*, which suggests an ending of their formal education and a beginning of the next chapter of their lives.

A comment frequently made by those considering retirement is "I don't think I'm ready to be a retiree." Many of these individuals just want to continue working. Others feel that *retired* means *at the end of the line, on the shelf, over the hill,* or *put out to pasture* (McCluskey 1989). Clearly these definitions rely on old models of retirement that no longer apply to retirement in this decade. Regardless of whether the term is appropriate, *retirement* is likely to stay. The task of our society is to give new meaning to the term so that one thinks of vitality and opportunity as part of the retirement experience.

Financial Security

A positive attitude is also related to an expectation of financial security. Although approximately 80 percent of employed adults aged fifty and older expect to have few financial problems in retirement (Atchley 1991), people contemplating retirement identify financial security as their greatest retirement concern. Increasingly, employees ask themselves whether or not they can afford to retire. Articles such as the one that appeared in *Fortune* magazine on July 31, 1989, offer little reassurance. The article in *Fortune* gave the following figures. An employee who is forty-five years old and whose income is $83,000 will need $1.2 million in financial assets to retire at age sixty-five without reducing his her standard of living. A 4.5 percent rate of inflation increases the financial assets this person will need to $2.8 million. Those who are thinking about retirement may be jolted by the popular press to reexamine their financial requirements for a secure retirement.

Acknowledging Losses

Individuals with positive attitudes towards retirement are likely to acknowledge that losses are often associated with retirement. As early as 1946, an article in *The Gerontologist* stated that a personal factor influencing retirement is the "real or anticipated *decrease* in status" and *reduced* comrade relationships" (Moore 1946:205).

As an instructor in retirement education, I have asked the following question to almost two thousand corporate middle-management employees attending retirement planning seminars, all of whom have been working for their companies for twenty-five to forty years: "What will you miss the most when you leave?" Employees consistently state that they will miss their friends and co-workers, the substance of their work, the contribution they are making, the opportunity to learn and travel, new challenges, being part of a respected company, working as a team member, and helping the company grow. Income is often omitted from the list; other times it is mentioned at the very end. Most people who are considering retirement have not thought about the role that work plays in their lives, and although discussing this issue is sometimes painful, they welcome the discussion.

Losses are part of any transition. One must give up something from the past to gain more or acquire something different in the future. The task for those planning for retirement is to consider substitutes that will compensate for aspects of their jobs that they value. For example, employees who thrive on the challenges of work may seek comparable rewards in retirement through volunteer opportunities or new employment opportunities, entrepreneurial activities, or activities that are personally rewarding, such as building a retirement home.

Fears about Retirement

Positive attitudes toward retirement are likely to be related to having few fears about the future rather than many. Some employees are afraid that retirement will change them from active and productive workers to sedentary people who are unsure of ways to spend their free time (Feit and Tate 1986). Others fear being treated as old people who are worthless. Shortly before his death Norman Cousins, former editor of *Saturday Review* and professor of medicine at UCLA, wrote, "The worst thing about being 75 years old is being treated as a 75-year-old" (Cousins 1990). Society views people of this age as no longer serving a useful purpose. Many others fear the unknown, and this inhibits them from making a decision about retirement. Such individuals often face their futures without goals or a sense of identity or purpose.

Although society may value work over retirement, not many people view retirement as negative (Cockerham 1991). Most people are not eager to work past the normal retirement age (Cockerham 1991) and actually look forward to retirement as a time of freedom to create a lifestyle of their choice.

Family Commitments and Relationships

Family considerations play an important role in retirement decisions. The increased number of women in the labor force, longer life expectancy, and the explosive growth of the segment of the population that is eighty-five and older is exerting new pressures on middle-aged adults who are contemplating retirement.

Considerations for Women

For women, in particular, the decision to retire is affected by family considerations (Vinick and Ekerdt 1989). For example, married women often time their retirement in response to specific family influences (Szinovacz 1987; Matthews and Brown 1987). One of these influences is when a woman's husband retires. A married woman usually retires early so that her retirement will coincide with her husband's. In fact, a husband's pension eligibility and the amount of his pension are major predictors of when a married woman will retire (Atchley 1991; Vinick and Ekerdt 1989; Campione 1987).

Another influence is the health of the woman's family. Women tend to retire more frequently than men when a spouse or other family member is ill (Matthews et al. 1987). Aging parents, in particular, present concerns that many adults had not previously considered. Although there is little if any data on this issue, the needs of an aging parent may either encourage or discourage a woman to retire. Women generally assume the role of family caregiver, and a woman may retire to provide in-home services and ongoing emotional support to an aging parent. On the other hand, at several retirement education seminars I have conducted, workers have stated that caring for an aging parent who lives in the same home discourages retirement. In these cases, the adult children want to continue working not only to receive income that will help them maintain their aging parents, but to retain their work-identified roles and balance their lives.

Single women tend to retire later than married women because they have fewer family considerations and must depend on their own pension incomes for retirement. Since their pensions are often inadequate because of low-paying jobs, single women are more likely than their married counterparts to remain working for their employers past age sixty-five (Atchley 1991).

Considerations for Men

Little has been written about the influence of the family on men's decision to retire. Occasionally men have to deal with difficult family situations that influence their retirement decisions. For example, a man who is responsible for a disabled or impaired wife faces retirement with a number of complex, often unresolved problems. It is difficult for such a man to define his retirement role and determine the choices he really has. Will he spend all of his time at home? Will the demands on him increase? Will he become the primary caregiver? How can he and his wife maximize their enjoyment of retirement as a married couple? Men have few places to turn to help them answer these questions.

Married men rarely retire as a result of the retirement decisions of their working wives. It is unclear whether the feelings or opinions of wives have a strong influence on men's retirement decisions (Matthews and Brown 1987). Wives of husbands who are considering retirement often express concern about the health status of their husbands. At the retirement planning seminars I lead, wives often indicate that they want their husbands to retire, particularly when their husbands have chronic or acute health problems. One wife was adamant about wanting her husband to retire, as he had been diagnosed with cancer not long before. But the husband resisted. Work was central to his life; it kept him productively occupied, involved him with colleagues, and prevented him from focusing on his illness.

Considerations for Couples

For working couples the decision to retire is especially complex. Husbands and wives tend to retire for different reasons. According to one author, many women are just beginning to "make their mark [in the workplace,] while men are leaving their mark" (Karp 1989:755). Therefore, husbands and wives may find it increasingly difficult to agree on the right time to retire if both want to retire together.

Communication with one another on career and retirement expectations is prerequisite to a "good" retirement decision for both parties. During a speech I once gave to a group of female CPAs a woman stood up and stated that her husband expected her to retire from the field of accounting and spend time in the kitchen baking pecan pies. In fact, he was looking forward to her new role. She declared that she had never liked baking even as a homemaker, detested pecan pies, and had no intention of become a retired CPA-turned-baker! It was obvious from this woman's comments and the vigor with which she expressed them that she and her husband had not been communicating well with each other and needed to improve their communication about their expectations of one another in order to achieve a mutually satisfactory retirement.

Husbands and wives who wish to make a joint decision to retire will also be influenced by external events. Aging family members will add to the complexity of their decision. According to one study, retired couples considered their retirement "spoiled" when they were responsible for the care of an elderly parent, often widowed, who lived with them. They reported a sense of missed opportunity, but felt they had no choice other than to care for the parent (Vinick and Ekerdt 1989).

The Meaning of Work

Occupational demands and the meaningfulness of work also influence the decision to retire. Different patterns can be seen among blue-collar workers, white-collar workers, and professionals. And the retirement decision is also influenced by a worker's level of identification with his or her career.

Differences between Blue-Collar Workers and White-Collar Workers

A number of studies support the finding that blue-collar workers tend to retire earlier than white-collar workers (Mitchel et al. 1988; Burtless 1987). Workers retire earlier from such occupations as mining, manufacturing, construction, and transportation than from professional industries, agriculture, and personal services (Burtless 1987). Blue-collar workers typically retire earlier because they are in jobs that are physically demanding, jobs that are more dangerous than white-collar jobs, and jobs that can cause injury and disability. Among men who are fifty-five and older, more blue-collar workers than white-collar workers retire because of health-related problems (Mitchel 1988).

How Professionals View Retirement

Professional workers have been neglected in the retirement literature (Kitty and Behling 1985). Karp (1989) has described how working professional men and women from fifty to sixty years old relate their work lives to the desirability of retirement. Those who are least likely to look forward to retirement have unfinished agendas at work, perceive retirement as financially unfeasible, are healthy, and are very satisfied with their jobs. Conversely, Kitty and Behling (1985) have found that professionals who are dissatisfied with their jobs due to limited autonomy, little mobility, and overwhelming bureaucracy within the company are likely to look forward to retirement.

The recent and ongoing mergers and acquisitions are good examples of why professionals (and others) may feel unhappy and insecure at work. New management is a factor in this insecurity. The managers of companies that have recently been involved in mergers are given the responsibility to create changes in management policies and practices for the purpose of increasing their companies' profitability. For many employees who are eligible for retirement, retiring is more attractive than trying to fit into the "new" organization. Leaving the workplace with a feeling of success and accomplishment is preferable to remaining and possibly becoming an outsider or even a failure. This feeling is particularly evident when new management is relatively young and mature employees have not been acknowledged by the new team.

Job satisfaction does not necessarily preclude professionals' looking forward to retirement (Atchley 1991). Many individuals enjoy their jobs and still want to retire. Perhaps the key to the desirability of the transition is related to the extent to which individuals identify with their careers.

Identification with One's Career

A person's job or profession is the most important feature of his or her social identity (Cockerham 1991). It contributes substantially to one's self-esteem, socioeconomic status, and satisfaction with life. This social identity often remains with individuals even after they leave the workplace. Often retirees refer to themselves as retired teachers, engineers, or machine operators rather than simply as retired.

In American society individuals are conditioned to set their life goals in occupational terms. At social gatherings individuals ask, "What do you do?" not "What have you read?" or "What are your beliefs?" (Halloran 1985:38). A fulfilling job or career is difficult to leave. Opportunities to create, exercise power and influence, gain respect, and make a contribution become the most significant values and objectives of an individual's life. The challenge for committed career professionals is to translate their values into meaningful new activities, such as volunteering, working for other employers, or working for themselves as consultants or entrepreneurs.

Individuals who strongly identify with their careers have more negative attitudes toward retirement than those who have little career identification (Dobson and Morrow 1984). For those who are still employed, Halloran (1985) has recommended the following steps to help them avoid the problems that may result from overly close identification with their work:

- Promote aspects of your life that are different from work. When someone asks what you do, respond without mentioning your job.
- Associate with individuals outside your work who have different career interests.

• Don't use your job to avoid dealing with interpersonal issues.
• Develop and maintain outside interests.
• Value and develop your individuality.

These steps provide opportunities to develop relationships, interests, and other forms of personal identification that are less dependent on one's work role.

DENYING THE REALITIES OF RETIREMENT

Workers frequently express their denial of the eventuality of retirement by procrastinating about planning. Some people fail to plan because they believe that retirement will take care of itself. They often believe that their retirement income will be adequate (without securing the data to validate such a belief), that doing very little can be a gratifying lifestyle, and that free time doesn't need to be managed. Others realize they should plan, but just haven't initiated the process.

Reasons for Such Denial

Workers give a number of reasons for not developing and implementing plans of action for retirement. First, they lack time because of commitments to and demands from work, family, and the community. Second, they believe that changing economic conditions are likely to make their plans less valid. Third, implementing a retirement plan suggests change, which many find difficult. Fourth, uncertainty about retirement and fears about the transition inhibit planning. Finally, many feel that retirement means they are becoming old and useless, so thinking about it conjures up negative images of aging that they want to avoid.

Consequences of Denial

The most obvious consequence of not planning for retirement is inadequate retirement income, which limits retirees' choices and opportunities. Another consequence is a meaningless retirement; the retiree has no reason to get up in the morning and has no feeling of self-worth or of fulfilling his or her personal needs, values, and objectives. A consequence that is apparent but is given little attention before retirement is the potentially negative impact of retirement on relationships.

Although the literature indicates that marital adjustment is not as big an issue in retirement as has been presumed, individuals attending retirement planning seminars eagerly discuss problems they anticipate in this area. Wives express concerns that their husbands will invade their space, will be around the house too much, and will want to do everything with them. Husbands indicate that they worry about too many requests that they assist with household chores. Most couples do not know how to begin discussing potential conflicts and believe that relationship problems in later life will take care of themselves.

A SUCCESSFUL PROGRAM TO PLAN FOR RETIREMENT

Leland Bradford, a pioneer in sensitivity training in the late 1940s who developed the National Training Laboratories, has used himself as an example of how *not* to retire.

Leland Bradford's Expectations of Retirement

Bradford was the CEO of an organization that he helped found and describes himself as a professional behavioral scientist who should have known better. This is how he describes his expectations of retirement:

> After 25 years of working under the strain of building an organization, or interweaving the ideas and needs of the key staff with a multiplicity of outside forces, I was ready for the beautiful promised land of retirement. I persuaded my wife to leave our lovely Georgetown home and move to North Carolina, where I could golf to my heart's content and enjoy relief from the stress of having to make daily decisions. I thought it would be just wonderful. (Bradford 1979a:103)

Bradford's Experience of Retirement

Bradford found retirement a terrible experience with emotionally destructive consequences. After retirement his emotions included feeling useless, unwanted, and disregarded; feeling lonely and missing work companions; feeling hopeless and unmotivated; feeling sad and angry at the loss of his previous power, influence, and recognition; and feeling resentful because many others view retirees as elderly and no longer powerful and attractive (Bradford 1979b).

Bradford's Retirement Training Program

As a result of this experience, Bradford developed one of the first retirement planning programs to enhance interpersonal relationships in retirement. The program, entitled "Preparing for Retirement: A Program for Survival," is designed to prepare employees for the emotional and psychological challenges of retirement. The program consists of five sessions, each lasting three hours, and includes such aids and activities as questionnaires, role plays, case studies, and checklists, along with a list of suggested readings. The program uses both a facilitator's manual and a participant's workbook.

An Example of One of the Sessions

The first session of Bradford's program is entitled "Facing the Reality of Retirement." Participants introduce themselves without mentioning their work. They complete a checklist regarding their expectations of retirement and describe in writing individuals who have had negative retirement experiences and those who have had positive ones. They simulate the last day of work before retirement and analyze the personal consequences of belonging or not belonging to a group.

Subsequent sessions focus on the use of time, on family relationships, on seeking psychological support, on including one's spouse, and finally, on how one might view the retirement experience after five years.

To avoid the emotional pitfalls of retirement, I recommend that your take the following steps:

1. Acknowledge the role of your work and the organization as providing you with both a sense of purpose and belonging and a degree of power and influence.
2. Indicate the "goodies" of work, i.e., why you have stayed with the company so many years. Which ones will you miss the most in retirement?
3. Determine how you will substitute for the losses you will experience as you leave the workplace.

4. Identify what makes life not only satisfying, but exciting to you.
5. If you like structure, plan to organize your time in retirement.
6. Acknowledge your needs for privacy in terms of both space and personal time, and plan accordingly.
7. Widen the number of personal interests that you can carry over to retirement.
8. Acknowledge that only you are responsible for creating a satisfying retirement.

If Bradford had completed his own program prior to retirement and gone through these eight steps, he probably could have avoided his own retirement crisis.

INITIAL STEPS ONE CAN TAKE TO BECOME READY FOR RETIREMENT

Establishing one's readiness to retire is a mid-life task. At a minimum, individuals who are preparing for retirement should try to answer the following sixteen basic questions, which I have adapted from C. Humple's (1985) *Retirement Designs:*

1. What are the sources of retirement income that I can count on?
2. What is my present net worth?
3. What will my assets be worth in retirement?
4. What benefits can I expect from Social Security?
5. What are my investment options?
6. Who can I turn to for investment advice?
7. How can I maintain the best possible level of functioning as I grow older?
8. How can I cope with the loss of friendships and human interaction from my job?
9. How can I create meaning and fun in my life?
10. What will I do with my time?
11. Will I want or need to work?
12. What are the retirement goals of my spouse or significant other?
13. What adjustments will I need to make in terms of my spouse or significant other?
14. What type of housing do I (we) want in retirement?
15. What can I do to make sure that my estate will be settled as I want it to be?

16. What are my commitments to and responsibilities for other family members?

There are no shortcuts in this process. Fortunately, resources are available that can help employees begin to answer these questions. They fall into three categories; professional services, public information, and seminars or classes.

Professional Services

Financial and estate planners, stock brokers, attorneys, and accountants provide information and analysis to help workers determine the affordability of retirement. For those considering new careers, career counselors are beginning to specialize in services for mature adults to assist them in assessing their strengths, abilities, and career opportunities. Agencies such as Project ABLE in Chicago and Career Encores in Los Angeles help match mature workers with employment opportunities. (See chapter 13 for more information.)

Public Information

Newspapers, periodicals, radio, and television represent a constant source of information on retirement in a number of areas, from financial planning to health promotion to the best place in America to retire. Additionally, brochures, computer programs, and audio and video cassettes address subjects such as finances, health, housing, and careers in retirement. This type of information is readily available from the American Association of Retired Persons (AARP), the National Council on the Aging (NCOA), and Retirement Advisors.

Seminars or Classes

Thirty to forty percent of large employers provide retirement planning seminars for their employees (Buck 1990; Morrison and Jedrziewski 1988). Community colleges, universities, and adult schools offer classroom programs that cover many aspects of retirement, such as financial and estate planning and career development. These programs are typically designed to increase workers' awareness about retirement planning, enhance their knowledge, and assist them to develop plans for retirement.

CONCLUSION

In the 1990s and beyond retirement will require early planning and thoughtful consideration of factors in addition to economics and health. Among them are attitudes towards retirement, family considerations, and the role and impact of work. Although most people have a rather favorable view of retirement, many still see it as an unknown negative. This negative attitude in itself becomes an obstacle to the planning process and the ultimate formation of decisions about retirement. Resources for planning are available, but they are meaningful only when individuals perceive these resources as relevant to their lives.

It is essential for the worker who is considering retirement to become aware of his or her vital role in the process of retirement planning. Only one person is responsible for creating and managing a successful retirement—the potential retiree. To be prepared for retirement, workers must assess their environments at work, at home, and in the community to capture the opportunities that will help them create a retirement experience that is meaningful for themselves and for those close to them.

REFERENCES

Atchley, R. C. 1991. *Social Theories in Aging.* Belmont, Calif.: Wadsworth Publishing Co.

Atton, H. 1985. "Psychology of Retirement." *British Journal of Occupational Therapy,* 48:375–378.

Bradford, L. P. 1979a. "Can You Survive Retirement?" *Harvard Business Review,* November–December:103–109.

Bradford, L. P. 1979b. "It's Time You Considered Preretirement Training." *Training/HRD,* June:52–55.

Braithwaite, V. A., T. M. Gibson, and F. Bosly-Craft. 1988. "An Exploratory Study of Poor Adjustment Styles among Retirees." *Social Science and Medicine,* 23:493–499.

Buck Consultants. 1990. "Firms Prepare Employees for Retirement." *Employee Benefit Plan Review,* June, 32–33.

Burtless, G. (1987). "Occupational Effect on the Health and Work Capacity of Older Men." In G. Burtless, ed., *Work, Health and Income Among the Elderly.* Washington, D.C.: The Brookings Institution.

Campione, W. A. 1987. "The Married Woman's Retirement Decision: A Methodological Comparison." *Journal of Gerontology,* 42 (4): 381–386.

Cockerham, W. C. 1991. *This Aging Society.* Englewood Cliffs, New Jersey: Prentice Hall.

Cousins, N. 1990. "Don't Tuck Me In." *The Los Angeles Times,* December 3.

Dobson, D., and P. C. Morrow. 1984. "Effects of Career Orientation on Retirement

Attitudes and Retirement Planning." *Journal of Vocational Behavior*, 24 (1): 73–83.

Ekerdt, D. J. 1986. "The Busy Ethic: Moral Continuity between Work and Retirement." *The Gerontologist*, 26 (3):239–244.

Ekerdt, D. J., B. H. Vinick, and R. Bosse. 1989. "Orderly Endings: Do Men Know When They Will Retire?" *Journal of Gerontology*, 44 (1):S28–S35.

Feit, M. D., and N. P. Tate. 1986. "Health and Mental Health Issues in Retirement Programs." *Employee Assistance Quarterly*, 1 (3):49–56.

Friedan, B., and M. Lazarus. 1985. "Opportunities: A Dialogue between Betty Friedan and Maurice Lazarus." In R. M. Butler and H. P. Gleason, eds., *Productive Aging: Enhancing Vitality in Later Life*. New York: Springer.

Halloran, D. F. 1985. "Viewpoint: The Retirement Identity Crisis—and How to Beat It." *Personal Journal*, May:38–40.

Humple, C. 1985. "Are You Ready for Retirement?" *Retirement Designs*. Los Angeles: C. Humple.

Karp, D. A. 1989. "The Social Construction of Retirement among Professionals 50–60 Years Old." *The Gerontologist*, 29 (6):750–760.

Kitty, K. M., and J. H. Behling. 1985. "Predicting the Retirement Intentions and Attitudes of Professional Workers." *Journal of Gerontology*, 40:219–227.

Matthews, A. M., and D. Brown. 1987. "Retirement as a Critical Life Event: The Differential Experiences of Women and Men." *Research on Aging*, 9 (4):548–551.

McCluskey, N. G. 1989. "Retirement and the Contemporary Family." *Journal of Psychotherapy and the Family*, 5 (1–2):211–224.

Mitchel, D. S., P. B. Levine, and S. Pozzebon. 1988. "Retirement Differences by Industry and Occupation." *The Gerontologist*, 28 (4):545–551.

Moore, E. H. 1946. "Preparation for Retirement." *Journal of Gerontology*, 1:202–212.

Morrison, M. H., and M. K. Jedrziewski. 1988. "Retirement Planning: Everybody Benefits." *Personnel Administrator*, January.

Szinovacz, M. 1987. "Preferred Retirement Timing and Retirement Satisfaction in Women." *International Journal of Aging and Human Development*, 24 (4):301–317.

Thompson, W. E. 1958. "Preretirement Anticipation and Adjustment in Retirement." *Journal of Social Issues*, XIV (2):35041.

Vinick, B. H., and D. J. Ekerdt. 1989. "Retirement and the Family." *Generations*, Spring:53–56.

"Will You Be Able to Retire?" 1989. *Fortune*, July 31.

5

Getting Ready to Retire: Preretirement Planning Programs

●

JANE W. COOPER

"Cheshire Puss" . . . Alice went on, "Would you tell me, please, which way I ought to walk from here?"
"That depends a good deal on where you want to get to," said the Cat.
"I don't much care where—" said Alice.
"Then it doesn't matter which way you walk," said the Cat.
"—so long as I get somewhere," Alice added as an explanation.
"Oh, you're sure to do that," said the Cat, "if you only walk long enough."

Lewis Carroll in
Alice's Adventures in Wonderland

When Alice begins to decide when, whether, how, and where to retire from work, she can feel as ill prepared to make a decision as she did in the midst of the woods of Wonderland. Retirement planning consultants, financial planners, benefits specialists, and other retirement advisors deliver messages like that of the Cheshire Cat: plan where you want to get to before you start. But the paths being suggested as alternatives diverge widely from one another, and the destination often seems indistinct, hidden in swirling mists and constantly moving farther away. Yet it doesn't seem as if it should be so difficult.

A college student doing research for a paper interviewed me about my work as a retirement planning consultant. "One thing my professor will want to know," she said, "is *why* does it take so much time and effort to figure out how not to get up early and go to work in the morning?" Many people ask the same question. Only a minority of retirees seriously plan for retirement, although most give it some thought in advance (Ekerdt 1989). While many reasons have been advanced for this, the "man in the street" often simply says, "People retire all the time. How can it be so complicated?" Or "My brother-in-law has had a great time this year. Just give me my numbers and show me the door."

As people look around them and see friends and colleagues retiring, the act of retiring from work often seems to be something people just *do*. However, common sense and the Boy Scout motto suggest a better course: be prepared. But the ability to be prepared depends on many factors: on the different needs and planning styles of individuals, on reports from friends and relatives, on what is available to help one become prepared, and on the skills needed to take advantage of the help.

Do retirement planning programs make a difference? Anecdotal evidence has long said, "Yes, of course." Documenting actual measurable effects has been more difficult, as reported by Ekerdt (1989), because there is confusion about the actual goals of programs for retirement preparation. Turnquist, Newsom, and Cochran (1988) have found that programs offered within six months of actual retirement have some positive effects on certain specific aspects of retirement, particularly those related to income. However, effective health planning and accumulation of resources take longer, and such planning should be done much earlier.

What do people need to know, when do they need to know it, and how can they learn it? What resources and programs are there to help people make retirement plans? In this chapter I will attempt to answer these questions.

NOT IN A VACUUM: THE DEVELOPMENT OF RETIREMENT TRAINING PROGRAMS

Individuals approach work and retirement from work from many directions and often with a great deal of baggage. What they hope to accomplish or believe they can do is structured not only by internal resources and life experiences, but also by what others are doing. "The era in which you were born can affect your view of the world, how you cope with your changes and the realities of the job market," says Betsy Jaffe (1991), who has explored how individuals can reshape their careers as the world in which they work changes in her book *Altered Ambitions*. But the "altered ambitions" of her book are equally those of retirement. *Retirement* is no longer either a concept that is unknown or an experience that is identical for all. The hopes and fears one has for retirement are influenced by the experiences of those who are already retired.

Early Programs

Even into the late 1930s, most older men who were able to work continued to do so—if they could find jobs. It was not until World War II that the prerequisites for supporting retirement as an option fully emerged: a productive industrial economy and adequate public and private pension systems. As the war ended, the idea of being retired was so new that little organized thought had been given to life beyond the assembly line or the back office. The rising economic tide of the 1950s and 1960s lifted the boats of retirees as well as workers. Pension plans, Social Security benefits, and postwar resale values of houses plus attractive prices for new sunbelt housing created opportunities that had been unimaginable to earlier generations. Frugal habits born during the Depression dovetailed nicely with low prices in expanding parts of the country as entrepreneurs strove to attract unexpected new market that retirees represented. Other chapters of this handbook address specific issues involved in the evolution of retirement from an opportunity for a few to a seeming entitlement for many.

Preretirement planning, to the extent that it existed in the early days of retirement, usually involved no more than employers' sitting down with employees on their last day to review pension and medical benefits and refer them to Social Security. Then in 1948, working independently of one another, Clark Tibbitts and Wilma Donahue at the University of Michigan began holding educational programs for older people and Ernest Burgess at the University of Chicago started developing preretirement education programs. In 1956 Woodrow Hunter at the University of Michigan offered the first union-sponsored preretirement education program in the country for the Upholsterer's International Union. The issues discussed had been raised by people who were already retired (Hunter 1968 and 1978). Retirement, it seemed, had not been an unalloyed pleasure for all. It was thought that possibly future retirees could avoid some of the blind alleys and the pitfalls that had been encountered by others if they could antici-pate them. And so the preretirement planning industry was born.

Early programs were directed toward those who were on the verge of actual retirement, which usually took place around age sixty-five. Hunter (1968) reflects this view, saying, ". . . older people are encour-aged to begin early to prepare for retirement. As we shall see, sixty is none too soon to start" (p. 4). While many of the topics covered in early programs sound like those covered in programs of the 1990s, the emphasis was very different. How could a man find ways to feel useful and productive in a society that was unfamiliar with the idea of retiring from work? The planning programs were primarily planned around the concerns of men, and women's issues were considered to be those of a spouse:

> Men eventually reach the age when they have to retire, and women must face their children growing up and establishing their own homes. It is not surprising, therefore, to have older people say they are no longer useful. (Hunter 1968:21)

Financial planning focused on "making do" with a reduced income. Retirement day was too late to begin looking for new sources of income, except possibly through part-time work.

Since those early programs were offered, countless men and women have retired from their jobs—some by choice and some because of the change that has occurred in the workplace during the latter decades of the twentieth century. Now more than one generation has gone through the entire retirement cycle, and the lessons of their experiences have surfaced in present-day retirement planning programs.

Changing the Focus

One of the comments most frequently heard in retirement planning programs is "I should have done this years ago." While of course individuals are free to start planning as early as they choose, most privately sponsored programs began to set lower age limits on attendance than they once had. Once retirement became a stage of life through which many had passed, people in the work force began to see earlier and earlier retirement as an entitlement. They could tolerate boring, unsatisfying, or demanding jobs if age fifty-five might bring retirement. Obviously age sixty or sixty-five would be too late to begin planning for retirement at fifty-five, so many programs began to allow participation at fifty-five or fifty, and some more forward-thinking organizations encouraged even earlier planning.

As the twentieth century draws to a close, the sense of entitlement that has become associated with retirement is being threatened. Many in the work force have become convinced that there is indeed life after work. Mergers, corporate downsizing, and budget cuts in the public, private, and nonprofit sectors have encouraged employees to find satisfaction in other areas of life and to look forward to retirement as a time to develop them more fully. But there are new realities: demographic changes that may require keeping people on the job longer, astronomical increases in health care costs, the probability of very long life spans, and less pension coverage than workers have expected. Once again ambitions are being altered by events. Retirement planning—whether independently by an individual or by a professional with a group—must respond to the changes.

WHAT PATH SHOULD ONE TAKE?

"I'm a widower," a company vice president said. "The money part of retirement is something I've planned out for years. But the idea of not working and being home alone scares me. How do I plan for *that?*" A female worker said, "We always planned on my retiring at fifty-five. But now, with two kids still at home who want to go to college and my mother living with us . . . well, it doesn't look so possible." These concerns are common.

There is no single best type of preretirement planning, just as there is no single best time or way to retire. While a good financial plan seems essential, it may not be the primary concern for someone who has always tracked finances, lived on a budget, saved for major expenditures, and enjoyed a long, successful career at a company with a generous pension plan. But the thought of unstructured time or unused skills can be disquieting to such a person. On the other hand, someone with a history of moving from job to job with marginal success may long for unstructured time but not know how to pay for it. A woman who entered the work force in midlife or later may not be thinking of retirement planning as planning to leave her job, but as a way to organize her future.

Financial planning has long been seen as the most basic topic to address in any retirement program. There are widely varying approaches to this. Because the growing field of preretirement planning attracts individuals from a broad spectrum of backgrounds and levels of knowledge, there are proponents of every approach to financial planning who are both skilled and ethical. There are also those for whom the financial fears of preretirees provide fertile soil for their own ventures. The content of financial planning units, whether in books or seminars, ranges from do-it-yourself estimates of income and expenditures, through introductions to such things as the impact of inflation on fixed income and the basic vocabulary of investment, to specific techniques for money management and financial planning.

An individual in the early or middle years of a career may begin with a self-assessment using some of the books or software packages now available. Seminars on planning can then be helpful in pulling together all the parts. Another approach is to take a financial planning seminar or midlife planning course and follow up independently on questions raised or new information gathered. Examples of these independent planning programs will be discussed later in the chapter.

In addition to financial planning, time and experience have brought increasing attention to a range of life-style issues that influence or are influenced by the decision to retire. While some people move toward the goal of retirement on well-traveled paths, others continue toward this goal along less obvious routes. No matter which route one takes, he same planning approaches, beginning in midcareer, are equally useful in making plans and anticipating change. Then the individual can determine how carefully to explore each path and which resources will be most helpful.

Retirement Planning Topics

Over time retirement planners have developed a generally accepted list of topics that individuals should consider as they begin to establish retirement objectives. The objectives, which should include whether, when, where, and how to retire, should also be open ended and flexible. Individuals whose retirement plans include another person should include that person from the beginning. Many a plan, though carefully worked out and made well ahead of retirement, has foundered when designed as a solitary exercise and presented as a *fait accompli*.

The topics most often included in retirement planning are as follows:

Life-Style Planning
• Attitudes toward work and retirement
• Life-style goals for retirement

Legal Issues
• Wills and estate planning
• Legal services
• Legal rights of the elderly
• Powers of attorney
• Titles, trusts, and property ownership
• Prenuptial agreements

Financial Planning

- Expenses (current and future)
- Sources of income
- Social Security
- Pension benefits
- Personal savings
- Investments
- Inflation
- Survivors' benefits
- Lump-sum benefits
- Insurance (life, health, and long-term care)
- Health care costs

Health and Wellness

- Nutrition
- Exercise
- Mental health
- Stress reduction
- Medication management
- Accident prevention
- Aging
- Sexuality
- Living wills
- Health care proxies
- Health maintenance
- Patient-physician relationships

Roles and Relationships

- Family roles
- Aging parents
- Husbands and wives
- Widowhood
- Retiring alone
- Caregiving
- Support systems
- Death and dying

Housing and Living Arrangements

- Moving or staying in one's home
- Geographical choices
- Housing options
- Owning versus renting
- The finances of retirement housing
- Shared housing

- Remodeling for the long term
- Continuing care facilities

Use of Time
- New careers
- Part-time work
- Volunteering
- Leisure activities
- Adult education
- Travel

CHOOSING A GUIDE

How individuals learn best varies. Howard McClusky spoke of the "teachable moment," the time when the learner is most ready, whether due to immediate self-interest or some other reason (1971). Many guides are available to help travelers on the journey to retirement. Some of the most readily available follow.

For Independent Learning
- Retirement books
- Newsletters
- Software programs
- Videotapes

For Group Learning
- Adult education courses
- College and university courses
- Company-sponsored programs
- Union-sponsored classes

For Group Leaders or Facilitators
- All of the above plus teaching guides and materials designed to support group leaders.

Independent Learning

Retirement Books

Books on retirement have begun to occupy many shelves of the "self-help" sections in bookstores. They range from the How-I-did-it-and-what-you-can-learn-from-me genre to professionally designed workbooks and academic treatises. For the self-starter there are seemingly infinite numbers of planning books with resource books in specialized areas to back them up. Often these books are especially helpful to people in their thirties and forties. They allow readers to selectively read bits and pieces depending on the areas in which they are interested and their level of interest at any given time. dipping in and out. They also raise provocative issues that readers may not have previously considered. And they usually contain forms and self-assessment checklists with recommendations for follow-on reading and action. The following is a representative sampling of some of the books that are readily available.

> *Comfort Zones: Planning Your Future.* Elwood N. Chapman. 2nd
> ed. Los Altos, Calif.: Crisp Publications, Inc., 1990.
>> An informal but comprehensive self-study guide with checklists, examples, forms, and facts. Provides an opportunity for the reader to assess his or her retirement readiness and personal needs.
>
> *Facing Our Future.* Jane M. Deren et al. Washington, D.C.: The National Council on the Aging, Inc., 1985.
>> A pair of books on financial and life planning for midlife women. One is a workbook that can be used as part of a group program or for individual self-assessment. The other is a leader's guide for use if the workbook is used with a group.
>
> *How to Plan for a Secure Retirement.* Barry Dickman, Trudy Lieberman, and the editors of Consumer Reports Books. Yonkers, N.Y.: Consumer Reports Books. 1992.
>> A comprehensive reference source for all ages that particularly focuses on four categories of retirement planning: income, health care, housing, and estate planning.
>
> *Looking Forward: The Complete Medical Guide to Successful Aging.* Isadore Rossman, M.D., Ph.D. New York: E. P. Dutton, 1989.
>
> *Over Fifty: The Resource Book for the Better Half of Your Life.* Tom and Nancy Biracree. New York: Harper Collins Publishers, 1991.
>> A guide to information and resources in all areas of retirement planning. It includes addresses, phone numbers, and the type of information or help to expect or ask for.
>
> *PREP Talk for Women.* The National Center for Women and Retirement Research. Southampton, N.Y.: Long Island University, 1989.
>> A series of handbooks on finances, employment, health, and social and emotional issues for midlife women.
>
> *Retiring Right.* Lawrence J. Kaplan. Garden City Park, N.Y.: Avery Publishing Group, Inc., 1990.

A comprehensive guide to financial planning for retirement, with personalized planning guides and work sheets. The book is clearly written, with glossaries of specialized words and phrases.

Retiring on Your Own Terms: Your Total Guide to Finances, Health, Life Style, and Much, Much More. James W. Ellison. New York: Crown Publishers, Inc., 1989.

A step-by-step guide to anticipating and managing planning needs.

Retirement Preparation. Helen Dennis. Lexington, Mass.: Lexington Books, 1984.

A guide written primarily for retirement planning specialists, but it is also helpful to individuals.

Taking Care: Supporting Older People and Their Families. Nancy R. Hooyman and Wendy Lustbader. New York: The Free Press, 1989.

A guide for those who find themselves facing the task of caring for elderly family members.

The Fifteen Factors of Retirement Success. Richard P. Johnson and Warren Jensen. Dubuque, Iowa: Randall/Hunt Publishing Co., 1989.

A book that identifies and explains factors instrumental to a successful retirement. Accompanied by an assessment instrument entitled the Retirement Success Profile.

The Price Waterhouse Retirement Planning Advisor. New York: Pocket Books, Simon & Schuster, Inc., 1990.

A readable guide with work sheets and practical information to help the reader plan the financial dimension of retirement.

The Second 50 Years: A Reference Manual for Senior Citizens. Walter J. Cheney et al. New York: Paragon House Publishers, 1992.

Information, tools, data, addresses, and ideas covering a wide range of issues of concern to people considering retirement.

The Touche Ross Guide to Financial Planning. John Connell, L. L. Dotson, W. T. Porter, and R. E. Zobel. Englewood Cliffs, N.J.: Prentice-Hall, Inc., 1987.

A guidebook to creating a personal financial plan, with strategies tailored to specific age groups.

Transitions: A Woman's Guide to Successful Retirement. Diana Cort-Van Arsdale and Phyllis Newman. New York: Harper Collins Publishers, 1991.

A how-to book for women contemplating retirement that employs a series of self-evaluation questionnaires for guidance and the experiences of other women as illumination.

You and Your Aging Parent. Barbara Silverstone and Helen Kandel Hyman. 3rd ed. New York: Pantheon, 1989.

A comprehensive and readable book that helps adult children identify and deal with the practical and emotionally loaded issues that arise as parents age.

You Can Afford to Retire! William W. Parrott and John L. Parrott. New York: Simon & Schuster, 1992.

A guide that walks the reader through the key financial issues of planning a secure retirement and answers the most commonly asked questions about financial planning.

Software Programs

As home computers have become common, software programs have been developed to allow individuals to make projections of their own retirement plans under a variety of circumstances. Most focus on financial planning issues, although some allow for the exploration of more subjective areas as well. Some of the best are listed below.

Discover for Retirement Planning. American College Testing Service, P.O. Box 168, Iowa City, IA 52243.

Uses exercises for personalized assessment in four areas of retirement planning: life-style, financial planning, physical well-being, and living arrangements.

FRED: The Friendly Retirement Education Database. Employee Benefit Systems, Inc., Dr. Timothy Prynne, P.O. Box 11485, Columbia, SC 29211.

Interactive software that provides a personal record in the areas of financial affairs, health, life-style, occupation, legal affairs, and records.

MERIT for Managing the Future. Decker & Associates, 3100 South Gessner, P.O. Box 771966, Houston, TX 77215.

Nolo's Personal RecordKeeper. Nolo Press, 950 Parker Street, Berkeley, CA 94710.

Helps the user organize and store important financial, legal, and personal information in more than two hundred categories.

RELOCATION Options. Martlet, Inc., P.O. Box 37, Herndon, VA 22070.

Conducts a dialog with the user to determine his or her preferences in the following areas: climate and environment, housing cost, cost of living, health concerns, senior services, recreation, and nearness to relatives and friends.

Survivors' Registry. Chuck Tellalian, P.O. Box 265, 9582 Hamilton Avenue, Huntington Beach, CA 92646.

Enables a potential retiree to build personalized retirement plan that takes into consideration both the financial and lifestyle aspects of retirement.

WillMaker. Nolo Press and Legisoft, Inc., Nolo Press, 950 Parker Street, Berkeley, CA 94710.

Uses a question-and-answer format to lead the reader through the steps of preparing a customized will that is legally valid in all states except Louisiana. Comes with a two hundred-page manual.

Newsletters

Newsletters and specific-issue newspapers offer up-to-date information on topics that directly affect aspects of retirement planning and retirement living. Some are ordered by subscription, and others are a benefit of membership in an organization. They allow individuals who have participated in formal group programs or who have used independent planning materials to review their plans regularly in light of new knowledge or changes in benefits, health issues, and tax policies. Some of the most useful are listed below.

AARP Bulletin. AARP Membership Services, P. O. Box 1600, Long Beach, CA 90801–1600.

A monthly paper that is sent as a benefit of membership in the American Association of Retired Persons, eligibility for which is set at age fifty.

Health After Fifty. The Johns Hopkins Medical Institutions, 55 North Broadway, Suite 1100, Baltimore, MD 21205.

A monthly newsletter that discusses health issues of particular interest to those over fifty.

Managing Your Finances: For People over Fifty. Jonathan Pond, Prentice-Hall, Englewood Cliffs, NJ 07632.

A monthly newsletter.

RetirementWise. Box IATSE, 55 Pringdal Avenue, White Plains, NY 10604–2309.

A monthly newsletter that provides information, data, suggestions, and resources for those who are retired or about to retire.

The OWL Observer. Older Women's League, 730 Eleventh Street NW, Suite 300, Washington DC 20001–4512.

A Bimonthly paper that is sent as a benefit of membership in the league. It addresses issues of concern to women in midlife and later.

Videotapes

New technology has encouraged the development of a variety of video-based programs for both individual and classroom use. The content and approach of video planning programs have evolved since the time of the "talking heads" with filmed scenarios occasionally inserted to stimulate discussion. Now video programs may include taped facilitator-led sessions with individual exercises to be done simultaneously with taped participants. The newest wrinkle has been interactive video, which requires and supports individual involvement rather than passive watching and listening. Technology does not come without cost, however, and content can become outdated rapidly unless it is quite generic. Two organizations that offer videotapes are as follows:

Menninger Management Institute, P.O. Box 829, Topeka, KS 66601–9908.
Offers *Planning for Creative Retirement: Exploring Psychological Considerations,* a videotape package with a facilitator guide and participant workbooks.
Financial Awareness Institute, 900 Jorie Boulevard, Suite 110, Oak Brook, IL 60521.
Offers participant books and a video on financial issues.

Group Learning Opportunities

"I thought this would be a boring class," said a participant in a retirement planning class. "But when I got here I realized that this is my *life* we're talking about. And how can I think that's boring?" In ever-increasing numbers retirement planning specialists are offering classes, lectures, seminars, and discussion groups preparing, informing, guiding, and supporting people in group settings. There can be real advantages to exploring retirement-related issues in a group. In a well-facilitated group individuals can share concerns and experiences, become comfortable with the universality of many issues, and have questions answered that they might not have thought of alone.

Retirement planning seminars are offered in a variety of settings under many auspices, with instructors or facilitators whose skills and knowledge range from limited to comprehensive. They can take the form of one-hour overviews of investment options or twenty or more hours of multidisciplinary classwork spread over a period of several weeks—or anything in between. They are offered by banks and investment companies in their facilities, by planners in public seminars, by community colleges and universities as part of their service commitment to the larger community, and by companies and unions for their own employees.

A retirement period that may encompass thirty or more years can require a different kind of planning as well as a different approach to work than that taken in previous decades. Some organizations have developed materials specifically for those who are planning for retirement in midlife. The National Council on the Aging designed the *Fortysomething: Life Planning Program* after many requests for a program that would permit a longer planning period than the organization's standard program, which was aimed at the age group around fifty-five. The National Center for Women and Retirement Research was established at Long Island University to help women begin to plan in midlife, because some research has suggested that women are less likely than men to do significant retirement planning (Block 1984).

Which type of program will be most appropriate is a subjective judgment at best. Certainly some of the questions an individual should ask are as follows:

- What kind of planning help is available to me through my place of employment?
- How much planning have I done already?
- When do I plan or hope to retire?
- What do I mean by *retirement?*
- What will the program cost?
- Will I be expected to buy something in return for participation?
- Is this program directed toward someone at my level of knowledge and sophistication?
- Does this program assume assets, language skills, or access to information that I lack?
- Will I be required to disclose private information?
- How much time will the program require of me, and can I devote that much time to it?

Adult Education and Community College Programs

In many communities adult education programs offered through the public schools or community college programs offer preretirement classes as part of their service commitment to the community. These classes may be offered as part of the regular curriculum, as special events, or in cooperation with other community agencies. The resources committed to such programs and the priority given to them by the administration will affect their content and quality, but the best of these programs are among the most comprehensive and student-oriented to be found. Such classes offer the advantages of learning in a group to individuals whose workplaces do not sponsor formal programs, to those who need a refresher or a place to start, and sometimes to people who are simply looking for a way to meet others in similar situations.

Typically such courses are taught on weekends or in the evening, sometimes over a period of weeks. They are usually coordinated by a retirement planning specialist who facilitates presentations by experts in a number of topic areas, such as financial planning, leisure activities, health care, and community resources. Because courses offered to the community at large draw diverse participants, certain job-specific topics, such as employee health and pension benefits, cannot be addressed except in general terms. However, such courses suggest ways of gathering more specific information on these topics and provide a framework for incorporating it into an individualized plan.

College and University Programs

Although many colleges and universities are extending a warm welcome for retirees who are choosing to go back to school, not all offer formal retirement preparation courses. Where such programs are available, they can usually be found in the Continuing Education department or its equivalent. In some schools these life planning, midlife planning, or retirement planning programs are described in the brochure or bulletin that announces all courses. In other places they may be announced in the newspaper or by means of posters and flyers.

At New York University in New York City, for example, courses are offered through the School of Continuing Education in the Center for Career and Life Planning. Classes described in the center's bulletin for this audience include the following:

• How to "Retire"
• Over 55? What's Next?
• Planning Second Careers
• Planning Today for Tomorrow

- Personal Financial Planning
- Planning for Elder Care
- Planning Retirement

Sponsored Programs

All the advantages of group learning apply to preretirement planning programs sponsored by one's workplace or union. In addition, the participants share a common experience in the workplace. These programs are presented by corporations, labor unions, nonprofit organizations, church organizations, public utilities, and government institutions. Some of these organizations provide such programs only for their employees/members and their spouses or partners. But some also occasionally offer programs that are open to the public.

In 1986 the American Society of Personnel Administration and the International Society of Preretirement Planners conducted a National Survey of Retirement Preparation Policies and Practices. This survey found that only about 40 percent of companies reported that they were familiar with or had offered formal retirement preparation programs (Morrison and Jedrziewski 1988). The primary areas addressed by such programs are still company pension plans, Social Security and Medicare, and company health plans. Most programs sponsored by the workplace have a minimum age for participation, usually age fifty or fifty-five. Morrison and Jedrziewski point out that such programs still do not pay significant attention to many issues of major concern, such as postretirement employment, health care, and long-term care. This fact reinforces the importance of the kinds of independent-study materials and community-based group programs described earlier.

Guides and Materials for Group Leaders or Facilitators

Most people who are asked to develop or lead preretirement planning programs, whether inside companies or as consultants, look to outside sources for many of their materials. What follows is a list of organizations and their offerings, including guides and materials designed for all kinds of programs and all levels of leader/facilitator sophistication. Some of these offerings are simple outlines and checklists; some are guides with work sheets, handouts, and slide or video supplements; and some are scripted session-by-session courses with leader training required before the program can be used. For more information, write to the organizations listed.

American Association of Retired Persons, 601 E Street NW, Washington, DC 20049.
> Leader training materials, participant workbooks, and supplemental materials.

Action for Older Persons, Inc., 30 West State Street, Press Building, Room 327-N, Binghamton, NY 13901.
> Participant workbooks. Coordinated leader training is offered through Life-Design Associates, 490 Stillwater Road, Greene, NY 13778

Crisp Publications, Inc., 95 First Street, Los Altos, CA 94022.
> Leader guides, participant books, and videos.

DAUCOR Resource Management, P.O. Box 1587, Lakegrove, OR 97034.
> Leader guides, participant books, and supplemental slides and audiotapes.

50 Plus, 850 Third Avenue, New York, NY 10022
> Leader training materials, booklets, participant books, and supplemental materials.

Manpower Education Institute, 715 Ladd Road, New York, NY 10471.
> Participant books.

National Council on the Aging, Inc., 409 Third Street SW, Washington, DC 20024.
> Leader training materials, participant workbooks, leader guides, and supplemental slides and audiotapes.

University Research Associates, 810 Parkway, #112, 44 Cook Street, Denver, CO 80206.
> Participant workbooks, supplemental materials.

WHO'S MISSING?

The discussions and descriptions of preretirement planning materials and programs in this chapter reflect a bias that is inherent in the planning process, which studies have supported. People who are better educated spend more time on retirement planning than do people who have less education, and members of minority groups spend less time planning than those in the white majority (Ferraro 1990).

Torres-Gil (1984) has written of the minority populations who are underrepresented in retirement planning programs. He has identified factors contributing to this underrepresentation, from culture and language to job level and income, and has suggested methods for reaching these audiences. Certainly the changing demographics of the work force suggest that all forms of retirement planning programs need to be reevaluated to make them more accessible.

CONCLUSION

Getting ready for retirement has long required more than picking up one's last paycheck, saying good-bye to co-workers, and shutting the plant or office door on the way out. There are many paths to retirement, and the wise traveler will select a destination, map out a route, and make some plans before setting out. Unlike many vacation trips, retirement does not lend itself to the "travel now, pay later" philosophy. What retirement planning programs offer, whether one undertakes them independently or as part of a group, is a structure for looking ahead.

Successful planning requires that one take personal responsibility for the trip, making decisions about when it will begin, what it will include, how much it will cost, and how it will be paid for. Like the Cheshire Cat, preretirement planning programs will not say, "This is where you should go," but only, "It depends a good deal on where you want to get to." Retirement planning programs can help individuals find the best paths to their personal destinations only if these programs are accessible. In some ways such programs have changed significantly over the past thirty-five years, but they have not changed enough to make them readily available to all who could use them. If the decision to retire is a complex one, more attention should be paid to these sources of help and direction.

REFERENCES

Block, Marilyn R. 1984. "Retirement Preparation Needs of Women." In H. Dennis, ed., *Retirement Preparation.* Lexington, Mass.: Lexington Books.

Carroll, Lewis. 1941. *Alice's Adventures in Wonderland.* New York: The Heritage Press.

Dennis, Helen. 1984. *Retirement Preparation.* Lexington, Mass.: Lexington Books.

Ekerdt, D. J. 1989. "Retirement Preparation." *Annual Review of Gerontology and Geriatrics,* 9:321–356.

Ferraro, K. F. 1990. "Cohort Analysis of Retirement Preparation, 1974–1981. *Journal of Gerontology: Social Science,* 45(1):S21–S31.

Goelzer, Patricia. 1989. "The Example of Retirement Planning at Weyerhaeuser." *Generations,* XIII (3):35–65.

Hunter, Woodrow W. 1968. *Preparation for Retirement.* Ann Arbor, Mich.: Institute of Gerontology, The University of Michigan-Wayne State University.

Hunter, Woodrow W. 1978. *Education for Retirement: A Bibliography.* Ann Arbor, Mich.: Institute of Gerontology, The University of Michigan-Wayne State University.

Hunter, Woodrow H. 1980. *Pre-retirement Education Leader's Manual*. Ann Arbor, Mich.: Institute of Gerontology, The University of Michigan-Wayne State University.

Jaffe, Betsy. 1991. *Altered Ambitions*. New York: Donald I. Fine, Inc.

McClusky, Howard Y. 1971. *Background and Issues: Education*. Prepared for the 1971 White House Conference on Aging. Washington, D.C.: White House Conference on Aging.

Morrison, Malcolm H., and M. K. Jedrziewski. 1988. "Retirement Planning: Everybody Benefits." *Personnel Administrator*, January.

Riker, H. C., and J. E. Myers. 1990. *Retirement Counseling: A Practical Guide for Action*. New York: Hemisphere Publishing Corporation.

Torres-Gil, Fernando. 1984. "Preretirement Issues that Affect Minorities." In H. Dennis, ed., *Retirement Preparation*. Lexington, Mass.: Lexington Books.

Turnquist, Philip H., W. B. Newsom, and D. S. Cochran. 1988. "More Than a Gold Watch." *Personnel Administrator*, January.

III

THE ECONOMIC CONDITIONS OF RETIREMENT

●

6

Social Security and Social Insurance Benefits: What to Expect and How to Obtain Them

●

NANCY J. ALTMAN

One hundred thirty-four nations have programs that provide old age and survivors' benefits. The programs are of three general types: universal programs, means-tested programs, and programs of social insurance (HHS 1989). The Old Age, Survivors, and Disability Insurance program in the United States, generally referred to as Social Security, is a form of social insurance. (The term *Social Security* is often used to include the Medicare program as well. In this chapter, however, it will be limited to the programs that provide cash benefits.)

Social Security, like similar programs around the world, is referred to as insurance because it contains elements of private insurance. Like private insurance, Social Security involves a pooling of risk. It insures against the contingency of lost earnings as the result of retirement, disability, or death. Also like private insurance, it generally provides benefits only to those who qualify by contributing to the system or by being dependents of contributors. Benefits are payable as the consequence of insured status, not as a result of financial need. The costs of the program are borne, for the most part, by employers, employees, and people who are self-employed.

Social Security and programs like it are referred to not simply as insurance, but rather as social insurance, because they contain features not generally found in private insurance. The protection they provide often reflects, in part, social concerns. For example, Social

Security offers extra protection to families with large numbers of dependents. Moreover, participation in Social Security, like most other programs of social insurance, is mandatory and virtually universal (Ball 1978; Myers 1985).

KINDS OF BENEFITS

Social Security provides cash benefits in the event of retirement, disability, or death. Full, unreduced, monthly retirement benefits are available starting at normal retirement age, which is currently age sixty-five. Actuarially increased delayed-retirement benefits, payable monthly, are available for those who retire after normal retirement age.

For workers under normal retirement age, actuarially reduced early-retirement benefits, also payable monthly, are available beginning at age sixty-two. In addition, monthly disability benefits are available after a five-month waiting period (Myers 1985; W&M 1991).

It should be noted that the normal retirement age is scheduled to be increased to age sixty-seven in the year 2027. The increase will occur gradually. Those born before 1938 will be unaffected. For those born in 1938, the normal retirement age will be age sixty-five and two months. The retirement age will increase by two months every year for five years, affecting those born from 1939 through 1942. In accordance with this schedule, the retirement age will increase to age sixty-six for those born in 1943.

The normal retirement age will remain age sixty-six for twelve years, applying to those born from 1943 through 1954. The age will then again slowly increase, two months every year, until the normal retirement age becomes sixty-seven for those born in 1960 or later.

The age at which Social Security retirement benefits are available, age sixty-two, is not scheduled to change despite the planned increase in the normal retirement age. The reduction in the benefit paid, however, will be greater for those with older normal retirement ages as a result of retiring early (Myers 1985; W&M 1991).

In addition to benefits for workers, Social Security provides auxiliary monthly benefits to family members of workers. These benefits include monthly payments to spouses, divorced spouses, and children of retired and disabled workers and to widows, widowers, children, and dependent parents of deceased workers (Ball 1978; Bernstein and Bernstein 1988; Kingson 1987). Social Security also provides a lump-sum death benefit of $255. On the death of a worker, the payment is made to a surviving spouse who was living with the deceased worker at the time of death or who qualifies for monthly survivor' benefits. If there is no eligible widow or widower, the payment is made to any children who are eligible for monthly benefits on the basis of the deceased worker's earnings record (Myers 1985).

ELIGIBILITY FOR BENEFITS

The Insured Status Requirement

In order for workers and their families to qualify for Social Security benefits, workers must be insured under the program. Workers become insured by obtaining the requisite quarters of coverage. Quarters of coverage are earned through employment in service that is covered under Social Security (Myers 1985).

Definition of *Covered Service* and *Covered Earnings*

Social Security is almost universal in its coverage. Nevertheless, certain categories of employment remain uncovered. For example, employees of state and local governments who are covered by their own retirement plans are covered under Social Security only if they and the governmental units for which they work so elect. Similarly, most civilian employees of the federal government who were hired before 1984 are not covered by Social Security (W&M 1991).

Moreover, some categories of employment have been covered under Social Security only relatively recently. Employees of nonprofit organizations, for example, have been covered under Social Security on a mandatory basis only since 1984 (Myers 1985).

All those covered under Social Security are required to contribute a percentage of their earnings up to a specified ceiling, known as the *maximum taxable earnings base*. Earnings so assessed are referred to as covered earnings. In 1993 employees are assessed 6.2 percent of their wages up to a maximum annual wage of $57,600. An additional 1.45 percent of wages up to a maximum annual wage of $135,000 is assessed for the hospital insurance portion of Medicare (Myers 1993).

Employers are required to pay a matching amount for their employees. The self-employed are assessed at a tax rate equal to the rate assessed against the employer and the employee in combination, but they may deduct half of the tax from their income for income tax purposes (Myers 1985).

Definition of *Quarter of Coverage*

Prior to 1978 a quarter of coverage was earned, in most cases, for every calendar quarter in which a worker was paid $50 or more in covered wages. Since 1978 quarters of coverage have been earned on an annual basis. That is, a worker earns a quarter of coverage, up to a maximum of four in any one year, if he or she earns the requisite amount of wages in covered employment, without regard to when over the course of the year the wages were actually earned (Myers 1985; HHS 1990).

In 1993 the amount necessary to earn a quarter of coverage is $590. A worker who earns covered wages of that amount, irrespective of when they are earned in 1993, is credited with a quarter of coverage; a worker who earns covered wages of at least $2360 any time in 1993 will be credited with the maximum of four quarters of coverage for the year (Myers 1993). The dollar amount is adjusted annually to reflect increases in average wages nationwide.

Determination of Insured Status

There are three types of insured status: fully insured, disability insured, and currently insured. The fully insured status provides the most complete protection. It provides eligibility for all types of old age and survivor' benefits.

If a worker is fully insured, disability insured status entitles the worker to disability benefits. Unlike other disabled individuals, people who are blind need only be fully insured to receive disability benefits. They are exempted from the requirement of being disability insured (Myers 1985).

Currently insured status provides the least comprehensive coverage. It simply entitles the families of deceased workers who are currently insured at the time of death, but not fully insured, to receive certain survivor' benefits. The benefits available are the children's survivor' benefits and their parents' survivor' benefits, described below. These families are also eligible for the lump-sum death benefit, described above.

Workers who have forty quarters of coverage are fully insured. In addition, workers are fully insured if they have a quarter of coverage, earned at any time, for every four quarters of coverage after 1950 (or the year in which they reach age 21, if later), and before the year in which they reach age sixty-two, die, or become disabled, whichever comes first. In order to be fully insured, a worker must have a minimum of six quarters of coverage.

Workers are disability insured if they have twenty quarters of coverage in the forty quarters immediately preceding the quarter in which the disability occurs. As an alternative, workers who are disabled before age twenty-four are disability insured if they have six quarters of coverage in the last twelve quarters before becoming disabled. Similarly, those who become disabled from age twenty-four through age thirty are disability insured if they have quarters of coverage that equal at least half the number of calendar quarters between when they reached age twenty-one and when they became disabled.

Workers are currently insured if they have six quarters of coverage during the thirteen calendar quarters ending with the quarter in which they die, become disabled, or retire (Myers 1985; W&M 1991).

Categorical Eligibility Requirements

Primary Benefits

In addition to satisfying the relevant insured status requirement, workers and their dependents must meet the categorical requirements in order to be eligible to receive Social Security benefits. Workers may receive monthly retirement benefits beginning as early as age sixty-two as long as they satisfy the retirement test, described below. Workers are eligible for monthly disability benefits at any age if they have a condition that meets the statutory definition of disability. *Disability* is defined, generally, as the inability to engage in any substantial gainful activity as a consequence of a physical or mental impairment. The impairment must be medically determinable and be expected to last for at least one year—or, if not, to result in death.

The definition of *disability* centers on the concept of substantial gainful activity. Workers who earn $500 or more a month are deemed to be engaged in substantial gainful activity and therefore are not considered disabled. A person who is not earning $500 or more is automatically considered disabled if his or her condition is specified as a severe impairment on a list maintained by the government. If the impairment is not on the list, a worker is considered disabled only if the impairment is so severe that it prevents the worker from engaging in any substantial gainful activity, considering the age, education, and work experience of the individual (Myers 1985; W&M 1991).

What qualifies as substantial gainful activity is determined using different criteria for people who are blind. Blind people may earn up to one-twelfth of the annual earnings limitation for those aged sixty-five through sixty-nine (see the section below on continued earned income), or $880 a month in 1993, before their work is deemed substantial. They are considered blind if their vision cannot be corrected to better than 20/200 in their better eye or if their visual field is twenty degrees or less even with a corrective lens (Myers 1993).

Auxiliary Benefits

If the retired or disabled worker has a spouse who is at least age sixty-two, the spouse is entitled to a spouse's benefit. A widow's or widower's benefit is available to a deceased worker's spouse who has reached age sixty or, if the widow or widower is disabled, age fifty. In addition, a spouse of any age is entitled to a benefit if he or she is caring for the retired, disabled, or deceased worker's child and the child (1) has not yet reached age sixteen or (2) is disabled and the disability occurred before the child reached age twenty-two.

Moreover, a divorced spouse is entitled to these same benefits if he or she was married to the retired, disabled, or deceased worker for at least ten years. Generally the divorced spouse must be unmarried to qualify. The one major exception is in the case of a widow's or widower's benefit, which is available as long as the remarriage occurred when the divorced spouse was at least age sixty.

Children's benefits are payable monthly to each unmarried child of a retired, disabled, or deceased worker if the child is (1) under age eighteen, (2) a full-time elementary or secondary student under age nineteen, or (3) a dependent disabled child of any age if the disability began before the child reached age twenty-two. These benefits are available to adopted children and stepchildren in addition to biological children.

Other categories of individuals who are entitled to monthly benefits are dependent parents, aged sixty-two or older, of deceased workers and, in very limited circumstances, dependent grandchildren. A grandchild can receive benefits on the basis of his or her grandparent's earnings record if the grandchild's parents are disabled or deceased and the grandchild has been living with and supported by the grandparent for at least a year. In addition, people born prior to January 2, 1900 are entitled to monthly benefits in some circumstances, even though they have not met the requirements for fully insured status, described above (Myers 1985).

AMOUNTS OF BENEFITS

Benefits payable to workers and their dependents are generally related to earnings. The basic benefit—the primary insurance amount or PIA—is calculated on the basis of a worker's average indexed earnings over his or her career. The auxiliary benefits payable to the worker's dependents are percentages of the primary insurance amount.

Primary Benefits

Because the Social Security Act has been amended many times over its history, a number of different methods of calculating amounts of benefits have been developed (HHS 1990). This section will describe the basic benefit computation method that will prevail over the long run.

As just stated, the primary insurance amount is based on career average earnings. If unindexed, however, career average earnings would be quite low since the average would contain nominal earnings from many years prior to the calculation.

To overcome this problem, Social Security could simply look at final earnings, as most private pension plans do. Final pay plans, though, can generate unfair results with respect to workers who have unusually high or low earnings immediately prior to retirement, disability, or death. Consequently, in order to achieve a result that approximates a final pay plan but without its problems, Social Security takes into account earnings received over a worker's career but indexes them to bring the nominal amounts into line with today's higher earnings levels.

Determination of Average Indexed Monthly Earnings

The earnings used in calculating levels of benefits are covered earnings—those on which Social Security taxes have been paid. Covered earnings for each year after 1950 (earnings prior to 1951 are calculated using a different method) are indexed up to two years before a worker reaches age sixty-two or is disabled or dies. For example, if a worker reached age sixty-two in 1992, his or her earnings for the years before 1990 are indexed. For the second year before the worker reaches age sixty-two—1991—and for all subsequent years, the actual unindexed earnings are used.

Earnings could have simply been indexed to take into account the effects of inflation. Instead, Social Security indexes earnings to reflect the increase in wages since the year in which they were earned. Technically, the result is achieved by multiplying the actual amount of the earnings by the ratio of (1) nationwide average annual earnings in the second year before a worker reaches age sixty-two or is disabled or dies to (2) nationwide average annual earnings in the year in which those earnings were actually earned.

For example, a worker who retired in 1992 at age sixty-five, and consequently turned age sixty-two in 1989, would have his or her earnings up to 1987 indexed. If that person had earned $6,000 in 1970, the $6,000 would be adjusted by multiplying it by the nationwide average annual earnings in 1987, or $18,426.51, divided by the nationwide average annual earnings in 1970, or $6,186.24. The result of that calculation, $17,871.77 would be considered the worker's earnings in 1970 for the purpose of calculating that worker's primary insurance amount, or basic benefit, under Social Security (Myers 1993).

Once earnings are indexed, a career average must be obtained. First, the number of years included in the average must be calculated. That number is the number of years between 1950 or the year in which the worker reached age twenty-one, whichever is later, and the year in which the worker reached age sixty-two, became disabled, or died, minus a certain number of drop-out years. With respect to retirement and survivors' benefits, the number of drop-out years is five. In the case of disability, the number of drop-out years depends on the year of onset of the disability. The maximum number is five for disabilities occurring after age forty-six.

For the purpose of calculating retirement benefits for those who reached age sixty-two in 1991 or thereafter, the number of years used in the calculation will generally be thirty-five. Those people will have turned twenty-one in or after 1950. The number of years after the year in which they reach twenty-one and before they reach sixty-two is forty. The number thirty-five is achieved by subtracting the five drop-out years. For those who turned twenty-one before 1950 or have become disabled or died before age sixty-two, the number of years used in the calculation is fewer than thirty-five.

Once the number of years is determined, the indexed earnings for that number of years are averaged. The highest earnings are used, which can be earnings from any year, including those before the worked reached age twenty-two and after he or she reached age sixty-one.

If a worker does not have sufficient years of earnings to total the number of years to be used in the calculation of the average, zeroes are used. The use of zeroes in the average causes workers with intermittent work records to have lower averages, and consequently higher proportionate benefits, as a result of the progressive benefits formula, described below than if the years of zero earnings were simply disregarded.

The resulting average is called the average indexed monthly earnings or AIME. (In doing this calculation, the result must be divided by twelve, as well as by the number of years, to obtain a monthly rather than a yearly average.) The AIME is necessary to determine the worker's basic benefit amount.

Determination of the Primary Insurance Amount

The basic benefit amount is obtained by inserting a worker's AIME into the appropriate benefits formula. The formula applicable to workers who reached age sixty-two, died, or became disabled (whichever occurred first) in 1992 is as follows:

90 percent of the first $387 of AIME,
32 percent of the next $1,946 of AIME, and
15 percent of AIME over $2,333 (Myers 1993).

The result is the worker's primary insurance amount or PIA.

The percentages in the benefit formula—90 percent, 32 percent, and 15 percent—remain unchanged from year to year. Only the dollar figures change. They are indexed annually to reflect the change in nationwide average wages. For 1993 the dollar figures are $401, $2019, and $2420, respectively (Myers 1993).

The benefit formula is progressive, much the way that the federal income tax is. The formula brackets earnings and replaces a larger percentage of earnings with respect to the lower brackets, or the first dollars earned, than with respect to the higher brackets, or the last dollars earned at higher earnings levels.

Workers who have earned higher salaries over their careers will receive benefits that are greater in absolute terms, but represent a smaller proportion of prior earnings than the benefits received by workers earning lower wages. It should be noted that low career averages can result not only from careers of low-paid jobs, but also from breaks in employment caused by unemployment, illness, accident, or other similar circumstances.

The benefit formula is progressive to assist those who have low career earnings as a result of breaks in employment or low-paying jobs. Since not all employment has been covered under Social Security, however, higher earners who have worked much of their careers in employment not covered under Social Security will inadvertently appear to be low earners for Social Security purposes.

To correct this problem, the Social Security benefit formula, described above is modified for workers who have pensions from noncovered employment. For workers who have fewer than thirty years of

Social Security coverage, the 90 percent factor in the Social Security benefit formula is reduced. The reduction depends on the number of years of covered service. For those with twenty or fewer years of Social Security coverage, the percentage used in the formula for the lowest band of earnings is 40 percent rather than 90 percent. In no event, though, is the Social Security benefit reduced to less than half the amount of the noncovered pension. It should be noted that this so-called windfall benefit provision, which was enacted in 1983, has been phased in over a five-year period and exempts a few categories of workers altogether (Myers 1985; W&M 1991).

The indexing of the dollar amounts in the Social Security benefit formula to changes in nationwide wage levels results in initial benefits that change over time at the same rate as average wages. Consequently, the indexing ensures that workers retiring in different years but with similar earnings records will have approximately the same percentage of earnings replaced by Social Security.

That is, low-income, steady workers, will receive monthly benefits that equal approximately 55 percent of their final wages whether they retire at age sixty-two this year or ten years from now; average-income workers will receive monthly benefits that equal approximately 42 percent of their final wages; and high-income workers—those earning at the maximum taxable wage base—will receive monthly benefits that equal approximately 25 percent of their final wages (Myers 1985). (It should be noted that these percentages vary slightly as a consequence of legislated changes in the normal retirement age and in the maximum taxable earnings base.)

A so-called special-minimum PIA is available as an alternative to the regularly calculated PIA for the benefit of workers who have worked many years at very low wages. The special-minimum PIA is based on the number of years worked rather than on levels of earnings. It is calculated by multiplying years of coverage in excess of ten, but not in excess of thirty (i.e., up to a maximum of twenty), by a flat dollar amount (Myers 1985; W&M 1991). (The definition of *year of coverage*) has been changed legislatively several times.)

The flat dollar amount is indexed and, as a result, changes annually. For the period from December 1992 through November 1993, the amount is $24.62. Therefore, the maximum size of the special-minimum PIA for that period is $492.50 (i.e., approximately $24.62 × 20).

Unless the special-minimum PIA is larger, a worker who retires and begins to draw benefits at age sixty-five or who is disabled receives the primary insurance amount as his or her initial benefit, adjusted for cost-of-living increases prior to its receipt. That is, a worker retiring at age sixty-five receives a PIA based on the benefit formula that was in effect when he or she reached age sixty-two three years prior. Cost-of-living adjustments that occur in those three years are applied to the PIA in calculating the worker's initial benefit.

Auxiliary Benefits

Generally, dependents receive a specified percentage of the worker's PIA. For example, a spouse who receives a spousal benefit starting at normal retirement age and an eligible child of a disabled or retired worker both receive benefits equal to 50 percent of the PIA. Children of deceased workers receive a benefit equal to 75 percent of the PIA. Widows and widowers claiming benefits at normal retirement age generally receive benefits equal to 100 percent of the PIA.

Certain limitations apply to the amounts just described. No one is eligible to receive more than the full amount of the largest benefit for which he or she is eligible. If, for example, a person qualifies for a benefit as a worker and also as a spouse, the person in effect receives the larger of the two benefits (although technically the person receives his or her own PIA, plus the excess if any, of the second benefit). A maximum family benefit, which is derived from an indexed formula, limits the amount one family can receive on the basis of one worker's earnings record. The limit is between 150 percent and 188 percent of the PIA. In addition, benefits payable to spouses and widows or widowers are generally reduced if that person is receiving a pension as a result of work in a government job that is not covered by Social Security.

ADJUSTMENTS TO AND WITHHOLDING OF BENEFITS

Early or Delayed Retirement

The benefits just described assume that payments to retirees commence at normal retirement age. Retired workers who claim benefits before normal retirement age receive a permanent reduction in the PIA. The reduction is approximately actuarially accurate to take into account the longer period over which benefits are expected to be paid. The benefit is reduced 5/9 percent per month for each of the first thirty-six months prior to the normal retirement age in which benefits are paid plus 5/12 percent per month for any additional months. For example, an individual whose normal retirement age for Social

Security is sixty-five would receive a permanent 20 percent reduction if benefits were to begin at age sixty-two. An individual whose normal retirement age is sixty-six would receive a permanent 25 percent reduction at age sixty-two.

Spouses' and widows' (or widowers') benefits are also reduced if they are claimed early. The rate of reduction differs slightly for different benefits, but the concept is the same.

For workers who choose to delay claiming benefits until after normal retirement age or who have benefits withheld as the result of the application of the retirement test, described below, their benefits are increased as a consequence of the delayed retirement credit. Workers who reached age sixty-five from 1981 through 1989 were entitled to an increase in the primary insurance amount of ¼ percent for every month beyond age sixty-five in which benefits were not received, up to a total of 3 percent for each year's delay.

Beginning for those who reached normal retirement age in 1990, the percentage adjustment is gradually being increased to bring it closer to the actuarially correct amount. The credit is increasing ½ percent year every other year, and the increase will continue until it reaches 8 percent for those who reach normal retirement age in the year 2009 (W&M 1991). (It should be noted that, starting in the year 2003, the age of normal retirement under Social Security will gradually increase, as described above, delaying the age at which the delayed retirement credit begins to apply.) The delayed retirement credit does not apply to the special-minimum benefit or to the various auxiliary benefits other than those for widows and widowers (Myers 1985).

Continued Earned Income

Workers who choose to continue to work after age sixty-two may nevertheless apply for Social Security benefits. Depending on the level of earnings, however, some or all of the benefits may be withheld. The provision for withholding benefits as the result of earnings—a provision known as the *retirement test* or the *earnings limitation*—has been controversial and misunderstood.

When the Social Security Act was enacted in 1935, Social Security was intended to be a retirement program. Consistent with that concept, the initial legislation required total cessation from "regular employment." Any earnings, no matter how small the amount, would result in the payment of no Social Security benefits whatsoever. This outcome was considered harsh. Consequently, in 1939 the program was modified to permit earnings of up to $15 a month without cessation of benefits (HHS 1990).

The retirement test or earnings limitation remains in the law but has been liberalized many times. Currently a beneficiary who is age seventy or older may earn any amount and still receive full Social Security benefits. Beneficiaries aged sixty-five through sixty-nine are entitled, in 1993, to earn $10,560 and still receive full Social Security benefits. Earnings above that exempt amount result in a reduction of $1 in Social Security benefits for every $3 of earnings. Beneficiaries under age sixty-five are entitled to earn $7,680 in 1993 without any withholding of benefits (Myers 1993). Earnings above that exempt amount result in a reduction of $1 in Social Security benefits for every $2 of earnings. The exempt amounts are indexed annually to reflect the increase in average nationwide wages.

To permit an individual to cease work in the middle of a year and begin to receive benefits at that time, a monthly test is applied, as an alternative to the annual test, for the initial year of the individual's receipt of benefits. The monthly test permits the payment of benefits for any month in which a beneficiary does not receive wages in an amount that exceeds 1/12 of the annual exempt amount and does not render substantial services in self-employment.

It should be noted that, for months in which benefits are withheld, higher benefits are paid later either through a recomputation at normal retirement age or through the operation of the delayed retirement credit, as described above. Moreover, a worker who has relatively high earnings after his or her AIME has been calculated will have his or her benefit recalculated using those higher earnings to replace lower earnings in earlier years.

Inflation

Benefits are adjusted every December to keep pace with price inflation. Because Social Security benefits are generally paid on the third day of the month following the month for which they accrue, the inflation adjustment is first reflected in the January check.

WHEN BENEFITS ARE TAXED

Up to half the Social Security benefits a taxpayer receives in a year may be subject to federal income tax. The need to include these benefits in taxable income applies only to people with higher incomes. The benefits are subject to tax if an individual's adjusted gross income and tax-free interest income, together with half the Social Security benefits received, total more than $25,000 in the case of a single taxpayer or $32,000 in the case of a married couple filing a joint tax return.

If a taxpayer is required, for federal income tax purposes, to include in income some proportion of Social Security benefits received, the amount to be included in income is the lesser of two amounts: (1) half the amount of benefits received or (2) half the excess of the individual's income as calculated in the preceding paragraph over the base amount of $25,000 or $32,000, whichever applies.

For example, a married couple filing jointly with an adjusted gross income of $24,000, tax-exempt interest income of $8,000, and Social Security benefits of $14,000 is required to include some portion of the Social Security benefits as taxable income. In that situation, the couple's adjusted gross income plus their tax-exempt interest income and half their Social Security benefits totals $39,000 (i.e., $24,000 + $8,000 + $7,000), exceeding the threshold of $32,000.

The amount to be include in income is determined by comparing half the amount of Social Security benefits received, in this case $7,000, to half the calculated amount over the threshold (i.e., half of $39,000—$32,000, or $3,500). Those two amounts, $3,500 and $7,000, are compared, and the lesser amount—in this case $3,500—is the amount to be included in taxable income. It should be noted that, if the couple's tax-exempt income had totaled $18,000 rather than $8,000, half the calculated amount over the threshold would have equaled $8,500 (i.e., half of $49,000—$32,000). In that case half the Social Security benefit, or $7,000, would be the lesser amount, and that would be the figure included in taxable income.

It is important to note that taxing up to half the Social Security benefits is not the same as taking away up to half of these benefits; rather, the applicable amount is simply added to taxable income. The tax is then assessed at the marginal income tax rate of the taxpayer. It is also important to note that the thresholds are not indexed, but rather remain constant over time.

HOW TO OBTAIN BENEFITS

Individuals can apply for benefits at any Social Security office. The location of the nearest office is listed in the phone book. To apply for benefits, a person can either walk into an office and wait or make an appointment in advance by dialing a toll-free number, 1 800 234–5772 (or, simpler to remember, 1 800 2345–SSA). Another option is to set up a telephone appointment by calling the toll-free number and file for benefits over the telephone. A claim filed in this way is called a *teleclaim*. Information is communicated over the telephone, and documents are transmitted through the mail.

It is advisable to apply for retirement benefits approximately three months before one wants to start receiving them. With respect to disability and survivor' benefits, individuals should apply as soon as they become eligible. This is true even though disability benefits do not begin until the sixth month following the onset of a disability. The disability determination process is extremely complicated, and a claim for disability benefits takes longer than any other type of claim to process.

Individuals are given some discretion in deciding the effective date for the commencement of their benefits. The best date to have benefits commence varies with circumstances. For a person who is retiring from a full-time career job at age sixty-five and does not plan to have any subsequent income from employment, it generally makes sense to file the claim so that benefits commence the month after retirement. For a person who continues to work part time after retirement, however, claiming benefits prior to the actual retirement date may result in the receipt of higher benefits during the first year. The reason for this outcome is complicated, involving the application of the retirement test, described above.

Until recently, one could apply for benefits that were effective retroactively for up to twelve months. In other words, an individual could apply for benefits on July 1, 1990, for example, that would have an effective starting date of up to a year before—July 1, 1989—and therefore be paid retroactively. As a consequence, if it were advantageous to claim benefits starting prior to retirement, this could be accomplished in the normal course of applying for benefits a few months prior to actual retirement. The retroactivity provision, however, has been restricted.

Under current law, retroactive benefits are limited to a maximum of six months, and then they are paid only if the benefits would not be reduced as a result of the retroactive application. For example, one could apply for benefits at age sixty-five and six months, but have the benefits start six months before, when he or she reached age sixty-five. In contrast, if one applied for benefits on his or her sixty-fifth birthday there could be no retroactive effective date, because benefits received before normal retirement age are actuarially reduced, as described above. As a consequence of the limitation of the retroactivity provision, it is prudent for a potential beneficiary to visit a Social Security district office as soon as he or she is eligible for benefits, even if this is well before the individual intends to retire. This will enable the future claimant to discuss with a Social Security representative the most advantageous time for benefits to commence.

An individual applying for benefits will generally be asked to furnish a variety of documents. The ones that will be sought depend on the circumstances of the claim. Nevertheless, the documents almost certain to be requested include the potential beneficiary's Social Security card; an original birth certificate (or a certified copy); a marriage certificate if one is requesting spousal benefits; children's birth certificates if one is requesting children's benefits; and the applicants most recent W-2 forms or, if self-employed, income tax return.

A person is entitled to receive a Personal Earnings and Benefits Estimate Statement at any time. This is a statement that lists an individual's earnings and contributions under Social Security, as well as an estimate of future benefits. An individual may acquire this statement by filing Form 7004, which can be obtained at any Social Security district office or by calling the Social Security Administration's toll-free number, stated above. Those aged sixty and over can also obtain the information simply by calling the toll-free number and providing the necessary information over the telephone. Beginning in 1995, these statements will automatically be furnished to all individuals who reach age sixty. Beginning in October 1999, these statements will automatically be provided on an annual basis to all workers covered under Social Security.

CONCLUSION

Social Security provides an important foundation of protection for beneficiaries. Most people need to supplement Social Security with private pensions and other savings in order to maintain their standards of living when their earnings cease. Nevertheless, Social Security provides a sound base on which to build.

Particularly during the 1970s and the early 1980s, newspaper accounts of the impending bankruptcy of the Social Security program generated fear among beneficiaries and contributors concerning the long-term soundness of the program. However, reports questioning the stability of the Social Security program are inaccurate and misleading.

The federal government has the power and ability to respond effectively to any projected shortfall in Social Security funds. The government can levy taxes to ensure the solvency of Social Security. Relatively small increases in the levels of payroll taxes, when imposed on all workers, generate substantial revenues for the program.

Similarly, because Social Security is such a large program covering so many people, minor changes in its structure can result in billions of dollars of savings. For example, rounding benefits up or down to the nearest dime or dollar in calculating benefits makes only a few cents' difference to pensioners every month, but results in millions of dollars in costs or savings to the program over just a few years.

The issue of whether Social Security is able to meet its obligations, then, is a political issue, not an economic one. As long as the program continues to be perceived as fair and important, Social Security should remain strong.

REFERENCES

Ball, Robert M. 1978. *Social Security: Today and.Tomorrow*. New York: Columbia University Press.

Bernstein, Merton C. and Joan Brodshaug Bernstein. 1988. *Social Security: The System That Works*. New York: Basic Books.

HHS. See U.S. Department of Health and Human Services.

Kingson, Eric 1987. *What You Must Know About Social Security and Medicare*. New York: Pharos Books.

Myers, Robert J. 1985. *Social Security*. Homewood, Ill.: Richard D. Irwin, Inc.

Myers, Robert J. 1993. "Summary of the Provisions of the Old-Age, Survivors, and Disability Insurance System and the Supplementary Medical Insurance System." Unpublished compilation.

U.S. Department of Health and Human Services (HHS), Social Security Administration 1989. *Social Security Programs Throughout the World-1989*. Washington, D.C.: U.S. Government Printing Office.

U.S. Department of Health and Human Services (HHS), Social Security Administration 1990. *History of the Provisions of Old-Age, Survivors, Disability, and Health Insurance, 1935–1990*. Washington, D.C.: U.S. Government Printing Office.

U.S. House of Representatives, Committee on Ways and Means (W&M) 1991, *Background Material and Data on Major Programs Within the Jurisdiction of the Committee on Ways and Means*. Washington, D.C.: U.S. Government Printing Office.

W&M. See U.S. House of Representatives, Committee on Ways and Means.

A number of explanatory publications are prepared by the Social Security Administration and are available at Social Security district offices. They can also be obtained by calling the Social Security toll-free number (1 800 234–5772).

7

Private Pensions

●

JOHN J. REGAN

Many people find that they must live on greatly reduced incomes after they retire. Social Security checks and lifetime savings may not be sufficient to meet their expenses of daily living. For those fortunate retirees whose employers had established pension plans, company pensions often fills the gap between income and expenses, and pensions have become an invaluable component of retirement income.

This chapter describes the rights of a worker who participates in an employer's pension plan. It explains how credit toward pension benefits is accumulated, how benefits are paid and taxed, and how certain changes, such as a divorce, the termination of a plan, or the employee's death affect his or her pension. In addition, it describes the rights of a worker's spouse to a share of the worker's pension. This chapter also discusses how a federal law known as ERISA (the Employment Retirement Income Security Act) regulates pension plans and provides tax breaks for workers who join such plans (Title 26, sections 401ff, and Title 29, sections 1001ff, United States Code).

TYPES OF PENSION PLANS

Pension plans are generally of two types: *defined benefit plans* and *defined contribution plans*. A defined benefit plan establishes a definite amount that will be paid to the participant at retirement (such as ten dollars per month for each year of service) or a formula that provides a certain amount (such as 19 percent of the worker's average pay at retirement multiplied by the number of his or her years of service).

During an employee's working years the employer is required to contribute to the plan's fund an amount sufficient to produce the promised level of payment when the worker retires. Sometimes the payment formula is stated as a percentage of the worker's salary, such as 50 percent of the average compensation for the three consecutive years of highest wages earned by the worker. Either way, the worker can estimate how much pension income he or she will receive at retirement.

As its name implies, a defined contribution plan obligates the employer to pay into the worker's account a specified amount each pay period, usually a percentage of the worker's earnings for that period. Some plans also require, or at least permit, the employee to make regular payments as well. These payments and their investment earnings are the funds that will be the source of the worker's pension at retirement. The employee can estimate the size of his or her pension by (1) projecting the amount of future contributions and accumulated earnings for the working years that remain before retirement and (2) determining how much monthly income this fund can be expected to produce during the retiree's and his or her spouse's lifetimes.

Some companies create pension plans to which the company contributes its own stock in lieu of a full or partial cash contribution. Other plans are sometimes known by the section of the Internal Revenue Code that regulates them, such as Section 401(k) plans or Section 403(b) plans. These plans are governed to a large extent by the same rules that are applicable to pension plans in general.

To better understand the rules concerning a company's pension plan, an employee should obtain a copy of the Summary Plan Description from the plan's administrator. The company's personnel office or the worker's union can usually supply the name of this individual.

MEMBERSHIP REQUIREMENTS

For an employee to join a company pension plan, the following standards must be met:

1. The pension plan must cover the employee's job description, such as "clerical employee" or "driver."
2. The worker must be at least age 21.
3. The employee must have worked one thousand hours in a year, which means forty hours per week for at least six months or twenty hours per week for a full year.

A worker receives credit for a "year of service" when he or she has worked at least one thousand hours for the employer during a year. Ordinarily, all years of service are counted in accumulating pension credits. However, sometimes credit for previous years of service can be suspended or even lost when a "break in service" occurs—i.e., when an employee works five hundred hours or less in a given year. Depending on how many such breaks occur over a certain period and on other rules of the plan, prior credit will be reinstated or canceled when the employee returns to work for the company. People who work between 501 and 1,000 hours in a year do not receive credit for a year of service, but neither do they incur breaks in service. Those who take maternity or paternity leave must receive credit for 501 hours of service for the year.

The method used to give credit for a year of service may vary among different plans. The starting point for the plan year may be the employee's first day of employment, or it may be the first day of the calendar year after being hired. Some plans then count every hour in the plan year for which the employee was paid, including holidays, vacations, and sick days. Other plans give credit for a year of service only if the employee is still working on each anniversary of his or her initial hiring. Regardless of the method chosen, however, the plan must count each year of service the employee has worked for the employer after age eighteen, even though the worker cannot join the plan until age twenty-one.

THE VESTING OF PENSION BENEFITS

A worker is entitled to receive a pension from his or her company's pension plan only when the pension benefits are "vested." All contributions that the worker makes to the pension account out of his or her wages are automatically vested. Questions about vesting arise only with respect to the employer's contributions. If benefits are vested, the worker will receive a pension even if he or she leaves the company to work elsewhere, but only when he or she reaches retirement age. These are known as *deferred vested pensions.*

Employers are permitted to choose between two options in creating rules concerning the vesting of their pension plans. Most plans demand that an employee work for five years for the company before earning the right to a pension. At the completion of those five years, the worker has a right to a pension at retirement based on the total contributions made to the plan by the employer and the employee and the employee's earnings as of that date. Subsequent contributions and their earnings are also vested, subject to the break-in-service rules. An employee who fails to work for the full five years loses all benefits except, as noted earlier, a return of the employee's own contributions.

The other option employers may choose for vesting their pension plans is to have the vesting phased in over a period of three to seven years. After three years of work, the employee is entitled to 20 percent of the fund that have accumulated in his or her account. This percentage increases by an extra 20 percent for each subsequent year of employment until it reaches 100 percent at the end of the seventh year.

Neither of these options for vesting applies to plans jointly sponsored by several employers and covered by a union contract. Such plans may require ten years of service before benefits are fully vested.

CALCULATING THE RATE AT WHICH A PENSION IS EARNED

After determining the working years that have been credited toward his or her pension, the employee will then want to know how much those years are worth in calculating his or her ultimate pension. This amount at a particular point during these years is known as the worker's *accrued benefit.*

If the plan is a defined contribution plan, the accrued benefit is the amount in the employee's plan account. This sum is usually the total of past contributions plus investment earnings. If the plan is a defined benefit plan, the accrued benefit can sometimes be computed by multiplying the number of years worked by either a percentage of the worker's current pay or a fixed dollar amount. Plans are permitted to favor employees who have long service, are older, or are higher paid, but the law requires a minimum rate of accrual for all workers under one of these three optional accrual formulas:

1. *The 3 percent rule.* Using this formula, if a worker joins the plan at the earliest possible entry age opportunity and works continuously until retirement age, at least 3 percent of the pension must accrue for each year of participation. For example, suppose that an employee joins a plan at age 22 and works continuously for 24 years, and that the plan's benefit at retirement is $500 per month. After 24 years the worker's accrued benefit will be $360 ($500 × >03 × 24).

   If the plan bases its benefits on an employee's compensation over a period of several years (e.g., 50 percent of the employee's average compensation for the three consecutive years of highest earnings), the accrued benefit is computed by assuming that the employee will continue earning his or her current wages. The average compensation for the stated period is multiplied by 3 percent and the total number of years the person has already worked. For example, suppose a worker joined the company plan at the earliest possible opportunity and worked at the company for 20 years. Suppose further that the plan will pay a pension equal to 50 percent of the average compensation for the three consecutive years of earnings. The worker's average earnings for the past three years is $20,000. Based on this average, the pension would be $10,000. The accrued benefit at the end of 20 years will be $6,000 ($10.000 × .03 × 20).

2. *The 133¹/₃ percent rule.* Under this rule, the accrual rate in a later year cannot exceed 133¹/₃ percent of the previous year's rate. For example, if a plan's benefits accrue at the rate of $15 per month for the first ten years of employment, the rate for later years cannot exceed $20 per month ($15 × 133¹/₃%).

3. *The fractional rule.* Under this formula, a worker who leaves a job must be given credit for the fractional portion of the full pension he or she would have been paid had the employee continued to work until normal retirement age. For example, suppose a plan's pension benefit at age 65 is set at $500 per month. An employee works for ten years, then quits at age 35. This person has earned 10/40 or 25 percent of the pension, or $125 per month ($500 × .25), which can be collected beginning when the worker reaches age 65.

Some plans integrate a plan member's Social Security benefits into the member's pension. This means that the pension payment will be reduced directly or indirectly by the amount of part of the person's Social Security benefit. Federal law requires that certain minimum pension benefits be paid by these integrated plans.

LIMITS ON CONTRIBUTIONS AND BENEFITS

Qualified pension plans enjoy tax advantages under federal law. Contributions to a plan that meets federal standards, as well as the investment earnings, are not subject to income tax liability until they are paid out as benefits. However, the amounts of the annual contribution and the annual benefit cannot exceed certain dollar amounts.

Generally annual contributions to a pension plan cannot exceed $30,000 or 25 percent of annual compensation, whichever is less. But many plans are subject to lower limits on the amount that can be contributed on a pretax basis. For example, the limit on an employee's contribution to a 401 (k) plan in 1993 is $8,994. The limit is $9,500 under salary reduction agreements for employees of public schools and certain tax-exempt organizations. The former figure is adjusted for inflation annually. These limits on pretax contributions operate, in effect, as limits on the benefits ultimately paid out, so no further benefit limits are imposed by law.

Defined benefit plans, however, are subject to a ceiling on benefits. This limit is the lesser of either $115,641 per year (1993 figure) or 100 percent of the employee's average compensation for the three consecutive years of highest earnings. This limit is adjusted downward for those who retire before age 65, but in no case will it fall below $10,000.

WHEN PENSION PAYMENTS BEGIN

The starting time for pension payments is when an employee reaches the "normal retirement age" set by the plan. This is usually the member's sixty-fifth birthday, although some plans use earlier ages. It is permissible, however, for a plan to require a worker to have been a plan participant for at least ten years. The plan also has the option of making the retiree wait until two months past the end of the plan year in which the person reaches age sixty-five.

Suppose a person is a participant in a company plan but leaves in middle age (e.g., at age forty-five) to take another job. If this person has vested benefits in that plan and has completed the minimum required number of years of service in that plan, he or she is entitled to receive benefits from that plan at the plan's normal retirement age (e.g., age sixty-five). Thus it is possible that an employee whose working career has encompassed several jobs and several different pension plans might qualify for separate pensions from each of them when he or she reaches retirement age. Moreover, if any of these plans offers early retirement to its members, this person will be entitled to start receiving benefits early under the same conditions as other persons currently working for the company as long as he or she satisfies these conditions.

Some pension plans offer disability benefits that begin earlier than retirement age. These benefits may continue as long as the worker is disabled, or they may convert to retirement benefits when the disabled employee reaches age sixty-five.

Employees who delay retirement by continuing to work beyond the plan's normal retirement age can delay the start of benefits as well, but not indefinitely. Pension payments must start no later than April 1 of the year after the year in which the employee reaches age 70½. For example, a worker whose seventieth birthday is August 15, 1995 will reach age 70½ on February 15, 1996, and therefore must begin receiving his or her pension by April 1, 1997.

The payout period for a retiree's pension cannot extend longer than the lives of the retiree and the designated beneficiary, nor can it extend for a period exceeding the life expectancy of the employee or the employee and the designated beneficiary. For example, an unmarried worker's life expectancy when he retires at age 65 is 20 years, while the combined life expectancies of the worker and his 56-year-old brother, his designated beneficiary, is 30.2 years. The retiree has the option of using his own life expectancy only, meaning that he must be paid 1/20 of his pension account in the first year of retirement. In each subsequent year, the fraction will become larger, with one subtracted from the divisor (e.g., 1/19, 1/18, 1/17, etc.) until the account has been fully paid out. Instead the retiree may use the combined life expectancies of himself and his brother (30.2 years), in which case he will have to draw only 1/30.2 of his account at retirement. The latter approach is used by those who do not need their full pensions for living expenses and who wish to provide an income for their beneficiaries. Extending the payout period may also move the retiree into a lower income tax bracket and thereby result in tax savings. The tables of life expectancies can be found in IRS Publication 939.

It is useful to note that the life expectancy chosen for the pension can be recalculated annually to take advantage of the fact that the recipient has survived one more year. For example, if the widower described above has used only his own life expectancy of 20 years at age 65 to calculate his pension payment, he can redetermine his life expectancy at age 66 and at the end of each subsequent year and recompute his pension accordingly. When he turns age 66, his life expectancy will still be basically 19.2 years, and therefore he can continue to receive only 1/19.2 of the account. The effect of recalculating life expectancy each year is to ensure that there will still be funds in the pension account until the retiree's death if he or she lives longer that the actuarial charts predicted when the person first retired.

Suppose the retiree dies after the pension has started but before the entire account has been distributed. The balance must be paid to the beneficiary at least as rapidly as it would have been paid under the method in effect when the retiree died. Or suppose the employee dies before the pension payments have started. Generally the law requires that the entire pension account be paid to the beneficiary within five years after the worker's death. However, the beneficiary has the option of stretching out these payments over his or her own life expectancy. These periodic payments must begin within twelve months of the end of the year of the worker's death. If the beneficiary is the employee's surviving spouse, the spouse has the additional option of deferring the starting date until the date on which the deceased employee would have reached age 70½.

HOW BENEFITS ARE PAID

Pensions can be paid in various ways, but the range of choices depends on the rules of a particular plan. The usual method of payment is in the form of monthly checks over the life of the retiree and his or her spouse (or sometimes another beneficiary). If payments are to be made for the life of the beneficiary alone, this method is commonly known as a *straight life annuity.* A variant guarantees a minimum payout period (e.g, ten years) to the beneficiary in case the retiree dies prematurely (this is known as a *straight life annuity with period-certain benefits*). If payments are to be made for the lifetimes of the retiree and another beneficiary (e.g., the retiree's surviving spouse), the option is often called a *joint and survivor annuity.*

The alternative to the payment of an annuity is a lump-sum payment of the entire pension account to the employee at retirement. If the plan is a defined contribution plan, the payment amount is the amount in the account. However, if the plan pays a defined benefit, the projected lifetime monthly payments are converted to their current lump-sum equivalent. If a plan offers the option of a lump-sum payout, the decision to accept it or not is generally the retiree's. The one exception is a pension account valued at $3,500 or less, which the plan may require the retiree to take as a lump sum. It is important to note that significant differences in income tax liability may result from a retiree's decision to choose an annuity or a lump-sum payment. These consequences are discussed later in this chapter.

PENSION RIGHTS OF SPOUSES

Federal law guarantees the spouse of a retiring plan member a share in the retiree's benefits. The retiree is required to receive the benefits in the form of at least a 50 percent joint and survivor annuity extending over the life of his or her spouse. Only if the spouse renounces this arrangement in writing at the time of retirement is it permissible for a plan to pay a straight life annuity to the retiree alone. The surviving spouse of an employee who dies before his or her pension payments begin has the same right to a pension as the spouse of a retiree.

To qualify for a pension, the spouse of a worker must have been married to the worker for one year before the worker begins receiving the pension or dies, whichever comes first. For example, suppose a worker retires while married and starts receiving his or her pension, but then divorces his or her spouse a short while later. If the couple has been married for a year before the start of pension payments, the divorced spouse continues to have a right to a joint and survivor annuity and will receive a pension after the retiree dies. Or suppose a couple marries on the husband's birthday. He retires six months later and starts his pension, but then dies just after turning sixty-six. His widow will have a right to his pension because she had been married to him for one year before his death, even though he had been receiving his pension for less than a year when he died.

How large will a surviving spouse's pension be? It need not be equal to the retiree's pension during his or her lifetime. The law requires only that the survivor receive a pension that is not less than 50 percent of the pension paid while both spouses were alive. For example, suppose that a worker is entitled to a monthly pension of $500 if it is to be paid for her lifetime alone. The benefit can be converted to its equivalent value as a joint and survivor annuity. Depending on the ages of the worker and her husband, the benefit may become $400 a month during the worker's lifetime, and $200 per month payable to the worker's husband after her death.

It is also permissible for the spouse to agree to convert the joint and survivor annuity to which he or she is entitled into a lump-sum payment or any alternative form of payment. The lump sum, of course, must be equivalent in value to the annuity. The retiree's spouse may not want the protection of the survivor's annuity because, for example, the spouse has a separate pension. In this case, the spouse must sign a statement indicating that he or she does not want the retiree's pension reduced. The result will be that the retiree will receive a full pension for his or her life, but after the retiree's death nothing will be paid to the surviving spouse.

A divorced spouse may also receive a share of a worker's pension during his or her lifetime by virtue of a court order as part of the divorce process, provided the marriage lasted for one year. If the employee has not yet retired but has passed the earliest retirement age permitted by his or her pension plan, a divorced spouse may ask the court to order that payments to him or her begin immediately as if the worker had retired.

PROTECTION OF THE PENSION AGAINST CREDITORS

Generally an employee is not permitted to transfer his or her benefits to a third party before receiving them. An exception to this rule, however, permits a retiree to transfer the right to no more than ten percent of his or her benefits to a third party as long as the retiree can cancel this arrangement at any time. The same rule prohibits a creditor from garnishing an employee's benefits, even if the person is due to receive a lump-sum payment instead of an annuity. Most courts also hold that pension benefits are protected from creditors if the employee declares bankruptcy.

PENSIONS AND FEDERAL INCOME TAX

One of the attractive features of a pension plan for an employee is that the employee does not have to pay income tax on his or her own contributions to the plan as they are earned or on the employer's contributions as they are made. Similarly, no tax is paid on the investment earnings of the contributions as they accumulate. But the tax liability is only deferred, not canceled. The moment of truth for the plan member arrives when the pension payments begin.

The general rule is that income tax must be paid on the portion of a pension payment that represents the payout of the untaxed contributions and their untaxed investment earnings. For example, if the pension was funded entirely by the employer, the entire payment will be taxable. If the pension is paid as an annuity, the IRS Form W-2P that is sent to each recipient at the end of the calendar year may indicate how much of the sum paid out during the previous year is taxable. If the IRS form does not specify the taxable portion, the retiree should consult the instructions accompanying IRS Form 1040 (the form used to report one's income tax) for details about calculating the taxable portion of the pension payments.

If an employee chooses to receive a lump-sum pension payment instead of an annuity, he or she has three choices for dealing with the income tax liability of this payout:

1. Roll over within sixty days of receipt all or part of the payout into another pension plan or an IRA account, thereby delaying payment of any income tax until the money is withdrawn from this new source at a later date.
2. Use the special lump-sum tax options (five-or ten-year averaging or treating the lump sum as long-term capital gains). Ten-year averaging is available only to employees born before 1936. The ability to treat the lump sum as long-term capital gains is available only to employees born before 1936 who participated in the plan before 1974. Five-year averaging is available to all employees who receive qualifying lump sums. However, employees born in 1936 or later cannot use five-year averaging unless the lump sum is received after age 59$\frac{1}{2}$;
3. Report the entire taxable portion of the payout as income for the year in which it was received, and pay income tax at regular rates on that portion. But note that, beginning in 1993, if the payout is not transferred *directly* into an IRA or another qualified pension plan, the employer must withhold 20 percent of the payout as income tax. The employee still has the option of having the lump sum paid directly to himself subject to the tax withheld. The employee can then roll it over to an IRA within the sixty-day grace period, but if he does so he must add to the rollover an amount equal to the 20 percent withheld by the employer to ensure tax-free treatment of the rollover. If he then rolls over the full amount, the amount of tax withheld by the employer from the lump-sum distribution should be claimed as a tax credit when the employee files his federal income tax form for that year.

   For example, an employee requests a $50,000 distribution from her pension plan. The plan will pay her only $40,000, with $10,000 withheld as income tax. If she then rolls over only the $40,000, she must pay income tax on the $10,000, thus entitling her to only a partial refund of that amount. On the other hand, if she takes the $40,000, comes up with an extra $10,000 on her own, and puts the total into an IRA within 60 days, she will avoid all income tax on the lump sum and will be entitled to a full refund of the $10,000 withheld.

Before making a choice among these options, the employee should consult a tax advisor. The tax rules on lump-sum distributions are extremely complicated, and federal law may impose additional tax liabilities on early or excess distributions.

PENSIONS AND STATE INCOME TAX

State income taxation of an employee's contributions to a pension plan and of distributions from a plan generally follows one of two models. Some states base their tax law on federal law and defer tax on contributions and investment income until the retiree receives them as payments. Others tax an employee's contributions at the time at which they are made, and therefore tax at distribution only that portion of the payment that is attributable to the employer's contributions and investment income.

A few states that tax pension benefits at distribution use a *3 percent rule* when the employee has made contributions toward the cost of the pension. Payments are taxed annually to the extent of 3 percent of the aggregate of the employee's contributions. The excess is excluded from gross income until the total amounts excluded equal the aggregate contributions. Thereafter, all payments are subject to tax in full. For example, suppose a retiree receives payments of $200 per month from his plan. Before retiring, he had contributed $5,000 toward the cost of his pension. In 1990 he received a total of $2,400. Of this amount, 3 percent of $5,000, or $150, was subject to tax. The balance of $2,250 was excluded from gross income. In 1991, again $150 was taxed and was $2,250 excluded. By the end of 1991 the retiree had received $4,500 of his total contributions tax free. Consequently, in 1992 only $500 (the balance of his contributions of $5,000 that were still to be recovered tax free) was excluded; the remaining $1,900 of his $2,400 pension was subject to tax. In 1993 and later, the full $2,400 will be treated as gross income each year.

In states using the 3 percent rule, lump-sum payments are generally taxed to the extent that they exceed the worker's total contributions, although some states have adopted the federal approach. Most states do not require tax withholding on pension payments, although voluntary withholding is permitted in most.

LOSING PENSION BENEFITS

It is possible for a person to lose all or part of his or her pension as a result of certain events or actions that he or she might take.

Return to Work

It is common for a retiree to consider taking another job after retirement. However, this step could result in a reduction or cutoff of his or her pension, so careful planning is necessary before such action. These are the rules for determining whether a retiree's pension will be affected by a return to work:

1. If the person is age sixty-five or over and will be working fewer than forty hours per month, it is permissible for the person to work for any employer without losing any pension.
2. If the person is age sixty-five or over but expects to work more than forty hours per month, the person can take a job with any employer except the company that sponsors the pension plan. However, if more than one company sponsors the plan under a union contract, the person will receive his or her full pension as long as he or she does not accept the type of job usually performed by members of that union in the region in which they usually work.
3. If the person is under age sixty-five and wants to return to work after retirement, he or she should check the rules of the pension plan concerning the cutoff of pension benefits.

Death of the Employee

Below are the rules about situations in which the death of an employee will affect the pension benefits of other persons:

1. Pension payments cease when an unmarried retiree dies while receiving a pension.
2. When a married pensioner dies, his or her surviving spouse will receive a pension worth half the benefits of the deceased unless the couple had agreed to a different arrangement.
3. When a married worker dies after the pension has become vested but before retirement, the surviving spouse will received a lifetime pension worth half of the accrued benefits, but payments will not begin until the year in which the deceased employee would have been eligible to start receiving benefits.
4. A surviving spouse will not receive a pension if the employee dies before benefits had become vested.

Divorce

When a worker divorces, his or her pension is an asset of the marriage; therefore a court may award a share of the pension to the divorced spouse. The marriage must have lasted for a year. However, the divorced spouse generally cannot begin collecting payments until the employee reaches the age at which he or she could receive the pension. At that point, payments to the divorced spouse can begin even though the worker has not yet retired.

PLAN TERMINATION

What are the rights of a worker who learns that his or her pension plan is being terminated? If the plan is a defined contribution plan, any money contributed to the plan on behalf of the worker belongs to the worker and must be paid to him or her. If the plan is a defined benefit plan sponsored by one employer, the employee's rights will depend on the reason for the plan's termination. A plan that ends for other than financial reasons must give the employee full payment of his or her vested benefits. Workers without vested benefits may get a small share of the pension fund if there is money left over after vested benefits have been paid out.

Workers who are members of single-employer defined benefit plans that close down because of financial distress (e.g., bankruptcy) will receive at least part of their pensions if the plan is insured by the federal agency known as the Pension Benefit Guaranty Corporation (PBGC). Federal law has established a priority system for allocating the plan's assets among plan members. The maximum coverage for an individual employee is a pension of $2,437.50 per month in 1993. However, many pension plans are not insured by the PBGC, such as those run by employers with fewer than 25 employees, by state or local governments, or by religious institutions; certain plans funded by union dues; and nonqualified plans for company executives. Also not insured are annuities purchased from insurance companies by pension plans when workers retire. These annuities represent an arrangement that creates risk for the retiree if the insurance company encounters financial difficulties.

Separate rules apply to the termination of plans run by more than one employer.

PROCEDURES FOR FILING CLAIMS

To file a claim for benefits, an employee should follow the procedures outlined in the Summary Plan Description. Generally the claim is filed with the employer's personnel department or with the insurance company administering the plan. If the claim is denied, the employee should consider appealing this decision, but legal assistance may be necessary unless the denial is based on a factual mistake that can be easily cleared up. A claimant who fails to receive a response to the filing of a claim within ninety days should assume that the claim has been denied and consider asking for a review.

RECOMMENDED READINGS

Bruce, Stephen R. 1988. *Pension Claims: Rights and Obligations.* Washington, D.C.: Bureau of National Affairs.

Canan, Michael J. 1991. *Qualified Retirement and Other Employee Benefit Plans.* St. Paul: West Publishing Co.

Coleman, Barbara J. 1989. *Primer on Employee Retirement Income Security Act.* Washington, D.C.: Bureau of National Affairs.

Perritt, Henry H., Jr. 1990. *Benefits Claims: Law and Practice.* New York: John Wiley & Sons.

Regan, John J. 1985, 1991. *Tax, Estate and Financial Planning for the Elderly.* New York: Matthew Bender & Co.

Regan, John J., and Michael Gilfix. 1991. *Tax, Estate and Financial Planning for the Elderly: Forms and Practice.* New York: Matthew Bender & Co.

8

Savings, Investments, and Individual Retirement Accounts

●

LAWRENCE R. MCCOOMBE

Retirees rely on the money they have saved and invested during their working years to supplement their payments from Social Security and pensions or annuities.

Managing these savings and investment resources wisely calls for three things: first, an understanding of basic investment vehicles; second, a strategy for choosing the investments that are most appropriate to the retiree's financial objectives; and third, if any of the investment portfolio is situated in individual retirement accounts (IRAs), an awareness of the special rules that apply to these accounts.

BASIC TYPES OF INVESTMENTS

There are just two ways to make money through investing. One is to lend money at interest, the other to buy something and later sell it at a profit. All investments fall primarily into one of these two categories, though some contain elements of both.

Debt Investments

Certificates of deposit (CDs), corporate and municipal bonds, U.S. Treasury securities, and agency securities are all debt investments or IOUs. The investor lends money to a bank, a corporation—even to the state or federal government—in exchange for a promise to pay a fixed rate of interest and to return the principal, usually at a predetermined future time.

Cash Equivalents

Debt securities that have no fixed maturity date and are accessible any time without penalty and without significant risk to principal or interest—passbook accounts, checking accounts, money market accounts, and money market mutual funds—are termed *cash equivalents*. The liquidity available in these accounts is gained by giving up the ability to lock in a fixed long-term interest rate. (While passbook accounts and some checking accounts usually carry fixed rates, they are ordinarily well below the fixed rate available for less liquid investments.) Because cash equivalents are instantly available, they are used as "parking places" for money between the sale of one investment and the purchase of another and as the investment vehicles of choice for funds to be tapped to meet personal financial emergencies.

Three Types of Risks

There are three types of risk in debt investments. One is the *risk of default*. The institution may be unable to keep its promise to pay interest and return principal. The greater the probability that the institution will renege on its promise, the higher the interest rate it must offer to attract investors. The safety of specific corporate and municipal bond issues from default is rated by Standard and Poor's Corporation and by Moody's Investors Service. Because bank investments are usually insured by the Federal Deposit Insurance Corporation (FDIC) for up to $100,000 per depositor (and another $100,000 for the depositor's IRAs in that bank), the risk of nonpayment is not nearly as high as for many nonbank investments—and neither is the interest rate.

Another risk is *interest rate risk*. The money invested is not available for other investments. Under most economic conditions, the longer the term of the investment, the more likely it is that another investment carrying a higher interest rate will become available at some time during that term. For this reason, long-term certificates of deposit and bonds usually offer higher interest rates than shorter-term investments with similar institutions. (This general rule does not hold true, however, if the current demand for credit that has produced a high short-term interest rate is expected to be temporary or if the rate of inflation is expected to decline during the term of the investment.)

The third type of risk to which all fixed income debt investments are subject is *purchasing power risk*, the risk that, even if the interest payments are made as promised, the dollars received will buy less than they would at the time of investment.

There is no such thing as a free lunch. Debt securities that offer very high interest when compared with similar securities of other institutions always entail greater degrees of risk. The baseline generally used for evaluating the risk of loss is the interest rate on short-term U.S. treasury bills. Since the treasury cannot default on its promise to pay, the rate of return on these securities is termed risk free. (Actually, it is free only of the risk of default. Interest rate risk and purchasing power risk attend *all* fixed-income securities.)

The degree to which the net return on a nontreasury investment exceeds this risk-free rate of return is a simple measure of the risk the investor is assuming. If treasury bills carry a 6 percent interest rate, for example, and company A issues five-year securities promising 6.5 percent while company B's five-year securities offer 7.5 percent, then it may be assumed that Company B is somewhat less likely to be able to pay the interest or to return the principal. On the other hand, if the treasury bills are paying 6 percent and companies A and B are offering 10.5 percent and 11.5 percent, both are so far above the treasury bill baseline that, unless inflation is expected to rise dramatically, both bonds may be assumed to carry substantial risk even though their interest rates are still only one point apart.

Bond Mutual Funds

Rather than personally evaluating and selecting specific fixed-income securities, many investors prefer to leave the choices to someone else by investing in bond mutual funds. It is then the fund managers who must do all the homework and make the decisions. A fund manager is not given carte blanche in making these decisions for the investors. He or she must abide by the fund's stated objectives and must adhere to the fund's declared methods for pursuing these objectives. Both the objectives and the methods are explained clearly in the fund's prospectus, which every potential investor receives.

The Secondary Market

With the exception of bank investments, debt securities whose maturity date is fixed may be sold before that date arrives. The sale is not to the issuer, but to another investor, and it is executed through a broker. Whether the investor selling the security will receive more or less than the amount he or she paid for it depends on what has happened to interest rates in the meantime and on whether the degree of risk associated with the issuing institution has changed. The closer the date of sale to the maturity date, the closer the sale price will be to the face value of the instrument, since whoever holds the instrument at maturity will collect the face value only, no more and no less.

In the case of a bank fixed-income investment (certificate of deposit), there is no secondary market through which to sell the investment. The investor can, however, present the certificate to the bank for redemption before its maturity date. Although federal law prescribes no penalty for early redemption, most banks do. The penalty is usually the loss of three to six months' interest on the instrument.

Tax Treatment

Interest the investor receives on debt securities is taxable with two exceptions: interest on treasury securities is not taxable by any state, and most municipal bond interest is not currently taxed either by the federal government or by the state where the bond was issued. If a security is sold for more or less than it cost the investor to acquire it, the profit or loss from the sale is treated under the rules that govern capital gains and losses. (A special provision applies to municipal bonds. Gains realized are treated as capital gains, but if a bond was purchased at a premium—that is, at an amount greater than its face value—no loss can be claimed if it is redeemed at its face value.) Notice that, although debt securities are purchased primarily for the promised interest payments, the possibility of gain or loss when they are sold in the secondary market makes them equity investments in this respect.

EQUITY INVESTMENTS

An equity investment represents the exchange of the investor's dollars for an ownership interest in something—a corporation, a parcel of real estate, a collectible, or some other asset. The investor makes this purchase because he or she believes (or at least hopes) that the value of the item will increase before it is sold.

The growth in value is, of course, guaranteed by no one and depends on a variety of factors. In the case of stock, for example, growth or decline in value may result from changes in society's need for the product or service the company sells, changes in the national economy, changes in the market position the company holds relative to others in the industry, or changes in the company's profitability, its management, or its indebtedness.

With all these influences on the value of the investment, it is clear that the investor in the company's stock is taking a far greater risk than the one who buys the company's bonds. The stockholder, after all, gets nothing until the bondholders (and other creditors) have been satisfied. On the positive side, whereas the bondholder is entitled only to the promised interest payments and the return of principal regardless of how much success the company achieves, the stockholder is an owner and participates directly and without limit in that success.

Besides participating in the growth (or decline) in the value of the business, stockholders may also receive dividends on the shares they own. Dividends represent the distribution of part of the profit the company has made. Newer, smaller companies usually reinvest their profits in research and development, equipment purchase, facilities acquisition, and other avenues intended to expand the business and make the company—and its stock—still more valuable. Older, larger companies whose initial growth took place long ago are more likely to regularly declare dividends as a way of attracting and rewarding stockholders, since the stock value itself is less likely to rise meteorically in the relatively short term.

Stock Mutual Funds

To eliminate some of the risk associated with holding the stock of just a few companies, many investors prefer the diversification offered by stock mutual funds. Because each fund invests in the stocks of many companies, the risk of dramatic loss through a major shift in the fortunes of the stock of one or two companies is greatly reduced. The diversification feature offers no protection, however, against market risk, the risk that the entire stock market (or that sector of it in which the particular mutual fund specializes) may experience a severe and sudden decline.

Stock mutual funds are quite varied in their objectives. Some buy stocks based on their potential for long-term growth alone; others aim for long-term growth plus a significant level of current income; still others focus on short-term, aggressive growth only; and so on. Information about a particular fund's objectives and how the fund manager pursues them is part of the fund's prospectus, which any potential investor should read carefully.

Tax Treatment

Growth or decline in the value of an asset has no tax effect until the property is sold. For federal tax purposes gains and losses from sales are treated as long-term or short-term capital gains and losses. Assets held for more than a full year before sale are long-term assets; otherwise they are short-term assets.

Under current tax law, short-term gains and losses for the year are netted against each other. The same thing is done with long-term gains and losses. If one of these calculations results in a gain and the other in a loss (a net long-term gain and a net short-term loss, for example), these two results are netted against each other, as in the example shown in table 8.1. In the example, the net short-term result is a loss of $1,500, the net long-term result a gain of $2,000. When the short-term loss is subtracted from the long-term gain, the final result is a net long-term capital gain of $500.

When the netting process is complete, any long-term gain remaining is taxed as ordinary income but, under current tax rules, cannot be taxed at a rate higher than 28 percent, no matter how high a rate applies to any of the investor's other income. If the gain remaining is short term, it is simply taxable as ordinary income with no tax advantage. If the netting calculation results in a long-term and/or short-term loss, up to $3,000 of the loss is deductible from income for the year. If the loss is greater than $3,000, the excess can be carried over to the next year's tax return.

The special treatment of long-term capital gains and capital losses changes from time to time as Congress modifies the law. In general,

TABLE 8.1. Netting Capital Gains and Losses

Short-Term Transactions	Purchase Cost	Sale Proceeds	Gain (Loss)
Company A	$2,000	$2,500	$500
Company B	10,000	8,000	(2,000)
Net Short-Term Loss: *($1,500)*			

Long-Term Transactions	Purchase Cost	Sale Proceeds	Gain (Loss)
Company C	$15,000	$12,000	($3,000)
Company D	7,000	12,000	5,000
Net Long-Term Gain: *$2,000*			
Net Long-Term Capital Gain ($2,000–$1,500): *$500*			

however, the rules encourage investors to take the risk of making an equity investment and holding the investment property for at least a year before selling it at a profit.

STRATEGIC CONSIDERATIONS

An investment strategy is a broad approach by which the investor intends to accomplish major financial objectives. For retirees, these major objectives are usually three: (1) to maintain an adequate emergency fund; (2) to provide regular income to meet ordinary living expenses, including a reserve to help maintain purchasing power in light of inflation; (3) to have money available for nonemergency special expenses. Other objectives, such as building an estate, going back to school, taking an extended vacation—the possibilities are endless—can usually be subsumed under one of the three main types.

Maintaining an Emergency Fund

Because money may be needed on very short notice, the investments chosen for the emergency fund must be highly liquid and must have a reliable value. Insured bank accounts and money market funds are typical choices because they carry a high degree of safety and are easily accessed when the money is needed. Financial planners usually recommend maintaining an emergency fund balance equal to three to six months of living expenses. However, that suggestion is geared to active workers, who may face the need for emergency cash presented by unemployment. If the retiree is free of the risk that his or her regular income may suddenly stop, the emergency fund can be somewhat smaller.

Providing Income to Meet Living Expenses

Money set aside to meet living expenses must meet both short- and intermediate-term needs. The investment selection should reflect this today-and-tomorrow approach. The short-term need is for regular income at appropriate times from investments whose value will not change suddenly and unpredictably. Certificates of deposit, AAA-rated bonds, treasury notes, and bonds and other highly rated fixed-income securities can provide this type of reliable, regular interest payment.

Retirees often select a number of small, separate investments with unequal terms to maturity rather than one or two large investments. The strategy of varied terms and staggered maturities accomplishes two things. First, since the maturity dates are different, this approach presents the opportunity to change or renew portions of the total investment frequently. If interest rates have risen, the retiree can select a new investment (or, in the case of a CD, renew the investment) at the higher rate and for a longer term. If rates are temporarily depressed, the retiree can select a shorter-term investment and wait for rates to rise. Second, holding some short-term and some longer-term investments keeps the retiree from finding himself or herself at the mercy of an unfavorable short-term interest climate and from tying up the whole investment for the long haul with no way of escape without losing principal or, in the case of CDs, sustaining an early redemption penalty.

Although the staggered maturity strategy can be helpful, it does not take inflation into account. If income needs are rising with inflation, receiving a fixed rate of interest on a fixed amount of principal means living with less purchasing power each year. In deciding how much to set aside for living expenses, the retiree will wish to consider a further strategy for maintaining that purchasing power. One approach to coping with inflation's erosion is to allocate a portion of the assets for use specifically as an inflation reserve. This amount can be invested in longer-term fixed-income securities or, less conservatively, in mutual funds or stocks—or in some combination of all of these. As inflation weakens the buying power of the existing interest-distributing assets, the retiree can cash in part of this reserve and move the proceeds into the staggered maturities portfolio, thereby creating a larger stream of regular interest income. This systematic conversion of the reserve assets can ensure that their original purchasing power is maintained.

Having Money Available for Nonemergency Special Purposes

For some retirees, having money available for special purposes is an optional objective; for others, it is an element that is essential for them to enjoy retirement; for a few, it is at least as important as being able to meet certain emergency needs. The degree of priority assigned to the objective of having funds available for special purposes should guide the retiree in choosing investment vehicles to fund it. If the objective is equal in importance to the objective of meeting some emergency needs and the expenditure itself will be in the near term, the very same investment types used for the emergency fund—cash equivalents—are appropriate. If the money will not be needed until some time in the intermediate or long-term future, investments like those used to fund the "today" portion of the living expense allocation—highly rated fixed-income securities—are likely to prove a better choice. The reinvestment of interest payments will keep up the purchasing power of the original amount invested.

If the special-purpose objective is seen as not quite as important as getting the roof repaired, a mix similar to that used for the "tomorrow" portion (the inflation reserve portion) of the living expense allocation—a mix of fixed-income securities and conservative-growth mutual fund shares—may fill the bill. This approach assumes, however, that the target date for spending the money is not inflexible. The growth rate of equity investments cannot be predicted with certainty. If the objective is truly of the optional type *and* if the retiree is both financially able to sustain substantial risk to the principal invested and personally able to postpone the objective until the funding is available, then a smaller investment in a combination of carefully selected growth mutual funds and common stocks may prove sufficient. A word of caution is in order: if the retiree views the objective as anything other than optional or if the principal may be needed for another more important objective, this last strategy is inadvisable.

INDIVIDUAL RETIREMENT ACCOUNTS

IRAs provide the opportunity to shelter the principal and earnings of retirement savings from tax until they are withdrawn from the account. The rules, restrictions, and requirements that apply to IRAs are intended to discourage account holders from using their IRAs for purposes other than the provision of retirement income. Of concern here are the rules governing rollovers, investments, and withdrawals later in life.

Rollovers

Most distributions from qualified employer-sponsored pension, savings, profit-sharing, or employee stock ownership plans are taxable. However, no income tax is immediately payable if the distribution is rolled over (deposited) into one or more individual retirement accounts. The rollover can be executed by either the employer or the retiree. Regardless of whether the rollover is executed by the employer or the retiree, the amount rolled over is not taxed until it is withdrawn from the IRA.

Federal law requires an employer to transfer the taxable portion of a rollover-eligible distribution directly to an IRA (or to another qualified benefits plan) designated by the retiree if the retiree requests the transfer. If the retiree does not request direct transfer, the distribution is subject to a 20 percent federal income tax withholding requirement. If the retiree chooses to receive the distribution and execute the rollover personally, the rollover must be completed within sixty days of receipt. The amount eligible for rollover is not changed by the 20 percent that is withheld before the distribution reaches the retiree. A taxable distribution of $100,000, for example, will have $20,000 withheld. The retiree will receive $80,000; however, the amount of the distribution remains $100,000. That is the amount eligible for rollover.

If the retiree rolls over less than the rollover-eligible amount, the remainder must be included in calculating his or her adjusted gross income for the year. In the example above, if the retiree rolls over only the $80,000 actually received, the remaining $20,000 of the distribution must be included in income. If the retiree rolls over the $80,000 received plus $20,000 from another source, however, the entire $100,000 will have been rolled over and no tax will be due on the distribution. The 20 percent withheld by the employer will then produce a refund when the retiree files that year's income tax return.

Federal tax law allows the retiree to roll over either the actual property received in the distribution or the proceeds from the sale of that property. This means that retiree is permitted to sell—but is not *required* to sell—any stock or mutual fund shares received in the distribution before making the rollover. Many IRA custodians will accept these assets "in kind"—that is, without requiring that they be converted to cash. Some custodians, however, refuse to accept anything but dollars when a rollover is made. Stock, then, can be sold or rolled over in kind. One transaction that is explicitly forbidden by the Internal Revenue Service (IRS) is the *substitution* of cash for other assets. The retiree may not simply keep the stock and roll over cash in its place.

The Payment of Excise Tax on Excess Contributions

The maximum amount that may be rolled over is the entire distribution minus any after-tax contributions included in it. For example, if an employee savings plan distributes $125,000 to an employee and that amount includes $25,000 of after-tax contributions the employee made to his account during his career, then $100,000 is eligible for rollover and $25,000 is not. If the retiree rolls over, in addition to the maximum amount, some or all of the after-tax portion of the distribution and allows the extra money to remain in the account past tax filing time for the year, there will be two tax consequences. First, an excise tax equal to 6 percent of the excess contribution will be imposed on the retiree. The 6 percent tax will continue to be assessed every year until an amount equal to the excess contribution has been withdrawn.

Note that up to $2,000 of the excess contribution may escape the excise tax if the retiree elects to recharacterize that amount as an IRA contribution from wages for the year, provided the retiree has wages of at least that amount for the year. This recharacterization may be repeated in subsequent years if the retiree continues to have wages of at least the amount being recharacterized. If the retiree has no wages, however, such recharacterization is impossible.

The second tax consequence that will result from the excess contribution is the conversion of the after-tax money that has erroneously been rolled over but not withdrawn in time into taxable money. When the excess contribution is withdrawn from the account, it is as fully taxable as any other IRA withdrawal would be. (The distribution of this money is also subject to the 10 percent early distribution tax if it is applicable.)

IRA Investments

An IRA is not a particular type of investment. It is simply a tax-deferral umbrella that can protect almost any type of investment from tax while it is held in the account. The IRA can be invested in certificates of deposit, money market funds, stocks, bonds, annuities— almost anything. However, a few types of investments are specifically prohibited: investments in which the IRA owner is dealing with himself or a related party (for example, by investing the IRA in the mortgage on his own house or selling property to the IRA); investments in collectibles other than certain U.S. gold and silver coins; and investments in life insurance policies.

The First Required Withdrawal

Beginning with the year in which an IRA owner reaches age 70½, federal law requires the owner to withdraw at least a certain amount from the account each year. This rule and the somewhat complex calculations that go with it are designed to make it likely that the IRA will last no longer than the lifetime of the owner or the owner and his or her designated beneficiary.

The minimum amount that must be withdrawn at age 70½ is determined by dividing the owner's remaining years of life expectancy (or the combined life expectancy of the owner and the designated beneficiary) into the balance of the IRA as of the start of the year. If the retiree owns more than one IRA, this calculation is done separately for each account. However, the actual withdrawal can come from any account or combination of accounts. Table 8.2 shows the calculation of the required withdrawal for three IRAs belonging to the same person.

For account A, containing $20,000 at the start of the year, the owner has designated no beneficiary. The minimum withdrawal is therefore based on the owner's life expectancy alone, which at age 70 is 16 years. The required minimum withdrawal is therefore $1,250 (20,000 divided by 16). For account B, containing $50,000, the designated beneficiary is the retiree's spouse, who is 67. The combined life expectancy of the owner and his or her spouse is 22.0 years, resulting in a minimum withdrawal of $2,273 ($50,000 divided by 22).

For account C, containing $30,000, the designated beneficiary is the retiree's nephew, who is 51 years old. Federal regulations prohibit the use of the *actual* age of any beneficiary who is more than ten years younger than the owner unless that beneficiary is the owner's spouse. The purpose of this rule is to keep retirees from setting up distribution patterns under which the lifetime withdrawals by the retiree are small, with most of the money distributed to the beneficiary after the owner dies. For this example, then, the nephew is treated as if he

TABLE 8.2. Calculating the first Required Withdrawal

	Account A	Account B	Account C
Balance	$20,000	$50,000	$30,000
Life Expectancy	16.0	22.0	26.2
Required Withdrawals	$1,250	$2,273	$1,145

were 60 years old—ten years younger than the owner. The combined life expectancy for people of ages 70 and 60 is 26.2 years, resulting in a required withdrawal of $1,145 (30,000 divided by 26.2).

The required withdrawals from the three accounts total $4,668 (1,250 + 2,272 + 1,145). This amount can be withdrawn from any account or any combination of accounts to meet the minimum distribution requirement.

The Deadline for Withdrawals

In general, required withdrawals must be made by the end of the year. The first required withdrawal, however, can be made as late as April 1 of the year *following* the year in which the account owner reaches age 70½. This postponement option is not available for succeeding years. If the first withdrawal is postponed until April, of course, two withdrawals will fall into that calendar year, one representing the postponed withdrawal for the year in which the owner reached age 70½ and one representing the required withdrawal for the second year, the year in which the owner reached age 71½. Both withdrawals are subject to income tax for the year in which the withdrawals actually occur.

Withdrawals in the Second Year and Beyond

After the first required withdrawal calculation has been made, the life expectancy used for the owner in succeeding years' calculations may be refigured or simply reduced by one each year. The life expectancy of the beneficiary may be treated in the same way, except that special rules apply to life expectancies for beneficiaries other than spouses. Rules governing the calculation of required withdrawals and the life expectancy tables that must be used are given in IRS Publication 590, *Individual Retirement Arrangements (IRAs)*.

The Penalty for Underwithdrawals

Not withdrawing at least the total required amount each year from age 70½ onward triggers one of the most severe penalties in federal tax law: an excise tax equal to 50 percent of the amount that should have been withdrawn but was not.

If the required withdrawal amount is $10,000, for example, and the retiree withdraws only $2,000, the amount of the underwithdrawal is $8,000 and the excise tax is $4,000. The excise tax has no effect on the taxability of the $8,000 when it is later withdrawn. It is treated as any other IRA withdrawal would be. The IRS has the authority to waive the excise tax if the retiree can show that the underwithdrawal resulted from ignorance or oversight. (Needing or not needing the withdrawal amount has nothing to do with it. The law has no requirement that the retiree *spend* the money, only that he or she withdraw it from the IRA and claim it as income for the year.)

RECOMMENDED READINGS

Individual Retirement Arrangements (IRAs). IRS Publication 590.

IRA Game Plans: Making the Rules Work for You. Pension Plan Guide no. 732 (March 1989). Chicago: Commerce Clearing House, Inc.

Mayo, Herbert B. 1991. *Investments: An Introduction*, 3rd edition. Chicago: The Dryden Press.

United Business Service Company. 1991. *Successful Investing*, 5th edition. New York: Simon and Schuster.

Wolf, Harold A. 1991. *Personal Financial Planning*, 8th edition. Needham, Mass.: Allyn and Bacon.

9

Early Retirement

●

NORMAN STEIN

Private employers in the United States began sponsoring pension plans in the late nineteenth century. Some of the earliest pension plans made provisions for some employees with long service to retire earlier than other employees. Today such provisions are common features of retirement plans, reflecting a trend toward generally earlier retirement, especially among white-collar and skilled blue-collar workers.

This chapter examines various legal and practical aspects of an employer's desire to sponsor a plan offering all or some of its employees the ability to retire earlier than the plan's normal retirement age. The first section of the chapter describes several common approaches to providing early retirement benefits, including so-called window programs that offer employees the opportunity to apply for such benefits during a specified period of time. The second section examines some of the factors that an employer will consider in determining whether to adopt such a program and designing one. The final section suggests a framework for employees to use in determining whether to participate in an early retirement program.

TYPES OF EARLY RETIREMENT PROGRAMS

Nonwindow Programs in Tax-Qualified Defined Benefit Pension Plans

The Employee Retirement Income Security Act of 1974 (ERISA) requires defined benefit pension plans to provide a normal retirement benefit, which is payable at a normal retirement age specified in the plan. Most plans set the normal retirement age at age sixty-five. But the majority of plans also allow some employees to elect to begin receiving benefits by retiring at earlier ages, generally after working for a specified length of time. These early retirement programs are as varied as the needs of the different employers who sponsor them.

The most basic distinction among early retirement programs is whether or not they subsidize the early retirement benefit. A nonsubsidized early retirement benefit has a present actuarial value equal to the present value of the plan's normal retirement benefit. This means that the amount of the monthly retirement annuity payable to an employee who retires early will be less than the normal retirement benefit. The reduction in the amount of the annuity reflects the extra costs to the plan of the early commencement date of the annuity (McGill and Grubbs 1989).

Computation of a nonsubsidized early retirement benefit thus requires the calculation of the normal retirement benefit, and then requires a reduction in the benefit so computed. A plan might specify a method of determining actuarial assumptions. (For example, a plan might provide that the actuary will determine mortality in accordance with the assumptions of a particular mortality table and determine the interest rate assumption by using the interest rate applicable to long-term government debt instruments. Or a plan might use the interest and mortality assumptions used for the purposes of funding the plan at the time an employee takes early retirement.) Alternatively, a plan might specify a set of fixed actuarial assumptions (for example, the UP-1984 mortality table and an interest rate of 6 percent) or a set of mathematical reduction factors reflecting the assumptions (for example, a 10.40 percent reduction of the normal retirement benefit for retirement at age sixty-four, a 19.5 percent reduction for retirement at age, and so on) (McGill and Grubbs 1989).

Generally reduction factors of the sort described are based on conservative interest assumptions or the interest assumption initially adopted by a plan used for funding purposes. The use of reduction factors can result in a benefit that penalizes an employee if the reduction factor is based on an interest assumption that is unrealistically low given the long-term interest rates available in the market. Conversely, the reduction factors might result in a subsidy of the benefit if the reduction factor is based on an interest assumption that is below the rates that are commercially available in a given year.

A plan might choose to subsidize early retirement benefits, i.e., make them more valuable than an employee's currently accrued normal retirement benefit. Generally such plans make eligibility for a subsidized benefit contingent on an employee's having reached a specified age and accumulated a specified number of years of service for the employer.

The most generous type of subsidized early retirement benefits are those whose annuity payments are not reduced at all relative to the accrued normal retirement benefit. Plans generally require that employees put in long years of service and reach a specified age to receive an unreduced early retirement benefit, e.g., thirty years of service and age sixty-two.

Plans may also provide a subsidized early retirement benefit that is reduced but not to the point at which it is actuarially equivalent to the plan's normal retirement benefit. Plans that offer a benefit with less than a full actuarial reduction typically do so by providing generous benefit reduction factors—for example, by using a reduction factor of 4 percent for each year prior to normal retirement age—which, in the view of most actuaries, would yield a subsidized benefit.

Generally a plan will offer a subsidized early retirement benefit only to an employee who elects it while still employed by the plan sponsor. The Internal Revenue Code, however, requires that a plan offering employees an early retirement benefit also offer an early retirement benefit to former employees after they have reached the plan's early retirement age. However, this benefit does not have to be subsidized.

In addition to the common forms of early retirement benefits, some plans offer special types of early retirement benefits. One such relatively common type is a *Social Security bridge benefit*, also known as a *Social Security supplement* or, more accurately, a *Social Security replacement benefit*. The purpose of this type of benefit is to provide additional income until an employee reaches the earliest age at which he or she is eligible for Social Security benefits or, alternatively, the age at which the employee becomes entitled to an unreduced Social Security benefit. When employees reach the age specified by their plans, the Social Security bridge payment ends. As a result, the retiree receives a roughly level stream of income throughout retirement.

Another specialized form of early retirement benefit is the disability benefit, which may allow an employee to begin drawing benefits after experiencing a total disability. Disability benefits may be subsidized but need not be. Most disability benefits reflect at least a modest subsidy over the accrued normal retirement benefit.

Window Benefit Programs

To meet specific needs, some employers offer generously subsidized retirement benefits to some or all of their employees who elect to retire during a specified period of time. These *window programs* will often do more than provide an unreduced early retirement benefit; they may also expand the group of employees eligible for early retirement and/or boost the size of the retirement benefit as calculated under the plan's formula.

A common way of increasing benefits in plans with benefit formulas based in part on years of service is to credit employees who elect the window benefit with additional years of service. (This method, along with treating employees as if they were a set number of years older than their true age, can also be used to extend eligibility to employees who are not yet eligible for early retirement, as in "five and five" plans.) Plans may also improve benefits by increasing them by a set percentage or by a flat dollar amount. Employees might also receive an additional sum of money, sometimes in a lump sum, in addition to their retirement benefits under the plan. It is also not uncommon for window programs to include employer-provided health insurance.

Window programs can be made available to all employees or only to specified groups of employees. The employer will specify the window period (the Older Workers Protection Act, enacted in 1990, generally prohibits a window period of fewer than forty-five days). The window program may be either unlimited—that is, providing benefits to all who apply—or limited to a specified number of employees. If the window enrollment is limited, the program will specify how employees are selected.

EMPLOYERS CONSIDERATIONS IN PROVIDING AND DESIGNING EARLY RETIREMENT BENEFITS

Nonwindow Programs

An employer might permit early retirement under a plan for a variety of reasons. Perhaps the most common reason finds its origins in the belief of some employers that workers over a certain age cease to be productive or that their compensation exceeds that paid to younger employees by a greater margin than does their productivity. Or an employer might believe that older employees create morale problems for younger employees, who find their promotion opportunities blocked by older workers. Early retirement programs, especially those offering subsidized benefits, encourage early retirement. (The desire to encourage retirement is also a reason that employers adopt retirement plans generally.)

Prior to enactment of the Age Discrimination in Employment Act (ADEA) in 1967, an employer could force employees to retire early if their supervisors believed that their productivity was sufficiently diminished. However, many employers eschewed this approach either because of the adverse effect it might have on morale or due to a moral concern for the older workers' welfare. With the passage of the ADEA, employers who were inclined to force the early retirement of some of its employees found their ability to do so diminished. Therefore, early retirement programs have become especially attractive to employers who believe it is in their interest to encourage some employees to retire early. This belief is probably the most common motivation for medium-sized to large employers' establishing early retirement programs, particularly programs offering subsidized benefits.

Employers may also decide to establish early retirement programs for other reasons. Some employers sponsor such programs because they believe they provide valuable, deserved rewards for employees who have provided long and faithful service. In some cases, market forces compel employers to offer early retirement programs in order to improve their competitive posture in the labor market. In other cases, a union may bargain for early retirement benefits. It is also possible that some smaller employers adopted subsidized early retirement programs primarily because ERISA's funding rules had permitted increased tax-favored contributions if the plan offered an early retirement benefit that was more valuable than the plan's normal retirement benefit.

There are countervailing considerations as well. Early retirement programs, at least those offering subsidized benefits, may substantially increase the costs of plans. Even when benefits are not subsidized, greater-than-anticipated utilization of early retirement by employees might pose cash-flow problems to some plans in which funding for benefits is not yet fully amortized.

Another significant consideration is the impact early retirement might have on the employer's work force. Especially with a highly trained work force, a significant number of employees' retiring early may prove costly to the employer because of the costs of both recruiting and training new employees. Moreover, it is difficult to make predictions about the utilization rates of an early retirement option;

various factors may suddenly and unpredictably increase the rate of early retirements for a particular industry or a particular employer.

An additional problem for some employers is that highly skilled employees may elect early retirement and then use their benefits to support themselves as they set up a business to compete against the employer (or to supplement salary payments from a competitor of the employer). However, in some circumstances it is possible for a plan to include a provision suspending the early retirement benefits of a retired employee who returns to employment (Department of Labor Regulations, 29 CFR, section 25.303-3).[1]

Window Programs

Once adopted, a nonwindow early retirement program is essentially out of the employer's control until and unless the employer amends the plan. Therefore, such a program may meet the employer's perceived long-term goals for its retirement plan, but it may not be a particularly effective instrument for effecting the employer's short-term goals concerning the size and/or demographics of its work force. Window retirement programs offer an employer the opportunity to use the retirement plan to meet such goals.

The most common reason for an employer to adopt a window program is the need to reduce its work force. Permitting employees to elect to retire voluntarily under a window program is often preferable to forcing terminations. In the absence of a window program, an employer will generally have limited options for scaling down the size of the work force. For example, the employer might terminate employees on the basis of least seniority. Often, however, this will be an unattractive option, as the employer may wish to retain relatively junior employees, whose compensation will be lower and whose productivity in some cases will be equal or superior to that of senior employees, especially in a relatively unskilled work force, where experience does not always add measurably to workers' productivity. In addition, terminating younger employees may have an adverse effect on the employer's reputation in the labor market.

The alternative to basing work-force reductions on seniority is to base them on individualized judgments about each employee's contributions to productivity and costs of compensation. Such judgments will often lead the employer to lay off more senior employees. Such an alternative, although inherently more attractive to some employers, is fraught with difficulties. Employers who are parties to collective bargaining agreements may be unable to reduce their work forces on any basis other than seniority. An employer may also feel a strong moral responsibility toward employees who have spent their careers with the employer and may also fear that laying off senior employees will create morale problems with the remaining members of the work force (who may better understand seniority-based layoffs) or problems for the employer's reputation in the community. Perhaps most significant, basing decisions on factors other than seniority has a tendency to spawn lawsuits under the ADEA.

Early retirement window programs provide an employer with the opportunity to encourage the retirement of older employees by offering them incentives to retire early. This accomplishes indirectly what the employer may have found difficult to accomplish directly. Or an employer may use early retirement windows simply to decrease the number of senior employees on the payroll and open opportunities for promoting and hiring younger employees, perhaps younger employees with better skills and training. In some senses, then, early retirement windows allow employers to circumvent the restrictions of the ADEA, raising troubling moral questions, to which I will return at the end of this section.

There is a sometimes powerful tax reason why an employer may decide to open a window program. An employer may have a substantially overfunded tax-qualified pension plan. The tax laws currently include excise taxes that make it expensive for an employer to take an asset reversion from the plan. But these assets may generally be used as part of an early retirement incentive program.

At least some empirical research has shown that window programs are effective in increasing the rate of retirements, especially among employees in their middle fifties to early sixties (Lumsdaine, Stock, and Wise 1990). This success, however, carries with it the seeds of a serious problem, as a window might encourage essential employees to retire. The window program can be targeted at divisions, plants, or classifications of employees, but it can be difficult to comply with tax requirements if a tax-qualified plan limits the plan to specifically named employees. However, one way to retain particular employees is to provide them incentives to stay, such as stock options or incentive bonuses. In addition, an employer can target specific employees through a plan that is not qualified for tax purposes.

Window programs also involve other problems, particularly in the area of compliance with a bewildering array of legal rules under the Internal Revenue Code, ERISA, and the ADEA (Hennessey 1991; Macy 1991). For example, the ADEA limits the amount of pressure a program may impose on employees to elect participation in a window. Some employers and consultants believe that imposing pressure increases the utilization of such programs. Indeed, some consultants note that window programs might be combined with prospective reductions in other employer-provided benefits, allowing employers to use both a carrot and stick (Macy 1991). However, if the pressure is too extreme the program may not be considered voluntary and thus will violate the ADEA. Among factors that are relevant in assessing whether a program is voluntary are the length of the period employees have to elect participation, the amount of pressure applied by supervisory personnel, and the appropriateness of other actions, such as the prospective reduction of benefits for employees who do not elect to participate.

The Internal Revenue Code places substantial limits on the design of window programs in order to achieve important social policy goals and to limit the opportunities for tax abuse. For example, section 415 of the code limits the maximum benefit from a defined benefit plan to a normal retirement annuity of an inflation-adjusted dollar figure, which is $115,651 for 1993. This figure is actuarially adjusted if the payment of benefits commences before the recipient reaches Social Security retirement age.

Section 411(d)(6) of the Internal Revenue Code[2] and section 204(g) of ERISA[3] prohibit plans from reducing or eliminating benefits, including early retirement benefits. (However, these sections permit plans to reduce or eliminate benefits on a prospective basis.) Treasury regulations indicate that in certain circumstances repeatedly offering window programs may cause the window to be propped open permanently, without regard to the time periods specified in the programs (Treasury Regulations, section 1.411(d)-4(c)).[4]

Window plans also raise issues regarding tax qualification with respect to the rules in the Internal Revenue Code (IRC) that prohibit plans from favoring highly compensated employees (IRC, section 401(a)(4))[2]; limiting social security integration (IRC, section 401(a)(5))[2]; requiring minimum participation (IRC, section 401(a)(26))[2]; establishing minimum funding standards (IRC, section 412)[2]; requiring that the rules for security bonds be applied to benefit improvements in underfunded plans (IRC, section 401(a)(29)[2]; requiring that pension benefits be definitely determinable (Treasury Regulations, section 1.401-1(b)(1)(i)[4]; restricting pension plans from providing layoff benefits (Treasury Regulations, section 1.401-1(b)(1)(i)[4]; requiring vesting for partial terminations (IRC section 411(d)(3))[2]; and mandating the use of a joint and survivor annuity as the normal form of plan benefit (IRC, section 411(a)(11))[2].

An important consideration, then, for an employer who decides to open a retirement window program is whether to do so in the context of a tax-qualified or a nonqualified plan. The rules applicable to tax-qualified plans apply to nonqualified plans only when there is a parallel ERISA rule. (For example, the rules relating to accrued benefits, funding, and joint and survivor annuities have ERISA analogues, although such rules are not applicable to certain unfunded plans for management—"top-hat plans"—or to unfunded plans designed to provide benefits in excess of the limitations imposed under section 415—"excess plans" (ERISA, sections 4(b)(5), 201(2), and 301(a)(9))[3], nor do they apply to plans that qualify as severance pay welfare-benefit plans (ERISA, section 301(a)(1), and 29 CFR, section 2510.3-2(b))[3]. However, there are ERISA fiduciary and disclosure rules that apply to most employee benefit plans other than "top-hat" plans.

Early retirement plans also raise issues under the ADEA. This act generally applies to employers with more than twenty employees. A significant 1990 amendment to the ADEA permits early retirement incentive programs that are consistent with the purposes of the ADEA. The legislative history provides examples that make it clear that a window program is consistent with the purposes of the ADEA if it increases the benefit on either a percentage or a flat dollar basis or if the plan recognizes additional years for purposes of age or service. A window program would be inconsistent with the purposes of the act if it were limited to employees under a certain age.

A plan may also violate the ADEA if it turns out to be a forced retirement program rather than a true optional retirement plan. In addition, the 1990 amendment provided rules governing waivers of ADEA rights, and some window programs make the election of such waivers a condition of participation. The election of such a waivers must be made voluntarily by an informed employee, and an employee must have at least forty-five days to consider signing such a waiver if it is in connection with an early retirement window plan.

Additional legal requirements apply when a group of employees has selected a bargaining representative recognized by the National Labor Relations Board. The employer must bargain with the bargaining representative before implementing an early retirement program. Moreover, a program must be consistent with any collective bargaining agreement unless the union agrees to amend it.

The Taft-Hartley Act requires some collectively bargained plans to be administered jointly by the employers and union representatives. Some jointly administered plans permit the trustees of the plans to amend their benefits. Such decisions cannot be arbitrary or capricious. Special rules under the Internal Revenue Code relieve plans from some of the legal requirements applicable to pension plans.

Window programs raise moral questions pertaining to age discrimination. Giving older employees an option to retire early with enhanced benefits does not, in itself, pose moral questions. However, forcing older employees to retire before they wish does, particularly when an employee has rendered long service to a particular employer. A window program, though voluntary in form, may feel like a forced retirement program if too much pressure is applied to the employee. Therefore, employers face moral concerns (as opposed to merely legal ones) in structuring early retirement windows.

THE EMPLOYEE'S PERSPECTIVE
OF EARLY RETIREMENT

Deciding when to retire involves a complex blend of financial and personal calculations. Unfortunately many employees lack the financial sophistication necessary to make informed decisions. Therefore, many employees would benefit from professional counseling when they are deciding whether to accept early retirement. Some corporations make such counseling available in group seminars, individual counseling sessions, or both. At their best, counselors will be familiar not only with the financial aspects of early retirement, but also with the psychological and personal dimensions of retirement.

Among the factors of a person considering early retirement should consider are the following:

1. How will early retirement affect the size of retirement benefits? Early retirement benefits, particularly in window programs, will often be more valuable than the normal retirement benefit accrued to date. However, under many plans continuing to work for the employer will increase the normal retirement benefit because such benefits are often based on service and final pay, both of which generally increase as the employee continues to work. This factor may be less important if the employee will accrue retirement benefits working for another employer, although the individual should carefully compare that projected benefit against the additional benefits that he or she would earn by continuing to work for the original employer. An employee should also determine what effect leaving the labor market will have on the amount of his or her Social Security benefits. In addition, an employee should learn whether electing early retirement benefits will affect other benefits offered by the employer or benefits available from state, local, and private agencies.

2. What are the employee's retirement plans? Does he or she plan to engage in leisure activities or community service or to continue to work, either self-employed or working for another employer? This is an important question not only in terms of financial planning, but also in terms of quality of life, because research indicates that retirees sometimes experience mental health problems if they do not have activities to replace work. A good question for prospective retirees to ask is: What will I do the day after I retire? If they cannot answer that question, they may not be ready to retire.

3. What are the employee's financial needs? How might those needs change over time? Other than funds to meet medical expenses, retirees often need less than 100 percent replacement of their income. This reflects not only the elimination of job-related costs, but also the fact that retirees will not be paying the Social Security payroll tax.

4. What are the employee's other sources of financial income? These might include Social Security, benefits from other government and philanthropic agencies, insurance contracts, pension benefits from other employers, and personal savings. Are any such sources currently available? Are any of them (other than Social Security) indexed to inflation? (Typically benefits from defined benefit plans are not.) If they are not, some assets should be set aside to enable the retiree to cope with future inflationary pressure on routine retirement expenses. The employee should also make a decision regarding when to begin receiving Social Security benefits and the effect early commencement will have on the amount of the benefits. The employee should additionally reassess his or her investment goals. After retirement, the safety of the investment rather than the maximization of income or aggressive growth is often paramount.

5. How will retirement affect the employee's taxes? Generally the employee will no longer pay Social Security taxes, and he or she may be in lower state and federal income tax brackets. Special tax rules might apply to employees who receive lump-sum distributions. State law may also provide certain exemptions or other types of income and property tax benefits for senior citizens.

6. What benefit options are available to the retiree under his or her pension plan? Which options are most valuable financially, and which are most compatible with the employee's own financial needs?

7. What are the feelings of the employee's spouse? These feelings are often undervalued as a consideration, although federal law generally requires spousal consent for retirement plan options that provide less spousal protection than a 50 percent joint and survivor annuity benefit.
8. How will the employee pay for health care? Some employers have health care programs for retirees, and early retirement windows often include such benefits. However courts have generally permitted employers to terminate these programs or reduce the benefits payable under them unless the employers have made binding contractual commitments otherwise. (Such a commitment is sometimes found in a collective bargaining contract or in a situation in which an employee, given a choice between a cash severance payment and medical benefits for retirement, chooses the medical benefits.) Employees should bear in mind that, although a person may elect actuarially reduced Social Security benefits at age sixty-two, Medicare will not commence until the employee reaches age sixty-five. In assessing whether to retire early, the employee will want to consider the value of the health benefits he or she is receiving as an employee.
9. How will early retirement affect the employee's ability to finance long-term care if that becomes necessary in the future?
10. In the event of an emergency, what resources are available to help the employee? These may include the employee's church, union, fraternal organization, and family.

CONCLUSION

Early retirement programs provide challenges (and opportunities) for both employers and employees. For an employer the challenge is to design a program that effects personnel strategies; for an employee, to evaluate the benefits and costs of the early retirement program offered. For both employer and employee, good communication is key. It is difficult for an employer to design a sound early retirement program without understanding employees' concerns and desires. It is equally difficult for an employee to evaluate an early retirement program without the employer's clear communication of the program's features, costs, and benefits.

NOTES

1. Department of Labor Regulations, 26 Code of Federal Regulations, sections 2500 and following.
2. Internal Revenue Code, sections 401 and following; 26 United States Code, sections 401 et seq.
3. Employee Retirement Income Security Act of 1974, Public Law No. 93-407, 88 Stat. 829, 29 United States Code, sections 1001 and following.
4. Treasury Regulations, sections 1.401-1 and following.

REFERENCES

Boren, G. 1991. *Qualified Deferred Compensation Plans*. Chicago: Callaghan & Co.
Hennessey, N. 1991. "Legal Issues Involving Early Retirement Incentive Programs." Meeting Materials, American Bar Association, Section of Taxation, May Meeting. Philadelphia: The American Law Institute-American Bar Association.
Lumsdaine, R., J. Stock, and D. Wise. "Efficient Windows and Labor Market Reduction." Working Paper no. 3369, National Bureau of Economic Research. Cambridge: Lumsdaine, Stock and Wise.
Macy, S. 1991. "Early Retirement Window Benefits in Qualified Plans." Meeting Materials, American Bar Association, Section of Taxation, May Meeting. Philadelphia: The American Law Institute-American Bar Association.
McGill, D., and D. Grubbs. 1989. *Fundamentals of Private Pensions*, 6th ed. Homewood, Ill.: Richard D. Irwin, Inc.

10

Converting Home Equity into Income

●

BRUCE JACOBS

The great majority of the elderly people in America head their own households. Rates of home ownership among them have been steadily increasing, from just under two-thirds in 1970 to more than three-quarters in 1989, when there were fifteen million elderly homeowners in the United States (U.S. Bureau of the Census 1973; U.S. Bureau of the Census 1991). While people with higher incomes are more likely to own their homes than those with lower incomes, a majority of elderly people with incomes below $10,000 (62 percent) are home-owners (U.S. Bureau of the Census 1991:334). More than four of every five older homeowners have paid off their mortgages and own their homes free and clear (U.S. Bureau of the Census 1991:344).

THE UNUSED ASSET

In addition to their consumption value and symbolic importance, homes represent the primary form of savings older people have amassed during their lifetimes. In 1988 the median net worth of all households of elderly people was $73,471. Without home equity (i.e., the value of the house minus any outstanding debt), this figure drops to $23,856 (U.S. Bureau of the Census 1990:6). Using earlier data, Friedman and Sjogren (1981) found that the median proportion of total wealth held in the form of home equity was 70 percent for all elderly homeowners and 83 percent for the single women (mostly widows) among them.

As is the case for all homes, the real value of homes owned by older

140

people has increased significantly (though not uniformly) over the last two decades. Expressed in 1989 dollars, the average value of these houses rose from $47,900 in 1970 to $96,000 in 1989. Median values went from $39,600 to $70,100 over the same period (U.S. Bureau of the Census 1973; U.S. Bureau of the Census 1991).

Significant levels of home equity are not limited to the wealthy. Jacobs (1986:497) found that in 1984 nearly a quarter of poor elderly homeowners had net home equity in excess of $50,000. (Of course, this figure would be higher today.) Among the reasons many older people are "house rich but cash poor" is the fact that widowhood is often accompanied by a substantial loss of income, even among those who have been in the middle class throughout their lives. In addition, some regions and metropolitan areas have enjoyed very high rates of inflation in home values over the past few decades. Therefore, some owners who struggled to buy their homes for under $25,000 in the 1950s now have ten times that amount or more tied up in their houses, even though their retirement incomes are quite modest.

For the most part, elderly homeowners have not used the assets they hold in the form of home equity to finance current consumption. This is true in part because they choose not to (or cannot) use either of the options most readily available to them—taking out "home equity loans" of the type marketed to all homeowners, or selling their houses and moving.

Those seeking home equity loans must qualify on the basis of their incomes rather than solely on the basis of their home equity assets. These loans are amortized over short periods and require monthly payments throughout the these periods. A high percentage of elderly homeowners who might want to borrow money would not have the requisite incomes to finance the loans during their retirement years.

There is a wide body of attitudinal and behavioral evidence documenting the reluctance of most older homeowners to leave their homes. While a relatively small minority will sell and move voluntarily, typically soon after retirement, these people tend to have more financial resources than the average person (Jackson et al. 1991). The fact is, a large majority of the elderly are very strongly attached to their homes, have not made plans to leave them, and intend to stay in them for as long as possible, preferably the rest of their lives (American Association of Retired Persons 1990; Jacobs 1985; Jacobs 1990).

Of course, a nontrivial number of older people are forced to leave their homes, usually late in their lifetimes. The primary reason is a declining capacity to function independently, often accompanied by a lack of available caregivers (Jackson et al. 1991; Speare et al. 1991). However, even in these circumstances many people make adjustments that allow them to remain in their homes (e.g., retrofitting their houses to accommodate their physical limitations or taking others in to live with them). Therefore, there is ample reason to believe that older homeowners who might want to use some of their home equity assets would prefer to remain in their homes if possible.

REVERSE MORTGAGES

Until fairly recently, it was not possible for elderly homeowners simultaneously to spend some of their home equity (if they so chose), remain in their homes, and not have to make monthly payments on a loan. Today, however, an expanding array of public and private programs allow many to do just that by means of *home equity conversion* plans, also called *reverse mortgages*. These plans differ in many ways, as discussed below. Yet they share the common characteristic that elderly homeowners can enjoy the use of their equity assets without having to make payments or move from their homes. On the other hand, these plans involve other risks for both borrowers and lenders (e.g., for borrowers, not having the equity to use for other purposes later on). These risks are discussed below.

Perhaps the best way to understand what a "reverse mortgage" does is to compare it with a conventional mortgage loan that is used to purchase a home. In the latter case, the borrower receives a lump sum at the start of the loan term (which is used to pay the former owner), and after this he or she makes monthly payments throughout the loan term (e.g., thirty years). At the end of the term, the borrower will have completely repaid the loan (including principal and interest). If the process were reversed, the lender would make monthly payments to the homeowner over the term of the loan, at the end of which the borrower (or the borrower's estate) would pay a lump sum to the lender, thus repaying the loan with interest. This reverse process is what happens in the case of a reverse mortgage.

With a reverse mortgage, as with a conventional mortgage, the house serves as collateral. However, an older homeowner need meet no income requirement for a reverse mortgage; only the value of the house is taken into account. This is appropriate for the simple reason that such a borrower is likely to have a fairly low income.

Over the term of a conventional mortgage, the home equity assets of the borrower are likely to accumulate, with appreciation in home value combining with a declining level of outstanding debt. Over the term of a reverse mortgage, however, the home equity assets held by the borrower will typically decline, since there will be a constantly increasing outstanding debt that combines principal (payments to the borrower) and interest on the entire sum. This decline may be partially offset if the value of the house appreciates substantially. (Some reverse mortgage plans require borrowers to commit a portion of this appreciation to repay the loan.)

In the simplest kind of reverse mortgage, equal monthly payments (loan disbursements) are provided to the elderly borrower over a fixed term, with a prespecified rate of interest. Principal and interest accumulate throughout the term, which is likely to be between five and twenty years, with the outstanding debt the highest at its end. However, there are a variety of important ways in which home equity conversion plans differ. Among them are the following:

1. Term of the loan. In contrast to loans with fixed terms (number of years), some reverse mortgages can extend as long as the borrowers remain in their homes or as long as they live. The latter have sometimes been called *reverse annuity mortgages.* However, such lifetime loan plans are not yet widely available. Another possibility is that loan disbursements cease at the end of a fixed period, but the loan need not be repaid until the borrower leaves the home. All else being equal, the longer the term of the loan, the less the monthly payment available to the borrower and the more equity that will be used to pay the interest on the debt.

2. Interest rate. Most reverse mortgages have fixed rates of interest, typically providing market rates of return to the lenders. In some public and nonprofit programs, however, the rate is set below (sometimes much below) that level. Obviously, the higher the rate of interest, the smaller the monthly checks to the borrower will be. Another arrangement allows the homeowner to pay interest in two forms. In addition to a fixed base rate, the owner pledges a portion of the house's future appreciation as interest, in effect resulting in a variable interest rate. In this case, the higher the appreciation, the higher the effective interest rate will be.

3. Stream of payments to the owner. Up to this point I have discussed a simple reverse mortgage in which payments are made monthly to the borrower throughout the term of the loan. However, a reverse mortgage loan may also involve a lump-sum disbursement at the beginning of the loan, much as a conventional mortgage does. Another option, which has become increasingly popular, is a *line of credit loan* that allows borrowers to specify both the size of disbursements (within limits) and their timing (Scholen 1992).

4. Portion of equity committed to repay the loan. All reverse mortgages end when the borrowers die (or before). Since the time of death is unknown at the inception of the loan, the total accumulation of principal and interest will vary from one borrower to another. In this sense, the amount of equity actually required to pay off a specific loan is not known beforehand. However, most home equity conversion plans will specify a maximum amount of outstanding debt that will be allowed. This is usually set as a percentage of the value of the house, which is most often estimated at the beginning of the loan, but sometimes includes future appreciation. In all cases, the home equity left after the loan is completely repaid remains with the borrower (or the estate). The higher the fraction of the home's value that is committed, the higher the amount of the loan disbursements.

5. Closing costs. As with conventional loans, typically a variety of charges are paid by the borrower (e.g., fees for lawyers and for a title search). In the majority of cases, these fees are folded into the loan as an initial disbursement and the borrower need not write a check to cover them. In some public programs there are few or no such charges. Obviously, the higher the initial disbursement to the borrower to pay fees, the smaller the among of future loan disbursements.

6. Mortgage insurance. The lender in a conventional loan sometimes requires mortgage insurance to guard against the possibility that the borrower will fail to make required monthly payments and that the value of the home will not cover the outstanding debt should the lender foreclose. If anything, reverse mortgages pose an even greater risk to the lender. This is because principal and interest continue to increase over the term of the loan. One reason many mortgage lenders have not embraced the notion of reverse mortgages has been the lack of protection against this risk. To address this concern, the federal government has launched the Home Equity Conversion Mortgage Insurance Demonstration, which authorizes the Federal Housing Administration to insure up to 25,000 loans through the end of the 1994 fiscal year (Scholen 1992; U.S. Department of Housing and Urban Development 1989). This program allows lenders throughout the nation to offer a variety of reverse mortgage loans to elderly homeowners with the knowledge that the federal government is assuming most of the risk of borrower default.

7. Purpose of the loan. Most reverse mortgages simply provide cash payments to borrowers, who may do as they please with

the proceeds. However, some government home equity conversion programs are for specific uses. The most popular of these is called *property tax deferral*. In several states (California, Oregon, and Wisconsin, among others) elderly homeowners are allowed to defer paying their property taxes until they sell their homes or their estates are settled. These loans are not called reverse mortgages, but in effect that is what they are. States make payments to the local taxing authorities, and are later reimbursed, typically at very low interest rates. Another popular form of home equity conversion for a specific purpose is also offered by the public sector, though mostly by local government agencies. In many localities around the nation, deferred payment loans are available to pay for necessary home repairs, weatherization, retrofitting, or other housing expenses (Scholen 1992). Of course, all reverse mortgage loans can also be used for these purposes.

One of the reasons for converting home equity to cash is to help offset health-care costs. This may be an option that is especially appropriate to address the long-term care needs of those at highest risk of having them (Jacobs and Weissert 1987).

THE POTENTIAL IMPACT OF REVERSE MORTGAGES

A variety of studies using different data sets have shown that home equity conversion could significantly increase the incomes of many elderly homeowners, especially those with limited incomes (Jacobs 1980; Jacobs 1986; Jacobs and Weissert 1987). In fact, the maximum payments that could be realized by elderly homeowners using one plan provided in the private sector did not vary much relative to the borrowers' incomes. For example, the percentage of owners who would receive more than $3,000 per year (in 1984 dollars) for as long as they stayed in their homes varied from a low of 25 percent of those with incomes below the official poverty line to 29 percent of those with incomes more than twice that high (Jacobs 1986:498).

This finding seems contrary to what one would expect to find. While some lower-income elderly homeowners have substantial home equity, on average the homes of these people are worth less than the homes of those with higher incomes (Jacobs 1986:497). Furthermore, the more equity one has to convert, the higher the potential monthly payments, all else being equal. Empirically, however, all else is not equal. Older homeowners who have low incomes are likely to share two qualities—being single and being age seventy-five or older. These characteristics combine to allow reverse mortgage lenders to guarantee higher monthly payments than would be the case if they were married or younger.

What is essential here is that, the smaller the number of years over which reverse mortgage payments are spread, the larger the amount of the monthly loan disbursements and the smaller the amount of interest owed at the end of the loan's term. This is analogous to what happens with conventional home mortgages. If one switches from a thirty-year loan to a fifteen-year loan, much less interest is paid; each check includes a higher portion of principal relative to interest.

When a homeowner who is sixty-five takes out a reverse mortgage guaranteeing payments as long as he or she remains in the home, the term is expected to be quite a bit longer than for a loan to a person who is seventy-five given the shorter life expectancy of someone that age. Similarly, if a couple must be guaranteed payments for as long as either is in the house, the term is expected to be longer than if the borrower were the same age, but single.

In short, the people who are best positioned to convert their home equity into a long-term income stream are single and among the oldest in the population. Those familiar with the demographics of aging know that a large majority of these people are women. While this is the profile of those who are likely to be the best positioned for home equity conversion, it is also the demographic profile of people who are most likely to need extra income. Levels of poverty among the aged are highest in this group, and the oldest of the old have the smallest amounts of assets other than home equity among the aged (U.S. Bureau of the Census 1990). In addition, those who are very old and alone are most likely to have long-term care needs and least likely to have readily available informal caregivers (Jacobs and Weissert 1987).

The impact of these demographic differences on the potential impact of home equity conversion can be dramatic. Jacobs (1986:499) found that the median increase in income that could be realized by single homeowners aged seventy-five or older was 58 percent. Poverty rates among this group could be lowered from 26 percent to 7 percent. In contrast, couples under the age of seventy-five could have their poverty rates lowered by only 2 percent.

The insight that is central to understanding the potential impact of reverse mortgages is the overlap between the profile of being best positioned to convert home equity and the profile of need for more income or health-care services. While this is a fortuitous circumstance, it also means that most elderly homeowners, who are younger than the profile group and more likely to be married, are not well situated to take out reverse mortgages.

SOME WORDS OF CAUTION

During the first decade or so in which home equity conversion plans have been available (albeit in just a few locations), a very modest number of older homeowners have availed themselves of this opportunity. Fewer than fifteen thousand reverse mortgages have been written by the dozen or so private plans that were available before the federal reverse mortgage insurance demonstration was launched. While well over one hundred thousand elderly homeowners have deferred their property taxes or taken out deferred payment loans for home repairs and the like (American Association of Retired Persons 1992), the total number of participants in all public and private plans represents a small portion of the potential market. Yet this should not be surprising. There are inhibiting factors on both the supply side and the demand side of this market.

Lenders have been reluctant to enter the reverse mortgage market for several reasons. Since reverse mortgages are new and sometimes complicated, lenders must invest substantial time in formulating and marketing their products without having a good idea of the potential interest on the part of consumers. Conventional mortgages appear to be surer and more profitable products to sell.

A second inhibition has been called the end-of-term problem. If a reverse mortgage is written with a fixed term at the end of which the loan is to be repaid and if the elderly borrower outlives the term and wants to stay in his or her home, the lender may be faced with an awful choice between foreclosing on a poor elderly person or taking a loss on the loan. If the home has appreciated sufficiently, its higher value might cover the outstanding debt later on, but it might not. The federal demonstration program is specifically aimed at reducing the end-of-term risk for reverse mortgage lenders, enabling them to offer these plans without great fear of large losses on loans taken out by borrowers who live a long time.

There are a variety of reasons elderly homeowners have been slow to take out these loans, especially those offered in the private sector. If the loans are somewhat complicated for lenders, they are all the more confusing to those who are likely to be in stressful situations and who have not made major financial decisions in quite a while. In addition, the age and marital status or low levels of equity of many elderly people simply preclude the possibility of their receiving large monthly payments from reverse mortgages. Equally important is the fact that most elderly people do not feel a strong need for more income (Harris et al. 1981:7). Finally, those elderly homeowners who remember the Depression have shown a substantial reluctance to take on any debt.

Reverse mortgage borrowers may have to face a variety of risks. Those who are not guaranteed the right to remain in their homes as long as they are able may face the other side of the end-of-term problem. More generally, the economic circumstances of the borrower may change in the future, with the homeowner regretting that he or she has already used the money for other purposes.

A related issue is the health of the homeowner. If the person loses functional independence, his or her ability to remain in the home may be severely threatened. While home equity can be used to pay for home care directly or for insurance premiums for long-term care (Jacobs and Weissert 1987), it might not be possible for some people to remain at home. If entry into a nursing home is necessary, home equity that has already been spent will not be available to help finance that stay.

Over the short history of the development of reverse mortgages, one issue that has been a source of confusion to some has been that concerning the tax implications of home equity conversion. However, there are only a few points to be made on this issue. First, payments made to elderly borrowers are loan disbursements and not income. Second, the accumulating interest on a loan can be deducted only in the year in which the loan is paid off, usually when the home is sold. It important to note that reverse mortgage borrowers rarely have sufficient incomes to worry about federal tax liabilities during the term of the loan. Finally, when the home is sold the deductible accumulated interest can be added to the once-in-a-lifetime deduction of $125,000 from the gain in the sale price of the home, thus canceling any tax liability for all but the most expensive homes.

There has been a fair amount of work done analyzing these and other risks for lenders and borrowers (American Bar Association 1991; Scholen 1991; Scholen 1992; Weinrobe 1990). Counseling potential reverse mortgage borrowers is a critical necessity. Advice and information are available from the AARP Home Equity Information Center, the National Center on Home Equity Conversion, and other local programs around the country. While a reverse mortgage can have a major positive impact on those in need, it is important for them to be reasonably sure that it makes sense for them in their current circumstances.

REFERENCES

American Association of Retired Persons. 1990. *Understanding Senior Housing for the 1980s.* Washington, D.C.: American Association of Retired Persons.

American Association of Retired Persons. 1992. "Progress and Challenges Mark 30 Years of Reverse Mortgage Lending." *Housing Report,* Spring: 4–6.

American Bar Association Commission on Legal Problems for the Elderly. 1991. *Attorney's Guide to Home Equity Conversion.* Washington, D.C.: American Bar Association.

Friedman, J., and J. Sjogren. 1981. "Assets of the Elderly as They Retire." *Social Security Bulletin,* 44:16–31.

Harris, L., et al. 1981. *Aging in the Eighties: America in Transition.* Washington, D.C.: National Council on Aging.

Jackson, J., C. Longino, Jr., R. Zimmerman, and J. Bradsher. 1991. "Environmental Adjustments to Declining Functional Ability." *Research on Aging,* 13(3):289–309.

Jacobs, B. 1980. "The Potential Anti-Poverty Impact of Reverse Annuity Mortgages and Property Tax Deferral." In K. Scholen and Y. P. Chen, eds., *Unlocking Home Equity for the Elderly.* Cambridge: Ballinger Books.

Jacobs, B. 1985. "Housing Policy for the Aged." In T. Tedrick, ed., *Aging: Issues and Policies for the 80's.* New York: Praeger.

Jacobs, B. 1986. "The National Potential for Home Equity Conversion." *The Gerontologist,* 26(5):496–504.

Jacobs, B. 1990. "Housing New York State's Elderly Population." In M. Wolkoff, ed., *Housing New York: Policy Challenges for the Year 2000.* Albany: SUNY Press.

Jacobs, B., and W. Weissert. 1987. "Using Home Equity to Finance Long-Term Care." *Journal of Health Politics, Policy and Law,* 12(1):77–95.

Scholen, K. 1991. *Home-Made Money: Consumer's Guide to Home Equity Conversion,* 3rd ed. Washington, D.C.: Home Equity Information Center, American Association of Retired Persons.

Scholen, K. 1992. *Retirement Income on the House.* Marshall, Minnesota: National Center for Home Equity Conversion.

Speare, A., Jr., R. Avery, and L. P. Lawton. 1991. "Disability, Residential Mobility and Changes in the Living Environment." *Journal of Gerontology: Social Sciences,* 46:S133–142.

U.S. Bureau of the Census. 1973. "Housing of Senior Citizens." *1970 Census of Housing.* Subject Report HC(7)-2. Washington, D.C.: U.S. Bureau of the Census.

U.S. Bureau of the Census. 1990. *Household Wealth and Asset Ownership: 1988.* Current Population Reports P-70, no. 22. Washington, D.C.: U.S. Bureau of the Census.

U.S. Bureau of the Census. 1991. *American Housing Survey for the United States in 1989.* Current Housing Reports H150/89. Washington, D.C.: U.S. Bureau of the Census.

U.S. Department of Housing and Urban Development. 1989. *Home Equity Conversion Mortgages.* Handbook 4235.1. Washington, D.C.: U.S. Department of Housing and Urban Development.

Weinrobe, M. 1990. *Home Equity Conversion for the Elderly: An Analysis for Lenders.* Washington, D.C.: Home Equity Information Center, American Association of Retired Persons.

IV
WORK AFTER RETIREMENT
●

11

The Job Market after Retirement

●

PHILIP L. RONES

Interest in older workers has escalated at the same time that older people have been continuing to make up a declining share of the work force. Such interest has been fueled by a wide range of events and issues. Among the factors leading to this growing focus on work and aging are the following:

- Federal law now prohibits discrimination on the basis of age against people age forty and over in such employment-related decisions as those concerning hiring, firing, retirement, and training. Before any such legislation existed, an upper age limit to employment (typically age sixty-five, the age of eligibility for full Social Security benefits) was an accepted part of American culture. Farmers or the self-employed might have worked to whatever age they desired (or were able), but wage-earning and salaried workers often faced mandatory retirement. Now, at least by law, older workers have equal rights to employment opportunities based on their abilities.
- The shift of employment out of manufacturing and into the service-based economy in recent decades has had a number of important ramifications. Primary among these have been dislocations for the many hundreds of thousands of people who have lost their long-held jobs as a result of this industry shift. Older workers are hardly protected against such job loss; they are most often displaced because of plant closings and moves, events against which seniority offers no protection. In addition, the pros-

pects for subsequent employment following displacement are relatively poor for older workers.

- The growing availability of retirement income over the past few
decades has allowed people to retire earlier and earlier, so that a
"typical" retirement age today (if such an age is meaningful) is
sixty-two, coinciding with the age at which workers first become
eligible for Social Security benefits. As a result, retirees of that
age or younger have at least several more years of good health following retirement than retirees did previously. In addition,
many retirees still leave the labor force with very low levels of retirement income. These factors result in a growing pool of older
people who might be interested in work or might be considered
available under the "right circumstances."

- Widowhood tends to leave the survivor, most often a woman,
with a very low level of retirement income. In 1990 the median
income for widowed women aged sixty-five and over was about
$8,689, and for widowed men it was $11,214 (Grad 1992). These
income levels compare with a median exceeding $20,000 for mar-
ried couples that age. Divorce leaves an individual in a similar
economic condition; the difference is that, while the likelihood of
widowhood has not been increasing, that of divorce has. In the
last twenty years the proportion of both men and women aged
fifty-five and over who are divorced has more than doubled—to
about 6 percent for men and 7 percent for women.[1] In coming
years this proportion is likely to grow further, leaving more and
more retirement-age people with a strong financial need to
work.

- Interest in the older worker, at least as it was reflected in the popular and business press, peaked in the late 1980s, as the economy
experienced an unusually long expansion. In that context—and
in view of the declining numbers of young people available to
join the work force—increasing attention was focused on older
workers as the solution to present and future labor shortages.
Employers also expressed increasing concern about the preparation and attitudes of younger workers. These factors together led
a few firms to launch well-publicized campaigns to attract older
workers. The recession of 1990–1991 largely put the issue of
shortages on hold. The long-term predictions, however, are still
operable: as a share of the working-age population, older people
will continue to increase—slowly for a while, and then rapidly
as the baby boomers begin reaching retirement ages between the
years 2005 and 2010. Their replacements will come from a shrinking pool of younger workers and, more and more, from among mi-

norities and immigrants, who may not have the preparation to compete for many of the available jobs.

For these reasons as well as others, employers have shown an interest that is growing (albeit slowly) in employing older workers at the same time that many potential workers, having "retired" at relatively early ages, have found themselves needing or wanting postretirement employment.

THE ISSUES INVOLVED IN COUNTING
RETIRED WORKERS

Ideally this chapter would outline the types of work opportunities available to retirees. However, such a seemingly simple task is actually quite impossible. The first problem (probably manageable) is identifying retirees from survey data on the employment characteristics of workers, a problem that will be discussed in more detail below. A more basic problem is that, other than measuring how many older retirees actually work, no data allow us to assess the actual or potential demand for the services of older workers. No national job vacancy survey exists. Also, employers typically do not advertise that they would consider (or prefer) older workers. Hence, reports of such targeted recruiting of older workers are more anecdotal than systematic, with mostly the same firms held up as examples of such targeted recruiting each year—The Travelers Companies, McDonald's, Days Inn, and only a few others.

While some jobs may indeed be available for older workers, these people may not apply for or accept them, either because of lack of information or because the types of jobs available—or the pay or working conditions associated with them—may not meet their requirements. Unless a retiree actually takes such a job, there is no way of identifying that job as an opportunity for a retiree.

Also, as mentioned, the "retired population" is quite difficult to define. Even a seemingly simple question, such as "What is the average age of retirement?" is virtually impossible to answer with precision, at least as it applies to the population in general. One must first define what retirement is. Is a nonworking sixty-year-old woman with no pension retired? What about a fifty-year-old employed man with a military pension? Or a sixty-six-year-old part-time consultant who receives Social Security and a private pension?

Approaches to defining *retirement* could focus either on labor force status or on pension receipt. In a simple definition based on labor force status, anyone above a certain age, say fifty-five, who is neither working nor looking for work could be considered retired. Regularly collected labor force data show that the median age of retirement— the age at which half the men are in the labor force and half are out— is sixty-two (Rones 1985). But if we use this concept, work among "retirees" is, by definition, impossible.

Moreover, such an exercise cannot be applied at all to women. One cannot necessarily assume that a sixty-two-year-old woman who is out of the labor force is retired. She may have had only a limited work history and may be ineligible for any pension. What would her "age of retirement" be?

A definition of retirement based on pension receipt can be equally problematic because some people receive pensions at very early ages and then continue to work full time for many more years. An extreme example is military personnel, who can retire after twenty years, while still in their late thirties or early forties. Assuming they were subsequently involved in other careers, these people certainly would not view themselves as retired.

In attempting to create a more meaningful view of postretirement employment for this handbook, data from the Current Population Survey (CPS) have been used to examine a combination of measures of pension receipt and labor force participation to identify the extent to which retirees work and the kinds of jobs they hold. In this survey, information on the employment status of the population is collected each month throughout the nation from a sample of about 60,000 households. The survey is conducted by the Census Bureau for the Bureau of Labor Statistics; it is the source of the unemployment rate, which is widely covered each month in the press. Each March an additional set of questions is asked about peoples' sources and levels of income during the previous calendar year. A combination of pension receipt (in this case, during calendar year 1989) and labor force status (in March 1990) was used to identify working "retirees"—that is, pension recipients who are employed.[2]

HOW MANY RETIRED WORKERS ARE THERE?

As shown in table 11.1, about fifteen million people aged fifty-five and over were employed in March 1990, and an additional half million were unemployed (looking and available for work). Of the nearly fifteen million older people who are actually employed, about four million were receiving pensions, including (not shown) nearly a million who were receiving two or more pensions (typically Social Secu-

TABLE 11.1. Labor Force Status in March 1990 by Pension Receipt in 1989, by Age and Sex (in Thousands)

Population[a]	Labor Force Participation Rate[b]	Employed	Unemployed	Total	Percent Full Time
Total, Pension and No Pension					
Both Sexes					
Total, 55 Years and Over	50,796	30	14,854	74	561	
55–61 years	14,889	63	9,030	85	363	
62–64 years	6,341	38	2,314	71	86	
65–69 years	10,126	22	2,149	53	67	
70 Years and Over	19,440	7	1,365	41	44	
Men					
Total, 55 Years and Over	22,334	39	8,439	81	363	
55–61 years	7,084	76	5,105	93	246	
62–64 years	2,917	46	1,299	83	56	
65–69 years	4,598	27	1,209	58	37	
70 years and over	7,736	11	825	42	25	
Women					
Total, 55 Years and Over	28,462	23	6,419	65	198	
55–61 years	7,805	52	3,925	74	117	
62–64 years	3,424	31	1,015	61	31	
65–69 years	5,529	18	940	47	3	
70 Years and Over	11,704	5	540	39	19	
Received Pension[c]					
Both Sexes					
Total, 55 Years and Over	33,085	13	4,273	45	178	
55–61 years	1,792	46	775	75	48	
62–64 years	3,817	21	749	38	43	
65–69 years	8,919	17	1,493	39	51	
70 Years and Over	18,557	7	1,255	38	36	
Men					
Total, 55 Years and Over	14,473	19	2,584	52	114	
55–61 years	1,300	50	612	80	42	
62–64 years	1,706	24	390	48	24	

TABLE 11.1 (Continued)

Population[a]	Labor Force Participation Rate[b]	Employed	Unemployed	Total	Percent Full Time
65–69 years	4,009	21	809	43	25
70 Years and Over	7,459	11	773	40	23
Women					
Total, 55 Years and Over	18,612	9	1,689	35	64
55–61 years	493	34	163	56	6
62–64 years	2,112	18	360	28	18
65–69 years	4,910	14	684	33	26
70 years and over	11,098	4	482	34	13
Received no pension					
Both Sexes					
Total, 55 Years and Over	7,711	62	10,585	86	382
55–61 years	13,097	65	8,255	86	314
62–64 years	2,524	64	1,565	87	44
65–69 years	1,208	56	656	86	16
70 Years and Over	883	13	110	73	8
Men					
Total, 55 Years and Over	7,861	78	5,855	94	249
55–61 years	5,784	81	4,493	95	204
62–64 years	1,212	78	910	92	32
65–69 years	589	70	400	88	12
70 years and over	277	19	52	67	2
Women					
Total, 55 Years and Over	9,850	49	4,730	76	134
55–61 years	7,313	53	3,762	75	111
62–64 years	1,312	51	655	80	12
65–69 years	619	42	256	82	4
70 years and over	606	11	57	79	7

[a] Civilian noninstitutional population.

[b] Civilian labor force as a proportion of population.

[c] Excludes people aged 55–61 who received only Social Security benefits, since those would be disability or survivors' benefits rather than retirement benefits.

Note: Due to sampling error, small estimates, particularly those less than 50,000, should be used with caution.

SOURCE: U.S. Bureau of Labor Statistics

rity and either a private or government pension). Labor force data for men and women in various age groups who are receiving pensions are summarized in table 11.2.[3]

Among this group of working retirees (here a retiree is defined as someone receiving a pension), slightly more worked part time than full time, and the proportion working full time decreased steadily with age. Full-time workers outnumber part-timers three to one among employed people from age fifty-five through age sixty-one. Part-time work becomes more dominant for people after age sixty-two because of a growing preference for leisure with advancing age, an improvement in an individual's (or family's) financial status as Social Security or other pension benefits become available, and the desire to keep earnings below the amounts allowable under Social Security regulations to avoid paying a very large penalty.

Older women receiving pensions are less likely than men to work at all, and the women who work are more likely to do so part time (see table 11.2). Very few women receive pensions prior to age sixty-two, so female pensioners are concentrated in the group aged sixty-two and over, for which part-time work is more attractive for the reasons outlined above.

TABLE 11.2. Labor Force Status in March 1990 of People Receiving Pensions[a] in 1989, by Age and Sex (in Thousands)

	Civilian Noninstitutional Population	*Participation Rate*[b]	Employed	
			TOTAL	PERCENT FULL TIME
Men				
55–61 years	1,300	50	612	80
62–64 years	1,706	24	390	48
65–69 years	4,009	21	809	43
70 years and over	7,459	11	773	40
Women				
55–61 years	493	34	163	56
62–64 years	2,112	18	360	28
65–69 years	4,910	14	684	33
70 years and over	11,098	4	482	34

[a] Excludes people 55–61 who received only Social Security benefits, since those would be disability or survivors' benefits rather than retirement benefits.

[b] Civilian labor force as a proportion of population.

SOURCE: U.S. Bureau of Labor Statistics.

INDUSTRIES IN WHICH RETIREES WORK

Examining the types of jobs held by retired workers requires an examination of both industry and occupational data. In most cases, people look for jobs in certain occupations; someone looking for a job as a secretary, for example, might be willing to work in any number of industries. In other cases, people look for work in certain industries (particularly when an area has only a small number of major employers), and they might be willing to work in a range of different jobs in those settings.

We will first examine the industries in which workers in various age/pension receipt categories are employed. As shown in table 11.3, full-time employed men aged fifty-five and older who are *not* receiving pensions (those we define as clearly not retired) have very much the same industry distribution as men aged twenty-five through fifty-four. Even among those receiving pensions, the industry distribution does not differ substantially from that of men who are not retired until age sixty-two. Compared with workers aged twenty-five through fifty-four, the pension recipients aged sixty-two through sixty-nine who are working full time are much more likely to be in agriculture and services and less likely to be in manufacturing and construction.

The large employment share in agriculture reflects at least three factors. First, many people living on farms farm only as a "second job" until they retire from their primary jobs. It is not until that time that the Current Population Survey counts them as farmers. Second, those for whom farming was always a primary job often work longer than people in other fields; they might not stop working until poor health forces them to do so. Third, it is likely that the pension benefits available to most career farmers is limited to Social Security and that the incidence of double pensions is quite low, serving as a strong financial incentive to continue working. (The unique case of farming will come up again later in the discussion of the extent of self-employment among retirees.)

Male pension recipients over age sixty-two who are working part time are distributed by industry in the same manner as other part-time workers. That is, trade, services, finance, insurance, and real estate account for nearly two-thirds of total employment. As is the case for retirees who are full-time workers, a relatively large share of those who are part-time workers are engaged in agricultural tasks.

The industry employment patterns of older women who are working full time (and receiving no pensions) are little different from those of younger workers. Relatively few women receive pensions prior to eligibility for Social Security, and those who do tend not to work. As a result, only about 160,000 female pension recipients that age worked in March 1990, compared with more than 600,000 men. Because of the small size of this group of women, no industry distribution is shown in table 11.3.

For women aged sixty-two through sixty-nine who are working full time, the distribution of employment by industry is still quite similar to that for women aged twenty-five through fifty-four. But employed female pension recipients that age, who are working part time, have an employment profile typical of part-timers of any age. Eighty percent work in trade and services. These part-time jobs tend to pay very low wages for workers of all ages, men or women. This is the only category in which the number of employed women actually exceeds the number of employed men.

An interesting point these data make is that, despite the well-publicized campaigns of some fast-food chains to recruit older workers, that type of work accounts for only a small proportion of employment of retired workers. As table 11.3 shows, eating and drinking places, among which fast-food restaurants are classified, employ a very small share of older people. That share is higher, however, for part-time workers than for full-time employees.

OCCUPATIONS OF RETIREES

It is not unusual for people seeking information about older workers to ask "What kind of work do older people (or retirees) do?" The occupational data presented in table 11.4 show a pattern similar to that of the industry data already discussed. That is, for nonretired workers over the age of fifty-five, occupational employment patterns are not much different from those of employees from age twenty-five through age fifty-four. As some workers retire (that is, begin to collect their pensions) but later take part-time jobs, the occupational distribution changes. However, with the exception of the large rise in the share who are farm operators and service workers, the change is not dramatic.

People aged sixty-two and older are very much underrepresented among technicians, probably because the jobs done by most technicians did not exist when the older workers began their careers. On the other hand, the proportion of older men and women who work in sales is higher than it is for younger groups, perhaps because of the availability of part-time employment in that field, the generally low level of physical demands, and the lack of prior experience needed for

Table 11.3. People Employed in March 1990, by Age, Sex, Industry, Full- or Part-time Status, and Pension Receipt in 1989

	Receiving No Pension, Working Full Time			Receiving Pension, Working Full Time		Receiving Pension, Working Part Time	
	25–54 years	55–61 years	62–69 years	55–61 years[a]	62–69 years	55–61 years[a]	62–69 years
Men							
Number Employed (in Thousands)	42,810	4,255	1,190	489	536	123	664
Percent Distribution:							
Total	100.0	100.0	100.0	100.0	100.0	100.0	100.0
Agriculture	2.9	4.3	4.6	2.2	15.5		11.1
Mining	1.2	1.0	0.5	0.8	0.7		0.3
Construction	11.4	10.0	9.7	4.7	7.0		6.2
Manufacturing	24.2	26.3	23.3	20.0	11.9		8.6
Durables	16.1	16.6	14.3	14.2	6.1		5.9
Nondurables	8.1	9.8	9.0	5.8	5.8		2.7
Transportation, Communications, and Public Utilities	10.2	9.3	8.0	10.3	5.1		6.6
Trade	17.0	15.2	14.8	14.7	15.8		24.1
Eating and Drinking Places	2.4	1.7	0.8	0.9	1.2		3.6
Finance, Insurance, and Real Estate	5.4	6.8	6.9	7.7	8.5		9.3

Services	21.9	22.5	26.7	31.6	28.1		31.5
Professional and Related	12.1	14.3	19.5	20.9	14.2		14.2
Public Administration	5.7	4.6	5.4	8.0	7.3		2.5
Women							
Number Employed (in Thousands)	29,853	2,805	733	92	326	71	718
Percent Distribution:							
Total	100.0	100.0	100.0	100.0	100.0	100.0	100.0
Agriculture	0.9	1.3	0.8		3.2		2.9
Mining	0.3	0.1	0.2		—		0.7
Construction	1.4	1.0	1.3		1.3		0.7
Manufacturing	16.1	16.9	14.4		11.1		5.1
Durables	8.1	8.4	6.9		1.9		1.2
Nondurables	8.0	8.5	7.5		9.2		3.9
Transportation, Communications, and Public Utilities	5.4	4.1	2.4		1.7		2.7
Trade	15.6	17.9	14.4		21.7		24.1
Eating and Drinking Places	3.3	3.9	2.1		3.5		4.3
Finance, Insurance, and Real Estate	10.3	8.5	8.3		10.5		4.7
Services	44.1	43.3	51.6		47.6		56
Professional and Related	33.1	32.7	41.0		31.3		36.7
Public administration	5.9	7.0	6.6		—		3.2

[a] Excludes people 55–61 who received only Social Security benefits, since those would be disability or survivors' benefits rather than retirement benefits.

Note: Distribution not shown when employment base is less than 200,000.

SOURCE: U.S. Bureau of Labor Statistics.

Table 11.4. People employed in March 1990, by Age, Sex, Occupation, Full- or Part-time Status, and Pension Receipt in 1989

	Receiving No Pension, Working Full Time			Receiving Pension, Working Full Time		Receiving Pension, Working Part Time	
	25–54 years	55–61 years	62–69 years	55–61 years[a]	62–69 years	55–61 years[a]	62–69 years
Men							
Number Employed (in Thousands)	42,810	4,255	1,190	489	536	123	664
Percent Distribution:							
Total	100.0	100.0	100.0	100.0	100.0	100.0	100.0
Executive, Administrative, and Managerial	15.3	17.5	20.1	21.5	17.7		10.5
Professional Specialty	13.2	15.1	18.6	11.2	12.1		7.0
Technicians and Related	3.5	1.7	0.7	3.2	0.7		1.1
Sales	11.2	11.6	14.3	11.0	13.6		18.3
Administrative Support	5.4	5.8	5.8	9.1	5.6		4.1
Service	7.7	7.1	5.9	13.3	12.4		17.2
Precision Production, Craft, and Repair	21.4	18.4	14.3	17.2	10.8		14.2
Operators, Fabricators, and Laborers	19.2	17.9	15.0	10.4	11.6		15.8

Farming, forestry, and fishing	3.2	4.8	5.3	3.0	15.6		11.8
Farm Operators and Managers	1.4	3.0	3.5	1.5	10.3		8.7
Farm Workers	1.6	1.5	1.6	1.3	5.0		2.9
Women							
Number Employed (in Thousands)	29,853	2,805	733	92	326	71	718
Percent Distribution:							
Total	100.0	100.0	100.0	100.0	100.0	100.0	100.0
Executive, Administrative, and Managerial	14.7	11.6	15.2		11.7		5.3
Professional Specialty	17.1	14.2	13.9		8.4		9.5
Technicians and Related	4.2	2.6	2.6		1.9		1.3
Sales	10.0	10.9	10.6		16.3		15.3
Administrative Support	29.2	28.3	32.1		22.4		27.9
Service	12.6	16.6	14.0		26.4		34.4
Precision Production, Craft, and Repair	2.5	3.1	2.6		1.8		8.5
Operators, Fabricators, and Laborers	9.1	11.7	8.3		8.0		3.6
Farming, Forestry, and Fishing	0.7	1.0	0.7		3.1		1.3
Farm Operators and Managers	0.3	0.5	—		0.3		2.1
Farm Workers	0.4	0.5	0.4		1.0		1.0

a Excludes people 55-61 who received only Social Security benefits, since those would be disability or survivors' benefits rather than retirement benefits.

Note: Distribution not shown when employment base is less than 200,000.

SOURCE: U.S. Bureau of Labor Statistics

people to switch into such jobs. A substantial representation of older workers in the services industry reflects similar factors. In addition, professionals and managers are among the most likely to defer retirement beyond age sixty-two.

Because there are several hundred occupations in the occupational classification system used by the Current Population Survey, no single occupation makes up more than a small share of total employment among the various groups of older workers. But the broad distribution of these workers across the occupational spectrum strongly suggests that jobs for older workers in general, or for retirees in particular, cannot easily be stereotyped.

SELF-EMPLOYMENT AMONG RETIREES

Perhaps the most important difference between older workers and their younger counterparts is in the incidence of self-employment. Employed men from sixty-two through sixty-nine years old are more than twice as likely as those from twenty-five through fifty-four to work for themselves, whether in an incorporated or unincorporated

TABLE 11.5. Incidence of Self-Employment Among Workers, by Sex, Age, and Pension Receipt (Numbers in Thousands)

	Wage and Salary Workers	Self-Employed Workers	Percent Self-Employed
Men			
25–54 years, no pension	38,262	6,433	4
55–61 years, no pension	3,483	1,007	2
62–69 years, no pension	905	402	31
55–61 years, pension[a]	490	122	20
62–69 years, pension	783	408	34
Women			
25–54 years, no pension	34,286	3,062	8
55–61 years, no pension	3,295	437	12
62–69 years, no pension	798	110	12
55–61 years, pension[a]	143	18	11
62–69 years, pension	864	170	16

[a] Excludes people aged 55–61 who received only Social Security benefits, since those would be disability or survivors' benefits rather than retirement benefits.

SOURCE: U.S. Bureau of Labor Statistics.

business. Even among men with no pensions, as shown in table 11.5, self-employment rates rise with age above age fifty-five.

The rise of self-employment with age occurs for several reasons:

Second Careers. Some people who retire use their skills to start small businesses (consulting businesses, for example, or those doing "odd jobs" such as carpentry, clothing alterations, or bookkeeping). Such an arrangement often affords people the flexibility they desire in "retirement."

Generational Differences. Men who are in the older age groups today started their careers at a time when self-employment was considerably more common than it is today. In 1963, 15.8 percent of all working men aged sixteen and over were self-employed. In 1990 that figure was only 10.5 percent. Therefore, these older men have carried their careers into retirement.

Agriculture. People who are in the older age groups today were more likely to have chosen farming as a career than were younger workers. In addition, many farmers do not retire in the usual sense. They are unlikely to have pension coverage other than Social Security and can, like other self-employed people, adjust their earnings and work effort to meet their health needs or their desire for increasing leisure.

The Nature of Self-employment. To the extent that owning one's own business is more personally satisfying, and may provide more flexibility (although it certainly does not always do so), self-employed people are more likely to continue working beyond average retirement ages.

Retention of a Second Job. People who had "side businesses" secondary to their primary jobs as wage-earning or salaried workers would have been identified in the CPS by their primary jobs. Many people retire from their primary jobs and are then, perhaps for the first time, counted as self-employed, even though they may have been in business for some time. Farming is a common second job in rural areas.

Self-employed people, then, are often the survivors, those remaining in their jobs after the wage-earning and salaried workers their age have retired, those who have continued in secondary jobs after retiring from "career" jobs, or those who have turned useful skills into new careers—or at least extensions of their previous careers.

JOB INTEREST AMONG NONWORKING RETIREES

What of the 35 million people aged fifty-five and older who are out of the labor force altogether? A widely offered argument is that a potentially large group of nonworking retirees is ready, willing, and able to work. But when the CPS interviewers ask those age fifty-five and over who are neither working nor looking for work whether they "want a regular job now, either full or part time," nearly 98 percent say no.

From these data it would seem that retirees who want to work do so or at least actively look for work since there are two hundred thousand unemployed people—jobseekers by definition—receiving pensions, while those who are out of the labor force simply do not want to work. Yet in 1990, the year of the CPS data used in this chapter, the Commonwealth Fund released the results of a well-publicized Louis Harris poll of older retirees that suggested otherwise. The study found that 1.1 million older men between the ages of fifty-five and sixty-four and women between fifty and fifty-nine were ready, willing, and available to work (The Commonwealth Fund 1990).[4] This figure is twice that reflected by the combined levels of unemployment and discouragement that were found by CPS interviewers, although it still represents a distinct minority of people who are out of the labor force.

Why the discrepancy? People who are neither working nor looking for a job have, by their absence from the labor force, demonstrated some level of commitment to not working. Therefore it makes sense that most say they do not want to work. One might presume that if they wanted to work they would be looking—although, admittedly, such a statement is simplistic given the wide range of reasons for which older people find themselves out of work. However, it may be the case that some substantial number of people would consider employment if more jobs were available that met the needs and desires of the potential older work force.

The questionnaire used by the Commonwealth Fund was quite different from that used in the CPS. It established the availability of jobs in a context of "Would you have continued work if . . . ?" The questions about whether an individual wanted to work were preceded by questions that, while they do not suggest Utopian work arrangements, introduced such options as working with reduced hours and responsibility, training for a different job at the employee's old salary, working if there were changes in the Social Security earnings test, and so on. The mere possibility of employment arrangements that were alternatives to those actually available (or perceived to be available) could be expected to elicit interest in work. People seem to be saying to the CPS interviewers that they do not want to work given their perception of the job market for older workers. That is, it is not their perception that acceptable jobs are available.

It is clear, by any measure, that most older people who are out of the labor force do not want jobs because of poor health, family responsibilities, or simple satisfaction with retirement. However, the potential pool of workers is probably fluid, subject to change as work opportunities increase in quantity and quality.

CONCLUSIONS

Perhaps more than anything else, the above discussion argues that people ask the wrong questions about work after retirement. The range of retired workers is amazingly broad—from the person working fewer than twenty hours a week in a minimum-wage job to an executive receiving a pension from one company and working full-time at another. The opportunities available to older jobseekers cannot (and should not) be generalized. A skilled individual with outstanding credentials in a field faced with labor shortages might have his or her pick of jobs, while a homemaker who has been out of the labor force for twenty years might find job-hunting (and job-getting) a frustrating experience.

In general, though, when older people want to continue working, they typically stay with what they know—their occupations and often their employers—and not just because of the comfort level. Getting started in a new occupation typically requires starting from the bottom, an unacceptable option for many potential workers. An individual's earning power tends to be greatest in a job in which the person has considerable experience, a "career job," especially with the person's long-term employer. That is one reason that occupational change is relatively uncommon among older workers and why the majority of workers withdraw from the labor force following retirement from a long-term employer.

The discussion presented above has suggested some of the major categories in which retirees tend to work in terms of industries and occupations. For example, part-time work is quite common in retail trade, certain services, and real estate, while it is unusual in manufacturing. And many professional, managerial, or skilled craft workers continue to work beyond retirement in a self-employed status. Some retirees even go into completely new fields, whether starting small businesses or getting training for "second careers."

As workers in the baby boom generation move toward the years in which they will be making retirement decisions, interest in this subject should continue to grow, particularly if the economy generates the level of job growth this country experienced during the last few decades. The discussion of the role of the older worker is an interesting one in a social and an economic sense, and it should become even more important in the future. But the individual retiree generally accepts employment only when his or her skills and goals match the services needed by a specific employer. Stereotyping the jobs "available" to retirees is generally not beneficial.

NOTES

1. Bureau of Labor Statistics, unpublished data.
2. For this we need to assume that someone receiving a pension in the prior year is still doing so in March of the current year, but such an assumption seems quite reasonable.
3. People aged fifty-five through sixty-one who were receiving only Social Security benefits were not counted as "pensioners" in this tabulation since those payments would be either disability or survivors' benefits rather than the retirement benefits in which we are interested.
4. The 1.1 million people met a series of criteria that were used to test their capacity to work and commitment to finding work:

> They were willing to work in available jobs; the jobs presented were among the top ten jobs employing men or women aged fifty-five to sixty-four that were anticipated to be among the fastest growing over the next decade.
> They needed jobs for financial reasons.
> They were physically capable of accomplishing key job tasks, such as using a calculator, driving a car, and reading a phone book.
> They were seeking work and had reasonable wage expectations.
> They were willing to accept difficult working conditions, including working alone, working on their feet, and working evenings and weekends.

REFERENCES

The Commonwealth Fund. 1990. *Americans Over 50 at Work Program*. Research reports 1 and 2. New York: The Commonwealth Fund.

Grad, Susan. 1992. *Income of the Population 55 or Older, 1990*. Washington, D.C.: Social Security Administration.

Rones, Philip L. 1985. "Using the CPS to Track Retirement Trends Among Older Men." *Monthly Labor Review*, February.

12

Alternatives to Conventional Work Patterns

●

SALLY COBERLY

As we approach the twenty-first century, businesses are worried about both the availability and the quality of workers in America (Hudson Institute and Towers Perrin 1990). The number of younger, entry-level workers has fallen off dramatically due to the low birth rates that produced the "baby bust" of the late 1960s and 1970s. As a result, some employers are facing a "youth squeeze" in the labor market as multiple firms compete for these workers (Doeringer and Terkla 1990). At the same time, many of those who are available are poorly educated and unskilled. It is estimated that every fifth new hire is both illiterate and innumerate, so it is not surprising that many employers must offer remedial training programs in basic reading, writing, and math (Richards 1990; Wiggenhorn 1990). Many employers believe that their problems with absenteeism and high turnover can be traced to the lack of the traditional "work ethic" among today's younger employees (The Daniel Yankelovich Group, Inc. (DYG) 1989; Doeringer and Terkla 1990).

These and other concerns are prompting increasing numbers of employers to rethink their employment policies and practices for existing workers and to consider alternatives to hiring young workers, such as hiring older workers and retirees. As a result some employers, such as McDonald's and Days Inns of America, are aggressively recruiting and hiring older employees. Others, such as Allstate, The Travelers Companies, and Polaroid, are offering "alternative work arrangements" that allow older employees to continue to work at reduced hours or that encourage retirees to come back to work on a part-time basis. Still others, such as IBM, are using flexible scheduling and work-at-home arrangements to allow middle-aged and older employees to balance work and family caregiving responsibilities.

While these companies are in the minority today (Herz and Rones 1989; Rix 1991; Rothstein 1988), the labor market woes described above suggest that the number of companies offering these alternatives to conventional work patterns will eventually expand as firms struggle to maintain competitive work forces in the 1990s and beyond (Belous 1990). Among a sample of firms offering part-time employment, for example, the most frequently cited objective for doing so was "to retain valuable employees" (Hewitt Associates 1991).

At the same time, some observers believe that the numbers of older employees and retirees seeking to exercise such options will also grow, particularly if adverse economic conditions threaten the value of pension benefits and savings or if traditional early retirement benefits, such as retiree health insurance, are eroded or eliminated. For example, 63 percent of a sample of a thousand working Americans indicated that they would postpone retirement until they became eligible for Medicare at age sixty-five if their employers did not sponsor health insurance for early retirees (Employee Benefit Research Institute 1990).

This chapter takes a closer look at alternative work arrangements for older workers and retirees by examining older workers' interest in alternatives to full-time employment, describing the characteristics of selected options, and providing examples of model programs currently offered by U.S. employers.[1] The chapter also discusses some of the factors that employers and older workers may wish to take into account in deciding to offer such arrangements or take advantage of them.

THE INTEREST OF OLDER WORKERS AND RETIREES IN ALTERNATIVE WORK ARRANGEMENTS

Surveys of older workers and retirees have consistently shown their preference for part-time work, particularly after age sixty-five (Harris 1981; Kraut 1989, McConnell, et al. 1980). And, in fact, the incidence of voluntary part-time work, including self-employment, increases dramatically among workers age sixty-five and older. In 1991, for example, nearly 53 percent of all workers age sixty-five and older were employed part-time, compared to only 18 percent of those ages 55 to 64 (Bureau of Labor Statistics (BLS) 1992). Not surprisingly, older women are more likely to be employed part-time than men; in 1991, nearly 60 percent of women age sixty-five and older were working part-time compared to 47 percent of their male counterparts (BLS 1991).

While the incidence of part-time employment is high among workers age sixty-five and older, most older workers have to change jobs to find such work (Quinn and Burkhauser 1990). For example, using data from the Social Security Administration's Retirement History Longitudinal Survey to track transitions from "career" employment to "bridge" jobs—jobs employees take after retirement from a career job but before they stop working entirely—Ruhm (1990) found that "partial retirement on the career job is an option available to relatively few workers" and that transitions almost always involve a "change of either industry, occupation, or both." Of course individual employers may offer informal part-time arrangements in order to retain valuable employees (Doeringer and Terkla 1990), but the limited availability of part-time jobs across all sectors may artificially restrict the choices of older workers who wish to remain with their current employers (Herz and Rones 1989). For example, only 27 percent of a representative sample of companies with fifty or more employees had made part-time jobs with benefits available to workers fifty and older; an additional 27 percent offered part-time jobs with no benefits (DYG 1989). Another study of a nonrepresentative sample of 435 employers found that, while 95 percent offered part-time jobs, the median percentage of part-time nonunion employees was only 5 percent (Hewitt Associates 1991). Job sharing was available in only 17 percent of manufacturing firms and 33 percent of nonmanufacturing firms that were surveyed. When large numbers of part-time jobs are available, they tend to be concentrated in the retail trade and in the health care and services industries.

While the overall availability of alternatives to conventional work schedules is still limited, there are enough creative examples to suggest that employers are becoming more responsive to the preferences of older workers and retirees. The following section describes these arrangements and provides examples of successful implementation in the workplace. Generally the focus is on options that involve less than full-time work. Some may be appropriate for both older employees and retirees, while others are limited to retirees. Because both workers and employers understand permanent part-time jobs in which employees work schedules involving partial weeks or partial days, these arrangements are not described.[2]

JOB SHARING FOR OLDER WORKERS AND RETIREES

Job sharing is a variant of permanent part-time work in which two part-time employees "share" a full-time job. Typically the job is split down the middle, with each employee working two and a half days a week, but other arrangements are possible to accommodate the preferences of both employees and their employer. For example one employee might work three days a week instead of two and a half to provide a half-day overlap.

Job sharing may be particularly appropriate when an older employee can be paired with a younger worker in a mentor capacity. For example, school districts have experimented with job sharing as a way to transition older teachers to retirement while providing valuable training and guidance for younger teachers beginning their careers (Paul 1988). Job sharing is also common in the health care and medical services industries which, because of the need for twenty-four-hour coverage in many instances, has aggressively adopted a host of flexible scheduling options for workers of all ages (Hewitt Associates 1991).

Unlike permanent part-time work, job sharing requires additional communication and coordination between the two partners to ensure continuity and follow-through. The advantage for an employer is that the job is approached with the insight, experience, and creativity of two employees rather than one (Coberly 1982).

RETIREES AS CONSULTANTS AND RETIREE JOB BANKS

Competitive pressures are forcing human resource managers to look for ways to increase the flexibility of their work forces (Belous 1990). Strategies include relying on either "contingent" workers—non-permanent employees—or permanent, part-time employees to meet fluctuating staffing requirements (Rupert 1991). The advantage of contingent workers is that they generally do not receive costly benefits and can be added or subtracted from the work force rapidly. The drawback of most contingent workers is that they are unfamiliar with the organization and its culture and may be unreliable due to a weak attachment to the labor force. However, using the firm's own retirees as consultants or using workers from a retiree job bank overcomes most of the problems associated with contingent workers by combining flexibility with familiarity and loyalty.

Many firms have been using retirees as consultants on an informal basis for some time. A number have begun to formalize and institutionalize this practice. For example, the Allstate Insurance Company established its CAT Program in 1987 to meet the added demand for agents' services when catastrophes such as hurricanes and tornados strike. About 120 retired agents are currently participating in the CAT Program. If called to the field to assist with claims, CAT Program agents are paid through a temporary employment agency, a move that protects the retirees' pension benefits from Allstate. The CAT Program is an example of an "on-call" retiree consultant option. In other cases employers negotiate directly with retiree consultants for a specific period of time or for the completion of a specific task or project.

The retiree job bank is another strategy for creating an internal contingent work force. Typically employers collect information about retirees' skills and work schedule preferences, and this information is matched to managers' requests for temporary help. Well-known examples of firms that operate retiree job banks include Bankers Life and Casualty, the Travelers Companies, and Wells Fargo Bank. Employers note that rehired retirees, in contrast to external temps, are familiar with the companies' procedures and corporate culture. Retiree job banks can also save money. Travelers estimates that it saves over $1 million annually on employment agency fees by operating its retiree job bank (Ginnis 1990).

It is important to note that the growth in the use of contingent workers has been a source of concern among some who fear the development of a two-tier work force, with the members of the two "tiers" increasingly separated by such issues as job security, access to training, and eligibility for benefits. While some older workers may be satisfied with the "marginal" status of many contingent jobs, it is important to remember that others will need "the same things as other workers" (Rupert 1991).

PHASED AND PARTIAL RETIREMENT OPTIONS

Phased and partial retirement options provide opportunities for older employees to experience greater amounts of leisure without entirely giving up their work roles. The two options are distinguished primarily by the duration of the period over while employees reduce their time at work. Typically phased retirement programs require employees to gradually reduce the amount of time they work over a set number of years. Partial retirement is essentially a part-time work arrangement with no set time limitation; programs may or may not allow employees to draw partial pension benefits to supplement their partial salaries (Olmstead and Smith 1989).

Varian Associates' Retirement Transition Program is a typical phased retirement program in which employees fifty-five and older with at least five years of service may reduce their hours over a three-year period. Although employees are allowed to return to full-time status under special circumstances, the program is intended to be a transition to retirement rather than a permanent part-time work arrangement.

A partial retirement approach is best illustrated by the California Public Employees' Retirement System (PERS) Partial Service Retirement program. Employees who meet age and service requirements may reduce their schedules by at least 20 percent and no more than 60 percent and receive a proportionate share of their retirement income. Employees may make downward adjustments in their time commitments each year; they may make upward adjustments only once every five years. Participation in the program is indefinite (California Public Employees' Retirement System 1984).

JOB REDESIGN AND JOB TRANSFERS

Sometimes older employees opt for retirement because of the mental, physical, or emotional stress associated with their jobs. Job redesign and job transfer options help employers overcome these problems by modifying the physical environment of a job, by removing the specific sources of stress associated with it, by lowering the demands of the job, or by providing new stimuli.

The Senior Employee Program at Xerox allows employees who meet certain age and service requirements to voluntarily transfer to jobs with less responsibility. Salary averaging and protection of pension benefits allows employees to take advantage of the program without sustaining significant financial losses (Levin and Kardos 1989). At AT&T, specially trained job accommodation specialists work with managers and supervisors to redesign jobs for employees whose performance may have fallen off due to problems associated with hearing or vision losses or with arthritis. Job redesign solutions include the modification of equipment, the addition of lighting, and the use of ergonomics in designing work stations.

Job transfers can also be effective antidotes to "burnout." At Baptist Medical Centers in Birmingham, Alabama, senior managers are routinely transferred to different positions within the company to keep their creative juices flowing (Cole 1989).

SECOND CAREERS AND VOLUNTEER OPPORTUNITIES

Although an employer's decision to establish a second career program or a volunteer program may stem as much from a desire to encourage retirement as from a desire to discourage it, these options seem to be legitimate topics in a discussion of alternatives to conventional work.

Second career programs are limited in number, but they appear to be most popular with high-technology firms that employ large numbers of scientists and engineers. For example, Polaroid's Project Bridge is a five-year experimental program that helps employees become elementary or secondary school teachers. The program combines an exploratory program focused on teaching with an accelerated degree program for those who decide to participate. In addition to paying a full year's salary and continuing the former employee's eligibility for health benefits while he or she is in school, Polaroid pays for tuition, books, and supplies (Washington Business Group on Health (WBGH) 1989).

For those who are not interested in salaried employment, volunteering can also be a way of easing the transition from work to retirement. At the Kollmoregen Corporation, older employees who meet the company's criteria for age and service eligibility can participate in a three-stage program in which they "gradually substitute volunteer work at a local community agency for their normal workload at the company" (WBGH 1989). Qualifying organizations are limited to those that are nonprofit, nonpolitical, and nonreligious.

FLEXIBLE WORK SCHEDULING AND WORK-AT-HOME OPTIONS

Perhaps the most popular "alternative work option" for workers of all ages is flexible work scheduling or "flextime," in which employees are able to adjust their starting and stopping hours as long as they put in full work days and are present during certain "core hours." For example, an employee may arrive at 7:30 a.m. and leave at 3:30 p.m. or arrive at 10:00 a.m. and depart at 6:00 p.m.

Although flexible work scheduling has long been popular with parents who must juggle work and child care arrangements, flextime is also gaining appeal among middle-aged and older workers who must balance work with "elder care" responsibilities, those associated with the care of older relatives. By adjusting their hours, these employees can perform extended caregiving activities in the early morning or the early afternoon. Several IBM plants are experimenting with a two-hour midday flex—an expanded window of time in the middle of the day that allows employees to provide assistance, such as preparing a meal or taking a parent or spouse to a medical appointment, and still return to work on time (Coberly 1991).

Work-at-home or "flex-place" policies that allow employees to spend part of the week working at home are also helpful to older workers with elder care responsibilities. IBM is experimenting with policies that allow employees on personal leaves of absence who want to work part-time to work at home. The work "must be suitable to be accomplished at home, and the employee must report to his or her regular work location at least four consecutive hours each week" (Coberly 1991).

CONSIDERATIONS FOR EMPLOYERS IN OFFERING WORK OPTIONS

In a 1983 study of alternative work options for older employees, the most frequently cited benefit of such options to employers "involved the ability of management to attract skilled older workers to their organizations and retain productive retirement-age workers" (Paul 1988). Today managers appear to be equally attracted to the flexibility that such options offer them to rapidly expand and contract the work force.

However, the use of older employees as "contingent" workers raises a number of questions. Is the use of contingent workers compatible with the firm's corporate culture? Will permanent employees raise issues of fairness and equity if older contingent employees receive no benefits? Will regular full-time employees feel threatened in terms of their own job security or the firm's commitment to its permanent work force? Frequent and clear communication with all employees about the goals, purposes, and structures of alternative work arrangements can help allay such concerns and ensure that the expectations of participants and management are in alignment.

Employers will also need to consider issues surrounding benefits in designing alternative work arrangements for older employees. One consideration is the number of hours retirees can work without jeopardizing their pensions. To encourage retirees to participate in its Retiree Job Bank, for example, Travelers doubled the number of hours its retirees could work before losing their pension benefits.

Perhaps the most basic decision an employer will have to make is whether or not to offer benefits at all and, if so, at what levels. While there is no right or wrong answer to this question, the issue of benefits must be carefully considered. Providing health insurance benefits for retirees participating in a job bank may not be an issue for a firm that already provides such benefits to all its retirees. On the other hand, the availability of health benefits may determine the success or failure of a program designed to attract older workers outside the firm's own pool of retirees.

Benefits are also an important consideration for older employees considering second career opportunities that require training or retraining. Few employees are likely to consider such options if they must bear the entire expense or if they lose health insurance benefits during the period of retraining.

Employers will also need to consider the extent to which programs should be geared or restricted to older employees and retirees or made available to workers of all ages. Many part-time options such as permanent part-time work and job sharing clearly appeal to workers of all ages, as do flexible scheduling and flex-place policies. Similarly, most second career programs appear to be available to younger as well as older workers, although a minimal years-of-service threshold may apply. And, because they help reduce disability costs, job accommodation and job redesign strategies, when available, are generally considered for employees of all ages.

Finally, in designing and implementing alternatives to conventional work schedules, employers will need to consider both short- and long-range objectives. Will the program be needed ten years from now when the demographics of the work force change? What will happen to employees' morale if programs are initiated and then terminated because they no longer meet management's objectives? Will a program such as phased retirement be used primarily as a vehicle for early exit from the work force today, but as a means of delaying retirement for participants ten years from now? While the future is always uncertain, employers can begin to assess the short- and long-range impacts of various options by looking at the current and projected demographics of the work force, past retirement patterns, and business trends.

CONSIDERATIONS FOR OLDER WORKERS
AND RETIREES

Before deciding to take advantage of alternative work arrangements, older employees and retirees will also need to carefully assess their needs and preferences. Factors to consider include the financial costs and benefits of participation, the mix of work and leisure provided, and the "permanence" of the decision to participate.

Clearly both older workers and retirees will need to carefully consider the financial implications of their decisions to participate in alternative work arrangements. Retirees will need to consider whether the level of anticipated earnings will reduce their Social Security benefits or jeopardize other pension benefits. Conversely, older workers considering part-time options will need to evaluate the impact of reduced hours not only on current income, but also on future pension benefits, which are often tied to previous earnings levels. Whether or not the work option provides other employee benefits such as health insurance may also be an important consideration for some older workers and retirees.

The desired balance between work and leisure is something that will vary from individual to individual and may be difficult to assess before participation has actually begun. For example, a retiree looking for twenty hours of work a week may be disappointed in a retiree job bank if most participants are called upon only once a month. To avoid misunderstandings and disappointment, it will be useful for the person considering this option to discuss expectations with the program staff and to interview other retirees currently participating in the program. Retirees who spend part of the year in another geographic location will also want to find out how such absences will affect their chances of being called.

Full-time employees considering phased retirement will want to consider not only whether the option provides the desired balance of work and leisure, but also how moving to part-time status will affect work assignments, scheduling, and other aspects of day-to-day work. For example, an older employee who is used to being involved in high-level day-to-day decision making may find it difficult to accept the fact that important decisions will be made in his or her absence.

Finally, some employees may find that their needs and preferences change over time. Perhaps filling two days of "time off" will not be as easy as they anticipated. Or perhaps the desire for full retirement has gained the upper hand. For many older employees and retirees, a change of heart will not be problematic. For example, participation in a retiree job bank can easily be ended by removing one's name from the data base. Some phased and partial retirement programs allow employees to return to full-time employment with little difficulty; others do not permit employees to increase their work time except under very stringent rules. The California PERS Partial Service Retirement program, for example, allows employees to increase their hours only once every five years! Clearly older workers and retirees considering alternative work arrangements will want to carefully consider the circumstances under which they are permitted to adjust their time commitments or terminate participation all together.

CONCLUSION

Alternatives to the nine-to-five, five-days-a-week work schedule are still the exception to the rule for many employers. Some, such as small businesses, have been using such options for years, often as a way to avoid paying costly benefits. Others have been reluctant to offer options because of opposition from unions, which have traditionally sought to protect full-time jobs at the expense of part-time opportunities. Still others simply have not taken the time to consider the needs and preferences of older employees and retirees.

The current middle-aging of the work force and the inevitable aging of the work force, however, suggest that increasing numbers of employers will begin to explore and offer alternatives to conventional work patterns in the 1990s and beyond. These efforts will undoubtedly be accelerated if older employees become more vocal in the workplace about their needs and preferences.

NOTES

1. More detailed information about many of the corporate examples presented in this chapter, as well as additional examples, can be found in S. Coberly, *An Employer's Guide to Older Worker Employment and Retirement Transition Programs* (Washington, D.C.: Washington Business Group on Health, 1991).

2. For an excellent discussion of how to use part-time options effectively in the workplace for workers of all ages, see Barney Olmsted and Suzanne Smith, *Creating a Flexible Workplace* (New York: AMACOM, 1989).

REFERENCES

Belous, R. S. 1990. "Human Resource Flexibility and Older Workers: The Employer's Point of View." In P. B. Doeringer, ed., *Bridges to Retirement: Trends in the Labor Market for Older Workers*. Ithaca, New York: ILR Press, Cornell University.

Bureau of Labor Statistics. 1992. *Employment and Earnings*, January.

California Public Employees' Retirement System. 1984. *Partial Service Retirement Brochure*. Sacramento: California Public Employees' Retirement System.

Coberly, S. 1982. "Alternative Work Arrangements." In D. Bauer, ed., *Significant Segment: A Technical Resource Manual*. Washington, D.C.: National Council on the Aging, Inc.

Coberly, S. 1991. *An Employer's Guide to Eldercare*. Washington, D.C.: Washington Business Group on Health (WBGH).

Cole, A. 1989. "Getting a Second Wind." *AARP News Bulletin*, February.

The Daniel Yankelovich Group, Inc. (DYG). 1989. *Business and Older Workers: Current Perceptions and New Directions for the 1990's*. Washington, D.C.: American Association of Retired Persons.

Doeringer, P. B., and D. G. Terkla. 1990. "Business Necessity, Bridge Jobs and the Non-bureaucratic Firm." In P. B. Doeringer, ed., *Bridges to Retirement: Trends in the Labor Market for Older Workers*. Ithaca, New York: ILR Press, Cornell University.

Employee Benefit Research Institute. 1990. *Public Attitudes on Retirement Age and Planning*. A national public opinion survey conducted by The Gallup Organization, Inc. Washington, DC: EBRI.

Ginnis, S. 1990. *The Changing Work Force in America*. New York: Fordham University Graduate School of Business Administration.

Harris, L. 1981. *Aging in the Eighties: America in Transition*. Washington, D.C.: National Council on the Aging.

Herz, D. E., and P. L. Rones. 1989. "Institutional Barriers to Employment of Older Workers." *Monthly Labor Review*, April.

Hewitt Associates. 1991. *Survey of Benefits for Part-time Employees*. Lincolnshire, Ill.: Hewitt Associates.

Hudson Institute and Towers Perrin. 1990. *Workforce 2000: Competing in a Seller's Market: Is Corporate America Prepared?* New York: Hudson Institute and Towers Perrin.

Kraut, A. I. 1989. "Retirees: A Flexible New Asset to Employers." *Jobs Today*, 1:69–72.

Levin, R. C., and J. F. Kardos. 1989. *Innovative Practices in the Provision of Retiree and Older Worker Health Benefits*. Washington, D.C.: Washington Business Group on Health.

McConnell, S. R., D. Fleisher, C. E. Usher, and B. H. Kaplan. 1980. *Alternative Work Options for Older Workers: A Feasibility Study*. Los Angeles: Ethel Percy Andrus Gerontology Center, University of Southern California.

Olmstead, B., and S. Smith. 1989. *Creating a Flexible Workplace*. New York: AMACOM.

Paul, C. E. 1988. "Implementing Alternative Work Arrangements." In H. Dennis, ed., *Fourteen Steps in Managing an Aging Work Force*. Lexington, Massachusetts: D.C. Heath and Company.

Quinn, J. F., and R. V. Burkhauser. 1990. "Work and Retirement." In R. Binstock and E. Shanas, eds., *The Handbook of Aging and the Social Sciences*, 3rd ed. New York: Academic Press.

Richards, B. 1990. "Wanting Workers." *The Wall Street Journal*, February 2.

Rix, S. E. 1991. *America's Aging Workforce*. Washington, D.C.: Public Policy Institute, American Association of Retired Persons.

Rothstein, F. R. 1988. "Older Worker Employment Opportunities in the Private Sector." In R. Morris and S. A. Bass, eds., *Retirement Reconsidered: Economic and Social Roles for Older People*. New York: Springer Publishing Company.

Ruhm, C. J. 1990. "Career Jobs, Bridge Employment, and Retirement." In P. B. Doeringer, ed., *Bridges to Retirement: Trends in the Labor Market for Older Workers*. Ithaca, New York: ILR Press, Cornell University.

Rupert, P. E. 1991. "Toward Employer Flexibility through the Employee Life Cycle: The Case for the Older Worker." In L. G. Perlman and C. E. Hansen, eds.,

Aging, Disability and the Nation's Productivity. A report of the 15th Mary Switzer Memorial Seminar. Reston, Va.: National Rehabilitation Association.

Washington Business Group on Health. 1989. *Together on Aging Newsletter.* Washington, D.C.: Washington Business Group on Health, Fall.

Wiggenhorn, W. 1990. Motorola U: When Training Becomes an Education. *Harvard Business Review*, July–August.

13

Job Placement and Referral Services for Working Retirees

•

DENISE D. JESSUP

- Orlando, a fifty-seven-year-old engineer, took an early retirement package when his company, an aerospace firm, lost several national contracts. Six months into retirement, he finds himself bored and seeking employment to provide structure for his life.
- Susan, sixty-two, considered herself "retired" when her husband of forty years retired. However, her recent separation has caused her to need additional income. Susan has been a homemaker for most of her life and is unsure of the value of skills in the job market.
- Gary, sixty-seven, retired from a job on the line of an auto parts manufacturing plant five years ago. He finds that his pension has not kept up with inflation, and although his income is still sufficient for his current needs, he is increasingly concerned about the future. He wants a part-time job to build more of a "nest egg."

There are common elements in these scenarios. Each portrays a person over fifty-five who is currently retired and seeking employment.

While often rewarding, the older person's job search can be particularly challenging due to lack of recent job-seeking experience, age discrimination, unfamiliarity with new technology, or lack of awareness of how to transfer one's job skills to a different industry than the one in which one has been working. Yet a variety of organizations and resources exist that can help older job-seekers, and some organizations have missions specifically to assist this segment of the labor force. The purpose of this chapter is to familiarize the reader with these.

The organizations and resources described below may be helpful to older people in two types of situations. First, currently employed mature people who are preparing for retirement and considering "retirement jobs" can use these resources to learn how to effectively conduct a job search, to gain a sense of the time involved in finding a new position, and to find out about the types of positions available. Second, unemployed retirees and older people who are about to lose their jobs but do not feel ready for retirement can use these resources to help them with active job searches. The assistance provided often includes training or one-on-one help with interviewing, writing résumés and coverletters, and filling out applications; supplying leads to job openings; and training potential workers in new job skills. In addition, some organizations have programs that provide group support and build self-esteem.

The organizations and resources described in this chapter can also support a job-seeker's own informal approach to the job search. From 75 to 80 percent of job-seekers use the informal networking approach to the job search (Merrill 1987). Networking involves informing one's own contacts about the job search. The goal is to develop additional contacts and find positions that have not been listed through the want ads or employment agencies. A combination of conducting an informal job search and using services for older job-seekers is an effective way to find the right job for one's retirement years.

Locating helpful organizations, whether they specifically target older workers or not, is not always an easy task. Many are independent organizations that are not affiliated with national networks. The names and types of organizations available vary from city to city. However, the types of organizations most likely to provide employment assistance services to older people are categorized below, with suggestions about how to locate organizations in each category. These organizations do not typically charge fees to older job-seekers unless noted.

NONPROFIT ORGANIZATIONS AND PROGRAMS

Employment Coordinating Organizations for Older Workers

A loosely affiliated group of eight nonprofit coordinating organizations operates model programs for older workers. These organizations, which often, but not always, include *ABLE* in their names, appear in Table 13.1. Most of these organizations are in major metropolitan areas, although some are statewide or in rural areas. Based

TABLE 13.1. Employment Coordinating Organizations for Older Workers

Arkansas

Arkansas ABLE
519 East Capitol Avenue
Little Rock, AR 72202
1 501 374–1318

California

Career Encores
5225 Wilshire Boulevard.,
  Suite 204
Los Angeles, CA 90036
1 213 933–9537

Illinois

Operation ABLE, Inc.
180 N. Wabash Avenue,
  Suite 802
Chicago, IL 60601
1 312 782–3335

Massachusetts

Operation ABLE of Greater Boston
World Trade Center, Suite 306
Commonwealth Pier
Boston, MA 02210–2004
1 617 439–5580

Michigan

Operation ABLE of Michigan
Crossroads Office Center
16250 Northland Drive, Suite 102
Southfield, MI 48075
1 313 443–0370

Nebraska

Operation ABLE of Southeast
  Nebraska
129 N. 10th Street, Suite 332
Lincoln, NE 68508
1 402 471–7064

New York

NYC Department for the Aging
Senior Employment Service
2 Lafayette Street, 15th Floor
New York, NY 10007
1 212 577–7597

Vermont

Vermont Associates for Training and
  Development
P.O. Box 107
St. Albans, VT 05478
1 802 524–3200

on the framework of Operation ABLE in Chicago, these organizations coordinate networks of local agencies that provide employment services to older adults. Generally they operate job lines that link older people and employers through their local networks. Most assist older workers of all skill levels. Some have special job-search services for older professionals. In 1987 employers listed more than 19,000 jobs with seven of these organizations. In the same year an estimated 8,900 older job-seekers found employment as a result of being referred to community employment and training services by these coordinating agencies (Charles Stewart Mott Foundation 1988).

Forty Plus Organizations

Another loosely affiliated network of independent organizations is called Forty Plus, which has eighteen chapters in the United States. In addition, one chapter is operating in Canada (Green 1991). A list of chapters appears in table 13.2. These are mutual membership organizations for people with professional or managerial experience. With a self-help focus, these organizations help members help themselves get jobs. Generally they charge initial membership fees and monthly fees and limit membership to people with previous incomes of a certain amount. In the Los Angeles chapter, for example, members pay $450 to join and $50 per month, and they must have had previous incomes in excess of $40,000. There is no paid staff, and volunteer work is required of members in order to operate these organizations. These organizations offer assistance in defining members' accomplishments and developing résumés, practice interviews, answering services, wordprocessing facilities and training, access to want ads and other publications, and support groups (Green 1991).

Nonaffiliated, Nonprofit Organizations for Older Workers

Numerous independent organizations throughout the country assist older workers. There is no national network of these organizations, and their names vary. The services offered by these organizations range from job referral only to numerous program options, including extensive training in new job skills. Their target groups within the population of older workers also vary; some organizations serve only job-seekers with low incomes who are in need of training, while others target professional job-seekers.

TABLE 13.2. Forty Plus Offices

California

Forty Plus of Northern California
744 Lockheed Street/P.O. Box 6639
Oakland, CA 94603–0639
1 510 430–2400
Fax 1 510 430–1750

Forty Plus of Southern California
3450 Wilshire Boulevard, Suite 510
Los Angeles, CA 90010
1 213 388–2301
Fax 1 213 383–7750

Forty Plus of San Diego
8845 University Center Lane
San Diego, CA 92122
1 619 450–4440
Fax 1 619 450–0303

Forty Plus of Orange County
23172 Plaza Pointe Drive, Suite 285
Laguna Hills, CA 92653
1 714 581–7990
Fax 1 714 581–4257

Colorado

Forty Plus of Colorado
5800 W. Alameda Avenue
Lakewood, CO 80226
1 303 937–4956
Fax 1 303 937–6050

Northern Division
3842 South Mason Street
Fort Collins, CO 80525
1 303 223–2470
Fax 1 303 223–7456, ext. 261

Southern Division
2555 Airport Road
Colorado Springs, CO 80910–3176
1 719 473–6220
Fax 1 719 633–4227, ext. 217

District of Columbia

Forty Plus of Greater Washington
1718 P Street, N.W.
Washington, DC 20036
1 202 387–1582
Fax 1 202 387–7669

Hawaii

Forty Plus of Hawaii
126 Queen Street, Suite 227
Honolulu, HI 96913
1 808 531–0896
Fax 1 808 538–7192

Illinois

Forty Plus of Chicago
28 East Jackson
Chicago, IL 60604
1 312 922–0285
Fax 1 312 922–4840

New York

Forty Plus of Buffalo
701 Seneca Street
Buffalo, NY 14210
1 716 856–0491
Fax 1 716 856–0449

Forty Plus of New York
15 Park Row
New York, NY 10038
1 212 233–6086
Fax 1 212 227–2974

Ohio

Forty Plus of Central Ohio
1100 King Avenue
Columbus, OH 43212
1 614 297–0040

TABLE 13.2 *(Continued)*

Pennsylvania

Forty Plus of Philadelphia
1218 Chestnut Street
Philadelphia, PA 19107
1 215 923–2074

Texas

Forty Plus of Dallas
13601 Preston Road, Suite 301E
Dallas, TX 75240
1 214 991–9917
Fax 1 214 991–9932

Forty Plus of Houston
2909 Hillcroft, Suite 400
Houston, TX 77057
1 713 952–7587
Fax 1 713 952–8829

Utah

Forty Plus of Utah
5735 Redwood Avenue
Murray, UT 84147–0750
1 801 269–4797

Washington

Forty Plus of Seattle
300 120th Avenue, N.W.
Building #7, Suite 200
Bellview, WA 98005
1 206 450–0040

Toronto, Canada

Forty Plus of Canada
920 Yonge Street, Suite 410
Toronto, Ontario, Canada M4W 3C7

Many of these organizations rely on funds from one or both of the two sources of government funds that target older job-seekers with low incomes. One source of such funds is the Senior Community Service Employment Program (SCSEP). This program was created by Title V of the Older Americans Act. In SCSEP programs older workers are typically placed in part-time subsidized positions, usually in non-profit or government organizations, and then assisted with transitioning to unsubsidized employment. To be eligible, older people must have family incomes below 125 percent of the national poverty level, which is adjusted annually by the Department of Health and Human Services. In 1992 a family of two had to have an income below $11,490 for one of its members to be eligible for SCSEP.

Ten "national contractors" are given SCSEP funds for nationwide programs that they operate themselves or subcontract to other organizations to operate. The national organizations include the American Association of Retired Persons (AARP), Green Thumb, the National Association of Hispanic Elderly, the National Center on Black Aged, the National Council on the Aging (NCOA), the National Council of Senior Citizens, the National Indian Council on Aging, the National Pacific/Asian Resource Center on Aging, the National Urban League, and the U.S. Forest Service (Gibson 1991).

The second source of government funds for older job-seekers is the Job Training Partnership Act (JTPA). Five percent of JTPA's Title IIA (adult) funds are set aside to assist older workers. Older job-seekers generally receive classroom or on-the-job training before being placed in unsubsidized employment. To be eligible, a job-seeker usually must have a family income below the national poverty level, or less than 70 percent of the lower living standard income level, which has regional variations (Larisch 1991). In 1992 the poverty level for a family of two is approximately $9,800 (Wilbanks 1992).

In September 1992 new legislation made major changes in JTPA that changed the way funds are allocated to programs for older workers. What used to be a 3 percent set-aside program is now a 5 percent set-aside program, although the amount of JTPA funds available for programs for older workers is not likely to change significantly due to complex funding formulas. It is also unlikely that there will be many changes that will significantly affect an older job-seeker's interaction with a local employment program for older people (Wilbanks 1992).

In an area that has no coordinating organization for older workers, the most effective way to locate these nonaffiliated organizations is to call the nearest Area Agency on Aging, which provides information about and referrals to services for older people, or a community information and referral line. In addition, the local Private Industry Council, which oversees JTPA programs, can provide information about JTPA programs for older workers.

The Displaced Homemakers Network

The original goal of this network, established in 1978, was to enable mid-life or older displaced homemakers to enter or reenter the world of paid employment and gain financial self-sufficiency. These organizations now serve displaced homemakers of all ages, and many have expanded to include life and career planning and personal development services. However, older women still make up a significant percentage of the network's client population. Services often include classroom training, job-search assistance, referrals to jobs, and seminars and workshops (Miller 1991). There are more than 1,100 Displaced Homemakers programs nationwide. The programs are funded by a variety of sources, and there is no standardization in organizational names. Therefore, the best way to locate the nearest program is to contact the national headquarters of the Displaced Homemakers Network at 1 202 628–6767 (Miller 1991).

AARP Works

The American Association of Retired Persons has developed a self-directed job-search program called AARP Works. Often implemented in conjunction with other community organizations, AARP Works is a series of eight workshops coordinated by AARP-trained volunteers. Job-seekers of all skill levels who are fifty and over are eligible for the program, which has served more than 5,000 people and is available at more than 80 sites across the United States. There is a small fee. To determine the nearest location of an AARP Works program, contact the Worker Equity Department at AARP's national headquarters, 601 E Street NW, Washington, D.C., 20049 (Ulrich 1991).

Programs Operated by Area Agencies on Aging and Senior Centers

There is a national network of 670 Area Agencies on Aging (AAAs), which may be nonprofit organizations or departments of city, county, or regional governments that provide services for older people. Not all AAAs operate programs for older workers. When they do, the programs are frequently supported by JTPA or Title V funds, and therefore serve only older job-seekers with low incomes. However, some AAAs have developed alternative employment programs with more lenient eligibility requirements. These programs have included a computer training and placement program for older workers, job fairs for older workers, networking events for older workers and employers, a conference about how to conduct a job search as an older worker, and a job line for older workers (Campbell 1991; Peterson 1991; Shoemaker 1991; Wallace 1991). Senior centers may also provide employment assistance. These centers are often best at linking job-seekers with temporary short-term employment, such as handyman jobs or opportunities to provide in-home child care or care for the frail elderly. The nearest Area Agency on Aging or senior center may be listed in the government section of the phone book or may be located through a community information and referral service.

Other Employment and Training Organizations

Other organizations also provide employment and training for older workers. These organizations may have general employment and training missions or may target special populations, such as ethnic groups or women. These organizations may have specific programs for older workers and/or may include older workers in their programs for all ages. Perhaps the most difficult to locate of all programs that provide such services for the elderly, these programs are not affiliated with any national network that is associated with programs for older worker, their names are not standardized in any way, and often they do not target older workers in their marketing efforts. One way to locate such organizations is through the information and referral services of Area Agencies on Aging.

PROGRAMS SPONSORED BY STATE AND LOCAL GOVERNMENTS

State Job Services

State-run job service departments provide services to job-seekers of all ages. Most services are not geared to professionals. However, some states have developed networking groups for professionals, and older job-seekers often constitute a significant percentage of those who join the groups. Though several states sponsor networking groups, there is no affiliation of these groups across state lines. Indeed, there appears to be little coordination among states, and there is no master list of networking groups sponsored by state job services (Dent 1991; Hartz 1991).

California is one state that sponsors networking groups, which are similar in organization to Forty Plus organizations, but do not charge fees. The twenty-four job clubs sponsored by the California Employment Development Department (EDD) are often called Experience Unlimited Job Clubs. They are voluntary self-help affiliations of job-seekers who volunteer to perform job-finding activities on EDD premises under the general direction of EDD staff members. The clubs' mission is "to provide enhanced job services to unemployed and underemployed professional, managerial, and technical skilled job-seekers." Twenty-one percent of the clubs' "members" are fifty-five or over (Hartz 1991).

The Arizona Professional Employment Network (AZPEN), which is sponsored by the Arizona Job Service, is similar to California's program. Services include workshops on the professional job search, referrals to professional jobs, networking practice, and linkages to support services. Approximately 30 percent of members are fifty-five or older (Bock 1991; Robinson 1991). Professional networking groups in other states can be located by contacting a state job services department.

City and County Services

City and county government agencies may also operate programs for older workers. Generally these programs are for low-income clients and are supported by JTPA and/or Title V funds.

FOR-PROFIT TEMPORARY AND OUTPLACEMENT SERVICES

While temporary organizations can provide valuable employment leads to older job-seekers and do not charge job-seekers for assistance, they are governed by their need to serve employers, not older job-seekers. That is, temporary services are operated by the fees they collect from businesses for providing temporary personnel, and they consider businesses their primary customers. The organizations listed in other categories above are governed by their missions to serve job-seekers.

National Temporary Services

Kelly Temporary Services, which is headquartered in Troy, Michigan, and has more than eight hundred offices nationwide, is probably the best-known temporary organization that has a recruitment focus on older workers. As part of its Encore program, Kelly has designed a recruitment brochure targeting older workers and another brochure explaining how work affects Social Security benefits. Kelly places people in clerical, light industrial, technical, marketing, and in-home caregiver positions. Nine percent of Kelly's work force is fifty or over. No special services are provided to Encore workers, but these mature workers tend to be very interested in the clerical skills training that is available to Kelly workers of all ages (Riesterer 1991).

Volt Temporary Services, whose offices are primarily in the West and Southwest, calls its program for older job-seekers Gateway. The program was designed to attract older workers who had opted for early retirement but were dissatisfied with it, along with older people who faced lay-offs (Ford 1991). Volt's services include tutorial programs to upgrade workers' clerical skills; referrals to temporary jobs;

the provision of some items that are needed for work, such as eye-glasses; and limited assistance in building confidence and developing interviewing skills. In addition, employers who have hired older temporary workers through Volt are encouraged to convert the older temporaries to permanent employees without the normal waiting period (Ford 1991).

Local Kelly and Volt offices can be located in the white pages of the telephone book. Other national temporary agencies, are also sources of employment for older people, even if they do not have programs designed to recruit older people.

Independent Local Temporary Services

Some small temporary services have created a market niche by providing businesses with older temporary workers or "experienced" temporary or permanent workers, who are often also older. For example, ACS Management Group, which has offices in Houston, Texas, and El Segundo, California, was created to supply business with older technical personnel on a temporary basis (Cates 1991). Another example is Mature Resources in Phoenix. This organization does not specifically mention age in its mission, which is to provide experienced, mature professionals to business on a contract or permanent basis. However, approximately 70 percent of the people Mature Resources has placed are fifty-five or over (Nelson 1991). Independent temporary agencies that are seeking to place older people may be located in the yellow pages under employment services. Organizations with words such as *mature* or *experienced* in their names are probably good bets.

Outplacement Services

Outplacement services offer services similar to those provided by the organizations described above. These services are generally paid for by a company when it is downsizing or laying off a portion of its work force. Older job-seekers whose companies provide outplacement services have the advantage of access to professionals who are aware of their companies' situations. Unfortunately, outplacement services are not available to the independent person who is seeking job-search assistance and, even if they were, their services would be prohibitively expensive for most unemployed people.

Clearly a variety of resources are available to older job-seekers.

Those who use the assistance available will probably be those who are better prepared to meet the challenges of the job search.

REFERENCES

Bock, J. 1991. Personal communication with current president of Arizona Professional Employment Network North Chapter, Phoenix, Ariz.

Campbell, P. 1991. Personal communication with representative of Atlanta Regional Commission, Atlanta, Ga.

Cates, D. 1991. Personal communication with president of ACS Management Group, El Segundo, Calif.

Charles Stewart Mott Foundation. 1988. *Coordinating Older Worker Programs: An Update and Guide to Mott Foundation Resources.* Flint, Mich.: Charles Stewart Mott Foundation.

Dent, W. 1991. Personal communication with representative to Arizona Department of Economic Security Employment and Training Administration, Phoenix, Ariz.

Ford, D. 1991. Personal communication with representative of Volt Temporary Services, Orange, Calif.

Gibson, G. 1991. Personal communication with representative of U.S. Department of Labor, Washington, D.C.

Green, J. 1991. Personal communication with representative of Forty Plus, Los Angeles, Calif.

Hartz, B. 1991. Personal communication with representative of California Employment Development Department, Sacramento, Calif.

Larisch, R. 1991. Personal communication with representative of U.S. Department of Labor, Washington, D.C.

Merrill, F. 1987. *Job Search Manual for Mature Workers.* Los Angeles, Calif.: Los Angeles Council on Careers for Older Americans (Career Encores).

Miller, J. 1991. Personal communication with executive director of Displaced Homemakers Network, Washington, D.C.

Nelson, D. 1991. Personal communication with representative Mature Resources, Phoenix, Ariz.

Peterson, J. 1991. Personal communication with representative of Seattle-King County Division on Aging, Seattle, Wash.

Riesterer, J. 1991. Personal communication with representative of Kelly Temporary Services, Troy, Mich.

Robinson, P. 1991. Personal communication with current president of Arizona Professional Employment Network East Chapter, Phoenix, Ariz.

Shoemaker, L. 1991. Personal communication with representative of Lewis Mason Thurston Area Agency on Aging, Olympia, Wash.

Ulrich, L. 1991. Personal communication with representative of American Association of Retired Persons Worker Equity Department, Washington, D.C.

Wallace, B. 1991. Personal communication with representative of East Central Florida Regional Planning Council, Winter Park, Fla.

Wilbanks, J. 1992. Personal communication with representative of Aging and Adult Administration, Arizona Department of Economic Security, Phoenix, Ariz.

V
LEGAL ISSUES

●

14

Age Discrimination in Employment: The Federal Age Discrimination in Employment Act of 1967

●

KENNETH L. J. MORSE

Older workers have faced discrimination in employment for many years. This discrimination has been the product of many factors, including the belief that older workers are less productive than younger workers and less able to learn new tasks or responsibilities (Jones and Herz 1989). The desire to cut down on labor costs, particularly in tough economic times, has often resulted in employers' terminating or forcibly retiring their senior, higher-paid workers and replacing them with younger, lower-paid workers. Older workers who lose their jobs are unemployed for longer periods of time than younger workers and are less likely to find other jobs.

It is precisely because of these problems that most states and some local governments have enacted laws prohibiting age discrimination in employment. These statutes, however, have differed greatly in terms of the age groups protected, the types of employer conduct prohibited, and the remedies available to victims of age discrimination in employment. It was not until 1967 that Congress enacted a law that prohibited age discrimination in employment. This law is the Age Discrimination in Employment Act of 1967 (ADEA).

The ADEA is a hybrid statute whose provisions were drawn from both Title VII of the federal Civil Rights Act of 1964 (Title VII) and the federal Fair Labor Standards Act (FLSA). Title VII prohibits discrimination on the basis of race, color, national origin, sex, or religion. The FLSA makes it unlawful for an employer to refuse to pay its employees minimum wages or overtime compensation. The substantive provisions of the ADEA, which define what conduct is unlawful, what defenses can be raised to a claim of discrimination, and what must be proven for a complaining party, the plaintiff, to prevail in a lawsuit, were derived from Title VII. The ADEA is enforced in accordance with the powers, remedies, and procedures of the FLSA. The federal agency responsible for enforcing the ADEA is the Equal Employment Opportunity Commission (EEOC).

The ADEA has three stated purposes: to promote the employment of older persons based on their ability rather than their age, to prohibit arbitrary age discrimination in employment, and to help employers and workers meet problems arising from the impact of age on employment. The primary focus of this chapter is on the ADEA and its provisions since it is the most comprehensive statute prohibiting age discrimination in employment.

INDIVIDUALS PROTECTED BY THE ADEA

The ADEA protects individuals forty and older (the protected age group or PAG) (Eglit 1992). As it was originally enacted in 1967, the ADEA applied only to individuals working for private employers. Since that time the ADEA has been expanded to cover individuals working for federal, state, and local governments. In 1984 the ADEA was amended to extend its protection to U.S. citizens working outside the United States. The ADEA applies not only to employees, but also to applicants for employment.

There are a number of groups that are exempted from the protection offered by the ADEA. The act exempts high-level executives and policy-making employees sixty-five or older who receive at least $44,000 per year in retirement benefits. EEOC regulations specifically exempt federal and state programs designed to encourage the employment of individuals with special employment problems, including the long-term unemployed, individuals with disabilities, members of minority groups, older workers, and youth. In addition, the age limits for entry into bona fide apprenticeship programs are not affected by the ADEA.

The 1986 amendments to the ADEA also created certain exemptions. Until December 31, 1993, state and local governments can enforce age limits for hiring and retirement that were in effect as of March 3, 1983, for employees of police, fire, and corrections department. Also until December 31, 1993, institutions of higher learning will be able to mandate the retirement at age seventy of individuals who are working under contracts of unlimited tenure.

Due to the way in which it defines the term *employee*, the ADEA also allows other specific exemptions. The act does not apply to state or local elected officials, to the members of their personal staffs, or to their appointees who are on a policy-making level.

ENTITIES THAT ARE SUBJECT TO THE ADEA'S PROHIBITIONS

Employers

For an employer to be covered by the ADEA, it must be engaged in an industry affecting commerce and must have twenty or more employees for each working day of twenty or more calendar weeks in the current or preceding calendar year. Except as noted above, the ADEA applies to federal, state, and local governmental employees.

Employment Agencies

Any person who regularly undertakes to procure employees for an employer, as well as the agent of such a person, fits the ADEA's definition of an employment agency and is covered by the act. The acts of an employment agency in procuring employees for employers are subject to the ADEA regardless of the number of individuals it employs.

Labor Organizations

For a labor organization to be covered by the ADEA, it must be in an industry affecting commerce. It must also have at least twenty-five members or maintain a hiring hall that procures employment opportunities for employees.

CONDUCT PROHIBITED BY THE ADEA

Employers' Conduct

It is unlawful for employers to refuse to hire, terminate, or otherwise discriminate against individual because of their age. The most common form of age discrimination lawsuit involves involuntary retirement or termination. Not only is it unlawful to discharge individuals because of their age; it is also unlawful to constructively discharge them by making their working conditions so intolerable that they are compelled to quit. Employers recognize that one way to reduce their labor costs is to get rid of their older, more highly paid workers. Corporate reductions in force have spawned considerable litigation.

Hiring discrimination against older workers, while common, is often more difficult to identify and prove than is involuntary retirement or termination. Saying that an older worker is "overqualified" often masks age discrimination. While older, long-term employees who are being terminated often have an extensive employment history to prove their competence, individuals who are denied employment often have no idea why they are not hired.

In addition to discrimination in hiring and termination, the ADEA prohibits age discrimination in promotions, demotions, training, and other terms and conditions of employment. Discrimination in the provision of fringe benefits is also generally unlawful. The cost of employing older workers is not a legitimate basis for terminating or otherwise discriminating against them. However, discrimination in the provision of benefits can be justified under the ADEA on the grounds that the employer, while not providing equal benefits, has expended an equal amount to provide those benefits to older and younger workers.

The Conduct of Employment Agencies

Employment agencies may not refuse to refer individuals or to classify or refer them for employment because of their age. For example, if an employment agency complied with an employer's request that the agency refer for employment only individuals under forty years of age, the employment agency as well as the employer would be in violation of the ADEA.

The Conduct of Labor Organizations

It is unlawful for a labor organization to exclude or expel from membership or to limit, segregate, or classify its members in a way that would deprive or tend to deprive members aged forty or older of employment opportunities. Therefore, if a labor organization agreed to a training program that did not allow employees over sixty to participate, it would have violated the ADEA. The ADEA also makes it unlawful for a labor organization to cause or attempt to cause an employer to violate the ADEA. Therefore, it would be unlawful for a labor organization to attempt to negotiate a lower mandatory retirement age for its members.

Retaliation

The ADEA makes it unlawful for a covered employer, employment agency, or labor organization to retaliate against an individual because he or she has opposed a practice made unlawful by the ADEA. The act also makes it unlawful to retaliate against an individual because he or she filed a charge of age discrimination or testified, assisted, or participated in any manner in an investigation, proceeding, or litigation under the ADEA. An individual does not have to be a member of the PAG to receive this protection. For example, if a young worker were terminated by an employer for testifying on behalf of an older co-worker who had filed a charge of age discrimination under the ADEA, the younger worker could sue for relief under these provisions (Eglit 1992).

Age-Discriminatory Advertising

The ADEA makes it unlawful for a covered employer, employment agency, or labor organization to print or publish any advertisement indicating a preference for or limitation on workers based on age. EEOC regulations make it unlawful to print or publish advertisements using wording such as "age twenty-five to thirty-five," "young," "college student," "recent college graduate," "boy," or "girl." An exception can be made if it can be shown that the specification or limitation would constitute a bona fide occupational qualification. For example, it would be lawful for a children's clothing store to hire only children as models.

PROVING AGE DISCRIMINATION

Age discrimination cases can be based on either disparate treatment or adverse impact. The Supreme Court of the United States has stated that a case of disparate treatment is one in which someone receives less favorable treatment than someone else because of a protected characteristic, such as age. A case of adverse impact is one in which someone has been subject to a policy that is not discriminatory on its face, but has an adverse affect on the individual because of a protected characteristic, such as being forty or older.

Proving Disparate Treatment

Direct Evidence

The simplest way to make a case of age discrimination is to provide direct evidence that a covered entity (an employer, employment agency, or labor organization) has relied on age in making an employment decision or referral. For example, if a school system has said that it would not hire anyone over thirty to be a teacher and has turned down an applicant over thirty, this is direct evidence of age discrimination. A similar case would be that of a labor organization that has said no member over sixty-five could be a union officer and has not allowed a person over sixty-five to run for a position as an officer. In another example, if an employment agency has run an advertisement seeking "individuals twenty-five to thirty-five years old" or "young, bright girls," such conduct would constitute direct evidence of age discrimination.

In such cases the employer, employment agency, or labor organization would be found to have violated the ADEA unless it could prove that it would have reached the same decision about an individual even if age had not been a basis for its action. For instance, the school system in the above example would not be found to have violated the ADEA if it could prove that it would not have hired the older applicant even if it had not discriminated based on age.

Circumstantial Evidence

In most instances there will be no direct evidence of age discrimination, and an individual will need to rely on circumstantial evidence to establish his or her case. Some examples of situations in which age discrimination can be inferred are a company has a reduction in force in which all employees terminated are fifty-five or older; a company with a large work force has no employees over age forty; or an employer has hired only individuals under forty although there has been a large number of applicants over forty.

In cases in which there is a basis for inferring that there has been age discrimination, it is still essential to understand what an individual must show in court to prove he or she is a victim of age discrimination. It is therefore important to have some understanding about the order and burden of proof in age discrimination cases under the ADEA.

Order and Burden of Proof

In cases in which there is believable, direct evidence of age discrimination, the defendant will be liable for discrimination unless it can prove that it would have taken the same action against the aggrieved individual despite his or her age.

For example, assume a woman aged fifty applies for a teaching position in response to an ad that reads "Wanted: certified teacher under thirty-five years of age" and is told that she has not been hired because of her age. If the employer does not hire her, the applicant might argue that she has not been hired because of her age. However, the employer could prevail even though there is direct evidence of discrimination if it could prove that the applicant lacked the required teacher certification. For someone to bring a successful age discrimination suit, the individual must be able to meet the job qualifications.

For a plaintiff or aggrieved individual to win a disparate treatment case, the individual must first make out what is called a *prima facie* case. To make out a *prima facie* case, the plaintiff must produce sufficient evidence of discrimination to support a finding of discrimination. If the plaintiff fails to do this, he or she will lose even if the defendant (employer, employment agency, or labor organization) does not offer any evidence. The courts have generally agreed on what must be demonstrated in an age discrimination case involving a claim of failure to hire because of age. In a case like that described above, in which a woman believes she has not been hired for a job because of her age, she must prove the following to make out a *prima facie* case: (1) that she is in the protected age group (forty or older); (2) that she has applied for the job and is minimally qualified; (3) that she has not been hired; and (4) that the employer continued to look for applicants with qualifications similar to hers.

Once an aggrieved individual has made out a *prima facie* case of age discrimination, the burden of proof shifts to the defendant. For a defendant to escape liability, it must articulate a legitimate nondiscriminatory reason for its actions. Once the defendant has articulated such a reason, the burden shifts back to the plaintiff to prove that the reason articulated by the defendant is pretextual or not worthy of belief.

For example, assume that the woman in the above example has

applied to teach chemistry to high school students and is rejected even though she appears to be qualified based on a job description provided by the school principal. This evidence should be sufficient to make out a *prima facie* case of age discrimination. However, if the principal states that the school is interested in hiring only someone with a Ph.D. and the applicant does not have a Ph.D., the defendant school will have articulated a legitimate, nondiscriminatory reason for not hiring the fifty-year-old woman.

There are a number of ways the unsuccessful applicant could prove this reason was pretextual. For instance, if the successful candidate for the position did not have a Ph.D., the school's justification would seem pretextual. Pretext could also be established if there was a witness who had been told by the school principal that he had not hired the fifty-year-old teacher because he could hire a recent college graduate for a much lower salary that he would have to pay the fifty-year-old applicant.

Direct evidence of age discrimination is important because it shifts the burden of proof to the defendant. In cases involving indirect or circumstantial evidence of age discrimination, the burden of proving discrimination always rests with the aggrieved individual, the plaintiff.

Proving Adverse Impact

Age discrimination lawsuits are brought less often on grounds of adverse or disparate impact than on grounds of disparate treatment because adverse impact is often difficult to identify and establish as a violation of the ADEA. Adverse impact claims involve systemic or institutional discrimination which, while facially neutral, have a more discriminatory impact on protected individuals (Bureau of National Affairs 1987).

Adverse impact theory has been applied in cases challenging facially neutral objective criteria. For example, in one case that was decided by the U.S. Second Circuit Court of Appeals, the court struck down a policy of not hiring teachers with more than five years experience. Courts have also applied the adverse impact theory in cases in which the subjective judgments of supervisors have been used in making layoff decisions. In a layoff case the court will seek to determine whether an employer has selected a disproportionate number of employees in the PAG (those forty or older) for layoff through the application of selective criteria.

The Use of Statistical Evidence to Prove Age Discrimination

The use of statistics may play an important part in proving liability in an age discrimination case. This is particularly true when there has been a large-scale reduction in force (RIF). Significant statistical disparities have been found to support *prima facie* cases involving discharge, layoff, and hiring. For example, aggrieved individuals who have been discharged as part of a RIF could establish a *prima facie* violation of the ADEA by showing a steep decrease in the average age of workers over time. However, the court or jury hearing the statistical evidence must still determine whether such evidence reasonably supports an inference of discrimination.

Mixed-Motive Cases

Complicated proof issues arise when a defendant has a number of reasons for its actions, only one of which is the individual's age. In such "mixed-motive" cases, the courts will attempt to determine whether age was a determining factor—that is, one that made a difference with respect to the outcome. For example, an employer might decide to terminate an older laborer because of performance problems and the employer's belief that the employee is too old for the job. If the individual can show that the employer would not have terminated him but for his age, the employer is liable for violating the ADEA even though the laborer's performance was part of the employer's motive for terminating him. If younger laborers with worse performance records have not been terminated, this would support the finding that age was a determining factor in the older laborer's termination.

DEFENDING ADEA CLAIMS

Several statutory defenses set forth in the ADEA provide that conduct that would otherwise be a violation of the ADEA is lawful. These defenses are the bona fide occupational qualification (BFOQ) defense, the reasonable factor other than age (RFOA) defense, the bona fide seniority system (BFSS) defense, and the bona fide employee benefit plan (BFEBP) defense.

The Bona Fide Occupational Qualification Defense

The ADEA permits discrimination when age is a bona fide occupational qualification that is reasonably necessary to the normal operation of a particular business (Eglit 1992). The United States Supreme Court has established a two-prong test for weighing a BFOQ defense (Bureau of National Affairs 1987). The first prong requires that a defendant claiming the BFOQ defense establish that there are particular qualifications that are essential to the operation of its business. The second prong requires that the employer prove that it has a factual basis for believing that either (1) all or substantially all of the individuals over the age limit would be unable to safely and efficiently perform the job duties in question or (2) determining the job fitness of older workers on an individualized basis would be impossible or highly impractical.

The Court has indicated that the BFOQ defense is to be narrowly construed. In evaluating a BFOQ defense, it is important to see whether the qualifications an employer claims older individuals lack are in fact abilities its younger employees or job applicants possess. The absence of uniformly applied standards of job fitness raises serious questions about the legitimacy of an employer's BFOQ defense.

Most of the cases in which employers have raised the BFOQ defense have involved police and fire departments. The EEOC brought more than one hundred lawsuits against state and local public safety departments that had maximum hiring ages and mandatory retirement ages. In almost all these cases, the public safety departments claimed that the age limitations were justified under the BFOQ defense. This litigation was a factor when Congress amended the ADEA in 1986 to allow police, fire, and corrections departments to continue to enforce such age limitations, if they were in effect as of March 3, 1983, until December 31, 1993 (Eglit 1992). This exemption has excluded more than one million public safety workers from the ADEA's protection.

The Reasonable Factor Other Than Age Defense

The ADEA permits age discrimination when the differentiation is based on a reasonable factor other than age (Eglit 1992). Factors that may be considered reasonable include production standards, performance on validated tests, and conduct or physical fitness requirements. For example, if a fifty-year-old man with a felony handgun conviction was denied a position with a police department, the department could reasonably claim an RFOA defense, asserting that the man was denied employment based on his prior felony conviction. Courts have found employees' misconduct or inability to communicate with management or an employer's lack of work for employees with certain skills to be reasonable factors other than age.

Where an employment practice such as a test has an adverse impact on individuals protected by the ADEA, EEOC regulations state that the RFOA defense will be valid only if the employer can show that the test is justified based on business necessity. When an employment practice uses age as a limiting criterion, the employer cannot use the RFOA defense.

The Bona Fide Seniority System Defense

Under the provisions of the ADEA it is not unlawful to observe the terms of a bona fide seniority system that is not a subterfuge to evade the purposes of the ADEA. This defense has infrequently been used in ADEA litigation. EEOC regulations provide guidance for determining whether a seniority system is bona fide (Eglit 1992).

The Bona Fide Employee Benefit Plan Defense

Prior to the Older Worker's Benefit Protection Act (OWBPA) of 1990, section 4(f) (2) of the ADEA provided a defense for discrimination in employee benefit plans that were not a subterfuge to evade the purposes of the ADEA (Eglit 1992). The courts uniformly held that the defendant employer had the burden of proving this defense, whose purpose was to allow employers to take into consideration the increased cost of providing certain benefits to older workers. It allowed employers to reduce benefits, such as retirement, pension, or insurance benefits, as long as the cost incurred by the employer on behalf of the older worker was equal to that incurred on behalf of the younger worker. Therefore, it was lawful to provide $10,000 in life insurance benefits to a sixty-five-year-old employee and $100,000 to a twenty-five-year-old employee as long as the money spent to obtain this benefit was equal for both workers.

However, in 1989 in the case of *Public Employees Retirement System v. Betts* the United States Supreme Court held that older workers could be denied benefits based solely on their age. Under this decision, it was the employee's burden to prove that an employer had used the benefit plan at issue for the purpose of discriminating in an area of employment that had nothing to do with fringe benefits (Eglit 1992). For example, an employee could prevail in an age discrimination case if it could be proved that the employer had reduced the employee's fringe benefits in an effort to get the employee to quit work.

The OWBPA provides that an employer may not give older workers less in benefits than it gives to younger workers unless the employer can show that the cost of the benefits directly increases with age (Eglit 1992). However, the OWBPA creates several significant exceptions to this rule. It provides that early retirement incentive programs are lawful if they are voluntary and consistent with the purpose of the ADEA. It specifically makes Social Security bridge payments and subsidized early retirement benefits lawful.

The OWBPA also allows employers to integrate their long-term disability benefits with pension benefits in two situations. An employer may reduce the long-term disability payments it makes to an individual by the amount of the pension benefits that individual has voluntarily elected to receive. The long-term disability benefits of a pension-eligible employee also may be reduced by the amount of the pension benefits for which the employee is eligible (Eglit 1992).

The OWBPA also allows for a reduction in pension payments when there is a plant closing, a layoff, or an "other contingent event unrelated to age." In such cases the severance benefits paid to an individual may be reduced by the value of any retiree health benefits or pension "sweeteners" that are paid to the employee (Eglit 1992).

The Discipline or Discharge for Good Cause Defense

The ADEA specifically makes it is lawful to discipline or discharge an individual for good cause (Eglit 1992). An individual's membership in the PAG does not protect that individual from a legitimate good-cause discharge. This defense frequently overlaps the reasonable factor other than age defense.

Waivers to ADEA Claims

The OWBPA sets forth the criteria the courts are to follow in determining whether an individual has made a "knowing and voluntary" waiver of any claim the individual may have had under the ADEA. When an individual has signed a waiver that meets these standards, the waiver will bar the individual from receiving relief on an age claim covered by the waiver.

FILING A CHARGE OF AGE DISCRIMINATION

When and Where to File a Charge

For an individual to seek relief from age discrimination under the ADEA, the individual must first file a charge with the EEOC within 180 days of the discriminatory act. In a state or locality that has a law or ordinance prohibiting age discrimination in employment and an agency to enforce the legislation (known as a *referral state* or or *referral jurisdiction*), an individual has 300 days within which to file the charge with the referral agency or the EEOC. An aggrieved individual cannot file his or her own ADEA lawsuit until 60 days have elapsed since the individual filed his or her charge; the statutory purpose behind this 60-day period is to give the EEOC time to attempt to resolve the charge short of litigation.

A charge of discrimination can be filed directly with one of the EEOC's district, area, or local offices. For more information about the closest EEOC office nearest or about the EEOC's policies and procedures an individual may call the agency's toll-free number, 1 800 669–4000.

The 180/300 days within which an individual must file a charge begins on the date on which the discriminatory practice is committed. The type of discrimination involved (e.g., hiring or discharge) may affect a court's determination of this date. In hiring cases a number of courts have held that the time period begins on the date on which the applicant could reasonably be expected to have known of the rejection of his or her application. For example, if a teacher is told on the first day of January that she will be fired on June first and that this decision is final, she will have 180 or 300 days from the first of January to file a charge. Given these constraints, it is prudent to file a charge within 180 days of first learning of the discriminatory act to avoid these procedural pitfalls.

What to Include in a Charge

A charge of discrimination should be typed or handwritten and should be signed by the charging party. The charge must identify the discriminating party and give a general description of the discriminatory act(s). An individual may file on his or her own behalf or may identify a class of aggrieved individuals.

INVESTIGATING AGE DISCRIMINATION CHARGES

Initiating an EEOC Investigation

The EEOC is the federal agency responsible for enforcing the ADEA. The EEOC may begin investigating an alleged violation when a charge of discrimination is filed by an individual. The EEOC may also begin an investigation when a charge is filed on behalf of a group. For example, if a union is aware that an employer is not allowing older workers to participate in training it is making available to its younger workers, the union may file a third-party complaint on behalf of those union members in the PAG who are affected by the company's policy. If an individual or group knows that a covered entity has violated the ADEA but does not want to file a charge, the information regarding the violation may be provided directly to the EEOC, which may initiate its own directed investigation. Thus, if an individual sees an age-based job announcement in the newspaper, he or she may give this information to a local EEOC office to conduct an investigation.

Internal EEOC Procedures

When a charge of discrimination is filed with the EEOC, there is usually an initial review of the claim to determine whether the charge identifies the discriminating official and the discriminatory act and meets the jurisdictional requirements (e.g., whether the employer has a sufficient number of employees to be covered by the ADEA).

After receiving the charge, the EEOC notifies the covered entity of the claim of discrimination and investigates the claim to determine whether there is reasonable cause to believe that the ADEA has been violated. The EEOC may attempt to resolve the claim before completing its investigation, but this is rarely done. In most cases the agency will investigate the claim by interviewing the charging party, obtaining and evaluating the covered entity's response to the claim, and reaching a conclusion concerning whether there is reasonable cause to believe the ADEA has been violated. If the agency finds reasonable cause, it must attempt to resolve the claim through conciliation before it can file a suit to enforce the ADEA.

LAWSUITS TO ENFORCE THE ADEA

Suits by the Equal Employment Opportunity Commission

Once the EEOC has found cause but has been unable to settle the case, it is authorized to bring a lawsuit challenging the discriminatory practice. The EEOC can bring suit based on an individual claim of discrimination or a class claim. Thus, if it has been alleged that an employer terminated its oldest, most senior workers as part of a reorganization, the commission could bring suit on behalf of all aggrieved individuals in the PAG.

Private Suits

An aggrieved individual has the right to bring his or her own lawsuit 60 days after filing a charge of discrimination (Eglit 1992). Private individuals can bring lawsuits based on individual or class claims. Group actions under the ADEA are covered by the "opt-in" provisions of the Fair Labor Standards Act. To become an ADEA plaintiff in an existing private lawsuit, the individual must consent in writing to be part of the suit, and the consent must be filed in the court in which the action has been brought (Eglit 1992). If an individual wants to pursue a private charge of discrimination, it is essential for the individual to file suit *before the EEOC files suit*. The filing of an ADEA lawsuit by the Commission bars the charging party from bringing his or her own ADEA suit.

Time Limitations on Filing Suits

Prior to the passage of the Civil Rights Act of 1990, an individual was required to bring an ADEA suit within two years of the alleged discrimination or three years of a willful violation of the ADEA. The Civil Rights Act of 1991, which went into effect for most employers on November 21, 1991, eliminated this time limitation. The ADEA, as amended, states that an aggrieved individual must bring suit within 90 days of receiving notice from the EEOC stating that it has completed its investigation of the case and determined that the individual has a right to file suit.

REMEDIES AVAILABLE UNDER THE ADEA

The Basis for Awarding Relief

The fundamental principle underlying the analysis of appropriate remedies in an ADEA case is that victims of discrimination should be restored to the economic position they would have occupied had it not been for the unlawful conduct (Eglit 1992). For example, if an individual has been fired because of age, that individual should be provided with back pay, reinstatement, retroactive seniority (if appropriate), and any other benefits he or she has lost as a result of separation.

Types of Relief Awarded

Courts may grant legal or equitable relief that would be appropriate to effectuate the purposes of the ADEA. In line with this authority, courts have ordered employers to hire individuals, provide them with lost fringe benefits (e.g., pension, severance pay, health benefits, or sick leave), pay them back pay, reinstate them, or promote them. If reinstatement is not feasible, courts have awarded *front pay*, compensation for what the plaintiff would have earned if he or she had not been terminated or denied employment (Eglit 1992). The EEOC has the authority to seek injunctive relief to bar future violations of the ADEA. The ADEA also provides for an award of *liquidated damages* or *statutory double damages* for willful violations of the ADEA. If for example, a court determined that an individual should be awarded $10,000 in back pay and that the violation was willful, it could award an additional $10,000 in liquidated damages. The ADEA does not provide for damages to be awarded for pain and suffering. As a result, an individual needs to determine, with the assistance of a lawyer, whether it is better to bring an action under state law in state court, where damages for pain and suffering may possibly be obtained, or under the ADEA.

It is also possible to obtain a preliminary injunction to prevent a future age discriminatory action. For example, if an employee is told he is to be terminated in 30 days, he can file suit in federal court and ask a judge to prohibit his retirement. If an individual seeks such relief less than 60 days after filing an ADEA charge with the EOC, he or she must work closely with the agency to allow it to attempt conciliation before the individual files suit. The EEOC can also initiate a lawsuit to obtain such preliminary relief on behalf of an individual.

OLDER WORKERS AND THE AMERICANS WITH DISABILITIES ACT

In October 1990 Congress enacted the Americans with Disabilities Act (ADA). This law, which prohibits discrimination in employment against individuals with disabilities, is an additional tool that may be used by older disabled workers to challenge discrimination they face in seeking or retaining employment.

Coverage

Employers with twenty-five or more employees that are engaged in industries affecting commerce were covered by the ADA as of July 26, 1992. As of July 26, 1994, the ADA will apply to employers with fifteen or more employees. The ADA also applies to employment agencies, labor organizations, and joint labor-management committees, as well as state and local governments.

Employment Prohibitions

The ADA prohibits any covered employer from discriminating against a "qualified individual with a disability" with regard to hiring, promotion, termination, pay, training, and other terms, conditions, or privileges of employment. An employer is required to make "reasonable accommodations" to the known physical or mental limitations of an otherwise qualified individual with a disability unless doing so would impose an "undue hardship." It is unlawful to use employment tests, qualification standards, or other selection criteria that disproportionately screen out individuals with disabilities unless they can be proven to be job-related and meet the business necessity standard set in the ADA.

Research has indicated that older workers and workers with disabilities have faced substantial obstacles to obtaining employment because of societal prejudice. Older workers with disabilities are especially vulnerable to such discrimination. The ADA is an important tool for challenging such discriminatory practices.

REFERENCES

Ageism: Prejudice and Discrimination Against the Elderly.
Bureau of National Affairs (BNA). 1987. *Older Americans in the Workforce: Challenges and Solutions.* BNA Special Report. Washington, D.C.: BNA.
Eglit, Howard C. 1992. *Age Discrimination.* Colorado Springs, Colorado: Shepard's/McGraw-Hill, Inc.
Hooper, Roy. 1989. "Working Late: The Railroad to Retirement." *Modern Maturity,* 34 (February–March):32.
Jones, Philip L., and Diane E. Herz. 1989. *Institutional Barriers to Employment of Older Workers. Monthly Labor Review,* 14 (April):112.
Palmore, E. B. 1990. *Ageism: Negative and Positive.* New York: Springer Publishing Company.
Schuster, Michael H., Joan A. Kaspin, and Christopher S. Miller. 1989. *Age Discrimination in Employment Act: An Evaluation of Federal and State Enforcement, Legal Processes and Employer Compliance: Final Report.* Syracuse, N.Y.: Syracuse University.
The Villers Foundation. 1987. *On the Other Side of the Easy Street: Myths & Facts About the Economics of Old Age.* Report of The Villers Foundation. Washington, D.C.: The Villers Foundation.
Weiss, Francine K. 1989. *Employment Discrimination Against Older Women: A Handbook on Litigating Age and Sex Discrimination Cases.* Report of the Older Women's League. Washington, D.C.: Older Women's League.

15

Estate Planning for the Older Person or Couple

●

DANA SHILLING

The estate planner's basic job is to combine legal documents and financial instruments such as wills, testamentary trusts, *inter vivos* (lifetime) trusts, "living wills," life insurance policies, joint ownership, and durable powers of attorney to distribute the client's property in accordance with the client's wishes in the most efficient and expeditious way possible at the lowest permissible tax cost. Usually considerations of tax cost focus on federal income taxes, gift taxes, and especially estate taxes. A number of states have no income or estate taxes, but in some states the burden of income, gift, estate, and inheritance taxes can be heavy enough to require additional planning. (An estate tax is imposed on the estate itself; an inheritance tax is imposed on heirs for the privilege of inheriting.) Furthermore, state tax rules do not always parallel the federal rules, so it may be necessary to balance savings on federal taxes against a higher state tax liability or vice versa.

CONSIDERATIONS FOR THE ESTATE PLANNER

On the most general level, the estate planning task is the same whether the planning client is twenty-one or ninety-one. However, senior citizens (those sixty-five and over) have special needs. Every estate planning decision must be reexamined not only in light of the tax consequences during the lifetime and after the death of the client, but in light of the possibility that either the transferor or the transferee of money or property will become incapacitated or need to apply for Medicaid. It may be necessary to sacrifice tax benefits to protect an impaired client or his or her Medicaid application—e.g., in a case in which minimizing the tax burden results in retention of income or assets in violation of Medicaid rules.

Sometimes estate planners without an adequate perspective of "elder law" inadvertently harm their clients by making recommendations that save taxes but lead to the depletion of their clients' estates to pay for health care (Strauss 1990). An older person making an estate or financial plan or a family caregiver should always inquire about the extent of the planner's background in issues pertaining to elder law and the steps the planner takes to keep that knowledge current. An attorney who does not have expertise in elder law should always advise a client to get an elder law attorney involved in the planning process; failure to do so could subject the attorney to malpractice liability if he or she gives bad advice because of lack of specialized knowledge.

Good plans safeguard the dignity and autonomy of the elderly as much as possible. Most older clients prefer to "age in place"—that is, remain at home, with suitable care—rather than being institutionalized. However, this preference is not always realistic, and sometimes the planner's job involves overcoming an older person's or family members' reluctance to use specialized housing or nursing home care when remaining in the community is detrimental to the older person's health or is not economically feasible.

In line with the client's wishes, the planner may advise the client to forego tax benefits (for instance, the exclusion of up to $125,000 in capital gains on the sale of the principal residence of a person over fifty-five) to maintain ownership of his or her home. If ownership of the home is transferred (e.g., to an adult child to avoid having a lien placed on the home by state Medicaid authorities), it may be worthwhile to give the older owner or owners life estates in the home so they will have a legal right to reside there for life. The use of life estates involves subtle tax and Medicaid questions, and it must be done carefully to comply with local real estate law.

AVOIDING DEPLETION OF THE ESTATE

The planner must integrate planning for the rest of the client's lifetime with planning for the client's death and after. Unless the client has a sound plan to pay for chronic medical care, he or she is likely to drain or deplete the savings of a lifetime. The planning strategies for funding that care will not be discussed here except to note that the estate plan should deal with the possibility of a reduction in the size of the estate. A person with $1 million in assets probably will not qualify for Medicaid no matter what planning measures are taken; he or she is likely to spend a great deal of money, perhaps several hundred thousand dollars, on long-term care insurance, home care, and/ or nursing home care. The people who expect to inherit this money will no doubt be disappointed!

The estate planner will probably recommend changing the distribution of the estate, perhaps by removing some bequests entirely so that the main beneficiaries will receive more or by stating bequests in terms of percentages of the estate rather than dollar amounts that the estate may not be large enough to satisfy. One reason wills should be periodically revised (with professional advice, of course) is to make changes to compensate for changes in the size of the estate.

OLD PEOPLE, OLD WILLS; THE IMPORTANCE OF UPDATING WILLS

For understandable psychological reasons, many people approach the whole process of estate planning with trepidation (Shaffer 1970; Schneiderman 1991). Many people never have wills drafted. Others retain wills that are legally defective. Married couples sometimes sign joint wills or mutual wills that have unintended contractual consequences and are harder to modify than wills signed on an individual basis. Yet others have wills that are legally valid and entitled to probate, but reflect outdated legal and/or factual assumptions because the individuals who made them are able to overcome the psychological barriers to the extent of making a will, but not enough to review the will or consult an estate planner for an updated plan. Tragically, some older people delay getting professional advice until their condition has deteriorated so much that they lack the capacity necessary to make a will or alter an old will.

Legislative changes can seriously influence estate planning. For example, unrevised wills made prior to 1981 reflect the limited availability of a "marital deduction"; since 1981 an unlimited marital deduction has been available in the federal system. Wills made before 1986 reflect the larger number of tax brackets and the sharper difference between the top and bottom brackets that existed prior to 1986, which justified elaborate devices to shift income to a lower bracket that are no longer worthwhile (Regan 1991).

Owners of closely held businesses sometimes engaged in elaborate "estate freeze" transactions to decrease the value of their stock in the businesses for estate tax purposes. In both 1987 and 1990 Congress took action to limit these freeze transactions, and in 1990 it also covered many other kinds of estate planning transactions by adding to the Internal Revenue Code a new Chapter 14, which has broad implications for trust planning and remainder transactions (Rothenberg 1992). In 1992 New York State made major changes in the surviving spouse's right to share in a deceased spouse's estate. Not only are these changes dramatic, but they do not parallel federal law, creating additional problems for planners.

Estate plans must also be updated in light of factual changes, such as children's growing up, divorce and remarriage, or the severe chronic illness of an intended beneficiary. Once one spouse dies, it is obviously appropriate for the surviving spouse to have a new will drafted based on a new estate plan (Acker 1992; Lemann 1992; Shumaker 1992).

CLIENTS' FEARS OF PROBATE

Estate planning clients frequently have an exaggerated fear of the probate process, and they often demand that the financial plan include a hefty revocable living trust. Revocable living trusts, like life insurance and joint property, are "will substitutes" that are exempt from the probate process (Gassman, Robinson, and Conetta 1992; Kasner 1992). Recent court decisions have also enhanced the viability of trusts containing life insurance policies as tax-saving mechanisms (Christensen 1992). Revocable trusts have their uses in planning, but they are no panacea.

Admittedly, probate is a time-consuming process that costs money, but it is not the horror that many clients seem to think it is. Setting up and administering a revocable trust also costs money. A client's fear of probate can be allayed by making sure that the estate has "liquidity"—cash to meet the family's needs until the estate is settled—in the form of life insurance and/or a separate account with several months' living expenses for each spouse. Steps can also be taken during the client's life to simplify the probate of the estate For instance, the planner can gather records and trace potential heirs.

REMOVING FUNDS FROM THE TAXABLE ESTATE

For older clients, the planner must not merely point out that the funds in a revocable living trust are not subject to the probate process, but also warn that the funds will be "available" for Medicaid purposes and that the trust's assets will be included in the trustor's taxable estate (Gardner 1991; Mazart 1991). To remove funds or property from the taxable estate, the owner must conclusively surrender control, either by making an outright gift or by placing the funds in an irrevocable trust over which the trustor has no control—or the minimal degree of control permitted by the Internal Revenue Code (Kruse 1991). The trustor retains control over the revocable trust, so it must be included in his or her taxable estate. Further limitations on Medicaid eligibility are likely to be imposed by Congress and state legislators in dire need of budget cuts.

Of course, inclusion in the taxable estate is not a concern if the estate is too small to be taxable. The general rule is that estates under $600,000 are entirely exempt from federal estate tax, although there may be state estate or inheritance taxes, and there may also be cases in which a smaller estate is subject to federal tax if extensive gifts were made prior to death. If the assets of a married couple are less than $1.2 million, federal estate tax on at least the estate of the first spouse to die can be avoided by "estate splitting." That is, transfers can be made from the wealthier spouse to the poorer so that each has an estate of under $600,000. This is feasible because there is no gift or estate tax on interspousal transfers. The surviving spouse might end up with an estate worth more than $600,000 unless he or she depletes the estate by spending money during widowhood, which is not unlikely considering the cost of chronic care. The survivor can usually escape taxation through conventional planning measures such as gifts, irrevocable trusts, and charitable contributions.

There is an unlimited marital deduction: that is, no gift or estate tax is imposed on a gift or bequest of any size from one spouse to the other. Admittedly, a very large marital bequest may merely delay the problem by making the "second estate" large enough to be taxable if the surviving spouse does not remarry and acquire another spouse for whom a marital deduction is available (Regan 1991; Streer 1991). One way to cope with this problem is by purchasing "second-to-die" life insurance, a policy on the joint lives of both spouses that doesn't pay benefits until the second spouse dies. The beneficiary can use the insurance proceeds to pay estate tax (Lyons 1991).

An outright bequest to the spouse clearly qualifies for the marital deduction. A person can also provide life income to his or her surviving spouse, meanwhile determining the disposition of the property after the surviving spouse dies, and still get the marital deduction, by following the Internal Revenue Code's rules for a qualified terminable interest in property (QTIP). For instance, an individual may establish a trust that pays income to the surviving spouse at least once a year. However, anyone who contemplates creating a QTIP should seek professional advice to see if doing this has negative consequences under state law.

Another common estate planning device is the "gifting program": a person desiring to reduce an estate (or reduce it below $600,000) will establish a practice of giving gifts. There is no gift tax on gifts of up to $10,000 per year per donee. If both spouses consent to the gift, up to $20,000 can be given to each donee yearly free of gift tax. Giving six such gifts a year for a period of eight years will do a good deal to reduce the size of an estate. However, it is almost certain that the gifts will be considered transfers for Medicaid purposes; and transfers made within the penalty period will delay Medicaid eligibility. The planner must balance the estate tax incentive against the Medicaid disincentive.

Actually, $600,000 is a rather modest figure. A couple that owns a home and has some investments and a healthy pension could easily accumulate that much. (It is important to realize that those who try to increase their estates by reducing the amount of pension benefits they draw during life will be subject to an additional excise tax on excessive pension accumulation in the estate.) Enough estate planning devices are available so that nearly all estates escape federal taxation. However, many more estates are subject to state estate and/ or inheritance taxes, so further planning steps may be needed to reduce or eliminate state tax.

KEEPING ASSETS IN THE ESTATE

Although the estate planner's objective is usually to reduce the size of the potentially taxable estate, there is at least one circumstance in which the planner for an elderly client may want to make sure an asset stays in the estate: when the asset (e.g., stock or real estate) has appreciated significantly and the heir wants a "stepped-up basis." For property other than money, *basis* is the value for tax purposes. (Despite inflation, money neither appreciates nor depreciates.) The donee of a gift has the same basis the donor had, but a person who inherits an asset has a "stepped-up" basis equal to the value of the asset when the testator died. The donee or heir must pay income taxes on the difference between the amount received from selling the asset and its basis. Therefore, the higher the basis, the smaller the difference and the smaller the tax liability. The general assumption is that assets appreciate over time, but this assumption may prove false in a recessionary economy. If values decline, recipients of depreciated assets prefer to be donees rather than heirs.

One strategy that works in a lot of plans is for elderly parent(s) to transfer the family homestead to a child before the Medicaid penalty period is predicted to begin, but retain (a) life estate(s) in the house, including the right to live there. If a life estate is retained, the gift is not complete enough for tax purposes to remove the home from the estate. Therefore, there is no gift tax at the time of the gift, and the child gets the basis step-up. Furthermore, because the home no longer belongs to the parent(s) by the time a Medicaid application is filed, Medicaid will not be allowed to put a lien on the home to recoup medical benefits provided to the parent(s). This example highlights an important principle: the Medicaid and tax systems do not always use the same definitions or arrive at the same conclusions, and transactions must be assessed from both perspectives without assuming that legal concepts will carry over from one to the other. However, strategies for home transfers may be cut back or eliminated by Congress or the legislators of a particular state.

MAKING SUITABLE PROVISIONS

Not only must provisions be made in a sound estate plan for the "objects of the testator's bounty," but provisions must be made in suitable form. When the beneficiaries are legally or practically unable to administer property because they are minors, the problem is handled by establishing a guardianship, by leaving money or property to them in trust, or by making transfers under state laws adopted pursuant to the Uniform Gifts to Minors Act or the Uniform Transfers to Minors Act.

Older clients typically (though not inevitably) have older spouses. Some older people suffer from mental or physical incapacity due to such causes as strokes, Alzheimer's disease, depression, or the consumption of too many medications. Others are not incapacitated, but factors such as the stress of bereavement and lack of investment experience make them unwilling to take responsibility for managing large estates. If the intended beneficiary cannot or will not manage the amount received, the planner must make other arrangements (Schlesinger and Scheiner 1991).

Perhaps the most common solution is for the desired amount to be left in trust rather than outright. The trustee will manage the investments and distribute trust income in accordance with the terms of the trust. The planning possibilities include giving the trustee discretion to determine when income will be distributed, how much will be distributed, and to whom it will be distributed and allowing the trustee to "invade" the trust principal and give it to a trust beneficiary, which may be permitted in accordance with conditions defined in the trust or according to the trustee's own discretion.

Creating and maintaining a trust has important gift, income, and estate tax implications. It is imperative that an individual seek professional advice on drafting a trust. The prudent estate planner will consider every estate planning device from the perspective of Medicaid as well as taxes. If an *inter vivos* ("living") trust is created, is it a "Medicaid-qualifying trust" that will delay Medicaid eligibility? Is creation of the trust a "transfer" for Medicaid purposes? Is the trust income or part or all of the trust principal "available" to either spouse for Medicaid purposes? Will the creation of a trust by one spouse affect the Medicaid eligibility of the other spouse (Longenecker 1990; Bagge 1992)?

If an heir is impaired or does not want to manage money and a trust is not desirable, an estate planning possibility is to limit provision under the will in favor of purchasing additional insurance to benefit the person who would otherwise be the heir. Life insurance can be paid out under "settlement options" so that the beneficiary receives a continuing stream of income rather than a large sum that may be difficult to invest wisely.

If the surviving spouse's Medicaid eligibility is the paramount consideration, a possible strategy is to limit or eliminate provision for the surviving spouse and pass the bulk of the estate directly to the children or other beneficiaries. For instance, if an individual is terminally ill and must make an estate plan that will be carried out in the near future, and if his or her surviving spouse will need long-term chronic care, it might be worthwhile to make sure that the surviving spouse will not inherit enough to preclude his or her Medicaid eligibility.

Prenuptial and postnuptial agreements can be used to waive claims on one's spouse's estate. Or, if a person inherits a sum from his or her spouse or anyone else that is inconvenient for Medicaid purposes, it may be possible to resolve the problem by waiving or disclaiming the amount, using it to purchase exempt assets, or having the money transmitted in a way that does not fall afoul of Medicaid prohibitions. A testamentary trust is not considered a "Medicaid-qualifying trust," so deriving an inheritance in this form does not have the same negative Medicaid effects as being the beneficiary of a living trust set up for one's own benefit or the benefit of one's spouse.

Medicaid applicants have an obligation to collect all assets to which they are entitled, so a waiver or disclaimer is likely to be considered a transfer. The planner's main option is to plan far enough in advance so the penalty period will have expired before any Medicaid application is made. The Internal Revenue Code prescribes the procedure that must be followed in order to make a disclaimer effective for tax purposes. Depending on the circumstances of the case, it may be possible to make a partial disclaimer or waiver rather than foregoing the entire inheritance. But the general rule is that no one can disclaim after receiving any benefits from an inheritance, so the disclaimer must precede actual receipt of the inheritance.

CHOOSING A FIDUCIARY

A fiduciary is a person or organization (e.g., a bank or trust company) responsible for administering funds that belong to someone else. In the elder planning context, the most common fiduciaries are executors, administrators, trustees, and agents under durable powers of attorney. Sometimes a legal document will contain detailed and explicit instructions for the fiduciary in an attempt to control the fiduciary's conduct in all situations. But it is more usual to grant the fiduciary anywhere from some discretion to total control over the investment and use of the funds under the fiduciary's power. In light of the potential for poor investment decisions or dishonesty on the part of the fiduciary, it is extremely important to make the right choice of fiduciary or fiduciaries.

There are strong arguments in favor of naming as fiduciary a spouse or close family member, either alone or in conjunction with other people or with a neutral observer such as an attorney, accountant, or bank trust department. But there are also counter arguments: it is not good practice to choose a fiduciary who is at all likely to die before or soon after a testator or trust creator or who is at risk of physical or mental impairment. In the case of a professional or corporate fiduciary, if one person dies, someone else will assume his or her professional role. So a professional or corporate fiduciary can provide continuity and investment expertise, but at the loss of some degree of personal interest and the literal cost of fees charged to the trust or estate.

In practical terms, it makes sense to have either a single fiduciary or an odd number of fiduciaries two or four fiduciaries can split evenly, preventing decisions from being made. A successor fiduciary is one named in advance in case the primary fiduciary is unable or unwilling to serve when needed. Naming successor fiduciaries is always good practice.

State laws set out the basic powers of fiduciaries. Other powers can be added if the documents are correctly drafted. Still other powers are permitted by the laws of some states but forbidden in others. The advantage of giving fiduciaries very broad powers (e.g., to invade trust principal, decide what to do with trust income, make gifts, and do tax, estate, and Medicaid planning) is that a flexible plan can be devised to meet a family's needs after a wealthy family member becomes incapacitated.

One risk of granting broad powers is that the fiduciary might engage in outright theft of a vulnerable person's funds. Another is that the fiduciary might exercise powers provided under the various instruments in a way that violates state law or public policy or that is unfair to other potential beneficiaries. For instance, if one child serves as fiduciary and makes gifts to herself and her children, excluding her siblings, such action may violate state law or create an unfavorable tax or Medicaid position for the parent.

MARITAL PLANNING VERSUS PLANNING FOR SINGLES

The estate tax and Medicaid systems operate on the tacit assumption that most people—and certainly most people entitled to relief from the harshest consequences of the legal system—are married. Therefore, married couples frequently are able to save income taxes by filing joint income tax returns, and there is an unlimited estate tax marital deduction. The Social Security Act contains elaborate provisions permitting the healthy spouse of a nursing home resident who receives Medicaid to receive a certain level of income and assets.

In order to get repayment for the medical care they have financed, a state Medicaid agency is entitled to place a lien on real property, including a home owned by a Medicaid beneficiary, but such a lien cannot be enforced on a homestead if the beneficiary's spouse, minor child, or disabled child continues to live there. It can be enforced at the death of a single, widowed, or divorced beneficiary or as soon as such a beneficiary becomes unable to return home from the nursing home where he or she is receiving Medicaid benefits.

A common (though by no means inevitable) demographic pattern is for husbands to be several years older than wives, with most of the couple's income, pension benefits, Social Security benefits, and assets derived from the husband's earnings. Coupled with women's longer life span, the result is a large number of widows who become sole owners of the couples' accumulated assets, as well as their late husbands' life insurance benefits.

This pattern has many implications. It can make it difficult for the husband to obtain Medicaid benefits because he may have excess income and resources that cannot be removed even with Medicaid planning. Even if the couple makes full use of the Medicaid spousal protection provisions, the healthy wife may not have enough funds to live comfortably in the community.

Furthermore, after the husband's death the widow may be exhausted by caregiving for her husband, and her inheritance may be too small to pay privately for the care she needs, yet too large for her to qualify for Medicaid. If at all possible, the husband's estate plan should take this possibility into account. It might be a good idea for him to make major bequests directly to the couple's children or other beneficiaries so that his wife's inheritance can be transferred or "spent down" so she can qualify for Medicaid. Furthermore, it might be a good idea for middle-aged or "young old" clients who are relatively healthy to buy long-term care insurance to cope with this possibility.

A properly drafted "QTIP" trust can benefit both the elderly surviving spouse and the testator's children. For Medicaid purposes, only the income—not the trust principal—belongs to the surviving spouse. In most states, Medicaid applicants can qualify if they "spend down" their excess income. If the QTIP produces more income than is desirable for the surviving spouse to receive in terms of Medicaid planning, the trustee may be able to change the trust's investments (within limits) to decrease income while maintaining the safety of capital—for instance, by investing in zero-coupon bonds.

The QTIP also works well in the not uncommon cases of divorce, remarriage, and friction between the second spouse and the children of the testator's first marriage. The surviving spouse gets income for his or her lifetime; the children get control of the trust property after the second spouse's death.

The above examples deal with the planning needs of a male testator making provisions for a surviving wife in the context of his own Medicaid planning. However, the estate planner must also be aware that the wife might need long-term care before the husband does and might die first, whatever their respective ages. A good plan cannot be usable in only one circumstance.

A very high percentage of nursing home residents are women—women who are widowed, divorced, or never married, many of whom have outlived their family support systems. Estate planning and Medicaid planning for unmarried women, who cannot use the marital deduction or Medicaid spousal allowances, are quite difficult. The counterbalance is that they need not meet the challenge of marital estate planning, making adequate provisions for the surviving spouse.

Single women with children usually (though not necessarily) want to make provisions for their children. Single women without children who have estates that are potentially federally taxable may want to implement a long-range "giving programs" with friends, nephews and nieces, or charities as beneficiaries. Because the Medicaid system focuses on transfers of assets, not on consumption, a single woman making a Medicaid plan may wish to increase her personal spending. If she is healthy, a cruise or European vacation may be enjoyable. If she has some health problems, but does not require the level of care provided by a nursing home, hiring a companion can provide reassurance.

HEEDING CLIENTS' WISHES

The most usual desire of a testator is to make sure that his or her spouse has adequate income for the rest of his or her life and that assets not required to support the surviving spouse pass to the couple's children and/or grandchildren. This desire can be implemented by making gifts during the testator's life; making outright bequests that take effect at the death of the testator,; or making dispositions for the life of the surviving spouse, then to the children, or through the surviving spouse's own gift-giving or will provisions. One powerful impetus for Medicaid planning is the desire to keep assets "in the family" rather than having them consumed by medical bills.

Not everybody, however, feels this way. The estate planner must find out the client's real wishes. Each spouse may have come to the marriage with substantial assets and not require a bequest from the other spouse. There may be a prenuptial agreement that limits the potential inheritance of one or both spouses. Each spouse may have been married before and have a primary estate planning objective of benefiting the children of the earlier marriage but not stepchildren, children of the other spouse's prior marriage.

Clients differ widely in their beliefs about Medicaid. To some, Medicaid planning is the equivalent of sound tax planning, a way to maximize the benefits legally available. To others, "going on welfare" is an indelible disgrace. The estate planner may believe (without substantiation) that the client wants a combined Medicaid and estate plan that will allow the client to be eligible for Medicaid and complete coverage of the client's medical needs by Medicaid in order to preserve the client's funds for his or her family; but the client may refuse to surrender autonomy by giving up control of his or her funds. Furthermore, the client may be unwilling to apply for Medicaid, may be unable to structure a plan leading to qualification, or may prefer to pay privately for some medical care, especially if access to high-quality nursing care of the type required by the client is much easier for private-pay patients than for Medicaid patients (U.S. GAO 1990). The client may be estranged from his or her relatives; the children may be affluent, so their inheritance is a low priority for the client.

One of the toughest ethical issues for the estate planner working with the elderly is who is the client, the testator alone or the testator's family? What is the planner's responsibility to the client, and what is his or her responsibility to society as a whole, and specifically to the public treasury in the form of its Medicaid budget (Donaldson and Severns 1991)?

A dynamic including anything from a sense of obligation to outright exploitation through terror may induce an elderly person to make gifts or testamentary provisions for his or her offspring. Testators who have more than one child usually want to treat their children fairly, but what is fair? Should each child get an equal provision, and should gifts the children have received before the testator's death be included in the computation? Should children receive more if they have financial problems and, if so, does this penalize the more financially successful siblings for their hard work?

If the testator lives with one of the children or if there is a caregiver child, fairness often requires compensation for the hard work of caregiving—especially if the child sacrifices income and career opportunities. But if the caregiver selects the estate planner, brings the parent/testator to the office, "interprets" what the planner says, and even answers the planner's questions, is an estate plan that favors the caregiver child the parent's own wish or the product of undue influence (Spriggs 1992)?

Whenever possible, the planner must speak to the testator alone to determine what he or she wants. This can be difficult, especially if the elderly client is sight-impaired, hearing-impaired, and/or confused or if the senior citizen is not fluent in English or has reverted back to a language spoken in youth. It is preferable to have an interpreter who is more objective than the caregiver child.

However difficult the task, the planner must find out what the client wants; advise the client of the consequences of those wishes; and do whatever the law permits to carry out the client's plan (Pennell 1992). As long as the client is competent, he or she is permitted to make dispositions that the estate planner considers unfair, generate additional tax costs, or have unfavorable Medicaid consequences. Once the planner has fully disclosed the risks, the decision is up to the client.

THE ISSUE OF COMPETENCY

What if the client is not competent? In legal terms, no one can make a contract unless he or she has "contractual capacity," an ability to understand the nature and implications of the transaction. No one can make or alter a will without "testamentary capacity," a knowledge of what one owns and who are the "natural objects of one's bounty"—generally speaking, one's family.

Adults are presumed to have capacity. However, a judicial conservatorship or guardianship proceeding may result in a determination of lack of capacity, in which case state law and the judge's decree must be consulted to see if the conservatee or ward retains the right to make or alter a will. Under some circumstances, the guardian or conservator will be permitted to take planning steps to reduce estate taxes and perhaps to promote Medicaid eligibility.

In most cases, there will be no judicial proceedings. The drafter of a will or trust must decide if the client is competent to understand and execute the document. Steps can be taken to enhance capacity. For instance, one can explain a document carefully, give the client a large-type copy, and schedule appointments—or even adjust medication—to promote alertness (Smith 1988; Strauss, Wolf and Shilling 1990; Pepe and Lindgren 1991).

After the testator's death, unhappy would-be heirs may challenge the will, claiming lack of capacity or undue influence. Proponents of the will (those offering the will for probate) should be prepared with testimony, perhaps even videotapes of the testator, showing that the testator understood the will and adopted it freely.

THE DURABLE POWER OF ATTORNEY

Although it is a part of planning for the client's lifetime rather than estate planning, the durable power of attorney (DPA) rates a mention here as a powerful, inexpensive, flexible, and valuable tool for planning. A power of attorney gives an agent the authority to perform acts (such as financial transactions) for the grantor of the power. A durable power of attorney remains valid even if the creator becomes incapacitated. A healthy elder can grant a DPA to a trusted child, friend, banker, or other agent who will then be able to pay bills, transact banking business, file tax returns, and take care of other matters the elder can no longer handle personally.

The agent's powers are quite broad, especially if the power of attorney is drafted so that it includes additional powers, such as the powers to make gifts and carry out tax, estate, and Medicaid plans, and this breadth allows for misuse. Even if the agent behaves properly, there is a loss of autonomy when someone else takes over financial tasks. Hence, most states allow a "springing" power of attorney that takes effect only when the grantor of the power becomes incapacitated. The key is selecting the right definition of incapacity. However, in many states a judicially appointed conservator or guardian has the right to revoke the DPA, and it may be revoked in the precise situation in which it was designed to be used! However, the court may find that appointing a conservator or guardian is unnecessary if the elder already has financial management mechanisms (such as a DPA, representative payment of Social Security benefits, and a trust) in place.

CONCLUSION

Failure to understand and confront issues of elder law can be detrimental to the older client's estate planning. Unless appropriate planning measures (such as insurance and Medicaid planning) are taken, it is very likely that the estate will be depleted by the cost of medical and nursing care for the chronically ill or mentally impaired senior citizen. Whatever remains to be inherited by the surviving spouse (if there is a surviving spouse) must be conveyed in a way that is useful to the survivor. The planner's goal is to integrate planning for the client's lifetime with planning for his or her death and after, to consider the special needs of each family member, and to preserve and convey wealth from generation to generation.

REFERENCES

Acker, Alan S. 1992. "Death Bed Tax Planning." *Tax Management Estates, Gifts and Trusts Journal,* 17 (2):55–62.

Bagge, Michael. 1992. "The Eye of the Needle: Trust Planning, Medicaid, and the Ersatz Poor." *New York State Bar Journal,* 64 (2):14–15.

Christensen, Burke A. 1992. "Irrevocable Life Insurance Trusts to the Rescue." *Trusts and Estates,* 131 (5):53–55.

232 *Legal Issues*

Donaldson, John E., and S. Severns. 1991. "Ethical Considerations in Advising and Representing the Elderly." In Proceedings, 3rd Annual Symposium on Elder Law, National Academy of Elder Law Attorneys (Orlando, Florida, May 15–18).

Gardner, H. 1991. "Designing Wills and Trust Instruments to Provide Maximum Flexibility." *Estate Planning*, 18 (3):138–142.

Gassman, Alan S., Charles F. Robinson, and Tami F. Conetta. 1992. "Living Trust Checklist." *The Practical Tax Lawyer*, 6 (4):89–96.

Kasner, Jerry A. 1992. "Reassessing the Joint Purchase as an Estate Planning Technique." *Tax Notes*, 55 (10):665–669.

Kruse, C. B. Jr. 1991. "Insulating Discretionary Trust Assets for Elders and Incapacitated Persons from Consideration by Medicaid and Other Public Support Providers." In Proceedings, 3rd Annual Symposium on Elder Law, National Academy of Elder Law Attorneys (Orlando, Florida, May 15–18).

Lemann, Thomas B. 1992. "Planning the Surviving Spouse's Estate." *Louisiana Bar Journal*, 39 (4):561–567.

Longenecker, R. 1990. "Planning for Medicaid Eligibility." *Tax Management Estates, Gifts and Trusts Journal*, 15 (3):131–141.

Lyons, P. J. 1991. "Factors to Analyze in Selecting a Second-to-Die Life Insurance Policy." *Estate Planning*, 18 (3):166–170.

Mazart, G. 1991. "Lifetime Planning." *New Jersey Lawyer*, 17 (1):28–32.

Pennell, Jeffrey N. 1992. "Ethics Concerns Are Being Addressed." *Trusts and Estates*, 131 (1):14–16.

Pepe, Steven D., and C. Lindgren, C. 1991. "Ethical Dilemmas in Elder Law: Working With Questionably Competent Clients." *ElderLaw Report*, 2 (10):1–6.

Regan, J. J. 1991. *Tax, Estate and Financial Planning for the Elderly*. New York: Matthew Bender.

Rothenburg, Richard S. 1992. "Business Freezes Under Chapter 14." *Journal of Taxation of Investments*, 9 (2):237–245.

Schneiderman, G. 1991. "The Creation of a Will is a Personal Matter." *Trusts and Estates*, 130 (2):68–70

Schlesinger, Sanford J., and B. J. Scheiner. 1991. "Planning for the Elderly or Incapacitated Client." In Rikoon, J. J., chairman, *Handling Your First Health Care Proxy and Living Will* 72–222. New York: Practicing Law Institute.

Shaffer, Thomas L. 1970. *Death, Property and Lawyers: A Behavioral Approach*. New York: Dunellen Publishing Co.

Shumaker, Roger L. 1992. "Estate Planning for the Newly Divorced." *Probate and Property*, 6 (2):16–17.

Smith, L. F. 1988. "Representing the Elderly Client and Addressing the Question of Competence." *Journal of Contemporary Law*, 14 (1):61–104.

Spriggs, Clare H. 1992. "Multi-Generational Representation."*Trusts and Estates*, 131 (1):17–23.

Strauss, Peter J. 1990. "The Geri-Hat Trick: Three Goals of Estate Planning for the Elderly." In John T. Gaubatz, ed., Proceedings of the 24th Annual Philip E. Heckerling Institute on Estate Planning. New York: Matthew Bender.

Strauss, Peter J., R. Wolf, and D. Shilling. 1990, 1992. *Aging and the Law*. Chicago, Ill.: Commerce Clearing House.

Streer, Paul J. 1991. "Estate Planning to Benefit the Medium-Sized Estate." *Estate Planning*, 18 (4):218–224.

U.S. General Accounting Office (GAO). 1990. *Nursing Homes: Admission Problems for Medicaid Recipients and Attempts to Solve Them*. GAO/HRD-90-135. Gaithersburg, Maryland: U.S. GAO.

16

Legal Planning for Incapacity

●

NANCY COLEMAN

By the year 2035, almost one quarter of the population of the United States (71 million) will be sixty-five or older (U.S. Senate et al. 1988). The federal government's Administration on Developmental Disabilities estimates that the population with developmental disabilities is currently 3.9 million. This population will increase because of improved survival rates of infants born with disabling conditions and increases in life expectancy.

This chapter looks at alternative decision-making tools used by the elderly and the increasingly frail population and by people with disabilities. Through guardianship and protective proceedings the courts have been used when "advance planning" has not been anticipated. This chapter describes protective services, guardianship, and the tools used for "advance planning." These tools include durable powers of attorney, living wills, and health-care powers or proxies.

Without advance planning directives, individuals who cannot make their own decisions will require the state to intervene and make those decisions on their behalf. In such instances, the state will intervene primarily through guardianship procedures or the use of protective services. Guardianships are generally involuntary, while protective services may be either voluntary or involuntary. Before any formal intervention is put into effect, the state must assess the individual's ability to make decisions.

INCAPACITY

The key question to planning or intervention is determining whether an individual is able to take care of his or her own affairs or person. Until recently the criteria used have been measures of incompetency. More recently there has been a shift away from examining a person's mental status and toward measuring his or her ability to function in society. Using the term *incapacity* to describe an inability to function in society may also alleviate the negative and all-encompassing connotation of the term *incompetency* (Anderer 1990). The term *incapacity* also lends itself to the notion of partial incapacity and partial disability, and it reflects the emerging trend in state statutes towards limited powers in guardianship.

PROTECTIVE SERVICES FOR THE ELDERLY

Since 1985 the area of adult protective services has radically changed. Previously state and local governments sought to protect children; at the end of the 1970s they began to apply some of the same principles to the protection of the elderly. It has been presumed that, if the state has an interest in protecting its vulnerable children based on its *parens patriae* role it has the same responsibility toward the vulnerable elderly. The state can intervene by voluntary and involuntary means. The latter is an action that is taken through either an administrative or a court procedure that is contrary to what the person who needs help wants.

The term *protective services* encompasses an interdisciplinary program of assistance to people with mental or physical disabilities who are not able to provide for their basic needs. These services are often labeled *preventive, supportive,* and *surrogate.* Preventive services are based on the early recognition of a need and the provision of information and encouragement toward independent living. Supportive services are based upon the provision of assistance and support so the individual can maintain self-direction and achieve the highest possible level of functioning. The services are coordinated by a caseworker who assesses each person's needs and arranges for the delivery of appropriate services. In many instances these services assist people in need who cannot identify or acquire necessary services and who might otherwise be unable to protect themselves from abuse, neglect, or exploitation.

Protective services are characterized by the surrogate function, that is, the legal authorization to act in the person's behalf. This is accomplished through the appointment of a surrogate decision-maker and/or the provision of services with or without the individual's consent through civil commitment, guardianship, or the appointment of a representative payee. *Civil commitment* is a process that allows for the treatment of mental illness by means of involuntary confinement to an institution. Because the process is used only for people who are a danger to themselves and others, it is of use to only a narrow cross section of those who might be considered mentally ill. Also of limited use is the appointment of *representative payees* for those who receive Social Security, Social Security Insurance (SSI), and veterans' benefits. The type of protective services that is helpful to the largest number of people is guardianship.

COURT-MANDATED GUARDIANSHIP

Interest in guardianship matters was catalyzed by a series of stories by the Associated Press (AP) in 1987. After numerous stories on abuses of the system appeared in the press, the AP conducted a study of the nation's guardianship system that culminated in a report entitled *Guardians of the Elderly: An Ailing System* (AP 1987). In addition, many local newspapers ran the AP stories on guardianship. State legislatures, as well as the U.S. Congress, have responded by holding hearings on guardianship and introducing legislative changes in the last few years. State legislation in this area has changed enormously.

Guardianship can be broadly defined as the process by which a court finds a person's incapacity so severe that the court gives the right to make decisions to another person. The standards for defining incapacity and the process for appointing a substitute decision-maker are generally left up to state statutes and processes.

Each state has statutes for some form of guardianship of adults and conservatorship of their property if they are not able to care for themselves without assistance. Many states have combined these provisions into a single statute. In its 1987 study the AP stressed that there were major problems in the administration of the various state guardianship statutes. The intent of guardianship is to ensure that incapacitated people are taken care of. However, there are limitations within the statutes that may prevent people from being taken care of properly.

Prior to the 1980s the courts, the state statutes, and those seeking guardianship thought in terms of *full* or *plenary guardianships*, by which types of decision making was accomplished for people with diminished capacity. However, it came to be seen that through such guardianships the courts were removing all rights and responsibilities from people under the guise of protecting them from perceived harm. Reforms beginning in the 1970s began to consider the fact that many individuals have partial or limited capacity to make decisions; they are capable of making some decisions by themselves, but need surrogates to help with other decisions. For example, an individual might be capable of deciding how much to spend on a piece of clothing, but not where to invest the interest received from a certificate of deposit. Another person might be able to understand the consequences of a gangrenous limb, but not be able to understand why a Social Security check has not come when it is being received by direct deposit.

Reformers saw that the type of intervention needed for each type of limitation needs to be different. Advocates argued for alternatives to full guardianship that would simply fill the function that a person had lost rather than imposing more control over the person's life than he or she might need. Guided by the principles of autonomy and least restrictive alternative, the reforms that were initiated in the 1980s focused on providing a method of determining what limitations existed (e.g., functional assessments) and developing mechanisms to address the limitations (e.g., durable powers of attorney for financial decisions, automatic bill-paying mechanisms, or health-care durable powers of attorney). Statutes began to mirror what the reformers were calling *limited guardianships*, which were put in place by courts guided by functional assessments of the capabilities of the persons in question. These limited guardianships allowed individuals protected by them to retain some control or autonomy over their own decisions.

Several states have changed their statutes to include alternatives to full guardianship, either through limited guardianship orders or other less restrictive planning tools. A number of social service organizations have developed money management programs (Zuckerman 1988) to provide for less intrusive intervention. Volunteer programs that encourage people to be representative payees for Social Security or Veterans Administration beneficiaries have blossomed throughout the country. Many are interested in attempting to develop alternatives, all of which have their advantages and disadvantages.

ALTERNATIVES TO COURT-MANDATED GUARDIANSHIP

Voluntary Guardianship

Some states have laws that allow individuals to voluntarily ask courts to appoint guardians over their property. This type of guardianship is generally known as a *voluntary guardianship*. These laws enable an individual who is aware of or concerned about his or her impending incapacity to plan for the management of his or her property prior to becoming incapacitated. A voluntary guardianship may be seen as an alternative to a full involuntary guardianship (Stiegel 1991).

Depending on an individual's circumstances, a voluntary guardianship may have advantages over other alternative measures such as living trusts or joint property management, which are discussed in the previous chapter by Dana Shilling. These include avoiding the stigma of being involuntarily declared legally incompetent, possibly having more control over the selection of the guardian, and having court oversight and monitoring of the guardian's actions. This could be particularly useful if the individual does not have anyone trustworthy to whom he or she can give a durable power of attorney or to add as a joint owner of property. Several alternatives allow an individual to maintain his or her autonomy. These include the durable power of attorney, the durable health-care power of attorney, and the living will.

Durable Power of Attorney

What Is a Durable Power of Attorney?

A traditional power of attorney is a written document in which one person grants authority to another to act on his or her behalf. For instance, the person may be planning an extended trip and may appoint a surrogate power of attorney to pay bills in his or her absence. In order to execute such a document the person must have capacity when the power of attorney is made. The person must remain legally competent for the power to stay valid, because by law the power is automatically invalidated when the person becomes incompetent. Although the law requires this to protect an incompetent person from being taken advantage of by a surrogate, a traditional power of attorney is of no use to a person who wants to plan in advance to authorize another to act if he or she becomes incompetent.

In response to this problem, all fifty states and the District of Columbia have passed laws allowing people to draw up durable powers of attorney (DPOAs). The difference between a traditional power of attorney and a durable power of attorney is that the latter generally remains valid if the principal becomes incompetent. This distinction is very important because it means that people can use durable powers of attorney to designate surrogates to make decisions and act for them if they become incapacitated at some later date. Because of this advance planning tool, a court may never need to appoint a legal guardian to make decisions and act for a person who is protected by a durable power of attorney (Collin 1991).

What Powers Are Conferred by a Durable Power of Attorney?

A durable power of attorney (DPOA) may have a number of different characteristics and confer various powers upon the surrogate. Depending on state law, those powers may be general or specific, may address money and property matters or health-care matters or both, and may become effective immediately (or in some states after a certain event. Therefore, these powers give a person greater flexibility to prepare a durable power of attorney that meets his or her specific needs.

A general durable power of attorney authorizes the surrogate to manage all of the person's monetary and property affairs. Alternatively, a special durable power of attorney gives the surrogate authority to act only in specified instances. The authority potentially granted under a DPOA gives the surrogate power to do such things as manage the person's bank accounts, sell or buy real estate or personal belongings, borrow money, hire and fire employees, bring legal actions, operate the person's business, give gifts, and create or modify a trust.

A person may want to make a durable power of attorney to authorize another person to make decisions about health care or other personal decisions on his or her behalf. Because the law regarding powers of attorney was developed to handle property and financial concerns, a DPOA is clear on such decisions; however, the state laws are less so about the types of personal decisions that can be made by a surrogate. Controversy may arise over decisions on health care and the placement of the principal in an institution (Collin 1991).

A DPOA may be effective immediately, or it may "spring" into effect at some later date. The latter form, known as a "springing" power of attorney, does not take effect until the person becomes incapacitated or upon the occurrence of a specific event stated in the power (e.g., hospitalization or placement in a nursing home). If incapacity is the criterion, the document should explain how incapacity is to be determined—for example, through certification of incapacity by two physicians. Some states do not allow springing powers (Collin 1991).

Who May Make a Durable Power of Attorney?

A durable power of attorney must be made while the person is legally competent to execute it. By virtue of their age, minors are not legally considered competent to execute documents. No standards exist on whether an adult is legally competent to make and sign a DPOA. The applicable legal standard is that the person making a DPOA must have the requisite capacity to understand the nature and significance of his or her act at the time the document is signed. State laws vary regarding requirements for witnessing and notarizing durable powers. A person who moves to another state or owns property in another state may need to execute a new DPOA in order to comply with the legal requirements of the other state.

May a Durable Power of Attorney Be Revoked?

A durable power of attorney may be revoked in four ways: (1) a competent person may revoke the power at any time; (2) the power is automatically terminated upon the principal's death or, in some states, when the surrogate is notified of the person's death; (3) in some states the DPOA may be automatically terminated if a guardian is appointed for the person who made the power; and (4) the DPOA may terminate after a specified amount of time has passed or once certain events have occurred—e.g., the death of the principal or the agent (Stiegel 1991).

ADVANCE DIRECTIVES

Other alternatives to court-mandated guardianship are advance directives. The Patient Self-Determination Act (PSDA), which was adopted by Congress in 1990 with an effective date of December 1, 1991, requires all Medicare and Medicaid provider organizations (specifically hospitals, nursing homes, home health agencies, hospices, and prepaid health-care organizations) to do five things: provide written information to patients at the time of admission concerning their rights under state law, maintain written policies and procedures with respect to advance directives, document in each individual's medical record whether or not the individual has executed an advance directive, ensure compliance with the requirements of state law, and provide for education for the staff and the community on issues concerning advance directives. The state must also develop and make available to providers a statement of the applicable state law. The purpose of the PSDA was to educate providers and consumers about advance directives and to encourage their use.

Two types of advance directives are living wills and health-care powers of attorney. These can be important for people of any age, but they are essential for older people.

Living Wills

A living will (sometimes called a natural death act) is a written statement of an individual's wishes regarding the use of specific medical treatments. The statement is to be followed if the person is unable to provide instructions at the time at which a decision needs to be made about his or her health care. Forty-eight states and the District of Columbia have living will laws that establish requirements and guidelines for the use of living wills. Generally those laws restrict the health-care decisions that can be directed through a living will to those concerning the use, withdrawal, or withholding of "life-sustaining" or "life-prolonging" procedures in the event of "terminal illness." Some states exclude artificial hydration and nutrition from the purview of a living will; other states leave that decision up to the individual or simply do not address the issue.

Health-Care Powers of Attorney

A health-care power of attorney (sometimes called a medical power of attorney or a health-care proxy) is a document in which someone (called the "person") authorizes another person to make health-care decisions on the person's behalf in the event that he or she becomes unable to do so. Because of the dispute about whether durable powers of attorney can be used to make health-care decisions if the state law does not specify that purpose, an increasing number of states have passed laws that clearly recognize health-care powers of attorney. As of June 1993, 49 jurisdictions had such laws.

Why Is a Health-Care Power of Attorney Useful?

A health-care power of attorney is useful for several reasons. First, it allows a person to designate in advance of illness or disability another person who can make health-care decisions on his or her behalf. This means that a person who loses the capacity to make or communicate decisions will still be able to control important decisions about his or her own health care. Second, if a person has not appointed a health-care agent, a health-care provider may make critical decisions about the person's health-care alone on behalf of the sick person. Those decisions might conflict with the person's wishes. Third, in some situations a health-care power of attorney may permit a person to avoid a guardianship proceeding. If a person has no health-care power of attorney, the health-care provider might ask a court to appoint a guardian to make decisions for the sick person. Fourth, a health-care power of attorney that includes a statement of a person's preferences regarding specific medical decisions may relieve family members or friends of some of the stress and conflicts that may arise if they have to make decisions on behalf of the sick person without any guidance as to what he or she wants.

What Should a Health-Care Power of Attorney Say?

The critical part of a health-care power of attorney is the designation of a surrogate to make health-care decisions for the person. Nothing else has to be included; the person can choose to rely completely on the judgment of the appointed agent. However, the person may want to be more specific in order to ensure that his or her wishes regarding health care are followed. To accomplish this, generally a health-care power of attorney may also include statements that define or limit the scope of the surrogate's powers and guidelines for decision making that the surrogate should follow. The person may also want to name successor surrogates in case the primary surrogate becomes unwilling or unable to act. However, a person should not name co-agents; if they cannot agree on decision, a guardianship may then become necessary. If a person opts to include guidelines for decision making in the health-care power of attorney, the level of specificity is a matter of choice. Specific preferences about the provision or withholding of certain medical treatments, including the artificial provision of food and water, may or may not be included in the document.

What Should Be Considered before Making a Health-Care Power of Attorney?

Before making a health-care power of attorney, a person should consider his or her values and thoughts about life and death. The person's values will shape the decision-making guidelines set forth in the health-care power of attorney, and these in turn will shape how the principal may experience a period of illness or disability and possibly the end of life. In order to determine those guidelines and to communicate them to an agent or family members and friends, it may be useful for a principal to develop a "values history" regarding medical decisions. The University of New Mexico has developed a values history that the reader might find useful (Gibson 1990).

Someone interested in making a health-care power of attorney needs to carefully select the surrogate, as the surrogate will have great authority over the person's health and personal care if he or she becomes incapacitated. Since there is no formal oversight or monitoring of an agent's decisions, it is crucial for a person to name a surrogate who can be trusted to make the same decisions that the person would make if capable of doing so. A person who wants to make a health-care power of attorney should explain his or her intentions to the potential agent and make sure that he or she is willing to serve as the surrogate and follow the principal's wishes.

Some states limit the effective duration of a health-care power of attorney, so a principal must make a new power after a certain number of years. A state's procedural requirements must be followed carefully to ensure the validity and effectiveness of the health-care power of attorney.

What Is the Difference between a Health-Care Power of Attorney and a Living Will?

A health-care power of attorney is different from and more flexible than a living will in three important ways:

1. A health-care power of attorney establishes a person to act as a surrogate if the person cannot act, but a living will does not. The advantage of appointing a surrogate is that, when a decision needs to be made, the agent can participate in discussions and weigh the pros and cons of treatment decisions in accordance with the person's wishes.
2. The health-care power of attorney applies to all medical decisions unless the person decides to include limitations. The living

will normally applies only to particular decisions that may need to be made near the end of one's life.

3. The health-care power of attorney can include specific instructions to the surrogate about treatments the person would prefer in certain instances and those he or she would not like or about whatever issues the person considers most important.

In theory, a living will could be combined with a health-care power of attorney (Sabatino 1989). However, state laws regarding the contents of the two documents or formalities for signing them must be compatible (Sabatino 1991).

CONCLUSIONS

Planning for one's own anticipated or unanticipated incapacity or disability is something that most people do not do. However, it is important in an ever-more-complex society to begin to do such planning. Through a variety of self-initiated mechanisms the law now allows an individual to control one's own affairs by delegating decision-making authority to an agent of the individual's choice. The devices used may be health care powers of attorney, durable powers for controlling finances, or more sophisticated mechanisms such as trusts. These devices give the individual personal control and avoid involuntary interventions by designating an agent as well as the range of decisions to be made. Designating who will make decisions before a person becomes disabled or incapacitated also allows the individual and his or her agent to discuss the values and criteria that the agent is to use in making any type of decision. Depending upon how complicated one's finances are and upon the nature of one's family relationships, it may be advisable to consult an attorney to make sure that all circumstances that might be peculiar to an individual are addressed.

REFERENCES

American Bar Association (ABA). 1989. *An Agenda for Reform*. Washington, D.C.: ABA Commissions on Legal Problems for the Elderly and the Mentally Disabled.

Anderer, Stephen. 1990. *Determining Competency in GuardianshipProceedings*. Washington, D.C.: ABA Public Service Division.

Associated Press (AP). 1987. *Guardians of the Elderly: An Ailing System*. Associated Press.

Collin, Francis J., John Lombard, Jr., Albert L. Moses, and Harley J. Spitler. 1991.

Drafting the Durable Power of Attorney: A Systems Approach, 2nd ed. Shepard's McGraw-Hill.

Gibson, Joan. 1990. "National Values History." *Generations,* 14.

Horstman, Peter. 1975. "Protective Services for the Elderly: The Limits of Parens Patriae." *Missouri Law Review,* 40:215.

Hurme, Sally. 1991. *Steps to Enhance Guardianship Monitoring.* ABA Commissions on Legal Problems of the Elderly and The Mentally Disabled.

Mitchell, Annina. "The Objects of Our Wisdom and Our Coercion: Involuntary Guardianship for Incompetents." *Southern California Law Review,* 52:1405. (1979)

Regan, John J. 1981. "Protecting the Elderly: The New Paternalism." *Hastings Law Journal,* 32:1111–1132.

Regan, John J., and Springer, Georgia. 1977. "Protective Services for the Elderly." A working paper prepared for the Senate Special Committee on Aging, 95th Congress, 1st session.

Sabatino, Charles P. 1990. *Health Care Powers of Attorney.* Washington, D.C.: ABA Commission on Legal Problems of the Elderly.

Sabatino, Charles P. 1991. "Surrogate Decision-Making in Health Care." *Health Care and Financial Planning Issues for the Elderly.* Washington, D.C.: ABA Division for Professional Education.

Stiegel, Lori. 1991. *Alternatives to Guardianship: Substantive Training Materials and Modules for Professionals Working with the Elderly and Persons with Disabilities.* Washington, D.C.: ABA Commission on Legal Problems of the Elderly and The Mentally Disabled.

U.S. Senate et al. 1988. *Aging America: Trends and Projections, 1987–1988 Edition.* Washington, D.C.: U.S. Senate, Committee on Aging, the American Association of Retired Persons, the Federal Council on Aging, and the Administration on Aging.

Zuckerman, Deborah. 1988. *Life Services Planning.* ABA Commission on Legal Problems of the Elderly and The Mentally Disabled.

17

Consumer Contracts for Continuing Care Facilities

●

CHARLES P. SABATINO

The following ad promises almost everything one could want in retirement living with health and long-term care services:

> Our "assisted living" concept gives residents plenty of freedom.
>
> Yet help is available 24 hours a day. Each resident has a personalized apartment with kitchenette, bath, cable hookup, and telephone. The monthly fee includes weekly housekeeping, three balanced meals a day, and 24-hour a day nursing supervision.
>
> [Our facility] provides conveniences of community living. A library, beauty/barber shop, laundry facilities, and a recreation room. And we are affiliated with ABC Nursing Home and XYZ Hospital if additional care is required. (Advertisement for Caton Merchant House 1990).

The ad is for a continuing care retirement community (CCRC,) and it claims that the community it is advertising offers comfort, freedom, and, above all, the security of knowing one's health needs will be met. But exactly what is being promised? What is the likelihood that the facility will keep its promises? And what is the risk to the individual or couple who chooses to enter this kind of retirement setting?

CONTINUING CARE RETIREMENT COMMUNITIES

Continuing care retirement community is the industry term for what was once more commonly called a life care community. These kinds of facilities have existed for a century or more. In their early days, they were commonly sponsored by religious or fraternal organizations for their members. Originally they promised care for the rest of one's life in return for the transfer of all one's assets. Essentially the initial transfer served as a prepayment for later services and care. In the last thirty years, improvements in life expectancy and the skyrocketing inflation of medical costs have made the economics of the original one-time payment model virtually impossible.

Today the conventional CCRC may be described as a retirement facility that provides shelter, care, and services, including nursing home services, for as long as one lives in the facility in return for a large one-time entrance fee and adjustable monthly fees. As we will see in a moment, the conventional CCRC is giving way to a more service-oriented concept that is not tied to any particular payment arrangement. The American Association of Homes for the Aging (AAHA) estimates that more than seven hundred CCRCs exist in the United States today, and the number is growing (AAHA and Ernst and Whitney 1987).

The physical plants of CCRCs run the gamut from urban high-rises to garden apartments or cottages around a separate nursing facility on a large campus. Nursing facilities may be on or off campus. In the latter case, the CCRC typically relies on some form of affiliation with a nearby nursing home, as in the ad above. The extent of the care and services provided in CCRCs is quite variable. The AAHA identifies three basic types of facilities, which are distinguished from one another by the care and services covered by the basic entrance fee and the monthly fees paid by residents: (1) all-inclusive or life care facilities, which provide long-term nursing care at little or no additional cost above the basic fees; (2) modified or continuing care facilities, which provide long-term nursing care at little or no additional cost for a limited period; and (3) fee-for-service facilities, which require residents to pay for most additional services as needed (AAHA and Ernst and Whinney 1987).

OTHER FORMS OF ASSISTED LIVING

The main problem with the conventional definition of CCRC and with the three levels of care described by the AAHA is that industry changes have been so dramatic in recent years that it is difficult to draw clear distinctions between CCRCs and the growing variety of other retirement housing options that offer some sort of assisted living package. The number of permutations of shelter plus services is daunting.

Developers are increasingly offering packages that differ in some respects from those of CCRCs—for example, by doing away with entrance fees and relying more on fee-for-service approaches. Normally CCRCs do not offer ownership arrangements, but rather contractual arrangements under long-term leases or occupancy agreements. Yet even some condominium developments have begun to "look" more like CCRCs by adding long-term health care packages that residents purchase through service agreements or "memberships." CCRC look-alikes are seen, too, in rental developments for seniors that offer health care or "assisted living" packages to tenants. The basic selling concept remains the same: a promise of security and services.

REGULATIONS FOR CONSUMER PROTECTION

The growth of the CCRC industry has not been without serious problems. Fisher (1985) notes that at least forty facilities in ten states have gone bankrupt since the mid-1970s. For residents, financial failure may mean the loss of life savings they have paid to facilities. Residents' claims are generally subordinate to mortgages, prerecorded liens, and other secured claims. A bankrupt facility is not likely to have much, if anything, left to repay residents after distributions are made to secured creditors.

One response to this risk has been the emergence of public regulation. CCRCs are now regulated to differing extents by statute in some thirty-five states, and the number is growing (AAHA 1991). Stearns, Netting, Wilson, and Branch (1990) distinguish three levels of regulation:

(1) Selective statutes, which isolate one or more specific problems encountered by residents of CCRCs and contain provisions to mitigate those conditions.

(2) Comprehensive disclosure statutes, which emphasize providers' obligations to inform consumers about facilities' policies and the providers' financial structure and operations. These statutes rely primarily on informed consumer choice as the main strategy for consumer protection.

(3) Comprehensive regulatory statutes, which include disclosure obligations as in (2) above, but also expand upon residents' rights and emphasize the obligations of states to review and monitor certain aspects of providers' activity. States are gradually moving toward this more comprehensive level of regulation.

Unfortunately, the fact that a state has a comprehensive regulatory statute does not necessarily mean that consumers can rest easy. Most of the statutes focus primarily on protection of the consumers' investments rather than on quality of care. And the narrow scope of regulation may leave many facilities uncovered. For example, since most states' definitions of CCRCs include the payment of entrance fees, facilities the AAHA would classify as fee-for-service facilities, which, require no entrance fees, may fall outside the regulations of these states. An increasing number of facilities now allow prospective residents to choose between paying an entrance fee or monthly fees only. This may lead to the anomaly that some residents within a facility are protected by state regulations while others are not.

Facilities or services that fall outside such regulations may or may not be covered by other state regulations governing long-term care. The most widely regulated service component in CCRCs is nursing home care. Nursing units in all CCRCs are subject to state nursing home regulations and also federal Medicare and Medicaid regulations if they participate in those programs.

Less certain is the degree of regulatory oversight of personal care and other health or social supports—often lumped under the term "assisted living" as in the ad at the beginning of the chapter. All states regulate facilities that are referred to as adult homes or as board and care, residential care, personal care, or domiciliary care facilities, among other terms. Some CCRCs may have separate floors or units that are specially licensed to provide this level of care. However, Coleman and Fairbanks (1991) argue that many CCRCs provide such services without being subject to regulation because of the definitional peculiarities of state law.

In most states, the state insurance commission or its equivalent is likely to be the primary agency that regulates CCRCs. While insurance commissions may have considerable expertise in financial oversight, they are usually poorly equipped to regulate quality of care. Health departments, state offices on aging, social services departments, and long-term care ombudsmen may all have some oversight responsibility for different aspects of CCRC operations. For other forms of assisted living, health and social services departments are likely to be the lead regulating agencies.

INDUSTRY STANDARD

Self-regulation of the CCRC industry began to emerge in 1985 under the leadership of the American Association of Homes for the Aging.

The association established the Continuing Care Accreditation Commission to operate a national accreditation program for CCRCs. The number of accredited CCRCs is still relatively small, numbering 125 according to the commission's January 1993 list. While accreditation is a positive indicator, not all consumer advocates consider it a reliable guide for prospective CCRC residents ("Communities for the Elderly." 1990). The accreditation commission has recently revised its standards in a continuing attempt to elevate the quality of the accreditation process (CCAC 1991).

Model regulations for different aspects of CCRC operation have been produced by a growing number of authoritative organizations. The Legislative Drafting Research Fund of Columbia Law School (1989) has produced a comprehensive model state regulation and commentary for CCRCs. The American Association of Homes for the Aging published a model act in 1980, but revised it as a set of guidelines rather than a model act in 1987 (AAHA 1987). These guidelines are subject to continuing revision. Other groups working on model standards or statutory language on specific issues affecting CCRCs include the National Association of Insurance Commissioners (1988), the American Institute of Certified Public Accountants (1990), and the American Academy of Actuaries (1987).

EVALUATING A CONTRACT WITH A
RETIREMENT COMMUNITY

Regardless of a state's regulations, or lack of them, the issues faced by prospective residents of CCRCs are similar. As a practical matter, the same questions should be considered by prospective residents of any type of retirement housing that offers a package of residential, supportive, and health care services, regardless of whether the facility characterizes itself as providing continuing care, residential care, assisted living, or care with some other label. The underlying contract issues concern protection of the consumer's financial investment and assurance that the individual will receive, and continue to receive, the accommodations and services that he or she expects.

The following checklist and commentary are divided into four sections: (1) the overall financial stability and expertise of the provider, (2) obligations and rights having to do with entrance fees and monthly fees, (3) the nature and extent of the accommodations and services being promised, and (4) the extent of residents' control and due process protections. The preferred answers are based primarily on the standards included in the model state regulation produced by the Legislative Drafting Research Fund of Columbia Law School, which is referred to below as the "Columbia Model."

It is unlikely that any facility's contract will contain all the preferred answers. However, by measuring responses against the preferred answers, prospective residents can compare facilities and better understand the benefits and risks of each. A facility's responses to these questions should be included in the terms of the contract.

CCRC CONTRACT CHECKLIST

A. Solvency/Expertise of the Provider. The questions in this section go behind the contract.

Question 1. The Provider. What is the identity of the provider, and what is its experience?

Preferred Response: The provider's identity and experience should be clear.

Comment: The provider is the person or entity that is legally and financially responsible for providing continuing care. Some facilities advertise that they are "sponsored" by nonprofit groups or churches that in reality may have no legal control or financial responsibility. Be wary if such illusory sponsorship is trumpeted in sales literature.

Prospective residents should receive information on the identity and business experience of the officers, directors, and managers of the organization and any key third-party service providers. It is also important to know whether there are any current or previous judicial or administrative proceedings to which they are party.

Question 2. Financial Soundness. What is the financial condition of the provider?

Preferred Response: At least two weeks prior to the execution of a resident contract (or a waiting list deposit agreement), the facility should provide extensive financial disclosure information.

Comment: The prospective resident should have disclosure materials reviewed by a knowledgeable attorney or accountant. It is worth the cost. While the content of these financial disclosures that is required varies from state to state, the Columbia Model suggests that they include, among other information, the following:

• Balance sheets and earnings statements for the last five years.
• An actuarial study with a ten-year demographic projection of the resident population and service costs and a calculation of the provider's actuarial assets and liabilities calculated over the expected lifetime of the residents.

- A projection of the sources and uses of funds for the next five years.
- Documentation of the utilization of health care services (especially differences between actual utilization and actuarial projections).
- Identification of any assets pledged as collateral. Disclosure of any late payments on mortgage loans or other forms of long-term financing.
- A statement of all reserve funds.

For facilities that are under construction, the developer should be able to provide a marketing study that evaluates the target population and the marketability of the product to that group, along with a feasibility study that evaluates the economic viability of the project. Both studies should be prepared by a reputable firm.

Question 3. Reserves. Does the facility maintain sufficient cash reserves to protect it against unexpectedly high operating costs?

Preferred Response: The facility should maintain a sufficient actuarial reserve or contingency reserve in liquid assets.

Comment: A reserve fund ensures that, if a financial crisis occurs, the residents' investments will still be protected. At least eighteen states require reserve funds. An actuarial reserve is calculated on an actuarial determination of future obligations. A sufficient actuarial reserve is the amount (in present dollars) by which future obligations that the provider has made under resident contracts are expected to exceed future revenues.

A contingency reserve is a more easily calculated liquid fund that is maintained in escrow to protect the provider against unexpected costs. The contingency reserve should be sufficient to cover the annual principal and interest on all debt that is due during the fiscal year, plus six months' normal operating expenses.

Question 4. Licensing and Accreditation. Is the facility licensed and accredited?

Preferred Response: All levels of care should be licensed, and CCRCs should be accredited by the Continuing Care Accreditation Commission.

Comment: Although licensure and accreditation do not in themselves guarantee financial responsibility or quality of care, they are positive threshold indicators.

B. Entrance Fees and Monthly Fees

Question 5. Entrance Fee. What is the entrance fee?

Preferred Response: No particular amount can be suggested as optimal. The amount depends on the geographic location, the type and size of the unit, the service package, and the extent to which the entrance fee represents prepayment for services delivered in the future.

Comment: Some facilities accept transfers of noncash assets as entrance fees. In these cases, it is important that the contract show the fair market value of all properties transferred.

One should be aware that facilities may charge other up-front fees that may or may not be regulated. The purchase of an ownership interest in a living unit is an entirely distinct interest that is subject to real estate laws. A waiting list deposit, which is intended to reserve one's future right to be considered for residence, should always be fully refundable and should be held by a licensed escrow agent in an interest-bearing account. Nonrefundable application fees should be less than two hundred dollars. The purchase of a "membership" package of services may or may not be treated as an entrance fee under state law. A number of facilities now provide a no-entrance-fee option under which prospective residents may choose to forego an entrance fee altogether, instead paying a higher monthly fee.

Question 6. Escrow. Is the entrance fee held in a protected escrow account?

Preferred Response: Yes. The entrance fee should be held in an interest-bearing account with a licensed escrow agent, protected from the facility's creditors, until the prospective resident's probationary contract period is completed (see next question).

Comment: Some states require that entrance fees be held in escrow only until a minimum percentage of units are built and contracted for by residents. Other states may require that entrance fees be held in escrow until the particular resident's unit is available for occupancy. The Columbia Model, reflected in the preferred response, provides more extensive protection for residents; it also requires assurance that there is an adequate reserve fund as a condition for the release of escrow.

Question 7. Cancellation. Under what circumstances does a resident have the right to cancel or rescind the contract?

Preferred Response: A probationary period of ninety days should be provided during which the resident has a right to terminate the contract and receive a full refund (less the cost of any care the resident has actually received).

Comment: Statutory minimum "cooling off" or "free-look" periods vary considerably. For example, Virginia requires seven days, Connecticut thirty, and California ninety.

Question 8. Refunds. Under what circumstances will the entrance fee be refunded to the resident or the resident's estate once the probationary period is over?

Preferred Response: The facility should, at a minimum, provide a formula for a pro rata refund of the entrance fee that is based on the resident's length of stay, regardless of whether the facility or the resident initiates the termination. Payment should not be conditioned upon reoccupancy of the unit.

Comment: Few states require any refund after the initial probationary period. However, many facilities have a declining refund schedule that is amortized at 1 percent or 2 percent per month. At a 2 percent decline per month, a resident's entitlement to a refund will totally expire after four years and two months. The Columbia Model suggests a pro rata refund formula that is derived by multiplying the entrance fee by a fraction whose numerator is the resident's life expectancy at the time at which the contract is terminated and whose denominator is the person's life expectancy at the time of admission. Some newer facilities now offer fully refundable entrance fees. One should note that fully refundable fees may be viewed as a loan to the facility and may result in imputed interest to the resident under IRS rules.

Question 9. Monthly Fee. What is the monthly fee?

Preferred Response: Monthly fees for all-inclusive CCRCs average about $1000 per month for one-bedroom apartments and $1150 for two-bedroom units ("Communities for the Elderly." 1990). An optimal fee for any individual depends on the person's particular needs, preferences, and available resources.

Question 10. Fee Increases. Under what circumstances can the monthly fee be increased and by what amount?

Preferred Response: It is rare for facilities or regulations to place a cap on periodic fee increases. However, increases should be limited to one per year, with thirty days' minimum advance notice. The contract should describe any automatic fee adjustments that will be made as a result of changes in levels of care.

Comment: Ask for documentation of the facility's record of fee increases for the previous five years and projected increases for the coming five years. Find out what happens if future fee increases exceed a resident's ability to pay. The facility should have a program that grants financial assistance to residents whose income becomes inadequate to pay increasing monthly fees and personal expenses. What is the extent of guaranteed assistance available and the track record of the program?

Question 11. Medical Expense Tax Deduction. How much health care is prepaid?

Preferred Response: The proportion of the entrance fee and monthly fees that constitute prepayment for future medical expenses should be specified, because residents may be entitled to medical expense tax deductions for this portion of the fees. Eligible medical expenses are defined by the IRS and normally include expenses such as home health care, nursing home care, and health insurance premiums.

Question 12. Living Unit. Is a specific description of the living unit included in the contract? To what extent can the resident modify or redecorate the unit? Can the resident move to another unit?

Preferred Response: The contract should identify the specific unit and the features and utilities included in the basic fee. For example, does the unit include wall-to-wall carpeting? Venetian blinds? Telephones? The facility should give residents reasonable flexibility to decorate or modify units. Residents should be permitted to move to other units for which they are otherwise qualified if they wish to do so.

Question 13. Changes in Household Composition. What happens if a resident marries, divorces, becomes widowed, or wishes to have a friend or family member move into the unit?

Preferred Response: The consequences of any changes in household composition should be clearly spelled out.

Comment: Changes in household composition may result in problems. For example, a new spouse of a resident may not meet the facility's age requirements. One should look for flexibility in such policies. While changes may have substantial cost implications, normally they should not result in forfeiture of the resident's right to occupy his or her unit. The prospective resident should also find out what restrictions the facility places on visitors, such as family members or friends, who are staying for short or extended periods of time.

C. Support Services and Health Care Services

Question 14. Service Definitions/Limits/Add-On Costs. What specific services are included under the contract with and without additional charge?

Preferred Response: Support services are difficult to enumerate in contracts because often they cannot be stated in precisely definable terms or units that one can quantify. One should examine the list of services included under the contract, their definitions, and their limits. It is especially important to inquire how the availability of services differs in independent living versus assisted living versus nursing home care. The contract should not grant the facility authority to cut back or eliminate services, and fee increases should be limited to one per year. The following outline may be helpful:

SERVICE CHECKLIST

The prospective resident should obtain the following information on each item:

1. A complete service description.
2. An explanation of limitations on the frequency, duration, location, or time of the service.
3. A statement of extra costs for which the resident may be responsible.

The types of services may include the following:

Housing/Social/Recreational:

a. Meal services
b. Special diets/tray service
c. Utilities
d. Cable television
e. Furnishings
f. Unit maintenance
g. Linens/personal laundry
h. Housekeeping
i. Recreational/cultural facilities and activities
j. Transportation

Health and Personal Care:

a. Physician services
b. Nursing services outside the nursing unit (e.g., assistance with medications)
c. Private-duty nursing
d. Dental and eye care
e. Personal care services (e.g., assistance with eating, dressing, bathing, toileting, etc.)
f. Homemaker/companion services
g. Drugs, medications, medical equipment, and supplies.

Question 15. Nursing Unit. If nursing home care is provided, is the nursing unit on the premises? If not, does the facility have a clear referral and admission relationship with a nursing home off the premises?

Preferred Response: If the facility relies on a referral arrangement with a nearby nursing home, the terms of that arrangement and the resident's right of access should be fully disclosed and clear.

Comment: The presence of a nursing home unit on the CCRC's premises may increase the likelihood of the availability of nursing services when they are needed and increase the facility's control over costs. Regardless of whether the nursing unit is on or off campus, the agreement should explain what happens if a bed is unavailable when the resident needs one.

Question 16. Medicare and Medicaid. To what extent can Medicare or Medicaid cover the cost of services provided in the CCRC?

Preferred Response: The contract should disclose the facility's participation, or lack of it, in Medicare and Medicaid. Any differences in optional or covered services for Medicare or Medicaid residents versus private-pay residents should be spelled out.

Comment: A facility's participation in Medicare and Medicaid provides additional assurance that residents will have access to services when they are needed, especially if they have exhausted their own resources. Medicare and Medicaid have not played a big role in CCRCs in the past, but as more CCRCs move toward fee-for-service models, residents are increasingly exposed to higher amounts of out-of-pocket expenses. Therefore, the need for some form of governmental subsidy or insurance is growing.

Question 17. Insurance. What types of insurance must residents carry?

Preferred Response: Insurance requirements and their likely costs should be identified and quantified.

Comment: Some facilities may require residents to enroll in special group insurance programs; others may require minimum private health coverage, such as Medicare supplemental insurance or long-term care insurance. One should also consider property and liability insurance. Even if they are not required, it is advisable to obtain them.

Question 18. Transfers Between Levels of Care. What are the criteria and procedures for determining when a resident needs to be transferred from independent living to assisted living or to the nursing unit? Who will be involved in that determination? How can the resident appeal that determination if he or she disagrees? When do transfers become permanent instead of temporary?

Preferred Response: Specific criteria should be spelled out in the contract and should include, in the absence of an emergency, a multidisciplinary evaluation and the meaningful participation of the resident and/or family. An appeals procedure should be available that ensures an independent review.

Comment: This cluster of questions is pivotal to a resident's sense of well-being, control, and independence. Yet contract provisions often leave the answers to questions of such monumental questions exceedingly vague or entirely within the discretion of the facility administrator.

Question 19. Quality of Care. What assurances of quality of care are contained in the contract? What are the qualifications of the health care providers? Are they Medicare-certified or licensed by the state? Are they trained and/or supervised by a reputable provider organization or other agency?

Preferred Response: Few contracts address this, although they should. Medicare certification and licensure do not, in themselves, ensure quality. Often a more accurate measure of quality is the extent to which the facility has an ongoing staff training program and a quality review process that includes substantial participation by residents.

D. Residents' Rights

Question 20. Residents' Control. What is the extent of residents' participation in management of the facility?

Preferred Response: The facility should support an active residents' council. It should inform the council of the facility's financial and operational status through quarterly or more frequent meetings (at which top management, board members, or owners are present) and invite input from the council regarding decisions that directly affect residents.

Comment: A number of state statutes give CCRC residents the right to self-organize, but few give residents any direct authority over the management of the facility. Michigan, Missouri, and Ohio give residents the right to appoint a representative to the board of directors, at least in an advisory capacity. Not surprisingly, facility owners generally oppose residents' participation on facility boards, considering such participation unwarranted interference in business.

Question 21. Grounds for Termination. When and how can the facility terminate the resident's contract and residency against the resident's wishes?

Preferred Response: The resident should have a lifetime contract or a lifetime right to renew the resident contract unless the provider can demonstrate "just cause" not to renew and the resident is given ninety days' notice and the right to a hearing to contest the action. The Columbia Model suggests the following definition of *just cause:*

(1) a reasoned determination in writing by the medical director and signed by the administrator of the facility attesting that a resident is a danger to him- or herself or others while remaining in the facility. Before such a determination is made, the provider shall

give the resident an opportunity to submit an evaluation by an independent physician selected by the resident or on the resident's behalf. The medical director shall consider the statement of the resident's physician and include a copy of it in the determination. The determination shall contain a statement of reasons why there is not less restrictive alternative;

(2) a material misrepresentation of information designated by the provider as admission criteria;

(3) a material breach by the resident of the resident contract; or

(4) an inability of a resident to pay periodic fees but only if the provider has not contracted to continue providing care in such a situation and the provider has earned the following:

(a) the resident's entire entrance fee;

(b) state or federal benefits received on behalf of the resident; and

(c) third party insurance benefits received on behalf of the resident. (Reference to come.)

Comment: At least fifteen states have "just cause" requirements for involuntary termination. In others, protections for residents are determined solely according to the terms of the contract and are often spelled out in fairly vague terms.

Question 22. Complaints. Does the facility have an effective grievance mechanism in place?

Preferred Response: A formal procedure for addressing complaints and a facility policy against retaliatory conduct should be acknowledged in the contact.

Comment: One should determine whether data on the number and outcomes of past complaints by residents is available, as it may provide a useful indicator of the quality of life for residents of the facility.

Question 23. Rules. Is there a handbook for residents or a similar document that contains other rules and policies that are not spelled out in the contract?

Preferred Response: Any ancillary rules or policies should be expressly incorporated into the contract.

Comment: In an effort to keep the contracts short and keep day-to-day management flexible, facilities may relegate certain policies— e.g., those governing visitors' parking rules, the use of community facilities, or safety rules—to supplemental documents. These materials should be provided prior to the execution of the contract, and they should not permit the facility to change or circumvent any of the terms of the contract.

Question 24. Injury to Person or Property. Does the contract waive or limit the liability of the resident or the facility for loss or damage caused by either?

Preferred Response: If the contract addresses these questions at all, it should not include a waiver of or a specific cap on the facility's own liability for negligence. One should also beware of waivers of the facility's liability for the negligence or wrongful acts of other residents or other third parties. Even in these instances, the facility may legally be deemed a contributing cause of the injury.

GETTING MORE INFORMATION

To learn more about CCRCs and locate facilities in your area, you may find the following resources helpful:

- The American Association of Homes for the Aging (AAHA) has published *The Consumer's Directory of Continuing Care Retirement Communities,* which profiles over three hundred not-for-profit retirement communities around the country and provides an overview of CCRC types, terminology, and features that consumers might want to consider. The directory is available for $19.95 from AAHA Publications, 901 E Street, NW, Suite 500, Washington, D.C. 20004, or you may call 1–202–508–9442 for further information.
- The American Association of Retired Persons maintains a computer data base of retirement housing, including CCRCs and facilities that offer assisted living, and it will provide a free printout for any geographic area. Request a printout (and specify the geographic area) from Membership Communications, AARP, 601 E Street, NW, Washington, D.C. 20049.
- State or local agencies on aging frequently prepare directories or guides on houseing options for older people and those with disabilities. You can almost always find the number of one of these agencies in your local phone book.

REFERENCES

Advertisement for Caton Merchant House. 1990. In the "Washington Family" advertising supplement. *The Washington Post,* October 17.

American Academy of Actuaries, Actuarial Standards Board. 1987. *Actuarial Standard of Practice No. 3: Relating to Continuing Care Retirement Communities.* American Academy of Actuaries, Actuarial Standards Board.

American Institute of Certified Public Accountants (AICPA). 1990. "Statement of Position 90-8: Financial Accounting and Reporting by Continuning Care Retirement Communities." Health Care Committee, Federal Government Relations Division, AICPA November 18.

American Association of Homes for the Aging (AAHA). 1991. *Summary of the Current Status of State Regulation of Continuing Care Facilities.* Revised July 11. Washington, D.C.: AAHA Publications.

American Association of Homes for the Aging (AAHA). (1987). *Guidelines for Regulation of Continuing Care Retirement Communities.* May 1987. Washington, D.C.: AAHA Publications.

American Association of Homes for the Aging (AAHA) and Ernst and Whitney. (1987). *Continuing Care Retirement Communities: an Industry in Action: Analysis and Developing Trends.* Washington, D.C.: AAHA Publications.

Coleman, N., and J. Fairbanks. 1991. *Licensing and New Board and Care for the Elderly.* St. Louis University Public Law Review.

"Communities for the Elderly." 1990. *Consumer Reports,* February.

Continuing Care Accreditation Commission (CCAC). 1991. *Handbook for Candidate CCRCs.* Washington, D.C.: CCAC.

Continuing Care Accreditation Commission (CCAC). (1993). *Accredited Facilities List.* Washington, D.C.: CCAC.

Fisher, W. 1985. "Continuing Care Retirement Communities: a Promise Falling Short," *George Mason Law Review* 8:47.

Legislative Drafting Research Fund of Columbia University Law School. December, 1989. *State Regulation of Continuing Care Retirement Communities: Model Language and Commentary.*

National Association of Insurance Commissioners. 1988. Draft Report of the Subgroup on Continuing Care Retirement Benefits.

Stearns, L., F. Netting, C. Wilson, and L. Branch. 1990. "Lessons from the Implementation of CCRC Regulation." *The Gerontologist,* 30:2.

VI
HEALTH CONDITIONS AND HEALTH CARE

●

18

Personal Habits and the Prevention
of Health Hazards

●

DAVID HABER

What comes to the minds of most Americans when the term *health care* is mentioned? In the minds of most people, *doctors, hospitals,* and *medications* are synonymous for *health care.* Few would think of the personal habits that characterize their lifestyles. Yet, as the oft-quoted Surgeon General's Report on Health Promotion and Disease Prevention cogently states, "A wealth of scientific research reveals that the key to whether a person will be healthy or sick, live a long life or die prematurely, can be found in simple personal habits . . ." (U.S. Department of Health and Human Services 1979).

Instead of thinking *doctors, hospitals,* and *medications,* Americans would be well advised to think *eat well, stay physically fit,* and *have some fun.* This simplified formula will not eliminate the prospect of doctor visits, hospital stays, and medication usage, particularly as people grow older, as more than 85 percent of older adults are afflicted with some degree of chronic disease (Cornoni-Huntley et al. 1985). But it can help us fulfill our potential for physical, cognitive, and emotional well-being even if we are coping with one or more of the hazards most commonly associated with old age: arthritis, heart disease, misuse of medications, and sexual dysfunction. Becoming informed about good health practices is the first step.

HEALTH EDUCATION FOR OLDER ADULTS

The amount of health information that has been bombarding us over the past decade has been enormous, and this information has been

263

pervasive. Most local television news programs have health segments, many newspapers have health sections, and magazine articles and radio programs on health education are abundant. Adding to the impact of this information are the not-so-subtle health messages that are communicated daily through advertising.

There is evidence to suggest that raising public awareness about the importance of lifestyle modifications to prevent disease has had a positive effect, such as on the incidence of heart disease. In 1989 the *Medical Tribune* reported that between 1970 and 1985 the annual number of deaths from heart disease declined 39 percent, in part due to public education about risk factors.

This news is encouraging to professionals, but at the same time we realize that more older adults could derive greater satisfaction from life if they would become more proactive and seek out more information about the link between lifestyle and health. A good starting point for the person who is so inclined is one of the more than twelve thousand senior centers around the country.

Sources of Health Education

A national survey revealed that 100 percent of the senior centers have some type of health screening program (Leanse 1985). In addition, most centers provide general health education seminars, exercise and nutrition classes, self-help groups, self-care programs, referrals to appropriate health services, or some combination of these services.

Senior centers are located in almost every community. They are broadly focused in their health education offerings and are also well connected to the medical community. More than 80 percent are linked to physicians, hospitals, or public health departments (Leanse 1985).

According to one recent survey, health promotion may not be an equally high priority among all senior centers and other organizations for the aging (Campanelli 1990). When the respondents to this survey were asked where they would locate information on health education and promotion, they identified state and local health departments, institutes of higher education, hospitals, other public service agencies, and voluntary organizations.

One voluntary organization in particular, the American Association of Retired Persons (AARP), will be highlighted in this chapter because of its wealth of free print and low-cost videocassette/slide materials that are both high in quality and easily available to the general public. A guide to locating services and resources is included at the end of this chapter.

Model Health Education Programs

There is no certain method for determining the quality of a health education program. It can be helpful, however, for an interested professional or older adult to gain access to a model program to see how it works. Some of these model programs have been developed with the aid of federal grants and other funding sources and have gone through program evaluations as well.

A useful directory entitled *Health Promotion and Aging* describes forty model programs around the country that can be adapted to local conditions, and it also provides references to more than two hundred additional programs. Another twenty-four model programs around the country are described in *Exemplary Contributions to Healthy Aging: Award Winners*. These programs were selected by a panel of experts through a cooperative project between AARP and the U.S. Public Health Service's Office of Disease Prevention and Health Promotion.

Two of the best-known older adult health promotion programs in the country are Growing Younger, a series of four two-hour workshops on exercise, nutrition, stress management, and medical self-care; and Growing Wiser, a series of four two-hour workshops on memory, mental alertness, coping with loss and life changes, and maintaining independence and self-image. In Boise, Idaho, where these programs originated, 10 percent of the city's older population has participated.

Another model program, Staying Healthy After Fifty, began as a research project for the W. K. Kellogg Foundation and was implemented by the American Association of Retired Persons, the Dartmouth Institute for Better Health, and the American Red Cross. The demonstration and research project, which was completed in 1988, involved 2,500 older adults from more than seventy communities nationwide including Asian, African American, and Hispanic communities. While the project did not address outcomes related to the physical health status of participants or their utilization of medical care, the older participants reported increased knowledge, improved self-care skills, and positive changes in health behaviors.

NUTRITION AND EXERCISE

The two health habits that are most likely to be included in a health education program, as well as the two personal habits that are of most concern to Americans, are nutrition and exercise. Interest in these two topics is well deserved since there is ample evidence from research that the adoption of good nutrition and exercise habits is important in preventing disease and promoting health.

Nutrition

The older people get, the more conscientious they become about their diets. One national survey reported that a higher percentage of adults age sixty-five and over—in comparison with adults in other age categories—"try a lot" when it comes to limiting sodium, limiting fat, eating enough fiber, lowering cholesterol, getting enough vitamins and minerals, and limiting sugar. About two-thirds of the older adults reported trying a lot versus half of the people in their forties (Harris and Associates 1989).

Though they are more concerned than other age groups, many older adults do not report success in controlling their eating habits. While only one of four Americans in their forties, for instance, report that they keep their weight within the recommended range, even fewer—15 percent—over age sixty-five report success in this area (Harris and Associates 1989).

The good news, though, is that the weight charts most older adults consult to find out their appropriate weight range are outdated. The ideal weights now recommended for older adults are higher than they used to be. In addition, studies from the National Institute on Aging have indicated that putting on some additional weight as we grow older is healthy (AARP 1987).

A study on in-hospital mortality, for example, reported that the lowest mortality rates in a retrospective review of 8,428 hospital admissions were among those patients considered moderately overweight. The authors speculated that perhaps the common tendency to gain weight in late middle life is natural, and perhaps this extra margin of nutritional reserve is beneficial during the stress of acute illness (Potter et al. 1988).

One of the challenges of practicing good eating habits is weighing the veracity of the many media announcements that capture our attention and often serve more to confuse than to enlighten. Newspaper headlines and television news programs have recently proclaimed the importance of bran. Then a report from a single research project with a small sample size was publicized questioning the importance of bran. But before much longer another announcement declared, once again, that bran was an important component of the diet.

In the spring of 1991 another issue captured the headlines: should the long-standing circle that depicted the four food groups be changed to a triangle? This issue was not merely a question of geometrical aesthetics. The equally divided circle implies that the four food groups—bread/cereal, vegetable/fruit, and milk/meat—are equal in value. The triangle, on the other hand, implies a hierarchy of value. There is more space—and consequently more emphasis—at the base of the triangle, which is devoted to breads and cereals. Higher up, with less space, are the vegetables and fruits, followed by dairy products and meat and, at the narrow apex of the triangle, the sinful fats, oils, and sweets.

After only a few weeks of national publicity, the U.S. Department of Agriculture dropped the triangle and returned to the circle diagram. There were some who accused the government of caving in to the dairy and meat industry. Supporters of the retraction, though, claimed that the triangle concept overlooked the recent surge in low-fat dairy products and leaner meats that made these foods more acceptable.

While the frequent controversies can be confusing, and sometimes amusing, they should not detract from the so-called bottom-line advice that guides most educated older adults. The best recipe for good nutrition is to eat with moderation and balance, to include plenty of fiber, and to avoid excessive fat and sugar.

Exercise

While the research findings are correlational rather than causal, there is nonetheless considerable evidence that regular exercise can reduce the risk of coronary heart disease, hypertension, colon cancer, and stroke; improve glucose tolerance and insulin sensitivity; preserve bone density; reduce obesity; enhance mental functioning; and decrease anxiety and depression (Gorman and Posner 1988; "Physical Activity, Physical Fitness, and Health" 1989). As a number of gerontologists have noted, if exercise could be encapsulated in a pill it would be the single most powerful medication a physician could prescribe.

The good news from several recent studies is that older adults do not need to become triathletes or engage in other high-intensity activities to reap the benefits of exercise.

For most older adults, a low-level walking program will provide sufficient intensity for a good fitness program (Paffenbarger 1986; Blair et al. 1989). For instance, an eight-year study of more than thirteen thousand people reported that walking briskly for thirty to sixty minutes every day was almost as beneficial in reducing the death rate as jogging up to forty miles a week (Blair et al. 1989).

This finding is important because the National Center for Health Statistics reports that walking has much greater appeal for older adults than high-intensity exercise. The national survey found that a smaller percentage of persons age sixty-five and over (27 percent) engage in vigorous activities than the general adult population (41 percent), while all age groups are equally likely to walk for exercise (41 percent) (U.S. Public Health Service 1985).

Usually considered an outdoor activity, walking is often abandoned in unfavorable weather. Prolonged hot or cold spells may sabotage a good walking program. Rather than stopping the activity because of the weather, adults would do well to consider walking indoors at their local shopping mall. Many older adults are finding that shopping malls are opening their doors early for walking clubs.

Walking is a popular example of an aerobic activity, i.e., an activity that involves rhythmic, repetitive, and continuous exercise. In the spring of 1990 a study of an anaerobic exercise program (which involves more intense breathing than an aerobic program) captured the headlines when ten frail nursing home residents ranging in age from eighty-six to ninety-six completed an eight-week training program. By working out with a weight machine these older adults increased their leg strength and consequently were able to walk 50 percent faster. One resident who had been unable to rise from a chair without the use of his arms was able to do so after the training (Fiatarone et al. 1990).

The importance of strength training for older adults is not only that it increases muscle mass, which can improve functioning, but that it increases bone density as well. When the skeletal frame is strengthened the likelihood of bone fractures from osteoporosis is reduced (Gorman and Posner 1988).

Whether interested in aerobic or anaerobic exercise, older adults should consult with their personal physicians before starting regular programs. It is also important to choose a pleasurable activity in order to sustain motivation, remember the warm-up and cool-down period, and emphasize regularity (at least three days per week and twenty minutes per day to strengthen cardiovascular capacity).

CHRONIC HEALTH CONCERNS

As noted earlier, few people escape chronic disease by the time they reach age sixty-five. By midlife an increasing number of persons are coping with arthritis, heart disease, cancer, stroke, lung disease, bereavement, hearing or vision impairment, or perhaps the stress of caregiving for someone else with a chronic impairment.

While addressing the full range of chronic impairments is beyond the scope of this chapter, we will look at two of the most common chronic conditions, as well as the ones that produce the greatest amount of limitation (Gorman and Posner 1988)—arthritis and heart *disease*. These two diseases account for about one-third of all days that the elderly spend in bed (*Aging America: Trends and Projections* 1987–1988). In addition, over half of the ten thousand prescription drugs available today are for arthritis and cardiac conditions (Ebersole and Hess 1990).

People who endure pain and experience limitations imposed by a chronic condition may be inclined to scoff at the simple admonition presented at the beginning of this chapter: eat well, stay physically fit, and have some fun. Yet there is evidence that they can positively affect the quality of their lives by making some changes in their personal habits.

Arthritis

It is estimated that everyone over age sixty has some degree of the most common form of arthritis, osteoarthritis; about 30 percent of older Americans recognize some of its symptoms. Osteoarthritis is the gradual wearing away of tissue around the joints of the hands, feet, knees, hips, neck, or back. Arthritic pain may vary from mild to severe, and it may come and go. While arthritis cannot be prevented or cured, the functioning of the arthritic joint can be improved and the pain often alleviated.

At more than one hundred local chapters of the Arthritis Foundation, a six-week course is offered that provides information on medications, exercise, nutrition, and the practical concerns of daily living for people with arthritis. The practical advice can range from tips on where to purchase Velcro®-modified clothing for those who have trouble dressing to the location of aquatic exercise programs.

These programs were developed at the Stanford Arthritis Center and have been implemented and evaluated over the past decade.

Participants are typically asked to pay a small fee for each course and the instructional materials. If enrolling in a complete program is not of interest, the local arthritis chapter will distribute free booklets on arthritis as well as information about most arthritis medications.

Heart Disease

Cardiovascular disease (including heart disease, hypertension, atherosclerosis, and angina) accounts for the highest percentage of doctor visits, short-stay hospital visits, and bed disability days of any disease (*Aging America: Trends and Projections* 1987–1988). Accounting for 600,000 deaths per year, heart attacks are the nation's number-one killer and are responsible for 45 percent of all deaths.

The good news is that between 1970 and 1985 the annual number of deaths from heart disease declined 39 percent (*Medical Tribune* 1989). Public education was given some of the credit for this decline, as during that period Americans had not only become more knowledgeable about the risk factors for heart disease—smoking, high blood pressure, obesity, and the consumption of sodium and fats—but begun to do something about it.

One of the fats that has received the most public attention over the past several years has been cholesterol. In 1985 the National Heart, Lung, and Blood Institute (NHLBI) set up the National Cholesterol Education Program (NCEP). The NCEP reported that sixty million American adults, including twenty-four million age sixty and over, had borderline or high cholesterol levels. Since the risk of cardiovascular heart disease rises sharply with the cholesterol count, a federal campaign to lower the cholesterol level was launched.

The implications of the research findings on cholesterol for older adults were far from clear. A major limitation on the studies that link the risk of heart disease to cholesterol level is whether data on middle-aged men can be extrapolated to older men or to women in general, since they have been studied much less extensively.

Should we worry more or less about cholesterol level the older we get? Some experts, like Dr. P. J. Palumbo, director of clinical nutrition at the Mayo Clinic in Rochester, Minnesota, endorse the more popularly held conception among health professionals—that older people can tolerate higher levels of cholesterol than the general adult population (AARP 1990).

Other experts, like Dr. William Castelli, director of the Framingham Heart Study in Massachusetts, believe that older adults may be even more vulnerable to the effects of high cholesterol levels than younger adults and that the standards should be more stringent, not less, for this population (AARP 1990).

The recently launched CRISP program (Cholesterol Reduction in Seniors Program), a new study sponsored by the NHLBI, will attempt to resolve the issue. Meanwhile, it is necessary for older adults to follow the advice of their physicians.

CONCERNS ABOUT MEDICATIONS

As previously mentioned, arthritis and cardiac conditions contribute significantly to the utilization of the more than ten thousand prescription drugs available today. Add to this prescription total an extraordinary number of over-the-counter medications being consumed, and it is not unreasonable to suggest that most Americans consider taking pills a normal part of growing older.

Given our increased vulnerability to chronic disease over time, it is not surprising that medication usage increases with age. Between 25 and 30 percent of prescription medications are utilized by the 12 percent of the population that is over the age of sixty-five. Older people turn to drugs to alleviate pain and discomfort as well as to provide a sense of security and control in sometimes frightening health situations. Drugs, however, can make matters worse as well as better. The potential for an older person to fall victim to serious adverse drug reactions is great.

About 15 percent of hospital admissions are for adverse drug reactions (Lamy 1986), and older adults suffer three times as many adverse drug reactions as the general population (Sloan 1986). In the community approximately 40 percent of the elderly may experience drug reactions (Lamy 1986).

To avoid adverse drug reactions, patients need to comply with their medication regimens, report unexpected side effects, and exercise caution with over-the-counter medications. Health professionals need to take good drug histories, carefully assess the dosage, communicate the rationale for the drug treatment as well as the expected response and common side effects, and monitor patients' reactions (Lamy 1981; Sloan 1986). However, both professionals and patients, tend to fall short of the ideal. Consequently, overmedication, drug interactions, and medication side effects are not uncommon.

One of the most effective strategies to prevent drug abuse is to not take the medication in the first place. Many Americans unthinkingly take pills to alleviate constipation, insomnia, indigestion, headaches, and other types of pain or discomfort. Diet, exercise, and stress management may be effective alternatives that do not pose the danger of medication side effects.

The reality is that 75 percent of all physician visits will result in the prescription of a drug (Kemper et al. 1985). And the older patient is the least likely to be a knowledgeable consumer of the drug that is being prescribed (American Board of Family Practice 1987).

For today's older adults, the many readily available booklets on medications are good consumer safety tools. These booklets remind medication consumers of important questions to ask their physicians and pharmacists, offer several medication-taking strategies to improve daily compliance with medication regimens, provide listings of generic equivalents, note commonly reported side effects of medications, or offer blank charts for listing all prescriptions and over-the-counter medications prior to visiting a physician.

SEXUAL CONCERNS

I began this chapter by stating the formula eat well, stay physically fit, and have some fun. Then I examined some ideas on nutrition and exercise, and left the fun for last. This order may also reflect the priorities of many older adults who grew up with a strong work ethic.

There are many ways for older adults to have fun once they have been encouraged. For example, there is playing with children, watching a sunset, feeding ducks, walking in the woods, and enjoying sexual intimacy. Playing, watching, feeding, and walking are not problematic for most older adults. Sexual intimacy may be more of a problem.

The following excerpt from a Harold Robbins novel is quoted in the book *Pathways* (Kemper et al. 1985): "We couldn't wait to get at each other. Our clothes made a trail up the stairs to the bedroom. We fell naked on the bed, tearing at each other like raging animals. Then we exploded and fell backward on the bed, gasping for breath" (p. 112). As Kemper and Associates conclude, it is doubtful that this passage was about older adults.

As we progress through the life cycle, the analogy of raging animals is less applicable to us in our sexual relationships. Sexuality becomes increasingly focused on warmth, sharing, touching, and intimate communication. This is not to suggest that older adults are asexual in the traditional sense. The majority of older couples, according to studies by the Duke University Center for the Study of Aging and Human Development, remain sexually active between ages sixty-five and seventy-five.

Nonetheless, as consumers of research it might prove more useful for us to pay less attention to the studies that emphasize physiological parameters and the frequency of sexual performance and more attention to the studies that report individual perceptions and experiences (Starr 1985). For instance, one study of eight hundred people between the ages of sixty and ninety-one found that 36 percent reported that sex was better over time, while 25 percent said it was worse (Starr and Weiner 1981).

Of course, the sexuality of some aging Americans can get waylaid by psychological factors such as depression, guilt, monotony, performance anxiety, and anger. And both young and old can be hampered by negative attitudes of their peers that reveal hostility toward the expression of sexuality in late life.

Yet another cause of sexual dysfunction is physical limitations. Arthritic pains, cardiovascular disorders, respiratory conditions, hormonal imbalances, and neurological disorders can interfere with sexual performance. In addition, various medications associated with these conditions can lead to sexual dysfunction (Ebersole and Hess 1990). But the most significant cause of sexual inactivity, particularly after age seventy-five, is widowhood or lack of opportunity. This problem is complicated when older adults are less accepting of alternative sexual practices.

To expand the options of an older adult, one intervention a family member might try is to arrange for a respected health professional to prescribe a reading of *The Joy of Sex* (Comfort 1972). In addition to presenting a wide variety of sexual ideas, Dr. Comfort describes other activities in which older people may engage in lieu of intercourse, such as fantasizing, masturbation, and touching.

The importance of touching became clear to me when I participated in presenting a yoga class that had been enthusiastically received by older adults at senior centers and congregate living facilities at ten nursing homes (Haber 1983; 1986; 1988). After a few unsuccessful attempts to engage the residents, we began each class with massage, either instructor-resident, resident-resident, or self-massage. At the same time we witnessed a dramatic increase in—there is not other word for it—*fun.* The residents enthusiastically awaited the remaining classes.

In summary, whether an individual is one of the majority of older adults who are coping with chronic health conditions or one of the fortunate few who are training for the Senior Olympics, the best advice is still the same—eat well, stay physically fit, and have some fun.

A GUIDE TO HEALTH SERVICES AND RESOURCES

Below are listed a number of resources to which one can turn for information on a variety of topics of interest to older people, including health education, nutrition, exercise, and specific diseases that especially affect older people.

Health Education

How does one locate a senior center or another community site where health education for older adults is offered? One way is by contacting one's state unit on aging or the local area agency on aging. These agencies are responsible for providing information, as well as coordinating the more than twenty thousand provider organizations that are involved in providing services for the aging around the country.

It may be difficult to locate one of the 57 state units on aging or one of the 672 area agencies on aging in the telephone book since there is no uniform name under which these organizations are identified. For help in locating the appropriate agency one may obtain the *1989–1990 Directory of State and Area Agencies on Aging* from the National Association of Area Agencies on Aging, 600 Maryland Avenue SW, Suite 208 West, Washington, D.C. 20024 (1 202 484–7520).

The preparation of a national directory of selected health promotion programs for older adults, entitled *Health Promotion and Aging*, was sponsored by the Administration on Aging and the U.S. Public Health Service (DHHS Publication No. (OHDS) 86-20950, ISBN 1-55672-001-7). It is distributed free of charge by the National Council on the Aging, Inc., 409 Third Street SW, Washington, D.C. 20024 (1 202 479–1200).

A monograph that recognizes model programs for older adults around the country, entitled *Exemplary Contributions to Healthy Aging* (July 1992), was developed as a cooperative project between AARP and the U.S. Public Health Service's Office of Disease Prevention and Health Promotion. It is part of the Healthy People 2000/Healthy Older Adults initiative, and it can be obtained at no charge from the American Association of Retired Persons, Health Advocacy Services, Program Coordination and Development Department, 601 E Street, NW, Washington, D.C. 20049.

The Growing Younger program, which has been described above, can be found in twenty-eight states. Complete program development packages for this program or its companion program, Growing Wiser, also described above, can be obtained at a nominal cost from Healthwise, Inc., P.O. Box 1989, Boise, Idaho 83701 (1 208 345–1161).

An important outgrowth of the Staying Healthy After Fifty project described above was the development of a curriculum for community programs that can be taught by trained volunteers. For more information, one may contact AARP, Health Advocacy Services, 601 E Street, NW, Washington, DC 20049 (1 202 434–2277).

Nutrition

For detailed advice and comprehensive materials on nutrition, older adults and health care practitioners can contact the National Dairy Council, 6300 North River Road, Rosemont, Illinois 60018–4233 (1 708 696–1020). The council provides printed materials, slides, videos, and films on nutrition. Especially relevant to older adults is the list of programs and materials that is annually published in the *Nutrition Education Materials* catalog, which includes the eight-page brochure *For Mature Eaters Only: Guidelines for Good Nutrition*.

In addition, AARP has several booklets on nutrition, two of which I have used quite successfully with groups of older adults: *Eating for Your Health* (PF 3400/2(590)-D12164) and *How Does Your Nutrition Measure Up?* (PF 4027(1287)-D12994). Up to ten copies are provided free of charge by AARP Publications, Program Resources Department/ BV, 601 E Street, NW, Washington, D.C. 20049.

Exercise

The National Organization of Mall Walkers (NOMW), which began in 1989, is a clearinghouse with two thousand members. NOMW President Tom Cabot reports that there are nearly three million mall walkers nationwide (AARP 1991). The overwhelming majority are age fifty and over.

An older adult who wants to exercise but is concerned about a health problem should be aware that there is a health foundation or professional association for people with practically any health condition that will provide free and useful information. If one cannot locate the appropriate organization in the telephone book, one should contact the state unit on aging or the area agency on aging.

Arthritis

If one cannot locate a local arthritis chapter, one may contact the national Arthritis Foundation 1314 Spring Street NW, Atlanta, Georgia 30309 (1 404 872–7100).

Heart Disease

For accurate, up-to-date information on cholesterol, contact the National Cholesterol Education Program, National Heart Lung and Blood Institute, Office of Information, Bethesda, Maryland 20205 or the American Heart Association, 7320 Greenville Avenue, Dallas, Texas 75231 (1 214 750–5300).

Medications

Perhaps as succeeding groups of older adults achieve higher educational levels, more will choose to become knowledgeable consumers. Those who are already interested may purchase the United States Pharmacopeial Convention's *Advice for the Patient* or any of a number of other drug information guides that are available at the neighborhood bookstore.

Two booklets that are especially good are provided free by AARP: *The Smart Consumer's Guide to Prescription Drugs* (PF 4297(389)-D13579) and *Using Your Medicines Wisely: A Guide for the Elderly* (PF 1436(1185)-D317). To order either or both, one should contact AARP Publications, Program Resources, 601 E Street, NW, Washington, D.C. 20049.

REFERENCES

AARP. 1987. *How Does Your Nutrition Measure Up?* PF 4027(1287)-D12994. Washington, D.C.:AARP.

AARP. 1990. *AARP Bulletin*, 31(3):2.

AARP. 1991. *AARP Bulletin*, 32(5):2.

Aging America: Trends and Projections. (1987–1988). Publication LR3377 (188)-D 12198. Washington, D.C.: U.S. Department of Health and Human Services.

American Board of Family Practice. 1987. *Rights and Responsibilities: Part II, the Changing Health Care Consumer and Patient/Doctor Partnership*. A National Survey of Health Care Opinions, Lexington, Ky.: American Board of Family Practice.

Blair, S., et al. 1989. "Physical Fitness and All-Cause Mortality: A Prospective Study of Healthy Men and Women." *Journal of the American Medical Association*, 262 (17):2395–2401.

Campanelli, L. 1990. "Promoting Healthy Aging." *Educational Gerontology*, 16(6):517–518.

Comfort, A. 1972. *The Joy of Sex*. N.Y.: Simon and Schuster.

Cornoni-Huntley, J., et al. 1985. "Epidemiology of Disability in the Oldest Old: Methodologic Issues and Preliminary Findings." *Milbank Memorial Fund*, 63(2):206.

Ebersole, P., and P. Hess. 1990. *Toward Healthy Aging: Human Needs and Nursing Response*. St. Louis: The C.V. Mosby Company.

Fiatarone, M., et al. 1990. "High-intensity Strength Training in Nonagenerians: Effects on Skeletal Muscle." *Journal of the American Medical Association*, 263(22):3029–3034.

Gorman, K., and J. Posner. 1988. "Benefits of Exercise in Old Age." *Clinics in Geriatric Medicine*, 4(1):181–192.

Haber, D. 1983. "Yoga as a Preventive Health Care Program." *The International Journal of Aging and Human Development*, 17(4):169–176.

Haber, D. 1986. "Health Promotion to Reduce Blood Pressure Level among Older Blacks." *The Gerontologist*, 26(2):119–121.

Haber, D. 1988. "A Health Promotion Program in Ten Nursing Homes." *Activities, Adaptation and Aging*, 11(1):75–84.

Harris, L., and Associates, Inc. 1989. *The Prevention Index '89: Summary Report*, Rodale Press, Inc.

"Physical Activity, Physical Fitness, and Health: Time to Act." 1989. *Journal of the American Medical Association*, 262(17):2347.

Kemper, D., et al. 1985. *Pathways: A Success Guide for a Healthy Life*. Boise, Idaho: Healthwise, Inc.

Lamy, P. 1981. "Special Features of Geriatric Prescribing." *Geriatrics*, 36:42–52.

Lamy, P. 1986. "Adverse Drug Reactions and the Elderly: An Update." In R. Ham, ed., *Geriatric Medicine Annual 1986*. Oradell, N.J.: Medical Economics Books.

Leanse, J. 1985. "The Senior Center as a Wellness Center." In Dychtwald, K., ed., *Wellness and Health Promotion for the Elderly*, 105–118. Maryland: Aspen Publication.

Medical Tribune. 1989. *Medical Tribune*, 30:20.

Paffenbarger, R., et al. 1986. "Physical Activity, All-Cause Mortality, and Longevity of College Alumni." *New England Journal of Medicine*, 314:604.

Potter, J. 1988. "In-Hospital Mortality as a Function of Body Mass Index: An Age-Dependent Variable." *The Journal of Gerontology: Medical Sciences*, 43 (3):M59–M63.

Sloan, R. (1986). *Practical Geriatric Therapeutics*. N.J.: Medical Economics Books.

Starr, B. 1985. "Sexuality and Aging." In M. Lawton and G. Maddox, eds., *Annual Review of Gerontology and Geriatrics*, vol. 5. New York: Springer.

Starr, B., and M. Weiner (1981). *Sex and Sexuality in the Mature Years*. New York: McGraw-Hill.

U.S. Department of Health and Human Services. 1979. *Healthy People: The Surgeon General's Report on Health Promotion and Disease Prevention*. 1979. Washington, D.C.: U.S. Government Printing Office.

U.S. Public Health Service. 1985. *National Health Interview Survey*. Advance Data 13. Hyattsville, Md: U.S. Public Health Service.

19

Medicare, Medigap, and Medicaid

●

STEPHEN L. ISAACS AND AVA C. SWARTZ

The purpose of this chapter is to describe the forms of health insurance and entitlements that are available to older people in the United States—Medicare, Medigap, and Medicaid.

Medicare is the U.S. government program that pays for much of the medical care of people aged sixty-five and older, rich and poor alike. It also covers the medical costs of some individuals with disabilities and those who need kidney dialysis or transplantation. When President Lyndon B. Johnson signed Medicare into law in 1965 he said, "No longer will older Americans be denied the healing miracle of modern medicine. No longer will illness crush and destroy the savings that they have so carefully put away over a lifetime." Today that fine sentiment falls short of reality.

Although Medicare gives a great deal of protection to the thirty-one million Americans who are sixty-five or over, it pays less than half of the average older person's health costs. This is because of what is *not* covered. Medicare does not cover most prescription drugs, the entire amount of hospital stays or doctors' bills, and many other health care costs of seniors. To get the additional coverage they need, many seniors buy insurance policies to supplement what is covered by Medicare. These policies, commonly called "Medigap" policies, are sold by commercial insurance companies and by Blue Cross and Blue Shield.

Neither Medicare nor Medigap policies cover custodial nursing or home health care. Seniors must pay for these kinds of care through long-term care insurance policies or out of their own pockets, often spending their life savings to cover the cost of nursing home care.

Once they become poor enough, they can qualify for Medicaid, a joint federal and state program that pays for the health care of indigent people.

MEDICARE

One of the most complicated laws ever written, Medicare changes almost every year. To find out the latest changes, consult the *Medicare Handbook*, which is published each year by the Health Care Financing Administration (HCFA) of the U.S. Department of Health and Human Services; call the Social Security Administration, the government agency responsible for providing information about the program at 1 800 772–1213; or contact one of the organizations listed near the end of this chapter.

Medicare is divided into two parts. Part A pays a portion of the cost of hospital care, skilled nursing care, home health care, and hospice care. Part B covers a portion of doctors' bills, outpatient services, and medical equipment and supplies. For eligible seniors, Part A does not cost a penny; it has already been paid for through a payroll tax. Part B is optional. A monthly "premium" is deducted from an enrollee's Social Security check.

Eligibility and Enrollment

People sixty-five or older who qualify for Social Security or railroad retirement benefits are eligible for Medicare. For most people, enrolling in Medicare is easy. They simply sign up during the seven-month enrollment period that includes the month during which they turn sixty-five and the three months preceding or following it. The best time to enroll is within the three months before turning sixty-five. Those who have applied for Social Security should receive Medicare cards automatically.

It is never too late to sign up for Medicare. An enrollment period is held between January 1 and March 31 every year. However, the federal government charges a 10 percent penalty for every year that the application has been delayed, and Part B coverage does not begin until the following July 1.

Those who take early retirement may sign up for Medicare upon reaching sixty-two, but benefits do not start until they turn sixty-five. For those who continue working past sixty-five and are covered by employers' health plans or who are themselves over sixty-five and are covered by the health plans of their spouses' employers, there are three options: (1) They may delay enrolling in Medicare until retirement (those who sign up within seven months of retirement are not assessed the 10 percent penalty described earlier). (2) They may enroll in both Medicare and their employers' plans, in which case their employers' plans, if twenty or more people are covered, provide primary coverage and Medicare provides secondary coverage. Or (3) they may turn down their employers' plans, in which case Medicare will be the sole source of coverage.

Elderly people with limited means may be eligible for the "Qualified Medicare Beneficiary" program, under which the state Medicaid program will pay Medicare premiums, deductibles, and co-payments. Those who are interested may contact the state Medicaid office for information or call 1 800 638–6833.

People who have not worked long enough to qualify for Medicare can buy it on their own by signing up during enrollment periods (the month of their sixty-fifth birthday and the three months surrounding it on either side, and the first three months of every year thereafter). There is a charge, however. Voluntary enrollment is open to anyone over sixty-five who is a resident of the United States and who is either a citizen or a lawfully admitted permanent resident who has resided in the United States continuously for at least five years preceding his or her application.

Coverage of Hospital Care under Medicare

Part A of Medicare covers most basic hospital costs, including the costs of a semiprivate room, meals, regular nursing services, blood beyond the first three pints, drugs, laboratory tests and radiology work billed by the hospital, and operating room charges. Hospitals are allowed to bill only for such extras as television, telephone, private nursing care, and a private room, unless it is medically necessary. The government contracts with insurance companies called *intermediaries* to administer Part A in different areas of the country.

Benefit Periods, Deductibles, and Coinsurance

Medicare does not pay for indefinite hospital stays. It places a cap on the length of time it covers and charges for part of a hospital stay through a system of deductible and coinsurance payments. The following discussion refers to the deductible and coinsurance amounts for 1993. They will probably be higher in subsequent years.

Medicare covers up to ninety days of hospitalization for each *benefit period* or *spell of illness*. A benefit period or spell of illness begins when a patient is admitted to a hospital and ends when he or she has been out of the hospital or a follow-up skilled nursing facility for sixty consecutive days.

Patients must pay the first $676 of their hospital expenses, which is called the *deductible*. After the deductible is satisfied, Medicare pays almost all hospital expenses for the first sixty days. Medicare covers the costs of an additional thirty days in the hospital during the same benefit period. However, for days sixty-one through ninety, patients must share the cost by paying $169 a day. This is called *coinsurance*.

In addition, every person covered by Medicare has the right to an additional lifetime reserve of sixty days of hospital coverage. The coinsurance for these days is $338 a day. These sixty days are not replaceable; once used, they are gone forever.

Table 19.1 describes coverage under Part A of Medicare.

Diagnostic Related Groups (DRGs)

When Medicare began in 1965, hospitals were paid on the basis of how much the services cost them. Somewhere along the line, health policy specialists realized that this system provided no incentive for hospitals to contain their costs. On the contrary, the more expensive their services, the better—and the more profitable. So Congress set about scrapping the old system and devising a new one that would encourage hospitals to reduce their costs—or even force them to. It came up with a system based on *diagnostic related groups* or DRGs and made it the law in 1982. The key features of this system are as follows:

- Hospitals are paid on the basis of the illness or injury for which a patient is admitted. Each illness or injury belongs to a particular DRG. There are about five hundred categories.
- The system specifies the number of days the average patient should be expected to stay for each DRG. The hospital is paid on the basis of this number of days.
- If the patient stays longer than the number of days allotted for the DRG, the hospital must absorb the additional costs from its own budget. If the patient is released early, the hospital is allowed to keep the money saved.

Even though DRGs offer an incentive to hospitals to discharge patients before they have fully recuperated—"sicker and quicker"— the law provides some protection to hospitalized Medicare patients.

TABLE 19.1. Medicare Part A: Hospital Insurance—Covered Services per Benefit Period

Services	Benefit	Medicare Pays[1]	You Pay
Hospitalization Semiprivate room and board, general nursing, and miscellaneous hospital services and supplies	First 60 days	All but $676	$676
	61st to 90th day	All but $169 a day	$169 a day
	91st to 150th day[2]	All but $338 a day	$338 a day
	Beyond 150 days	Nothing	All costs
Posthospital skilled nursing facility care You must have been in a hospital for at least 3 days and enter a Medicare-approved facility, generally within 30 days after hospital discharge.	First 20 days	100% of approved amount	Nothing
	Additional 80 days	All but $84.50 a day	$84.50 a day
	Beyond 100 days	Nothing	All costs
Home health care	Medically necessary skilled care, home health aide services, medical supplies, etc.	Full cost of services; 80% of approved amount for durable medical equipment	Nothing for services; 20% of approved amount for durable medical equipment
Hospice care Available to terminally ill	As long as doctor certifies need	All but limited costs for outpatient drugs and inpatient respite care	Limited cost sharing for outpatient drugs and inpatient respite care
Blood	Blood	All but first 3 pints per calendar year	For first 3 pints[3]

[1] The amounts are for 1993 and are subject to change each year.

[2] Sixty reserve days may be used only once; they are not renewable.

[3] To the extent the blood deductible is met under one part of Medicare during the calendar year, it does not have to be met under the other part.

Source: National Association of Insurance Commissioners and Health Care Financing Administration.

Upon admission, each patient should receive an Important Message from Medicare that says, "According to Federal law, your discharge date must be determined solely by your medical needs, and not by DRGs or Medicare payments."

Sometimes hospitals try to discharge patients before they feel they are fully recovered by sending them a Notice of Noncoverage. These are not eviction notices; rather, the hospital is saying that Medicare will not continue to pay for hospital care. Patients can stay, but they must pay on their own.

There are ways in which a patient may protest a Notice of Noncoverage. First, the patient or a friend or family member may discuss the situation with the doctor. A doctor can be an important ally, so it is important for the doctor to be on the patient's side. Second, the patient may ask to see the hospital's patients' representative. Many hospitals, especially those in urban areas, employ trained personnel called patients' representatives or patients' advocates to deal with patients' problems and complaints. Finally, the patient may appeal the Notice of Noncoverage to the appropriate peer review organization (PRO). PROs are organizations set up by federal law to monitor cost containment efforts and quality of care under Medicare. Part of their job is to review complaints of patients who believe they are being sent home prematurely. Medicare has set up a formal procedure for complaints to a PRO, and patients should take advantage of it.

The Notice of Noncoverage will state how to file an appeal. Merely by lodging a protest, a patient will gain two additional days in the hospital. The patient or his or her representative should time the appeal on the basis of whether the doctor agrees or disagrees with the hospital's decision to release the patient. If the doctor and the hospital disagree, an appeal should be made immediately. The hospital cannot submit a bill until the third day after receipt of a Notice of Noncoverage. If the doctor and the hospital agree on the discharge, an appeal should be made by noon of the next working day (Monday through Friday excluding holidays) after the Notice of Noncoverage is received. The PRO has one working day to rule on an appeal, and a patient cannot be charged until the following day.

Leaving the Hospital

Under the Medicare law, each patient leaving a hospital should be given a discharge plan that covers further care such as home health care, skilled nursing care, or hospice care. Most hospitals have a discharge planner—often a social worker—who can help arrange further treatment outside the hospital.

Coverage of Skilled Nursing Care under Medicare

Seniors who need nursing home care only to help them walk, eat, or bathe should not look to Medicare to pay for it. Medicare considers these services custodial services and will not pay for them. However, Medicare pays for care only in skilled nursing facilities; these tend to be high-tech sites where specially trained staffs work under doctors' orders. Most nursing homes are not skilled nursing facilities.

To qualify for Medicare coverage of skilled nursing care, the following criteria must be met:

- A patient must have been hospitalized for at least three consecutive days, not counting the day of discharge, and transferred to the skilled nursing facility within thirty days of discharge.
- Skilled nursing or skilled rehabilitation services must be needed on a *daily* basis. A doctor must certify that the patient needs, and is receiving, these services every day. The need must continue. Once a patient no longer needs daily skilled nursing or rehabilitative care, Medicare stops paying the bill. Committees from the facility and the insurance company that is serving as the intermediary monitor the need for skilled services.
- The care must be provided in a Medicare-certified skilled nursing facility.

Medicare covers up to one hundred days of skilled nursing care in each benefit period. It pays the first twenty days completely. There is a coinsurance payment of $84.50 a day for days twenty-one through one hundred. The nursing facility bills Medicare directly. If the facility believes a service is not covered, it must let a patient know in writing. About one out of five times the nursing facility is wrong, and Medicare will pay for the service. Patients should have the nursing facility bill Medicare if there is any doubt about whether a service is covered. If Medicare denies payment, a patient will have to pay the nursing facility directly.

Coverage of Home Health Care under Medicare

Medicare pays the cost of skilled nursing care; physical, speech, and occupational therapy; and care by home health aides that is delivered at home under certain conditions. Medicare does not pay for round-the-clock nursing care or for such home care services as cleaning, cooking, and shopping. To qualify for Medicare payment of home health care, a person must meet these criteria:

• The patient must be homebound. This means that the patient can leave home only infrequently or with the assistance of another person or a mechanical aid such as a wheelchair.
• The patient must be under the care of a doctor who approves an individualized treatment plan.
• Care must be provided by a Medicare-certified home health care agency.
• The patient must need skilled nursing or physical or speech therapy on a part-time or intermittent basis.

How Medicare defines *part-time* or *intermittent* is hard to understand and even harder to explain. According to Diane Archer, executive director of New York City's Medicare Beneficiaries Defense Fund, generally an individual "must need skilled services less than five days a week and as little as once in sixty days. Medicare will then cover up to thirty-five hours a week of skilled nursing care, care by a home health aide, or therapy services. Ms. Archer says, "Care can continue indefinitely as long as it is medically necessary." Medicare will also cover up to five or six hours a week of daily skilled nursing services for a finite period. There is no requirement that a person be hospitalized first in order to be eligible for Medicare's home health care benefits. The home health agency bills Medicare directly for the full cost of services, but there is a twenty percent co-payment for durable medical equipment such as hospital beds, ventilators, or oxygen tents.

Coverage of Hospice Care under Medicare

Hospice care is for the terminally ill. It aims to relieve pain and provide comfort, generally in a patient's home or the home of a family member, although there are also inpatient hospices. Eligibility is based on the following criteria:

• A doctor must certify that the patient is terminally ill, meaning that the patient is expected to live six months or less.
• The patient must choose to receive hospice benefits instead of standard Medicare benefits.
• Care must be provided by a Medicare-certified agency.

If these conditions are satisfied, Medicare pays all of the costs of hospice care, except for a small amount toward the cost of drugs, and five days of inpatient care in a facility to provide respite to the home hospice care worker. Medicare will pay for two ninety-day periods of hospice care. This can be followed by a thirty-day period and another extension period, which may last indefinitely if necessary.

Coverage of Doctors' Bills and Other Medical Costs under Medicare

Part B of Medicare covers part of the costs of doctors' bills, medical equipment and supplies, other outpatient care, and laboratory tests. Congress and the Health Care Financing Administration determine what services are covered. Claims are reviewed and paid by insurance companies that are designated as Medicare *carriers* to administer Part B in specific areas. The list of what is covered and what is not may change somewhat from year to year. Pap smears and mammograms were not covered for a long time, but now they are.

Medicare Part B pays part of the cost of physicians' services and those of other health providers such as nurse-midwives and clinical psychologists. Part B also pays a large part of the reasonable cost of other medically necessary services and supplies, including the following:

- Drugs that a doctor or nurse must administer.
- Outpatient hospital services, including those of the emergency room.
- Laboratory and diagnostic tests.
- Prosthetic devices, braces, and artificial limbs.
- Durable medical equipment, such as wheelchairs or crutches.
- Physical, occupational, or speech therapists' services.
- Ambulances under certain conditions.
- Kidney dialysis machines, supplies, and services.
- Blood for outpatient use after the first three pints.
- Home health care (for beneficiaries who do not have Part A).

Medicare will not pay for prescription drugs; routine dental, hearing, vision, and foot care check-ups; and most chiropractic visits and immunizations.

Paying for Services under Medicare Part B

Medicare Part B does not pay the total amount of doctors' bills. Every year patients must pay the first $100 of their medical bills. They pay this *deductible* amount once per year, not per visit or per procedure. Once the deductible has been paid, Medicare covers 80 percent of the scheduled amount. Patients must pay the remaining 20 percent, called *coinsurance.*

Under Medicare, some doctors accept *assignment;* they agree to accept the amount that Medicare approves as the entire amount of the bill. Medicare sends the doctor 80 percent of the approved charge; patients must pay the remaining 20 percent. Doctors who accept assignment are listed in a U.S. government book entitled *The Medicare Participating Physician/Supplier Directory.* Medicare carriers, the Social Security office, area agencies on aging, and many senior citizens' centers have copies.

Many doctors do not like to accept assignment. They feel that Medicare compensates them such so poorly that it is hardly worthwhile to treat Medicare patients. However, it can be advantageous to patients to find doctors who accept assignment, as seeing such doctors can save patients money, and it probably cuts down on paperwork. Even doctors who do not normally accept assignment make exceptions in individual cases.

In 1992 the government began a new system of paying doctors and other health professionals. It establishes a fee schedule that specifies the amount a doctor can charge for any diagnostic procedure or treatment. Doctors who do not accept assignment can charge a fee greater than Medicare allows for their services. This is called *balance billing.* Under federal law, a doctor can levy an excess charge up to a maximum of 15 percent of the amount Medicare allows for a service. (Some states have a lower maximum or forbid balance billing altogether.) Let us say that an internist sends a bill for $1,100 and Medicare allows $1,000 for the treatment. Assuming that the deductible had been paid, Medicare would pay $800 for the treatment (80 percent of $1,000) and the patient would pay the $200 coinsurance plus the physician's excess charge of $100, which is less than the $150 maximum (15 percent of $1,000) that could be charged under Medicare law. Whether a doctor accepts assignment or not, it is his or her responsibility to bill Medicare directly for services rendered.

Table 19.2 summarizes the services covered under Part B of Medicare.

Health Maintenance Organizations

Medicare gives seniors the option of joining what it calls "coordinated care plans," health maintenance organizations (HMOs) or similar

TABLE 19.2. Medicare Part B: Medical Insurance—Covered Services per Calendar Year

Services	Benefit	Medicare Pays[1]	You Pay
Medical expense Physicians' services, inpatient and outpatient medical and surgical services and supplies, physical and speech therapy, diagnostic tests, durable medical equipment, etc.	Medicare pays for medical services in or out of the hospital.	80% of approved amount (after $100 deductible)	$100 deductible plus 20% of approved amount (plus excess charges up to 15% of approved amount)
Clinical laboratory services	Blood tests, biopsies, urinalysis, etc.	Full cost of services	Nothing for services
Home health care	Medically necessary skilled care, home health aide services, medical supplies, etc.	Full cost of services; 80% of approved amount for durable medical equipment	Nothing for services; 20% of approved amount for durable medical equipment
Outpatient hospital treatment	Unlimited if medically necessary	80% of approved amount (after $100 deductible)	Subject to deductible plus 20% of approved amount
Blood	Blood	80% of approved amount (after $100 deductible and starting with 4th pint)	For first 3 pints plus 20% of approved amount for additional pints (after $100 deductible)

[1] The amounts are for 1993 and subject to change each year.

Source: Health Care Financing Administration.

groups that have contracted with the government to serve Medicare beneficiaries. An HMO provides a comprehensive range of services in return for a fixed monthly fee. Seniors who join an HMO must use its doctors except in emergencies and can see specialists only if a primary physician authorizes it. At an HMO, there are no deductibles and coinsurance payments. The Part B premium goes to the HMO, which may also charge a monthly fee in lieu of deductibles and coinsurance.

Appealing Adverse Medicare Decisions

The little-known secret about Medicare is that over 60 percent of the people who challenge the amount of a Medicare payment by filing an appeal get more money. Anyone whose claim is turned down or who receives less money than he or she is due should not hesitate to file an appeal immediately. There is a six-month time limit. The reason a claim was rejected is noted on the Explanation of Medicare Benefits (EOMB), a form sent by the insurance carrier to describe what happened to the claim.

Anyone who wishes to appeal an adverse decision should take the following steps:

- Write a short letter to the carrier asking that the claim be reviewed, attach it to a copy of the EOMB, and send it to the Medicare carrier whose address is listed in the EOMB. The carrier will assign a person other than the one who reviewed it originally.
- If the claim was turned down for a specific reason or the carrier needs more information, ask the doctor to answer the carrier's questions and explain why the treatment was medically necessary. As in other cases, the doctor can be a patient's strongest ally.
- Medicare provides three additional appeal levels. If the amount in dispute is $100 or more, the patient has a right to a formal hearing with the insurance carrier. If the amount in dispute is at least $500, a dissatisfied patient can appeal to a lower-level court. Finally, if the amount in question is more than $1,000, one has the right to appeal to a U.S. district court.
- Contact one's state or national legislators. A letter of inquiry from a senator, representative, or assemblyman often works wonders.

Reporting Fraud and Abuse

People who are overcharged or billed for services they have never received can fight back. The first step is to get in touch with the source of the problem—which might be a doctor, a hospital administrator, or a supplier of medical equipment—to make sure that an honest mistake has not been made. If this contact does not lead to satisfactory results, a patient may report the matter to the insurance company that handles Medicare claims in the area. Copies, not the originals, of relevant documents such as bills and EOMBs should be enclosed.

The Inspector General of the U.S. Department of Health and Human Services has a Medicare fraud and abuse hotline. One may write to the Inspector General at P.O. Box 17303, Baltimore, Maryland 21203–7303 or call 1 800 368–5779.

MEDICARE SUPPLEMENT (MEDIGAP) INSURANCE

Since there are so many holes in Medicare coverage, two out of three seniors now buy some kind of Medicare supplement (Medigap) policy. These policies pay for deductibles, coinsurance, charges in excess of Medicare's approved amount, and various services and supplies that Medicare does not cover.

The Options

Until recently, Medigap policies were unregulated. As a result, many seniors were victimized by slick salesmen who promised everything and delivered nothing. Then in 1990 the U.S. Congress passed a law that addressed many of the tawdry practices that had characterized the sale of Medigap policies. This legislation ordered the National Association of Insurance Commissioners (NAIC) to come up with ten model policies and required the states to pass laws that make these the only ones that may be sold. The insurance commissioners complied in 1991, and the states have adopted the NAIC guidelines as the law since then.

Under these guidelines, which apply to all Medigap plans except employer-sponsored ones and those sold in Massachusetts, Minnesota, and Wisconsin (which have their own strict laws), each company must offer a core plan that covers many of the basic gaps in Medicare. For hospitalizations, the core plan must cover the daily coinsurance for days sixty-one through ninety and the lifetime reserve days. Moreover, it must cover an additional 365 days after the Part A benefits have been exhausted. For doctors' bills, it must cover the 20 percent coinsurance. For blood transfusions, it must cover the monetary cost of the first three pints of blood.

Beyond this core package, companies may offer up to nine other plans that pay for a variety of services not covered by Medicare. Such plans may cover the deductible for hospital care and doctors' services, skilled nursing care coinsurance, prescription drugs, excess doctors' charges (those above the Medicare will pay), and foreign travel. Table 19.3 summarizes the ten standardized Medicare supplement plans.

The 1990 law provided other types of protection for consumers. It made it illegal for an insurance agent to sell duplicate Medigap policies. Under the law, an agent must get a written statement of the policies customers already own, and customers must state in writing that they plan to drop their current coverage. An agent found in violation faces a fine of upto $25,000 and five years in jail.

The law also prohibited an insurance company from turning people down for a Medigap policy—even if they have preexisting health conditions—if they apply within six months of enrolling in Medicare Part B. Although seniors may not be denied coverage, an insurance company may impose a six-month waiting period before coverage begins for preexisting conditions. However, an insurance company may not require a waiting period for people who are switching from other Medigap policies that they have held for six months or longer.

Ten Tips on Buying a Medigap Policy

Even with the protection provided by federal and state regulations, seniors should exercise caution when buying Medigap policies. The following ten points can guide potential buyers of Medigap policies:

1. Do not change policies unless it is really necessary. Most people do not realize that an insurance agent earns a huge commission on the sale of a new policy—up to 50 percent of the first year's premiums—and a much lower commission on continuations. As a result, agents have a great incentive to sell new policies whether people need them or not.

2. Request an Outline of Coverage and the NAIC/HCFA buyers' guide. The Outline of Coverage is a summary description of what the policy covers and how much it costs. The National Association of Insurance Commissioners and the federal

TABLE 19.3. Medicare Supplement Standards

Ten different policies, labeled A to J, are available under the standards. The core package is included with all options.

	A	B	C	D	E	F	G	H	I	J
Core[1]	◆	◆	◆	◆	◆	◆	◆	◆	◆	◆
Skilled nursing home	—	—	◆	◆	◆	◆	◆	◆	◆	◆
Hospital deductible	—	◆	◆	◆	◆	◆	◆	◆	◆	◆
Doctor deductible	—	—	◆	—	—	◆	—	—	—	◆
Excess doctor charges	—	—	—	—	—	80%	—	100%	—	100%
Foreign travel	—	◆	◆	◆	◆	◆	◆	◆	◆	◆
At-home recovery	—	—	—	◆	—	—	◆	—	◆	◆
Prescription drugs[2]	—	—	—	—	Basic	—	—	—	Basic	Ext.
Preventive screen	—	—	—	—	—	—	◆	—	—	◆

[1] The core package includes payment of the patient's 20% share of coverage for doctors' services; the patient's per-day contribution to hospital bills for the 61st through 90th day; the patient's contribution for blood; and coverage for up to a year in the hospital if Medicare benefits are exhausted.

[2] The basic coverage pays half the cost of prescription drugs up to $1,250 a year after a $250 deductible is met; the extended coverage is the same, except that the upper limit is $3,000.

SOURCE: National Association of Insurance Commissioners.

Health Care Financing Administration publish a booklet entitled *Guide to Health Insurance for People with Medicare.*

3. Do not be pressured into buying. With yearly premiums ranging from $400 to well over $1,000, people need time to think about the purchase of such a policy. High-pressure tactics are the refuge of the desperate.

4. Fill out the application personally or have a friend do it. In the past, unscrupulous agents filled out applications and omitted vital medical information from applications. This practice is illegal, but watch out for it anyway.

5. Be sure to include all the health information requested by the company. Companies may refuse to pay the claims of anyone who lies or omits important information. Honesty can save money and future aggravation.

6. Pay premiums by means of checks made out to the insurance company. Never pay cash. And never make the check payable to the agent. More than one has skipped town with the money.

7. Do not be fooled by companies that imply they are associated with the government or by sales pitches by celebrities. Neither Medicare nor any branch of the government sells or endorses private insurance policies. It is against the law to make such a claim. As for celebrities, remember that they are actors or athletes or whatever, not insurance experts.

8. Take advantage of the "free-look" provision. A buyer has thirty days to look over a Medigap policy. If the buyer is not happy with it, the company must refund the premium. To cancel, one should send a letter and the policy to the insurance company, not the agent, by certified mail, return receipt requested.

9. Check the financial health of the insurance company. As some insurance companies have gone the way of the S&Ls, it is vital to check the financial health of a potential insurer. The companies whose business it is to rate insurers are A. M. Best (1 900 420–0400, $2.50 per minute); Standard and Poor's (212 208–1527); Moody's Investors Service (1 212 553–0377); Duff & Phelps (1 312 368–0377); and Weiss Research (1 800 289–9222, $15 per report). The same information is also available at some public libraries. Buy only from a company that is given a top rating by two of these firms.

10. Remember, Medigap policies do not cover nursing home care, at least not the kind of custodial care that most people mean when they think about nursing homes. To get insurance protection for custodial care, a senior must buy a separate "long-term care insurance" policy.

Where to Turn for Help

Many states have volunteer-run programs to help seniors understand Medicare and Medigap. The state insurance department is the organization to contact for information. Other sources of assistance are area and state agencies on aging, senior citizens' centers, and organizations that help and advocate on behalf of the elderly.

A number of not-for-profit organizations are available to help Medicare beneficiaries. They include the following:

Medicare Beneficiaries Defense Fund
1460 Broadway
New York, NY 10036
1 212 869–3850

Greater Boston Elderly Legal Services
102 Norway Street
Boston, MA 02115
1 617 536–0400

Medicare Advocacy Project
520 South LaFayette Park Place
Los Angeles, CA 90057
1 213 383–4519

Legal Assistance to Medicare Patients
P.O. Box 258
Willimantic, CT 06226
1 203 423–2556

The Center for Health Care Law
519 C Street, NE
Washington, DC 20002
1 202 547–5262

Center for Medicare Advocacy, Inc.
P.O. Box 171
South Windham, CT 06266
1 203 456–7790

Senior Citizens Legal Services
343 Church Street
Santa Cruz, CA 95060
1 408 426–8824

Medicare Advocacy Project
P.O. Box 887

Springfield, VT 05156
1 802 885–5753

Medicare Advocacy Project
606 Minnesota Building
St. Paul, MN 55101
1 612 228–0771

Advocates for Medicare Patients Project of Legal Services for the
Elderly, Inc.
P.O. Box 2723
Augusta, ME 04338
1 207 289–2287

In addition, legal services groups can often help decipher Medicare. The National Senior Citizens' Law Project (1 202 887–5280 or 213 482–3550) or the Legal Counsel for the Elderly Program of the American Association of Retired Persons (1 202 434–2139) can provide the name of a nearby group.

MEDICAID

Every day one out of twenty people over the age of sixty-five wakes up in a nursing home. Of those over eighty-five, the number rises to one out of five. A study published in the *New England Journal of Medicine* indicated that nearly half of all people who are sixty-five will spend at least some time in a nursing home, and a quarter will spend more than a year.

Medicare does not cover custodial care in a nursing home. However, Medicaid does. Medicaid is a health program for the poor that is funded by both the federal and state governments. National policy is set by Congress, but the program is administered by the states. Once a person becomes sufficiently impoverished, Medicaid can pick up the costs of nursing home care. The bills of six out of ten people in nursing homes are paid by Medicaid.

Married Couples and Medicaid

For a person in a nursing home to qualify for Medicaid, his or her assets (house, bank accounts, and stocks) and income (retirement benefits, interest, and dividends) must fall below a certain level, which is set by the states. This level is very low, a few thousand dollars or less. In the past, with nursing homes charges running up to $50,000 annually, many couples quickly ran through their life savings and sank into poverty.

Changes in the Medicaid law that went into effect in 1989 give married couples some protection. When calculating their assets, they may exclude the value of their home plus some other items, the most important of which are a car, wedding and engagement rings, and household goods. They may also exclude half their savings up to a maximum level set by the states, ranging from $14,000 to $67,000 (it rises every year). As a practical matter, this means that the spouse who still lives in the community can avoid nearly total impoverishment by keeping the home, some money, and the other items listed above. The rest, with the exception of a small living allowance, goes to pay for nursing home care.

Single People and Medicaid

The law favors married couples. The situation is worse for the 80 percent of Americans who are single or widowed when they enter nursing homes. Unless a single person takes advantage of the legal ways to protect his or her assets, almost all of them will go to the nursing home. This includes a home in most states, unless the plan is for the person to return there. A single person may keep a small monthly allowance and get credit toward payments the nursing home makes for Medicare, other health insurance premiums, and medical expenditures not covered by Medicare or Medicaid. In half the states a nursing home resident can get an allowance, for up to six months, to maintain a home in anticipation of returning there.

Transferring Assets: The Thirty-Month Rule

Under the law, people who give away or sell their assets for less than their fair market value within thirty months of applying for Medicaid are assumed to have done so in order to qualify for the program. Their applications will be denied for a period of time. The length of time that an applicant is excluded from Medicaid depends on the value of the assets transferred and the cost of a nursing home. The government divides the value of the assets transferred by the average monthly cost of a nursing home. The maximum time a Medicaid application can be denied is thirty months.

Protecting Life Savings

Despite the penalty for transfers made within thirty months of applying for Medicaid, there are legal ways to shield assets so that they will go to loved ones rather than a nursing home. Since they involve intricate areas of state and federal law, an individual should consult an attorney who is experienced in estate planning and Medicaid. Among the legal ways to protect assets are the following:

- Take advantage of the transfers that are allowed by law. Parents may give their house to a son or daughter who cared for them there for at least two years prior to admission to a nursing home. An elderly person may give assets to his or her blind or disabled child. A married person may transfer title to a house to his or her spouse.
- Increase the value of a home, the one big asset that is exempt. Seniors can think about paying off a mortgage, adding home improvements, or even buying new homes.
- Give a trustworthy person a durable power of attorney. This allows another person to make financial decisions on behalf of an older person entering a nursing home and can be used to protect the senior's assets.
- Set up a Medicaid trust. By doing this, seniors put their assets into a separate legal entity, called a trust, which is managed by a trustee—perhaps a son or daughter—for their benefit. However, seniors must give up control of the assets in the trust, and it must be irrevocable.
- Get a divorce. This alternative is clearly a last-ditch one. Although in most states a wife must pay the nursing home costs of her husband, an ex-wife has no such obligation.

Finding a Knowledgeable Lawyer

Seniors should first ask friends and family members for recommendations. If they are unable to identify a lawyer who is experienced in Medicaid, the state bar association should be able to help. Seniors should ask for the names of lawyers who are leaders of the elder law section or who specialize in legal problems of the elderly. Advice on finding the right lawyer can be provided by the National Academy of Elder Law Attorneys, 655 N. Alvernon Way, Suite 108, Tucson, Arizona 85711 (1 602 881–4005).

20

Health Care Options for the Elderly

•

MONIKA WHITE AND DOTTIE THOMAS CEBULA

Other chapters in this book discuss health care insurance issues and options for older adults related to Medicare, Medicaid, Medigap, and long-term care. This chapter describes managed health care mechanisms with an emphasis on health maintenance organizations (HMOs) and the Social Health Maintenance Organization (Social HMO), a special demonstration program that was funded by the federal government.

BACKGROUND

Once an individual reaches the age of sixty-five, Medicare becomes the predominant type of health insurance. Most other types of insurance now incorporate or "wrap around" Medicare, including Medigap, retirement, and managed care plans. For instance, HMO membership, among the fastest growing health care mechanisms for the elderly, can be financed through Medicare. Acceptance of Medicare assignment by other managed care plans such as hospital-based group programs and independent physician associations (IPAs) is also on the rise. For some, of course, fee-for-service health care continues to be a preference because it allows for the most individual choice of provider.

Health Care Utilization and Costs

The majority of elderly people are well and independent and lead active, quality lives. Contrary to popular belief, more than 50 percent

of adults over eighty live independently and care for themselves totally (Institute of Medicine 1991). But those older adults who need
health care utilize considerably more services than younger people.
They average eight physician visits per year versus five for the general
population, three times as many hospital admissions, and twice the
prescription drug consumption (Persily and Albury 1991). According
to Densen (1991), 84 percent of the elderly saw a physician and 26
percent were in a hospital at least one time during 1986.

Over the past decade, health care costs for the elderly have
increased dramatically. In 1977 costs totalled $45.2 billion ($1,856
per capita). By 1987 costs for the care of older adults rose to $162
billion ($5,360 per capita). The 1987 Medicare costs alone amounted
to $75 billion, and this figure is expected to double by the year
2020. It is estimated that Medicare costs will reach $79 billion by
the end of 1993 for nearly thirty-two million recipients (Friedland
1990). Individuals paid $2,394 for health care in 1988 compared
to $966 in 1980; this amount is expected to triple in the next ten
years (Institute of Medicine 1991; Schneider and Guralnik 1990). Figures 20.1 and 20.2 reflect health care expenditures and how they are
financed.

FIGURE 20.1. Health Care Expenditures

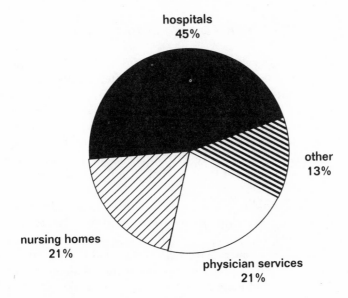

1984 data from Institute of Medicine, 1991:7.

FIGURE 20.2. Health Care Financing

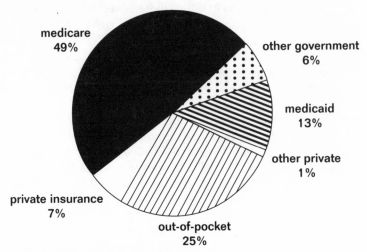

1984 data from Institute of Medicine, 1991:7.

The demographics and economics described above demonstrate that health care for the elderly is likely to be a major issue in the future. Adequate access to medical care is already a significant problem for almost thirty-three million Americans of all ages who are unable to find affordable health insurance (Todd et al. 1991:2503).

The Shift from Acute to Chronic Care

Discussion about health care and the elderly will inevitably shift from acute to chronic illness. Chronic illnesses are often accompanied by or result in intermittent or ongoing problems with daily activities such as dressing, bathing, shopping, cooking, or transferring—e.g., from bed to a chair or from a wheelchair to the toilet (American Hospital Association 1982). It is estimated that more than half of those over sixty-five have difficulty with at least one such task. Table 20.1 illustrates the 10 most common chronic conditions among the elderly.

According to T. Franklin Williams, M.D. (1991), former director of the National Institute on Aging, the medical conditions that are most likely to affect disabled people eighty-five and over are dementia, arthritis, and vascular disease. With the exception of those who meet Medicaid income requirements, the custodial, nonmedical services needed to care for individuals with these conditions do not fit the eligibility criteria of most types of acute care insurance coverage.

FIGURE 20.3. The Ten Most Common Chronic Conditions in the Elderly

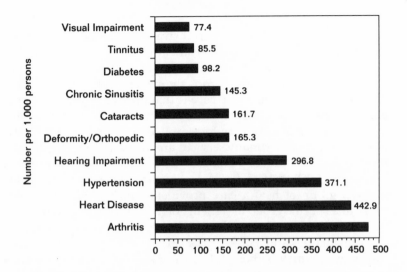

1987 data from Persily and Albury, 1991:18.

A number of recommendations are being proposed that combine acute and long-term care benefits, but to date only the Social Health Maintenance Organization (S/HMO) developed by Brandeis University and San Francisco's On Lok program have been implemented. In these programs a broad range of medical, health, social services, and long-term care services are provided under a capitated financing system involving both Medicare and Medicaid. No private pay system is yet in place.

The Clinton administration is proposing major changes in health care delivery systems, including the development of *health alliances,* groups of doctors and hospitals that would be formed to provide benefits through a number of health plans. President Clinton would like all Americans to join one of these health plans, which would be financed through a combination of payroll costs and employee contributions. Coverage for the elderly is expected to incorporate home and community-based care as well as nursing home and hospice benefits. Members of the administration are advocating that Medicare remain intact and that the elderly be able to switch to health alliance plans if they wish to do so (Older Americans' Report 1993). In the face of great debate and controversy, any new health care programs are expected to be phased in slowly, with a definite emphasis on managed care.

MANAGED CARE

Managed care is a term for the overall strategy to reduce health care-costs for employers, insurers, government, and consumers by directing consumers to the most cost-effective medical care. In managed care plans, risk is transferred from the payer to the provider. The most common form of managed care is that provided by health maintenance organizations (HMOs). HMOs are responsible for providing inpatient and ambulatory care for enrollees at a fixed monthly premium regardless of how many services are utilized (Jonas 1992).

Another major form of managed care is the preferred provider organization (PPO). *Preferred provider organization* is the term used to describe a group of health care providers who provide discounted services to a specific group of patients on a fee-for-service rather than a prepaid basis. Therefore, unlike an HMO, a PPO is not at financial risk for high utilization of services. PPOs vary according to their sponsors, which may be hospitals, insurers, groups of physicians, or others (Gabel and Ermann 1985).

The movement to managed care stems from employers' insistence on offering "triple-option" insurance plans including several indemnity plans, HMOs, PPOs, and fee-for-service plans (Youkstetter 1990:2268). When such plans are offered through one insurance group, cost savings can be realized (Health Resources Information Services 1987:3). The managed care approach is being encouraged by the Health Care Financing Administration (HCFA) for Medicaid recipients. HCFA is offering waivers to states to test greater access to medical care without greater costs (AHA, Hospitals 1991).

Health Maintenance Organizations

In an HMO, delivery and financing of care are integrated. Care is given to an enrolled population through specified providers who are organized for this purpose. Payments are made to the HMO prior to service utilization, thus establishing a budget from which to draw as needed. This mechanism provides an incentive for the efficient use of these resources (Gold 1991:289). In order to receive benefits, enrollees must receive services from the specified providers who have agreed to discounted fees that are not to exceed a predetermined amount. Unlike the more traditional indemnity insurance plan under which the enrollee is usually responsible for the difference between what the insurance company pays and what the provider charges (most often

20 percent), the HMO charges each enrollee a nominal co-payment (commonly five or ten dollars) for physician visits or medications (Youkstetter 1990).

HMOs are based on early models of prepaid health plans created in the 1920s and 1930s for specific groups of workers. One of the first was developed in the city of Los Angeles, which arranged with Doctors Ross and Loos to provide health services for its workers at a predetermined fixed fee. A few years later, E. F. Kaiser became interested in applying the model for his construction workers and began what was to become the Kaiser Permanente Medical Care Program (Thorpe 1986).

With the passage of the 1983 Federal HMO Act (P.L. 93-222) prepaid group health plans began to be seen as a national alternative to the traditional fee-for-service plans. The term *health maintenance organization*, coined by Dr. Paul Ellwood, was popularized with the passage of this act. HMOs offer a combination of prepaid health care services and health insurance. HMOs were designed to emphasize preventive care, reduce regulation, and maximize consumers' choice. However, the HMO Act was so open and contained so few definitions that it was feared that the costs of HMOs would not be competitive with those of existing health plans, and very few plans were developed. The act has been modified over the years by removing many of the disincentives and clarifying much of the terminology.

There were 236 HMOs in 1980 (Gold 1991), 390 by 1985 (Thorpe 1986), and 550 by 1986 for a 12 percent market share (Health Resources Information 1987). HMOs have gained in popularity and have steadily increased their numbers of enrollees. Membership in HMOs is expected to reach fifty million during the 1990s.

Until the 1980s HMO membership was not an accessible option for Medicare beneficiaries, but now the government is encouraging enrollment. Although only about 5 percent of Medicare beneficiaries were enrolled in HMOs by 1988, the numbers are increasing. In 1990 the percentage had grown to 6.7 percent—nearly 2,140,000 individuals (Williams and Torrens 1993). HMOs must provide all of the services that Medicare offers. Many HMOs also provide additional services and supplies such as routine physicals, eye examinations, prescriptions, hearing aids, prescription eyeglasses, and dental care.

While there are variations in fees, services provided, eligible populations, and staffing, HMOs focus on preventive care, health promotion, and health maintenance while controlling costs. Coe (1987:315), utilizing a description by H. Luft of four components shared by all HMOs, characterizes them as organizations that (1) assume a contractual responsibility to provide a specified range of services, (2) serve a defined population of subscribers (consumers) who are voluntarily enrolled in the program, (3) require a fixed payment in advance independent of use of services, and (4) assume part of the financial risk of providing services to subscribers.

The notion that consumers have choices about health insurance presumes that they have enough information to make informed decisions about which plans would provide high-quality care at moderate costs. This notion also assumes that the primary issue for the U.S. health care system is cost containment; thus, competition is needed to hold down costs. Consumers are not always well enough informed to make sound decisions about purchasing health care plans or to determine reasonable costs. In reality, physicians play a major role in decisions about health care resource allocation (Jonas 1986).

Types of HMOs

There are three basic types of HMOs. In a staff/group plan, physicians are employed by the HMO to provide health care exclusively to plan members. The physician, as an employee of the HMO, receives either a salary or a fixed fee per patient seen or per unit of time (known as *capitation*). In a closed panel, physicians own the HMO or are paid under capitated rates and provide services to members on a contractual basis. The physicians may also see many patients from other HMOs. In an individual/independent practice association (IPA), physicians see HMO members as well as non-HMO patients in their own private or group speciality practices. The physicians may be paid on a prepaid fee or a capitation basis. An HMO may also contract with multiple physician groups (Thorpe 1986; Feldman et al. 1990). When contracts involve several provider groups, the relationship is sometimes referred to as a network model (Gold 1991:289).

Most plans serving the elderly are Medicare HMOs, which means that they have contractual arrangements with Medicare to provide health care for Medicare beneficiaries who enroll with them. They are essentially the same as other managed care programs that operate on a prepaid, capitated basis and require their enrollees to utilize specified providers (Wolfson and Levin 1991).

Quality of Care in HMOs

Despite numerous studies addressing such factors as costs of care and types of care arrangements, the issues related to quality have yet to be determined because the precise elements that most influence high-quality care are unknown (Thomas and Kelman 1990:91). Although health care spending has been rapidly increasing since the late seventies and is continuing its climb into the nineties, there has been no comparable increase in health outcomes (Institute of Medicine 1991:95).

While studies regarding the quality of care of HMOs versus fee-for-service organizations have shown mixed results, some trends are becoming apparent. Early studies of HMOs showed that they "tend to have proportionately more highly educated physicians and are more likely to use accredited hospitals" (Thorpe 1986:177). Later studies have reached opposing conclusions on whether HMOs underprovide necessary medical services or overprovide (Thorpe 1986). Research on such measures as lost workdays, disability work loss, and length of illness show that HMO enrollees have fewer losses. One study of more than 1950 firms that offered HMO coverage to employees showed that HMOs cost employers 17 percent less than traditional plans (American Hospital Association 1991).

Consumers have voiced concerns about a number of issues related to quality of care. Among them are waiting time for appointments, a perceived lack of access to a broad range of medical specialties, the high turnover of physicians, access to or length of waiting time for elective surgery, marketing practices, and obstacles to disenrollment. Elderly consumers especially have complained of incomplete information or misinformation regarding Medicare when joining HMOs.

The Future of HMOs

HMOs can no longer be viewed as a passing fad or trend. Medicare benefits are expanding and attracting increasing numbers of seniors. According to one report on Medicare HMOs, the trend toward enrollment in HMOs by seniors will continue because of several factors: enrollees pay no premiums, no additional supplements are necessary, benefits increasingly include drug coverage, no underwriting or screenings are required, enrollees can switch to other plans if desired, and paperwork is greatly reduced (Coile 1992:2). Thorpe and associates say that HMOs "have become mainstream health care, no longer an experimental alternative" (1986:179). Futurist Kenneth Abramowitz predicts that "HMOs are the future. . . . HMOs are the equivalent of putting the country on a budget. . . . America will come to its senses and realize that it has no choice but to accept budgeted health care" (Anderson 1991:41).

HMOs are a small but growing component of the health insurance market. In order for them to remain competitive they will need to adequately address consumers' and employers' costs, cost-containment policies, and quality-of-care issues and must serve the range of patients from young to old, rich to poor, and well to sick.

SOCIAL HEALTH MAINTENANCE ORGANIZATIONS

The Social Health Maintenance Organization, known as a Social HMO, was a demonstration program that was originally funded by the federal Health Care Financing Administration (HCFA) in 1980 under Public Law 98-369, section 2355. The model, developed by Brandeis University, is a prepaid health plan under a single organization that provides a full range of acute and long-term care (LTC) services for its elderly members. Socials HMO applicants must meet four eligibility requirements: they must (1) be sixty-five years of age or older, (2) reside within a specified catchment area, (3) have required no institutionalization for at least thirty days prior to applying, and (4) be not already covered under existing Medicare programs such as those for hospice care or end-stage renal disease.

A key component of the Social HMO model is the need for participants who reflect a balance of the well and the at-risk or vulnerable elderly. The avoidance of adverse selection is necessary because Social HMOs are at financial risk. So far, according to Newcomer and Harrington's evaluation research (1990), it appears that adverse selection is not a major problem. In the early phases of the demonstration project it was discovered that provider organizations experienced a dilemma when the reimbursement rates to maintain high-risk clients in their own homes were higher than when these clients were institutionalized. The formula was corrected to remove this disincentive (Greenberg 1985). A major difference between the Social HMO and the traditional HMO is that the Social HMO is paid 100 percent of the fee based on local demographics, while the traditional HMO gets 95 percent (Griffin 1992:8).

Benefits and Services

The Social HMO offers a full range of services and supplies, including acute care hospital and outpatient services, rehabilitation, case management, transportation, drugs, adult day care, home health care, personal care, and inpatient skilled nursing services, which are provided for a limited number of days annually. A case manager assesses a frail or disabled client's needs for services, authorizes payment, and sets up and coordinates the range of services often needed to prevent or delay institutionalization. The case manager continues to monitor the services to ensure quality service delivery and the appropriateness of services in case the needs of a client change.

Social HMOs offer benefits for the eligible frail or disabled elderly up to a fixed annual or lifetime amount. Usually co-payment is required for some or all services. Services are paid for by pooling funds from Medicare, Medicaid, and members' premiums.

The goal of Social HMOs is to maximize the independence of the elderly and provide in-home and community-based services to prevent unnecessary and costly institutionalization. Social HMOs have received Medicare and Medicaid waivers in order to extend services beyond the traditional range of basic Medicare benefits.

Social HMO Demonstration Sites

Since 1985 four organizations have been developing Social HMO model health plans: Seniors Plus, sponsored by the Ebenezer Society and Group Health, Inc., in Minneapolis-St. Paul, Minnesota; Elderplan, sponsored by the Metropolitan Jewish Geriatric Center Inc., in Brooklyn, New York; Seniors Plus II, sponsored by Kaiser Permanente in Portland, Oregon; and the SCAN Health Plan, sponsored by the Senior Care Action Network in Long Beach, California. Full risk was assumed by the sites in 1987 (Griffin 1992:8).

In 1990 the Congressional Omnibus Reconciliation Act [Public Law 100-203, section 4018, and Public Law 101-508, section 4207(b)(4)] provided for the continuation of the four existing Social HMO sites through at least 1995 and for the expansion of the demonstration project to an additional four sites in the near future. The goals of the second generation of Social HMOs include refining marketing strategies and benefits to extend access to new target populations including elders in rural areas, expanding and developing the role of case management in integrating acute and long-term care services, and refining reimbursement and enrollment mechanisms, including the expansion of Medicaid's involvement (America Health Consultants 1991).

HEALTH CARE IN THE FUTURE

Both the structure and the financing of today's health care system primarily address the acute care needs of younger individuals.

Changes in the current system are essential if the health care needs of the aging baby boomers are to be met. As one researcher has noted,

> There is a pressing need for non-institutional models of care, where appropriate; for integrated programs that offer acute, chronic and social services; for training of skilled gerontological physicians, nurses and other providers; for meaningful health promotion and preventive care for seniors who have been largely ignored by health education; and for a serious commitment to research on the diseases of aging (Friedman 1991:36–37).

Congress is considering several proposals, including recommendations for the reform of Medicaid, Medicare, and long-term care. In 1991 Dr. Louis Sullivan, then-secretary of the U.S. Department of Health and Human Services, outlined the reforms needed: more equity of premium rates between small and large businesses, tax credits so individuals with modest incomes can buy insurance, and methods to discourage employer-paid, high-cost benefits, such as taxing health insurance premiums above a predetermined amount as income to the employee (Dunkin 1991).

The American Medical Association (AMA) proposes that Medicare be prefunded beyond its payout amount so that investment income can be generated, thus decreasing taxes for this purpose. The AMA also suggests that during individuals' working years a combination of employees' and employers' tax contributions be made to a catastrophic plan that would enable age-eligible individuals to purchase comprehensive health insurance policies through a voucher system. Others suggest that all full-time employees and their families should be covered by health insurance through their employers and that this can be accomplished by creating tax incentives and risk pools that would enable small businesses to participate (Todd et al. 1991:2505). Others, like Coile, predict that "a comprehensive continuum of benefits and services will come to dominate the industry" (1987:14). Many proposals incorporate recommendations for managed care models that would coordinate financing as well as services.

Research is needed to better understand a number of issues: public and private sector health insurance arrangements and the problems faced by those who are underinsured, overinsured, or uninsured; the relationship between finances, health care access, and health status; and how types of care and services are shaped by both financing and regulations (Institute of Medicine 1991). Schneider and Guralnik warn that cost containment strategies will not impact future health care financing given the increase in the number of elderly people and the projected numbers of people and costs associated with such diseases as Alzheimer's. A better way to decrease costs would be to approach today's diseases as polio and tuberculosis were approached in the past—with support for research, prevention, and cure (1990:2340).

Health care programs and insurance policies are complicated. Older consumers are often confused about what coverage they have or whether to change to an HMO program. Assistance is available to help older people analyze programs and select the appropriate ones or to obtain information. Many states have the Medicare Advocacy Program (MAP), which furnishes information about Medicare and HMOs. Most area agencies on aging can help older people locate insurance counseling programs for the elderly, and many hospitals have special personnel who assist patients with insurance matters. The American Association for Retired Persons (AARP) and the National Council on Aging (NCOA) also have useful materials available.

Health care for the elderly requires major restructuring given the current and projected growth of the population and their needs. The challenge is to design a system that encompasses preventive, acute, home, and community services, both short- and long-term, into an affordable, accessible whole to serve today's elderly and future generations of the elderly. As noted by Dr. Fernando Torres-Gil, who was appointed Assistant Secretary of Aging in 1993 under the Clinton administration, "Long term care needs to be defined better and must be offered as a continuum of care that provides people the choices to draw on institutional care, whether hospital, nursing facilities or hospice, as well as home and community-based care. It must include housing, transportation, rehabilitation and other social and supportive services (*Older Americans' Report* 1993).

REFERENCES

America Health Consultants. 1991. "SHMOs Prepare for a New Generation." *Case Management Advisor*, 2:54–60.

American Hospital Association, The Office on Aging and Long-Term Care. 1982. *The Hospital's Role in Caring for the Elderly: Leadership Issues*. Chicago, Ill.: The Hospital Research and Educational Trust.

American Hospital Association. 1991. "Employers' Costs for HMOs below Indemnity Plans: Poll." *AHA News*, 27(33):3.

American Hospital Association. 1991. "State Managed Care Initiatives Spur Medicaid Policy Debates." *Hospitals*, August:46–52.

Anderson, H. J. 1991. "Health Care's Changing Face: The Demographics of the 21st Century." *Hospitals*, April:36–43.

Coe, R. M. 1987. "Health Maintenance Organizations." In G. Maddox, ed., *The Encyclopedia of Aging*. New York: Springer Publishing Company:315–316.

Coile, R. C., Jr. 1987. "Overview: Environmental Forces and Trends." In C. J.

Evashwick and L. J. Weiss, eds., *Managing the Continuum of Care.* Rockville, Md.: Aspen Publishers, Inc.

Coile, R. C., Jr., ed. 1992. "Why Seniors Will Enroll in Medicare HMOs." *HOSPITAL Strategy Report*, 4(6):2.

Densen, P. M. 1991. *Tracing the Elderly through the Health Care System: An Update.* AHCPR Monograph. Washington, D.C.: U.S. Department of Health and Human Services, Public Health Service, Agency for Health Care Policy and Research.

Dunkin, M. W. 1991. "Dr. Louis Sullivan: Daring to Make a Difference." *Arthritis Today*, 5(3):30–35.

Feldman, R., J. Kralewski, J. Shapiro, and H. C. Chan. 1990. "Contracts between Hospitals and Health Maintenance Organizations." *Health Care Management Review*, 15(1):47–60.

Friedland, R. B. 1990. *Facing the Cost of Long Term Care.* Washington, D.C.: Employees Benefit Research Institute.

Friedman, Emily. 1991. "Health Care's Changing Face: The Demographics of the 21st Century. *Hospitals*, April:36–43.

Gabel, J., and D. Ermann. 1985. "Preferred Provider Organizations: Performance, Problems and Promise." Springfield, Md.: National Technical Information Services. Reprint from *Health Affairs*, 4(1).

Gold, M. 1991. "Health Maintenance Organizations: Structure, Performance, and Current Issues for Employee Health Benefits Design." *Journal of Occupational Medicine*, 33(3):288–297.

Greenberg, J. N., W. N. Leutz, and R. Abrahams. 1985. "The National Social Health Maintenance Organization Demonstration." *The Journal of Ambulatory Care Management*, 8(4):32–61.

Griffin, A. 1992. Hospitals and Long-Term Care Financing. Unpublished monograph. Pasadena, Calif. Huntington Memorial Hospital, Senior Care Network.

Health Resources Information. 1987. *The Many Faces of Managed Care.* Wall Township, N.J.: American Business Publishing.

Institute of Medicine. 1991. *Extending Life, Enhancing Life: A National Research Agenda on Aging.* Washington, D.C.: National Academy Press.

Jonas, S., ed. 1986. *Health Dare Delivery in the United States*, 3rd ed. New York: Springer Publishing Company, Inc.

Jonas, S. 1992. *Introduction to the U.S. Health Care System.* New York: Springer Publishing Company.

Kongstvedt, P. R., ed. 1989. The Managed Health Care Handbook. Rockville, Md.: Aspen Publishers, Inc.

Newcomer, R., C. Harrington, and A. Friedlob. 1990. Awareness and Enrollment in the Social/HMO. *The Gerontologist*, 30:86–94.

Older Americans' Report. 1993. *Older Americans' Report*, 17(24):185.

Persily, N. A., and S. R. Albury. 1991. "The Growing Elderly Population and Health Care Utilization." In Persily, N. A. (ed), *Eldercare: Positioning Your Hospital for the Future.* Chicago, Ill.: American Hospital Publishing, Inc., 11–32.

Schneider, E. L., and J. M. Guralnik. 1990. "The Aging of America: Impact on Health Care Costs." *Journal of the American Medical Association*, 263(17):2335–2340.

Thomas, C., and H. R. Kelman. 1990. "Health Services Use among the Elderly under Alternative Health Service Delivery Systems." *Journal of Community Health*, 15(2):77–92.

Thorpe, K. W., J. L. Thorpe, and N. Barhydt-Wezenaar. 1986. "Health Maintenance Organizations." In S. Jonas et al., *Health Care Delivery in the United States*, 3rd ed. New York: Springer Publishing Company, 166–182.

Todd, J. S., et al. 1991. "Health Access America: Strengthening the U.S. Health Care System." *Journal of the American Medical Association*, 265(19):2503–2506.

Williams, S. J., and P. R. Torrens. 1993. *Introduction to Health Services.* Albany, N.Y.: Del Mar Publishers.

Williams, T. F. 1991. "Caring for an Aging Population." Keynote address, 1991 Series, Critical Issues for HMO Medical Directors, Part II, Cambridge, Mass., July 24–26.

Wolfson, J., and P. J. Levin. 1991. "Financing for Eldercare Health Services." In N. A. Persily, ed., *Eldercare: Positioning Your Hospital for the Future.* Chicago, Ill.: American Hospital Publishing, Inc., 115–154.

Youkstetter, W. D. 1990. Health-Insurance Products and Plan Options. *American Journal of Hospital Pharmacy,* 47 (October):2265–2269.

21

Private Long-Term Care Insurance

●

LAWRENCE J. KIRSCH

The nearly two million long-term care insurance (LTCI) policies that have been sold to date by private insurers are designed to provide financial protection against the potentially catastrophic expenses of nursing home care, home care, and certain other noninstitutional services.[1] Current estimates suggest that 22 percent of people sixty-five and older will incur at least $50,000 (1989 dollars) in nursing home and at-home care expenses during their remaining lifetimes (M. Cohen et al. 1991). The full weight of this burden can be appreciated if one considers that, in 1988, 38 percent of all people in this age group (and 52 percent of all women) had net worths of less than $50,000. Based on current experience, actuary Stephen Goss has calculated that a woman with $50,000 of assets at age sixty-five currently stands a 25 percent chance of spending at least the same amount on out-of-pocket nursing home expenses during her remaining lifetime (Goss 1990).

The amount of money insurers will ultimately pay out in long-term care benefits is still very much in question, mostly due to inconsistent forecasts of future long-term care utilization. Current statistics suggest that, while half of the population now turning sixty-five will probably never enter a nursing home, 15 percent will be light users (i.e., utilizing sixty days or less of such care throughout their lifetimes), and the remaining third will have moderate to long stays. At current rates, more than a fifth of all persons turning sixty-five will ultimately reside in a nursing home for one year or more. Approximately 16 percent will utilize 365 or more home care visits during their remaining lifetimes (Polniaszek and Firman 1991).

But these statistics may change. Experts concede that evolving definitions of disability and changing patterns of long-term care delivery, altered economic conditions, increased longevity, and different attitudes toward family caregiving might well influence future levels of long-term care utilization and resulting insurance payouts.

Although a handful of insurers began to offer LTCI in the 1970s, the market did not really become significant until the middle of the following decade. The first generation of policies was widely criticized for high cost, limited benefits, and overly restrictive conditions. Newer products on the market tend to provide a more comprehensive range and level of benefits and less onerous conditions of use. While these improvements undoubtedly decrease the risk that a person who uses nursing or home health services will file an insurance claim that is denied, they fall far short of eliminating that risk altogether.[2]

Some consumer organizations, including Consumers Union, Public Citizen Health Research Group, and United Seniors Health Cooperative, have developed criteria they believe would make for more useful LTCI coverage. Among other things, they advise potential purchasers to look for policies that (1) offer nursing home benefits and a range of home care benefits, (2) provide protection against catastrophic levels of long-term care expense, (3) offer the best possible hedge against the erosion of coverage due to inflation, (4) minimize artificial barriers to the receipt of benefits, (5) provide nonforfeiture benefits to safeguard the equity policyholders have accumulated in their LTCI policies, and (6) have defined upper limits on periodic premium increases (*Consumers Reports* 1991; Public Citizen Health Research Group 1991; USHC 1991). If policies with these features were readily available, consumer analysts might be more enthusiastic about the value of private long-term care insurance. Because they are not, a substantial number of analysts still advise consumers to exercise extreme caution.[3]

THE FUNDAMENTAL PROBLEM OF RISK IN LONG-TERM CARE INSURANCE

Long-term care insurance is still too risky to be attractive to the vast majority of consumers. To gain general policyholder acceptance, future policies will have to provide more adequate and predictable coverage and greater stability of premiums. Right now a basic question in the long-term care insurance market right is this: just how much predictability do consumers feel they need, how much will they be willing to pay for it, and, conversely, how much risk are insurance companies prepared to assume for themselves? If a satisfactory balance is not reached on this crucial question of how the risks of long-term care expense are to be distributed between consumers and insurers, the outlook for LTCI is apt to be very bleak.

Currently one of the most promising vehicle for arriving at a consensus on this crucial issue is the LTCI Consumer Protection Bill (H.R. 438) introduced by Representative Ron Wyden in 1993. A Senate bill cosponsored by Senators Kennedy and Hatch, S. 2141, takes a slightly different approach to resolving these problems but represents another viable vehicle.

In this chapter we will consider just why it is that the distribution of risk is so problematical in the market for long-term care insurance. We will then propose some criteria that consumers, insurers, regulators, and legislators might consider in the coming dialog over how a reasonable balance might be struck between competing needs. We will also explore how pending federal legislation addresses these issues.

Why Is Long-Term Care Insurance So Risky?

Time is perhaps the most important source of risk in the market for long-term care insurance. Over time, economic, political, and technological conditions change, as do social values and attitudes. For the insurance company, the job of predicting what impact all of these factors will have on the use and price of long-term care is fraught with great uncertainty. Considering that the majority of people who buy individual LTCI policies this year and ultimately go on to use them will not submit their first claims for at least ten or fifteen years to come, insurers face a long time horizon.

Unlike standard health or Medicare supplement insurance programs (which are basically priced on a pay-as-you-go basis), LTCI is heavily prefunded. Today's premiums are set and reserved to meet claims that the insurer expects to receive in the reasonably distant future. If private insurers could predict future patterns and costs of long-term care with greater certitude or if they could limit their risk by writing gap-filling coverage rather than first-line protection, perhaps the long time horizon might not be quite so daunting.

Insurers legitimately worry about miscalculating future costs. Because long-term care insurance is still so new, actuarial cost experience is still incomplete. The insurance company's prime concern is that the particular group of policyholders it enrolls today may ultimately need more costly long-term care services than it has provided for in its premium calculations.[4] Since a miscalculation of this sort may not become apparent to the insurer for a long period of time, companies genuinely fear that such financial errors may compound themselves.

In view of these concerns, many long-term care insurers are apt to adopt defensive strategies in such core areas as underwriting, policy design, and pricing. This fact has important implications for consumers. It means that insurers will tend to use medical testing or questionnaires and age restrictions to safeguard themselves against enrolling individuals they perceive to be at high risk; they will want to control their financial liability by putting an upper limit on annual or lifetime payments to individual policyholders, by restricting the scope of benefits offered, and by using various gatekeeping mechanisms and coverage limitations to deter the use of what they define as *ineligible* services; and they will be disinclined to fully index insurance benefits to keep pace with inflation or to return to disenrolling policyholders the full amount of their built-up equity, or to cap premium increases.

Time is also a major risk factor for policyholders. Whereas the insurance company is concerned about having underpriced its product, consumers' principal worries are that the insurer will raise future premiums to an unaffordable level or fail to pay claims or that inflation will erode their insurance protection.

Once policyholders have been issued coverage, it becomes more costly and difficult for them to withdraw. Consumers who wish to surrender their insurance outright or to switch to another (say, less costly) insurance policy face two potentially costly deterrents.

First, they may expose themselves to the risk of foregoing coverage, either temporarily or on a permanent basis. This could happen if their chosen (successor) company imposed new waiting periods or precluded coverage for preexisting illnesses.[5] Since the likelihood of developing a preexisting illness increases with age, this type of risk is not unimportant (Liu et. al. 1990).

Second, if the policyholder discontinued coverage (or allowed the policy to "lapse" in insurance parlance), he or she would generally forfeit all built-up equity in the policy. A person who purchased a typical policy at age seventy-five and has held it for ten years may have built up $12,000 to $14,000 in cash value—all of which would be relinquished if the policyholder discontinued coverage at age eighty-five (Shikles 1990). The NAIC has been attempting to address this issue for several years (Ad Hoc Actuarial Group 1992A). In that forum, insurers and consumers have been divided over the need for a mandatory nonforfeiture benefit as well as the design of such a benefit.

These examples show that buyers and sellers of LTCI are both subject to significant amounts of risk, financial and otherwise. In the worst case, these risks could lead to insolvency for insurers and to the loss of expected insurance coverage, built-up equity, and free choice of insurance products for policyholders.

How Is LTCI Risk Distributed between Insurers and Consumers?

If buyers or sellers of LTCI think that the level of risk is excessive or the distribution between the two parties is inequitable, it is not likely that a durable market relationship can exist. The LTCI Consumer Protection legislation introduced by Representative Wyden attempts to address both aspects of the risk problem by reallocating certain burdens between insurers and consumers in a more rational and equitable way and by creating indirect incentives for risk reduction.

The Wyden bill addresses five fundamental areas of consumer uncertainty: (1) adequacy of coverage, (2) affordability, (3) accumulated equity, (4) settlement of claims, and (5) continuity of benefits. Table 21.1 summarizes the consumer risks addressed in this bill and indicates how each is distributed in LTCI policies that conform to the minimum standards adopted by the National Association of Insurance Commissioners in December 1991.

In two of the five areas indicated in Table 21.1, the policyholder alone is at risk. In a third area, continuity of coverage, insurers are generally at risk. And in the remaining areas, claims administration and adequacy of coverage, the risks would be shared between the parties.

One way to analyze this distribution is to test each risk against prevailing *standards of fairness* applicable to personal insurance transactions. Three standards are appropriate to this analysis.

The first may be called the standard of *knowledge*. It holds that, if a risk is known to one party but not the other, the party with superior knowledge should be the risk bearer. The effect of this standard is to create an incentive for the most knowledgeable party to mitigate risk. Actions taken by the party with superior knowledge in order to balance the scales, e.g., disclosure, consumer counseling, or education, may or may not be an effective form of risk mitigation.[6]

The second is the standard of *control*. It is governed by the principle that risks should be borne by the parties in proportion to their

TABLE 21.1. Risk and Risk Allocation in the LTCI Market

Risk to Policyholders	*Who Bears Risk?*
1. Adequacy of Coverage Proportion of actual LTCI costs may erode due to inflation of medical care.	Risks shared. Insurer must offer voluntary inflation protection.
2. Affordability Annual premiums may increase without limit.	Policyholder bears full risk.
3. Accumulated Equity Forfeiture of equity if policy lapses.	Policyholder bears full risk.
4. Claims Settlement Coverage may be affected by changing claims settlement practices.	Shared. Practices may become more restrictive or more liberal.
5. Continuity Added cost, loss of coverage, and/ or additional underwriting may occur if policies are voluntarily switched.	Insurer bears risk. Successor company cannot require new waiting periods, medical underwriting, and other exclusions.

ability to avoid, minimize, or spread their impact. Thus, if one party has the ability to effectively control a risk that the other party would have no option but to accept, the controlling party should bear the complete burden of risk.

The third standard imposes upon the insurer the responsibility to satisfy the *reasonable expectations* of the average policyholder even if they should exceed the insurer's obligations as set forth in the language of the policy itself.[7] Thus, enforcement by the insurer of a particular limitation or policy restriction may be deemed unfair or unconscionable if the typical policyholder has a reasonable expectation that the benefit will be paid (Keeton and Widdis 1988). (This goes beyond the well-known rule that any ambiguity in the language of the policy will be strictly construed against the insurer.)

HOW COULD LTCI RISKS BE DISTRIBUTED FAIRLY?

The remaining pages of this chapter will discuss the provisions of the Wyden bill that bear on the distribution of the five risks already reviewed and will comment on them from a perspective of *fairness*.

Adequacy of Coverage: Inflation Protection

To help keep pace with increasing long-term care charges, the legislation requires insurers to provide mandatory inflation protection. Daily payment levels and maximum annual and/or lifetime benefit limits are to be increased annually by at least 5 percent compounded. While there is no guarantee that a 5 percent compound inflation provision will completely safeguard the future purchasing power of any given policy, it will provide 63 percent more protection than the policyholder would have with a policy without any inflator by the tenth year and 108 percent by the fifteenth year of uninterrupted coverage.[8]

To provide a visual illustration of the relationship between observed increases in long-term care payments and two alternative amounts of inflation protection, figure 1 graphs the annual rate of increase in the average per-diem reimbursement rates (1978–1986)

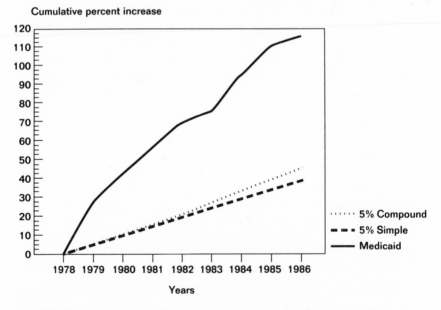

FIGURE 21.1. Cumulative Percent Increase in Medicaid Payment Rates vs. Inflation Protection.

for the services of Medicaid intermediate care facilities (ICFs) versus a 5 percent simple and 5 percent compound rate of increase.[9]

The graph demonstrates that, for all but one year, actual rates of increase exceeded the 5 percent inflator; it also indicates that the cumulative increase in ICF per-diem rates was 114 percent as compared with 40 percent for the simple 5 percent inflation factor and 48 percent for the 5 percent compound inflator.

The Wyden proposal appears to represent a compromise between a mandated, more fully guaranteed approach to inflation protection, such as indexing the inflator to the medical component of the consumer price index (CPI), versus a more voluntary approach, such as requiring that a separate inflation rider be made available to policyholders who wish to purchase one.[10] From a point of view of fairness, since insurers do not seem to have a decisive advantage over consumers with respect to knowledge or control, an inflation protection mechanism that allocates a limited amount of risk to the policyholder would seem to be justified.[11]

A very important unresolved issue is the incremental cost and demand for inflation protection (AARP 1992). Since the added costs of protection will be passed on to consumers through higher premium charges, it is vital to test consumers' opinions of different options. Admittedly, this will be a difficult task to accomplish with reliability. Special care and perhaps unique approaches may be required to obtain good information. In approaching consumers on this matter, it will be crucial to make sure that they understand that without inflation protection the value of coverage purchased today will deteriorate over time. Thus, whatever LTCI policies they may have chosen will be less useful when and if they are ultimately called upon. At the same time, they must realize that inflation protection will make LTCI more costly and may, therefore, increase the burden of keeping their coverage in force when they most need it.

The Affordability of Premium Increases

To increase the affordability and predictability of future premiums, the Wyden proposal follows a Delaware requirement that insurers specify on their policy forms an upper limit on annual rate increases. No maximum ceiling is established in the legislation. Nor, on the other hand, does the bill adopt suggestions that LTCI policies be issued exclusively on a "noncancellable" (i.e., fixed premium) basis for all policyholders or for people over a certain age.[12]

While the Wyden bill offers policyholders a reasonable amount of protection against sharp annual price increases, it stops short of capping premiums over the term of the policy. Hence, under this proposal consumers would have no way of gauging in advance the long-term affordability of coverage.

In September 1992 the NAIC adopted for exposure the proposal of a 5 percent annual cap on premium increases without any lifetime limits. Consumers' groups favored a 5 percent annual ceiling coupled with a 50 percent lifetime limitation. In general, insurance companies opposed rate limitations, annual or lifetime, on the grounds that long-term cost estimating is still too precarious (NAIC 1992).[13] It is quite possible that the NAIC exposure draft will be modified before it is adopted in final form.

In summary, the Wyden bill incorporates one of a number of mechanisms for enhancing premium predictability and affordability by shifting some portion of the risk now borne by policyholders to insurers. In general, a sharing of risk would seem to be consistent with the fairness criteria specified earlier. Insurers do not have full knowledge of long-term utilization trends, and they are exposed to unpredictable external factors such as new legislative requirements.[14] At the same time, they have superior knowledge and more control than consumers over other rate-related risk factors. Precisely how this set of risks should be divided is far from clear. Nor is it clear just how willing consumers will be to pay for the added certainty of an annual cap or some other measure.

Nonforfeiture of Accumulated Equity

To protect policyholders who may discontinue their LTCI coverage at some point against the outright loss of built-up equity, the Wyden bill requires that carriers continue to pay benefits at a reduced level or to offer policyholders some other prescribed form of compensation. The task of fleshing out the details of this provision is left up to a standards-setting body, most likely the National Association of Insurance Commissioners.

Many analysts believe that a substantial proportion of policyholders will discontinue their coverage and that the incremental cost of providing any of several reasonable forms of nonforfeiture benefits will therefore be quite high. In a study commissioned by the American Association of Retired Persons (AARP), it was estimated that sixty-five out of one hundred people buying LTCI coverage at age sixty-five will voluntarily drop their policies by the time they reach seventy-five (AARP 1992).

To some extent, high lapse rates are induced by insurance companies' actions. Rate increases, the obstruction of voluntary policy upgrades, and churning by insurance agents are among the causal factors. *Churning* is a practice whereby an agent periodically issues new (revised) coverage in order to earn (high) first-year commissions. To the extent that reforms, initiated by insurers themselves or in response to the Wyden bill or similar legislation, get at the root causes of high lapse rates, nonforfeiture protection may ultimately become less expensive.[15]

Since the extra premium cost of indemnifying all lapsing policyholders could make coverage virtually prohibitive for many people, the sounder public policy strategy might be to combine strong preventive and/or corrective measures with mandatory nonforfeiture benefits targeted at policyholders of long duration, say five to seven years or more.[16] In September 1992 the NAIC learned from its ad hoc actuarial group that one type of nonforfeiture, a shortened benefit period policy, could be written for a sixty-five-year-old policyholder holding LTCI (including inflation protection) for five years for just over $1,000 (Ad Hoc Actuarial Committee 1992B).

From a perspective of fairness, the proposal would shift at least some of the risk from policyholders to insurers. In that sense, it would be consistent with the criteria developed before.[17] Whether or not LTCI consumers would wish to support this or similar policy enhancements and their costs is still an open question. But the major consumer organizations involved in LTCI reform have unanimously endorsed the concept of mandatory nonforfeiture protection in the NAIC forum.

Claims Settlement Practices

Insurance companies enjoy considerable discretion with respect to the adjudication of claims. A study by Rice and colleagues has provided the first information available on the quantitative impact of differing claims settlement practices on policyholders' liability (Rice et al. 1991).

The legislative proposal approaches claims settlement in two ways. First, it requires companies to use uniform definitions, terminology, and formatting that will be developed by an independent standards-setting body. This is an important provision that should reduce the bewildering variety of special terms and small-print exclusions that critics have decried for years.

Second, it specifically addresses the tricky problem of eligibility for home care services. At present, companies employ a variety of gatekeeping mechanisms to determine the appropriate use of noninstitutional care. Some require physicians' certification of medical necessity; others use functional impairment measurements. The bill has deemed it most appropriate to use a functional assessment scale (e.g., Activities of Daily Living) as the gatekeeper. While it does not mandate coverage beyond any particular level of impairment, it does require that a uniform measuring device be used.[18] It also provides an appeals process. Over time, this should help remove some of the subjectivity that now plagues the claims' settlement process.

Continuity of Coverage

In states that have not adopted the NAIC standards, a policyholder risks being penalized for switching from one insurer to another or even between policies within the same company. Penalties take various forms, including additional medical underwriting, new waiting periods, preexisting illness exclusions, and higher premiums.

The proposal addresses a number of common contingencies such as the continuation of benefits, conversion from group to individual coverage, replacement of coverage by a new carrier, and upgrading of policies. In each case, the bill works to free up the policyholder and to prohibit unwarranted restraints. Thus, for example, a (successor) insurer issuing a replacement policy would not be allowed to impose new waiting periods or preexisting condition exclusions on a policyholder who has met these conditions under a prior policy. (This mirrors the NAIC model standard.) Although the Wyden proposal may not be comprehensive, it makes it more realistic for consumers to comparison shop and to upgrade or downgrade coverage free of onerous penalties.

CONCLUSION

No matter how they are measured, the risks facing issuers and purchasers of private long-term care insurance are staggering. The prospect of making durable, long-term commitments in an environment as changeable and difficult to foresee as this one requires considerable courage. In the long term it may prove to be impossible, and the risks may overwhelm the market.

While the rules of the game currently in play are imbalanced and in need of reform, it is only fair to recognize that consumer protection could conceivably lead to problems of its own. As insurers take on more of the risks now allocated to consumers, due attention must be paid to pressures on insurers' solvency and safety.

In the long run, perhaps a more viable role for private long-term care insurance would be as a supplemental program analogous to the successful Medigap model, with the public sector bearing a substantial amount of risk. Depending on how the basic federal program was designed, private insurers could offer consumers deeper coverage (e.g., higher benefit limits or lower deductibles) or an expanded range of covered services (Congressional Budget Office 1991). By circumscribing the insurer's risk in this way, it is likely that the policyholder would emerge a winner as well.

NOTES

1. Unlike Medicaid, LTCI does not require individuals to deplete (i.e., spend down) their assets to achieve eligibility. Hence, it has been particularly attractive to persons interested in estate preservation.

2. *Consumer Reports*, for example, concluded a review of LTCI policies with the following sobering statement: "If you find this report leaves you with miserable alternatives, that's because long-term care policies aren't good enough" (*Consumer Reports* 1991). And former North Dakota Insurance Commissioner Earl Pomeroy, an outspoken advocate of market reform, recently surprised the insurance industry and consumers with a pessimistic assessment of the current status of the market. According to Pomeroy there is a fundamental question of fairness in the LTCI market; too many policies are being sold to people who cannot afford to keep up their payments, and too many consumers are destined to get nothing when they are economically driven to drop their coverage (NAIC Long-Term Care Insurance Task Force 1992). Pomeroy referred to a buyer survey which showed that one-third of LTCI purchasers had household incomes of $20,000 or less and a quarter had assets valued at less than $30,000 (HIAA 1992).

3. For several years, the National Association of Insurance Commissioners (NAIC), assisted by a consumer-insurer advisory committee, has been working to develop a set of model minimum LTCI standards for adoption by state legislatures and insurance departments. The NAIC has had mixed results, and the states have been slow to adopt the latest versions of the model legislation. In response, pending federal legislation would set a timetable for the development of comprehensive national LTCI standards and would require states to enact them.

4. The insurer must also forecast the number and the demographics of people who will discontinue their coverage (voluntarily or due to death) before they file for benefits. This is a major problem in the context of LTCI.

5. In states that have adopted the NAIC Long-Term Care Insurance Model Regulation, section 21 would prohibit the imposition of new waiting periods or preexisting illness exclusions to the extent that the new policy was similar to the one it replaced.

6. Adler and Pittle (1984) provide a well-reasoned argument concerning the

limits of consumer education as it relates to issues of uncertainty. This is separable, however, from the question of whether an insurer's failure to disclose a material fact to a policyholder is "unfair or deceptive."

7. *Van Orman v. American Ins. Co.*, 680 F.2d 301, 3rd Cir. 1982.

8. There has been some debate on the issue of compound versus simple rates of increase. The equivalent figures on a noncompounded basis would be 50 percent and 75 percent.

9. The Medicaid data reflect average per diem rate increases for the U.S. as a whole. (Swan 1988).

10. The model LTCI regulation promulgated by the NAIC (as of December 1991) requires that insurers *offer* a minimum level of inflation protection to those policyholders who wish to purchase it.

11. This is not to say that the specific proposal crafted by Representative Wyden is necessarily ideal. For instance, some may feel that a fixed 5 percent inflator puts too much of the burden of risk on the policyholder. Others would argue that a fully indexed (e.g., CPI-based adjustment) is too risky to insurers who face strong consumer pressure for stable premiums. Another of many feasible alternatives would be to require that the annual increase in payments and benefit limits be set at the actual CPI or a given compounded inflation factor, whichever was less.

12. Consumers Union has recommended a fixed premium guarantee for all policyholders, possibly beginning with those over a particular age. United Seniors Health Cooperative recommended a limited guarantee for persons over age seventy-five in its 1991 study (United Seniors Health Cooperative, June 1991). More recently, United Seniors and Consumer Health Advocates have supported a somewhat more complex rate stabilization approach that would kick in when policyholders are at younger ages.

13. Certain insurers have indicated a willingness to consider some type of annual or multiyear premium limit, but have been adamantly opposed to a lifetime cap.

14. In fashioning rate stabilization mechanisms, appropriate recognition must be given to the threat of insurer insolvency. If an insurer has to absorb cost overruns for a protracted period of time, there is a chance that reserves will be depleted. Some carriers may safeguard against this simply by capping their maximum premium increases at a high level; others may see fit to incorporate an additional allowance for reserves in their premiums.

15. Gordon Trapnell, an actuary who has studied LTCI, extensively, believes that widespread, predatory pricing practices lead to high lapse rates. He refers to the deliberate "low-balling" of initial premiums (to make the first sale) which are then followed by substantial rate increases. He argues that such pricing practices should be curbed (NAIC Long Term Care Insurance Task Force 1991). The NAIC is working on this issue.

16. While this strategy would have the obvious disadvantage of exposing some relatively large number of people to the risk that each might lose some rather small amount of accumulated equity, it could have the positive effects of making nonforfeiture benefits less costly and of targeting them to persons who had the most to lose. Wiener and Harris (1991a) make the point that the value of nonforfeiture benefits to short-term policyholders is illusory since they will not have accumulated much equity. Trapnell argues that nonforfeiture benefits should be targeted at younger policyholders who have had coverage for at least five to ten years (NAIC 1991). These and other nonforfeiture options plainly require further analysis—for example, to determine their distributional impact.

17. An insurance industry representative has taken the opposite position, saying, "LTC insurance is designed to protect an estate and should not be designed to

force the transfer of the investment responsibility from the policyholder to the insurer" (Weller 1991).

18. Definitions and measurements of disability vary. Some analysts estimate that more restrictive definitions can reduce the eligibilty for benefits by as much as 41 percent (Wiener and Harris 1991a).

REFERENCES

American Association of Retired Persons (AARP). 1992. *Inflation Protection and Nonforfeiture Benefits in Long-Term Care Insurance Policies: New Data for Decision Making.* Washington, D.C.: AARP, June.

Ad Hoc Actuarial Group, National Association of Insurance Commisioners (NAIC). 1992a. *Final Report on Nonforfeiture Benefits.* NAIC.

Ad Hoc Actuarial Group, National Association of Insurance Commissioners (NAIC). 1992b. *Report on Shortened Benefit Period.* NAIC.

Adler, R., and R. Pittle, 1984. "Cajolery or Command: Are Education Campaigns an Adequate Substitute for Regulation?" *Yale Journal on Regulation,* 1.

Cohen, M. et al. 1991. "Long-Term Care Financing Proposals: Their Costs, Benefits and Impact on Private Insurance." Health Insurance Association of America (HIAA). *Research Bulletin,* January.

Congressional Budget Office. 1991. *Policy Choices for Long-Term Care.* Washington, D.C.: Congressional Budget Office, June.

Goss, S. 1990. "Who Should Buy Long-Term Care Insurance? What Type of Policy Makes Sense?" *Contingencies* 2(4).

"Gotcha! The Traps in Long Term Care Insurance." 1991. *Consumer Reports,* June.

Health Insurance Association of America. 1991. News Release, May 30.

Health Insurance Association of America. 1992. Statement on Who Buys Long-Term Care Insurance: Results of a National Sample. Long Term Care Insurance Task Force, National Association of Insurance Commissioners, March 31.

Keeton, R., and A. Widdis. 1988. *Insurance Law.* St. Paul, Minn: West Publishing.

Liu, K., et al. 1990. "Morbidity, Disability, and Long-Term Care of the Elderly: Implications for Insurance Financing." *The Milbank Quarterly* 68(3).

National Association of Insurance Commissioners, Long Term Care Task Force. 1992. Minutes, Meeting of September 22.

Polniaszek, S., and J. Firman. 1991. *Long-Term Care Insurance: A Professional's Guide to Selecting Policies.* Washington, D.C.: United Seniors Health Cooperative.

Public Citizen Health Research Group. 1991. *Health Letter* 7(12).

Rice, T., et al. 1991. "The Effect of Owning Private Long-Term Care Insurance Policies on Out-of-Pocket Costs." *Health Services Research* 25 (6 February).

Rivlin, A., and J. M. Wiener. 1988. *Caring for the Disabled Elderly: Who Will Pay?* Washington, D.C.: Brookings Institution.

Shikles, J. 1991. Long-Term Care Insurance: Risks to Consumers Should be Reduced. Statement before the Subcommittee on Health, U.S. House Ways and Means Committee, April 11.

Swan, J., et al. 1988. "State Medicaid Reimbursement for Nursing Homes, 1978–86." *Health Care Financing Review,* 9(3).

Trapnell, Gordon. 1991. Presentation to the NAIC Long-Term Care Insurance Task Force, March 13.

United Seniors Health Cooperative (USHC). 1991. *Eight Recommendations for Improving Private Long-Term Care Insurance.* Washington, D.C.: USHC (1991).

Van Gelder, S., and D. Johnson. 1991. "Long-Term Care Insurance: A Market Update." HIAA *Research Bulletin,* January.

Van Orman v. American Ins. Co. 1992. 680 F.2d 301, 3rd Cir. 1982.

Weller, W. Statement of the Health Insurance Association of America on Long-Term Care Insurance Non-Forfeiture Values. Presentation to the NAIC Long-Term Care Task Force, March 13, 1991.

Wiener, J. M., and K. Harris 1991. "High Quality Private Long-Term Care Insurance: Can We Get There From Here?" *Journal of Aging and Social Policy,* 3(3).

Wiener, J. M., and K. Harris "Regulation of Private Long-Term Care Insurance", Statement before the Health Subcommittee, U.S. House Ways and Means Committee, April 11, 1991.

VII
HOUSING AND
ENVIRONMENTS
●

22

Aging in Place or Moving: The Multiple Meanings of Retirees' Housing

●

STEPHEN M. GOLANT

The word "home" simply tells us that any man's personal world has a centre. . . . The centre represents to man what is known in contrast to the unknown and somewhat frightening world around. It is the point where he acquires position as a thinking being in space, the point where he 'lingers' and "lives" in the space.   *(Norberg-Schulz 1971:19)*

In somewhat abstract language, Norberg-Schulz tells us that people's residential accommodations are critical focal points around which they organize their everyday behaviors and experiences. The residential setting has special significance to American retirees. More than a place in which they satisfy their usual shelter and security needs, it is also where they must cope with all their manifestations of growing old, from changes in how they use their time to the difficulties they have doing things and getting around. The dwelling is often the setting in which these milestones are first played out. A fall on the stairs or the physical signs of housing neglect will often alert others to a retiree's vulnerability.

To help them deal with their changing life-styles and capabilities, retirees can select from a variety of housing-related solutions. In so doing they must make a fundamental decision—whether to stay in their current dwellings of many years (i.e., age in place) or move to new locations and perhaps to very different types of accommodations. Many of the factors that they must weigh—such as dwelling and moving costs, dwelling size and design, crime rates, the characteristics of neighbors, the closeness to needed stores and services, and climate—are the concerns of all age groups. Additionally, they must consider the desirability of housing features, locations, and services that have special relevance to their stage in life. Their decision making is complicated, however, because they are often unfamiliar with the options presented to them and have difficulty assessing the suitability and quality of these options and because the alternatives are not consistently available in all localities.

The choices they have made over the past two decades reveal much about what they value most about their residential situations and the challenges they have confronted in realizing them. Even as they have found solutions to their housing problems, they have sometimes also irreversibly and undesirably altered some of the most valued qualities of what they once considered "home."

SOME UNIQUE PERSONAL CONSIDERATIONS

Certain events in retirees' lives often are catalysts for their housing reassessments. Stopping a full-time job may be pivotal because a residence that is accessible to a place of employment is no longer necessary. Rather, the neighborhood and the community are evaluated in terms of how well they accommodate new leisure and recreation activities. Retired men may find that their more frequent presence in the dwelling results in new marital conflicts having to do with their intrusion into the "private" domains and activities of their wives. A loss of regular salary may make it financially stressful to cover the usual costs of upkeep.

When physical or mental disabilities afflict retirees, they may have difficulty performing even the most routine household- and dwelling-related chores. A once acceptable house or apartment design may become inappropriate. When their disabilities are of such severity that they cannot perform even the most basic of life's activities (e.g., eating, bathing, moving in and out of beds or chairs, getting groceries, or managing financial matters), they confront the real threat of having to leave their familiar accommodations.

The changing circumstances of other significant people in their lives may profoundly influence the suitability of their residential situations. A child's move to another state or the death of an especially friendly neighbor may eliminate the social advantages of a long-occupied address. The death or institutionalization of a husband may result in the widow's perceiving her house for the first time as too big—as a lonely and insecure place. She may have to assume an unaccustomed responsibility for its physical upkeep. She may find her new financial situation inadequate to deal with the continually rising costs of utilities (heating and cooling), property taxes, and insurance. A remaining mortgage or a rising rent may constitute an intolerable burden and result in her curtailing expenditures on other consumer goods and services. If she cannot drive and had relied on her husband for automobile transportation, she will be suddenly without a highly flexible form of mobility. The neighborhood is evaluated in a totally new light (Golant 1984).

SOME UNIQUE SOCIETAL RESPONSES

Virtually every sector of society—private (for-profit interests), non-profit (charitable, religious, and fraternal groups and foundations), and public (federal, state, and local governments)—has offered housing solutions that are designed to address these new personal circumstances. Tables 22.1 and 22.2 classify these societal responses according to whether they encourage the retiree to move or to stay put.

Encouraging Residential Moves

The societal responses that encourage residential moves can be divided into four subgroups (table 22.1). Retirees can avail themselves of conventional housing alternatives produced by the private sector that are smaller, easier, and less expensive to maintain (e.g., townhouses, condominiums, and manufactured homes). These more manageable shelter opportunities are also often the mainstay of planned active retirement communities catering exclusively to the leisure behaviors of retirees.

Three types of government programs make it financially attractive for retirees to move. Government-subsidized housing programs offer the lower-income retiree apartment accommodations at more affordable rents than they could otherwise find. Selling a home is made less expensive by a tax code provision that reduces the amount of capital gains tax retirees must pay on profits they realize by selling their homes. A third program facilitates residential moves by lower-income retirees in a somewhat convoluted way. It enables owners of board-and-care homes who cater to a more physically impaired and poorer retiree population to charge affordable monthly rents. Their occupants typically rely on Supplemental Security Income or SSI (a federal program) along with supplemental monthly incomes from their state governments. These income sources, the lifeblood of the board-and-care enterprise, are turned over to its operators.

TABLE 22.1. Societal Responses Encouraging Residential Moves by Retirees Differentiated by Their Usual Level of Independence

Levels of Independence Responses	*Independent*	*Semi-independent*	*Dependent*
Private[a] Shelter Strategies			
Active adult planned retirement communities	X		
Smaller and less demanding conventional dwellings	X		
Townhouses	X		
Condominiums	X		
Manufactured Housing	X		
Apartments	X		
Single-room occupancy hotels	X		
Financial Strategies			
Low-rent government-subsidized rental accommodations	X		
One-time capital gains tax exclusion on home sale	X		
State supplements to recipients of SSI[b] living in board-and-care homes		X	
Household Strategies			
Availability of child's or sibling's residence	X	X	
In spare "bedroom"	X	X	
In accessory apartment or in-law suite	X	X	
In ECHO (elder cottage housing opportunity) or granny unit	X	X	
Residence shared with unrelated housemate	X	X	
Group Shelter Strategies			
Emergency shelter	X		
Congregate housing	X	X	

TABLE 22.1 *(Continued)*

Shared housing or small-group communal living (agency-assisted or -managed)	X	X	
Assisted living or assisted care facilities	X		
Board-and-care or foster care homes		X	
Continuing care retirement community (CCRC)	X	X	X
Nursing home care			X

[a] Refers to whether the dwelling has its own separate entrance and locked door rather than to its organizational auspices.

[b] Supplemental Security Income

Adopting less conventional household arrangements also encourages residential moves by retirees. They can share the dwellings of family members or friends who can accommodate them in a "spare bedroom"; in an accessory apartment or "in-law suite"—a garage, basement, sunroom or other part of an existing house that is architecturally converted to resemble a hotel suite with its own kitchen and bathroom facilities and its own separate entrance; or in an "elder cottage housing opportunity" (ECHO), a very small separate and removable residential building located on the same lot as the single-family dwelling.

The private and nonprofit sectors have developed a variety of group housing options for retirees who are reluctant to live alone or who are having some difficulty preparing their own meals, maintaining their own households, or performing everyday activities. In some of these, retirees are still able to maintain conventional self-contained apartments; in others, they must share their bedrooms and cannot lock their doors. in most, the residents regularly eat at least one of their meals in an on-site central dining room facility or sometimes merely a communal kitchen. They may receive residential services (e.g., housekeeping) and some level of personal assistance and nursing care, but it is short of the intensive skilled care found in nursing homes. The most notable of these variously labeled alternatives are adult congregate housing (Gordon 1988; Streib 1990); shared group (communal) living (Streib, Folts, and Hilker 1984); residential care facilities, including board-and-care, foster care, and assisted liv-

TABLE 22.2. Societal Responses Facilitating the Aging in Place of Retirees Differentiated by Their Usual Level of Independence

Responses	Levels of Independence		
	Independent	*Semi-independent*	*Dependent*
Financial Strategies			
Reverse mortgages (some plans FHA-insured[a])	X		
Sale-leaseback plans	X		
Home equity loans	X		
Mortgage interest and property tax deductions	X		
Property tax relief programs	X		
Rent subsidies linked to current residence	X		
Home energy and weatherization assistance programs	X	X	
Household Strategies			
Family caregiving assistance		X	X
Residence of elderly person shared with housemate	X	X	
Elderly-initiated shared arrangements	X	X	
Agency-assisted shared matches	X	X	
Accessory apartment conversions to accommodate housemate	X	X	
Home-Based Service Strategies			
Home nursing care		X	X
Home personal or custodial (nonmedical) care	X	X	X
Home modification and repair programs	X	X	
Home-delivered meals	X	X	X
Special transportation and escort services	X	X	X
Home monitoring and alert services	X	X	X
Telephone reassurance and friendly visiting programs	X	X	X

TABLE 22.2 *(Continued)*

Personal emergency response systems	X	X	X
Information and referral	X	X	X
Case management		X	X
Life care at home	X	X	X
Community-Based Service Strategies			
Congregate meals in community sites	X	X	
Respite care		X	X
Adult day care		X	X
Senior centers	X	X	
Group Shelter Strategies			
Congregate and personal care for existing residents of government-subsidized rental housing		X	
Assisted living facility in congregate housing facility		X	
Assisted living facility on CCRC[b] campus		X	

[a] Federal Housing Administration

[b] Continuing Care (Life Care) Retirement Community

ing facilities (Eckert, Namazi, and Kahana 1987; Mor, Sherwood, and Gutkin 1986); and continuing care (or life care) retirement communities (Sherwood, Ruchlin, and Sherwood 1990; Tell et al. 1987).

Encouraging Aging in Place

The five categories of aging-in-place strategies illustrate the diverse ways in which retirees can be helped to "stay put" (table 22.2). The financial strategies are designed either to increase the monthly incomes of poor retirees (e.g., reverse mortgages or home equity loans) or to make more affordable the cost of owning or renting a dwelling (e.g., property tax relief or subsidized rent). The household strategies involve the introduction of another person into the retiree's dwelling, such as through the regular visits of a family member or the full-time occupancy of a boarder or live-in helper. These people can assist retirees with their household chores, provide them with personal assistance, offer companionship, and in the case of live-in boarders supply an additional source of income in the form of monthly rent. A number of agencies will match retirees with people unrelated to them—both younger and older—who are willing to share the accommodations of retirees.

TABLE 22.3. The Home as a Setting in Which Formal Care Is Delivered: The Example of Hawaii's Nursing Home without Walls

Tolerated Disabilities and Chronic Conditions	Tolerated Problem Behaviors	Manageable Nursing Needs and Patient Conditions
Inability to:	Refusing to participate in programmed activities	*Nursing Needs:*
Make own bed		2-hour positioning
Clean own room	Refusing to take prescribed medicine	2-person transfer
Feed self		Hoyer lift
Bathe/clean self	Refusing to bathe	Special diet
Help with transfer	Refusing food and drink	Bolus feeding
Get out of bed	Complaining all the time	Suctioning
	Tracheostomy cannula care	
Chronic Conditions:		IV therapy
Incontinence		Oxygen
Confusion		Insulin injections
Depression/crying		Indwelling catheter
		Colostomy/ileostomy care
Patient Conditions:		
Less than 6 months to live		
Aspiration		
Cmatose		

SOURCE: Modified from Braun and Rose 1989.

Home- or community-based care delivered by paid personnel and professionals (formal care) can compensate for virtually every difficulty that retirees confront in their attempt to remain independent in their dwellings. Various organizational strategies have been developed to administer these services and benefits. Assistance can range from the most simple and elementary, such as help with washing dishes, to the most specialized and technologically sophisticated, such as the most skilled nursing. Retirees can potentially receive as much care in their homes as they would in a nursing home. Hawaii's Nursing Home Without Walls (NHWW) program, which was established in 1983, is one example of such a comprehensive home care program (table 22.3). It accommodates retirees with a wide range of disabilities, problem behaviors, and specialized nursing needs (Braun and Rose 1989). On-site services are sometimes also available for retirees who are already living in group housing accommodations that allow them to remain in their current accommodations rather than having to move to even more supportive housing situations.

The Availability of These Options

These retiree-oriented housing and service options are not equally available in all states and their urban and rural localities. Thus, a "good" location in which retirees might live obviously implies much more than an attractive climate or whether everyday goods and services are accessible by foot, car, or public transportation.

Some communities have an adequate supply of government-subsidized low-rent apartment housing units, and their waiting lists are largely nonexistent or extremely short; in other places a wait of one to two years is the norm. Some municipalities have less restrictive neighborhood land-use zoning ordinances that make it easier to introduce shared household and group shelter accommodations or to develop manufactured home subdivisions with their more affordable homes.

Some communities possess more hospitable business climates and present greater opportunities to groups interested in developing retiree housing accommodations. In some localities more than others there are religious, charitable, and civic nonprofit groups, concerned private individuals, and progressively minded corporations and public agencies that have the experience, skills, and adeptness to access and package government funding sources.

Merely characterizing a service or facility as "available" or "unavailable" may also be deceptive. The mere presence of adult day care, home care, congregate housing, or public housing in a locality offers few guarantees that specific accommodations or services will actually be offered. These programmatic labels can be ambiguous (McCaslin and Golant 1990). Adult day care programs, for example, do not all serve retirees with significant mental disabilities (e.g., Weissert et al. 1989). Congregate housing facilities deal differently with retirees who incur needs for personal assistance. State government programs define differently who is eligible for their "low-income" benefits. Even when a locality's housing programs or services are appropriate, retirees may be unable to use them if they do not have the financial means or they encounter a barrage of bureaucratic obstacles and hassles.

An option's presence does not reveal anything meaningful about its quality or effectiveness. Retired consumers are better protected in some states than in others that have statutes and regulatory bodies that define minimum standards of shelter and care in congregate housing facilities, board-and-care homes, and continuing care retirement communities (see chapter 17). Some localities have more comprehensive matching services for home sharing than others (e.g., they continually monitor the success of the sharing arrangements) or more generous property tax abatement programs.

These examples only hint at the extent to which options are not similarly available to all retirees seeking solutions to their current housing difficulties.

HOW HAVE RETIREES REACTED TO THESE OPTIONS?

Retirees have reacted more favorably to those housing-related alternatives that most resemble conventional living arrangements, allow them to remain in their current dwellings, least threaten their independent, private living styles (Wister 1988), and least subject them to out-of-the-ordinary bureaucratic requirements.

When they have moved to less conventional residential settings, it is because they are attracted to these places' overall style of living (as in the case of adult retirement communities), are forced to confront the realities of their personal health or income limitations, lack families or friends from whom they are able or willing to elicit help, or are responding to culturally inspired family traditions (as is the case for retirees with ethnic or racial affiliations who move in with their grown children).

Retirees' desire to stay put appears to be as strong as ever. About two out of every ten persons aged sixty-five and older move (change their address) in any five-year period, down from the 1950s, when almost three out of every ten older people moved (Golant 1990). In 1986 and 1989 the American Association of Retired Persons (AARP) carried out nationwide surveys of older adults (in 1986, those over the age of fifty-nine; in 1989 those over the age of fifty-four). The AARP reported (American Association of Retired Persons 1990:8), "Older Americans are more likely to want to "age in place," with 86% of those surveyed in 1989 wanting to stay in their present home and never move, compared to 78% in 1986."

The Importance of the Familiar

The residential inertia of retirees is partly explained by their desire to live in familiar settings and their unwillingness to confront change in their environments (Golant 1984). They develop strong social attachments and emotional connections to their long-occupied places and are reluctant to disturb established family and friendship networks. These long-term residential associations are the sources of significant memories. Knowing the people, houses, streets, stores, doctors, landmarks, and how to get about increases their feelings of control and competence. Conversely, not having to be preoccupied with learning and adapting to new environments frees them to explore other aspects of their surroundings and life with greater creativity and abandonment. Campbell, Converse, and Rodgers (1976) offer yet another interpretation. They argue that over time older persons progressively accommodate to their residential situations, lower their aspirations, and in so doing less frequently contemplate other housing alternatives.

Economic Considerations

The poor financial situations of many retirees may discourage them from changing addresses. Appropriate rental and homeowner ship options may be too costly, or they may be unable to afford moving their belongings from one place to another. Thus they view the occupancy of a "better" place as an unattainable goal. On the other hand, the improved economic status of other retirees may have allowed them to postpone or avoid residential moves that they otherwise would have made. For example, retired home owners can better cope with their rising property taxes, utility costs, insurance, and home repair costs and renters with their rising rental charges—all these housing items very sensitive to inflationary pressures.

The Importance of Home Ownership

Retirees have especially equated homeownership with private, autonomous, and self-reliant living. Most (over 80 percent) own their homes free and clear and move less frequently than renters. In the 1980s over 75 percent of older households owned their dwellings, up from 70 percent in the 1960s. Among retirees aged sixty-five to seventy-four an even higher 79 percent were owners. This rate significantly drops only after the age of seventy-five, but it still remains high (70 percent). Even when they are cash poor, retired homeowners reluctantly participate in any loan plans that threaten their occupancy rights or their financial control over their dwellings. They often view the equity in their homes as a "last-resort" security blanket. Furthermore, they seek the right to bequeath their homes to their heirs. This helps explain why most retirees express little interest in reverse mortgage plans that, by drawing down their equity in their homes, allow them to receive monthly cash payments over some specified period.

When the upkeep of their current homes has demanded more time, energy, or money than they can afford, retirees have sought out less onerous homeownership alternatives such as townhouses, condominiums, or manufactured homes. As of 1987 about 6 percent of older home owners were occupying manufactured housing (mobile homes), and 5 percent were in condominiums or cooperatives (U.S. Department of Commerce 1990).

Maintaining Conventional Living Arrangements

Whether owners or renters, retirees tenaciously seek to keep their conventional living arrangements. In the 1989 AARP national survey (American Association of Retired Persons 1990) only 17 percent of the respondents indicated that they would ever consider moving in with a family member and only 3 percent responded that they presently were seriously considering this option. The actual living arrangements of older people are consistent with these preferences (U.S. Bureau of the Census 1991). Compared with the 1950s or 1960s a higher percentage of the current (1990) older population is living alone (16 percent of males and 42 percent of females), and a smaller percentage is living with a relative other than a spouse (8 percent of males and 16 percent of females). As Hooyman and Lustbader (1986:253) observe, "[Older people] accustomed to arranging their possessions in the same way for years or who jealously guard their privacy may prefer to endure loneliness or high housing costs rather than accept intrusions on their personal habits."

When their physical and mental vulnerabilities demand that they receive assistance, retirees are initially likely to turn to family and then, but much less frequently, to friends, often only one person is involved: among the married, this is usually the spouse; among those who are not currently married, it is a child, usually a daughter, secondarily a son, and then a friend (Chappell 1991).

Among the old with disabilities that restrict at least one of their everyday activities, about 75 percent depend exclusively on such care-giving, while nearly 90 percent rely at least in part on this informal assistance. Thus, when retirees avail themselves of formal care, it is usually to supplement rather than to replace the help provided by family or friends (Soldo 1985; Soldo, Wolf, and Agree 1990). As much as possible, aging in place is kept a family affair.

Only when retirees are in their later 70s and have more serious debilitating health problems do they demonstrate a greater propensity to live with family other than a spouse. This is especially true for older women. In 1990 17 percent of women aged seventy-five to eighty-four and 28 percent of women eighty-five and over lived with such a relative (U.S. Bureau of the Census 1991). This living arrangement was also more prevalent among blacks and Hispanics because of the importance of family ties to these racial and ethnic groups. In 1988, for example, 31 percent of black women and 34 percent of Hispanic women aged sixty-five and older lived in a household with relatives other than their spouses (U.S. Senate 1989).

Sharing a household with someone unrelated is even less popular, although the number of human service agencies arranging such matches is larger than ever. The incidence of this household arrangement has declined since the 1950s (Mindel 1979), although it became more prevalent during the 1980s. In 1990 only 2.2 percent of people over the age of sixty-five (whether male or female) shared a household with people unrelated to them (U.S. Bureau of the Census 1990). This household arrangement was again more prevalent among blacks and Hispanics, especially women (U.S. Senate 1989).

Postponing Group Housing Occupancy
As Long As Possible

Most retirees delay their entry into group housing until they reach
their late 70s—and older (see table 22.1 and chapters 24 and 25). This
partly explains why retirees over the age of seventy-five have higher
moving rates than those aged sixty-five to seventy-four. It is seldom
merely the presence of other compatible older people that motivates
their selection. Those moving to these accommodations recognize
that they need help (or that they are about to) managing their own
households or preparing their own meals, or they feel insecure about
living alone without supervision. The occupants of group housing
facilities are dominated by unmarried women who either do not have
children to assist them or who prefer not to be a burden on their
children. In the parlance of the private sector, "need" rather than
"life-style preferences" drive these people.

The observation made by Streib, Folts, and Hilker (1984:58) after
studying the familylike communal living arrangements of a well-run,
high-quality shared group housing facility is insightful:

> The majority came because their failing health, increasing frailty,
> or sensory losses made living alone impossible, or because someone
> they had been living with died or became too disabled to care for
> them. They did not come because they shared the "family" ideology
> of the organizers, although some later began to share this ideology,
> or because they had any interest in forging new possibilities in
> human relationships. They came because they had to, and most
> would have preferred to be able to live completely on their own
> again.

Choices of Poor Retirees

The housing options selected by poor retirees undoubtedly speak
more to their income constraints than to their preferences. Most pri-
vate-sector alternatives designed for elderly occupants are simply not
affordable. The poor are especially over-represented in at least two
types of housing. At the end of the 1980s, about 43 percent of federally
assisted low-rent housing units were occupied by older people (U.S.
Congressional Budget Office 1988). Given the long waiting lists for
these accommodations in some communities, these occupancy rates
would probably be even higher if units were available. The poor are
also over-represented in board-and-care group homes. These low-cost

accommodations offer some personal assistance to those elderly people (usually in their late 70s and early 80s) who are dependent on Social Security or Supplemental Security Income.

THE UNIQUE CONSEQUENCES OF THESE HOUSING ALTERNATIVES

Virtually all the options identified in figures 1 and 2 can constitute excellent residential solutions. There are many good examples of caring, family-oriented board-and-care or foster home accommodations. Well-trained and thoughtful staff administer many low-rent housing projects. The high-end continuing care retirement community can offer a resortlike atmosphere that is responsive to independent and dependent residents alike. Living in the home of a married child can be a workable and satisfying experience. Participation in adult day care programs can be therapeutic to the impaired and give relief to family caregivers. A live-in helper can postpone the need for the assistance offered in more supportive group housing accommodations.

As these and other residential alternatives deviate more from the conventional, however, retirees must necessarily accept more restricted life-styles and relinquish some of their autonomy, privacy, or individual rights (Golant 1991, 1992). Parmelee and Lawton (1990:468) go so far as to argue that older people's goals of simultaneously achieving both security and autonomy may be elusive.

The intrusions may be small or subtle. The management of even the best-run and benevolent congregate housing or continuing care retirement facilities must impose rules and regulations that can be construed as inhibiting. They must of necessity closely monitor the physical and mental conditions of their occupants to ensure the appropriateness of their accommodations. Some violation of individual privacy is inevitable. Retirees in even the most attractive senior-citizen low-rent housing projects may find their social situations intolerable because they previously culled their acquaintances and friendships from the nonelderly. If these low-rent projects are also accommodating people who are physically or mentally impaired, the financially deprived but otherwise active resident may find it depressing to continually deal with these frail people.

The loss of autonomy is often more blatant. Retirees may achieve the greater amount of help and security offered by the assisted living facility only by accepting cramped one-room quarters in which their doors can never be locked. Occupants of board-and-care homes may find themselves physically neglected and scorned by an uncaring, indifferent or overworked staff.

Physically impaired retirees who are trying to stay in their own homes may find they have lost control over their very own living situations. The retiree sharing part of her house with a younger housemate may have to deal with a continued parade of boyfriends. Power-hungry and abusive home-aid workers may treat the frail retiree with disdain. The financial burden of maintaining a home may expose the retiree to the unrelenting demands of a collection agency.

Even the well-meaning daughter who takes her mother in may unwittingly provide too much assistance. She may introduce a hospital bed into the home when one is not really needed or order a harness to facilitate walking when a strong arm would suffice. Langer (1983:285) elucidates the dilemma:

> Simply helping people may make them incompetent. While meaning well, it communicates to the person that he or she is not able to do whatever it is for him- or herself. If the person faces no difficulty, if there are no challenges, large or small, feelings of mastery are precluded.

When family caregivers elicit additional help from formal service providers, they run the risk of experiencing yet another unintended and unpleasant consequence. They can unsuspectingly introduce into the home setting the very qualities of nursing home life that they consider so abhorrent (Gubrium and Sankar 1990). The most conventional-looking dwelling can be transformed into a mini-nursing home. The retiree is treated not as a mother or father, but as a "patient" who must follow highly structured medical and therapeutic regimens and whose privacy is secondary. The family caregiver adopts a very paternalistic attitude, often "overruling a person's autonomy for that person's own good" (Kane 1988:28).

CONCLUSION

American society has presented its retirees with a wide and sometimes bewildering array of residential choices to address their changing personal needs and life-styles. These have allowed them both to remain in their long-standing residences and to move elsewhere, sometimes to very different housing accommodations. Retirees have found, however, that these alternatives are not equally available. Sometimes they simply are not found in a specific locality; in other instances their costs are too high or their eligibility requirements and bureaucratic features too restrictive.

Retirees have most favored those housing options that least deviate from the conventional and the familiar. Only when they experience highly disruptive personal circumstances do they consider those options that infringe on their accustomed living styles. Even as these residential alternatives have addressed their emerging needs, they have also altered their most basic and treasured meanings of home.

REFERENCES

American Association of Retired Persons. 1990. *Understanding Senior Housing for the 1990s.* Washington, D.C.: American Association of Retired Persons.

Braun, K. L., and C. L. Rose. 1989. "Goals and Characteristics of Long-Term Care Programs: An analytic Model." *The Gerontologist,* 29:51–58.

Campbell, A., P. G. Converse, and W. Rodgers. 1976. *The Quality of American Life.* New York: Russell Sage.

Chappell, N. L. 1991. Living Arrangements and Sources of Caregiving. *Journal of Gerontology: Social Sciences,* 46:S1–S8.

Eckert, J. K., K. Namazi, and E. Kahana. 1987. Unlicensed Board and Care Homes: An Extra-Familial Living Arrangement for the Elderly. *Journal of Cross-Cultural Gerontology,* 2:377–393.

Golant, S. M. 1984. *A Place to Grow Old.* New York: Columbia University Press.

Golant, S. M. 1990. Post-1980 Regional Migration Patterns of the U.S. Elderly Population. *Journal of Gerontology,* 45:S135–S140.

Golant, S. M. 1991. "Matching Congregate Housing Settings with a Diverse Elderly Population: Research and Theoretical Contributions." In L. W. Kaye and A. Monk, eds., *Congregate Housing for Elderly: Theoretical, Policy and Programmatic Perspectives.* New York: Haworth Press, 21–38.

Golant, S. M. 1992. *Housing America's Elderly: Many Possibilities, Few Choices.* Newbury Park, Calif.: Sage Publications.

Gordon, P. 1988. *Developing Retirement Facilities.* New York: John Wiley.

Gubrium, J. F., and A. Sankar, eds. 1990. *The Home Care Experience.* Newbury Park, Calif.: Sage Publications.

Hooyman, N. R., and W. Lustbader. 1986. *Taking Care: Supporting Older People and Their Families.* New York: The Free Press.

Kane, R. A. 1988. Case Management: Ethical Pitfalls on the Road to High-Quality Managed Care. In K. Fisher and E. Weisman, eds., *Case Management: Guiding Patients through the Health Care Maze.* Chicago: Joint Commission on Accreditation of Healthcare Organizations.

Langer, E. J. 1983. *The Psychology of Control.* Beverly Hills, Calif.: Sage.

McCaslin, R., and S. Golant 1990. "Assessing Social Welfare Programs for the Elderly: The Specification of Functional Goals." *Journal of Applied Gerontology,* 9:4–19.

Mindel, C. H. 1979. "Multigenerational Family Households: Recent Trends and Implications for the Future." *The Gerontologist,* 19:456–463.

Mor, V., S. Sherwood, and C. Gutkin 1986. A National Study of Residential Care for the Aged. *The Gerontologist,* 26:405–417.

Norberg-Schulz, C. 1971. *Existence, Space, and Architecture.* New York: Praeger.

Parmelee, P. A., and M. P. Lawton. 1990. "The Design of Special Environments for the Aged." In J. Birren and K. W. Schaie, eds., *Handbook of Psychology of Aging,* 3rd ed. San Diego: Academic Press, 464–488.

Sherwood, S., H. S. Ruchlin, and C. C. Sherwood. 1990. "CCRCs: An Option for Aging in Place." In D. Tilson, ed., *Aging in Place: Supporting the Frail Elderly in Residential Environments.* Glenview, Ill.: Scott, Foresman, & Co., 125–164.

Soldo, B. 1985. "In-Home Services by the Dependent Elderly." *Research on Aging,* 7:281–304.

Soldo, B., D. A. Wolf, and E. M. Agree. 1990. *Journals of Gerontology: Social Sciences,* 45:S238–S249.

Streib, G. F., W. E. Folts, and M. A. Hilker. 1984. *Old Homes-New Families: Shared Living for the Elderly.* New York: Columbia University Press.

Streib, G. F. 1990. "Congregate Housing: People, Places, Policies." In D. Tilson, ed., *Aging in Place.* Glenview, Ill.: Scott Foresman, 75–100.

Tell, E., et al. 1987. "Assessing the Elderly's Preferences for Lifecare Retirement Options." *The Gerontologist,* 27:503–509.

U.S. Bureau of the Census 1991. "Marital Status and Living Arrangements: March." *Current Population Reports,* Series P-20, no. 450. Washington, D.C.: U.S. Government Printing Office.

U.S. Congressional Budget Office 1988. *Current Housing Problems and Possible Federal Responses.* Washington, D.C.: Superintendent of Documents.

U.S. Department of Commerce 1990. *American Housing Survey for the United States in 1987.* Current Housing Reports, H-150–87. Washington, D.C.: U.S. Government Printing Office.

U.S. Senate, Special Committee on Aging 1989. *Aging America: Trends and Projections.* Serial No. 101-E. Washington, D.C.: U.S. Government Printing Office.

U.S. Senate, Special Committee on Aging. 1990. *Developments in Aging: 1989,* vol. 1. Washington, D.C.: U.S. Government Printing Office.

Weissert, W. G., et al. 1989. "Models of Adult Day Care: Findings from a National Survey." *The Gerontologist,* 29:640–649.

Wister, A. V. 1988. "Privacy, Independence, and Separateness in Living Arrangement Selection among the Elderly." *Environments,* 20:26–35.

23

Community and Neighborhood Issues

●

NANCY J. CHAPMAN

This chapter outlines some of the issues that planners and advocates must consider when creating neighborhoods and communities for an aging population. A community's built environment, including the location of land uses, the availability of housing alternatives, and the adequacy of pedestrian systems, has a direct bearing on the ability of older people to maintain their independence. An enabling environment for an older population offers a variety of housing options to suit different needs and preferences, a variety of transportation options, quality neighborhoods, and freedom from victimization and fear of crime.

Although we often think of older people moving to retirement communities or specialized housing as they age, the vast majority of older people age in place in their previous housing, often single-family homes. The single-family residence is the most common and preferred housing for older people in America. Sixty-five percent of those over age sixty-five own their homes, and most choose to continue living in those homes as they age. Recent housing projections show that home ownership is both more common among the elderly than among the population as a whole and likely to increase in the future (Newman 1986). However, national housing policy to address the housing problems of older people has focused almost entirely on multiple-family housing, including publicly assisted housing, congregate care, and life care facilities.

Most older people living in U.S. metropolitan areas are now growing older in suburban neighborhoods. Nationally, 26 percent of the nation's elderly (those over the age of sixty-five) lived in the suburban ring in 1960, and this percentage increased to 39 percent in 1980. In 1977, for the first time a greater number of elderly people lived in the suburban ring than in central cities (Fitzpatrick and Logan 1985; Golant 1990). This trend is significant because it concentrates older people in low-density suburban areas and small towns that are difficult to access without a car.

ZONING REGULATIONS

One barrier to creating alternative forms of housing and land use within communities is zoning regulations. Zoning regulations are tools used by planners and adopted by the local community that influence the availability, design, and location of various kinds of housing and the mix of residential, commercial, industrial, and recreational land uses. Lands are zoned for allowable uses and densities; zoning does not generally change lot by lot, but is designed to ensure that lands with similar uses are grouped together. Residential zoning is largely single-family zoning, with multiple-family dwellings used as buffers or transitions to commercial and industrial zones.

Among the zoning obstacles to developing innovative housing options are the separation between single-family and multiple-family housing, the separation between residential and neighborhood commercial uses, limitations on siting manufactured housing, limitations on siting multiple-family housing, and the definition of the family. In addition, subdivisions often specify a minimum house size, further limiting the diversity of options available within the neighborhood.

Zoning for the Single-Family Home

Certain alternatives within single-family housing that have the potential to serve older persons, particularly accessory apartments, home sharing, ECHO housing, and home occupations, are often limited or unavailable in communities due to zoning regulations. The issues that arise will be discussed briefly, but an extended discussion and sample ordinances can be found in the report by Pollak and Gorman (1989).

Accessory Apartments

Accessory apartments are created by subdividing a large house to form smaller apartments. Such units may benefit older people by allowing them to live with their children, but in separate units or by allowing them to develop rental units in unused space in their homes that may be exchanged for rent or assistance. Historically, most zoning codes have not allowed the subdivision of housing in single-family zones.

Accessory apartments represent a controversial housing alternative due to neighborhood concerns about rentals, traffic, and overburdened schools. These issues can be addressed by zoning codes that place an emphasis on maintaining the single-family appearance of such structures, requiring off-street parking, and limiting the size of accessory apartments. From a community perspective, the lower cost of converting an existing dwelling compared to constructing new rental housing creates the potential for affordable rentals. In some cases ordinances have restricted occupancy in accessory apartments to persons who are elderly or have disabilities. The specific form taken by the ordinance will depend on the concerns of the particular community, such as the need to provide affordable housing or to house a specific population.

Home Sharing

Home sharing may become a planning issue when a group of older adults, perhaps six or more individuals, choose to share a home. Local zoning restrictions that impose limits on the number of unrelated people who are allowed to live together in a single-family residence (usually four to six) may make it impossible for a group of older adults to develop this type of housing alternative. Family definitions determine who qualifies as a "single family" and is eligible to live in housing in a single-family zone.

If shared housing for the elderly is designed for the frail elderly who need assistance from outside staff, or if it is run for profit, it generally must be located in multiple-family or commercial zones. Then the zoning issues for specialized housing for the elderly that are discussed in the next section come into play.

ECHO Housing

ECHO (elder cottage housing opportunity) housing is a self-contained, usually removable housing unit that is placed on the same lot as an existing single-family dwelling. It is typically used to allow elderly parents to live close to and receive assistance from their children. Although the elderly parents and their adult children might be considered an extended family, ECHO housing is not generally permitted in single-family zones. Communities are concerned that the units could be converted to use by unrelated households after their use by extended family members was no longer needed.

Most ordinances that allow ECHO housing specify minimum lot sizes and maximum lot coverage; adding a unit is clearly not likely to be feasible in sections of a municipality with very small lots. Ordinances may also specify where the second unit may be sited on the lot, the size and design of the unit, how it is to be connected to sewage and water, and parking requirements. One approach to countering resistance to ECHO housing is zoning that grants occupancy to a specific person rather than to the unit (Hare and Hollis 1983). The unit might be leased from a local agency and would be removed when no longer needed. Granting the permit to a specific individual makes it feasible to eliminate many zoning requirements.

Home Occupations

"Home occupations" allow residents to provide services or manufacture products in their homes. They offer the potential both to meet the needs of the disabled elderly and to provide income to the more able (Hare and Price 1985). Examples include allowing in-home or "family" day care for disabled adults in residential neighborhoods as an analog to family day care provision for children and allowing "bed and breakfast" inns that can provide income and social contact for older homeowners. Ordinances can reduce the impact of these on the neighborhood by limiting the number of day care recipients or roomers to two to four.

Zoning for Specialized Housing

Jurisdictions can use a variety of zoning devices to promote the development and control the siting of multiunit congregate facilities for older adults and other forms of special housing (see table 23.1). Although arguments for and against special zoning for the elderly have appeared in the planning literature (Hopperton 1986; Shifman 1983), communities are more and more commonly adopting comprehensive ordinances for housing for the elderly (see Pollak and Malakoff 1984). The devices listed in table 23.1 can encourage well-planned housing for the elderly in a variety of ways. The planned unit developments, flexible density zoning, and cluster zoning may each encourage developers to include multiple-unit housing for the elderly in what might otherwise have been a development of single-family units only. These

TABLE 23.1. Zoning Devices to Encourage Specialized Housing for the Elderly

Zoning Device	Application
Special Permit	Allow multiunit housing in appropriate residential area subject to review and approval of each proposal if it complies with specific standards.
Floating Zone	Has listings of permitted uses and detailed standards covering development, but location of zone is not determined until an application is submitted.
Planned Unit Development	Allows unified rather than lot-by-lot development of an area. Jurisdiction approves a comprehensive plan rather than presetting standards.
Overlay Zone	A zone superimposed over an existing district and used as a supplemental zoning regulation. Could be used to identify suitable areas for multiunit housing for the elderly.
Incentive Zoning	Encourages development by offering incentives, such as density bonuses. The bonus allows the developer to build a larger number of dwelling units on a given site than would otherwise be permitted, provided that certain criteria are met.
Inclusionary Zoning	Mandatory set-asides can be used to encourage housing for the elderly. Set-asides might require that all new housing developments include minimum numbers of units for sale or rent to low- and moderate-income residents.
Flexible Density Zoning	Allows the developer to vary the location and density of development on a particular site as long as the average density does not exceed the maximum density limit. Could construct high- and low-density housing on one site.
Cluster Zoning	Allows approval of a subdivision with variation in the location of buildings and uses, the types of buildings, and the design of the project. May allow structures to be built in close groups in order to maintain open space.
Site Plan Review	Allows a jurisdiction to require site planning and design review of development proposals.

Adapted from Pollak and Malakoff 1984.

may increase the availability of affordable housing and of smaller units suitable to older persons. They also have the advantage of locating apartments in a residential setting giving future generations of elderly people more options to remain in familiar neighborhoods while moving to smaller apartments or condominiums as their needs change.

Incentive zoning has been used to encourage developers to locate specialized housing for the elderly in suitable locations and to develop designs that meet the needs of the elderly. The bonus allows a developer to build a larger number of dwelling units for the elderly on a given site than would otherwise be permitted, provided that the developer meets certain criteria. In San Diego, for example, the bonus is connected to affordability and regulations regarding access to the disabled. That is, the developer is offered the option of building at a greater density than the existing zoning would allow if a given number of housing units meet city low-income affordability criteria and access requirements. Clackamas County, Oregon, ties its density bonus program to access and proximity to services. A development plan is rated on a point system that rewards locating a housing project for the elderly in close proximity to a transit service and to facilities such as parks, groceries, pharmacies, laundries, and senior activity centers.

TRANSPORTATION ALTERNATIVES

The ability to be mobile and to move easily from place to place is critical to older people if they are to remain independent and experience a sense of control over their lives. Although many think first of buses when they think of transportation for the elderly, older people, like the rest of the population, rely largely on the automobile for transportation (see table 23.2). Whether as a driver or a passenger, 70 percent of the trips made by those aged 85 or older were by car in 1977. That percentage increased to 79 percent in 1983—a large change in only six years. This growing reliance on the automobile is the result of the growing percentage of the older population who have driven throughout their lives, and to the increasing location of the elderly in low density suburbs due to the "graying of suburbia" (Fitzpatrick and Logan 1985).

Unfortunately, some of the disabilities that become more probable as we age also prevent many older people who are quite able to remain in their own homes from driving. Older people are concentrated in suburban and rural areas, and these lower-density areas are

TABLE 23.2. Distribution of Trips per Person by Age and Mode
of Transportation

Year	Mode	Percentage by Age			
		65–74	*75–84*	*85+*	*All Ages*
1977	Private Vehicle	83.1	75.8	70.1	83.8
	Public Transportation	3.2	3.4	3.3	2.5
	Taxi	0.3	0.2	0.7	0.2
	Walk	2.2	20.7	25.9	9.3
	Other	1.2	0.5	0.0	4.2
1983	Private Vehicle	86.4	84.0	78.8	84.7
	Public Transportation	2.8	2.0	3.7	2.4
	Taxi	0.1	0.7	0.0	0.2
	Walk	9.8	12.6	13.7	8.9
	Other	0.9	0.7	3.8	3.8

SOURCE: Transportation Research Board 1988.

difficult to access without a car. Shopping and services are typically spread out along arterial highways and separated by large parking lots; they are difficult to reach either on foot or by bus. Although there is evidence that older people may relinquish their role as driver when their health declines (Jette and Branch 1992),those who have no other driver or alternative form of transportation may continue to drive longer than they safely can.

The distance older people travel in driving to shop, to visit family and friends, to attend church, or to see the doctor is such that on average none of these destinations can be reached on foot in less than an hour one way (Rosenbloom 1988). Providing mass transit as a total solution to the problem of transportation for the elderly is also clearly not feasible. To increase the mobility and access to safe transportation of the elderly, all modes of transportation must be reassessed and adapted for the older population.

Older People as Drivers

Although older people are the age group least at risk of traffic accidents or death when measured by accidents or deaths per thousand persons in their age group, this figure is somewhat misleading because older people travel fewer miles per year than people in other age groups. If we look at accidents per million miles driven, the accident rate at intersections for the group aged seventy-five and older is the highest of all age groups (Stamatiadas, Taylor, and McKelvey 1991); the overall accident rate of this group is exceeded only by that of the group from fifteen through nineteen years of age (Transportation Research Board 1988). Some of the increase in accident and fatality rates with age is likely to be due to physical changes. For example, older people are more likely to have deficits in visual acuity and peripheral vision, greater susceptibility to glare, and poorer night vision and ability to focus than people in other groups. They find it harder to detect messages related to driving in the visual clutter of other signs, and they take longer to make decisions based on the information they receive. Many older drivers do not have enough time or distance to respond to visual cues; they may have trouble negotiating complex intersections or merging with high-speed traffic. Another cause of the increased fatality rate with age is the frailty of the older population.

There are many policy changes that can increase safety for older drivers and passengers, some of which must be made at the state and national rather than the local level. For example, seat belt laws and the installation of air bags would reduce the incidence of injury and death among older people involved in accidents. Revisions of national standards for signs and procedures for licensing drivers have recently been recommended by a special report on transportation in an aging society by the Transportation Research Board (1988). Other changes can be implemented at the local level. These include the following:

- Adding lines to the edges of roads to make it easier to guide a car under the glare of oncoming headlights.
- Increasing the luminance of major signs, such as those on freeways, and increasing the size of the letters to a standard of one inch per forty feet of viewing distance rather than one inch per fifty feet.
- Standardizing the color and location of traffic signs so that they are easier to find among the visual clutter and using multiple signs or advance signing (e.g., Stop Ahead; Ash Street Next Signal) where appropriate.
- Improving the maintenance of signs and painted traffic lines on streets and highways.
- Creating separate left-turn lanes and traffic signals with separate left-turn phases to reduce accidents at intersections (the advantages of which must be weighed against the associated costs of slowing the traffic flow, and increasing the distance that pedestrians must cross).

- Reconsidering the "sight-distance triangles" used in designing intersections to allow older drivers to see approaching cars far enough away to make decisions to pull into traffic safely.
- Encouraging driver education programs for older drivers that help them identify and adapt safely to their physical abilities and the modern transportation system. Both the American Association of Retired Persons (AARP) and the American Automobile Association (AAA) offer driver retraining programs.

Older People as Pedestrians

Walking is the second most important mode of transportation among older people (see table 23.2). Older people without drivers' licenses make between 20 and 40 percent of all of their trips by walking (Rosenbloom 1988). The changes with age that are most likely to affect the pedestrian are inability to walk long distances; inability to walk quickly; need to use a cane, walker, or wheelchair that limits access; and problems with balance. Those over the age of seventy show by far the highest rate of pedestrian fatalities compared with those in other age groups. It is not clear whether this death rate is due to the greater proportion of older people walking or to their greater likelihood of being injured if they are involved in accidents.

Communities need to consider ways to make pedestrian travel more attractive and practical, as well as safer. Some options include those listed below:

- Providing a mix of land uses so that neighborhood services can be located within walking distance of many homes. This may include planning carefully for the inclusion of neighborhood service districts in suburban locations.
- Assessing the overall adequacy of the pedestrian system. Are there continuous sidewalks throughout the community, including along major roads, for access to buses and services? Is there pedestrian access from neighborhoods and housing complexes for the elderly into neighboring shopping plazas?
- Are there clearly protected pedestrian walkways within large parking lots?
- Providing amenities for pedestrians in conjunction with sidewalks. These include well-designed benches where shoppers and walkers can pause to rest, clean public restrooms, and adequate lighting of pathways and stairs.
- Designing crosswalks and walk signals to accommodate people

with disabilities and older people with slower walking speeds. It is estimated that about one-third of the population, mostly older people, walk more slowly than is taken into account by the typical design guideline of four feet per second. Crosswalk signals should be timed to three feet per second at intersections that are heavily used by older persons. To decrease their impact on traffic, signals can be pedestrian-activated and pedestrian refuge areas can be built in the medians of wide streets.

Older People as Users of Public and Specialized Transit

Public Transit

Public transportation is currently the third most frequent mode of transportation for the elderly (see table 23.2), but frequency of use has fallen among those under the age of eighty-five in recent years. Current use levels are as much a consequence of the absence of alternatives to the automobile as of user preference. Public transit is more widely used by people of all ages in New York and Chicago than in Los Angeles and in the compact city of San Francisco than in the sprawling city of San Antonio (Carp 1988). In general, however, those who drive are the only group of elderly people who are satisfied with their ability to get around (Carp 1988).

Dissatisfaction with public transit stems from the difficulty older people find in getting where they want to go on the bus, fear of crime on public transit and on the trip to and from the bus, and problems of getting on the bus and riding it. For example, among a sample of elderly and disabled residents of Houston, 50 percent lived within two blocks of a bus stop, but 60 percent lacked sidewalks between their home and the bus stop. 71 percent lacked curb cuts, and 76 percent lacked bus shelters (Gilderbloom and Rosentraub 1990).

The growing suburbanization of the older population increases the difficulty involved in providing transportation alternatives to those who can no longer drive. Martin Wachs (1979), in a study of the Los Angeles area, found that about one-half of the elderly in Los Angeles County were living in areas with densities lower than fourteen people per acre. An Urban Mass Transit Association study showed that bus transit is feasible only in areas with thirty to forty or more people per acre.

Communities need to assess the adequacy of their public transit systems, and they should aim to do the following:

- Make access to public transit safer and more convenient. Bus stops should be clean and well lighted, and they should have benches protected from the weather. Buses should have low steps with well-marked edges, well-designed visible handholds, and rear doors that are easy to open.

- Purchase wheelchair-accessible buses and be sure that light rail lines are wheelchair-accessible. Emphasize providing accessible public transit to areas with a high proportion of elderly and disabled residents.

- Analyze the travel behavior of the elderly in planning bus routes. The traditional emphasis on the suburban-to-downtown commuter no longer serves many commuters, and it is particularly unlikely to meet the travel needs of the elderly.

Specialized Transit

Specialized transit includes such special transportation as dial-a-bus or van systems provided or subsidized by the public and private nonprofit sectors, as well as private alternatives such as taxis. Like public transit, special transit, dial-a-bus, and small van systems will be difficult to provide outside central city areas without a high level of subsidy (Wachs 1979). The Urban Mass Transit Association study cited above estimated that a dial-a-bus service must serve ten to fifteen people per acre to be feasible. Providing transportation in rural areas, where a high proportion of the elderly are poor, is particularly problematic.

As intercity bus lines decrease their routes in rural areas and as many small towns lose even the most basic services needed on a weekly or monthly basis, transportation becomes a critical issue. Communities need to take the following steps:

- Find innovative ways to provide special transit, including using taxis and volunteer driver programs as well as small vans and buses. Fixed-route buses cannot adequately serve low-density suburban areas because the stops are likely to be too far from the average older person's home. Demand-responsive services such as those provided by subsidized taxis and volunteer services may prove to be necessary alternatives to fixed-route and dial-a-bus transit for those who need transportation on weekends or at short notice, who cannot sit very long or need assistance door to door rather than curb to curb, or who need transportation to destinations not covered by specialized transit.

- Coordinate volunteer programs with the rest of the transportation system. For example, a variety of volunteer programs available in the community may meet only specific needs, such as medical travel or shopping, or may cover only specific geographi-

cal regions. Some communities are developing transportation systems that coordinate the special transit (dial-a-bus) and volunteer programs by means of central telephone referral systems.
- Develop statewide interconnected rural transit systems that are coordinated across county lines.

WHAT MAKES A NEIGHBORHOOD APPROPRIATE FOR OLDER PEOPLE?

Characteristics that increase older adults' satisfaction with a neighborhood include a convenient location (Lawton and Kleban 1971; Hunt and Ross 1990), the kind of people in the neighborhood (Ward, LaGory, and Sherman 1988), a high percentage of older people (Rosow 1967), a low perceived crime rate (Jirovec, Jirovec, and Bosse 1984), and a lack of such nuisances as noise, trash, and abandoned buildings. Unfortunately, these characteristics do not always come together. Many neighborhoods that are rich in transit options and in stores and services that are attractive to older people are in deteriorating or high-crime sections of a city (Burby and Rohe 1990). Burby and Rohe argue that neither convenient services nor living in an age-segregated building offsets the negative impact of a high-crime neighborhood.

As such areas revitalize or "gentrify," there is concern that older persons are disproportionately being forced out by rising rents and taxes and by the destruction of low-cost housing options such as single-room occupancy (SRO) hotels. Although a recent study of revitalizing neighborhoods that were part of the Urban Homesteading Demonstration Project (Varady 1986) showed that older residents were neither hurt nor helped more than younger residents by the changes in the neighborhood, Singelakis (1990) argues that his research in New York and similar work in other major cities has shown that there is disproportionate displacement of low-income elderly people due to condominium conversion and loss of SRO units.

Distance to Services

Living in an area close to needed services becomes more important as transportation options become limited. Carp and Carp (1982) found that older adults identified thirteen resources that a majority would like to have located within easy walking distance of home in an ideal situation. The most desired resources were a bus stop, a favorite grocery store, a bank, and a library. Other resources these people found desirable were their own church, a senior center, a favorite grocery store, their own doctor's office, a favorite restaurant, a favorite beauty shop, a congregate meal, and a fire station. But only the bus stop would be located by the majority within one block of their homes in an ideal environment.

Restaurants, churches, and beauty/barber shops are the social amenities used most frequently by older residents of public housing (Christensen and Cranz 1987). Smith (1991) found that inner suburbs were the most advantageous locations for grocery shopping among elderly residents of Winnipeg. Competitively priced supermarkets were located within walking distance of inner suburb residents; 25 percent of these elderly residents walked to shop for groceries compared with 9 percent of those living in the central city and 4 percent of those living in the outer suburbs. In summary, the ideal environment is one with services conveniently close but not so close as to increase traffic and noise.

Age Homogeneity

The desirability of living in housing or a neighborhood with a high percentage of other older people has been a subject of considerable debate. Some studies have found that living with others the same age in apartments and neighborhoods increases how often neighbors talk to or rely on each other for help (Lawton and Nahemow 1979; Rosenberg 1970; Rosow 1967); others have found that it has no effect or decreases interaction (Chapman and Beaudet 1983). There is also evidence that older people who choose housing with a higher percentage of older residents may do so because they place more value on being close to friends and age peers than do those who choose age-mixed housing (Hunt and Ross 1990).

Age homogeneity may be more closely associated with older people's satisfaction with a neighborhood in the central city than in suburban and rural locations (Ward, LaGory, and Sherman 1988). In addition, it is most likely to be important for those accustomed to relying on their neighbors for social contact, such as ethnic groups with a history of living in tight-knit communities. It is also important for older people whose mobility has declined and who are no longer able to maintain contact with a widely scattered network of family and friends. As a higher proportion of women join the work force, the older residents of a mixed-age neighborhood are likely to find themselves isolated during the day, left behind in a virtual ghost town.

Crime and Fear of Crime

Victimization

Although the mass media have tended to characterize older people as frequent victims of crime and as occupied by fear of crime (Fattah and Sacco 1989), careful research has shown that older people tend to be crime victims less often than younger people. Fattah and Sacco (1989) have summarized the literature, concluding that rates of both personal crimes and crimes against property tend to be lower for older people. National statistics show that the elderly are burglarized in their homes at one-half the rate of other groups and are victims of violent crime at one-fifth the rate of younger groups. Only rates of personal theft with contact (such as purse-snatching and pickpocketing) and fraud may be higher among older adults.

Lawton and Yaffe (1980) noted that urban public housing projects for the elderly tend to be selectively located in high-crime areas within cities. They found that victimization rates were higher in larger communities and in projects where young and old were mixed indiscriminately; separating age groups by floors, buildings, or projects decreased the victimization equally.

Fear of Crime

The estimates of fear of crime among the elderly vary widely, from 23 percent choosing *crime* from a list of potential personal problems to 1 percent spontaneously mentioning crime as a major worry (LaGrange and Ferraro 1987). One reason gerontologists have been concerned about older people's fear of crime has been the possibility that fear causes older people to restrict their activities and become isolated. The results of research regarding the existence of a relationship between fear of crime and behavioral restriction are mixed. Indeed, Lawton and Yaffe (1980) found that older public housing residents who had been victimized actually increased their mobility three years later. Akers et al. (1987) found little relationship between being crime victims and fear of crime among older people.

Fear of crime is associated with a number of personal and environmental characteristics. Women, the poor, and those in poor health are particularly likely to show a high fear of crime (Golant 1984; Yin 1985). Fear of crime is higher in neighborhoods that are urban and deteriorating and have a high percentage of poor, black, or older residents (Ward, LaGory, and Sherman 1986). A number of studies have shown a decrease in fear of crime with an increase in the age homogeneity of a housing project or neighborhood (Akers, LaGreca, Sellers, and Cochran 1987; Lawton and Yaffe 1980); others have found an increase (Ward, LaGory, and Sherman 1986). It may be that the social and structural supports found in planned age-homogeneous communities increase the sense of safety. Without those supports, an increase in age peers may only spread fear about crime. Finally, as predicted by the theory of defensible space (Newman 1972), older people who feel more control over their territory also are less fearful of crime (Normoyle and Lavrakas 1984). Newman has theorized that building designs that increase residents' sense of ownership of shared spaces (e.g., lobbies, hallways, and building grounds) and allow residents to watch over these spaces in the course of their daily lives decrease the incidence of residential crime. These would be likely to increase the residents' sense of control over their personal and shared territory.

COMMUNITY PLANNING

In order to create communities that are better suited to our aging population, the perspective of aging should infuse the planning process. It may be the focus of a special initiative, such as that of the city of Richmond and Henrico County, Virginia, or of the Maryland-National Capital Park and Planning Commission. These communities have identified the priority needs of older adults, and in the latter case the master plan for the community was altered to encourage the development of group homes and the reuse of former schools as housing for the elderly, to allow accessory apartments and bed-and-breakfast establishments in residential zones, and to improve pedestrian transportation throughout the area.

A community that wishes to incorporate a perspective of aging in the planning process must examine the problems now being faced by older adults and reflect on the challenges the community will face as it ages. Issues that merit consideration include the following:

- Demographics. Is the community aging? To what extent, where, and why? Is the aging due to the aging in place of the current population, the immigration of older people, or the outmigration of the young? Each of these has different implications for the needs of the aging population.
- Housing. What is the match between housing supply and need? Is there a full range of housing options, and are they affordable? Are these options located in areas that are well served by transportation options?

- Mobility/accessibility. To what extent can older adults maintain mobility when they can no longer drive?
- Economic development. How do the demographic characteristics of the community, particularly the older population, influence local economic development? If attracting older people appears to have a positive impact on economic development in the short run, will communities be prepared for the increased service needs of these retirees as they age?
- Serving older adults. How will land use and development patterns affect the ability of the community to provide services? Not only transportation, but all in-home social services will prove more difficult and expensive to provide to a low-density community than to one with a higher density.
- Participation of older adults. How can older people be most effectively involved in local planning efforts? Many planning meetings are held in the evening, when many older people prefer not to travel, or in locations that are difficult to reach.
- Gaining support. What opportunities exist for obtaining support for a focus on older adults within the planning process? Many of the changes that would serve older residents would be equally welcome to others in the community. Environments that are difficult for older people to negotiate are also difficult for parents with children in strollers and for people who use wheelchairs or who have diminished vision. Children and adolescents as well as older people find their mobility limited if they are unable to drive.

An encouraging trend is the growing interest among planners and urban designers in creating communities that are less dependent on the automobile and that allow more flexible and varied housing types within neighborhoods. Among these are Peter Calthorpe's concept of "pedestrian pockets" (Kelbaugh 1989). These are zones of redevelopment or new development located around light rail or bus lines and designed to facilitate pedestrian access. The pockets cluster housing, neighborhood services, and workplaces within walking distance of each other. A related concept is Andreas Duany's "traditional neighborhood development" (see Boles 1989), a redesign of the suburb that is pedestrian-oriented, allowing mixed uses within walking distance. These new directions in planning are supportive of children, teenagers, and families as well as the elderly, and thus may attract wide support if people are able to envision an urban form that is supportive of a wider range of family types and transportation options.

REFERENCES

Preparation of portions of this chapter was supported by Administration on Aging Grant No. IOAT0019/01. The author would like to thank Deborah Howe and Sharon Baggett for their collaboration on that grant.

Akers, R. L., A. J. LaGreca, and J. Cochran. 1987. "Fear of Crime and Victimization among the Elderly in Different Types of Communities." *Criminology*, 25:486–505.

Boles, D. D. 1989. "Reordering the Suburbs." *Progressive Architecture*, May:78–91.

Burby, R. J. and W. M. Rohe. 1990. "Providing for the Housing Needs of the Elderly." *Journal of the American Planning Association*, 56:324–340.

Carp. F. M., and A. Carp. 1982. "The Ideal Residential Area." *Research on Aging*, 4:411–439.

Carp, F. M. 1988. "Significance of Mobility for the Well-Being of the Elderly." In Transportation Research Board, ed., *Transportation for an Aging Society: Improving Mobility and Safety for Older Persons*, vol. II:1–20. Washington, D.C.: National Research Council.

Chapman, N., and M. Beaudet. 1983. "Environmental Predictors of Well-Being for At-Risk Older Adults in a Mid-Sized City." *Journal of Gerontology*, 38:237–244.

Christensen, D., and G. Cranz. 1987. "Examining Physical and Managerial Aspects of Urban Housing for the Elderly." In V. Regnier and J. Pynoos. eds., *Housing for the Aged: Design Directives and Policy Considerations*, 105–132. New York: Elsevier.

Fattah, E. A., and V. F. Sacco. 1989. *Crime and Victimization of the Elderly.* London: Springer-Verlag.

Fitzpatrick, K. M., and J. R. Logan. 1985. "The Aging of the Suburbs: 1960–1980." *American Sociological Review*, 50:534–539.

Gilderbloom, I., and M. S. Rosentraub. 1990. "Creating the Accessible City: Proposals for Providing Housing and Transportation for Low Income, Elderly and Disabled People." *American Journal of Economics and Sociology*, 49:271–282.

Golant, S. M. 1984. *A Place to Grow Old: The Meaning of Environment in Old Age.* New York: Columbia University.

Golant, S. M. 1990. "The Metropolitanization and Suburbanization of the U.S. Elderly Population: 1970–1988." *The Gerontologist*, 30:80–85.

Hare, P. H., and L. E. Hollis. 1983. *ECHO Housing: A Review of Zoning Issues and Other Considerations.* Washington, D.C.: American Association of Retired Persons.

Hare, P. H., and G. Price. 1985. "Services Begin at Home." *Planning*, 55 (September):25–26.

Hopperton, R. 1986. "Land-Use Regulations for the Elderly." In R. Newcomer, M. P. Lawton, and T. O. Byerts, eds., *Housing an Aging Society: Issues, Alternatives, and Policy*, 229–233. New York: Van Nostrand Reinhold.

Hunt, M. E., and L. E. Ross. 1990. "Naturally Occurring Retirement Communities: A Multi-Attribute Examination of Desirability Factors." *The Gerontologist*, 30:667–674.

Jette, A. M., and L. G. Branch. 1992. "A Yen-Year Follow-up of Driving Patterns among the Community-Dwelling Elderly." *Human Factors*, 34:25–31.

Jirovec, R. L., M. M. Jirovec, and R. Bosse. 1984. "Environmental Determinants of Neighborhood Satisfaction among Urban Elderly Men." *The Gerontologist*, 24:261–265.

Kelbaugh, D., ed. 1989. *The Pedestrian Pocket Nook: A New Suburban Design Strategy.* New York: Princeton Architectural Press.

LaGrange, R. L., and K. F. Ferraro. 1987. "The Elderly's Fear of Crime." *Research on Aging*, 9:372–391.

Lawton, M. P., and M. H. Kleban. 1971. "The Aged Resident of the Inner City." *Gerontologist*, 11:277–283.

Lawton, M. P., and L. Nahemow. 1979. "Social Areas and the Well-Being of Tenants in Housing for the Elderly." *Multivariate Behavioral Research*, 14:463–484.

Lawton, M. P., and S. Yaffe. 1980. "Victimization and Fear of Crime in Elderly Public Housing Tenants." *Journal of Gerontology*, 35:768–779.

Newman, O. 1972. *Defensible Space*. New York: Macmillan.

Newman, S. 1986. "Demographic Influences on the Future Housing Demand of the Elderly." In R. Newcomer, M. P. Lawton, and T. Byerts, eds., *Housing in an Aging Society: Issues, Alternatives and Policy*, 21–32. New York: Van Nostrand Reinhold.

Normoyle, J., and P. J. Lavrakas. 1984. "Fear of Crime in Elderly Women: Perceptions of Control, Predictability, and Territoriality." *Personality and Social Psychology Bulletin*, 10:191–202.

Pollak, P. B., and A. N. Gorman. 1989. *Community-Based Housing for the Elderly*. Report No. 420. Washington, D.C.: American Planning Association, Planning Advisory Service.

Pollak, P. B., and L. Malakoff. 1984. *Housing Options for Older New Yorkers: A Sourcebook*. Ithaca, N.Y.: Cornell Cooperative Extension and the New York State Office for the Aging.

Rosenberg, G. S. 1970. *The Worker Grows Old*. San Francisco: Jossey-Bass.

Rosenbloom, S. 1988. "The Mobility Needs of the Elderly." In Transportation Research Board, ed., *Transportation for an Aging Society: Improving Mobility and Safety for Older Persons*, vol. II, 21–71. Washington, D.C.: National Research Council.

Rosow, I. 1967. *Social Integration of the Aged*. New York: Free Press.

Shifman, C. 1983. *Increasing Housing Opportunities for the Elderly*. Report No. 381. Chicago, Ill.: American Planning Association, Planning Advisory Service.

Singelakis, A. T. 1990. "Real Estate Market Trends, and the Displacement of the Aged: Examination of the Linkages in Manhattan." *The Gerontologist*, 30:658–666.

Smith, G. C. 1991. "Grocery Shopping Patterns of the Ambulatory Urban Elderly." *Environment and Behavior*, 23:86–114.

Stamatiadis, N., W. C. Taylor, and F. X. McKelvey. 1991. "Elderly Drivers and Intersection Accidents." *Transportation Quarterly*, 45:377–390.

Transportation Research Board. 1988. *Transportation for an Aging Society: Improving Mobility and Safety for Older Persons*. Washington, D.C.: National Research Council.

Varady, D. P. 1986. *Neighborhood Upgrading: A Realistic Assessment*. Albany, N.Y.: State University of New York Press.

Wachs, M. 1979. *Transportation for the Elderly: Changing Life-Styles, Changing Needs*. Berkeley, Calif.: University of California Press.

Ward, R. A., M. LaGory, and S. R. Sherman. 1986. "Fear of Crime among the Elderly as Person/Environment Interaction." *The Sociological Quarterly*, 27:327–341.

Ward, R. A., M. LaGory, and S. R. Sherman. 1988. "The Environment for Aging: Interpersonal, Social, and Spatial Contexts." Tuscaloosa, Ala.: University of Alabama.

Yin, P. 1985. *Victimization and the Aged*. Springfield, Ill.: Charles C. Thomas.

24

Housing Options for Active and More Independent Retirees

●

STEPHEN M. GOLANT

Where people live throughout most of their adult lives is strongly dictated by the location of their workplaces. Retirement removes this residential constraint or at the very least allows for new residential choices for those who still seek part-time employment. The recently retired also acquire a new block of unstructured time for leisure and recreation activities, pursuits to which the current dwelling, neighborhood, or community may be ill suited. For both these reasons the long-occupied residence may come under new scrutiny as a place to live.

Active, relatively healthy, and independent retirees can select from several different residential strategies (table 24.1). Most decide not to move. When they do move, it is usually to dwellings only a short distance away (Golant 1987). A very small group moves to countries outside the United States. A larger but still small group moves to residences in different states, sometimes in an entirely different part of the country (Golant 1990). Some of these retirees are "snowbirds," however; they live in warmer states during the fall and winter months, but still retain their original residences, to which they return during the spring and summer months.

This chapter focuses on one small subset of this group of retired movers (whose choices are represented by items with asterisks in table 24.1). They permanently move from their current dwellings and settle in planned communities or neighborhoods exclusively marketed to and occupied by retirees. These communities may be found

TABLE 24.1 Residential Decisions of Active Independent Retirees

Decision about Moving

Remain in current dwelling.
* Relocate elsewhere.

Decision about Country Destination

* Relocate within United States.
Relocate to destination outside United States (e.g., Mexico, Central America, Spain, France, or South America).

Decision about State Location in the U.S.

Move within same state.
Move to different nearby state.
Move to different state in different region of the country.

Decision about Locality in the U.S.

Move to metropolitan (more urban or suburban) place.
Move to nonmetropolitan (more rural or small town) place.

Decision about Permanence of Move

* Permanent Migrant Move: Sell or end rental lease of existing residence and purchase or rent another.
Temporary "Snowbird" Move: Maintain current residence and purchase or rent second dwelling (including the leasing of space for recreational vehicle) in another locality for less than 12 months of the year.

Residential Destination: Organizational Aspects

Unplanned residential setting designed for all age groups.
* Planned residential setting exclusively marketed to and occupied by active retirees.

Planned Residential Settings: Site Plan

*Retirement New Towns
* Retirement Villages
* Retirement Subdivisions

Planned Residential Settings: Ownership Arrangement and Dwelling Type

Recreational vehicle
Rented unit (e.g., low-rise or high-rise apartment, duplex)
Conventional single-family dwelling
Conventional attached dwelling (e.g., townhouse)
* Manufactured home on lot that is owned
* Manufactured home on lot (pad) that is rented
* Condominium or cooperative

---

* Of primary interest in this chapter

close to where these retirees used to live, but often they are in a different part of the country.

This chapter considers the distinguishing features of these active adult communities and their appropriateness for retirement living. Manufactured homes, condominiums, or cooperatives are considered separately because they present somewhat unique dwelling ownership arrangements in these communities.

SETTLEMENT CHARACTERISTICS OF PLANNED RETIREMENT COMMUNITIES

Active adult retirement communities, also known as retirement villages or retirement towns, are the products of private, profit-minded developers that are specifically serving a healthy, independent, and active older consumer market (age fifty and over). These age-segregated residential settlements contain some of the largest planned concentrations of retirees. In this category are settlements that range from subdivisions of fewer than five hundred homes built on tracts of less than 175 acres to small towns containing twenty-five thousand homes spread over nine thousand acres. They contain a wide range of conventional dwelling types, including single-family detached houses, row houses, townhouses, or manufactured (mobile) home units, condominiums, cooperatives, and rental apartment units.

The strongest growth of retirement communities was in the 1960s and 1970s. They have continued to increase in number, but their growth has slowed and the newer projects have tended to be smaller. While some of the most well-known developments are found in traditional sunbelt and western retirement states, they are also situated in the midwestern, eastern, and northwestern parts of the country (e.g., in states such as Illinois, New Jersey, and Washington), often within easy (automobile) access of large metropolitan populations (e.g., Chicago, New York, and Philadelphia). Because their development can require the acquisition of large tracts of land, they may be located on relatively less expensive acreage on the urban fringe or in relatively isolated rural areas (Heintz 1976). Politically, they are administered as incorporated municipalities, subdivisions, or freestanding villages.

Though ownership is the norm in these communities, their dwellings can vary greatly in price and luxuriousness. These can range from under $40,000 for a manufactured home unit in a mobile home park to over $300,000 for a high-end single-family home in an amenity-rich retirement town. While age restrictions are sometimes informally enforced by the selling or renting practices of the owner or developer, in most instances the older age composition of these communities is enforced through deed restrictions or through special land-use zoning classifications.

Many of these communities, but certainly not all, will have extensive outdoor recreational facilities (e.g., for golfing and swimming). Medical facilities, nursing homes, and congregate housing facilities can be found in a few of these developments, usually in the more long-established communities that have responded to the needs of their aging populations. These services are also present in some newer communities to improve their marketability. One private research survey reports "an increasing trend toward developing congregate care or continuing care facilities either within or adjacent to active adult communities" (Kenneth Leventhal and Co. 1990:41). However, these support facilities are not central to the identity of these planned retirement settlements; nor are they the primary reason that retirees are attracted to them.

With the exception of the scheduling of recreational and leisure-oriented events, very little structure is imposed on the lives of the retired residents who live in these developments. They eat, sleep, and come and go as they would in any ordinary community setting. Even the extent of security arrangements varies greatly from one setting to another. While many such developments are surrounded by walls or fences or accessed through guarded gates, others have few such safety features.

THE ATTRACTION OF SUCH COMMUNITIES TO RETIREES

Characteristics of Residents

Retirees are usually married and in their late fifties and early sixties when they move into these settlements. In a survey of twelve upscale retirement communities (Kenneth Leventhal and Co. 1990) it was found that the average age of the occupants was sixty-three and that the ages mostly ranged from sixty to sixty-seven. The occupants were predominantly white and in the middle-to upper-middle income brackets (their minimum annual income typically was $25,000), and they had larger than average net worths ($273,000, reflecting savings, investments, and property ownership). Their minimum net worth was $150,000.

On the whole, this is a better educated group of people who are more likely to have worked for themselves or in professional and managerial positions (Sherman 1971). A small percentage may still work full time or part time. Generalizations must be made carefully, however. There are also lower-end retirement communities that attract a more moderate-income population with a wider range of occupational backgrounds.

GEOGRAPHIC ORIGINS OF RESIDENTS

Retirees who select these communities often have moved across state lines, usually from one of five to ten feeder states. Still, the majority of a retirement community's occupants usually are drawn from its own state's population; this is especially true in a development's beginning years (Kenneth Leventhal and Co. 1990). These patterns may vary regionally. While retirement communities in Arizona and California attract older people from locations in the midwest and east, other developments in California, some in Florida, and many in New Jersey and Illinois draw large segments of their residents from the populations living in their own states.

Life-Style Opportunities

Retirees are not attracted to these communities because they are concerned about their frailty or because they are greatly dissatisfied with their current homes. Indeed, these retirees usually do not have unmanageable or intolerable housing problems. At most they will complain about oversized homes that they are finding too expensive, time consuming, or exhausting to maintain.

What is significant to this group is the promise of a residential setting that is consistent with how they want to spend their leisure and recreational time. This may involve a continuous stream of golf and card playing or simply a low-maintenance residential setting occupied by others who share a common retirement orientation.

In the vernacular of the private developer, this is a wants-driven, not a needs-driven, older consumer group. The size of the retiree population that is attracted to these active communities is small, however, and constitutes less than 3 percent of the population that is age sixty and over.

Features of Retirement Communities

The residents of these retirement communities often express an antipathy to urban life as manifested by its older housing, deteriorating neighborhoods, higher crime rates, pollution, bad neighbors, and crowded and noisy streets (Sherman 1971; Heintz 1976). In contrast, they find appealing the more suburban- or rural-like settings of these adult communities, their uncongested physical layout, their newer and similarly styled dwellings, and their relatively homogeneous group of occupants (Golant 1980).

Residents feel they are getting a lot or a "good deal" for their money (Heintz 1976). They are lured by the economically priced package of attractive housing, neighborhood, and recreational features. Less upscale communities with smaller-sized single-family attached housing units with minimal outside lawns and grounds to maintain are particularly appealing to active but somewhat older retirees (those in their late sixties and early seventies).

A favorable year-round sunny climate is a further inducement, though not a feature of all communities. Better weather is linked with more prevalent outdoor activities, the greater ease of getting around, fewer upkeep problems (e.g., with snow and ice) and the prospects of better personal health (e.g., relief from chronic conditions such as asthma and arthritis).

Even while substantial percentages of these retirement settlements' occupants have friends and relatives who live in the same state, proximity to these people is not a major motive for living there. People who have family members living near their retirement communities do not identify them as the key reason for their location choice (Gober and Zonn 1983).

Similar Ages of Residents

Retirees generally avoid pointing to the ability of these communities to support a life-style "apart and separate from younger people" (Kahana and Kahana 1983:216) as a major determinant of their decisions to move to them. Rather, they emphasize the importance of living with persons of similar social and economic backgrounds. At the same time, however, they will vigorously defend the age restrictions in their retirement developments (Mangum 1973; Heintz 1976). They also hold more positive views about "old age" and thus are less concerned than others their age about how living in a "retirement" community will affect their image. Other retirees will value the age homogeneity of these places because they will not be continually compared with younger persons. As Rosow (1967:265) suggests, an older person will "not stand out so markedly from his neighbors, so it is easier for him to deny his age and flatter himself in accordance with the norm of youth."

Distinctive Personalities of Residents

Retirees who relocate to these active adult retirement communities display values that are at odds with some interpretations of old age. Rather than maintaining the status quo in their familiar dwellings, they "pull up stakes" to partake of a new form of residential living. It is for this reason that they are believed to possess more adventurous personalities and to have a more positive orientation to the future than many of their peers (Kahana and Kahana 1983). They have probably sought out and successfully coped with new roles, responsibilities, and situations throughout their lives.

How Retirees Learn about These Developments

Many have their first contacts with such developments as a result of earlier vacation experiences or the location of a second home near the retirement community. Others hear secondhand from friends, neighbors, or relatives who have visited or settled in these places (Golant 1980). For example, in the Sun City, Arizona, retirement community 72 percent of the households had earlier heard about this alternative from these informal sources, 16 percent had heard about the community through the media (i.e., advertising), and about 10 percent had discovered it by traveling through or living within the area. The overall impression is that favorable "word-of-mouth" communications are most instrumental in making retirees aware of this alternative (Gober and Zonn 1983).

DIFFERENCES IN SITE PLANS

While similar in many ways, active adult retirement communities come in many varieties. Hunt and his colleagues (1983) have distinguished three categories of active adult retirement developments: retirement new towns, retirement villages, and retirement subdivisions.

Retirement New Towns

The largest and most upscale planned residential developments are literally small towns or cities. They are often the homes of more affluent retired populations. The sizes of these communities can be impressive. Southern California's Leisure World contains almost thirteen thousand homes (with more than twenty thousand residents) spread over two thousand acres. Arizona's Sun City contains more than twenty-five thousand homes (with more than forty-six thousand residents) located on more than eight thousand acres.

Among the earliest established of planned developments, these larger communities also contain some of the oldest retiree populations. For example, retirees in Leisure World in southern California and Sun City, Arizona, both opened in 1960, have an average age of over seventy (Kenneth Leventhal and Co. 1990).

Single-family detached homes and townhomes are common dwelling types in these communities. However, retirement towns exist that are comprised exclusively of manufactured home units, and these towns are comparable in most ways except for their lower housing costs.

The major attraction of these communities is their extraordinarily abundant indoor and outdoor recreational and leisure opportunities. These largely self-contained communities also usually include extensive arrays of shopping, restaurant, religious, and financial facilities and services. Some also contain an impressive range of health care and medical facilities. Of the three types of retirement communities, they are also the most likely to have more supportive housing options (nursing homes, continuing care retirement facilities, and congregate housing facilities) in or near their developments to accommodate their older retired residents.

The responsibility for managing a retirement town will either be retained by its developer (through its management company) or turned over to its residents. In either case, a large staff is often employed and various resident associations are elected to oversee the community's various recreational activities and its security, fire protection, and upkeep efforts. Residents are typically charged a monthly fee to cover these administrative costs. The level of volunteer activity by the residents also tends to be high.

Retirement Villages

These settlements are situated in more urbanized areas and are located on as much as twelve hundred or as little as one hundred acres of land. Typically occupied by between one thousand and five thousand retirees, these developments are much smaller than retirement towns. Prototype villages include Maryland's Leisure World and Leisure Village in New Jersey.

Such developments may be dominated by one type of similarly priced housing units (e.g., manufactured homes) or contain a mix of both higher- and lower-priced accommodations. Thus, these communities are accessible to a wider mix of income groups than are usually found in retirement towns.

Retirement villages, like retirement towns, offer wide arrays of recreational facilities and maintenance services. Residents pay a monthly fee to cover administrative costs. Unlike retirement towns, however, these developments are not designed to be self-contained and their residents usually rely on commercial and financial establishments adjoining their borders or in nearby urban areas. In particular, extensive medical and health care facilities are usually not available, although emergency medical services, medical clinics, and laboratory facilities staffed by physicians, dentists, and technicians may be located in these developments. In more recent years the owners of some retirement villages, though certainly not all, have yielded to their aging residents' demand for more supportive housing accommodations by building rental adult congregate housing facilities or continuing care retirement facilities in or near their developments.

Retirement Subdivisions

These residential communities are sited on much smaller amounts of acreage than retirement towns or retirement villages, usually within an urban center. Their retiree populations number only in the hundreds. While most developments are occupied by people over age fifty, age restrictions are less stringent in others, which may be limited only to persons over the age of eighteen. They are usually dominated by smaller and less expensive detached single-family homes, townhouses, or manufactured homes. Their land uses and dwelling designs give them the appearance of typical suburban subdivisions, and thus they are often indistinguishable from surrounding residential developments.

Like most suburban subdivisions, these developments generally lack shopping, medical, or financial facilities within their boundaries. Thus, an automobile is usually essential to access the closest shopping center. These retirement locales offer no special housing facilities to address the needs of their retired residents who have difficulty living independently.

The recreational facilities in these developments are much less extensive than those in retirement towns or retirement villages, often consisting of only a clubhouse or recreation center with space for hobbies, crafts, bingo, cards, and other passive indoor activities. Outdoor facilities typically include shuffleboard courts and a swimming pool.

Pointing to their relatively lower-cost housing and more limited recreational facilities (resulting in lower monthly maintenance fees), Hunt et al. (1983:257) have referred to these developments as "the bargain retirement communities." One result is that the retirees living in these developments are often less affluent than those found in the other types of developments. Their smaller dwellings and easy-to-maintain grounds also attract more people in their late sixties and seventies.

STRENGTHS AND WEAKNESSES OF
RETIREMENT COMMUNITIES

On the Positive Side

A number of arguments are presented by proponents of communities planned exclusively for retirees:

- An age-homogeneous residential setting presents retirees with good opportunities for friendships with people who have similar life concerns and backgrounds.
- These residential settings allow retirees to avoid a society that seems excessively preoccupied with the desirability of youth, the rewards of employment, and the joys of child raising (Golant 1985). Retirees in these age-segregated settings can literally create their own social worlds and surround themselves with others who value their worth and are more sensitive to what it means to grow old. Occasional visits with children are one thing; continually confronting the playing and screaming of neighbors' insensitive and uncaring children is quite another.
- Retirees in these communities are more likely to learn of pro-

grams and benefits (ranging from health maintenance to income tax changes) that affect their lives. Centrally situated recreation or community buildings will often contain bulletin boards and other "message centers" filled with relevant information (Golant 1985).

- The presence of a relatively large concentration of age-homogeneous residents with similar life-styles makes it possible to provide a more extensive array of leisure and recreational programs at lower cost (because of economies of scale) than would be available in conventional communities.
- These planned residential concentrations of better-educated and single-minded retirees can serve as a political base from which to influence the outcomes of local voting referendums. Thus their occupants can more effectively exercise their rights and voice their opinions. Button and Rosenbaum (1990), for example, found that older people living in planned retirement communities in Florida had high voter turnouts and were more likely to vote against school bond and tax issues than were the residents of other areas. Planned retirement communities offer their occupants relatively unchanging, ordered, and predictable settings and life-styles (Golant 1984). This is in contrast with conventional neighborhoods in which the population makeups, dwellings, and land uses can change unexpectedly and for the worse. This greater sense of certainty can be valued highly in a society that is perceived as rapidly changing and sometimes intolerant of its elderly citizenry.

On the Negative Side

Equally cogent reasons are given for the lack of appeal of these active adult retirement communities:

- Many retirees view unfavorably a residential setting that is so preoccupied with organized leisure and recreational activities. They shy away from a recreation-driven life-style in which residents are always supposed to be "on the go" and "just relaxing" is frowned upon. Others are disconcerted by the perception that everyone and everything is organized into "cliquey groups" and "scheduled activities."
- Retirees often object to living in an age-segregated or age-homogeneous residential setting. They see such communities as having all the negatives of minority ghettos in general, and geriatric ghettos (implying disease and illness) in particular. Many retir-

ees do not want to be identified with the "old", nor do they want
to be continually surrounded only by persons of their own age.
- Many older people reject any residential situation that is
"planned" and labelled as a "community," preferring a less ordered and less homogeneous assemblage of people and activities.
- Older people often find the idea of pulling up stakes and "starting over" in a brand-new community a stressful and undesirable
way to spend their old age. Many retirees have difficulty establishing new friendships and relating to a completely new group
of people.
- Most retirees are unable to afford the costs of these alternatives.
- Retired people who are members of ethnic or racial minority
groups may be dismayed and put off by the poor representation
of their populations in these communities.

The Experiences of Retirees in These Communities

Most retirees who currently live in these communities favorably evaluate their residential situations. Their dwelling turnover rates are
low, and it is usually only the demands of poor health or a family
crisis that cause them to move. Other retirees are less fortunate. They
feel restricted by the rules and regulations of their communities and
by the administrative styles of their management teams. Others feel
that the developers have failed to deliver what they promised. Still
others have to endure undesirable administrative changes when their
communities change ownership or management.

In a new community where housing sales are slower than predicted, the developer may be reluctant to relinquish the control of
management to a resident association, fearing interference with marketing and sales efforts. Thus residents have a limited say in running
their community. Residents may experience other problems when
the developer does leave. The small groups of residents who assume
leadership and control the handling of general administrative issues,
the use of buildings' common areas, and the community's recreational and leisure activities (several resident associations may be
operating in the same community) may be accused of incompetence,
of misusing management funds, or of holding views inconsistent with
those of the majority of the retired residents. The community may
find itself divided into factions, each with its own views and policy
orientations. Residents who take leadership positions may be seen
"as being more instigators of discord than harmony" (Streib, Folts,
and La Greca 1985:409). In practice, "these active persons can cause

a lot of mischief by stirring up trouble, attempting to escalate trivial issues into big causes, and hampering effective self-government by parliamentary maneuvers" (Streib, Folts, and La Greca 1985:409). In the majority of communities these disputes are handled internally, but cases of lawsuits over control of retirement communities are becoming more common.

The Last Home?

Retirees must come to grips with the strong possibility that an active adult community will not be their final place of residence. These communities are not especially appropriate places for the physically and mentally frail. More supportive housing accommodations are usually unavailable except in the largest of these communities. This in itself is hardly a reason to reject this residential life-style, since the majority of retirees spend many happy years in these developments. But, like older residents living in conventional neighborhoods, retirees contemplating this alternative must recognize that they may eventually have to move to more supportive residential accommodations.

THE SIGNIFICANCE OF OWNERSHIP ARRANGEMENT AND DWELLING TYPE

The appropriateness of a retirement community may depend less on its occupants' age homogeneity or on its leisure and recreation orientation than on its ownership arrangements and dwelling types. Manufactured home parks (as distinct from manufactured home subdivisions), condominiums, and cooperatives offer some unique advantages and disadvantages to retirees.

Manufactured Homes

Still also referred to by their earlier "mobile home" labels, these factory-built structures usually remain on the sites to which they are initially transported. Their principal attraction is that they are affordable. Even after the add-on costs for site preparation and improvements (e.g., foundations, tie-downs, concrete driveways and walks, porches, awnings, and landscaping), they are priced significantly lower than comparable conventional single-family dwellings

(Mathieu 1986). About 6 percent of the population age sixty-five and older occupies these units, and most (90 percent) own them. Compared with older homeowners generally, their occupants are more likely to be white and less affluent and to live alone (U.S. Department of Commerce 1990).

This dwelling type can convey strikingly different images. On the one hand, there are double-wide (multisection) structures with shingled roofs, natural wood siding, and aesthetically attractive external designs that are located in carefully designed and landscaped manufactured home retirement subdivisions. Affixed to permanent foundations and sited on individual, retiree-owned lots (and thus taxed as real property), they can be virtually indistinguishable from conventional single-family homes. Their occupants have the same legal and financial status as other retirement community home owners.

On the other hand, there are relatively unattractive single-wide, metal, flat-roofed structures that are sited haphazardly and closely packed in mobile (manufactured) home parks. While the retired occupants may own their units, they only rent or lease their pads (the land on which their units are sited) from a single park owner—often on a monthly basis. About 77 percent of older manufactured home owners do not own their lots (U.S. Department of Commerce 1990). As owners of their units, but not of their lots, they have far more restricted legal and financial rights than do other owners of more desirable manufactured units. Community leaders often view these residential parks as undesirable, and they are relegated to traffic-congested roadside commercial or industrial districts of urban areas or their outlying fringe areas (Chernoff 1983).

Unique Issues That Face Retirees in Manufactured Home Parks

Retirees who occupy manufactured home parks can experience a number of serious problems (Sheldon and Simpson 1991). By far the greatest threat is the prospect of their parks being sold to realize land profits (Streib, La Greca, and Folts 1986). Where once the land around a manufactured home park was vacant, over time it may have become surrounded by rapidly expanding suburban subdivisions or industrial parks. The mobile home park now occupies highly valuable land.

Retirees who do not own their individual lots must also confront the prospects of large, frequent, and unexpected increases in rental fees. A shortage of mobile home park locations (because of restrictive zoning practices) has resulted in some park owners' increasing their rents as much as 50 percent to 60 percent annually.

According to Sheldon and Simpson (1991:6):

> [The park owners may also charge] excessive fees to install appliances, washing machine fees, trash fees, pet fees, maintenance fees, recreational fees, late charges and bounced check charges. . . . One common fee is extra charges when guests visit or additional people live in the unit, or even when a tenant has a large immediate family.

A park owner may also pay for the utility costs of the tenants and then bill them at an inflated price. The occupants may be powerless in such situations.

Residents who are forced to leave a park because of its sale or are financially stressed because of exorbitant rent increases can find themselves in a unique dilemma as home owners. The value of their homes may be lost entirely if their units cannot withstand the rigors of transportation to another site or if the other parks will not accept older units. If relocation is a possibility, they may find the costs of moving their units extreme—$10,000 or more (Sheldon and Simpson 1991). If they try to sell their homes to others, the high park rents will lower the homes' marketability (and thus their selling prices). Assuming they have an option to stay put, "mobile home owners who are unsatisfied with one park often have no alternative but to 'grin and bear it' " (Association of American Retired Persons 1988:3).

Retirees may find that parks have a host of regulations and rules that can crimp their life-styles. In some parks, frail older people are prevented from having live-in helpers because of limitations on the number of people living who may live in the home or rules preventing the sharing of households with nonrelatives.

Park maintenance is often identified as a problem (Sheldon and Simpson 1991). Among the complaints are septic tanks that back up, roads that fall into disrepair, and poorly maintained recreation buildings.

Mobile home parks vary as to whether they have such problems. One multistate survey found widespread problems such as "unreasonable park rules and regulations, evictions without good cause, harassment of tenant organizations and retaliatory evictions, as well as unfair restrictions on the sale or transfer of the home or tenancy" (Sheldon and Simpson 1991:ii).

How protected older tenants are from the unfair practices of manufactured home park operators will depend on whether they have written leases spelling out their rights. Unfortunately, the unit owners' property rights often are subordinate to those of the park owners. State statutes also vary greatly as to the protection they offer residents.

Condominiums and Cooperatives

Opportunities to own condominiums or cooperatives, ranging from the modest to the luxurious, can be found in all categories of retirement communities. Most are units in mid- and high-rise apartments; however, various types of dwellings can be owned as condominiums or cooperatives, including mobile homes and townhouses.

Home ownership is defined somewhat differently in a cooperative than in a condominium (Gordon 1988; Clurman, Jackson, and Hebard 1984). Occupants of condominiums legally own their individual units (e.g., apartments). In contrast, a cooperative project is organized as a corporation that operates the entire development (the building, its dwelling units, and its common areas) for the benefit of its residents. Tenants do not directly own their individual (apartment) units, but rather own shares of stock in the corporation, with the number of shareholders equalling the number of units. A shareholder is usually given the right to exclusive occupancy of a particular apartment unit (i.e., granted a proprietary lease in perpetuity). This right is retained as along as the household meets the conditions of membership, abides by its rules, and pays the appropriate share of its operating costs and fees.

In both forms of ownership the residents share ownership rights of certain common areas of the building and grounds (the lobby, hallways, exterior walls, roof, parking areas, utility buildings, and inside and outside recreational and social areas). A homeowners' association composed of elected residents (a board of directors) assumes the task of managing the common or "outer" living areas. This group develops annual budgets for the residential complex, establishes the amount of the monthly fees, arranges for proper insurance and legal coverage of the project, and arranges for the usual management tasks to be performed.

Typically the occupants of each unit are assessed a monthly fee to pay for the usual maintenance tasks and insurance protection of the common areas. The amount usually varies according to the sizes of the units such that occupants of larger two-bedroom units pay more than occupants of one-bedroom units. Some part of the monthly maintenance fee may also be placed in a reserve fund to cover the costs of large or unusual maintenance expenses (e.g., replacing the building's roof, repainting the building's hallways, or replacing the carpeting in the common areas). When the reserve funds are insufficient, residents are required to make "one-time" lump payments to cover the costs of these periodic maintenance problems. These payments may be substantial and sometimes unexpected. This is not necessarily a problem provided the assessment of such payments is not a regular occurrence and the residents are alert to the possibility. There is, however, always a risk that some retired residents will feel financially burdened.

Unique Advantages and Disadvantages of Condo and Coop Living

Condo and coop living may be especially attractive to retirees who seek relief from everyday home owners' tasks such as cutting grass, removing snow, removing garbage, cleaning a pool, and fixing leaking pipes or a damaged roof. These buildings also often have good crime security precautions.

Relief from these responsibilities of home ownership, however, comes only with a price. Inevitably there is some sacrificing of individual rights because the upkeep of the building (i.e., its common areas) is no longer strictly under a resident's control. Residents may disagree about the necessity of painting a recreation area, resurfacing a parking area, or enlarging a swimming pool deck. Arguments may arise over whether the building is well kept or there are sufficient parking spaces for guests. Residents may be restricted from physically modifying their dwellings (e.g., enlarging doors for wheelchairs or knocking out an interior wall). They may find disagreeable rules that prevent them from having pets, guests, or permanent live-in helpers. Residents may also face constraints regarding to whom they can sell their units and, in the case of cooperatives, prospective buyers may have difficulty obtaining conventional mortgages.

Ironically, some of these dissatisfactions have little to do with the unique aspects of condo or coop ownership, but rather are associated with high-rise living. Previous home owners who have lived in single-family dwellings most of their lives may find that multifamily building occupancy requires them to tolerate higher noise levels, unfriendly or incompatible neighbors, insect problems (as in the case of living next door to someone with an infested apartment), or the sharing of common facilities, such as a laundry room.

Certain consumer abuses also can be linked with these homeownership arrangements. There is no shortage of documentation of older consumers' suffering injustices in their dealings with condo developers who produced shoddily constructed projects or who violated their management promises.

CONCLUSION

Even though they constitute a distinctive residential option for American retirees, active adult retirement communities are not all the same. Their housing accommodations differ as to their types, costs, and ownership arrangements. They offer vastly different opportunities for shopping, service, medical, leisure, and recreation. What they have in common is their appeal to a relatively small segment of the active, relatively healthy retiree population that is willing to leave familiar surroundings for the promise of a distinctive residential lifestyle. Such retirees are drawn by these communities' planned and controlled features, their attractive housing and amenities, their economic value, their relatively homogeneous populations, their organized recreational opportunities, and their well-maintained grounds. Paradoxically, some of these very same features are the basis on which others reject this alternative.

Most retirees in these communities evaluate their housing situations positively. However, others express dissatisfaction with how they are managed. Specifically, they feel that their administrative fees are excessive, their regulations and rules are unreasonably restrictive, and they infringe upon residents' ownership and legal rights.

REFERENCES

American Association of Retired Persons (AARP). 1988. *AARP Housing Report*, April–May.

Button, J. W., and W. Rosenbaum. 1990. *Community Involvement and Voting Among the Aging in Local Elections: A Final Report*. Submitted to Aging and Adult Services Program, Florida Department of Health and Rehabilitative Services.

Chernoff, S. N. 1983. "Behind the Smokescreen: Exclusionary Zoning of Mobile Homes." *Washington University Journal of Urban and Contemporary Law*, 25:235–268.

Clurman, D., F. S. Jackson, and E. L. Hebard. 1984. *Condominiums and Cooperatives*. N.Y.: Wiley.

Gober, P., and L. E. Zonn. 1983. "Kin and Elderly Amenity Migration." *The Gerontologist*, 23:288–294.

Golant, S. M. 1980. "Locational-Environmental Perspectives on Old-Age Segregated Residential Areas in the United States." In D. T. Herbert and R. J. Johnston, eds., *Geography and the Urban Environment*. N.Y.: Wiley, 257–294.

Golant, S. M. 1984. "The Effects of Residential and Activity Behaviors on Old People's Environmental Experiences." In I. Altman, M. P. Lawton, and J. Wohlwill. eds., *Elderly People and the Environment.* New York: Plenum, 239–278.

Golant, S. M. 1985. "In Defense of Age-Segregated Housing." *Aging,* 348:22–26.

Golant, S. M. 1987. "Residential Moves by Elderly Persons to U.S. Central Cities, Suburbs, and Rural Areas." *Journal of Gerontology,* 42:534–539.

Golant, S. M. 1990. "Post-1980 Regional Migration Patterns of the U.S. Elderly Population." *Journal of Gerontology,* 45:S135–S140.

Gordon, P. 1988. *Developing Retirement Facilities.* N.Y.: John Wiley.

Heintz, K. M. 1976. *Retirement Communities.* New Brunswick, N.J.: Rutgers, Center for Urban Policy Research.

Hunt, M. E., A. G. Feldt, R. W. Marans, L. A. Pastalan, and K. L. Vakalo. 1983. "Retirement Communities." *Journal of Housing of the Elderly,* 1:1–278.

Kahana, E., and B. Kahana. 1983. "Environmental Continuity, Futurity, and Adaptation of the Aged." In G. D. Rowles and R. J. Ohta, eds., *Aging and Milieu.* New: Academic Press, 205–228.

Kenneth Leventhal and Company. 1990. *Opportunities for Developing Active Adult Communities.* Los Angeles: Kenneth Leventhal and Co.

Mangum, W. P. 1973. "Retirement Villages." In R. R. Boyd and C. G. Oakes, eds., *Foundations of Practical Gerontology.* Columbia, S.C.: University of South Carolina Press, 237–250.

Mathieu, R. 1986. "Manufactured Housing: The Industry in the Eighties." *Construction Review,* 32:2–17.

Rosow, I. 1967. *Social Integration of the Aged.* New York: Free Press.

Sheldon, J., and A. Simpson. 1991. *Manufactured Housing Park Tenants: Shifting the Balance of Power.* Washington, D.C.: American Association of Retired Persons.

Sherman, S. R. 1971. "The Choice of Retirement Housing among the Well-Elderly." *Aging and Human Development,* 2:118–138.

Streib, G. F., W. E. Folts, and A. J. La Greca. 1985. "Autonomy, Power, and Decision-Making in Thirty-Six Retirement Communities." *The Gerontologist,* 25:403–409.

Streib, G. F., A. J. La Greca, and W. E. Folts. 1986. "Retirement Communities: People, Planning, Prospects." In R. Newcomer, M. P. Lawton, and T. Byert, eds., *Housing an Aging Society.* New York: Van Nostrand, 94–103.

U.S. Department of Commerce. 1990. *American Housing Survey for the United States in 1987.* Current Housing Reports, H-150-87. Washington: U.S. Government Printing Office.

25

Housing with Assistance: Opportunities for the Less Independent Retiree

●

PATRICIA S. TAYLOR AND
LEONARD F. HEUMANN

Today there are many options for assisted independent living. The average retiree may have a difficult time identifying and choosing among the diverse living arrangements now available. This chapter describes the negative and positive attributes of seven of the most popular types of housing options for assisted independent living that are found in the United States. These housing options give retirees life-style choices on a continuum that ranges from staying put in a conventional house or apartment with the help of visiting support added as needed to moving to intentionally built facilities with increasingly less private space and/or more on-site support staff. The seven residential options described are (1) conventional houses and apartments, (2) accessory apartments, (3) shared housing, (4) retirement communities and independent living facilities, (5) board-and-care homes and assisted living facilities, (6) congregate housing, and (7) continuing care facilities.

A major assumption underlying this chapter is that retirees who are frail but well are seeking housing designed to help them retain maximum independence, providing support only at the margin of need. All seven of these housing options provide frail but well retirees some degree of flexibility in tailoring support to their personal needs and tastes.

FACTORS TO CONSIDER IN SELECTING ASSISTED LIVING HOUSING

To describe how the seven housing options differ, each will be discussed relative to the following factors: (1) housing costs, (2) formal support, (3) informal support, (4) potential for aging in place, (5) provision of support at the margin of need, (6) age-integrated living, (7) private versus communal style of living, and (8) preservation of the overall dignity of the resident. We will first define these eight factors, which constitute the framework for evaluating each housing alternative.

Housing Costs

Housing costs include the costs of rent or mortgage payments, utilities, and daily living expenses. The necessity to modify housing to accommodate more sever or multiple dependencies as the retiree ages often creates a costly and unplanned expense.

Formal Support

The availability and variety of support services, both privately purchased and publicly subsidized, as well as their costs, must be considered. Formal support services include meal preparation, housekeeping, transportation, budget counseling, and personal care services. In the least supportive environments, these services might be obtained and coordinated solely by the retiree or his or her family; in more supportive housing programs services may originate off site but be provided with the assistance and coordination of trained staff; and, in the most supportive settings, the support is provided by on-site staff. As people become more frail and need more formal support in settings that rely on visiting service providers, these services may become hard to coordinate and too costly or difficult to provide, placing the resident in jeopardy of an unwanted and even traumatic move.

Informal Support

Regardless of the type of housing chosen, most frail elderly people continue to get, and prefer, support from family and friends. One of the misconceptions of moving to housing facilities with on-site support services is that the retiree will no longer need or want help from family and friends. Some elderly people choose retirement housing with no on-site support assuming their families are, or will be, their primary sources of support. This may work out well while a retiree's dependencies are minor, but the family may become overloaded and its resources in time and money may be depleted as the retiree becomes more dependent. Housing that allows for more independent living may have long waiting lists for rent-subsidized units, or the management may have a policy not to take in residents at an advanced level of frailty even though it will allow younger residents to age in place to that level of dependency.

Potential for Aging in Place

The selection of housing should include a consideration of not only the retiree's support needs, life-style, and tastes *at the point of entry*, but also the degree to which the housing can accommodate changing future needs. Some types of housing offer a full range of options for assisted living short of constant nursing surveillance, while others offer a very narrow range. Most types of housing, through the addition of physical modifications and the hiring of support service providers, can be made to accommodate dependent people. However, the costs of physically modifying single houses and delivering support to widely dispersed locations may become prohibitive. In some types of living facilities (conventional apartments, for example), management policy may forbid the needed modifications or residential zoning policy may legally prohibit such accommodations. These factors can force frail people to relocate to more supportive housing when they are least able.

Provision of Support at the Margin of Need

While all seven housing options that will be presented provide some flexibility in service delivery, some are less flexible than others. In particular, where the housing option relies on off-site visiting service providers, residents must often take the services as provided. In some cases, this may mean that residents get more support than they want or that they are ineligible to receive certain services until they reach a specified level of dependency. Ongoing appraisal of multiple support services received from different providers is necessary to ensure that the services needed are being received and that the services received are appropriate. Without such appraisal, support can be inappropriate or incomplete or can interfere with the retirees' own efforts to retain functional independence.

Age-Integrated Living

Some retirees want to live among their peers and avoid contact with younger people. Others want housing that is as close as possible to conventional living, intermixed with the housing of younger people. Although some experts favor age-integrated housing (Hennig 1992), age-segregated retirement communities remain popular.

Private versus Communal Style of Living

One of the concerns of retirees selecting housing is how much space in various housing options will be private space that is under their control compared with communal space that they must share. At one end of the spectrum, represented by the conventional home, the entire dwelling unit is private space. At the other end, represented by some board-and-care facilities, a retiree's private space may be little more than a bed and a dresser in a shared bedroom. In between are many combinations of private living space and shared common space.

The Overall Dignity of the Resident

Another concern is the dignity of residents, or the ways in which their self-esteem, independence, and life-style are supported by a housing choice. How much control are individuals permitted to have over their lives? Accommodation of preferences, choice and scheduling of activities, and maintenance of preferred amounts of social interaction are all important to the quality and dignity of life.

AN EVALUATION OF SEVEN POPULAR
HOUSING OPTIONS

In the remainder of the chapter we define each type of housing, then evaluate it in terms of the factors described above. The factors are grouped into negative attributes, mixed or relative attributes, and positive attributes for each housing option.

Conventional Houses and Apartments

For a few people, staying put in their preretirement homes is not desirable because the buildings are substandard, the neighborhoods are no longer desirable, or the homes are linked to bad memories of preretirement life. For most people, however, the ideal retirement environments are the homes in which they are currently living. If one chooses this option, one retains all the comforts, familiarity, and control desired with none of the distress of moving and adapting to a new setting. It is possible to grow frail and stay in conventional housing with the help of formal and informal services. There are also real risks and costs involved.

Negative Attributes

The disadvantages of conventional housing as one loses functional independence are numerous. Visiting support is not always available. Housing barriers such as steps, narrow doorways, poor lighting, and poor security may make daily living quite hazardous. Other problems may include long walking distances to reach shops, public transportation, and friends and the growing costs and difficulty of maintaining and managing the property. Any combination of these factors may retard a retiree's efforts to live independently and may force a move at a time when the retiree is least able to adjust to the move. The fewer resources a frail person has, the greater the risk of staying put in a conventional house or apartment.

Mixed Attributes

When looking at housing options, most older people think that staying put means they will have no new housing costs. Because over 60 percent of all older people in the United States already own houses with no mortgage payments or low payments, staying put seems very economically prudent. However, home owners need to determine what it is going to cost to live in their homes if and when they become more functionally dependent, then plan for the time when the costs of staying put will outweigh the benefits of moving to more supportive accommodations. Maintenance costs, utilities, and taxes may take ever-increasing portions of income. Renters may not be allowed to make modifications and may face frequent or unexpectedly steep rent increases.

People often believe that formal services, such as housekeeping or personal care, can be added whenever they are needed. However, arrangements for formal services often pose a number of problems. Not all communities can provide all forms of services. The range, quality, and reliability of services vary dramatically from place to place and are very hard to come by in some inner city neighborhoods and most rural areas. If subsidized services are needed, there may be long waiting lists. Formal services are often reduced or nonexistent on evenings and weekends. As more services are needed, coordination among the services is required or quality of life may suffer. The costs of formal support for very dependent persons in independent houses and apartments are high because of the time and expense of support specialists' traveling between dispersed clients.

Too often elderly people assume that family and friends will be available to care for them—without asking the future caregivers or planning the needed care with them. The more one intends to rely on informal care, the more planning is needed. Informal support is likely to be incomplete in terms of the types of services offered, and the burdens on the care providers over the long term are likely to be high.

Programs that can assist the informal caregiver include elder day care and respite care programs. Elder day care allows a frail person to be dropped off during the day, freeing the informal caregiver, who continues to provide night and weekend support. Respite care can provide service-rich temporary housing for the retiree when the informal caregiver is unable to accommodate him or her for a period ranging from a few weeks to a few months. Respite care can offer the caregiver a vacation or provide support to meet some episodic need of a frail person that the caregiver cannot, such as providing care during recovery from influenza or a broken hip. While these programs are excellent, they are not available in ample supply, leaving many caregivers with no relief and causing some to abandon their support roles.

The popular assumption is that staying put offers a high degree of social integration and age integration because the retiree stays connected with traditional social networks. However, neighbors are also aging and moving away. Neighborhood environments can deteriorate physically and become dangerous, or they can undergo rapid social change, leaving the elderly in an unfamiliar milieu.

Older people who are outgoing and functionally able will maintain active social lives by staying put in stable neighborhoods. For many, the loss of roles as spouses and employees changes their social networks and can result in increasing isolation at home in detached single-family houses.

Positive Attributes

Despite the risks, staying put in their preretirement homes offers retirees the major advantage of continuing life with the accustomed amount of private space, even if it is too much space to clean or care for. Most elderly people seem willing to accept the trade-off of retaining their own homes while incurring some loss of financial and functional independence and the increasing burdens of maintaining their houses.

In the United States such a high value is placed on living in one's own home that aging there provides a greater sense of worth and dignity than aging in any other type of housing. This appears to be true even if the quality of support and daily life is sacrificed somewhat. The older person and his or her family must weigh how much sacrifice is too much. The authors have witnessed cases in which older people have lost so much control over their treasured homes that they have retained only nominal ownership of expensive, socially isolated, and support-deficient environments.

Most of this discussion has centered on the pros and cons of staying put for home owners. Renters are typically much more at risk in staying put. Renters lack the investment resource of owning a home and may be subject to sudden and sharp rent increases. In some areas gentrification and condominium conversion pose threats to older people who want to stay in convenient and familiar neighborhoods at rents that are affordable. Another problem can be the refusal of landlords to eliminate barriers as tenants become more frail. On the positive side, renting in buildings with large elderly populations often means that neighbors can help each other, landlords are accommodating, and visiting services can take advantage of economies of scale (Hunt and Ross 1990).

Accessory Apartments

An accessory apartment is "the addition of a unit to a residential structure in a way that does not fundamentally alter the internal layout or plan of the existing dwelling or dwellings" (Gellen 1985:3). The conversion of part of a home to an accessory apartment is often nonstructural in nature, such as "the blocking off of a doorway, or adding a partition wall" (Gellen 1985:4) and thus may be done, and undone, with minimal expense and effort. The conversion of a home to include an accessory apartment can include structural modifications, such as the addition of rooms to the rear of a house or the construction of a second story, which are much more costly.

Accessory apartments have often been equated with "in-law" apartments occupied by widowed parents of relatively young homeowners. However, Rudel (1984) reported that older homeowners between fifty-one and sixty-seven were the most likely to consider accessory apartment conversion; furthermore, the occupants of these apartments were frequently younger relatives of the homeowner, most often a married son or daughter and his or her spouse or a divorced daughter with children.

An accessory apartment provides two possibilities for the retiree. In the first instance, the retiree may convert his or her existing home to provide the accessory apartment. In this case, Both Rudel's work in New York and Gellen's in California suggest that conversion is most frequently done for additional income, although the provision of space for relatives or companionship is also a motive for conversion by the retiree. In the second instance, an accessory apartment in the home of a relative or a nonrelative provides the retiree with a lower-cost rental alternative to a conventional apartment (Rudel 1984).

One variant of accessory housing that has not been tried very often in the United States is ECHO (elder cottage housing opportunity) housing (Mace and Phillips 1984). An ECHO unit is a temporary cottage or mobile home that is moved into the backyard of a single-family lot. In the most typical case, an elderly parent occupies the temporary unit, while the single-family house is occupied by his or her children. The single-family house may be one owned by the retiree who is handing it down to family members or one that is owned by the son or daughter. This arrangement offers the elderly member of the household the dignity of independent living with family support nearby. The problems of this option include the initial cost of the ECHO cottage, the fact that many lots are not large enough for a cottage, and the zoning laws of many places, which prohibit this arrangement.

Positive and Mixed Attributes

Accessory units have many of the same positive and mixed attributes as conventional housing. However, the retiree as homeowner sacrifices some space and privacy for additional income, companionship, nighttime security, or more convenient informal support. Of course, the accessory arrangement need be no more personal than that of any two households living in conventional rental apartments. For the retired homeowner who is considering a conversion, local zoning and building codes may prohibit or restrict accessory apartments or may add substantially to the costs and taxes (Gellen 1985; Rudel 1984). For the retiree who rents or occupies an ECHO unit, this option may provide lower rent, as well as the advantages of companionship and informal care.

Shared Housing

The term *shared housing* covers a diverse set of housing options that range from family settings to quasi-institutional settings. *Home sharing*, one kind of shared housing, is defined as "a living arrangement in which two unrelated individuals share a single family home owned by one of them" (Danigelis and Fengler 1990). Others include larger groups in their definitions; for instance, Cram (no date) defines *shared housing* as a situation in which two or more unrelated persons live together as a "family of choice" in a dwelling in which each has some private space while sharing common areas.

An alternative conceptualization of shared housing stresses the relationship between social service agencies and the housing of people in shared residences. Using this classification, Jaffe and Howe (1988) distinguish three kinds of shared housing: (1) shared housing that is developed without the intervention of a social service agency, (2) shared housing promoted by an agency that assists individuals in finding suitable candidates with whom to share, but is not actively involved in managing the residence, and (3) group homes that are actively managed by a social service agency.

Shared housing, whether defined in terms of interpersonal relationships or agency involvement, may take any number of forms. For example, an elderly person may seek a house sharer of any age to provide additional income or may trade a room, offering low rent to a person in exchange for companionship, help with household chores, or personal care.

Two elderly people may form a shared household in order to provide each other with social and personal support and to share housing costs. Renters also may share housing for these reasons. Rosabeth Kanter (1972) found an apartment building in Florida in which a number of renters rent their own apartments and also share the rent of a common apartment that serves as a community center where they can eat communal meals and socialize.

A third type of shared housing involves a group of three to ten people who arrange to buy or rent a house together. In some shared housing, such as the Share a Home program (Streib, Folts, and Hilker 1984), staff may be hired to provide housekeeping, meal preparation, and other services.

Arrangements for shared housing may be made privately or with various levels of support from social service agencies. Agency involvement may be limited to referring potential house sharers, interviewing and placing house sharers, providing or coordinating social and welfare services to the shared household, or, in the case of some agency-sponsored group homes, actively managing the entire household as well as providing various personal, social, or health-related services (Streib et al. 1984).

House sharing is not for everyone, however. Jaffe and Howe (1988) report that rates of matching vary greatly among agencies and that from 10 percent to 75 percent of applicants may drop out without being matched. Few matches are successful in the long run: 30 to 90 percent of all agency matches end within three months (Jaffe and Howe 1988). There is a high potential for failure. Furthermore, local zoning laws and regulations may prohibit or restrict house sharing.

Positive and Mixed or Relative Attributes

The one positive attribute is that home sharing can considerably lower housing costs for elderly home owners, renters, or a group of elderly tenants sharing the rent. There is also a potential for lowering the costs of support services through pooled informal care, living a very engaged and active life integrated with peers in a shared household, and achieving integration with the larger society.

Privately arranged home sharing leaves the burden of arranging formal support on the retiree and/or the house sharer. Some agencies will assist people in making support arrangements, while other housing "brokers" may provide some services themselves, such as providing counseling when matches are less than amicable (Streib et al. 1984).

A good match between people whose needs are complementary and whose life-styles are compatible can greatly extend the possibilities for aging in place in conventional housing. A poor match can actually make independent living more difficult. In many cases, living alone and relying on visiting service providers can result in better support at the margin of need than a well-meaning but inept live-in acquaintance. In the best cases, well-matched house sharers can provide wonderful support and companionship.

Home sharing has a potential for keeping a retiree in a house or apartment in a residential neighborhood that he or she knows with a new friend to share expenses, experiences, and outings. Home sharing is therefore a way to retain and even increase one's level of social engagement and integration. In some cases, however, home sharing can be even more isolating if a person is unable to get along with a limited selection of home sharers. In a successful match, shared housing preserves a noninstitutional style of living, but failure of the match may hurt the self-esteem of the participants and even impair their functional independence.

Retirement Communities and Independent Living Facilities

Retirement communities and independent living facilities (ILFs) range from leisure-oriented villages or neighborhoods to single buildings housing healthy, independent retired people. This is the first housing option on the continuum that requires the retiree to move and adjust to a new environment and new neighbors. The concentration of elderly people is quite large in these facilities, as they range from an average of 80 to 120 apartments or bungalows in the ILFs to retirement communities that may take the form of new suburban villages of forty-five thousand retirees, such as Sun City, Arizona. The vast majority of these retirement communities are private market ventures in which the residents buy or rent their units, and therefore they are affordable only to people with incomes in the middle or higher range.

The biggest single attraction of these facilities is the provision of a secure, easy-to-maintain unit with ample opportunity for social enjoyment with age peers. The biggest drawback is that they are designed for and cater to healthy, independent people and may actually prohibit people from remaining if they exceed a minimal threshold of physical or mental dependency (e.g., inability to manage their own finances and/or walk without a four-prong cane or walker).

Mixed and Negative Attributes

Despite the popularity of retirement communities and ILFs, we do not rate them highly for elderly people who are frail. These facilities, conceived for active, independent people, do not make it easy for frail people to receive either formal or informal supports, to age in place, to receive support at the margin of need, or to live in an age-integrated setting. The costs of some leisure-oriented communities can be quite high, involving the costs of purchasing a house or apartment, maintenance fees, fees for the central activity (such as golfing), and purchase of additional social services.

The relative isolation of many retirement communities may affect the availability of both formal and informal supports and visits from friends and relatives. The size and remote location of some retirement communities, and the size and austere appearance of some ILF buildings, can further discourage visits. Availability of formal support services may depend on the willingness of management to provide the services or to permit common spaces to be used by outside vendors. However, residents of minimal-service retirement communities can form informal support networks among themselves. Some vendors may make their services available to residents once the concentration of elderly people produces enough demand to ensure economies of scale.

The potential for aging in place is quite variable. Most retirement villages or ILFs were designed for independent living, but some are converting to provide congregate support as the residents age. It is very important to discuss local policies and future plans with the management and to carefully read the lease or purchase agreement to determine eviction and transfer policies. Some places may require full independence; if it is lost, the retiree must leave.

The possibilities for support at the margin of need in retirement communities or ILFs are likely to be poor, since such support is often not provided on site, may be discouraged by the management, and may not be easily available in isolated suburban new towns.

Retirement communities are typically highly age-segregated. In some, residents may be actively discouraged from having their grandchildren or families visit. On the other hand, some developments make special provisions for visitors, such as offering playgrounds or even having units available to accommodate daytime or overnight visitors. Because of this variability, one must scrutinize each scheme carefully before purchasing.

Positive Attributes

Many retirees want to maximize their functionally independent years and worry about how they will handle functional dependencies if and when the need arises. If that is the case, this housing option is a positive one. The private living units, common grounds, lobbies, social activity spaces, laundry facilities, crafts, hobby and recreation spaces, and possibly restaurant(s) and visitors' accommodations are usually very nice. For the retiree who can afford the costs and wants excellent security, social controls, a barrier-free environment, and socialization almost exclusively with other young, healthy retirees, retirement communities or ILFs offer the desired style of living.

Surveys of these facilities show that residents are happy and that their sense of social worth and dignity is similar to or better than that of active retirees living in conventional housing. However, we must warn potential buyers that increasing frailty, decreasing income, and decreasing activity may lead to social isolation and cause residents to hide frailties from the management for fear of eviction.

Other Types of Housing in This Category

The previous discussion has emphasized private retirement schemes because they are the most numerous. Also included in this category is subsidized housing for elderly people with low and moderate incomes—public housing, Section 8 rent-subsidized housing, Section 202 low-rent housing for the elderly and handicapped, and numerous state-run programs, all of which together house close to seven hundred thousand people over the age of sixty-five nationwide.

Even though the majority of this housing is designed for people who are independent, many schemes provide for aging in place by encouraging and coordinating visiting support services and/or adding congregate support services (see the next section). A 1988 study of the Section 202 program, which houses over two hundred thousand elderly people, shows that 28 percent of the local nonprofit sponsors have made at least a partial conversion to congregate services to help their tenants age in place (Gayda and Heumann 1989). The majority of the residents in these facilities say they have never lived in nicer accommodations with such high-quality security, social interaction, and friendships. By and large, subsidized housing for the elderly provides great dignity, but waiting lists are typically very long: an average of eight to ten years in Section 202 housing in 1988 (Gayda and Heumann 1989).

Congregate Housing

The term *congregate housing* may be used to describe a wide range of living situations, from an apartment building with a restaurant to an institutionally organized group home. More usually, congregate housing is defined as

> a multiunit apartment building in which the apartments all have bathrooms and kitchens or kitchenettes, and where the management provides some supportive services, such as a dining room where residents can obtain at least one meal a day, optional housekeeping, transportation, and twenty-four-hour watch service. Usually there is common space for residents to engage in social, educational, and other group activities, and often management arranges for other services—such as health monitoring or a beauty parlor that are desired by the residents. (Streib 1990:76)

Congregate care is sometimes synonymous with assisted living or residential care homes, which provide some personal care beyond that of room and board (Mor, Sherwood, and Gutkin 1986); however, this type of facility is not covered in this section.

Important considerations in choosing congregate housing include the amount and kind of on-site services provided, such as the number and style of meals and the amount of personal care, transportation, security, and emergency aid, and which services are included in the monthly rent and which are available for purchase.

Positive Attributes   Unlike the housing options described previously, congregate housing is designed to accommodate the frail elderly. Additional positive attributes include the availability of formal supports, including support at the margin of need, and the potential for aging in place.

The One Negative Attribute   Congregate housing is clearly a step closer to institutional living than the options previously described. Congregate facilities can house totally independent people, but they will also admit and retain residents who are facility-bound and chairfast, but not in need of regular nursing care. Congregate facilities often house eighty or more residents, and they have larger on-site support staffs than the options described earlier. They can become age-segregated facilities whose residents may increasingly turn inward. Some countries such as Sweden and Israel are designing housing with congregate services and common space exclusively for elderly residents, but are also mixing units for elderly people into complexes for younger families so residents are not so isolated from the larger society (Shtarkshall 1992).

Mixed Attributes   Private-market congregate housing is the most common variety, and, while it is not cheap, some large markets are actually overbuilt and prices have come down. Considering that full congregate services include rent, thirty meals per month, housekeeping services, transportation, and social and recreational activities, costs are quite reasonable. A check of current prices in the midwest found that most big-city units with full congregate services charged about $1,200 to $1,400 per month, with costs as low as $800 per month in smaller cities and as much as $2,600 in the most luxurious accommodations. Currently there are few subsidized congregate facilities, especially in smaller cities and towns, but those that exist provide excellent services at very reasonable prices (Heumann 1991).

Informal support is similar to that available to residents of retirement communities and ILFs: it depends on whether the facility is located close to family and friends, whether the physical design makes it easy for outsiders to visit, and whether the management welcomes and encourages informal supports. In most facilities the style of living is very close to that in a conventional apartment building, and visitors feel at home in the common space or the residents' apartments. In other schemes the apartments are small studios with no private kitchens and common space is limited to minimal and overused multipurpose rooms that make visitors feel unwelcome.

Positive Attributes   Formal support in congregate housing is usually very good, since many services are available on site and are either included in the housing contract or available for purchase. The management of congregate housing does not usually provide personal care, although it generally assists in arranging private personal care services for individuals in need. In the best cases, congregate facilities offer just about everything a person will need throughout the aging process short of full-time nursing care. Many facilities understand the need to provide services at the margin of need so that residents' skills at independent living do not atrophy.

One of the best ways to evaluate a congregate facility under consideration is to focus on the meal service and the quality of food. If a potential resident does not like the food, the way and setting in which it is served, and the social atmosphere, he or she will probably not be very happy in the facility. The potential resident should look for restaurant-style rather than cafeteria-style meals with menu choices for the main meals, residents' input on entree choices, accommodations for special diets, flexible hours for the serving of meals, and the freedom to cook some meals on one's own or to take all meals in congregate fashion. If the management has designed the meal service to meet the marginal needs and desires of the residents, it is very likely that all services are well designed and delivered with the recipient in mind rather than the service provider.

Board-and-Care Homes

Board-and-care home is one of a number of terms used for facilities that offer "the provision by a nonrelative of food, shelter, and some degree of protective oversight and/or personal care that is generally nonmedical in nature" (Newcomer and Grant 1990:103). People who reside in board-and-care homes are usually very frail upon entry and are in need of more personal care and sometimes more nursing care than residents in any type of housing discussed thus far.

Board and care may be provided in a number of settings. Some settings are more like traditional boarding houses, while others attempt to provide a family-type setting for the retiree. The worst may be more like small-scale institutions than like private homes. Unfortunately, the research literature concentrates on facilities licensed or regulated by state programs (e.g., Mor, Sherwood, and Gutkin 1986), so very little is known about the residents of or the conditions in the many unlicensed and unregulated facilities that exist. Namazi, Eckert, Kahana, and Lyon (1989) investigated unlicensed board-and-care homes in Ohio. They found that most of these "facilities" were private homes, the number of residents in each home tended to be small, and few of the homes provided "family" atmospheres.

Mixed and Negative Attributes

Board-and-care options provide relatively little private space, perhaps the least of any option discussed in this chapter. In some board-and-care arrangements, the retiree does not even occupy a private bedroom. The amount of common space is also far less than in most congregate facilities: sometimes the only rooms outside the bedroom available to the resident are the bathroom, the dining room, and a sitting room.

The availability of both formal and informal support varies greatly depending on the management, the community, and the program. Organized programs have high levels of both formal and informal support. In unregulated, private board-and-care homes, the residents may live very isolated lives and the managers may make little effort to obtain support services for the residents.

The amount of dignity one retains after moving into a board-and-care facility greatly depends on the attitudes of the care providers, the quality of the program providing the placement (if any), and state regulations. Foster care providers may see themselves either as mere providers of housing or as loving family surrogates (Namazi et al. 1989).

Positive Attributes

Board-and-care residences are usually attractive to lower-income retirees who have little informal support available. Most residents of
board-and-care homes rely mostly on Social Security and Social Supplemental Income (SSI) for income (Mor, Sherwood, and Gutkin
1986). At the low cost end of the range, there are homes for the
very frail that provide the bare minimum of support. More expensive
board-and-care homes may try to provide—and often succeed in providing—personalized, even affectionate care. Some board-and-care
operators really adopt the small number of boarders they care for and
provide a semblance of family (Namazi et al. 1989).

The success of aging in place will depend on the levels of support
available, the resident's health, and the policies and preferences of
the management, but these programs are designed to care for people
who are very frail from the start. Oregon's assisted living facilities are
trying to provide the routine nursing care necessary at the lowest
possible prices and in a more congenial environment than that found
in a nursing home (Wilson, Ladd, and Saslow 1988). Since the residents of board-and-care homes are typically quite frail, the important
concern is whether the residents are receiving all the care and support
services necessary, not whether support is provided at the margin
of need.

The small size of board-and-care facilities, which are often existing
or converted houses in residential neighborhoods, provide an excellent opportunity for very frail people to stay in the residential community they know, where they are near friends and neighbors and are
cared for by a younger surrogate family (Namazi et al. 1989; Sherman
and Newman 1988). The location and size of many board-and-care
homes offer at least the possibility of participation in the community,
although the evidence is unclear whether residents of this type of
housing are better integrated into the community than residents of
other housing options (Sherman and Newman 1988).

Continuing Care Retirement Communities

Continuing care retirement communities (CCRCs) are described by
the American Association of Homes for Aging (1988) as having the
following characteristics:

> . . . long-term contracts for residence, services, and health care;
> intention to remain in the community and for the contract to re-

main in effect over a lengthy time period, often the retiree's life; housing and nursing care under coordinated management at one location; and guarantee of at least access to health care service; and, in the best cases, full coverage of nursing care costs.

Continuing care facilities are typically larger than congregate care facilities, often with 225 to 250 apartments or more. Services that might be expected from a continuing care or life care facility include those available in congregate housing plus personal care services, home health care that is provided to the individual unit, sheltered care that is available in a unit outside the individual apartment, and skilled nursing care that is offered in a unit on the grounds (Alperin and Richie 1990).

Sherwood, Ruchlin, and Sherwood (1990) have detailed the kinds of contract plans usual in CCRCs. One type of plan covers the residential unit, services for the residence (maintenance, etc.), recreation or other amenities of the retirement center, and health care services at a specific cost, which is usually paid as an entrance fee or an endowment and monthly payments. In the second type, the costs of the living unit, the housing services, and amenities are included, but the cost of health care is paid at a per diem rate and only *access* to health services is guaranteed with residence in the community. There are many variations that fall between these two extremes. Continuing care facilities are especially appropriate for retirees who know that their health will be failing in the future and want to choose their own housing while they are still able, not leaving difficult choices to be made by their children.

Negative Attributes

The monthly costs and/or the initial entry fee or endowment have to be the greatest drawback of this housing option. The risk to owners of continuing care facilities is great because they are guaranteeing people care for the rest of their lives. Therefore, the endowments are substantial, ranging from $20,000 to $80,000 plus the amount of monthly rent and other costs that are not covered by the housing contract, which can increase each year. Despite such substantial initial payments, these facilities occasionally go bankrupt, leaving some residents without resources because they invested everything in the endowment thinking the move to the continuing care facility would be their last housing move. In the United States there are no publicly subsidized continuing care communities, so this option is available only to people with upper middle and higher incomes.

Mixed and Positive Attributes

All necessary formal support is available. The retiree just needs to be aware of which services are included in the monthly fees and which may be purchased as options. The location and broad market area covered by such a large facility may mean old friends and relatives live too far away to provide informal support. However, all indications are that, because of the large number of fairly homogeneous middle- to upper-class residents who have all made similar life commitments to this housing, residents make many new friends who provide them with informal support.

Of course, aging in place is the primary goal of this housing option, and great care is taken to provide most support at the margin of need. Because the residents are paying for services up front, most take all meals and all housekeeping services from the day they move in.

This style of living seems to be very attractive because the residents get good-sized apartments that they retain for the rest of their lives. Even if they need to go into the nursing unit, some facilities will maintain their apartments on the chance they can return. This model seems to give those who choose it a great deal of satisfaction and the security of knowing that they will never have to make another move, and this results in a higher potential for aging with dignity. The only risks are that the owner may fail to stay solvent or that a resident may no longer like the housing after a few years and want to move out. In either case, the entry fee or endowment may be forfeited wholly or in part.

SUMMARY AND CONCLUSIONS

In summary, staying put in conventional housing maximizes the private style of living most people prefer and provides great personal dignity so long as the risks of a frail person living alone can be overcome with care and repair support services. The elderly owner or renter of an accessory apartment may sacrifice space and privacy for more income or lower housing costs and better informal support and security. Shared housing definitely keeps down the cost of housing. It can also provide informal support and companionship, but these depend on successful matches between home sharers. Retirement communities and independent living facilities are not highly recommended for retirees who want to stay put if and when they become more dependent, because these facilities are designed to house only people who are independent. Some of these facilities are being adapted to meet the support needs of their aging residents, so careful screening is necessary. Congregate housing has become the most popular form of intentionally built apartments with on-site services. While some of these facilities can be highly age-segregated and can cause residents to turn inward, many are designed to provide comprehensive support at the margin of individual need and offer the highest level of dignity for aging tenants. People entering board-and-care housing are often already quite dependent. Most licensed board-and-care facilities provide decent support at relatively low costs. Continuing care programs are designed to be the last housing choice a retiree need make, because they provide private apartments, flexible support services, and, if needed, full nursing care at one site. However, guaranteeing the full range of support for life is quite expensive, and new models of payment and services are evolving.

In choosing one of the supportive housing options, potential residents are committing to residential settings and life-styles that are quite different from what they knew in their preretirement lives. Retirees and their families must carefully scrutinize these facilities and the attendant lifestyle options. The commitments to communal living required by these environments are great, and the costs of leaving in emotional, resettlement, and financial terms are usually higher than the costs of any housing choices made by younger independent persons.

The seven housing options presented in this chapter are all evolving and spinning off new variants. While the United States still does not have the variety of options found in some countries, the choices available in most urban areas today are quite diverse. Unfortunately, the lower one's income and the smaller one's informal support network, the fewer the housing choices and the more difficult it is for frail people to evaluate their choices.

REFERENCES

Alperin, D. E., and N. D. Richie. 1990. "Continuing/Life Care Facilities and the Continuum of Care." *Journal of Housing for the Elderly*, 9:125–130.

American Association of Homes for the Aging. 1988. *National Continuing Care Directory*. Washington, D.C.: American Association of Retired Persons.

Cram, L. L. (no date). "Shared Housing." *Guide on Aging*. Columbia, Mo.: Missouri Gerontology Institute.

Danigelis, N. L., and A. P. Fengler. 1990. "Homesharing: How Social Exchange Helps Elders Live at Home." *The Gerontologist*, 30:162–170.

Gayda, K., and L. F. Heumann. 1989. *The 1988 National Survey of Section 202 Housing for the Elderly and Handicapped, House of Representatives Select Committee on Aging*. Washington, D.C.: Government Printing Office.

Gellen, M. 1985. *Accessory Apartments in Single Family Housing.* New Brunswick, N.J.: Rutgers University, Center for Urban Policy Research.

Hennig, C. 1992. "An Integrated Physical and Social Plan to Prevent the Marginalization of the Frail Elderly at the Neighborhood Level." In L. F. Heumann and D. Boldy, eds., *Aging in Place with Dignity: International Solutions Relating to the Low Income and Frail Elderly.* New York: Praeger Press.

Heumann, L. F. 1991. "A Cost Comparison of Congregate Housing and Long Term Care Facilities for Elderly Residents with Comparable Support Needs in 1985 and 1989." In L. W. Kaye and A. Monk, eds., *Congregate Housing for the Elderly: Theoretical, Policy, and Programmatic Perspectives.* New York: Haworth Press.

Hunt, M. E., and L. E. Ross. 1990. "Naturally Occurring Retirement Communities: A Multiattribute Examination of Desirability Factors." *The Gerontologist,* 30:667–674.

Jaffe, D. J., and Howe, E. 1988. "Agency-Assisted Shared Housing: the Nature of Programs and Matches." *The Gerontologist* 28:318–324.

Kanter, R. M. 1972. *Commitment and Community: Communes and Utopia in Sociological Perspective.* Cambridge, Mass.: Harvard University Press.

Leather, P., and S. Mackintosh. 1990. *Monitoring Assisted Agency Services: Home Improvement Agencies—An Evaluation of Performance,* part I. London: Department of the Environment.

Mace, R. L., and R. H. Phillips. 1984. *ECHO Housing: Recommended Construction and Installation Standards.* Washington, D.C.: American Association of Retired Persons.

Mor, V., S. Sherwood, and C. Gutkin. 1986. "A National Study of Residential Care for the Aged.: *The Gerontologist,* 26:405–417.

Namazi, K. H., J. K. Eckert, E. Kahana, and S. M. Lyon. 1989. Psychological Well-Being of Elderly Board and Care Home Residents. *The Gerontologist,* 29:511–516.

Newcomer, R. J., and L. A. Grant. 1990. Residential Care Facilities: Understanding Their Role and Improving Their Effectiveness. In D. Tilson, ed., *Aging in Place: Supporting the Frail Elderly in Residential Environments,* 101–124. Glenview, Ill.: Scott, Foresman.

Rudel, T. K. 1984. "Household Change, Accessory Apartments, and Low Income Housing in the Suburbs." *The Professional Geographer,* 36:174–181.

Sherman, S. R., and E. S. Newman. 1988. *Foster Families: A Community Alternative in Long Term Care.* New York: Columbia University Press.

Sherwood, S., H. S. Ruchlin, and C. C. Sherwood. 1990. "CCRCs: an Option for Aging in Place." In D. Tilson, ed., *Aging in Place: Supporting the Frail Elderly in Residential Environments,* 125–164. Glenview, Ill.: Scott, Foresman.

Shtarkshall, M. 1992. "Aging in Place and Public Sheltered Housing in Israel with a Special Focus on Age Integration." In L. F. Heumann and D. Boldy, eds., *Aging in Place with Dignity: International Solutions Relating to the Low Income and Frail Elderly.* New York: Praeger Press.

Streib, G. F. 1990. "Congregate Housing: People, Places, Policies." In D. Tilson, ed., *Aging in Place: Supporting the Frail Elderly in Residential Environments,* 75–100. Glenview, Ill.: Scott, Foresman.

Streib, G. F., W. E. Folts, and M. A. Hilker. 1984. *Old Homes—New Families: Shared Living for the Elderly.* N.Y.: Columbia University Press.

Wilson, K., R. Ladd, and M. Saslow. 1988. "Community Based Care in an Institution: New Approaches and Definitions of Long Term Care." Paper presented at the 41st Annual Scientific Meeting of the Gerontological Society of America, November, 1988, San Francisco, Calif.

26

Where Retirees Prefer to Live: The Geographical Distribution and Migratory Patterns of Retirees

●

CHARLES F. LONGINO, JR.

Dr. Robert Butler, former head of the National Institute on Aging, has been quoted as saying, "The best place to retire is the neighborhood where you spent your life" (Boyer and Savageau 1987). For most people who are retiring, this statement is probably sound advice. The retiree's house represents an accumulation of a lifetime, a comfortable, secure, and familiar setting in which friends visit and to which children return for holidays; ties to the community, the neighborhood, tavern, clubs and church are secure and socially rewarding; opportunities to indulge recreational interests and to be useful are within driving distance and plentiful enough to match the life-style the retiree desires in retirement; and the climate in which the retiree has lived for years poses no serious health problems. Under these circumstances, why would anyone think of moving? In any recent five-year period, people of retirement age are only about half as likely to make long-distance moves as is the U.S. population as a whole (Flynn et al. 1985). So the initial answer to the question implied in the title of this chapter is that people tend to stay put when they retire.

Like boats to a mooring, people are tied to their environments by investments in their property, by the many community contexts in which they find meaning, by friends and family whose proximity they value, by the experiences of the past, and by life-styles that weave these strands together into patterns of satisfying activity. Any life-style requires for its existence a unique combination of environmental resources, and a retirement life-style is no exception to this rule.

A minority of retired people seek to change their life-styles in such a way that a change of territory is required, and some find that they must relocate in order to maintain their desired life-styles because the environments around them have changed. In the paragraphs that follow, the relationship between retirement and geographic mobility will be examined, with particular emphasis placed on the kinds of people most likely to move, where they tend to move, and how they adjust to their changed environments. Then such mobility will be viewed in the context of the life course after retirement.

WHO ARE THE RETIREES MOST LIKELY TO RELOCATE?

The retirees who are most likely to relocate are those who have the fewest moorings; those whose desired retirement life-styles are not compatible with their present community, neighborhood, and housing environments; those who are homesick for other places and times; and those with the economic, health, and psychic resources to move (Wiseman 1980; Longino 1986). We shall look at these one at a time.

Work itself is a major community mooring; it ties us, within community distance, to the place of our employment. If a retiree has no other strong ties to the community, one would expect that retirement alone might be enough to motivate a move. If some local friends move when they retire, they model the process and their leaving may loosen ties further. As children leave for college or jobs, community ties are also loosened. It is not unusual to hear a retiree explain a move by saying that he or she had "no reason to remain," followed by a litany of loosened or lost moorings (McHugh 1984, 1990; Oldakowski and Roseman 1986).

The weakening of ties to a place may make moving easier, but it is seldom the major factor behind a move. It becomes more important when combined with a clear image of a retirement life-style that calls for a different environment. Images of retirement are drawn primarily from leisure or vacationing experiences when one expects retirement to fit the model of an extended vacation. One's childhood summer camps and family vacations have a powerful influence on images of one's life-style in retirement. Unsurprisingly, the most popular retirement locations are overwhelmingly in or near places that attract tourists and vacationers (Longino 1990a).

There may be a darker side, however, to the idealization of retirement life-styles and environments. These may be formed partly as opposite projections of negative experiences. An obvious example of this process is the yearning to retire in a setting that has a climate with none of the bad aspects of one's own. If the climate in which one lives is too cold, then the ideal place would be warm. Perhaps this accounts in part for the sunbelt retirement pattern and for the fact that native Floridians tend to seek out cool summer places, such as western North Carolina, as retirement sites. The danger in letting such fantasies guide our retirement planning is that such fantasies never broadly consider our basic needs, but only our frustrations.

There also can be a large measure of nostalgia in our retirement life-style fantasies, which can be sirens' songs from previous times and places. The attempt to recover satisfying memories of one's past may underlie many attempts to return to an earlier setting or one that seems like it in some important ways.

Serow and I (1992) argued from the results of a regional analysis that those returning to their states of birth fall into two categories: provincial return migrants and counterstream return migrants. The hypothesis of provincial return migration, or migration for a job when one is young, ultimately followed by a return to one's roots after retirement, has been an appealing notion to theorists (Wiseman and Roseman 1979; Wiseman and Virden 1977). The advantages are obvious: the retiree gains a lower cost of living (Serow et al. 1986) in a location where experience in the world and greater retirement income give the retiree a higher status than relatives who never left, thus elevating his relative status. This provincial migration pattern is one of the enduring prototypes of retirement migration in the United States. Although it is no more frequently seen among retirees than among younger migrants on the whole, return migration is somewhat more characteristic of retirement migration among African Americans (Longino and Smith 1991).

Counterstream return migration is a return to one's state of birth when one is older and more dependent on the care of others, presumably members of one's extended family. Thus for some retirees migration is a cyclical process, first attracting them to places where they can approximate their idealized life-styles and later returning them to family caretakers when their dependency increases.

We must not lose sight of the fact that retirees vary in terms of the resources they need to relocate. These resources may be categorized broadly as economic, health and psychic. There is a substantial range of economic well-being among people who relocate in retirement. On the whole, long-distance movers are better off economically than those who do not move or those who move short distances, perhaps because of the economic resources needed to make such a move. An economic bonus also follows when one moves to an area with a lower cost of living.

Health makes a difference two ways (Patrick 1980). Being in good health can encourage an early retirement move. When asked, retirees often justify moving by saying that they want to do this while they are in good health and can enjoy their new life-styles. On the other hand, Jackson, Zimmerman, Bradsher, and I (1991) found that even a moderate decline in functional health when one is over age seventy can trigger a change of living environments. This process is accelerated when it is combined with widowhood (Bradsher et al. 1992).

Psychic resources are those that provide the inner strength or freedom necessary for one to take the risks involved in moving. Retirees who have the most frequently experienced residential relocation during their working years best understand the positive and negative sides of these residential and community transitions. For them, the prospects of such transitions generate fewer doubts and fears. Strong community moorings carry an emotional cost. They reduce one's ability to move even when income and health resources are abundant.

Cuba (1984, 1987) argues that "selves" can be relatively mobile, as can "bodies." Moving oneself physically to another community does not necessarily mean that one also moves emotionally. Some migrants never put down roots, but remain emotionally moored to their former communities. Perhaps the less mobile "self" is the one more likely to return "home" upon retirement and the mobile self is more likely to make moves to exotic places based on life-style choices (Cuba 1989; Longino 1989a).

Retirees who make interstate moves may be collectively described by looking at their average characteristics (Longino 1989b, 1990a). Mobile retirees tend to be married, younger retirees who are in good health and to have better-than-adequate economic resources. They are less likely than others their age to work or to rent their dwellings. These general tendencies, however, cover many major differences that allow one to distinguish several types of retired migrants.

The largest number represent a type that may be called amenity migrants, who have the most economic and societal resources and are driven primarily by life-style issues. They are psychically mobile and often plan for retirement moves years or decades before retirement. There are also dependency migrants, whose moves are motivated largely by health-related issues. They tend to be older and more often widowed, although not necessarily poorer than the average older migrant. Return migrants, those who return to their states of birth, fall into both categories. On the average, there are higher proportions of African Americans (Longino and Smith 1991) and Hispanic Americans (Biafora and Longino 1990) in this category. Finally, return migrants are attracted to big-city life in retirement in lower proportions than members of other groups.

CHARACTERISTICS AND DIFFERENTIAL FEATURES OF RETIREMENT HAVENS

Where do retirees concentrate geographically, and what do these places tend to have in common? Before focusing on individual settings, it is important to understand the national patterns of retirement migration.

The earliest study of migration-stream patterns of retirees (Friedsam 1951) examined interregional moves between 1935 and 1940. Friedsam reported that the Pacific coast and south Atlantic regions were the most frequent destinations of older interregional migrants and that migrants to the south Atlantic came mostly from east of the Mississippi. These findings have been remarkably stable through the years.

A census question on mobility asks where a person lived five years before the census. The periods before the 1960, 1970, and 1980 censuses showed very similar patterns. Half of the interstate migrants, regardless of their points of origin, were flowing in high proportions to only seven of the fifty states. Florida dominated the scene, receiving about one-fourth of all interstate migrants aged sixty and over during all three decades. California, on the other hand, maintained its second position throughout. Arizona, Texas, and New Jersey held either third, fourth, or fifth places in both 1970 and 1980 (Rogers and Watkins 1987).

Although only Florida, California, and Arizona attracted several unusually large streams from states outside their regions, the major recruitment areas were different (Flynn 1980). It is as if a great divide stretched south from Lake Michigan and created two drainage systems of interstate migration by older people: east to Florida and west to Arizona and California. This is the same regional pattern Friedsam (1951) glimpsed in the 1940 census. New York contributed over 14 percent of all older interstate migrants during the periods 1965–70 and 1975–80, making it the leading sending state in both periods.

The twelve sunbelt states have been studied collectively as a retirement destination (Biggar 1979, 1984; Biggar, Cowper, and Yeatts 1984). These states contained one-third of the national population but attracted 56 percent of all elderly migrants during 1975–80. In addition, two-thirds of the sunbelt states increased their proportional share of older migrants between 1970 and 1980 (Biggar 1984).

Regional (as opposed to national) retirement destinations are places that attract unusually large proportions of retirees from adjacent states, but not from farther away. Several such regional destinations form a chain stretching from New England to the Pacific Northwest (Cuba and Longino 1991). Established tourist industries in coastal, lake, or mountainous territories already existed in these states. From east to west the chain of regional migration destinations included coastal New England, the New Jersey coast (the largest and oldest regional center), certain zones in the mountainous Appalachian region that stretches from Pennsylvania to northern Alabama (particularly western North Carolina), and the mountainous Ozarks region that overlaps northern Arkansas and southern Missouri. The resort areas of southern and western Nevada receive migrants in large numbers from California, and the Washington-Oregon coastal region, benefiting from warm Pacific currents, attracts migrants from farther inland and from California. This chain of regional centers may alter the national migration patterns at some point in the future if it becomes a buffer to the larger flows farther south to the more popular Sunbelt destination states.

Reference volumes that offer advice about places to retire (Boyer and Savageau 1987; Dickinson 1986, 1987) are very helpful when giving the potential migrant additional information about places in which he or she is already interested. In the end, however, most retirees who relocate do not go to the places that are most highly rated in these books, and they are probably no worse off for it. Their motivations and selections are most often based on individual experience and personal considerations (Longino 1989a).

ADJUSTMENT AND LIFE-STYLES

Adjustment centers around the idea of place identity, the process by which the mobile "self" comes to identify a place as "home." There are two types of mobile retirees in this regard: those who merge into the social fabric of the local community and those who remain aloof from the natives and affiliate socially primarily with other migrants.

A fruitful example of the transition to membership in the local community is found in descriptions of retired migrants in Cape Cod (Cuba 1989). Those who moved to the cape had regularly visited, some even as seasonal residents. Few moved there without having established this pattern of preretirement visitation. The migrants' initial identity, therefore, was as seasonal visitors. As they lived there throughout the year, in some there was a gradual shift in identity occurred for some, from visitor to resident (Cuba 1989). Their understanding of the nature of the community changed from one that was pleasure-oriented, characterized by what happens during the "tourist season," to one that was more productively oriented, characterized by what goes on in the' off season." Some of these migrants with changed identities eventually avoided tourists altogether and complained about them as loudly as those who had been born in the community.

The Center for Creative Retirement in Asheville, North Carolina, conducts leadership seminars in several towns where there are concentrations of recent retirees who have moved from other states. The purpose of these seminars is to acquaint the retirees with the history and demographic characteristics of their new communities, to introduce them to the leaders of the communities, and to match their interests and skills with the communities' needs and the structures that exist to meet those needs. In this way, the center serves as a broker between retirees who want to become integrated into their new communities and the communities themselves. This process often founders without some systematic attempt to facilitate the civic rooting of retired transplants.

Migrants of the second type yield to a strong temptation to form their own ties with one another and to integrate very little into the larger indigenous community that surrounds them. This "enclave" mode of adjustment is especially characteristic of retirees who are in planned communities where the emphasis on a leisure-orientated lifestyle may not differentiate them from retirees who are seasonal residents or even tourists. It is also common outside these enclaves (Longino et al. 1980). Whether there is a shift in identity, therefore, depends largely upon one's choice of life-style in retirement. And choice of life-style depends to some extend upon the migrant's personality needs and values.

Retired newcomers to small towns in regional retirement settings tend to base their new place identities on somewhat different criteria than do younger migrants (Cuba 1992). Retirees tend to identify with a place because of their historical vacationing connections and their retirement dwellings, while younger newcomers base their identification with the place more on their relations with family and friends. Younger migrants tie into the community more easily than do retirees because they can connect through their workplaces and their children's schooling. Therefore, retirees are more vulnerable than younger migrants to being stigmatized as "outsiders" by the natives.

Without making a concerted effort to break through the local xenophobia, migrants with no kinship ties to traditional rural communities tend to be relatively rootless in such communities, building their important social ties with other migrants in the neighborhoods, churches, and voluntary associations and, in so doing, perpetuate their separateness (Longino 1990b).

In this context, adjustment issues become life-style issues. The key to successful adjustment is the successful matching of one's desired retirement life-style to a retirement location and the accommodations that are found in one's new environment. This is why one should perform a rigorous and ruthlessly honest life-style self-inventory before settling on a location. Climate and natural beauty always rank high on the list of reasons retirees choose new places to live (Longino 1986), but their long-term satisfaction is more strongly influenced by whether they can do the things and be the people they want to do and be in retirement.

One's fantasy about the ideal retirement life-style becomes an obstacle in this process of discernment. Golf or deep-sea fishing may be enjoyable tourist activities, but unless one is a serious golfer of fisherman, the golf course and marina may get little use after the first year, while the absence of a well-run library or a nearby airport or the unavailability of cable television may become the foci of considerable grumbling and regret.

If the retiree intends to live in the new residence throughout the year, not just during the tourist season, living in the area temporarily for at least one off season is strongly recommended. When the visitors have left, the retiree may find an entirely different environment there, both socially and climatically, a world that may not appeal to the retiree.

Some retirees who are strongly moored to their preretirement communities may have the best of both worlds by settling in a regional retirement center less than a day's drive from "home" so they can visit often with family and friends from home. Cuba and I (1991) found that this was true for many Cape Cod retirees, for whom maintaining old social ties after retirement was very important.

REASONS FOR RELOCATING AND FOR RETURNING FROM THE SUNBELT

It is a mistake to think that retirement migration involves only one move soon after retirement, although this is the move that people approaching retirement think about the most. A broader understanding of the issue of relocation in retirement requires a more expansive view of the life course.

Litwak and I (1987) proposed that there are three types of migration by the elderly that are associated with different periods in the life course, and they developed a typology of moves. The first move that many retirees make has been called "amenity" migration (Wiseman 1980). If retirees make this move, it tends to closely follow retirement; movers are often married couples in good health with better-than-average financial resources (Longino et al. 1984), and they appear to be motivated primarily by life-style considerations. Not many such moves are a required part of the life course. If retirees make such a move, they tend to do so early in retirement.

The motivation for the second type of move arises when older retirees develop chronic disabilities that make everyday household tasks difficult to perform. A spouse provides help in and motivation for performing these tasks. Therefore, the motivation for this second type of move is usually compounded when the deficits of widowhood and disability are combined. As this happens, if older retirees live at a distance from a person who is available to provide help and if they cannot adequately adapt their living environments, they must move to get the help they need.

This is not necessarily the second in a sequence of moves in an individual's life. It may be the first and only move a person makes, or the need for such a move may be preempted by death. However, people who make this type of move have a higher median age than those making postretirement amenity moves, and in that sense it is the second move of the typology. The aggregate population profiles of older migrants in the stream and counterstream from New York to Florida seem to fit this interpretation (Longino 1984; Flynn et al. 1985). Most retirees who move from New York to Florida seem to be making the first type of move, while a large proportion of those who move from Florida to New York are making the second type of move.

Limited family resources motivate the third basic type of move, from more or less exclusive care by family to institutional care. When older people suffer from more severe forms of chronic disability, institutional care is crucial. The motivation may be slight for the first type of move, stronger for the second, and the strongest for the third.

Contingency planning is the lesson of this typology for retirees considering retirement moves. The first move may not be the last. Some new homes in Sun City near Phoenix, Arizona, have attached one-bedroom apartments that can accommodate an older parent who needs the watchful care of a retired child or the early middle-aged child who is between jobs or spouses and needs emergency shelter and support. This kind of housing flexibility has been developed with thoughtful and realistic consideration of the complexity of migration patterns throughout the life course.

SUMMARY AND CONCLUSION

Most retirees prefer to continue to live in their preretirement settings because of their local economic and social ties, the experiences of their past, and satisfying life-styles they have adapted to that environment. For these retirees, there may be no compelling reason to move. A minority of retirees want to change their life-styles to be more in keeping with their dreams of retirement, and this requires a change of territory. In this chapter the relationship between retirement and geographic mobility has been examined, and particular emphasis has been given to the kinds of people most likely to move, where they tend to move, and how they adjust to their changed environments. It has been argued that retirement relocation makes more sense when viewed from the perspective of the retiree's life course, because retirement may last for a long time and call for different kinds of environmental adjustments.

The retirees who are the most likely to relocate are those who have the fewest ties to the local community and whose desired retirement life-styles require residential change, those who want to return to places of fond memories and old relationships, and those with the health, economic, and psychic resources to move. Amenity migrants are those who desire life-styles that emphasize comfort and pleasure, usually defined in the context of leisure. The majority of those who move great distances from their preretirement homes fall into this category, and many locate in more pleasant climates. Dependency migrants are motivated largely by health-related issues. They tend to be older and more often widowed, although not necessarily poorer than amenity migrants. Return migrants, those returning to their states of birth, may fall into the amenity or dependency category, but they want something extra, familiar settings.

Nationally, mobile retirees concentrate in the sunbelt. Regionally, they concentrate in the mountain, lake, and coastal locations with strong tourist traditions. Amenity migrants are strongly represented in these places because dependency and return migrants tend to scatter more randomly.

Adjustment often depends on how people feel about their new places of residence—whether and how soon they come to consider it home. There are two primary adjustment strategies, one that emphasizes merging into the social fabric of the local community and one that emphasizes remaining aloof from the natives and affiliating primarily with other migrants. Either can be successful strategies. Challenges such as environmental and life-style change can stimulate personal growth in retirement at any stage of the life course.

REFERENCES

Biafora, F., and C. F. Longino, Jr. 1990. "Elderly Hispanic Migration in the United States." *Journal of Gerontology: Social Sciences*, 45:S212–S219.

Biggar, J. C. 1979. "The Sunning of America." *Population Bulletin*, 34:3–41.

Biggar, J. C. 1984. " The Greying of the Sunbelt: A Look at the Impact of U.S. Elderly Migration." *Population Trends and Public Policy*. October.

Biggar, J. C., D. C. Cowper, and D.E. Yeatts. 1984. "National Elderly Migration Patterns and Selectivity, 1955–1960, 1965–1970, and Decade Trends." *Research of Aging*, 6:163–188.

Boyer, R., and D. Savageau. 1987. *Retirement Places Rated*. Chicago: Rand McNally and Company.

Bradsher, J. E., C. F. Longino, Jr., D. J. Jackson, and R. S. Zimmerman. 1992. "Health and Geographic Mobility among the Recently Widowed." *Journal of Gerontology: Social Sciences*, 47:S261–S268.

Cuba, L. J. 1984. "Reorientations of Self: Residential Identification in Anchorage, Alaska." *Studies in Symbolic Interaction*, 5:219–237.

Cuba, L. J. 1987. *Identity and Community on the Alaskan Frontier*. Philadelphia: Temple University Press.

Cuba, L. J. 1989. "Retiring in Vacationland." *Generations*, 13:63–67.

Cuba, L. J. 1992. "Aging Places: Perspectives on Change in a Cape Cod Community." *Journal of Applied Gerontology*, 11:64–83.

Cuba, L. J., and C. F. Longino, Jr. 1991. "Regional Retirement Migration: The Case of Cape Cod." *Journal of Gerontology: Social Sciences*, 46:S33–S42.

Dickinson, P. A. 1986. *Sunbelt Retirement*. Washington, D.C.: AARP.

Dickinson, P. A. 1987. *Retirement Edens Outside the Sunbelt*. Washington, D.C.: AARP.

Flynn, C. B. 1980. "General versus Aged Interstate Migration, 1965–1970." *Research on Aging*, 2:165–176.

Flynn, C. B., C. F. Longino, Jr., R. F. Wiseman, and J. C. Biggar. 1985. "The Redistribution of America's Older Population: Major National Migration Pattern for Three Census Decades, 1960–1980." *The Gerontologist*, 25:292–296.

Friedsam, H. J. 1951. "Interregional Migration of the Aged in the U.S." *Journal of Gerontology*, 6:237–242.

Litwak, E., and C. F. Longino, Jr. 1987. "Migration Patterns among the Elderly: A Developmental Perspective." *The Gerontologist*, 27:266–272.

Longino, C. F., Jr. 1984. "Returning from the Sunbelt." In Abraham Monk, ed., *Returning from the Sunbelt: Myths and Realities of Migratory Patterns among the Elderly*, 7–21. Columbia University in the City of New York: The Brookdale Institute on Aging and Adult Human Development.

Longino, C. F., Jr. 1986. "Personal Determinants and Consequences of Independent Housing Choices." In R. J. Newcomer and M. P. Lawton Eds.. *Housing in an Aging Society*, 83–93. New York: Van Nostrand Reinhold.

Longino, C. F., Jr. 1989a. "Migration Demography and Aging." *Gerontology Review*, 2:65–76.

Longino, C. F., Jr. 1989b. "Rating Places: A Demographer Thinks Aloud about Retirement Guides." *Generations*, 13:61–62.

Longino, C. F., Jr. 1990a. "Geographic Distribution and Migration." In R. H. Binstock and L. K. George, eds., *Handbook of Aging and the Social Sciences*, 3rd ed., 45–63. San Diego: Academic Press.

Longino, C. F., Jr. 1990b. "Retirement Migration Streams: Trends and Implications for North Carolina Communities." *Journal of Applied Gerontology*, 9:393–404.

Longino, C. F., Jr., J. C. Biggar, C. B. Flynn, and R. F. Wiseman. 1984. *The Retirement Migration Project: A Final Report to the National Institute on Aging*. Coral Gables, Fla.: University of Miami Center for Social Research in Aging.

Longino, C. F., Jr., D. J. Jackson, R. S. Zimmerman, and J. E. Bradsher. 1991. :The Second Move: Health and Geographic Mobility." *Journal of Gerontology: Social Sciences*, 46:S218–S224.

Longino, C. F., Jr., K. A. McClelland, and W. A. Peterson. 1980. "The Aged Subculture Hypothesis: Social Integration, Gerontophilia and Self-Conception." *Journal of Gerontology*, 35:758–767.

Longino, C. F., Jr., and W. J. Serow. 1992. "Regional Differences in the Characteristics of Elderly Return Migrants." *Journal of Gerontology: Social Sciences*, 47:S38–S43.

Longino, C. F., Jr., and K. J. Smith. 1991. "Black Retirement Migration in the United States." *Journal of Gerontology: Social Sciences*, 46:S125–S132.

McHugh, K. E. 1984. "Explaining Migration Intentions and Destination Selection." *Professional Geographer*, 26:15–25.

McHugh, K. E. 1990. "Seasonal Migration as a Substitute for, or Precursor to, Permanent Migration." *Research on Aging*, 12:229–245.

Oldakowski, R. K., and C. C. Roseman. 1986. "The Development of Migration Expectations: Changes throughout the Lifecourse." *Journal of Gerontology*, 41:290–295.

Patrick, C. H. 1980. "Health and Migration of the Elderly." *Research on Aging*, 2:233–241.

Rogers, A., and J. Watkins. 1987. "General versus Elderly Interstate Migration and Population Redistribution in the United States." *Research on Aging*, 9:483–529.

Serow, W. J., D. A. Fournier, and D. W. Rasmussen. 1986. "Cost of Living Differentials and Elderly Interstate Migration." *Research on Aging*, 8:317–327.

Wiseman, R. F. 1980. "Why Older People Move: Theoretical Issues." *Research on Aging*, 2:482–529.

Wiseman, R. F., and C. C. Roseman. 1979. "A Typology of Elderly Migration Based on the Decision-Making Process." *Economic Geography*, 55:324–337.

Wiseman, R. F., and M. Virden. 1977. "Spatial and Social Dimensions of Intra-Urban Elderly Migration." *Economic Geography*, 53:1–13.

VIII
INDIVIDUAL AND
FAMILY LIFE
●

27

Family Life in Retirement

●

JUDITH TREAS AND MICHELE SPENCE

Our families help us sustain meaning and navigate change throughout our lives. Because relations with friends, co-workers, and neighbors depend on common interests and day-to-day proximity, they may not last much beyond retirement or a move to Florida. Family ties, however, are lasting bonds based on deeper feelings of affection, duty, and shared identity. Retirees are embedded in a life-long network of spouses, grown children, grandchildren, siblings, aging parents, and other kind. They are caught up in the family give-and-take of gifts, services, information, advice, social support, and companionship. In later life, kin may become a meaningful focus for activity, efforts, and attention—one that generates gratification along with occasional aggravation. Family members also serve as a bulwark against the problems of aging. This chapter sketches family patterns associated with the second half of life. We begin with the married couple and then turn to intergenerational and other kin relations.

MARRIED LIFE

Despite higher divorce rates and delayed marriage, the fact that people are living longer means Americans are spending more years married than ever before. In 1800 women averaged about twenty-seven years in marriage; today they are married for thirty-five years (Watkins et al. 1987). Women tend to outlive men on average, and this is reflected in higher rates of widowhood at older ages. As table 27.1 shows, 83 percent of men from fifty-five to sixty-four years of age are

TABLE 27.1. Marital Status (Percentages) by Age and Sex, 1989

	55–64	65–74	75–84	85 and over
Men				
Never Married	5.6	4.9	4.6	3.2
Married[a]	83.1	81.1	72.7	52.6
Widowed	3.3	8.9	19.7	42.1
Divorced	8.0	5.1	2.9	2.1
Total	100.0	100.0	100.0	100.0
Women				
Never Married	4.4	4.5	5.8	5.6
Married[a]	68.2	53.2	29.6	10.0
Widowed	18.0	36.6	61.5	82.3
Divorced	9.4	5.7	3.0	2.1
Total	100.0	100.0	100.0	100.0

[a] Includes separated from spouse.
SOURCE: U.S. Bureau of the Census 1989.

married, as are 68 percent of women in this age group. By the time they are age eighty-five and older, most men (53 percent) are still married while only 10 percent of women are. Less than 6 percent of men and women have never married, while fewer than 10 percent are divorced. In sum, most older men lead married lives, as do most women under seventy-five. However, most women seventy-five and older are widows.

Marriage is the most important family relationship for most older married people. If anything, marriage plays a more important role in the lives of older husbands than in the lives of older wives (Chappell 1990). Although both husbands and wives see their mates as companions, a husband is more likely than a wife to rely on his spouse as a confidante. Women, who typically maintain closer relations with friends and other kin, are less emotionally dependent on the marital relation. Because wives usually take the lead in orchestrating couples' contact with kin, widowers and other single men are at a distinct disadvantage in terms of interaction with their relations. Of course, women's broad network of intimates may be a mixed blessing, offering more social support, but also exposing them to more conflict and unpleasantness (Antonucci 1990).

A man is also more likely than a woman to depend on a spouse to cope with illness and disabilities in later life. Since husbands tend to be older than wives, they are usually the first to fall seriously ill, and a man is more likely to have a surviving spouse to tend him.

When husbands do care for wives, they are typically very old themselves, but children, particularly daughters, are more likely to pitch in and help when their mothers require care. Caring for a severely impaired elderly person is stressful (Chappell 1990). Those caring for spouses say they miss how he or she used to be; feel depressed; worry about how care would be provided if they, too, got sick; and find the physical demands of caregiving difficult. Some caregivers, however, point to positive consequences of caregiving, such as feelings of accomplishment or even an improved marital relation.

Retirement Living

Retirement is a challenging life-style change for many couples. Since the decision to retire is often influenced by the health and resources of a spouse, retirement is a family decision. In fact, retirement may have consequences for the broader kin network; the retired are freer to enjoy a second honeymoon, relocate closer to offspring, or run errands for an aging parent.

As married women increase their participation in the labor force and as men retire earlier, more and more middle-aged couples are retiring at about the same time in order to spend more active leisure time together (Szinovacz 1989). Retired couples participate in joint leisure activities (e.g., walking, gardening, watching television, and visiting friends and family), but they do not necessarily share the same level of interest in activities (Atchley and Miller 1983; Dorfman and Heckert 1988). For couples who have celebrated a golden wedding anniversary, leisure activities have been associated with more general satisfaction with life (Condie 1989). An exception is "relaxing and taking it easy," which older couples see as their least fulfilling activity and one that has proved to be related to a low level of satisfaction with life.

Reactions to the sudden togetherness at retirement are varied. Valued aspects of this togetherness are reduced work pressure, more free time, and more opportunities for leisure activities. Retirement also imposes new strains, however. Rural housewives whose husbands have retired have pointed to reduced income, lack of routine, and increased workload as problems, perhaps compounded by health declines (Dorfman and Hill 1986). Having a husband underfoot is a common complaint among wives (Rapoport and Rapoport 1975; Szinovacz 1989), as noted by the wife who lamented, "I married him for better or for worse, but not for lunch."

While little is known about the effect of wives' retirement, women may experience more problems than do men. Adjusting to a full-time role as housewife can prove difficult for someone used to the routine, rewards, and sociability of paid employment (Szinovacz 1989). Other changes of later life may also affect married life. Both partners are less satisfied with life when one is in poor health (Atchley and Miller 1983; Brody et al. 1987). When wives are called on to care for elderly parents, husbands also report strain and disruption (Kleban et al. 1989). Wives, in particular, see elder care as having a negative effect on their marriages.

In the face of changes, couples may be called upon to renegotiate marital roles. Consider the division of household tasks. Retired couples share more household tasks and exhibit more egalitarian patterns of housework than do working couples (Brubaker 1985; Dorfman and Heckert 1988). Household chores still seem to be divided along traditional gender lines (Keating and Cole 1980; Szinovacz 1989). A major change like the wife's illness is apt to demand a redistribution of household responsibilities between spouses.

Decision-making among older couples is marked by egalitarianism. Joint decision-making increases significantly after retirement, especially when it comes to decisions concerning finances, trips, and running the household. Perhaps husbands take a more active part in making household decisions to compensate for their loss of earnings and occupational status. Alternatively, couples may simply have more time together to share and discuss decisions.

The Empty Nest

Time together without children in the home is a relatively recent stage of the life cycle. In 1900 this empty nest stage lasted about two years on average; more recently, the typical couple could expect to spend thirteen years together after launching their last child (Glick 1977). Rather than finding the empty nest stressful, many parents look forward to its freedom and privacy (Barber 1989). Mothers, given a chance to indulge their interests, find their adult children contribute to their sense of well-being. For many couples, the empty nest enhances satisfaction with their marriage.

Of course feelings of sadness, loneliness, or even regret may also occur when children finally leave home—a situation dubbed the "empty nest syndrome." Mild depression, worry, and dissatisfaction are not uncommon, especially among mothers who have been very protective and highly involved in the lives of their children. Fathers, especially those with fewer children and a highly nurturing orientation, also experience some unhappiness in the transition to the empty nest (Lewis Freneau, and Roberts 1979). Fathers, for example, sometimes regret not taking more time to interact with children when they were still at home (Barber 1980). On the whole, the transition to the empty nest involves complex reactions for both mothers and fathers. Serious manifestations of the empty nest syndrome are not as widespread as previously thought and do not pertain exclusively to women.

In the face of high divorce rates, housing costs, and unemployment, some adult children either delay moving out or move back to the parental home. The "full" or "cluttered nest" takes older couples by surprise. Problems develop over the comings and goings of adult children and the use of household resources. The presence of an adult child may thwart parents' desire for privacy and renewed intimacy.

Marital Relations

Most older people say their marriages are happy ones. The low divorce rate for older Americans suggests that older couples are happier couples, if only because the most troubled marriages are not likely to last into old age. Evidence about the relationship between age and marital happiness is mixed (Medley 1977; Ade-Ridder and Brubaker 1983). Earlier studies reported a relentless decline in marital happiness after an initial period of satisfaction—a pattern attributed to disenchantment following unrealistic expectations for happiness. More recent studies have found a curvilinear pattern—a low during the child-rearing years followed by an increase in happiness. Many older couples report that their postchild-rearing years have been the happiest in their married lives. Other studies find neither a continual decline nor a curvilinear pattern; rather, marital quality remains fairly constant over the life course.

Older couples report more positive interactions with less negative sentiment (e.g., sarcasm, disagreements, and criticism) than younger couples (Treas and Bengtson 1987). They also have different views on love. Younger couples give more weight to sexual intimacy, passion, and communication, while elderly couples stress emotional security, loyalty, and a mutual investment in the relationship (Levinger 1974; Reedy, Birren, and Schaie 1981). Indeed, most studies of long-term marriages find that commitment is a basic ingredient of marital stability, along with agreement on life goals, being best friends, humor, playfulness, and good conflict management skills.

Despite a decreased emphasis on sexual intimacy, many couples continue to enjoy satisfying sexual relations well into old age. Over half of all older married couples are sexually active, with the frequency of sexual intercourse ranging from three times a week to once every two months (Newman and Nichols 1970; Garza and Dressel 1983). Advancing age is associated with less sexual activity, and significant declines occur after age seventy-five. Both spouses usually attribute declines in the frequency of sexual intercourse to the husband. Other expressions of affection—cuddling, touching, and holding hands—may become more important for older couples. Good sex is not strongly associated with overall marital satisfaction and stability in late-life marriages. Among younger couples, there is a correlation between the severity of marital problems and sexual discord, but sexual problems have less effect on the marital satisfaction of older couples (Garza and Dressel 1983).

INTERGENERATIONAL RELATIONS

Kin figure more prominently in the lives of older people than in those of younger adults. Older people show higher levels of "kin embeddedness." They are more likely to socialize with kin, to name them as people who can be counted on, and even to prefer friends they have met through family members—perhaps because they are freer to choose their associates once school, work, and active parenting no longer structure their day-to-day contacts (Rossi and Rossi 1990:69). If kin are favored over friends, certain categories of family relations are also regarded as more important. Americans feel especially obliged to celebrate the joys (and to lend a hand with the troubles) of their parents and children.

Next to the marital bond, the closest ties are up and down the generational ladder. Claims made on kin depend on age. Younger retirees, especially those who are well off and healthy, tend to be actively involved in the lives of both older and younger generations. Although parents of retirees are usually old enough to need some assistance, aging parents of aging children die off. In the area of Albany, New York, 40 percent of women aged fifty-five to fifty-nine reported that they had living parents, but the figure fell sharply to 29 percent among those from sixty to sixty-four (Spitze and Logan 1990a). Similarly, children eventually grow up and move out on their own. Therefore, few retirees are apt to be caught in the middle between the pressing needs of dependent parents and dependent children. With advancing age, they may even find that the tables turn; they need and get more help from their children than they can give in return.

Support for Aging Parents

Over most of the adult life course, the exchanges between younger and older generations are fairly even. Both generations give and receive emotional reassurance, practical services, and financial assistance. As people age, however, feelings of obligation to children drop off more sharply than those to parents (Rossi and Rossi 1990:225). Daughters help both self-sufficient mothers and mothers who depend on them for services; it is just that dependent mothers get more help (Walker and Pratt 1991). In other words, providing support for aging parents (and parents-in-law) is an intensification of ongoing efforts rather than a new pattern of help.

Greater need prompts more help. For example, widowed or divorced mothers are more likely to get financial and household help from offspring than older moms who are still married (Hoyert 1991). Parents mostly get assorted practical services and emotional support. Given the growing financial independence of retirees, children are rarely called on to provide housing or regular financial assistance. Americans have come to see public assistance for old and young as a universal entitlement—not an indicator of the indifference of kin (Treas and Spence 1989). Indeed, the preference of most older people is for self-reliance and "intimacy at a distance."

How much help parents get depends on whether children are available to help out. Today more people sixty-five and older have at least one surviving child (86 percent in 1984 versus only 82 percent in 1962), although very large families have certainly become less common than they once were (Crimmins and Ingegneri 1990). People with more children get more help. All things being equal, older people with three or more children report more visits, get more help, and are more likely to live with children than parents with one or two children (Spitze and Logan 1990b).

Of course, having more children raises the odds that a child will be living close enough to visit and help out regularly (Crimmins and Ingegneri 1990). Not surprisingly, older people whose children live far away see less of their offspring. Over time, older Americans have become less and less likely to have children living nearby. To be sure, people seldom make their homes with grown children today. Although 28 percent of older Americans lived with children in 1962, only 18 percent did so by 1984. Those who live apart are also less and less apt to have children living in the same neighborhood. In 1962, 47 percent said they lived within ten minutes of offspring, but only 40 percent lived this close in 1984.

Whether children are sons or daughters also determines how much help older parents receive. All things considered, daughters provide markedly more support to older parents than do their brothers. This difference reflects women's special kin-keeping role, not that they have more time available due to less paid work (Stoller 1983). Having a daughter turns out to be the key to getting some kinds of support. Visits, telephone calls, and help with activities of daily living (e.g., housework, bathing, and money handling) are all associated with having one or more daughters (Spitze and Logan 1990b).

Sons pitch in by helping with more tasks when there are no sisters to take over. Men who are only children or who have no sisters spend about as much time in parent care—and experience as much caregiver stress—as their female counterparts (Coward and Dwyer 1990). What sons and daughters do for aging parents tends to differ, nonetheless. Sons give occasional advice and money, but daughters provide the more time-consuming and emotionally demanding services such as giving comfort, doing chores, and remembering special gifts (Rossi and Rossi 1990).

Although the number, gender, and proximity of children are important, the tenor of intergenerational relations is shaped by how the older and younger generations feel about one another. The legacy of earlier parenting plays itself out in the emotional lives of older people. For example, grown offspring who remember their parents' marriage as happy are closer to them emotionally. When the generations share core values (e.g., general outlook, political views, and religious beliefs), they also feel closer to one another (Rossi and Rossi 1990). Mothers and daughters seem better able to forgive and forget their differences, but fathers and sons sometimes carry conflicts into old age. Men's relations are especially vulnerable to strains of the past. In their later years divorced fathers, for example, are less likely than other fathers to keep in touch with their children or to name them as sourcees of support (Cooney and Uhlenberg 1990; Bulcroft and Bulcroft 1991).

The research is not entirely consistent, but it appears that African-American families provide for elderly family members to a somewhat greater extent than do white families. Although older blacks are less likely than their white counterparts to live with a spouse, they are more likely to live with children and grandchildren (Taylor 1988). Elderly Hispanics are also more likely to live with other family members (Markides and Mindel 1987), and the exchange of aid and services is generally higher among Hispanics than among non-Hispanics. These findings tend to hold even when socioeconomic status is taken into account.

Support for Grown Children

Older parents give as well as getting. Mothers and daughters, who maintain especially close ties, exchange the most help (Rossi and Rossi 1990). What individuals of each generation contribute depends on their needs and resources. Older parents give more than their share of job leads, advice, and money to grown children and are rewarded with comfort, special gifts, and help with chores and illness. In Hispanic families the older generation maintains a certain amount of influence over family decisions and plays a strong role in the transmission of ethnic culture and heritage.

Parental attention and resources are directed disproportionately toward children with the greatest needs (Aldous 1987). These include unmarried children, especially those who are divorced with children of their own. Because money is tighter for working-class families, they are more likely than their middle-class counterparts to provide one another with services rather than financial support. Older minority parents are very supportive of grown children, especially when it comes to child rearing.

Shared housing is one example of continuing parental support of grown offspring. Because the average age at the time of first marriage has risen, more and more grown children still live at home. Because divorce has become commonplace, more children move back in with parents once their marriages have ended. The older generation usually expresses satisfaction and positive feelings about joint living arrangements, but some circumstances are associated with more conflict (Aquilino and Supple 1991). When a child is unemployed and economically dependent, when there are grandchildren at home, or when an offspring returns home after a divorce, relations are more troubled.

THE BROADER NETWORK OF KIN:
SIBLINGS AND GRANDCHILDREN

Although marital and intergenerational relations are especially close, the family lives of older Americans encompass many other kin as well. A careful study of kin obligations found that people feel almost as obliged to provide financial aid to sons- and daughters-in-law as to their own children (Rossi and Rossi 1990). These intimates are followed by another set of kin who are related by blood and marriage—grandparents, grandchildren, siblings, stepchildren, and parents-in-law. Stepparents generate somewhat fewer feelings of obligation. More peripheral kin (e.g., aunts and uncles, nieces and nephews, and cousins) inspire only limited feelings of responsibility—akin to those felt for such nonrelatives as friends and neighbors.

Brothers and sisters play a unique role in the lives of older people, if only because their relationship draws on shared experiences of childhood and a common genetic heritage. No other family relationships are as enduring. Most older Americans have at least one living sibling. Of course, since women live longer, a surviving sibling is often a sister.

Some siblings are immersed in one another's lives—frequently visiting, socializing, and helping out. Others may get together only on an occasional holiday if at all. This is because the sibling bonds are voluntary. American culture does not demand close ties between siblings, and Americans feel less obligation toward their siblings than toward their parents and children (Rossi and Rossi 1990). How much contact brothers and sisters have depends on how close they live to one another, how close they are emotionally, and how obligated they feel personally to interact with their siblings (Lee, Mancini, and Maxwell 1990).

Contact with siblings is relatively limited in early and middle adulthood when jobs and children demand time and attention, but caring for a parent in the second half of life may once again involve siblings in a common task. Although some relations are marked by life-long conflict and competition, siblings often grow closer as they grow older. Siblings are seen as welcome and accepted members of older people's social worlds. While providing much less aid than offspring do, brothers and sisters often serve as back-ups in emergencies. They contribute in various ways to the support of older people, and their help is especially important to the childless elderly.

Siblings are most important as sources of companionship and emotional support. Their many years of shared living uniquely enable them to interpret earlier events and place old relationships in perspective (Goetting 1986). In fact, feelings of anger, resentment, and envy that once separated siblings diminish by old age (Gold 1989). To be sure, sisters are closer than brothers at all ages. Brother-sister pairs fall somewhere in between, but they are less likely to report negative sentiments like envy and resentment—even in old age—than are same-sex pairs (Gold 1989).

While grandchildren surely enrich the lives of their grandparents, a certain amount of ambiguity surrounds this role of later life. Depending partly on the wishes of parents, partly on their own life-styles and self-concepts, grandparents tend to carve out fairly predictable styles of grandparenting (Brubaker 1985b; Cherlin and Furstenberg 1986). For example, remote grandparents may develop a ritualistic, impersonal type of relationship. Others want to do what is morally right for their grandchildren and wish to act as good role models. Still others indulge their grandchildren and develop more companionate relations. In extended African-American households grandmothers, who often adopt parentlike relations with grandchildren, see themselves as bulwarks against drugs, crime, and other ills that befall low-income youth; for example, a grandmother who regularly checked up on grandchildren at school earned the nickname "Sergeant" (Cherlin and Furstenberg 1986). Whatever the relationship, a key function of grandparenthood is, as Hagestad (1985) puts it, "being there"—bringing intergenerational continuity and support.

Recent social trends have given rise to a more active role for many grandparents. Grandparents have always provided child care, but divorce, teenage pregnancy, and economic instability have resulted in many grandparents' actually raising their children's children. In 1989 nearly three million children lived in households headed by grandparents. One-third of those households consisted of "skipped-generation families" in which neither of the child's parents was present (Boddie 1991). The rise of divorce has stimulated in the formation of grandparents' rights groups. Most states have passed some sort of legislation providing visitation rights for grandparents and sometimes even great-grandparents (Werner 1991).

CONCLUSION

The special relations that bind kin are measured in treasured heirlooms passed from generation to generation, in golden anniversaries toasted, and in gifts toward down payments on first homes. They are seen in everyday events—a lawn watered for vacationing relatives, a warm hug, a hot casserole, and red tape cut through.

Most older men as well as most women under seventy-five are married. Spouses stand at the center of the family network, especially for older men who rely on wives as confidantes and caretakers. Couples often find marriage happiest in the second half of life, although they are also apt to confront changes (the empty nest, retirement, and disability) that call on them to renegotiate aspects of their relationship. Commitments to parents and children are also keen.

Over most of the life course, the exchange between generations is fairly balanced, with each giving and receiving according to recources and needs. However, advancing years may require children to help out more. More frequent interaction and help come from having more children, especially daughters, who reside nearby. The amount and type of contact and assistance between aging parents and grown children also depend on the quality of the intergenerational relationship built up over a lifetime. Other relations such as grandchildren and siblings also play a part in family life in retirement.

REFERENCES

Ade-Ridder, L., and T. H. Brubaker. 1983. "The Quality of Long-Term Marriages." In T. H. Brubaker, ed., *Family Relationships in Later Life*. Beverly Hills, Calif.: Sage Publications.

Aldous, J. 1987. "New Views on the Family Life of the Elderly and Near-Elderly." *Journal of Marriage and the Family* 49:227–234.

Antonucci, T. C. 1990. "Social Supports and Social Relationships." In R. H. Binstock and L. K. George, eds., *The Handbook of Aging and the Social Sciences*. New York: Academic Press.

Aqilino, W. S., and K. R. Supple. 1991. "Parent-Child Relations and Parents' Satisfaction with Living Arrangements when Adult Children Live at Home." *Journal of Marriage and the Family*, 53:13–27.

Atchley, R. C., and S. J. Miller. 1983. "Types of Elderly Couples." In T. H. Brubaker, ed., *Family Relationships in Later Life*. Beverly Hills, Calif.: Sage Publications.

Barber, C. E. 1980. "Gender Differences in Experiencing the Transition to the Empty Nest: Reports of Middle-Aged and Older Women and Men." *Family Perspective*, 14:87–95.

Barber, C. E. 1989. "Transition to the Empty Nest." In S. J. Bahr and E. T. Peterson, eds., *Aging and the Family*. Lexington, Mass.: Lexington Books.

Boddie, E. 1991. "Raising Your Children's Children." *New Choices*, 31:18–21.

Brody, E. M., M. H. Kleban, P. T. Johnsen, C. Hoffman, and C. B. Schoonover. 1987. "Work Status and Parent Care: A Comparison of Four Groups of Women." *The Gerontologist*, 27:201–208.

Brubaker, T. H. 1985a. "Responsibility for Household Tasks: A Look at Golden Anniversary Couples Aged 75 Years and Over." In W. A. Peterson and J. Quadagno, eds., *Social Bonds in Later Life*. Beverly Hills, Calif.: Sage Publications.

Brubaker, T. H. 1985b. *Later Life Families*. Beverly Hills, Calif.: Sage Publications.

Bulcroft, K. A., and R. A. Bulcroft. 1991. "The Timing of Divorce: Effects on Parent-Child Relationships in Later Life." *Research on Aging*, 13:226–243.

Chappell, N. L. 1990. "Aging and Social Care." In R. H. Binstock and L. K. George, eds., *The Handbook of Aging and the Social Sciences*, 3rd edition. New York: Academic Press.

Cherlin, A. J., and F. F. Furstenberg, Jr. 1986. *The New American Grandparent*. New York: Basic Books.

Condie, S. J. 1989. "Older Married Couples." In S. J. Bahr and E. T. Peterson, eds., *Aging and the Family*. Lexington, Mass.: Lexington Books.

Cooney, T., and P. Uhlenberg. 1990. "The Role of Divorce in Men's Relation with Their Adult Children after Midlife." *Journal of Marriage and the Family,* 52:667–88.

Coward, R. T., and J. W. Dwyer. 1990. "The Association of Gender, Sibling Network Composition, and Patterns of Parent Care by Adult Children." *Research on Aging,* 12:158–181.

Crimmins, E. M., and D. G. Ingegneri. 1990. "Interaction and Living Arrangements of Older Parents and Their Children: Past Trends, Present Determinants, Future Implications." *Research on Aging* 12:3–35.

Dorfman, L. T., and D. A. Heckert. 1988. "Egalitarianism in Retired Rural Couples: Household Tasks, Decision Making, and Leisure Activities." *Family Relations,* 37:73–78.

Dorfman, L. T., and E. A. Hill. 1986. "Rural Housewives and Retirement: Joint Decision-Making Matters." *Family Relations,* 35:507–514.

Garza, J. M., and P. L. Dressel. 1983. "Sexuality and Later-Life Marriages." In T. H. Brubaker, ed., *Family Relationships in Later Life.* Beverly Hills, Calif.: Sage Publications.

Glick, P. C. 1977. "Updating the Life Cycle of the Family." *Journal of Marriage and the Family,* 37:5–13.

Goetting, A. 1986. "The Developmental Tasks of Siblingship over the Life Cycle." *Journal of Marriage and the Family,* 48:703–714.

Gold, D. T. 1989. "Generational Solidarity: Conceptual Antecedents and Consequences." *American Behavioral Scientist,* 33:19–32.

Hagestad, G. O. 1985. "Continuity and Connectedness." In V. L. Bengtson and J. F. Robertson, eds., *Grandparenthood.* Beverly Hills, Calif.: Sage Publications.

Hoyert, D. L. 1991. "Financial and Household Exchanges between Generations." *Research on Aging,* 13:205–225.

Keating, N., and Cole, P. 1980. "What Do I Do with Him 24 Hours a Day? Changes in the Housewife Role after Retirement." *The Gerontologist,* 20:84–89.

Kleban, M. H., E. M. Brody, C. B. Shoonover, and C. Hoffman. 1989. "Family Help to the Elderly: Perceptions of Sons-in-Law Regarding Parent Care." *Journal of Marriage and the Family,* 51:303–312.

Lee, T. R., J. A. Mancini, and J. W. Maxwell. 1990. "Sibling Relationships in Adulthood: Contact Patterns and Motivations." *Journal of Marriage and the Family,* 52:431–440.

Levinger, G. A. 1974. "A Three-Level Approach to Interaction: Toward an Understanding of Pair Relatedness." In T. Houston, ed., *Foundations of Interpersonal Attraction.* New York: Academic Press.

Lewis, R. A., P. J. Freneau, and C. L. Roberts. 1979. "Fathers and the Postparental Transition." *Family Coordinator,* 28:514–520.

Markides, K. S., and C. H. Mindel. 1987. *Aging and Ethnicity.* Beverly Hills, Calif.: Sage Publications.

Medley, M. L. 1977. "Marital Adjustment in the Post Retirement Years." *Family Coordinator,* 26:5–11.

Newman, G., and C. R. Nichols. 1970. "Sexual Activities and Attitudes in Older Persons." In E. Palmore, ed., *Normal Aging.* Durham, N.C.: Duke University Press.

Rapoport, R., and R. N. Rapoport. 1975. *Leisure and the Family Life Cycle.* London: Routledge and Kegan Paul.

Reedy, M. N., J. E. Birren, and R. Schaie. 1981. "Age and Sex Differences in Satisfying Love Relationships across the Adult Life Span." *Human Development,* 24:52–66.

Rossi, A. S., and P. M. Rossi. 1990. *Of Human Bonding: Parent-Child Relations Across the Life Course.* New York: Aldine de Gruyter.

Spitze, G., and J. Logan. 1990a. "More Evidence on Women and Men in the Middle." *Research on Aging,* 12:182–198.

Spitze, G., and J. Logan. 1990b. "Sons, Daughters, and Intergenerational Social Support." *Journal of Marriage and the Family,* 52:420–430.

Stoller, E. P. 1983. "Parental Caregiving by Adult Children." *Journal of Marriage and the Family,* 45:851–858.

Szinovacz, M. 1989. "Retirement, Couples, and Household Work." In S. J. Bahr and E. T. Peterson, eds., *Aging and the Family.* Lexington, Mass.: Lexington Press.

Taylor, J. T. 1988. "Aging and Supportive Relationships among Black Americans." In J. S., Jackson ed., *The Black American Elderly.* New York: Springer.

Treas, J., and V. Bengtson. 1987. "The Family in Later Years." In M. B. Sussman and S. K. Steinmetz, eds., *Handbook of Marriage and the Family.* New York: Plenum Press.

Treas, J., and Spence, M. 1989. "Intergenerational Economic Obligations in the Welfare State." In *Aging Parents and Grown Children.* Lexington, Mass.: Lexington Books.

U.S. Bureau of the Census. "Marital Status and Living Arrangements: March 1989." *Current Population Reports.* Series P-20, no. 445. Washington D.C.: U.S. Government Printing Office.

Walker, A. J., and C. C. Pratt. 1991. "Daughters' Help to Mothers: Intergenerational Aid versus Caregiving." *Journal of Marriage and the Family,* 53:3–12.

Watkins, S. M., J. A. Menken, and J. Bongaarts. 1987. "Demographic Foundations of Family Change." *American Sociological Review,* 52:346–358.

Werner, E. E. 1991. "Grandparent-Grandchild Relationships amongst U.S. Ethnic Groups." In P. K. Smith, ed., *The Psychology of Grandparenthood.* London: Routledge.

28

Retirement and the American Woman

●

SARA E. RIX

Uppermost in the mind of everyone who approaches old age is the matter of financial security. Maintaining preretirement living standards, coping with the expense of a catastrophic illness, and avoiding the exhaustion of one's resources are concerns that few retirees can ignore.

Money worries are by no means gender-specific, but ensuring financial security in later life is a more elusive goal for women than it is for men. Older women's substantially higher poverty rates, smaller pension benefits, and greater dependence on Social Security are stark evidence of this. Women are understandably less likely than men to have confidence in their ability to prepare financially for retirement (Mathew Greenwald and Associates 1991).

GENDER DIFFERENCES IN INCOME IN OLD AGE

As of 1991, older women had a median income of $8,189, just under 60 percent of the $14,357 median income for men (U.S. Bureau of the Census 1992b, table 24). Over 90 percent of these women were collecting Social Security benefits that averaged $531 a month, three-fourths of the $713 average benefit paid to men (Social Security Administration, unpublished data). That same year only 22 percent of women aged sixty-five or older, compared to 49 percent of older men, were receiving income from pensions other than Social Security. Again, women's benefits were substantially lower, averaging $5,186 for the year, or 53 percent of the $9,855 average benefit paid to men (U.S. Bureau of the Census, unpublished data from the Current Population Survey for March 1991).

Figures such as these might not be so troublesome if women's Social Security and pension resources were always augmented by the resources of a spouse. By virtually any financial measure—total income, assets, home ownership, ownership of property other than a home, and net worth—aging couples are better off than their non-married counterparts (e.g., see Sherman 1985 for a discussion of assets among newly retired Social Security beneficiaries; see also U.S. Bureau of the Census 1989, table 26, for the assets of older families and unrelated individuals).

It is ironic that women are financially handicapped by the fact that they are far less likely than men to grow old with a spouse at their side, and yet it was caring for a husband and children earlier in life that contributed to many women's inability to accumulate substantial retirement benefits of their own. Women's greater life expectancy (by nearly seven years at birth and nearly four years at age sixty-five), coupled with the tendency of men to marry younger women, means that most women can expect to outlive their husbands. Three out of four men aged sixty-five or older, but only two out of five women, are married (U.S. Bureau of the Census 1992a), a difference that quite naturally plays itself out in living arrangements: older women are more than twice as likely as older men to be living alone.

For older women, living alone often means living in poverty. Overall, aged women are nearly twice as likely as older men to have incomes below the official poverty level (15.5 percent and 7.9 percent, respectively, in 1991). However, the poverty rate for older women living alone (27 percent in 1991) is more than five times that of older married women (5 percent [U.S. Bureau of the Census 1992c, table 6]). Although some of these women were poor when younger, losing a spouse is a critical factor in the impoverishment of perhaps as many as three-fourths of poor widows who had not been poor when their husbands were alive (Hurd and Wise 1989; see also Bound et al. 1991 and Holden, Burkhauser, and Feaster 1987).

WOMEN'S RETIREMENT

Despite women's growing labor force participation rates, their work experiences, employment choices and opportunities, and lifetime earnings differ from those of men and translate into retirement benefits that are generally inferior. Over their careers, women spend less time than men in the paid labor force and most earn substantially less. Therefore, millions of women remain economically dependent in retirement on a spouse's work record. As a result, there is a question in the minds of many as to whether women really "retire" in the sense that men do.

THE ROLES OF WOMEN

While there can be little doubt about the generally disadvantaged financial status of many older women, what is not known is whether women are even cognizant of the long-range consequences of their work/family decisions or whether economic calculations dominate their choices. Many still feel that women who choose to be homemakers for whatever reason or who move into and out of the labor force are making a conscious decision to tie themselves to the income and retirement benefits of someone who *is* in the work force.

Choices women make about family and work responsibilities may be best for nearly everyone involved over the short run, but they might not be in the best interest of women over the long haul (e.g., see Sorenson and McLanahan 1987). Though measuring the long-term costs of homemaking or caregiving is fraught with methodological problems, common sense says that caregiving that reduces paid work effort will have a negative impact on retirement income. Several efforts to more precisely estimate the costs indicate that the impact can be sizable (Bureau of National Affairs 1990; Kingson and O'Grady-LeShane 1990; O'Rand and Landerman 1984).

The financial penalties for homemaking and caregiving are among the reasons that women's advocates have been arguing for changes to the nation's retirement income system that would recognize homemaking and caregiving as socially necessary and desirable activities whose value extends well beyond the family. The more recent view of homemaking and child rearing as "occupations" that may merit remuneration other than spousal benefits is a product of post-1960s thinking, particularly among those sensitive to women's issues, who see a retirement-income system based only on paid work as unfairly penalizing women. Calls for radical overhaul of the retirement system, particularly Social Security, rest on the assumption that multiple role demands, coupled with occupational segregation and continuing wage inequities, will continue to undermine women's efforts to achieve a financially secure old age.

Female labor force participation rates, which have been increasing for all age groups under sixty-five (see table 28.1), may leave observers with a misleading impression about the intensity and continuity of women's labor force attachment and hence about women's eligibility for decent retirement benefits. For example, look at the figures for women between the ages of fifty-five and sixty-four, who are at or nearing retirement age. Even though most of these women are not yet eligible for retirement benefits, most of them are not in the labor force either and were not necessarily there when they were younger (table 28.1).

Labor force absences are likely to be characteristic of retirement-age women for many years to come. For example, among forty-five- to fifty-nine-year-old mothers in the National Longitudinal Survey, interrupted careers were the norm: only one in five had been in the labor force "fairly continuously" between the time they had first reentered and the time they were reinterviewed in 1982 (Shaw 1988:57–58).

Even among younger women, lifetime employment prospects do not match those of men. To be sure, labor force participation rates have risen dramatically for age groups succeeding the group that is fifty-five to sixty-four years old today, and growing proportions of women are remaining in the labor force during their child-rearing years. Nonetheless, one out of every four twenty-five- to thirty-four-year-old women was not in the labor force in 1990, and many of those who were employed were working less than full-time. As of 1979–80, a twenty-five-year-old woman had an estimated work life of twenty-four more years, nine fewer than a man of the same age; at all ages through sixty, when differences narrow, rates of labor force withdrawal are far higher for women (Smith 1985).

Even if each individual absence is relatively short, repeated spells away from work can add up to large numbers of years out of the labor force (Shaw 1988). The Census Bureau estimates that working women

TABLE 28.1. Labor Force Participation Rates of Women by Age, 1950–1990 (in Percentages)

Age	1950	1960	1970	1980	1990
25–34	34.0	36.0	45.0	65.5	73.6
35–44	39.1	43.4	51.1	65.5	76.5
45–54	37.9	49.9	54.4	59.9	71.2
55–64	27.0	37.2	43.0	41.3	45.3
65+	9.7	10.8	9.7	8.1	8.7

SOURCE: U.S. Bureau of Labor Statistics 1985 table 5; U.S. Bureau of Labor Statistics 1991, table 3.

in 1984 had spent nearly 15 percent of their potential work years away from work, mainly for family reasons, in contrast to working men, whose absences totaled less than two percent of their potential work years (U.S. Bureau of the Census 1987a). Among women, work absences rise sharply with age, but even the youngest in the Census Bureau sample had already lost five percent of their potential work years.

While much of the work loss experienced by middle-aged women is attributable to time spent rearing children, more and more women may find themselves pulled back into the home by the demands of elder care, especially as their parents' life expectancy increases. Thus, their hopes to accrue good Social Security and pension benefits by moving into and/or up in better-paying jobs may again be dashed as their work opportunities are limited by elder care responsibilities. At present, total withdrawal from the labor force to provide elder care is relatively rare, although caregivers resort to other forms of work accommodation, such as reduced hours or leave without pay (Gibeau 1988; Stone and Short 1990; U.S. House of Representatives 1987).

SOCIAL SECURITY AND WOMEN

No assessment of the status of women in retirement is complete without a discussion of the contribution that Social Security makes to women's financial well-being. There is considerable concern in some circles about the adequacy and equity of that contribution. Older women may not, for the most part, get much in the form of private pension benefits, and income from other sources may be generally modest (e.g., Sherman 1985), but almost all older women receive Social Security benefits that constitute a sizable portion of their total income. Just under half (46 percent) of the aggregate income of older widowed, divorced, and never-married women comes from Social Security, a figure that has changed barely at all since the mid-1970s (Social Security Administration 1979, table 28, and 1992, table VII.2). For some 20 percent of these women is it apparently the *only* source of income.

Because Social Security benefits are based on work histories and earnings and because women typically work and earn less than men, women's benefits from their own work tend to be lower than men's. However, the system is nondiscriminatory, treating workers comparably who have comparable work and earnings records. The issue of equity or fairness arises predominantly in the case of married women whose eligibility for Social Security benefits may be based either on their own or on their husbands' work records.

A married woman with paid work experience may find herself qualifying for Social Security benefits in one of what is technically three ways but, in fact, works out to only two: [1]

1. On the basis of her husband's (or, if married for at least ten years, her ex-husband's) work history and earnings record. This beneficiary receives a spousal benefit that, if she begins collecting at age sixty-five, amounts to 50 percent of her husband's retired worker benefit.
2. On the basis of her own work history and earnings record. This beneficiary has worked long enough and earned enough to receive retired worker benefits. If she is married or has been married, this means that her own worker benefit is higher than her spousal benefit.
3. On the basis of her own and her spouse's work histories and earnings records. This Social Security beneficiary has worked long enough to qualify for benefits as a retired worker, and she is eligible for spousal benefits as well. She is what is known as *dually entitled.*

Dually entitled beneficiaries collect only one benefit. According to the technical definition, a dually entitled beneficiary receives her own retired worker benefit plus the difference between that benefit and her spousal benefit. Her own smaller benefit is, in a sense, "topped off" by the larger benefit. When a woman is classified as "dually entitled," however, her spousal benefit is *always* larger than her own retired worker benefit. If the latter were larger, she would be classified simply as a retired worker, in spite of the fact that she might also qualify for a spousal benefit.

Upon applying for Social Security benefits, many women with paid work experience discover that their spousal benefit is larger than their own retired worker benefit. This can be the case for women who (1) have had a history of low or relatively low-wage work, (2) have worked intermittently, and/or (3) have returned to work in midlife after years in the home. Because a husband's benefit is generally based on a substantially longer work life and higher wages, a woman often finds that 50 percent of his benefit is larger than 100 percent of her own.

Despite women's growing labor force attachment, there has been virtually no change in the proportion of married beneficiaries who collect benefits based their own work experience: 38 percent in 1988 and 39 percent in 1960. What has changed is the proportion eligible for benefits solely as "dependent" spouses, which had dropped to 40 percent in 1988 from 57 percent in 1960. Over the same period, the proportion of women who are dually entitled had risen from 4.5 percent to 22 percent (Lingg 1990). In sum, the proportion of married beneficiaries who, for Social Security purposes, might as well never have worked for pay has not decreased at all over the past three decades.

Moreover, today's female dual beneficiaries are actually getting *less*, on average, as retired workers than they were getting more than twenty years ago. In 1970, 79 percent of the average dually entitled wife's total benefit was her retired worker benefit; by 1990 that figure had dropped to 64 percent (Social Security Administration, undated, table 84; Social Security Administration 1991, table 5.G3).

Staying at home is one of the reasons that a woman's spousal benefit may be higher than her retired worker benefit. The impact of remaining at home may be indirect, in the form of limiting employment opportunities, or it may be direct, in the form of shortening work histories and lowering lifetime earnings (O'Rand and Landerman 1984). Because Social Security benefits are based on earnings, years of no earnings may lower average lifetime earnings and result in lower Social Security benefits. Up to five of a worker's lowest earning years (known as the "drop-out" years) are deducted from his or her work record, which raises average wages and, consequently, retirement benefits. Applicants who spend time out of the paid labor force for any reason, including family care, may find that years of zero earnings, perhaps more than five, are the ones deducted from the benefit formula, thus lowering the benefit. This caregiving "penalty" applies almost exclusively to women.

With their paid work, of course, dually entitled married women are adding to the family's monthly income, accumulating work experience, and perhaps saving for retirement and acquiring the right to private pension benefits. In addition, recent work experience and an earnings record of one's own are especially desirable in the event of marital dissolution. Yet many beneficiaries who have worked for pay object to the fact that they seem to get nothing at retirement for the taxes they paid during their working years. If the equity principle embodied in the Social Security system means that benefits people receive ought to bear some relationship to their contributions (Beedon 1991), the equity of the system for married working women, compared to women who embraced the homemaker role, can be called into question.

WOMEN AND PRIVATE PENSIONS

Women who are able to supplement their Social Security with private pension benefits are in an enviable financial situation compared to their peers. Combined average income from Social Security and pensions for older women in 1984 was over 70 percent higher than the average income from Social Security alone (U.S. Bureau of the Census 1987b), a difference that "points up the importance of older women being able to move into jobs that provide pensions" (Shaw 1988:73). It also highlights the importance of women's remaining in those jobs until they earn a nonforfeitable right to receive benefits or vest.

Although most older women today do not receive private pension benefits, both the number and the proportion of women who are entitled to survivor benefits and pension benefits based on their own employment can be expected to increase. Help to widows came in the form of the Retirement Equity Act (REA) of 1984.

Widows and Pensions

By passing the REA, Congress acted to lower the odds that the loss of a husband's private pension would propel a widow into poverty. Up until then, private pension benefits really belonged only to the spouse on whose work record and earnings the benefits were based. Workers were obligated neither to provide survivor benefits to their spouses nor to inform them that they had not elected such benefits. Since the selection of a single life annuity over a joint and survivor annuity resulted in the payment of higher benefits during the life of the retired worker, many survivors were left out in the cold.

The Retirement Equity Act did not mandate survivor benefits, but it did require that spouses be fully informed about and in agreement with any decision to forego those benefits. Both spouses must now agree *in writing* to waive the right to survivor benefits; otherwise the benefits are automatic.

The REA appears to have had a positive impact on survivor benefit selection rates (Davis and Snyder 1990). In question, however, is just how much it has improved or will improve the financial status of widows. The General Accounting Office (GAO) has estimated that, had the REA been in effect in the early 1980s, survivor benefits would have been left to at most 100,000 more women in the Social Security Administration's New Beneficiary Survey, an increase of 17 percentage points in the number of potentially entitled widows (U.S. General

Accounting Office 1988). Especially disquieting is the observation that the REA would have done little for the poorest of widows because their husbands were likely not to have any pension coverage at all.

Even when workers have a choice, opting for survivor benefits may not be the best decision for everyone. Couples may need the higher benefit that a single life annuity provides, or survivors might expect to receive income from other sources, such as insurance or private pensions of their own. In many instances, too, the benefit would be so small that it would likely have little impact on financial well-being. GAO found, for example, that a 50-percent survivor benefit would have averaged less than $200 a month for widows of high-income couples and less than $70 for widows of the lowest-income couples (U.S. General Accounting Office 1988).

Although relatively little is known about how couples go about deciding among survivor options, it appears from the GAO research that both the size of the survivor benefit and its significance to the widow as a source of income are particularly influential factors in the decision to elect the benefit. That benefit is undoubtedly important to many widows. Nonetheless, augmenting a widow's income through survivor benefits is only one component of promoting a more financially secure old age for women.

Women Workers and Pensions

Women's entitlement to private pension benefits in their own right has been on the rise in recent years. In 1979 only seven million working women, less than one in six, were entitled to employer-provided pension benefits on their current job. By 1988 that was the case for some thirteen million working women, or about one in four (Piacentini 1989). These are women who, even if they change jobs or leave the labor force, can expect to receive something from their pension plans upon reaching retirement age.

Of course, in order to become entitled to pension benefits workers have to participate in pension plans. The Retirement Equity Act included a number of provisions designed to make it easier for women, in particular, to do this. For instance, break-in-service rules for vesting were liberalized; the minimum age requirement for pension plan participation was lowered, and the years of service counted for vesting purposes were increased. However, before women can benefit from the REA, they must find jobs that are covered by private pensions. As of 1988, just 54 percent of all working women were employed in pension-covered jobs, a slight increase from 52 percent in 1979 (Piacentini 1989).

A worrisome fact is that, over the past decade, pension participation rates for working women have remained stagnant at about 38 percent (Piacentini 1989). While it is reasonable to predict that many women in covered jobs will eventually participate and vest in their employer's plan, job mobility, structural changes in the work force, and the continued work absences experienced by many women also make it certain that in the future millions of retired women will collect little or nothing in the way of pension benefits.

Pension coverage, participation, and entitlement rates are lower in low-wage, part-time, and nonunionized jobs, as well as in jobs in smaller firms—all jobs more likely to be held by women than by men. Women are also less likely than men to be employed in high-pension industries such as durable manufacturing or transportation and public utilities, and they are more often found in service industries in which coverage is less prevalent. The fact that most job growth in recent years has been in service industries does not augur well for rapid private pension expansion. Nor does the growth of the contingent work force, which includes part-timers, temporary workers, and leased employees.

Contingent workers get less in benefits than permanent, full-time employees, and many of them have to pay for whatever "benefits" they may want or need. The flexibility of scheduling inherent in contingent work has obvious appeal to caregivers and other workers who might prefer less than full-time, year-round work, and employers respond favorably to the potential for reducing labor costs. Both factors point to further increases in contingent employment, regardless of its long-term financial impact on workers.

Pension coverage for women is greater in male-dominated *industries* than for women in the total work force, although this favorable development does not appear to be the case among women in male-dominated *occupations* (Korczyk 1990). It may be, as Korczyk (1990) tentatively suggests, that increases in pension coverage among women in recent decades have been more the result of women's moving into male-dominated industries than of the expansion of pension coverage to female-dominated industries.

Women's shorter job tenure also affects their participation in employer-provided pension plans. To vest in a pension plan, a worker must have participated in that plan for a minimum period of time. The 1986 Tax Reform Act requires plans to provide full vesting after five years of service or partial vesting over a period of time until full vesting is achieved in seven years, a change designed to increase vesting rates for both men and women.

Korczyk (1990) reports that, when there are controls for worker and job characteristics, job separation rates are similar for men and women. Even so, long tenure is less common among women than among men. In fact, men are about 50 percent more likely than women to have been at their current jobs for at least ten years (U.S. Bureau of the Census 1987a).

The reduction in vesting periods may leave workers with an unwarranted sense of security about future retirement benefits, but early vesting is of little value without job longevity. When all is said and done, higher pension benefits accrue to workers who stay the longest with a single employer, since benefits based on formulas incorporating years of service and final years of salary reward employees whose wages have increased over many years. Workers who leave after a short tenure, even though vested, may receive very little in the form of pension benefits based on unindexed wages earned early in their careers.

As of 1984, 55 percent of working women and 45 percent of working men had been on their current jobs for less than five years (U.S. Bureau of the Census 1987a). Some of these workers will remain at work long enough to vest, but others will not.

Unvested workers who change jobs may eventually vest in a subsequent plan. They may also be eligible for a lump-sum pension distribution from their former plan, which—to ensure its availability in retirement—should be rolled over into another retirement vehicle or some other savings instrument. Unfortunately, however, workers tend to consume their lump-sum distributions. According to Korczyk (1990), only about one-fifth of women who receive lump-sum distributions roll over any of the distribution into other retirement vehicles.

PLANNING FOR RETIREMENT

Despite projections of improvements in their economic status (Commonwealth Fund Commission on the Elderly Living Alone 1987; Reno and Rader 1982; "Women and Social Security" 1985), many older women will remain economically vulnerable. An anticipated drop in poverty rates will not be anywhere near as pronounced among older women living alone as among couples, warns the Commonwealth Fund Commission for the Elderly Living Alone (1987), which predicts that a higher percentage of elderly widows living alone will be poor in 2020 than were poor in 1987.

Bleak as the future may look for some groups of elderly women, others should do very well indeed. Dual-career couples are one group that can generally view the future with optimism. The same should be true for substantial numbers of never-married women who are taking advantage of career opportunities closed to their mothers and grandmothers. There is little cause for concern about women in the professions, women in corporate board rooms, or women who have fought their way into high-paying, traditionally male occupations. Instead concern should focus on the majority of women, the 70 to 80 percent who remain concentrated in female-dominated occupations—the secretaries, waitresses, clerks, and department store personnel—and/or who fulfill the roles of homemaker and caregiver at some point in their lives. For the most part, these are not high-earning, upwardly mobile, career-oriented women, however important their jobs may be to them.

As long as women remain the primary caregivers to children and, increasingly, the elderly, their paid work attachment stands to suffer. Restricted labor force activity limits employment opportunities and reduces earnings, access to benefits, and ultimately retirement income. Raising the standard of living for many older women in the future will require that they give more thought to the consequences of how they manage their paid work and family responsibilities. Financial planners and advisers have an obligation to make it clear to women how decisions about family and work—including occupational choice and work scheduling—affect later work opportunities and ultimately retirement benefits.

In some respects, this chapter on women and retirement could be considered guilty of perpetuating an outdated and stereotypical view of women and families. The fact is that few families today conform to the type whose needs are most adequately met by Social Security—the lifelong single-earner couple. Households and families are increasingly diverse, and over the course of their lives women (and men) are likely to find themselves in a variety of household and family constellations that will affect their retirement status. Few data are available on the impact that being a single parent—whether divorced, widowed, or, increasingly, never married—has on future well-being or on how best to help these parents plan for retirement.

The retirement prospects of the growing number of minority women, including recent immigrants, should also be studied, as should the prospects of women in other types of nontraditional families in which they may find themselves (Holden 1989).

Legislators and other policymakers can expect continued pressure to make changes in the retirement-income system to eliminate inequities experienced by women and to enhance their retirement-income status. Because it is the largest and most important source of retirement income for women and because it is a public program, Social Security will be the focus of greatest pressure.

In all probability, any changes in Social Security will be relatively modest in impact. Consequently, what Social Security replaces now in the form of income is what it will replace in the future. Women who want or need more will have to seek out other sources of income, a rather daunting prospect for those women who are not now employed in jobs covered by private pensions. Unless something can be done to reverse the extraordinarily low rates of savings in the United States, income from this source will not carry many retirees very far.

Thus, for the large majority of older women, especially those dependent on Social Security, retirement security will continue to be an elusive goal. For these women, and for millions of men like them, longer work lives will be one of the only income guarantees available.

NOTES

The author wishes to thank Laurel Beedon and Judith Hushbeck for their careful review of and insightful comments on this chapter. They bear no responsibility for any remaining shortcomings.

1. For ease of reading and because this is a chapter on women, the following discussion on dually entitled beneficiaries focuses on women. It should be stressed, however, that the same rules apply to men, although relatively few men collect benefits based on a wife's earnings.

REFERENCES

Beedon, L. 1991. "Women and Social Security: Challenges Facing the American System of Social Insurance." *AARP Issue Brief*, 2.

Bound, J., G. J. Duncan, D. S. Laren, and L. Oleinick, L. 1991. Poverty Dynamics in Widowhood. *Journal of Gerontology: Social Sciences*, 46(3):S115–S124.

Bureau of National Affairs, Inc. 1990. *Retirement Income versus Family Responsibility: 10 Ways to Protect Working Women's Pension Benefits*. Special Report no. 29. Washington, D.C.: Bureau of National Affairs.

Commonwealth Fund Commission on Elderly People Living Alone. 1987. *Old, Alone and Poor*. Baltimore, Md.: The Commonwealth Fund Commission on Elderly People Living Alone.

Davis, G. G., and D. C. Snyder. 1990. *Pension Equity Issues*. Remarks presented at the Annual Meeting of the Gerontological Society of America, Boston, Mass.

Gibeau, J. 1988. "Working Caregivers: Family Conflicts and Adaptations of Older

446 *Individual and Family Life*

Workers." In R. M. Morris and S. A. Bass, eds., *Retirement Reconsidered: Economic and Social Roles for Older People*, 185–201. New York: Springer.

Holden K. C. 1989. "Economic Status of Older Women: A Summary of Selected Research Issues." In A. R. Herzog, K. C. Holden, and M. M. Seltzer, eds., *Health and Economic Status of Older Women*, 92–130. Amityville, N.Y.: Baywood.

Holden, K. C., R. V. Burkhauser, and D. J. Feaster. 1987. *The Timing of Falls into Poverty after Retirement and Widowhood*. Paper presented at the Annual Meeting of the Gerontological Society of America, Washington, D.C.

Hurd, M. D., and D. A. Wise. 1989. "The Wealth and Poverty of Widows: Assets before and after the Husband's Death." In D. A. Wise, ed., *The Economics of Aging*, 177–200. Chicago: University of Chicago Press.

Kingson, E. R., and R. O'Grady-LeShane. 1990. "The Effects of Caregiving on the Retirement Incomes of Women." Mimeo. Chestnut Hill, Mass.: Boston College.

Korczyk, S. M. 1990. *Pension Portability Issues Affecting Women*. Revised. Washington, D.C.: U.S. Department of Labor, Pension and Welfare Benefits Administration.

Lingg, B. A. 1990. "Women Beneficiaries Aged 62 or Older, 1960–1988." *Social Security Bulletin, 53* 7, 2–12.

Mathew Greenwald & Associates. 1991. *National Taxpayers Union Foundation: Survey on Retirement Confidence*. Draft. Washington, D.C.: Mathew Greenwald and Associates.

O'Rand, A. M. 1984. "Women. In E. B. Palmore, ed. *Handbook on Aging in the United States*, 125–142. Westport, Conn.: Greenwood.

O'Rand, A. M., and R. Landerman. 1984. "Women's and Men's Retirement Income Status." *Research on Aging*, 6(1):25–44.

Piacentini, J. S. 1989. "Pension Coverage and Benefit Entitlement: New Findings from 1988." *EBRI Issue Brief*, 94.

Reno, V., and Rader, D. A. 1982. "Benefits for Individual Retired Workers and Couples Now Approaching Retirement Age." *Social Security Bulletin*, 45(2):25–31.

Shaw, L. B. 1988. "Special Problems of Older Women Workers." In M. E. Borus, H. S. Parnes, S. H. Sandell, and B. Seidman, eds., *The Older Worker*, 55–86. Madison, Wisc.: Industrial Relations Research Association.

Sherman, S. R. 1985. "Assets of New Retired-Workers Beneficiaries: Findings from the New Beneficiary Survey." *Social Security Bulletin*, 48(7):27–43.

Smith, S. J. 1985. "Revised Worklife Tables Reflect 1979–1980 Experience." *Monthly Labor Review*, 108(8):23–30.

Social Security Administration. Undated. *Social Security Bulletin Annual Statistical Supplement, 1971*. Washington, D.C.: U.S. Government Printing Office.

Social Security Administration. 1979. *Income of the Population 55 and Over, 1976*. SSA Publication no. 13-11865. Washington, D.C.: U.S. Government Printing Office.

Social Security Administration. 1991. *Social Security Bulletin Annual Statistical Supplement, 1991*. Washington, D.C.: U.S. Government Printing Office.

Social Security Administration. 1992. *Income of the Population 55 or Older, 1990*. SSA Publication no. 13-11871. Washington, D.C.: Social Security Administration.

Sorensen, A., and S. McLanahan. 1987. "Married Women's Economic Dependency, 1940–1980." *American Journal of Sociology*, 93:659–687.

Stone, R. I., and P. F. Short. 1990. "The Competing Demands of Employment and Informal Caregiving to Disabled Elders." *Medical Care*, 28(6):513–526.

U.S. Bureau of the Census. 1987a. *Male-Female Differences in Work Experience, Occupation, and Earnings: 1984*. Current Population Reports, Series P-70, no. 10. Washington, D.C.: U.S. Government Printing Office.

U.S. Bureau of the Census. 1987b. *Pensions: Worker Coverage and Retirement Income, 1984.* Current Population Reports, Series P-70, no. 12. Washington, D.C.: U.S. Government Printing Office.

U.S. Bureau of the Census. 1989. *Money Income of Households, Families, and Persons in the United States: 1987.* Current Population Reports, Series P-60, no. 162. Washington, D.C.: U.S. Government Printing Office.

U.S. Bureau of the Census. 1992a. *Marital Status and Living Arrangements: March 1991.* Current Population Reports, Series P-20, no. 461. Washington, D.C.: U.S. Government Printing Office.

U.S. Bureau of the Census. 1992b. *Money Income and Poverty Status in the United States: 1991.* Current Population Reports, Series P-60, no. 180. Washington, D.C.: U.S. Government Printing Office.

U.S. Bureau of the Census. 1992c. *Poverty in the United States: 1991.* Current Population Reports, Series P-60, no. 181. Washington, D.C.: U.S. Government Printing Office.

U.S. Bureau of Labor Statistics. 1985. *Handbook of Labor Statistics.* Bulletin 2217. Washington, D.C.: U.S. Government Printing Office.

U.S. Bureau of Labor Statistics. 1991. *Employment and Earnings,* 38:1. Washington, D.C.: U.S. Government Printing Office.

U.S. General Accounting Office. 1988. *Retirement Income: 1984 Pension Law Will Help Some Widows but Not the Poorest.* GAO/HRD88-77. Washington, D.C.: U.S. General Accounting Office.

U.S. House of Representatives. 1987. *Exploding the Myths: Caregiving in America.* A study by the Subcommittee on Human Resources of the Select Committee on Aging, Committee Publication no. 99–611.

Women and Social Security. 1985. *Social Security Bulletin,* 48(2):17–26.

29

Adaptation to Retirement Among the Never Married, Childless, Divorced, Gay and Lesbian, and Widowed

●

ROBERT L. RUBINSTEIN

In this chapter we review the retirement concerns of retirees in what at first glance may appear to be several distinctive social categories: the never married, the childless, the divorced, the gay and lesbian, and the widowed. At the very least, these social categories are linked by their shared difference from a culturally normative model of life course and family cycle development. To be sure, the retirees in these social categories have the same set of concerns that affect all retirees. But due to their special circumstances, they may be unusually vulnerable during retirement and their retirement periods may require special considerations and planning.

Retirement is both a life course transition and a state of being (Logue 1991). It is also identified with aging, although the two are not synonymous. Retirement may be a state of being that represents or denotes the lifestyle of the young old or the old young as they age or as they are in transition from the world of work. For whatever reason, it appears hard to think of the old old, those eighty and above, as retired, because we do not "naturally" think of the advanced elderly as workers.

This chapter serves as a foil to the popular literature on retirement that presumes a normative, culturally idealized retirement experience that focuses on a married couple (usually after the child-raising years) that has done some financial preparation and assumes a lifestyle associated with leisure and leisure-based friendships.

However, technical literature presents a more complex view of American retirement even among such married couples (Bradsher et al. 1992; Crystal et al. 1992). And indeed, this complexity can be extended to those whose lifestyles and marital and parental status are nonnormative. These include retirees who have never married; those who are married but childless; those who are widowed and divorced, childless and otherwise; and retiring gay men and lesbian women, whether once married or currently married, childless or not.

In this chapter I explore some of the dimensions of the retirement experiences and life-styles of people in these social categories. In doing so, I draw in part on the existing specialized literature in this area; as one might expect, it is not voluminous. I will also draw on some studies in gerontology on people in these social categories and on interviews I have conducted over the last decade with retirees in these marital, parental, and social categories. As you will see, the issues that most structure the lives of all retirees—retirement preparation and transition, activities and leisure, finances, health, social support, and work and volunteerism—clearly and centrally affect retirees in these categories; however, people in each category discussed here have distinctive retirement concerns. The primary purpose of this chapter is to describe these special concerns.

RETIREES WHO HAVE NEVER MARRIED

Some five to seven percent of people who are now retirement age have never married. Among the individuals in this group there are two distinctive profiles, that of "career" women with a relatively high level of education or occupational achievement and that of more poorly educated men with uneven career histories.

Women Who Have Never Married

For women who have never married, retirement can represent an especially significant personal transition. Like other retirees, many never-married women have experienced a long-term immersion in a single job or career. Keith (1989), reviewing the very few studies of the work orientation of never-married women, has found that work assumes a greater importance in the lives of women in this category than in the lives of single men and other women. Indeed, for many in this category, employment has been the central focus of their adult lives (Braito and Anderson 1983).

Despite the importance of work to these women, they are subject to the same disadvantages experienced by other women at retirement in terms of employment, discrimination, and finances. Yet, unlike other women, the never married have usually had no counterbalance to work in the form of a family life and children. This is not to say that they have had no involvement with the children of siblings and others; some studies of never-married women report such involvement (Simon 1987; Allen 1989; Rubinstein et al. 1991). However, such involvement, although rewarding in many ways, is often contingent on their relatives' time demands and say-so and, as I have found in my research, is often viewed by the women as uncertain for these and other reasons (Rubinstein et al. 1991). However, many have had a more significant involvement with parents as they and their parents have aged and as caregiving has become necessary.

For women who have never married the work arena has often functioned as an environment that is both confidence-affirming and the center of generative behavior—that is, behavior that is supportive or nurturant of the younger generation. "Career" women of retirement age have disproportionately been involved in jobs that demand interpersonal caring and nurturance: teaching, nursing, office supervision, and the like. Often their relationship with younger employees or clients has been semiparental. Never-married women are often quite articulate about the generative functions of their work. While they may desire and long to relinquish specific duties through retirement, they may find it difficult to adjust to the loss of some of the psychological elements of the work relationship, and this difficulty in adjusting may emerge only with time and with the absence of the work environment.

As Keith notes (1989), the few studies that have examined unmarried women's transition to retirement do not support the conclusion that this transition is negative or provide information on the differential effects of retirement on the formerly married and the never married. Most women who have never married appear to be satisfied with retirement (see Keating and Jeffrey 1983). However, there is a contrasting view that retirement is more difficult for never-married women than for others (Ward 1979). In Simon's (1987) study of fifty elderly women who had never married, she found that twenty-three had retired voluntarily, but the majority (twenty-seven) had retired involuntarily, before they wanted to, because of their own illness, because of family caregiving responsibilities, or because they had reached the legal age limit and were forced out. Those who had been forced out were extremely vocal in their protests of unfairness. Further, many who had retired voluntarily developed second careers, and twenty-two of the fifty continued in part-time work after formal retirement.

The economic transition at retirement for these women as a group can be difficult and clearly represents, a downward adjustment. Simon noted the realistic economic perceptions of the women she interviewed and their "foresighted adaptiveness." Many, realizing in midlife their potential for future economic difficulties, made adjustments in savings or sought, upon retirement, to share a household. Some work has focused on how these women, as caregiving daughters, made economic contributions to their parents' household. Most in my sample lived alone (Rubinstein et al 1991). Some 44 percent of the women interviewed by Simon lived below the poverty level (in 1983).

Men Who Have Never Married

Only a few studies have examined the life-styles of older men who have never married, and little is known about their transitions to retirement. As has been noted elsewhere (Rubinstein 1986), to the extent that these men follow a pattern, there is a significant group that has been viewed as outsiders or loners who are marginal to society, while others have been seen as as more well educated and sophisticated.

The men in the first group have generally experienced uneven work histories, often in insecure jobs with no pension benefits. Many derive their only income from Social Security. Therefore, their retirement may be contingent on lack of work opportunities, or they may follow a profile of taking irregular part-time jobs to augment a poor retirement income. Retirement in any formal sense may be entirely health-driven, when they can no longer work effectively. Chronic problems these men are likely to experience in retirement are poverty and social isolation. Indeed, retirement may represent a transition to a secure and certain, though low, income. An ongoing lack of social skills and exposure to health dangers among unskilled and semi-skilled blue-collar workers may contribute to poor health maintenance in their retirement years.

While for unmarried older women the role of worker may have been central to identity and retirement is therefore seen as a threat to identity, for men with checkered occupational careers the role of work in identity may be less overt, but the effects of its termination equally significant. Counselors and others need to be sensitive to these situations and the role of work in lives that may be socially circumscribed in distinctive ways.

For never-married men who are well educated and affiliated with professional or middle-income groups, the transition to retirement and retirement life present the same sorts of concerns that affect all retirees who are middle class and above. They are more concerned than married men with income sufficiency, health maintenance, and the need for adequate social support. And, like never-married women, they may need to address concerns relating to the latent psychological functions of work.

Counselors and others need to be sensitive to the situations described above and to the role of work in lives that may be socially circumscribed in distinctive ways.

Both men and women who have never married face similar difficulties in later life, including the potential for insufficient income and concern about issues of future care in the face of health problems. Because these people have no children and their relations with younger generations may be limited, the need to maintain preexisting social relations and to enhance and replace social ties as friends begin to age and die is paramount in retirement. Women are generally more effective in establishing and maintaining social relations than are men. The lack of social skills may especially affect older men. Little is known about the relations with other generations of older men who have never married. The potential for a close identification of self with work also suggests that the psychological gratifications of work may be long lasting and unaddressed in retirement without acquisition of a suitable substitute, although part-time work or volunteerism are possible substitutes.

THE WIDOWED

Widows

The social adaptations of older widowed women have been extensively studied and described (Lopata 1973, 1979, 1987), although their adaptations to retirement have been less so (Szinovacz 1982). A widow may experience both her own and her husband's retirement as well as her husband's death. As described below, the possibilities of this potentially complex set of events are significant for the retirement life and experience of the widow.

General factors that have been identified as contributing to the satisfaction and well-being of retired widows include adequate income and health, adequate ability and support to absorb household functions formerly undertaken by the husband, and adequate social support. Insufficient income may be a serious problem for retired older widows. For example, in 1980 nearly 60 percent of widows over the age of sixty-five had incomes of $5,000 or less (Grad 1983). In a more recent analysis of the links between poverty and widowhood, Bound and colleagues (1991) found that widowhood drops one's standard of living nearly 20 percent and forces 20 percent of women into poverty. However, they also documented the long-term volatility of this profile and noted that two-thirds of the widows who enter poverty will leave it in five years, most generally through employment.

Bound and colleagues (1991) found that income level prior to widowhood is the strongest predictor of objective economic status after widowhood. However, the perceived adequacy of income may be especially important for widows, who may feel vulnerable in many ways (O'Bryant and Morgan 1989). One image of older widows is that they lack knowledge and experience of financial matters, although O'Bryant and Morgan (1989) have challenged this notion.

It is fairly clear that any negative financial effects widows may experience in the transition to retirement, no matter when they are widowed, may be counteracted by careful retirement planning and preparation. In a study of three hundred widowed women aged sixty and older, O'Bryant and Morgan noted that fewer than half the sample reported financial decline since their husbands' deaths. Because economic status is not fully related to income level, the perceived level of economic well-being can depend not only on the women's economic status prior to widowhood, but also her own expectations about what will happen to her financially in widowhood (1989:249). Many widows feel that home ownership is their most significant form of financial protection in retirement and in later life. Currently, widowed persons account for 47 percent of the "economically advantaged retirees," a label that describes those with incomes more than twice the poverty level (Longino and Ullman 1988).

The significance of social support and social relations to older retired widows has been amply demonstrated (Neale 1987). For example, Dorfman and Moffett (1987) found that, while adequacy of income and frequency of help from friends were significantly correlated with retirement satisfaction for older married women, maintenance of preretirement friendships and frequency of visits with friends predicted life satisfaction for widowed women.

One issue that is significant but remains obscure is how retirement is timed for both spouses relative to spousal death. Often widows say that they and their husbands had hoped to have a longer time together in retirement, but in fact had a short and unfulfilled co-retirement that ended tragically and prematurely without much shared

retirement time. Interestingly, nearly all the popular self-help literature and much of the technical literature on widowhood fails to address issues of retirement. Widowhood itself is a category that can
include a wide variety of ages and situations. Unlike never-married
status, widowhood has little direct effect of the amount of social
support one will receive in retirement. Certainly the implications of
widowhood are different for a woman who is widowed in her forties
while still raising her children and consequently increases her work
participation until retirement at age sixty-five and a woman who
returns to work after raising her children at age fifty-five, retires at
age sixty-five, and spends a meaningful period of co-retirement with
a husband who survives into his early seventies.

For both widows and widowers the experience and quality of retirement are likely to be quite different if the spouse's death has
occurred quite a while prior to retirement, if the spouse's retirement
and death occur after retirement (and as a condition of life as a
"young old" person), or if both spouses have co-retired and lived into
their eighties and one dies as an "old old" person.

In the first instance, by retirement the widowed person will no
doubt have faced and dealt with his or her economic circumstances
and the loss of the spouse's living skills and will have had time for
adjustment and healing. As gerontological research pointed out early
on, younger widows and widowers have more time to establish alternatives or to replace what is absent in life after the spouse's passing.

If widowhood occurs after retirement, and presumably at a time of
greater age, the situation is quite different and the sudden adjustment
to the multiple effects of age, loss, health problems related to loss,
reduced income, and changing activities can be difficult if not overwhelming. Many women who are widowed after both they and their
spouse have retired still manage to build a new life for themselves.
This is testimony to great tenacity and vitality and to the strengths
often found in widows' mutual support and relationships (Silverman
1986).

Widowers

The timing of retirement relative to widowhood is critical to widowers, perhaps even more than to widows, because widowed men are
likely to display a greater amount of inflexibility in adapting to roles
in retirement that were formerly handled by the wife.

While the same issues concern widowers that concern all retirees
(income maintenance, health, time use, social support, and activities),

social support in retirement is an especially critical concern for widowers. Despite a popular image to the contrary, older men tend not to remarry; their life expectancy is less than that of their spouses, and their terminal decline generally begins earlier. For those men who do survive spouses, little is known about the dynamics and timing of retirement and caregiving by men to their infirm spouses.

For most men, work has been an important arena, if not the major arena, for social contact and friendships. With retirement, men lose not only the efficacy of self that is represented by work, but a large number of social contacts as well. Retiring men are well aware of stories, true of not, of men who died soon after retirement, men who either worked themselves to death or who were cut off from their major source of personal identity and efficacy and were effectively "blocked" as persons in some way.

Yet with the death of a wife men often feel as if they are "set adrift," as one widower put it. In most marriages the wife has functioned as the social organizer and instigator, and the ability to act socially is difficult for many older men. Sad, with time on their hands, and in the absence of social contacts and the wife's mediating role, many widowers can find retirement difficult. The difficulties most commonly mentioned by widowers include the development and maintenance of social relations, resocialization to the single role, and emotional difficulties. Retired widowers may seek part-time work as a form of self-validation and a way of increasing income and being useful. While some remarry and become active in social programs of various sorts, many suffer from health, nutritional, and self-maintenance problems and from isolation and loneliness.

The Childless

While retirement is often viewed as an individual phenomenon (a person retiring from a long-term job), in fact, retirement clearly affects the family as well. A good deal is known about how retirement shapes marital relations at home. Certainly the image of the newly retired, overinvolved husband who reinvents domestic routine, much to the consternation of his wife, is well known. Not knowing what to do with oneself at home can be troubling until one can develop a new postretirement pattern of home life.

How retirement affects children who may be grown and out of the house is less clear. Certainly the diminution of income at retirement must affect perceptions by children who are still in some way economically dependent on their parents of the help they may be able to obtain from their parents. Retirement may also bring with it economic fears on the part of the retiree, an incipient sense of the possibility of future economic dependency on children and thus probably the first instance of the resolve "not to be a burden" on adult children. With retirement, the generations enter a decades-long negotiation about resources, support in later life, dependency, and inheritance.

Yet some 20 percent of older Americans do not have children. Either they never had children, or the children died. One's marital status—never married, currently married, widowed, separated, or divorced—has implications that affect the experience and meaning of childlessness in later life and after retirement. Results of a recent study (Henretta, Chan, and O'Rand 1992) suggest that, for men at least, having no children in the current marriage is one of several reasons that a man may wish to retire.

The new retiree, either singly or as part of a couple, must view the absence of children anew. Elsewhere I have suggested that, for childless adults as well as for those with children, the meaning of one's life situation must be reevaluated at every stage of life and at the occurrence of every major event (Rubinstein 1988). Retirement, a significant life transition, is a venue for such a reexamination.

In such a review, three themes are salient. First, childlessness may be viewed in the context of the emerging and unfolding issues of independence and support in later life. For example, extended interviews with childless older women, nearly all of whom were retirees, showed that, while many had come to terms with being childless earlier in life, a variety of issues about childlessness had newly emerged in the later years. These were brought out by concerns about future care, generativity, and finitude—the sense of the impending end of life.

Second, the life-style of retirees may cause them to see themselves negatively because of their childless status. For example, the social arenas and relations of retired widows—neighborhood-based affiliations, retiree groups or programs, senior centers, retirement communities, and the like—while emphasizing orientation to present-day activities and self-development in retirement, often use discussions of children and grandchildren as the raw material of social performance. Childless elders may newly experience feelings of alienation and stigmatization and may develop strategies for confronting them. Johnson and Catalano (1981) have noted the close attachments childless older couples often form with one another and have described a sense of social inversion or isolation that may accompany this childless status.

Third, in mid-life childless adults may have sought psychological replacement or adjustment to the lack of children in their work settings. With retirement, issues that have been submerged for decades may surface. Retirement from a main job may precipitate involvement in part-time work for both economic and psychological reasons or immersion in some type of volunteer activity as a means of psychological fulfillment.

The Divorced

It is very difficult to assess the impact of divorce on retirement. Indeed, most standard books about aging and retirement fail to discuss this topic. While only about 5 percent of those who are now age sixty-five and older are divorced, clearly the percentage of older adults who are both retired and divorced will increase.

Once again the matter of timing is critical; if one is divorced early, it allows for recovery from the event prior to other transitions such as retirement. There is little doubt that divorce is destructive to all participants and, even if it opens new opportunities and allows one to "undo" an event that "never should have occurred," it can be difficult in the extreme for all affected.

The effects on retirement of a divorce that has occurred in early adulthood or mid-life is less significant than a divorce that occurs near or after retirement. Relatively few people get divorced after age sixty, and this is especially the case of divorce from an only spouse. As we noted in our discussion of widowhood, the co-occurrence of two such profound life changes is likely to have many stressful effects. While some may long for divorce after a lengthy and unsatisfying marriage, the actual decision to divorce and the process of divorce are likely to be difficult. This may especially be the case for older wives, who may lack the work experience, independent retirement income, familiarity with the outside world, and potential mate pool of men.

Divorce prior to the retirement years is more common, and the financial and social effects cannot only be well anticipated, but there is often enough time to alter financial plans to ensure a more certain economic future. Divorce at or after retirement will complicate the difficult transition in a variety of ways.

First, the co-occurrence of these two events will greatly alter the retiree's image of what retirement is or can be. A lengthy marriage that ultimately ends in divorce has no doubt included considerable conflict between partners over the years. Should a lengthy marriage end in divorce, it is unlikely that the divorcing spouses will have developed an image of retirement that is fully satisfactory to both parties and will remain so through the transition of divorce. Whatever planning has gone into actualizing an image of what retirement is to be, this is likely to require considerable change; indeed, it may necessitate a return to the work force by one or both spouses to augmented their income.

Divorce can be quite difficult financially and, from locality to locality, will involve a variety of legal provisions. The division of income, assets, and benefits may become complex. Income will now be required to support two households. The psychological issues are also profound. To the extent that retirement was once viewed as an opportunity, this view may now be compromised; to the extent that retirement was viewed with a sense of trepidation, this sense is now bound to be magnified.

The social effects of divorce are also great. The identity of the couple in relation to other couples, former work acquaintances and friends, children, and all other friends and acquaintances is compromised, and the former partners must now newly negotiate the nature of their relationships as individuals.

Gay Men and Lesbian Women

There is a lack of literature on retirement among gay men and lesbian women. Consequently, in the discussion that following I will outline some of the issues, but I will be unable to present any detailed findings. Berger (1982), in discussing older homosexual men, presents portraits of men who believe that retirement can be an opportunity and briefly discusses issues of adjustment, community involvement, status, satisfaction, and finances. In the present discussion, I will rely on a small number of interviews with older gays and lesbians pertaining to retirement issues.

Clearly gay and lesbian retirees face the same transition difficulties and adjustment problems as all other retirees, as well as concerns about income sufficiency, social support, satisfaction with activities and the transition to a senior lifestyle. Yet because of the social stigma attached to their sexual orientation and the generally persecutory stance of society toward homosexuality, a number of special concerns relative to retirement must be mentioned. These include the role of work in personal identity, community involvement, commitment to relationships, family relationships, and retirement goals and aims.

As one's identity has evolved in adulthood, it has likely evolved in the context of a work identity, including such components as the degree of satisfaction with one's work and the degree of satisfaction with the presentation of one's identity to co-workers and others as gay or lesbian. Those for whom maintaining secrecy or privacy about this aspect of their social identity has been a struggle in the work arena or in the face of a single unpleasant supervisor will no doubt look on retirement as a blessed relief or even an opportunity for openness.

Yet again, having chosen a particular job and having persevered through social hardships and occupational infighting may indicate a great deal of personal attachment to the job situation, the income, some co-workers, the type of work, the clients, or the satisfaction one derives from the job. One may have to grapple with the loss of all these positive aspects of employment upon retirement. Some work environments may have provided openness and acceptance of diversity. The loss of such a safe haven for one's identity (regardless of the other problems of the work setting) may have profound personal ramifications, since after retirement daily life may no longer provide such a setting. Of course, some may feel no special attachment to their work or to co-workers, and for them the importance of work to life may never develop as an issue.

If gays or lesbians are to experience retirement as part of a long-standing committed couple, the retirement period will be significantly different from any other period. As is the case for any dedicated couple, having one or both members around the house can increasingly lead to tension. Similarly, the timing of retirement for each partner is an issue that may affect the quality of life in retirement. The implications of two job holders retiring on the same day is different from that of their retiring a year or two apart in terms of income maintenance, activities, maintaining the home, social relations, and the like. The couple must make decisions about retirement goals and aims in common with respect to shared interests and predilections.

Very little is known about whether gays and lesbians retire to care for a partner who is infirm or, if so, how. The legal ramifications of caregiving for gays and lesbians must be explored in each locality. Recent cases that have been discussed in the national media have included conflicts over the rights and interests of families and partners who are providing care. When an infirm partner has children, conflicting interests may arise between those children and the well partner, and these will need to be anticipated and explored with legal counsel.

If a geographic move is anticipated upon retirement, it is clear that one must thoroughly explore the ramifications on one's life-style, including openness of identity. While certain communities or localities may be known to be either directly supportive of gays or lesbians or at least neutral in attitude, others may simply be unknowns; an effort should be made to assess their suitability for retirement. Since active discrimination against gays and lesbians appears to be on the rise in the United States, unfortunately such a scouting process appears to be increasingly necessary. If a couple sees involvement in a gay or lesbian community as a necessity or a goal, retirement venues may be limited.

With retirement may come changes in relationship not only between partners, but also in relations with partners' family members. Some families may have denied or refused to acknowledge the retiree's sexual orientation and life-style, making the co-retirement of both partners especially difficult for family members to handle. In contrast, in the cases of some older men and women, partners' families appear to have been more accepting as the relationship has become lengthier. If the partners have children from previous marriages, income diminution at retirement may cause questions to surface regarding children's expectations of income, as in any adult parent-child situation.

CONCLUSIONS AND PRACTICAL IMPLICATIONS

The members of the social categories discussed here share a number of characteristics. As retirees, they have the same concerns that affect all retirees: income adequacy, health, social relations, and activities. As retirees, they are also linked by their differences and by the fact that they do not fit the normative image of the aging American family at retirement. Yet those in each category have special needs and concerns, which are briefly outlined in this chapter. A number of issues have also been mentioned about which knowledge is currently lacking and future research is required.

The materials presented in this chapter indicate that the specific context of retirement must be understood if problems and difficulties that arise upon retirement are to be effectively handled. Certainly the short list of retirement concerns mentioned here affect all retirees. But these concerns have ramifications in areas that are largely related to and shaped by antecedent social structural and interpersonal factors (Szinovacz and Washo 1992; Logue 1991).

Retirement difficulties must be examined and dealt with in a context that includes income, health, social relations, time use, and activities.

REFERENCES

Allen, K. A. 1989. *Single Woman/Family Ties: Life Histories of Older Women.* New York: Sage.

Berger, R. M. 1982. *Gay and Gray: The Older Homosexual Man.* Urbana, Ill.: University of Illinois Press.

Bound, J., G. Duncan, D. Laren, and L. Oleinich. 1991. "Poverty Dynamics in Widowhood." *Journal of Gerontology: Social Sciences,* 46:S115–S124.

Bradsher, J., C. Longino, D. Jackson, and R. Zimmerman. 1992. Health and Geographic Mobility among the Recently Widowed. *Journal of Gerontology: Social Sciences,* 47:S261–268.

Braito, R., and D. Anderson. 1983. "The Ever-Single Elderly Woman." In E. Markson, ed., *Older Women: Issues and Prospects.* Lexington, Mass.: Lexington Books.

Crystal, S., D. Shea, and S. Krishnaswami. 1992. "Educational Attainment, Occupational History, and Stratification: Determinants of Later-Life Economic Outcome." *Journal of Gerontology: Social Sciences,* 47:S213–221.

Dortman, L., and M. Moffett. 1987. "Retirement Satisfaction in Married and Widowed Rural Women." The Gerontologist, 27:215–221.

Grad, S. 1983. *Income of the Population, Age 50 and Over.* United States Department of Health and Human Services, Social Security Administration, Publication 13-11871. Washington D.C.: U.S. Government Printing Office.

Henretta, J. C., C. Chan, and A. M. O'Rand. 1992. "Retirement Reason versus Retirement Process: Examining the Reasons for Retirement Typology." *Journal of Gerontology: Social Sciences,* 47:S1–S7.

Johnson, C., and D. Catalano. 1981. "Childless Elders and Their Social Supports." *The Gerontologist,* 21:610–618.

Kart, C., C. Longino, and S. Ullman. 1989. "Comparing the Economically Advantaged and the Pension Elite: 1980 Census Profiles." *The Gerontologist,* 29:745–749.

Keating, N., and B. Jeffrey. 1983. "Work Careers of Ever-Married and Never-Married Retired Women." *The Gerontologist,* 23:416–421.

Keith, Pat M. 1989. *The Unmarried in Later Life.* New York: Praeger.

Lingg, B. A. 1990. "Women Beneficiaries Age 62 and Older, 1960–1988." *Social Security Bulletin,* 53:2–12.

Logue, B. J. 1991. "Women at Risk: Predictors of Financial Stress for Retired Women Workers." *The Gerontologist,* 31:657–665.

Longino, C., and S. Ullman. 1988. *The Economically-Advantaged Retiree: State Statistical Profiles.* Coral Gables, Fla.: University of Miami, Center for Social Research on Aging.

Lopata, H. 1973. *Widowhood in an American City.* Cambridge, Mass.: Schenkman.

Lopata, H. 1979. *Women as Widows: Support Systems.* New York: Elsevier.

Lopata, H. 1987. *Widows. Volume II: North America.* Durham, N.C.: Duke University Press.

Neale, A. 1987. "Widows in a Florida Retirement Community." In H. Lopata, ed. *Widows. Volume II: North America.* Durham, N.C.: Duke University Press.

O'Bryant, S., and L. Morgan. 1989. "Financial Experience and Well-Being among Mature Widowed Women." *The Gerontologist,* 29:245–251.

Rubinstein, R. 1986. *Singular Paths: Old Men Living Alone.* New York: Columbia University Press.

Rubinstein, R. 1987. "Childless Elderly: Theoretical Perspectives and Practical Concerns." *Journal of Cross-Cultural Gerontology,* 2:1–14.

Rubinstein, R., B. Alexander, M. Goodman, and M. Luborsky. 1991. "Key Relationships of Never Married, Childless Older Women: A Cultural Analysis." *Journal of Gerontology: Social Sciences*, 46:S271–S278.

Silverman, P. 1986. *Widow-to-Widow*. New York: Springer.

Simon, B. 1987. *Never Married Women*. Philadelphia: Temple University Press.

Szinovacz, M., 1982. *Women's Retirement: Policy Implications of Recent Research*. Beverly Hills, Calif.: Sage.

Szinovacz, M., and C. Washo. 1992. "Gender Differences in Exposure to Life Events and Adaptation to Retirement." *Journal of Gerontology: Social Sciences*, 47:S191–196.

Ward, R. 1979. "The Never Married in Later Life." *Journal of Gerontology*, 34:861–869.

30

Caregiving to Older Relatives

●

NANCY R. HOOYMAN

Family caregiving for the elderly affects the experiences of a growing number of retirees, since families provide 80 percent of the in-home care to older relatives with chronic illness. It is estimated that 5 million adult children currently care for aging parents and 2.2 million individuals provide care to other older relatives. Given the extent and necessity of family caregiving, long-term care of an older relative is a normative experience—predictable, expected, and nearly universal, something that nearly all families will do in their lives—but for which they generally are unprepared (Walker and Pratt 1991; Scanlon 1988; Brody 1985).

Increasingly, service providers presume that families will provide the majority of in-home care. Older people who receive familial assistance while living in the community typically use fewer home-based formal services than their counterparts without such support (Ward, Sherman, and LaGory 1984). If families were not providing such care, nearly 10 percent of older people living in the community would require nursing home placement, tripling the number of elders in nursing homes (Brody 1981, 1985). In fact, it is estimated that the cost of replacing the care currently provided "free" by family members would be, at a minimum, $9.6 billion and perhaps as high as $17.5 billion (Paringer 1983).

This chapter focuses on two consequences of family caregiving for individuals during the retirement years: (1) the burdens of caregiving and the resultant disruption of plans and relationships for spouses in the presumed "golden years" and (2) the economic costs of caregiving across the life span that result in lower retirement income and benefits, particularly for older women.

Gender differences are a central consideration in examining these consequences, since women, who comprise 80 percent of the family caregivers to the elderly, are more often than men both unpaid and underpaid providers of care as well as recipients of care (Older Women's League 1989; Stone, Cafferata, and Sangl 1987). Numerous studies document a well-defined caregiving hierarchy: the primary caregiver is most often a spouse, followed by an adult child, and in both cases is usually female (Older Women's League 1988; Stone, Cafferata, and Sangl 1987; Brody 1985). During their retirement years wives are more likely to be primary caregivers than husbands, daughters than sons, and sisters than brothers. Of all family caregivers, 23 percent are wives, 29 percent are daughters and daughters-in-law and 20 percent are other more distant female relatives (Abramovitz 1988; Older Women's League 1989; Stone, Cafferata, and Sangl 1987 Brody 1987).

More than 33 percent of all disabled men who are over age sixty five and living in the community are cared for by wives, compared to only about 10 percent of older women who are cared for by husband: (Brody 1981; Barusch and Spaid 1989; Tennstead, McKinley and Sul livan, 1989). For older women, daughters are the most frequently mentioned sources of support, followed by husbands (41.2 percen and 21.6 percent respectively) (Coward, Horne, and Dwyer 1992). Ir most instances, the caregivers themselves are vulnerable, averaging fifty-seven years of age, with over 30 percent in fair or poor healtl and over 30 percent having low incomes (U.S. House of Representa- tives 1987; Older Women's League 1989). In part this pattern reflects demographic realities: women live longer than men, are more likely to experience physical and mental impairments that require care, and tend to marry older men, thereby increasing the likelihood that they will become caregivers to disabled husbands.

This pattern also reflects societal expectations that caregiving is women's work. Although some male caregivers, particularly husbands over age sixty-five, are "unsung heroes," men are less likely than women to be involved in direct personal care and routine housekeeping. Instead, they tend to perform indirect, intermittent, male-stereotypic tasks, such as financial management and home maintenance (Brody 1985; Matthews and Rosner 1988). Sons, in particular, generally assume primary responsibility only when a female relative is unavailable, while daughters provide more intensive care to older people with higher levels of dependency and for longer time periods (Stoller 1992; Tennstedt, McKinley, and Sullivan 1989). This division of labor is consistent with the pattern of men's involvement in child care and housework; men perform about one hour of housework for every two hours performed by women. Even when women and men are equally involved in economic activities outside the home, the domestic division of labor is rarely equal (Lee 1992). In fact, this pattern has not shifted dramatically in the past three decades, and it is unlikely to do so in the near future, despite the growing numbers of women in the paid labor force and despite apparent changes in attitudes toward gender-appropriate tasks (Montgomery 1992; Lee 1992).

SOCIAL AND DEMOGRAPHIC TRENDS THAT IMPACT FAMILY CAREGIVING

Before examining these gender inequities in terms of the burdens experienced by family caregivers during retirement, the social and demographic factors that underlie the increasing demands upon families will be highlighted. These trends particularly impact the young old, those in their sixties, who are likely to be faced with caregiving responsibilities along with the transition to retirement.

The primary demographic factor is the increase in life expectancy and the resultant growth of the population over age sixty-five from 4 percent in 1900 to 12 percent currently. Almost four out of five individuals can now expect to reach age sixty-five, at which point one has better than a 50 percent chance of living past age eighty (U.S. Senate Special Committee on Aging 1992).

Another demographic trend is the increasing diversity among the elderly, with the most rapid growth among the oldest old, those in their eighties. The percentage of the oldest old, who are most likely to have chronic health problems, will escalate in the next few decades, particularly when the baby boomers reach advanced old age by the year 2050; we can expect a 500 percent increase in the oldest old within sixty years (U.S. Senate Special Committee on Aging 1992). The delay in the onset of morbidity and the need for care among the rapidly growing oldest old will pose caregiving dilemmas for the young old, who may also be facing both life-style and socioeconomic changes entailed by retirement.

Although this dramatic growth in the numbers of "senior boomers" will challenge the young old generation, future generations of the elderly are likely to be healthier until advanced old age and more financially secure than current generations of the elderly, thereby postponing the need for care. On the other hand, the very old will be women, since women's life expectancy is predicted to remain greater than men's (U.S. Bureau of the Census 1990; Rossi 1985). And women will continue to be characterized by lower income, a higher incidence of chronic disease, and a greater probability of living alone than their male counterparts—all trends that have significance for future retirees.

Another demographic change underlying the growing demands upon family caregivers during middle and early old age is the growth of the multigenerational family. The increase in life expectancy, as well as patterns of earlier marriage and childbearing in some generations, have resulted in more four- and five-generation families. Among adult children, over 80 percent of middle-aged couples who may also be experiencing retirement have at least one living parent, compared to fewer than 50 percent in 1900. Forty percent of adult children in their late fifties have a surviving parent, as do 20 percent in their early sixties, 10 percent in their late sixties, and 3 percent in their seventies. Changing multigenerational dynamics are reflected in the fact that 10 percent of people over age sixty-five have a child who is also over sixty-five, so they may be both children and grandparents at the same time. By the year 2000 four-generation families will be the norm, and more young old generations will face caring for the oldest old (U.S. Senate Special Commission on Aging 1992).

What is unknown is the extent to which multigenerational family members in the future will live with or near each other. Currently most older people with children do not share intergenerational households, but they live less than an hour away from at least one child. In fact, less than 3 percent of older people live in multigenerational households composed of parents, children, and grandchildren (U.S. Senate Special Committee on Aging 1992), although ethnic minority elders are more likely than their white counterparts to reside in extended households (Taylor and Chatters 1991). However, due in part to the poor economy of the past decade and the growth of the number of single mothers, the number of children who are living in three-generational households has doubled from 1.3 million in 1980 to 2.3 million in 1990 (U.S. Bureau of the Census 1990).

Even when family members do not live near or with each other, multigenerational ties tend to be characterized by affection and socio-emotional closeness; there are patterns of reciprocal support, which flows from those with more valued resources, such as money and good health, to those with less. At various points older parents provide substantial support to younger generations, especially financial assistance and help with child care, and they step in during crises, such as divorce or early widowhood faced by their adult children. When the oldest generation experiences chronic health problems, widowhood, or divorce, the direction of the flow of support generally changes, with younger generations assisting parents, grandparents, or great-grandparents.

Differences in socioeconomic class and ethnicity tend to affect the nature and frequency of support. For example, middle-class adult children typically provide more emotional support, financial assistance, and coordination of services, while lower-income children tend to perform the caregiving tasks themselves. Although ethnic minority families have typically been portrayed as providing extensive support throughout extended family networks, economic necessity may be a more important factor than norms of obligation or affection (Rosenthal 1986).

The proportion of older people in families has increased faster than the pool of younger family members. The current generation of frail older people, who reached childbearing age during the Depression, had low marriage and birth rates, resulting in proportionately fewer adult children to assist with their care in old age. People now entering old age, who gave birth to the baby boom generation, will have more children to look to for care. But this increase in the number of potential caregivers is temporary. By 2005 there will be 180 middle-aged people for every 114 over age sixty-five; but by 2025 that ratio will be 100 to 253 (Older Women's League 1989). This decrease in the number of potential caregivers reflects not only declines in fertility, but also an increase in the proportion of nonmarried persons and childless couples.

Another effect of increased life expectancy combined with reduced fertility is that for the first time women can expect to spend more years caring for an older parent than for a dependent child (U.S. Senate Special Committee on Aging 1992). Similarly, the average married couple has more living parents than children for the first time in history. The average American woman can expect to spend eighteen years caring for an older family member compared to eight years in 1900, and she can currently expect to spend seventeen years caring for children (Older Women's League 1989; Stone, Cafferata, and Sangl 1987).

Today children do not expect the loss of parents until the second half of adulthood, and the death of a child is no longer an anticipated part of family life; in contrast, more than half of the children born in 1910 and who survived to age fifty had experienced the death of a parent of sibling by their early teens. For current generations of middle-aged women, the death of a mother may occur close to the daughter's retirement age. These changes mean that a growing proportion of parents and children will share such critical adulthood experiences as retirement and widowhood.

These changes in birth rates, life expectancy, and the incidence of four- and five-generation families have meant an increase in vertical intergenerational ties and a decline in horizontal relationships (e.g., those with siblings and cousins). Individuals in a multigenerational family interact in the framework of a much more complex set of family identities than is seen when there are only two generations, those of parent and child. For example, who is responsible for a great-grandparent who falls and needs daily care—the grandparents, who may themselves be frail; the parents, who may be facing retirement; or the grandchildren, who are often in school or employed?

The increase in the complexity and the vertical links that cross generational lines, along with a decreasing number of horizontal relationships within generations, has created a "beanpole" family structure (Bengston, Rosenthal, and Burton 1990). As noted above, within this structure middle-aged and young old children will be even more likely to care for more than one elderly relative in the future. And they will be less likely to have siblings or cousins with whom they can share such care tasks. At the same time, as a result of reduced fertility rates there are fewer individuals within the younger generations in whom retired people can invest emotionally, making intergenerational relationships that include retired people more emotionally intensive (Hagestad 1986). This means that those in the young old or middle generations will continue to have a strong sense of obligation to care for parents or grandparents.

Of this current and declining pool of younger caregivers, middle-aged and young old daughters have traditionally been responsible for elder care, especially for parents and parents-in-law. But their ability to care for the oldest old over longer periods of time is increasingly affected by the multiple and often conflicting demands of paid work. In fact, conflicts between elder care and employment are more pervasive for young old caregivers than are the conflicts between elder care and child care (Cantor 1991; Stone and Kemper 1989). Middle-aged women now comprise the largest category of employed women; 69 percent of women aged forty-five through fifty-four are employed, as are 75 percent of those aged thirty-five through forty-four (U.S. Bureau of the Census 1988). Most women are employed out of economic necessity, either because of widowhood or divorce or because their families need or have come to depend upon two incomes. Yet, when faced with caregiving demands, they are more likely than their male counterparts to have to quit their jobs or reduce their hours of employment, thereby diminishing their income.

Cross-generational demands are increasing not only because the oldest generation with chronic illness is expanding, but also because the younger generation often does not leave home. Many young old individuals who are facing the prospect of retirement experience pressures to financially and emotionally assist both their parents and their young adult children. Rather than a time of financial freedom, retirement is a time of new financial demands; the "empty nest" that has previously been characteristic of early retirement is being filled both by frail elderly parents and by "boomerang" kids—young adult children who are launched and leave home briefly, but then return home because of divorce, unemployment, child-care needs, inability to purchase a house, the need to pay debts, or personal problems, including drug and alcohol addiction. In fact, the number of unmarried adults aged eighteen to thirty-five who are living with their parents has increased steadily since 1960, while the median income for those fifteen to twenty-four has increased. In 1987 over 50 percent of unmarried adults aged eighteen to twenty-four lived at home, compared to 43 percent in 1960 (U.S. Bureau of the Census 1988).

Not only are young old parents caring for adult children who return home, but 90 percent of middle-aged women have at least one child at home, compared to 66 percent in 1900. Accordingly, some young old women are still responsible for dependent children. These factors have created the phenomenon of "women in the middle" or "the sandwiched generation," people who face the triple burden of maintaining employment and providing care to both younger and older generations (Brody 1985; Miller 1981).

These multiple and sometimes conflicting demands are particularly complex because they involve different generations and can expand dramatically within a relatively short period of time. In fact, for many women caregiving extends across the life course, from caring for children in young adulthood to caring for older parents in middle age and the young-old years to caring for husbands in old age. This career of caring can negatively affect older women's economic status in retirement, as will be examined below.

In a growing number of instances, young old individuals may not only be assisting their grown children emotionally and financially, but also may be caring for young grandchildren. This is especially likely when their adult children are struggling with divorce or alcohol and drug addiction, as is the case with the current crack cocaine epidemic. Approximately three million children now live with their grandparents, and in a third of these cases neither parent is present. In fact, the incidence of caregiving by grandparents has doubled in the last decade. Although it occurs in all racial groups, it is especially

470 Individual and Family Life

pronounced in the African-American community, where 13 percent of children are cared for by grandparents, compared to 3 percent of Hispanic children and 2 percent of Caucasian children (Minkler and Roe 1991). Women who had looked forward to retirement, the "empty nest," and having financially independent children who could provide them with gifts or money may instead be caregivers to three or four generations and be faced with illness, sleepless nights, and locating day care for both children and older relatives.

Accordingly, caregiving relationships across generations may be even more complex because of the growth in rates of divorce, remarriage, and blended or reconstituted families. Over 50 percent of all marriages contracted during the 1970s are estimated to end in divorce—and it is these individuals who will reach old age and retirement around the year 2020. A high proportion will remarry, but it is estimated that 44 percent of these marriages will also end in divorce (Martin and Bumpass 1989; Reiss and Lee 1988; Pratt and Kethley 1988). Therefore, young old adults may not only be caring for their biological parents and current parents-in-law but, if divorced, may be emotionally tied to the parents of their former spouse.

Looking toward the future, it is unknown to what extent younger members of "blended" families and those who are unrelated by blood but joined by years of sharing familial responsibilities will assume the role of caregiver. Conflicting loyalties to in-laws, former in-laws and one's own parents will undoubtedly complicate the distribution of time, attention, and financial resources across generations.

Another type of caregiving relationship that affects retirement experiences is that of gay and lesbian partners (Pratt and Kethley 1988). Gay and lesbian caregivers have to confront many of the same issues that long-term heterosexual partners do, such as the disruption of retirement plans by a partner's illness or role changes in response to illness, but they also face particular legal obstacles and homophobic attitudes among providers of health and human services and other family members.

Despite the complex and extensive caregiving relationships that many young old retirees may face, the majority experience satisfaction from their roles within the expanded kin networks of multigenerational families. Most grandparents and great-grandparents, for example, derive considerable emotional satisfaction from their interactions with younger generations, even when they are the primary caregivers to grandchildren or great-grandchildren. However, with the continuing decline in birth rates, increase in life expectancy, changing family structures, growing racial and socioeconomic diversity of the population, and declining economic conditions, young old adults can no longer anticipate or plan for a retirement uninterrupted by the demands of cross-generational caregiving.

CAREGIVING BURDENS AND RETIREMENT

As noted throughout this book, retirement poses numerous adjustments for spouses, even for those who eagerly anticipate and plan together for retirement. Partners must adjust to more free time and leisure with one another, reduced income, and their own decreasing energy. An adjustment that is rarely planned for, however, is the type necessitated by the illness of a partner or parent.

Even though caregiving has been called a normative experience, most individuals do not plan for the impact of a relative's illness upon their retirement, largely because the onset of the need to care for an older relative can rarely be accurately predicted. In addition, most people do not even want to consider the possibility of becoming caregivers to older relatives. Yet often all it takes is a moment and a single nightmarish surprise—a fall and a broken hip, a stroke, or an unexpected diagnosis of Alzheimer's disease—to dramatically change one's retirement plans.

Caught in circumstances beyond their control, families are likely to enter into caregiving arrangements believing that their short-term assistance can help their older relative "get better." But most of the time the situation does not improve. Instead, it frequently becomes one of increasing dependency, decline, and relentless care. The unpredictability of care tasks, the uncertainty of prognosis, and the resultant need to continuously redefine what is considered a normal life intensify the stress of caregiving. Not surprisingly, caregivers may see themselves forsaking their golden years—their time to enjoy life to the full as a reward of their labor—and resent the dramatic change in their retirement plans (Robinson and Thurnher 1979).

Many family caregivers do experience personal growth, rewards, and closer relationships as a result of performing their tasks. Family members may discover new strengths and ways of relating to one another, for example. However, most caregivers experience some costs, which are heightened by the low status and unpredictable nature of their care tasks. Caregiving is generally performed in isolation from other adults, requires twenty-four-hour maintenance, and is all-consuming and progressively more demanding. Even caregivers who derive satisfaction from their role may find their tasks burdensome because of the lack of societal support and rewards for caregiving.

Physical Costs

The physical costs of caregiving are greatest for those caregivers, usually women, who provide the majority of personal hands-on care for highly impaired older persons—lifting or turning, preparing extra meals, and cleaning two homes. These costs are also greatest for those who are caring for highly impaired elders. Of the elderly receiving care, 58 percent are homebound, 38 percent are bedridden, and 24 percent are confined to wheelchairs. Their average age is seventy-seven, and 25 percent are at least eighty-five years old. The spouses of such severely impaired elderly people tend to be old themselves, with diminishing physical resources available for providing care (Stone, Cafferata, and Sangl 1987).

The caregivers' capacity to meet their older relatives' needs fluctuates with their own well-being; 16 percent of caregivers report that their health has declined since they began to provide care (Braithwaite 1990; Pruchno and Patashnik 1989; Satariano, Minkler, and Langhauser 1984; Cantor 1983; Johnson and Catalano 1983). Not surprisingly, due to physical stress, health problems are more common among spouse caregivers than among their age peers or other types of caregivers (Rabin, Mace, and Lucas 1982; Snyder and Keefe 1985). Their health problems include constant fatigue, stomach disturbances, loss of appetite, headaches, weight changes, and in some cases higher morbidity rates. Caregivers also tend to use prescription drugs more than twice as often as the rest of the population (Haley et al. 1987; George and Gwyther 1986). Yet even when an older wife becomes ill, she will generally neglect her health and continue to care for her disabled husband (Wilson 1990).

In addition, most caregivers do not utilize formal services to reduce physical stress. In fact, about 50 percent provide care without any outside assistance, and less than 10 percent are assisted by a community agency or other paid service providers. Of those who do receive supplemental assistance from either informal helpers or formal services, husbands and sons are more likely to do so than wives and daughters (Montgomery and Borgatta 1989; Stone, Cafferata, and Sangl 1987).

One reason for such gender inequities in service provision is the gender-specific impact of a spouse's disability upon the division of household labor (Stoller 1992). When a wife is ill or disabled, husband caregivers must assume responsibility for more household chores than in the past. The incapacity of a husband means that wife caregivers take on more responsibility for male-stereotypic tasks, such as yard work, household repairs, and financial management. However, since wives traditionally perform the majority of domestic work, assuming responsibility for her husband's tasks has little overall impact on the total workload of a caregiving wife (Stoller 1992; Rexroat and Shehan 1987). On the other hand, when a wife is ill or disabled a husband-caregiver must perform more household chores with which they generally have had little prior experience. Therefore, a wife's illness results in more reorganization of household activities than a husband's (Stoller 1992). In fact, Brubaker and Kinsel (1988) argue that it is illness rather than retirement per se that typically causes couples to alter preretirement patterns in the division of household tasks.

Societal expectations regarding women's role as caregivers may also explain why service providers are more likely to offer in-home services to husbands than to wives (Stoller 1990, 1992; Polansky 1985). Men's involvement in caregiving is viewed as an unexpected expression of compassion rather than as simply their "work." Therefore, their caregiving efforts, however minimal, are more likely to be acknowledged and rewarded by others than are women's (Waerness 1985).

Despite the greater support that is generally extended to husband caregivers, married women are institutionalized more frequently than married men. This gender difference suggests that husbands may not be as dependable as wives in providing long-term care and that husbands and wives may have different tolerance thresholds at which the demands of caregiving overwhelm their capacity (Hess and Soldo 1985; Stoller 1990, 1992).

Sons are also more likely than daughters to be provided with supportive services and to withdraw when caregiving demands escalate to include routine household chores and personal care (Montgomery 1992). In fact, daughters caring for frail parents receive the lowest level of community services of any caregivers (Wright 1983; Stoller 1990). Not only do sons feel less personally obligated and expect to provide less hands-on care, but this attitude may be supported by other female relatives who expect only "circumscribed" or "sporadic" assistance. In turn, sons are likely to feel that the caregiving role is a greater imposition, even when they are providing less intensive care than their female counterparts (Stoller 1990).

Elders' attitudes may also perpetuate such gender biases. Older care recipients frequently have strong feelings about what constitutes family care and who should provide such care. For example, mothers who are living with adult children assist their sons with household tasks more than they help their daughters. Mothers are more likely to turn to daughters than sons for assistance, even when both sons and daughters are available (Matthews and Rosner 1988; Wright 1983; Lee 1992).

Emotional Costs

For many caregivers, the greatest stress may be produced by the tangled web of emotional burdens they experience—feeling alone, lacking privacy, sacrificing leisure and recreation, foregoing their own plans, and receiving little support from friends (George and Gwyther 1986). Women are more likely to experience the disruption and loss of their friendship networks, since throughout their lives women depend upon friendships for support more than men do (Lee 1992). When these networks are altered by caregiving, many women experience a "support gap," giving more support than they receive. Caregivers often talk of feeling like prisoners or say that they are drowning in tasks at the same time that they are dealing with the emotional strain of a relative's becoming more dependent (Fengler and Goodrich 1979; Crossman, London, and Barry 1981). These emotional burdens frequently intensify when long-held retirement plans for leisure and enjoyment are drastically disrupted.

Caregivers often experience conflicts with their spouses, children, and siblings, and the relationship between the caregiver and the care receiver may be negatively affected. Wives have been found to experience more depression and deterioration of the marital relationship than have husbands (Wilson 1990). The history of the caregiver's personal relationship with his or her older relative, the fear that the relative will die, and the caregiver's own sense of vulnerability all become intertwined, creating a kaleidoscope of feelings—ambivalence, love, anger, guilt, and resentment.

Women caregivers tend to experience higher levels of emotional stress and depression than their male counterparts, even when they perform similar tasks for the same amount of time (Biegel, Sales, and Schulz 1991; Horowitz 1985; Barusch and Spaid 1989; Fitting et al. 1986; Young and Kahana 1989; Pruchno and Resch 1989). In Brody's study (1981) of three generations of women, 75 percent of the women in the middle generation felt guilty and inadequate for not doing enough, even though these women provided extensive care.

Throughout their lives women tend to have stronger and more intense vertical ties to kin than do men, which results in a greater sense of psychological responsibility for others' well-being and more difficulty maintaining the emotional distance that may be needed to manage caregiving problems. More likely to respond to others' difficulties by absorbing their concerns themselves, women caregivers tend to suffer distress when they cannot relieve the suffering of their older relatives (Brody et al. 1983; Brody et al. 1987; Stoller 1992; Abel 1990). In contrast, men are less likely than women to feel personally responsible for their parents' emotional well-being or to experience guilt from not doing more. They are also better able to distance themselves physically and emotionally from the person receiving care, focusing primarily on economic and concrete tasks (Robinson and Thurnher 1979; Wethington, McLeod and Kessler 1988).

Differences in socialization may also explain why women caregivers experience more emotional stress than male caregivers. From childhood more women are socialized to respond first to others' needs and to sacrifice their own interests. Greater internalization of an injunction to care is central to women's identity; many women judge themselves according to an ethic of responsibility (Walker 1992; Gilligan 1982). As a result, women caregivers may believe that they should be able to perfectly manage all the caregiving responsibilities themselves as proof of their love, competence, and loyalty to their parents or their marriage vows. Failure to do so may cause women to feel guilt and to be unable to set limits on their own and others' expectations about how much care they should provide (Lewis and Meredith 1988). Excessive caregiving and refusing offers of help while complaining that no one assists them may be motivated by women's perception of caregiving as the primary basis of their identity and power in their relationship with the person receiving care and what gives the relationship meaning for the woman. Guilt, perhaps stemming from anger at the person receiving care for becoming ill, past conflicts, or disappointment at changed retirement plans, also frequently underlies excessive caregiving.

In contrast, men tend to define themselves as recipients of care or as instrumental agents—for example, as the person who writes the check for formal services, but not as the hands-on caregiver (Matthews and Rosner 1988). Men generally respond to attachments to others by supporting them economically (Walker 1992).

Explaining women's greater distress from caregiving in terms of these differences in socialization is not intended to blame women or discredit their experiences. Women's socialization to an ethic of caring and to bonds of attachment can be strengths. But the costs of the ethic of caring must also be acknowledged. Given the socialization of many women, a decision to care is not necessarily rational or always freely made. Rather, it is made within a framework of widely held assumptions that caregiving is women's work and that, in the end, caring for others should take precedence over other types of labor.

Another source of emotional stress for wives is that the responsibilities of caring for disabled husbands in old age may be an extension of caregiving throughout the life course. Caregiving is thus not a new activity or a single time-limited episode for many older women, but is a continuation of what they have always done. They may see meal preparation, housework, and laundry not as elder care tasks per se, but simply as responsibilities that they have had to perform throughout their lives (Pruchno and Resch 1989). In contrast, older husbands who are caregivers are more likely to continue their own outside interests and to seek respite by leaving their wives unattended for periods of time (Miller 1987). Viewing caregiving as another "job," husband caregivers are more likely to approach it in a businesslike, instrumental fashion, which may minimize the emotional stress they experience (Dwyer and Seccombe 1991).

Financial Costs

Financial costs include not only the direct expenses of elements of care, such as medical care, modifications to the home, or the hiring of help, but also the indirect costs of lost income, foregone employment opportunities, missed or modified work hours, or used-up vacation benefits (Rimmer 1983; Gibeau and Anastas 1989). People who are serving as caregivers during retirement are probably adjusting to living on a fixed income, not having calculated the additional costs entailed by care.

However, to focus only on the immediate loss of income and the direct costs of extra expenses is to underestimate the long-term financial loss to caregivers (Rimmer 1983). In old age many women caregivers are faced with living on a low income as a result of years spent out of the labor force to provide dependent care for children, then for parents and parents-in-law, and finally for a disabled husband. One of the greatest costs for such women is lower retirement benefits and resultant low income in old age, even though their caregiving services have been essential to the economy of the family (Abramovitz 1988).

After devoting their lives to attending to others' needs, many women, particularly minority women, face years of living alone on low incomes, with inadequate medical care, and with their own welfare depending on the care of younger female relatives or underpaid care attendants (Glazer 1990; Fengler and Goodrich 1979). For example, older women currently comprise nearly 70 percent of the low-income elderly; over 16 percent of older women live below the poverty line, and women over age seventy-five who are living alone, especially women of color, form the poorest group in our society.

Women's total average retirement benefits are 73 percent of men's (Older Women's League 1990). And despite the increased number of women in the paid work force and the relatively greater economic affluence among younger women, in the future older women are predicted to remain significantly poorer than older men. When today's twenty-five-year old woman retires after having been employed for as long as thirty-five years, she can expect to receive, on average, the same retirement benefits—adjusted only for inflation—that her mother received, even though she will have paid more into Social Security. In fact, it is predicted that 70 percent of baby boom women will outlive their husbands by fifteen years but that they will earn, on average, only two-thirds the pay of their husbands. In the year 2030, 60 percent of women will also have had five or more years of zero earnings averaged into the calculation of their Social Security benefits (Older Women's League 1990).

This grim economic outlook is due to a number of factors. One is the limited number of options for in-home care coupled with the spend-down requirements under Medicaid, which force many women to become impoverished by providing care on their own (Osterbusch, et al. 1987). However, a primary reason for this grim outlook is that women are more likely than men to interrupt employment throughout their life spans in order to care for dependents of all ages. The average woman spends nearly one-half of her life fulfilling the role of family caregiver to dependents.

Women now average 11.4 years out of the paid labor force to provide care, while men average 1.3 years (Older Women's League 1989, 1990, 1991). For most women such discontinuities carry severe economic costs, since years of lower or no earnings reduce women's Social Security benefits and minimize the likelihood of their receiving private pensions. This is because pension systems benefit traditional male work patterns that are not disrupted by care responsibilities. For many young old women, leaving the work force to care for a husband during his final illness amounts to early retirement given the low probability of reemployment among older workers (Schulz 1988).

Women working full time are four times as likely to be primary caregivers as are men. Yet they are also more likely than their male counterparts to quit their jobs, rearrange their work schedules, or reduce their hours of employment rather than limiting their caregiving activities (Stone and Kemper 1989; Brody et al. 1987). Sons are the least likely caregivers to quit their jobs in order to provide care (Stone, Cafferata and Sangl 1987). Employed women provide an average of sixteen hours of care a week compared to ten hours for employed male caregivers (Travelers Insurance Company 1985). In other words, women caregivers deal with their multiple responsibilities by sacrificing free time, modifying employment demands, and maintaining rigid schedules, not by reducing their hours of caregiving (Gibeau and Anastas 1989; Stone, Cafferata, and Sangl 1987). As long as women continue to assume more care responsibilities, are paid on average less, and live longer than men, these biases will take an enormous toll on women's retirement income in the next century.

In fact, current policies that rely on "cost-efficient" informal family care of the elderly exacerbate the already disadvantaged position of women by not accounting for the unobserved costs associated with care (Osterbusch et al. 1987). Society considers the unpaid labor of women to be "low cost" to individuals families and communities because not all the costs of this labor are assessed, such as lost contributions to a retirement plan and the lost potential for financial equity in interpersonal relationships. In sum, many women sacrifice their financial independence and well-being to meet their perceived social obligation to be unpaid caregivers (Finch and Groves 1983; Glazer 1990).

Practical Implications

Given the physical, emotional, and financial costs of care, particularly for women in retirement, and the demographic and societal changes that are likely to increase the burdens faced by family caregivers, what are some practical implications for both professionals and the elderly themselves?

As a first step, the young old need to plan for such caregiving responsibilities. Ideally, as part of retirement planning individuals should openly discuss finances, living arrangements, and care responsibilities with older relatives before an emergency arises. Such discussions can help prevent caregiving from being a burden. Fortunately a growing number of corporations, such as IBM, AT&T, and Travelers, are providing information and referrals that can assist employees with planning and managing elder care (Scharlach, Lowe, and Schneider 1991).

Once families are faced with caregiving demands, they need to be assured that they are not alone and do not need to "do it all" on their own. Advocacy for caregivers is essential to insure that the growing number of resources from agencies and the corporate sector, such as respite, education, support groups, day care, and in-home help, are accessible to all families (see the end of this chapter for a list of practical resources). As the central providers of social and health care to the elderly, families are entitled to these resources. Such services must be viewed not as a luxury or an add-on, but as essential to the caregiver's well-being and his or her long-term ability to provide care. Families cannot keep giving indefinitely, but must be able to answer the question "What about you?" and give themselves permission to take care of themselves. Burned-out caregivers cannot provide quality care.

Caregivers also need to be encouraged to ask for help from relatives and friends and to devise ways to divide tasks equitably among family members. They need to set realistic limits on the amount of care they can provide. As noted earlier, excessive caregiving often stems from guilt. Yet caregivers need not feel guilty about what they wish they could have done; they should learn to accept what they cannot do as well as what they can do. In some instances, it may be most appropriate for the caregiver to do less, not more.

Accordingly, professionals need to clarify their own values regarding family responsibility and recognize that the best form of care will vary with both the caregiver's and the care receiver's needs. This includes acknowledging when placement outside the home is the best alternative, then working with the caregiver during the transition to nursing home care.

However, as professionals seek to provide services, such as education, support, and respite for caregivers, they must be careful not to inadvertently intensify the burdens experienced by caregivers. Educational programs have been found to increase the caregivers' knowledge and skills, but not necessarily to reduce the level of their stress (Biegel, Sales, and Schulz 1991). Some interventions, such as time management training, presume that increased efficiency at task performance is an antidote to the stresses of multiple care demands (Clark and Rakowski 1983). But efficiency is a misplaced standard of caregiving. Economizing on the amount of time required to change an incontinent person's bedding does not substantially minimize the stress of performing this task several times a night year after year. Nor do models of efficiency offer solutions to the constant vigilance required to prevent a cognitively impaired person from wandering. Instead of asking what is the most efficient and cost-effective way to keep an older person alive, the central question should be what is the best way to care for him or her (Sommers and Shields 1987).

Well-intentioned interventions may intensify the burdens of caregiving if families must locate respite care and transportation on their own in order to participate in education or support groups. Accordingly, such groups may reach only caregivers who have the time and resources to attend and who are already connected to services, not those who are the most isolated, particularly low-income older women of color, who are experiencing the greatest stress and the most need for services. Although education and support groups can provide opportunities for caregivers to ventilate and problem solve, they do not necessarily reduce their stress (Haley et al. 1987; Toseland and Rossiter 1989; Zarit, Anthony, and Boutsellis 1987; Biegel, Sales, and Schulz 1991). Similarly, clinical/direct service interventions, such as counseling and behavioral/cognitive stimulation, may modify objective stressors, but not reduce levels of anxiety or depression or improve the caregiver's functioning (Biegel, Sales, and Schulz 1991).

SUMMARY

In the next several decades retired individuals will face family caregiving duties that are often impossible demands. It is essential that they be given choices about how to care for older relatives. Resources must be available, both in the community and in the workplace, to support those who choose to assume the role of primary caregiver. If caregivers are asked to meet complex multigenerational demands—and if they agree—they must be rewarded and supported in ways that take account of current social and demographic trends. As our society confronts the challenges posed by a growing number of older and retired individuals, the issue of family care must also be addressed to ensure that caregiving work is equitably shared and valued and that individuals are able to receive and to give to others the care that they want and need.

Resources for Family Caregivers
ORGANIZATIONS

Many of these organizations have publications related to elder care.

Alzheimer's Association
70 East Lake Street
Suite 600
Chicago, IL 60601

American Association of Retired Persons
601 E Street, NW
Washington, DC 20049

Children of Aging Parents
2761 Trenton Road
Levittown, PA 19056

Family Survival Project
44 Page Street
Suite 600
San Francisco, CA 94102

Older Women's League
666 11th Street, NW
Suite 700
Washington, DC 20001

Women Who Care
Marin Senior Day Services
Box 692
Mill Valley, CA 94941

CORPORATE ELDER CARE PROGRAMS

The Travelers Insurance Companies
Older Americans Program
National and Community Affairs
One Tower Square
Hartford, CT 06183

IBM
Elder Care Consultation and Referral Service
Employee Benefits
2000 Purchase Street
Purchase, NY 10577–2597

Bank of America
Elder Care Referral Program
180 Montgomery Street
San Francisco, CA 94137

Partnership for Elder Care
Philip Morris
CARE Program
100 Park Avenue
New York, New York 10017

REFERENCES

Abel, E. K. 1987. *Love Is Not Enough: Family Care of the Frail Elderly*. Washington, D.C.: American Public Health Association.

Abel, E. K. 1990. Informal Care for the Disabled Elderly: A Critique of Recent Literature. *Research on Aging*, 12:139–157.

Abramovitz, M. 1988. *Regulating the Lives of Women: Social Welfare Policy from Colonial Times to the Present*. Boston: South End Press.

Barusch, A., and W. Spaid. 1989. "Gender Differences in caregiving: Why Do Wives Report Greater Burden?" *The Gerontologist*, 29(5):667–676.

Bengtson, V. C., C. J. Rosenthal, and C. Burton. 1990. "Families and Aging: Diversity and Heterogeneity." In R. H. Binstock and L. K. George, eds., *Handbook of Aging and the Social Sciences*, 3rd ed. New York: Academic Press, 263–287.

Biegel, D., E. Sales, and R. Schulz. 1991. *Family Caregiving in Chronic Illness*. Newbury Park, Calif.: Sage.

Braithwaite, V. 1990. *Bound to Care*. North Sydney, Australia: Allen & Unwin.

Brody, E. 1981. " 'Women in the Middle' and Family Help to Older People." *The Gerontologist*, 21(5):471.

Brody, E. 1985. "Parent Care as a Normative Family Stress." *The Gerontologist*, 25(1), 19–29.

Brody, E., P. Johnsen, M. Fulcomer, and A. Lang. 1983. "Women's Changing Roles and Help to Elderly Parents: Attitudes of Three Generations of Women." *Journal of Gerontology*, 38(5):597–607.

Brody, E., M. Kleban, P. Johnson, C. Hoffman, and C. Schoonover. 1987. "Work Stress and Parent Care." *The Gerontologist*, 27(2):201–208.

Brubaker, T. H., and B. Kinsel. 1988. "Who Is Responsible for Household Tasks in Long Term Marriages of the Young Old Elderly?" In L. Ade-Ridder and C. Hennon, eds, *Lifestyles of the Elderly: Diversity in Relationships, Health and Caregiving*. New York: Human Sciences Press.

Cantor, M. 1983. "Strain among Caregivers: A Study of Experience in the United States." *The Gerontologist*, 23(6):597.

Cantor, M. 1991. "Family and Community: Changing Roles in an Aging Society." *The Gerontologist*, 31:337–346.

Clark, N., and W. Rakowski. 1983. "Family Caregivers of Older Adults: Improving Helping Skills.: *The Gerontologist*, 23:637–642.

Coward, R., Horne, C., and Dwyer, J. 1991. "Demographic Perspectives on Gender and Family Caregiving." In J. Dwyer and R. Coward, eds., *Gender, Families and Elder Care*. Newbury Park; Calif.: Sage.

Crossman, L., C. London, and C. Barry. 1981. "Older Women Caring for Disabled Spouses: A Model for Supportive Services." *The Gerontologist*, 21:464.

Dwyer, J., and R. Coward. 1992. *Gender, Families and Elder Care*. Newbury Park, Calif.: Sage.

Dwyer, J., and Seccombe, K. 1991. "Elder Care as Family Labor: The Influence of Gender and Family Position." *Journal of Family Issues*, 12(7):229–247.

Fengler, A. P., and N. Goodrich. 1979. "Wives of Elderly Disabled Men: Hidden Patients." *The Gerontologist*, 19(2):175.

Finch, J., and D. Groves. 1983. "Introduction." In J. Finch and D. Groves, eds., *A Labour of Love: Women, Work and Caring*, 1–10. London: Routledge and Kegan Paul.

Fitting, M., P. Rabin, M. Lucas, and J. Eastham. 1986. "Caregivers for Dementia Patients." *The Gerontologist*, 29(4):449–465.

George, L. K., and L. P. Gwyther. 1986. "Caregiver Well Being: A Multidimensional

Examination of Family Caregivers of Demented Adults." *The Gerontologist,* 26:253–259.

Gibeau, J., and J. Anastas. 1989. "Breadwinners and Caregivers: Interviews with Working Women." *Journal of Gerontological Social Work,* 14(1–2):19–40.

Gilligan, C. 1982. *In a Different Voice.* Cambridge, Mass.: Harvard University Press.

Glazer, N. Y. 1990. "The Home as a Workshop: Women as Amateur Nurses and Medical Providers." *Gender and Society,* 4:479–499.

Hagestad, G. 1986. "Women and Grandparents as Kin-Keepers." In A. Pizer and L. Bonte, eds., *Our Aging Society: Paradox and Promise.* New York: W. W. Norton.

Haley, W., E. Levine, B. Berry, L. Brown, and G. Hughes. 1987. Psychological, Social, and Health Consequences of Caring for a Relative with Senile Dementia. *Journal of American Geriatrics Society,* 35(5):405–411.

Hess, B., and B. Soldo. 1985. "Husband and Wife Networks." In W. J. Sauer and R. T. Coward, eds, *Social Support Networks and the Care of the Elderly,* 67–92. New York: Springer Publishing Company.

Horowitz, A. 1985. "Sons and Daughters as Caregivers to Older Parents: Differences in Role Performance and Consequences." *The Gerontologist,* 25:612–617.

Johnson, C. L., and D. J. Catalano. 1983. "A Longitudinal Study of Family Supports to the Impaired Elderly." *The Gerontologist,* 23:612–618.

Lee, G. 1992. "Gender Differences in Family Caregiving: A Fact in Search of a Theory." In J. Dwyer and R. Coward, eds., *Gender, Families and Elder Care.* Newbury Park, Calif.: Sage.

Lewis, J., and B. Meredith. 1988. *Daughters Who Care: Daughters Caring for Mothers at Home.* London: Routledge.

Martin, T. C., and L. L. Bumpass. 1989. "Recent Trends in Marital Disruption." *Demography,* 26:37–51.

Matthews and Rosner. 1988. "Shared Filial Responsibility: The Family as the Primary Caregiver." *Journal of Marriage and the Family,* 50:185–195.

Miller, B. 1987. "Gender and Control among Spouses of the Cognitively Impaired: A Research Note." *The Gerontologist,* 27:447–453.

Miller, B. 1990. "Gender Differences in Spouse Caregiver Strain." *Journal of Marriage and the Family,* 52:311–322.

Miller, D. 1981. "The 'Sandwich' Generation: Adult Children of the Aging.: *Social Work,* 26(5):419–423.

Minkler, M., and K. Roe. 1991. "Preliminary Findings from the Grandmother Caregiver Theory." Oakland, Calif.

Montgomery, R. 1992. "Gender Differences in Patterns of Child-Parent Caregiving Relationships." In J. Dwyer and R. Coward, eds., *Gender, Families and Elder Care.* Newbury Park, Calif.: Sage.

Montgomery, R. and E. F. Borgatta. 1989. "The Effects of Alternative Support Strategies on Family Caregiving." *The Gerontologist,* 29:457–464.

Noelker, L., and R. Wallace. 1985. "The Organization of Family Care for Impaired Elderly." *The Journal of Family Issues,* 6(1):23–44.

Norton, A. J., and J. E. Moorman. 1987. "Current Trends in American Marriage and Divorce." *Journal of Marriage and Family,* 49:3–14.

Older Women's League. 1989. *Failing American's Caregivers.* Washington, D.C.: Older Women's League.

Older Women's League. 1990. *Heading for Hardship: Retirement Income for American Women in the Next Century.* Washington, D.C.: Older Women's League.

Older Women's League. 1991. *Paying for Prejudice.* Washington, D.C.: Older Women's League.

Osterbusch, S., S. Keigher, B. Miller, and N. Linsk. 1987. "Community Care Policies and Gender Justice." *International Journal of Health Services,* 17:217–232.

Paringer, L. 1983. *The Forgotten Costs of Long-Term Care.* Washington, D.C.: The Urban Institute.

Polansky, E. 1985. "A Feminist Analysis of Hospital Discharge Planning: Women as Caregivers of Disabled Family Members." Presented at the Annual Program Meeting of the Council on Social Work Education, Washington, D.C.

Poulshock, S. W., and G. Diemling. 1984. "Families Caring for Elders in Residence: Issues in the Measurement of Burden." *Journal of Gerontology: Social Sciences*, 39:230–239.

Pratt, C. K., and A. J. Kethley. 1988. "Aging and Family Caregiving in the Future: Implications for Education and Policy." *Educational Gerontology*, 14:567–576.

Pruchno, R. A., and S. L. Patashnick. 1989. "Caregiving Spouses: Physical and Mental Perspectives." *Journal of American Geriatrics Society*, 37:697–705.

Pruchno, R. A., and N. Resch. 1989. "Husbands and Wives as Caregivers: Antecedents of Depression and Burden." *The Gerontologist*, 29:159–165.

Reiss, I. L., and G. R. Lee. 1988. *Family Systems in America*, 4th ed. New York: Holt, Rinehart and Winston, Inc.

Rexroat, C., and C. Shehan. 1987. "The Family Life Cycle and Spouses Time in House Work." *Journal of Marriage and Family*, 49:735–750.

Rimmer, L. 1983. "The Economics of Work and Caring." In J. Finch and D. Groves, eds, *A Labour of Love: Women, Work and Caring*, 131–147. London: Routledge and Kagen Paul.

Robinson, B., and M. Turnher. 1979. "Taking Care of Aged Parents: A Family Circle Transition." *The Gerontologist*, 19:586–593.

Rosenthal, C. J. 1986. "Family Supports in Later Life: Does Ethnicity Make a Difference?" *The Gerontologist*, 26(1):19–24.

Rossi, A. 1985. "Gender and Parenthood." In A. Rossi, ed., *Gender and the Life Course*. Hawthorne, N.Y.: Aldine.

Satariano, W. A., M. A. Minkler, and C. Langhauser. 1984. "The Significance of an Ill Spouse for Assessing Health Differences in an Elderly Population." *Journal of American Geriatrics Society*, 32:187–190.

Scanlon, W. J. 1988. "A Perspective on Long Term Care for the Elderly." *Health Care Financing Review, Annual Supplement*, 7–15.

Scharlach, A., B. Lowe, and E. Schneider. 1991. *Elder Care and the Work Force.* Lexington, Mass.: Lexington Books.

Schulz, J. 1988. *The Economics of Aging*, 4th edition. Belmont, Calif.: Wadsworth.

Snyder, B., and K. Keefe. 1985. "The Unmet Needs of Family Caregivers for Frail and Disabled Adults." *Social Work in Health Care*, 10:1–14.

Sommers, T., and L. Shields. 1987. *Women Take Care: The Consequences of Caregiving in Today's Society.* Gainesville, Fla.: Triad Press.

Spitze, G., and J. Logan. 1990. "More Evidence on Women and Men in the Middle." *Research on Aging*, 12:182–198.

Stoller, E. P. 1990. "Males as Helpers: The Roles of Sons, Relatives and Friends." *The Gerontologist*, 30:228–235.

Stoller, E. P. 1992. "Gender Differences in the Experiences of Caregiving Spouses." In J. Dwyer and R. Coward, eds., *Gender, Families, and Elder Care.* Newbury Park, Calif.: Sage.

Stoller, E. P., and L. L. Earl. 1983. "Help with Activities of Everyday Life: Sources of Support for the Noninstitutionalized Elderly." *The Gerontologist*, 23(1):64.

Stone, R., G. L. Cafferata, J. and Sangl. 1987. "Caregivers of the Frail Elderly: A National Profile." *The Gerontologist*, 27(5):616–626.

Stone, R., and P. Kemper. 1989. "Spouses and Children of Disabled Elders: How Large a Constituency for Long-Term Reform?" *The Milbank Quarterly*, 67:485–506.

Taylor, R., and L. Chatters. 1991. "Extended Family Networks of Older Black Adults." *The Journals of Gerontology*, 46(4):S210–S218.

Tennstead, S., J. McKinlay, and L. Sullivan. 1989. "Informal Care for Frail Elders: The Role of Secondary Caregivers." *The Gerontologist*, 29:677–683.

Toseland, R. W., and C. M. Rossiter. 1989. "Group Interventions to Support Family Caregivers." *The Gerontologist*, 29:438–448.

Travelers Insurance Company. 1985. *A Survey on Caregiving Responsibilities for Older Americans*. Hartford, Conn.: The Travelers.

U.S. Bureau of the Census. 1990. "Marital Status and Living Arrangements." *Current Population Reports*, Series P-20, no. 1450. Washington, D.C.: U.S. Department of Commerce, March.

U.S. Bureau of the Census. *Statistical Abstract of the United States: 1988*, 10th ed. Washington, D.C.: U.S. Government Printing Office.

U.S. House of Representatives. 1987. *Exploding the Myths: Caregiving in America*. U.S. Government Printing Office.

U.S. Senate Special Committee on Aging. 1992. *Aging America: Trends and Projections: 1991 Edition*. U.S. Department of Health and Human Services.

Waerness, K. 1985. "Informal and Formal Care in Old Age—What Is Wrong with the New Ideology of Community Care in the Scandinavian Welfare State Today." Paper presented at the Conference on Gender Divisions and Policies for Community Care, University of Kent, Canterbury, England.

Walker, A. 1992. "Conceptual Perspective on Gender in Family Caregiving." In J. Dwyer and R. Coward, eds., *Gender Families and Elder Care*. Newbury Park, Calif.: Sage.

Walker, A. J., and C. C. Pratt. 1991. "Daughters' Help to Mothers: Intergenerational Aid versus Caregiving." *Journal of Marriage and the Family*, 53:3–12.

Ward, R. A., S. R. Sherman, and M. LaGory. 1984. "Informal Networks of Services for Older Persons." *Journal of Gerontology: Social Sciences*, 45:229–237.

Wethington, E., J. McLeod, and R. Kessler. 1988. "The Importance of Life Events for Explaining Sex Differences in Psychological Distress." In R. Barnett, L. Biener, and G. Baruch, *Gender and Stress*, 144–159. New York: Free Press.

Wilson, V. 1990. "The Consequences of Elderly Wives Caring for Disabled Husbands." *Social Work*, 35:417–421.

Wright, F. 1983. "Single Carers: Employment, Housework, and Caring." In J. Finch and D. Grover. *A Labor of Love*, 89–105. London: Routledge and Kegan Paul.

Young, R., and E. Kahana. 1989. "Specifying Caregiver Outcomes: Gender and Relationship Aspects of Caregiving Strain." *The Gerontologist*, 29:660–666.

Zarit, S., C.R. Anthony, and M. Boutsellis. 1987. "Interventions with Caregivers of Dimentia Patients: Comparison of Two Approaches." *Psychology of Aging*, 2 (3):225–232.

IX
COMMUNITY INVOLVEMENT, LEISURE, AND PERSONAL GROWTH
●

31

Recreation and Leisure

•

JOHN R. KELLY

The common canard is that those in retirement have no valued social roles. Those who do not die from the shock of being nonpersons without productive positions or schedules face lives of emptiness. Time is a measureless void, both frightening and shapeless. Except for some seasonal gardening, retirement becomes a kind of vegetative state without goals or meaning. In cold climates a few sad souls sit around tables in senior centers crocheting doilies and exchanging tales of the good old days. In the sunbelt they sit around the pool exchanging the same tales augmented by tales of sun damage and the sport of insect swatting.

A summary of this drab picture is that retired older people have nothing worthwhile to do. The assumption is that, in a production-oriented society dominated by a work ethic, retirement is little more than a prelude to death. Further, in order to mitigate this sad state it is necessary to provide a special set of time-filling activities in segregated places to fill the void. Note the assumptions inherent in this picture: First, prior to retirement most adults center the meaning as well as the timetables of their lives around their jobs. Second, they have no other significant commitments or relationships. Third, retirement forces them out of the gracious environments of employment. And fourth, they lack the flexibility to adapt to change.

ACTIVITY IN ORDINARY RETIREMENT

Fortunately, relatively few retired men and women would recognize themselves in this sad picture. Almost everyone has seen or read of the marvelous "old folks" who are organizing multicultural festivals, starting innovative pollution-free businesses, and snowshoeing across the Himalayan tundra at age eighty-four. Few retired adults recognize anything relevant to their lives in those tales, either. Nor do most retirees find that trips to upscale retirement resorts in glamorous locales are remotely possible on their budgets. In between the 5 to 10 percent who can afford expensive options and the 15 to 20 percent who are severely limited by poverty are the majority of ordinary folks for whom retirement is one more phase in the journey of life in which most have already had to cope with a series of transitions and traumas (Kelly 1987). Retirement is one more change, generally foreseen and usually anticipated.

Retired adults often comment on how busy they are. "I don't know how I had time for work" is a common reflection. What do these ordinary people do in retirement? An interview study of the twenty-five men and women who had retired from a food-processing plant in the midwest focused on their own accounts of activity as well as their resources and relationships (Kelly and Westcott 1991). These people had left routine jobs and were without the special resources of a college education or financial affluence. Except for the few who had health problems or had recently suffered the loss of a spouse, they were getting along reasonably well. Life was full and viable, if not spectacular. A common story emerged from most of the interviews, a general profile of ordinary retirement for unexceptional people.

The profile begins with a decision to retire several years before the age of sixty-five. The people described by the profile are "aging in place" in the community and homes that were their physical and social environments before retirement. The overall image is one of continuity—in relationships, values, and patterns of activity. The blocks of time opened up by retirement afford the opportunity for a planned car trip or two and the completion of a couple of projects. "At first I did a lot of work around the house" was a common description of the first months. After completing that initial agenda, they settled into routines that were built around the relationships, interests, and commitments that had paralleled their work for years, often for most of their adult lives.

Positive elements include a sense of freedom, blocks of time for travel and other activities, not having to get up early in the morning, and reduced pressure. One man specified relief from "setting the clock at 5:30." Another asserted, "It's good just not to be so tired so much of the time." A relatively active man summarized the new freedom he had when he said, "I can do what I want to do when I want to do it." The retired workers in this case study have not done quite as much traveling as they had anticipated. Their plans for becoming active in one or more community organizations have not materialized. The picture of their activities is one of continuity, doing the kinds of things they did before retirement, but they have days and weeks free for things that take a chunk of time. There have not left many plans unfulfilled, because most of their plans were rather vague to begin with.

For those with only a high school education, the range of leisure interests seldom extends far beyond the immediate. For those with intact marriages and other family members accessible, the family is the center of the social world. This is reflected in their value priorities. Family and home in some combination are first in importance. Men are more likely to be engaged in projects around home. Women spend more time in family interaction. Both, however, are generally "family-focused" in their orientations and values. Trips are usually family visits. Family celebrations punctuate their yearly schedule. For those who are married, the husband or wife is the usual companion for most activities as well as the main confidant. Other kin are also important. A recently widowed woman referred to her "precious grandchildren" just one state away. If nearby, children and grandchildren are a regular part of the social routine; if distant, their homes are the most common destinations for trips. Distance is the main factor in patterns of interaction among members of extended families.

Financial conditions are neither lavish nor extremely limited. For those who lived their entire lives on modest incomes, a modest retirement is not a great change. For those in reasonable health, satisfaction with retirement tends to be fairly high. For most, life is as good as it has ever been, if not quite all that had been hoped. Unlike many whose work has greater elements of autonomy and variety or who are forced out of high-status positions, these retired factory hands leave the workplace for good, and they have no desire for part-time employment, even if they have left the plant in their mid-fifties. Their jobs were routine and demanding and were defined instrumentally, primarily as a source of necessary income.

The activity patterns described by the profile revolve around a core of relatively accessible and low-cost engagements. The "ordinary" retired watch television, regularly if not always intensively. They talk to others in their households and get together with immediate family as well as friends. They do some entertaining, usually informally. Get-togethers with friends may involve card games, eating out inexpensively, or just spending the evening together. As one man said, "I just do what comes along."

Around the home, most do some reading, at least of newspapers and magazines. Gardening and yard work are common in the summer, sometimes as satisfying commitments and sometimes as chores. Men usually have some little project in the offing. Women more often seek out conversation with family and friends. Religious activity is the most common organizational activity outside the home and is significant for a minority of the retired. Most women have a hobby, usually a traditional women's handcraft. Almost half the men go fishing regularly in season, although several admitted that they do less fishing than they had anticipated. Special engagements for a half dozen include regular square dancing or bingo. Men are somewhat more likely to head out in the car and women to talk on the telephone. Going shopping is common for all. And none participate in any form of age-designated "senior" activity. Why not? They report that their lives seem fairly full.

What takes the place of the structuring of work schedules and the everyday familiarity of work associates? For the most part, the retirees described by the profile have constructed new routines around a core of companions and activities. The regularities are punctuated or highlighted by occasional special events, often involving some travel. However, routines are synchronized with television schedules, regular involvement with other family, and the everyday tasks of living.

Ordinary retirement seems rather predictable. Are there no surprises or idiosyncratic patterns? Of course there are exceptions. Three of the blue-collar men interviewed play golf regularly in season. One woman is involved in a special volunteer program in a nursing home and a man in prison tutoring. A man with a college education is working on a book of crossword puzzles. Another builds radio-controlled airplanes but does not fly them himself.

No two retirees are just alike, but the similarities seem to overshadow the differences. The stories told by this small number of retired workers are consistent with the results of other research (Kelly 1987). For those with intact families and viable health, their core of activities is focused on home and family, even when the quality of the relationships is less than perfect.

These men and women are in early retirement. As each year passes, more will experience losses in their social networks and in their own abilities. The "active old" will enter a period of transition that requires more and more adaptation to limits. Nevertheless, any approach to activity in retirement begins with the fact that most men and women are at least relatively engaged and satisfied and are going on with most of the things they did before retirement. Whatever the losses related to leaving their work roles, they seem to be more than compensated by the release from routines and demands.

CONTINUITIES OF RETIREMENT

There are individuals who are so invested in their work that life loses meaning without it. There are some who have to reinvest in activity that resembles work in order to cope with retirement (Ekerdt 1986; Kaufman 1993). Maintaining a sense of worth and even productivity is a central theme of satisfying retirement, even when the context of activity that yields such a self-definition shifts away from the workplace. The old image of the trauma of retirement has given way to one that stresses the normal transition that is expected and taken in company with companions of one's age group. The new image is that of the "active old" who have to make time in their schedules for anything new or extraordinary. "Continuity theory" (Atchley 1989, 1993) has replaced models of disengagement as well as those that focus on activity itself. Continuity encompasses who people are as well as what they do (Kelly 1993).

For all people who are of retirement age, the journey of life has had its zigzags. Some directions have been blocked, some surprising opportunities opened, and some lines of action diverted. Through that journey, however, there are continuities of the self who has learned a variety of skills, social repertoires, and self-definitions that carry over from one situation and time to another. As social actors, we become largely consistent in terms of who we are and how we act, in our identities and styles of behavior.

In the same way, there is consistency over time in our relationships and activities. Death, divorce, geographical moves, and other events disrupt our social tapestries. We add and subtract activities as our resources, opportunities, associations, and interests change. Nevertheless, there are commitments—to others and to activity investments—that persist through the years. Especially in relationships and activities to which we have sustained a commitment, we tend to manage our lives toward continuity. When skill-based activity such as fishing or playing chamber music is central to our sense of life's meaning, then usually sustain involvement into retirement. Further, such activities continue as the basis for companionship and friendship.

Any perspective that assumes that at some magical or cataclysmic time, age sixty-five or any other, we become different people is quite false. For the most part, even when recognizing incremental and inevitable change, we see ourselves as the same person who was fifty-five a few years ago and forty-five only a decade before. We do not categorize ourselves by age, but know ourselves in the continuity of an "ageless self" (Kaufman 1986).

The implications of this continuity of selfhood for leisure and recreation are manifold:

- First, there is a likelihood that most older adults will go on doing most of the things they have done before with most of the same associates.
- Second, while revised activities are not precluded, it is likely that changes will build on previous satisfactions, associations, and skills rather than require leaping into something entirely new.
- Third, any opportunities that require radical redefinitions of the self are unlikely to attract much interest. This is especially true when the redefinition involves a category with negative connotations such as "old" or "senior." The self that is getting older, especially in the relatively active early retirement years, is the same person as before, more "ageless" than defined primarily by age.

IS THERE "EXTRAORDINARY RETIREMENT"?

People are characterized by their diversity. The error of accepting negative stereotypes about "retirees" should not lead to the inverse mistake of defining almost everyone as "ordinary." Economically, there are the upscale affluent as well as the disinherited marginal and poor. Culturally, there are those who are bound to prescriptive lifestyles as well as those who are experimental—the conventional and the risk takers. There are even a few whose lives revolve primarily around their work or their leisure.

There are extraordinary retirees who have the financial means and initiative to move to a friendlier climate for all or part of the year. At the upscale end of the market are those with the wealth to purchase condominiums or homes in richly appointed communities that are usually on water and offer private golf courses and other recreational facilities. Restricted by cost to the affluent, they attract those accustomed to country club amenities and social life. They continue to be on the move, often spending part of the year in former environments as well as in travel. They are able to purchase a full set of opportunities for leisure as well as the privacy of a recreation-based residential enclave.

More common are the "snowbirds" and migrants who move to retirement areas or developments in Florida or the Southwest on a budget. Some may choose a locale with a number of retirees from their snowbelt community. Others take advantage of the concentration of the active old to form new friendships in activity-based groups. They tend to develop activity patterns that are responsive to the opportunities of the new environment. Such retirement areas and developments have their own life cycles as the initial settlers age, become frail, and die or are moved nearer to family caregivers.

At the other extreme are the retirees who struggle to survive due to histories of irregular or low-income employment. They have no pensions or savings, only the limited income of low-level Social Security. Their lives are dominated by the problems of the bills already on the table and the devastation that can be wrought by acute health costs. Their lives also demonstrate continuity in their day-to-day strategies of survival.

The affluent are important markets for upscale provisions. The poor are significant targets for life-sustaining programs. Most retirees, however, stay in the communities and neighborhoods where they have lived before. Further, their values and routines reflect their histories despite some reorientations related to preparation for retirement.

In a study of preretirement and retired older adults in the prototypical community of Peoria, Illinois (Kelly 1987), two life-styles were found to be far and away the most common. The first type was practiced by "balanced investors," who found meaning in a combination of family, work, and leisure. They found at least two of these three aspects of life important enough to take some priority in their allocation of resources. Their identities were not limited to a single role, but took on a balanced configuration appropriate to their period in the life course. The second common life-style was practiced by the "family focused," who tended to organize their lives around family roles. Usually with less education than "investors," they defined their lives primarily in terms of home and family. They valued work and leisure in terms of their contribution to the expression and strengthening of family bonds.

The retired replace work demands and opportunities by expanding their other commitments, especially those involving the family. The lives of retirees with a balanced investor type of life-style included somewhat more resources and variety than those of the "ordinary" retired factor workers described earlier. They are more likely to allocate financial and time resources based on an articulated set of values. Further, although their lives are seldom spectacular in terms of unusual commitments, they have made decisions about activities and relationships that are worth maintaining, cultivating, or renewing. They are most satisfied with their later years when they achieve a balance of caring and sharing relationships and meaningful activity.

However striking is the tendency toward continuity in later life, it does not preclude shifts in emphasis or even a resocialization into new roles and commitments. There are radical changes in the life courses of many adults, but life tends to be more a matter of building on foundations and composing with familiar themes than turning to the utterly new. As a consequence, those with the fullest and most diverse base on which to build are best able to respond to the opportunities of retirement.

Retirement brings significant change, all emphasis on continuity notwithstanding. The most obvious change is in the structure of time. The week is no longer dominated by employment obligations. This opens blocks of time to be reallocated for new routines or special events. While travel is the most obvious possibility, commitments to developing new friends, caring for grandchildren or neighbors, or redeveloping a demanding skill are not unusual. There is also a flexibility in timetables that permits more spontaneous response to unplanned opportunities.

Two parallel possibilities may be developed for the use of leisure time. The first is to utilize leisure to reconstitute a fundamental structure for time. Freedom from incessant demand does not imply a total lack of regularity. Most retirees rebuild some structure in their timetables. Complete voids are no more satisfying than demand saturation. New commitments to leisure activity and groups may be combined with a reengagement with former skills and identities. The second possibility is to retain enough openness that it is possible to respond to the immediacy of a lovely afternoon, an unexpected invitation, or a random impulse.

Extraordinary retirement is partly a matter of recognizing the opportunities that are released by the new life situation. If ordinary retirees tend to be relatively satisfied with their lives, then what is special about being more than ordinary? The answer may be surprising.

REQUISITES AND PREREQUISITES
OF SATISFYING RETIREMENT

What characterizes those who are doing more than getting along reasonably well in their later years? Are there marks of extraordinary retirement?

The "prerequisites" of satisfying retirement are almost self-evident. They are functional health and economic viability (Palmore 1979). Without those fundamental conditions, everything else is difficult or impossible. No community program, service, support, or association can replace these prerequisites. At issue is what is most significant when those two conditions are met. In a longitudinal study, group and physical activity for both men and women and solitary activity for women were the most salient factors that distinguished those with a high level of satisfaction in later life (Palmore 1979). A causal model of of analysis identified health, socioeconomic status, and activity as the three primary factors that produced satisfaction (Markides and Martin 1979). In a review of thirty years of research, Larson (1978) found that, following health, social activity accounts for the greatest differences in life satisfaction.

Other research has identified some refinements in the importance of activity. Especially among older persons, the quality rather than the quantity of relationships is most significant (Tobin and Neugarten 1961; Conner, Powers, and Bultena 1979; Kelly, Steinkamp, and Kelly 1986, 1987). One issue is the extent to which leisure and social activity make a direct contribution to life satisfaction rather than serving as a context for social interaction and integration. This issue was addressed directly in a study of women who were retired from employment or had always been homemakers (Riddick and Daniel 1984). Leisure activity was found to have the strongest direct effect on life satisfaction, followed by income and health. In a different study, level of leisure activity accounted for 6.2 percent of the remaining variation in life satisfaction after the 11.8 percent of health, occupational status, education level, age, gender, and marital status were entered (Kelly, Steinkamp, and Kelly 1987).

A number of explanations have been offered for the consistent finding that social and leisure activity make an independent contribution to well-being in later life. One holds that engagement in activity is itself important to a balanced and satisfying life (Cutler and Hendricks 1990; Longino and Cart 1982). Lemon, Bengtson, and Peterson (1972) suggest that informal leisure provides a context for significant social interaction. They further argue that frequent participation in fewer salient activities contributes more than does a wide range of activities. Atchley (1989) proposes that leisure enables retired people to continue roles that they have valued earlier. This view of engagement in meaningful activity defines leisure as an arena for the development and expression of valued identities in which one may gain some degree of competence, achievement, and recognition (Havighurst 1961; Rapoport and Rapoport 1976; Gordon, Gaitz, and Scott 1976; Kelly 1983).

In summary, there seems to be ample evidence that leisure and recreation are important elements of the quality of life in retirement. Further, there are indications that some kinds of activities contribute more than others and that quality is more important than quantity. A summary of the early findings of the Yale Health and Aging Project (Elder 1991) points to the importance of genetic endowment and then adds this: "But if staying involved with other people and keeping up your tennis game turns out to be even part of the answer, it just may be the closest humankind will ever get to the fountain of youth."

ALTERNATIVE THEORIES OF ACTIVITY

In the 1961 volume edited by Robert Kleemeier, *Aging and Leisure*, a number of authors went beyond presentations of what older people did to analyze the relationship of changes in economic and family roles in retirement to the meanings of nonwork activity. In particular, the chapter by Robert Havighurst entitled "The Nature and Value of Meaningful Free-time Activity" examined the dimensions of values found in a range of leisure engagements. He and others in the Kansas City Study of Adult Life found that leisure is multidimensional in meanings, varied in forms, and interwoven with family and community roles. "Balanced" and home-centered life-styles at high, medium, and low levels of activity were in part indexed by measures of social status.

The Reduction Model

From the same study, Cumming and Henry (1961) proposed their "disengagement theory," which has usually been placed in opposition to views of aging that stress activity and continuity. Disengagement is based on the dual findings that older people tended to be less involved than younger people in activity outside the home and that both tended to be relatively satisfied with this situation. The argument was then developed that some withdrawal from activity is functional for older people who need to concentrate their resources and energies on activity that is appropriate and satisfying for their stage of life.

It is certainly true that advancing age is correlated with lower rates of activity and even a constriction of interests (Havighurst 1961). In a more recent study, lower rates of participation were found for each older age category in travel, outdoor recreation, and exercise and sport (Kelly, Steinkamp, and Kelly 1986). For those over seventy-four, there were also lowers rates of participation in community organizations, cultural activity, and even home-based activity. There appears to be a constriction process that narrows the range of activities in terms of spatial location as well as number in later life. However, participation in two kinds of activity—social activity and family leisure activity—remain relatively high. Continuity is demonstrated in the "core" of relatively accessible and informal leisure that makes up the ongoing, day-to-day center of activity.

This constriction in the range of activity was also reported in a time-diary study (Lawton 1987). Increasing age was associated with more time spent alone eating, resting, relaxing, and engaging in at-home religious activity rather than in more active engagement outside the home. In a Houston-area study, the pattern of constriction associated with age held for such activities as dancing, movies, sports and exercise, outdoor recreation, travel, reading, cultural productions, and spectator sports to a greater degree than for social interaction, entertaining, volunteer work o, and cultural consumption (Gordon, Gaitz, and Scott 1976).

The Engagement Model

Constriction, however, may be an adaptation to conditions rather than a preference. Gordon, Gaitz, and Scott (1976), for example, suggest that energy reductions and the relinquishing of some social roles lead to some constriction in the frequency and range of one's participation in activity, but that the "meaningful integration" of sharing and interaction remain central for those in the retirement years. Further, self-definitions with valued identities are significant and are often supported by engagement in leisure.

Maddox (1968) reports on a longitudinal study in which it was found that declining health reduces the capacity to engage in many kinds of activity. The decline, however, tends to be gradual for those without traumatic loss of ability. Further, the declines are more gradual for activities such as reading, participating in cultural activities, entertaining, conversation, home enhancement, and other types of in-home and social activities than for events that are physically demanding (Gordon, Gaitz, and Scott 1976; Kelly, Steinkamp, and Kelly 1986). Even travel and participation in community organizations are markedly lower only for those in age categories associated with frailty. Older people continue to engage in activity that brings them together with valued other persons and in which they feel comfortable with their abilities. The stability of golfing rates suggests that even outdoor activity can continue to attract those with the developed skills, resources, and companions.

The reduction model, then, is supported when the sole measure is frequency of participation by activity type. A life course approach that is based on continuity, however, suggests an engagement model of adaptation and choice. When activity is associated with perceived quality of life, older people are more likely to focus on those activities and relationships that they believe contribute most to their lives. Those most satisfied with their lives in later years are those who have maintained engagement with meaningful activities and associations. Overall age-related lower rates of participation in many kinds of recreational activities obscure the relative stability in rates of participation in activities that are appropriate, possible, and satisfying to older people. Activities are selected rather than simply reduced, at least until the time when frailty severely limits the possibilities.

LEISURE THAT MAKES A DIFFERENCE

The approach toward leisure in retirement that is being developed here has the following theses:

1. The activity patterns of retired men and women are characterized by considerable continuity with the activities and relationships that have been meaningful to them in their preretirement years.
2. Retirement, then, involves a reconstruction of patterns of involvement based on previously established competencies and associations to accommodate the new freedom from demand.
3. The image of the "active old" is more accurate than one of voids of time and commitment, despite a pattern of age-related constriction in activity.
4. Retired adults are social actors who are selecting valued engagements that have proven satisfying rather than disengaged

pawns sliding into voids of meaninglessness and low level of satisfaction with life.

A primary issue, then, is that of resources and opportunity. What do retired men and women need in order to develop satisfying lifestyles with adequate levels of engagement? What are the factors that really make a difference?

In general, the two complementary elements of satisfying retirement beyond the prerequisites are activity and community, regular and meaningful engagement in doing things that are satisfying and sharing life with people through interaction and involvement. For most older people, both the activity and the relationships are an extension of histories that have been developed through the life course.

Retirement Activity

Does it make any difference what kinds of activity older adults participate in? Is bingo as satisfying as volunteer service, television as satisfying as golf, or gardening as satisfying as travel? One answer to this question would be that almost any pattern of regular action and interaction that provides a sense of meaning and brings retirees into association with friends and family would fulfill the requirements. Some research, however, indicates that those with the highest levels of satisfaction participate in certain kinds of activity. In the Peoria study there were significant differences in activities that contributed to satisfaction among people in different age groups (Kelly, Steinkamp, and Kelly 1986). For those aged forty to sixty-four, regular travel and participation in the arts and other cultural activity distinguished those with the highest level of perceived quality of life. Social and travel activity marked those aged sixty-five to seventy-four with the highest level of satisfaction. For those seventy-five and older, family and home-based activities were most salient. What is suggested is that the activity should be whatever provides the greatest stimulation and social involvement within the pattern of constriction that develops in later years.

In the longitudinal Duke study, activity outside the home, social and physical, marked the retirement-aged men and women with the highest level of satisfaction with life (Palmore 1979). The two critical dimensions seem to be challenge and social integration. In addition, for women, who are more likely to live alone than men, solitary activity that is involving or challenging is significant.

Another approach identified the kind of activity often referred to as "serious leisure" (Stebbins 1979). This is activity that demands skill, attention, and commitment. Serious leisure has a career of inauguration, development, and demonstrated competence. It usually involves its devotees, "amateurs," in regular interaction with groups in which association is built around common action. Those engaged in serious leisure make this commitment a central element of their identities. In retirement, these identities may claim even greater centrality. A Canadian study of time use and associations in later life found that those who were extraordinarily satisfied with their lives were those engaged in serious leisure (Mannell 1993). They experienced both the sense of community with their companions and the sense of competence produced by meeting the challenge of the activity (Csikszentmihalyi 1990).

Again, the two critical elements that make activity significant seem to be challenge and community. Challenge is stimulating, involving, and even exciting. Facing a challenge—physical, mental, or social—requires concentration and effort. Meeting the challenge requires a demonstration of skill. The outcome is twofold: the immediate involvement and the consequent sense of ability and worth. Community is commonly developed in the process of such engagement. Bonds are formed not by mere proximity or being entertained, but by common action, especially in activities that require exchange and reciprocity to form relationships of communication, sharing, and trust.

The forms of activity that combine the two critical elements are almost infinite. They may focus on physical, mental, aesthetic, or social tasks and challenges. They may involve outcomes that can be seen and appreciated, that are shared or more individual, that are of recognized social value or more private. They represent commitments that become central to life's meaning over time. They are the "extra" that may lift retirement above the ordinary.

Examples are endless. Retirees run, dance, fish, play softball, produce plays, counsel, teach, write, experiment, explore, learn, and organize. They sculpt in metal or wood, throw pots or create stained glass, rebuild old cars or train dogs, landscape or decorate, coach or provide care. What makes the activity significant is that the engagement is regular and demanding and involves some kind of community. It calls for continued learning and development, for assessment and commitment. And usually it has some connection with previously valued identities.

Such "serious leisure" is not all of anyone's retirement activity. A balanced leisure style also includes disengagement and relaxation, activity that is low-intensity as well as demanding, appreciation as well as creation, being alone as well as sharing. The ordinary patterns of living are there as well, especially in the day-to-day associations of home, family, neighborhood, and friends. But the extraordinary is the something more that highlights the ordinary, that makes the self someone special—a person of ability sharing with others. And it is the highlights that produce extraordinary enjoyment in the routines of retirement.

IMPLICATIONS FOR PROGRAMS AND RESOURCES

It is evident that retirees are not waiting around out there for just about anything to fill their time. In an analysis of more than thirteen thousand people aged sixty and above in the 1984 National Health Interviews, it was found that the proportion who regularly participate in "senior center" programs is quite low (Kelly and Reis 1991). Some 86.9 percent never go to senior centers, and 92.7 never eat at centers. In general, the percentage of those over sixty who are regularly engaged in any specific type of age-designated program is about 1 percent. If there was ever an accepted myth that desperate retirees would flock to just about any program, that presumption has been exploded. The issue yet to be resolved concerning such programs is the extent to which they serve and support those most bereft of economic and social resources rather than the more resourceful "active old."

The reasons older people give for not participating in age-designated programs are consistent with the engaged image of ordinary aging. The most common explanation older persons offer is that they are too busy (McGuire, Dottavio, and O'Leary 1986). These reasons also testify to the negative images of "senior" activity programs as low-quality programs that attract individuals of low ability who would not be interesting companions. For the most part, in order to attract older participants programs must project a quite different image—one of quality, interest, and value. Just filling time is not attractive to most retirees. Even ordinary retirement is too full to be devoted to boredom. Most retirees have to make a place in their schedules for any new activity.

The negative image of programs for seniors is related to the redefinition of the self required by participation in such programs. Even though older people recognize the reality of age and loss, in general they do not reclassify themselves as "old," "senior," or "golden." They are the same persons who guided and taught children, improved homes, fulfilled the demands of jobs, and shared life with friends.

Any program that requires a negative redefinition of the aging self runs counter to continuities of identity. When such a program also requires entering an age-segregated and unfamiliar environment, the psychological price of admission is too high. This resistance also reflects a common confusion between activity programs and programs that offer services to seniors that is intensified by locating them in the same place.

A pilot study of those who were participating in a number of recreational programs for older adults found that they were primarily attracted by a reputation of high quality (Schneider 1989). They were willing to cross the barriers of age and place segregation because the leadership of an exercise, arts, or educational program was known to be excellent. Most participants had personal histories of community activity and had often been brought along by friends. This emphasis on quality may also account for the rapid growth of the Elderhostel program, which offers educational stimulation, travel, and companionship at a reasonable price. The appeal is not the "elder" designation or the age segregation, but the combined quality and affordability.

What this analysis seems to suggest is that the "senior" market for activity opportunities is much more diverse than many programs have acknowledged. There are many retirees who seek travel opportunities at a variety of costs and in a variety of social contexts. Some want to be led and protected, but many do not. Some travel on a budget, while others are expanding the upscale travel market. Styles of travel differ for retirees as well as for their children and grandchildren. The business term is *market segmentation*, which refers to the identification of the market not by age alone, but according to social and economic resources and developed life-styles and tastes. Increasingly travel businesses are identifying diverse market segments *among* adults in later life.

The same diversity is demonstrated by responses to public programs (which are distinct from service and support programs. There are many indications that over-fifty softball and "century" doubles tournaments in tennis are expanding, but relatively few adults are active in sports past the age of forty. Bach choirs and festivals attract older people with developed skills and tastes, but there is a demand for sing-alongs as well. Duplicate bridge attracts some, and bingo others. Continuity with previous patterns of participation is one clue to attracting participation. Recognizable quality is another. The criterion of success is not percentages of participation in programs, but the provision of unique opportunities that consistently attract and engage people with a diversity of personal histories.

One community response to the perspective presented here would be to recognize that retirees are still people who will direct their lives by engaging in a balance of activity that is at least relatively satisfying. Why not just accept ordinary retirement as it is? The problem is that "ordinary" is not all that it might be. Those who are doing better than OK are those involved in communities of challenging activity. They have more than routines that fill the day; they have commitments that yield a sense of competence and community. They have that "something more" that transforms the ordinary into the extraordinary. The process of constriction that characterizes later life may at least be delayed by opportunities that are both possible and satisfying.

Should not all older people have the opportunity and resources for such engagement? The good news is that planners and developers in both the market sector and the public sector are recognizing the significance of the "active old" and the possibilities of providing for them. The problem is that they often do not know what to offer or how to attract participation. The analysis developed up to this point provides some guidelines:

1. Build on continuities. Older people have built up their own repertoires of abilities, their histories of meaningful engagements, and their priorities. Useful opportunities will build on previous histories of significant and satisfying activity. The activities, locales, and associations offered should be familiar rather than requiring that older people go to different age-designated places with different age-segregated people. Programs should build on the continuities of the "ageless self" rather than the discontinuities of being "old." Further, since diversity characterizes leisure styles and commitments in earlier adult years, it may be expected to continue into retirement. One answer to the question "What do seniors want?" is "Quite a variety!"

2. Emphasize quality. The premise is that retirees allocate resources, including time, much as they have before. Any commitment has to been seen as worth it. Programs for older adults should have leadership recognized as the best, be offered in locales associated with quality, and gain reputations for challenging abilities rather than accommodating the lowest levels.

3. In most situations, there is no need to designate programs by age at all. Scheduling alone will tend to attract those who are now free from usual work timetables. Since there is no reliable correlation between age and ability in most activities, there is

no inherent reason why skill-based activities need to be strictly age segregated anyway. Nor need the locations be limited to "senior centers." Discussion groups in libraries, sports and exercise groups in recreation centers, and art classes in schools and colleges are connected with images of quality. And the market sector is quite open to the possibilities of using facilities during the work week as well as making them available as travel accommodations in the off season to those who are retired. The attraction is quality at a price, not segregation by incompetence.

4. All this does not mean that opportunities may not take into account limitations in mobility, communication, and social ties that many acquire with age. The decremental process leading toward frailty may call for activity contexts that are closer to the life conditions of ordinary people who are at some stage of that process. Nevertheless, quality and continuity remain principles that support dignity as well as ability.

SUMMARY

In the life course studies of leisure activity that have been discussed, two main dimensions of motivation have been found. The first is more individual: the opportunity to develop, build, and demonstrate competence. People want to relax, rest, escape, and withdraw at times. But the engagement they find most significant offers the challenge of action. The second dimension of motivation that draws consistent engagement is social, the expression of community.

To be able and to be related to others—these are the elements that most often draw people of any age into consistent activity. And in later life it is such activity that makes the difference between an ordinary and an extraordinary retirement.

REFERENCES

Atchley, Robert. 1989. "A Continuity Theory of Normal Aging." *The Gerontologist*, 29(2):183–189.

Atchley, Robert. 1993. "Continuity Theory and the Evolution of Activity in Later Adulthood." In J. Kelly, ed., *Activity and Aging*. Newbury Park, Calif.: Sage.

Conner, Karen, E. Powers, and G. Bultena. 1969. "Social Interaction and Life Satisfaction: An Empirical Assessment of Later Life Patterns." *Journal of Gerontology*, 34:116–121.

Csikszentmihalyi, Mihaly. 1990. *Flow: the Psychology of Optimal Experience*. New York: Harper and Row.

Cumming, E., and W. Henry. 1961. *Growing Old: the Process of Disengagement.* New York: Basic Books.

Cutler, Stephen, and J. Hendricks. 1990. "Leisure and Time Use across the Life Course." In R. Binstock and L. George, eds., *Handbook of Aging and the Social Sciences,* 3rd edition. New York: Academic Press.

Ekerdt, David. 1986. "The Busy Ethic: Moral Continuity between Work and Retirement." *The Gerontologist,* 26:239–244.

Elder, Sharon. 1991. "The Secrets of Successful Aging." *Yale Alumni Magazine,* April:24–29.

Gordon, Chad, C. Gaitz, and J. Scott. 1976. "Leisure and Lives: Personal Expressivity across the Life Span." In R. Binstock and E. Shanas, eds., *Handbook of Aging and the Social Sciences.* New York: Van Nostrand Reinhold.

Havighurst, Robert. 1961. "The Nature and Value of Meaningful Free Time Activity." In R. Kleemeier, ed., *Aging and Leisure.* New York: Oxford University Press.

Kaufman, Sharon. 1986. *The Ageless Self: Sources of Meaning in Later Life.* New York: New American Library.

Kaufman, Sharon. 1993. "Values as Sources of the Ageless Self." In J. Kelly, ed., *Activity and Aging,* Newbury Park, Calif.: Sage.

Kelly, J. R. 1983. *Leisure Identities and Interactions.* London: Allen and Unwin.

Kelly, J. R. 1987. *Peoria Winter: Styles and Resources in Later Life.* Lexington, Mass.: Lexington Books.

Kelly, J. R. 1993. *Activity and Aging.* Newbury Park, Calif: Sage.

Kelly, J. R., and Reis, J. 1991. "Identifying Senior Program Participants." *Journal of Park and Recreation Administration,* 9:55–64.

Kelly, J. R., M. Steinkamp, and Janice Kelly. 1986. "Later Life Leisure: How They Play in Peoria." *The Gerontologist,* 26:531–537.

Kelly, J. R., M. Steinkamp, and Janice Kelly. 1987. "Later Life Satisfaction: Does Leisure contribute?" *Leisure Sciences,* 9:189–200.

Kelly, J. R., and G. Westcott. 1991. "Ordinary Retirement: Commonalities and Continuity." *International Journal of Aging and Human Development,* 32:81–89.

Kleemeier, Robert. 1961. *Aging and Leisure.* New York: Oxford University Press.

Larson, Reed. 1978. "Thirty Years of Research on the Subjective Well-Being of Older Adults." *Journal of Gerontology,* 16:134–143.

Lawton, M. Powell. 1987. "Activities and Leisure." In M. Lawton and G. Maddox, eds., *Annual Review of Gerontology and Geriatrics.* New York: Springer.

Lemon, B. W., V. Bengtson, and J. Peterson. 1972. "An Exploration of the Activity Theory of Aging." *Journal of Gerontology,* 27:511–523.

Longino, Charles, and C. Kart. 1982. "Explicating Activity Theory: A Formal Replication." *Journal of Gerontology,* 37:713–722.

Maddox, George. 1968. "Persistence of Life Style among the Elderly: A Longitudinal Study of Life Patterns of Social Activity in Relation to Life Satisfaction." In B. Neugarten, ed., *Middle Age and Aging.* Chicago: University of Chicago Press.

Mannell, Roger. 1993. "High Investment Activity and Life Satisfaction: Commitment, Serious Leisure, and Flow in the Daily Lives of Older Adults." In J. Kelly, ed., *Activity and Aging.* Newbury Park, Calif.: Sage.

Markides, K., and H. Martin. 1979. "A Causal Model of Life Satisfaction among the Elderly." *Journal of Gerontology,* 34:86–93.

McGuire, Francis, D. Dottavio, and J. O'Leary. 1986. "Constraints to Participation in Outdoor Recreation across the Life Span." *The Gerontologist,* 26:538–544.

Palmore, Erdman. 1979. "Predictors of Successful Aging." *The Gerontologist,* 19:427–431.

Rapoport, Rhona, and Robert Rapoport. 1976. *Leisure and the Family Life Cycle.* London: Routledge and Kegan Paul.

Riddick, Carol, and S. Daniel. 1984. "The Relative Contributions of Leisure Activity and Other Factors to the Mental Health of Older Women." *Journal of Leisure Research*, 16:136–148.
Schneider, Cynthia. 1989. "Senior Program Participation." Unpublished M.S. thesis. University of Illinois at Urbana-Champaign.
Stebbins, Robert. 1979. *Amateurs: On the Margins between Work and Leisure*. Newberry Park, Calif.: Sage.
Tobin, Sheldon, and B. Neugarten. 1961. "Life Satisfaction and Social Interaction of the Aged." *Journal of Gerontology*, 16:344–346.

32

Leisure Opportunities, Leisure Resources

●

RICHARD D. MACNEIL AND MICHAEL L. TEAGUE

For most people, retirement represents a transition from a life dominated by work-oriented schedules and activities to one dominated by schedules and activities that reflect personal choices and preferences. Debate over the retiree's ability to handle this newfound freedom occupies a significant place in much of the retirement literature. Despite this debate, one fact is abundantly clear: leisure is a critical issue associated with adjustment to the retirement years.

This chapter provides an overview of the significance of leisure in the life of the retiree. It is divided into two main sections. The initial section provides a perspective of the concept of leisure and discusses its potential impact upon the life satisfaction of older adults. The second portion presents a brief guide to leisure opportunities and resources in four broad areas: (1) educationally oriented activities, (2) recreational travel, (3) health-oriented activities, and (4) service activities and volunteering. The names and addresses of key resource organizations and associations are provided for reference.

LEISURE AND LIFE SATISFACTION: WHAT IS THE CONNECTION?

In the previous chapter John R. Kelly provided a thoughtful review of research which suggests that leisure is critical to an overall perception of life satisfaction among retirees. To understand why this is true, it is important to have a clear understanding of the meaning of leisure.

The concept of leisure is perhaps best understood by considering the origin of the word itself. It derives from the Latin *licere*, which means *to be permitted*. Implicit in this meaning is the notion of personal freedom, the license to do what one wants, when one wants. In this context *leisure* refers to both freedom *from* (work, chores, and so on) and freedom *to* (do as one chooses).

The Greek word for leisure, *scholé*, is the origin of the word for school or scholar in many modern languages. As used by Plato, *scholé* referred to the ultimate purpose of education, to liberate one from the toil of work. Once free from unnecessary labor, humans could participate in distinctly human forms of activity such as contemplative thought, creation, or appreciation of the arts. To the Greeks, involvement in these experiences represented leisure.

The Greek conceptualization of leisure has been largely forgotten since the Industrial Revolution. Replacing the Platonic notion of leisure have been concepts that define leisure in terms of time or diversionary activity. In the first context, the term *leisure time* has become synonymous with unobligated time, the "free" time left over after the necessary tasks of life (i.e., working, eating, and sleeping) have been completed. In this context the identifying quality of leisure is the period of time in which one engages in it. Thus mowing one's lawn, washing one's clothes, and similar tasks are commonly considered forms of leisure if one participates in them during one's otherwise unobligated hours.

In the second context leisure is identified in terms of the activity in which one engages rather than in terms of the time of engagement. Most people would have no trouble responding to the request, "Name your favorite leisure activities." This perspective assumes that leisure refers to freely chosen, nonutilitarian activities that provide enjoyment and satisfaction to the participant. The underlying assumption is that the enjoyment we associate with leisure is inherent in the activity itself.

However, we encounter a dilemma when we attempt to explain the findings reviewed by Kelly in the preceding chapter, which link leisure satisfaction with a high level of life satisfaction in studies of older adult populations. If leisure is merely unobligated time, why is it that all retirees do not have a high level of life satisfaction? Or for that matter, why is it that unemployed or underemployed individuals who cannot find satisfactory employment usually have low levels of life satisfaction?

If leisure is defined as nonessential activity, how might we explain the fact that a particular activity may be identified by a participant as leisure at one time, but as work, a chore, or drudgery at another time? For instance, satisfaction in a game of tennis may be thought of as leisure when one is playing up to his or her perceived skill level or in the company of friends, but it does not seem like leisure if one is playing poorly or is playing with others whose company one does not enjoy. The activity (tennis) has not changed, but the perception of leisure has. So again we ask, what might account for the finding that leisure is a vital contributor to perceived life satisfaction in retired adults?

In an effort to resolve this quandary, the authors propose an alternative way of looking at leisure. Rather than conceiving of leisure in terms of time or activity, we may more appropriately view it in relation to an individual's emotional and cognitive response to an activity or experience. Thus we may conceive of leisure as an emotional condition within an individual that flows from a feeling of well-being and self-satisfaction. This condition is characterized by feelings of mastery, achievement, success, personal worth, and pleasure.

What is the source of the feelings described above? Neulinger (1981) and Iso-Ahola (1980) have suggested that the most distinguishing features of leisure involvement are the perception of freedom/personal choice on the one hand and involvement motivated by intrinsic rather than extrinsic factors on the other. In other words, the underlying characteristic of a leisure experience is the perception of personal control. Leisure is what one does because one wants to do it. As an intrinsically motivated behavior, it is done simply for its own sake. The feelings of well-being and self-satisfaction that are produced are the result of an awareness of potential pleasure stemming from associated feelings of competence and control over one's life.

We may now have the answer to our initial question, why might leisure be a vital contributor to the life satisfaction of retirees? Studies conducted using older adults as subjects have consistently produced findings which indicate that personal perceptions of control may be influenced by the provision of choice (Langer and Rodin 1976; Rodin and Langer 1977; Mannell, Zuzanek and Larson 1988; Shary and Iso-Ahola 1989). More significantly, three studies, one conducted by Peppers (1976), another by Ray (1979), and a third by MacTavish and Searle (1991), have shown that perceived control over activity choices can have a positive influence on life satisfaction among older adults.

Iso-Ahola and Weissinger have summarized the evidence as follows:

> Empirical research leaves little doubt about the fact that intrinsically motivated leisure is positively and significantly related to psychological or mental health. Those who are in control of their

leisure lives and experiences and feel engaged in and committed to leisure activities and experiences are psychologically healthier than those who are not in control over their leisure lives and feel detached and uncommitted. (1984:41)

THE CHALLENGE OF LEISURE

In a speech at the Eighth Annual National Wellness Conference, Kenneth Pelletier highlighted a study conducted in Canada using four thousand people aged sixty-five and over. The researchers did extensive medical and psychological testing of the subjects at age sixty-five and then tested them again five years later. One purpose of this work was to attempt to identify those factors which were most predictive of the subjects' being alive and healthy at age seventy. It turned out that none of the medical parameters was particularly predictive, nor were the psychological factors. The most predictive factor was the answer to the simple, open-ended question, "What do you think your life is going to be like in the next five years?" Those people who were optimistic, involved in many activities, and looking forward to the future were healthy and alive five years later. This was the case even if they had clearly debilitating, supposedly terminal, medical conditions (Pelletier 1984).

This study holds many implications for individuals nearing retirement. One of the most important of these concerns is the retiree's expectations regarding leisure and the unobligated time associated with retirement. It would seem that health and well-being are enhanced by a perception that the true challenge in retirement is not simply to find experiences to fill time, but to find personally fulfilling experiences.

Basic to this notion is the acceptance of the ideas that leisure is not synonymous with idleness or diversion and that leisure is not the inevitable result of spare time, a holiday, a vacation, or retirement. Instead, the leisure state results from concentration, stimulation, and involvement in personally satisfying experiences. To be "at leisure" literally means to be involved in experiences that give meaning to one's life.

LEISURE OPPORTUNITIES, LEISURE RESOURCES

In thinking about leisure involvement in retirement, it is helpful to keep two thoughts in mind. First, it is essential to realize that a distinct "retirement personality" does not exist. As Atchley's (1989) "continuity theory" suggests, there is consistency over time in our relationships, activities, and preferences. Thus any attempt to plan for leisure in retirement should begin by identifying the kinds of involvement that have been meaningful and enjoyable throughout one's adult life. This process of self-exploration may be completed on an informal basis, perhaps using one of the several leisure assessment guides available (e.g., *Plan Now For Your Retirement: Free to Do, Free to Be*, Retirement Services, Inc., 1975; *Leisure Wellness*, McDowell 1982). Alternatively, a leisure self-evaluation is usually one component of "formal" preretirement education programs such as the Retirement Planning Program (sponsored by the National Council on the Aging, Inc.), the Andrus Pre-Retirement Education Project (sponsored by the Ethel Percy Andrus Gerontology Center, University of Southern California), or the Industrial Relations Program (sponsored by the University of Chicago).

It should also be emphasized that, while being "actively involved" is the essence of leisure, the word *activities* is not completely appropriate since it suggests the notion of physical action. While we should be aware of the consequences of complete inactivity, there are many forms of leisure involvement that may be personally stimulating and satisfying, but require minimal levels of physical activity. This is significant in light of research which indicates that the leisure activities of most individuals become more sedentary, home-centered, and informal as they advance through the retirement years (MacNeil et al. 1987).

While it is probably true that informal, home-centered activities are the largest contributors to the leisure repertoires of adults of all ages, it appears that participation in recreational activities that require extensive expenditures of physical energy diminishes with age. However, this generalization must be tempered by the knowledge that the leisure patterns one displays in younger adulthood are more predictive of one's leisure patterns in retirement than is the simple passage of chronological time.

The remaining pages of this chapter highlight leisure opportunities and resources in four broad areas.

Educationally Oriented Activities

We should be well aware of the fallacy of the adage "You can't teach old dogs new tricks." The healthy older adult can learn, and many desire to continue to learn. Educational activities provide retirees with the opportunity to exercise their interests and curiosity. Moreover, as was shown by the Canadian study cited earlier (Pelletier 1984), there is a strong intuitive appeal to the idea that continued involvement in educationally oriented activities can contribute to a longer, healthier life.

Education, in some form, is available to everyone. It can vary from classes in a university to field trips offered by local environmental groups to study migrating birds. Educational television programs, correspondence courses, and audio and video materials distributed by libraries allow even the homebound older adult to participate. In some instances the purpose of educational activity may be to obtain a formal degree or certificate. More commonly, the retiree may pursue an interest for its own sake by reading, going to lectures, joining study groups, or just engaging in discussions with friends.

Opportunities for educational involvement have proliferated in recent years. Adult education classes offered by high schools, community colleges, and universities often allow retirees to take classes and pursue degrees at reduced fees. Educational programs at senior centers are very popular, as are the activities of special-interest groups like the Audubon Society and the Sierra Club, the YMCA and YWCA, museums and art galleries, craft guilds and associations, churches, and so on. Two very successful programs that are specifically aimed at the continued education of older adults are the Elderhostel Program and the Institute for Retired Professionals. In Charlottesville, Virginia, the Marriott Corporation and the University of Virginia have built The Colonnades, a specialized adult community with a focus on lifelong learning.

Several books that highlight educational possibilities for retirees include *You Are Never Too Old to Learn* (Cross and Florio 1978), *The Best Years Book* (Downs and Roll 1981), *The Life Long Learner* (Gross 1977), and *Prime of Your Life* (Michaels 1983). The Institute of Lifetime Learning, managed by the American Association of Retired Persons (AARP), is a prime resource concerned with a broad spectrum of educational opportunities for retired people. Finally, information about home study/correspondence courses may be acquired through the National University Continuing Education Association, University Without Walls, and the National Home Study Council. (The addresses for these organizations and others mentioned in this chapter are found at the end of the chapter.)

Recreational Travel

In the United States the consumer market of those aged fifty and older has been described as relatively affluent, with substantial per capita discretionary income; growing at a substantial rate; and comprising a market that is relatively untapped and underrecognized. According to Dychtwald (1989:268), "Although they represent only 25 percent of the total U.S. population, Americans over 50 now have a combined annual personal income of over $800 billion and control 70 percent of the total net worth of U.S. households—nearly $7 trillion of wealth." This rising prosperity among older adults is an evolutionary product of an aging population, economic changes, life-style changes, and attitude changes.

Many older adults now have the wealth and time to explore a variety of new leisure and recreational opportunities. Country clubs, recreational vehicles, senior centers, longevity centers, theme-focused retirement communities, and life care community facilities are but a few examples. The one market, however, that has received considerable attention is the travel industry. A study by AARP and the U.S. Travel Data Center of the mature traveler found that travelers aged fifty and older accounted for 30 percent of all travel, 30 percent of passenger air travel, 72 percent of trips in recreational vehicles, 34 percent of package tours, and 32 percent of all hotel room bookings (Todd 1989:58).

The travel industry is one of the few American enterprises that responds to the marketplace with considerable plasticity. This plasticity is well illustrated by the travel options marketed to the mature consumer. World-class cruises extending two weeks or longer have been specifically marketed to wealthy older adults. Low-cost motor coach tours for older tourists who are better able to afford "budget excursions" have also found favor. Amusement industries like Disney have tried to "woo" older adults by providing off-peak senior discounts. Major airlines offer older adults senior passes for domestic travel at a flat fee. The federal government offers "golden age passports" for entry into all national parks and recreational facilities. Nightingale Travel Attendant agencies have emerged to provide company for older adults who do not like to travel alone. Society Expeditions sponsors trips to such exotic destinations as Antarctica, the Amazon, and Tibet. Retirement communities such as Sun City and Villa Marin provide travel advice as well as extensive recreational facilities. Some communities are catering to older adults by developing life-style towns; for example, William Hill in Providence,

Rhode Island, is a complete New England village of the mid-eighteenth century. Quality International, the world's third largest lodging chain, created an upper-level management position to oversee marketing and sales efforts directed at mature consumers.

Health-Oriented Recreational Opportunities

Old age has a bad reputation in American society. For example, if one asks children about older adults, they are likely to respond that they have heart attacks at age eighty and die, are crippled and use canes, talk funny, cannot remember anything, go to church a lot, watch television a lot, and reside in rest homes. These negative views may also be shared by older adults themselves and by health-care professionals. George Burns complains that too many older adults practice playing old by adopting sedentary life-styles and self-defeating attitudes. Some health professionals assume that to be old is to be sick; they greet discomfort with such statements as, "Well, what do you expect at your age?" (Evans and Rosenberg 1991).

We cannot deny that growing old is unhealthy. More than 80 percent of older adults suffer from at least one chronic condition, and almost 50 percent report two or more such conditions (e.g., arthritis and diabetes). Approximately 24 percent of elderly people living in the community suffer from one or more chronic conditions that are severe enough to prevent them from performing one or more major daily life activities (U.S. PHS 1989). Moreover, the prevalence of chronic conditions and their subsequent impact on daily life functions accelerate greatly as age increases beyond seventy-five years. Underlying the prevalence of chronic conditions in late life is the knowledge that optimal health is not entirely in the hands of older adults.

Because the American population is living longer, health professionals now recognize the need to address the issues of vitality and dependence in later life. The foundation for addressing this need is captured in the recently published Public Health Service (PHS) report entitled *Promoting Health/Preventing Disease: Year 2000 Objectives for the Nation.* One chapter of this report specifically addresses vitality and independence in later life. The overall goal of the report for older adults is to reduce the average number of disability days by 20 percent—for example, to reduce thirty days to less than thirty days. Health promotion programs at state and community levels, changes in clinical practices, challenges to older individuals, and increased accumulation of knowledge through research are emphasized.

Resources for spearheading efforts to promote health to the aging have exploded since the mid-1980s. The Year 2000 Health Objectives Report will encourage even more resource development. An all-inclusive review of these resources is impossible. Rather, our intent is to direct the reader's attention to several popular resources and publications and to association membership activities that can help older people keep abreast of resource development. Healthwise, Inc., has developed several health promotion programs for older adults; among them are programs based on the books *Growing Wiser: The Older Person's Guide to Mental Wellness* (1989) and the *Growing Younger Handbook* (1986). The U.S. Department of Health and Human Services has published such useful publications as *A Resource Guide for Injury Control Programs for Older Persons* (1985), *A Resource Guide for Nutrition Management Programs for Older Persons* (1985), and *A Resource Guide for Drug Management for Older Adults* (1985).

Books and pamphlets that are particularly useful include Kimble and Lange's *Health Promotion for Older Adults: Planning for Action* (1989, American Hospital Association), Dychtwald's *Wellness and Health Promotion for the Elderly* (1986, Aspen Publishers, Inc.), and Teague and McGhee's *Health Promotion: Achieving High-Level Wellness in the Later Years* (1992, Brown and Benchmark). Professional journals of interest include the *Journal of Aging and Health: Topics in Geriatric Rehabilitation*, and the *American Journal of Health Promotion*.

The reader is especially encouraged to consult professional associations and government agencies for assistance. The National Council on the Aging, Inc., has a special branch that is specifically concerned with health promotion programs for older adults. The American Cancer Society; American Heart Association; American Diabetes Association; Arthritis Information Clearinghouse; National Heart, Lung, and Blood Institute; and Consumer Health Information Corporation publish a number of publications on health promotion for the aging. The Administration on Aging has created a National Resource Center on Health Promotion and Aging, which is located at AARP. Finally, the reader is encouraged to consult the AARP publication *Perspectives in Health Promotion and Aging*, which may be obtained by contacting the National Resource Center on Health Promotion and Aging, AARP.

Service Activities and Volunteering

One of the most popular forms of leisure involvement among retirees is volunteering. It is estimated that 22 percent of Americans over age sixty-five do volunteer work. The reasons for volunteering vary. Some retirees do it to meet people and some to keep active or to fulfill a sense of duty, but most volunteer because it provides them with a sense of satisfaction (AARP 1988).

Volunteer programs offer many benefits to the public. Communities benefit from the availability of free or low-cost manpower. Many volunteers possess special skills or training that would be costly for the community to provide otherwise. In addition, the presence of volunteers often allows for increased individualization of human service programs, which is a factor known to increase their effectiveness. Many of our finest public organizations (e.g., the Red Cross, the Peace Corps, the Boy Scouts, Goodwill, and many others) would be severely impaired without the services provided by volunteers.

The range of volunteer opportunities is enormous. There are large national programs and small local ones. There are programs that demand commitment in excess of twenty hours per week, and others with no time requirements at all. Most volunteers participate at the local level. Community clubs, churches, museums and libraries, hospitals, political action groups, nursing homes, and charitable organizations usually all make use of volunteers. Local senior centers, area agencies on aging, and the state division of aging usually maintain current lists of possibilities. The Volunteer Talent Bank at AARP also matches available volunteers with local community organizations seeking assistance.

General information about national volunteer programs can be acquired through Volunteer: The National Center for Citizen Involvement or the Commission on Voluntary Service and Action. In addition to these general sources of information, some of the major national volunteer programs include the following: ACTION, the Foster Grandparents Program, Big Brothers/Big Sisters of America, Goodwill Industries of America, the Peace Corps, Retired Senior Volunteer Corps (RSVP), the Service Corps of Retired Executives (SCORE), the Senior Companion Program, the United Way of America, Volunteers in Service to America (VISTA) and American National Red Cross. (The addresses of the national offices of these organizations are found at the end of this chapter.)

SUMMARY

During the past century retirement has changed from an ideal realized by only a very few individuals to a reality experienced by most members of our society. Retirement has become an expected event in the American life cycle. Initial concerns that the process of retirement would impose "a new and negatively valued burden upon the elderly" (Bell 1976:51) have given way to research efforts dedicated to identifying the "best" way to maximize one's potential for personal satisfaction during the retirement years. In these research efforts leisure has emerged as a highly predictive variable contributing to positive adjustment among retirees (Palmore 1979; Ragheb and Griffith 1982; Mancini and Orthner 1980; Riddick and Daniel 1984).

The first objective of this chapter was to present a rationale for these findings. In an effort to do that, we defined leisure as an emotional response to an experience or activity that is characterized by feelings of mastery, self-satisfaction, achievement, and success. We suggested that the leisure condition is the result of a perception of personal control over one's life. To be "at leisure," as we define it, means to be intensively involved in experiences that are personally meaningful and fulfilling.

Our second objective was to present a brief overview of leisure opportunities and resources available to retirees or individuals considering retirement. This segment of the chapter was subdivided into four broad areas: educationally oriented activities, recreational travel, health-oriented recreational opportunities, and service activities and volunteering.

In final analysis, retirement must be considered one of the most challenging periods of the human life cycle. How well one is able to meet this challenge may largely depend upon one's perception of leisure in his or her life. We hope that this chapter has helped the reader understand the significance of leisure as a component of the psychological well-being of retirees and that it has provided useful suggestions and ideas that may contribute to rewarding leisure involvement.

A WORD OF CAUTION

Despite the "rosy" picture of leisure and retirement presented in the preceding pages, one must not ignore the fact that retirement still catches many Americans by surprise. Many Americans are unprepared for retirement and unsure of where to turn for competent advice. James Dickenson, in a special 1991 supplement to *The Retirement Letter*, acknowledged these characteristics of retirement:

> You've got the fight of your life on your hands. Politicians, bureaucrats, bankers, brokers, and tax collectors are planning to make a meal of your nest egg—but that's just the beginning: . . . Inflation

pilfers your wealth one dollar bill at a time. . . . Congress mugs you with repeated sneak attacks on social security and Medicare benefits. Failing banks and S&Ls threaten to embezzle your savings (p. 2).

Dickenson's description of building a secure and rewarding retirement is accurate. Individuals who have retired or are planning retirement need sound advice on financial investments, health insurance, housing alternatives, and leisure and recreational opportunities. Two resources that may prove particularly beneficial are *The Retirement Letter* and the fall 1989 issue of *Money Guide*, entitled "How to Finance a Comfortable Retirement." Additional retirement resources include Leland Bradford's Preparing for Retirement: A Program for Survival, the Andrus Gerontology Center's Pre-Retirement Education Project, and the University of Chicago's Industrial Relations Program.

The reader is also encouraged to consult the National Council on the Aging's retirement program and magazines such as *Dynamic Years*, published by Action for Independent Maturity, and AARP's *Modern Maturity*. Retirement consumers may turn to Sears's club for people over fifty, called Mature Outlook, for advice. Retiree clubs, retiree associations, annuitant clubs, and twenty-five-year clubs sponsored by corporations have also become important bridges between work and retirement. The Hello Neighbor program of Florida Power and Light and the Telephone Pioneers of America are premier examples of retiree clubs. Finally, the reader may consult an article by Stroves (1984) for a review of a variety of sport and recreation organizations that may be of interest to older adults.

Addresses of Organizations Cited in This Chapter

American Association of Retired Persons (AARP)
601 E Street NW
Washington, D.C. 20049

Commission on Voluntary Service and Action
475 Riverside Drive, Room 1126
New York, NY 10027

Elderhostel Program
100 Boylston Street
Suite 200
Boston, MA 02116

Institute for Retired Professionals
66 West 12th Street
New York, NY 10011

National Center for Citizen Involvement
P.O. Box 4179
Boulder, CO 80306

National Council of Senior Citizens
925 15th Street NW
Washington, D.C. 20005

National Home Study Council
1601 18th Street NW
Washington, D.C. 20009

National Parks and Recreation Association
2775 South Quincy Street, Suite 300
Arlington, VA 22206

National University
Continuing Education
One Dupont Circle, Suite 360
Washington, D.C. 20035

University without Walls
Provident Bank Building
P.O. Box 85315
Cincinnati, OH 45201

Addresses of National Offices of Volunteer Programs
ACTION
1100 Vernon Avenue NW
Washington, D.C. 20525
1 800 424–8867

American National Red Cross
17th and D Streets SW
Washington, D.C. 20006
1 202 737–8300

Big Brothers/Big Sisters of America
117 South 17th Street, Suite 1200
Philadelphia, PA 19103
1 215 567–2748

Foster Grandparents Program
1100 Vernon Avenue NW
Washington, D.C. 20525
1 800 424–8867

Goodwill Industries of America, Inc.
9200 Wisconsin Avenue NW

Washington, D.C. 20014
1 301 530–6500

Peace Corps
806 Connecticut Avenue, N.W.
Washington, D.C. 20525
1 800 424–8580

Retired Senior Volunteer Program
1100 Vernon Avenue NW
Washington, D.C. 20525
1 800 424–8867

SCORE
1441 L Street, Room 100
Washington, D.C. 20416
1 202 653–6279

Senior Companion Program
1100 Vernon Avenue NW
Washington, D.C. 20525
1 800 424–8867

The United Way of America
801 North Fairfax Street
Alexandria, VA 22314

VISTA
806 Connecticut Avenue NW
Washington, D.C. 20525
1 800 424–8580

REFERENCES

American Association of Retired Persons. 1988. *Attitudes of Americans over 45 Years of Age on Volunteerism.* Washington, D.C.: American Association of Retired Persons.

Atchley, R. 1989. A Continuity Theory of Normal Aging. *The Gerontologist,* 29(2):183–189.

Bell, B. D., ed. 1976. *Contemporary Social Gerontology: Significant Developments in the Field of Gerontology.* Springfield, Ill.: Charles C. Thomas.

Campanelli, L. C., and S. P. Bagley. 1990. "An Objective Look at the 'Year 2000 Objectives for the Nation.' " *Topics in Geriatric Rehabilitation,* 61:1–5.

Cross, W., and W. Florio. 1978. *You Are Never too Old to Learn.* New York: McGraw-Hill Book Company.

Dickenson, P. 1991, August. *Retirement Health Builder.* Special Supplement to the Retirement Letter, 1:21.

Downs, H., and R. Roll. 1981. *The Best Years Book.* New York: Delacorte Press.

Dychtwald, K. 1989. *Age Wave.* Los Angeles, Calif.: Jeremy P. Tarcher, Inc.

Dychtwald, K. 1986. *Wellness and Health Promotion for the Elderly.* Rockville, Md.: Aspen Publishers.

Gross, R. 1977. *The Life Long Learner.* New York: Simon and Schuster.

Hunnicutt, B. K. 1990. "Leisure and Play in Plato's Teaching and Philosophy of Learning." *Leisure Sciences,* 12:211–227.

Iso-Ahola, S. E. 1980. *The Social Psychology of Leisure and Recreation.* Dubuque, Ia: William C. Brown.

Iso-Ahola, S., and E. Weissinger. 1984. "Leisure and Well-Being: Is There a Connection?" *Parks and Recreation,* 18(June):40–44.

Kimble, C. S., and M. E. Lange. 1989. *Health Promotion Programs for Older Adults.* Chicago, Ill.: American Hospital Publishers, Inc.

Langer, E. J., and L. Rodin. 1976. "Effects of Choice and Enhanced Personal Responsibility for the Aged: A Field Experiment in an Institutional Setting." *Journal of Personality and Social Psychology,* 342:191–198.

MacNeil, R., M. Teague, F. McGuire, and J. O'Leary. 1987. "Older Americans and Outdoor Recreation: A Literature Synthesis." *Therapeutic Recreation Journal,* 211:18–25.

MacTavish, J., and M. Searle. 1991. "Older Individuals with Mental Retardation and the Effect a Physical Activity Intervention on Selected Social Psychological Variables." *Therapeutic Recreation Journal,* 25(2):55–71.

Mancini, J., and D. Orthner. 1980. "Situational Influences on Leisure Satisfaction and Morale in Old Age." *Journal of the American Geriatrics Society,* 281:466–471.

Mannell, R., J. Zuzanek, and R. Larson. 1988. "Leisure States and 'Flow' Experiences: Testing Perceived Freedom and Intrinsic Motivation Hypotheses." *Journal of Leisure Research,* 20:289–304.

McDowell, C. 1982. *Leisure Wellness.* Eugene, Ore.: Sun Moon Press.

McGinnis, M. 1989. *Promoting Health/Preventing Disease: Year 2000 Objectives for the Nation.* Office of the Assistant Secretary for Health, Office of Disease Prevention and Health Promotion. Washington, D.C.: Government Printing Office.

Mancini, J., and D. Orthner. 1980. "Situational Influences on Leisure Satisfaction and Morale in Old Age." *Journal of the American Geriatrics Society,* 28:10, 466–471.

Michaels, J. 1983. *Prime of Your Life.* Boston: Little, Brown and Company.

Neulinger, J. 1981. *To Leisure: An Introduction.* Boston: Allyn and Bacon.

Palmore, E. 1979. "Predictors of Successful Aging." *The Gerontologist,* 19:427–431.

Pelletier, K. 1984. Longevity: Fulfilling our Biological Potential. In J. Opatz, ed., *Wellness Promotion Strategies.* Dubuque, Ia.: Kendall/Hunt.

Peppers, L. G. 1976. "Patterns of Leisure and Adjustment to Retirement." *The Gerontologist,* 16:441–446.

Ragheb, M., and C. Griffith. 1982. "The Contribution of Leisure Participation and Leisure Satisfaction to Life Satisfaction of Older Persons." *Journal of Leisure Research,* 14(4):295–306.

Ray, R. O. 1979. "Life Satisfaction and Activity Involvement: Implications for Leisure Service." *Journal of Leisure Research,* 11:112–119.

Retirement Services, Incorporated. 1975. *Plan Now for Your Retirement: Free to Do, Free to Be.* Eugene, Ore.: Retirement Services Incorporated.

Riddick, C., and S. Daniel. 1984. "The Relative Contribution of Leisure Activities and Other Factors in the Mental Health of Older Women." *Journal of Leisure Research,* 16:136–148.

Rodin, L., and E. J. Langer. 1977. "Long Term Effects of a Control Relevant Intervention with Institutionalized Aged." *Journal of Personality and Social Psychology,* 35(12):897–902.

Shary, J., and S. E. Iso-Ahola. 1989. "Effects of a Control-Relevant Intervention on Nursing Home Residents' Perceived Competence and Self-Esteem." *Therapeutic Recreation Journal*, 23:7–15.

Strovas, J. 1984. "Seniors Walk away from Sedentary Life." *The Physician and Sports Medicine*, 12(4):144–152.

Teague, M. L., and V. L. McGhee. 1992. *Health Promotion: Achieving High-Level Wellness in the Later Years*. Dubuque, Ia.: Brown and Benchmark.

Todd, B. 1989. "Marketing to Older People." *Generations*, 13(3):58–60.

Tomb, D. 1984. *Growing Old: A Handbook for You and Your Aging Parent*. New York: Viking.

U.S. Public Health Service (PHS). 1989. *Promoting Health/Preventing Disease: Year 2000 Objectives for the Nation*. Washington, D.C.: U.S. PHS.

33

Lifelong Education and Personal Growth

●

ROGER HIEMSTRA

Why is it important to have a chapter on lifelong education and personal growth? For one reason, the number of older people in the United States continues to grow; there has been nearly a 21 percent increase in the group aged sixty-five and older since 1980, compared to only 8 percent for the group under sixty-five (American Association of Retired Persons 1990). Courtenay (1989) indicates that this growth, combined with increasing educational levels, simply means that today there are more potential learners at retirement time. Covey (1983) cites improving health and health care, more free time, and earlier retirements as factors contributing to the importance of lifelong education and the need for personal growth opportunities. Brockett and Hiemstra (1991), Estrin (1986), Hiemstra (1975, 1976b, 1985), and Ralston (1979, 1981) also have demonstrated that seniors spend many hours annually engaged in self-directed learning activities, suggesting that a real desire for lifelong education exists.

Learning opportunities for older people are available in various settings, such as senior centers, churches, labor unions, clubs, libraries, schools, Y programs, colleges (including community colleges), and universities (Courtenay 1989; Waskel 1982). Brockett and Hiemstra (1991), Hiemstra (1980), Okun (1977), Peterson (1983), and Ventura-Merkel (1982) are some authors who have documented such learning activity and related implications for planning programs, recruiting learners, and teaching elderly people.

This interest and involvement in lifelong education has caught the attention of many organizations and officials. For example, Robert Maxwell, former president of the American Association of Retired

Persons (AARP), stressed education and training for older adults during his two-year term (Maxwell 1991). The theme of the 1991 conference of the Association for Continuing Higher Education was "Renaissance of the Individual: The Older Learner in the Next Century." New York State's officials are developing a comprehensive state policy on aging that includes educational elements (Center 1989). The U.S. Senate's Special Committee on Aging has compiled information on educational opportunities for older adults to guide future policy and legislation (A. A. Fishman, personal communications, April 23, 1991).

Considerable past research has verified that most adults can experience personal growth and learning throughout life until physiological, psychological, or sociological barriers intervene (Clough 1992; Hiemstra 1975; Moody 1986; Peterson 1983). Some declines in learning performance can take place when various barriers develop, but the overall picture is optimistic: "Although researchers and educators had concluded that age-related decline generally occurred, some are now suggesting that cognitive stability can continue throughout the adult years and that growth is possible with continued education and a supportive environment" (Peterson 1983:90).

Many such supportive environments have been created. For example, Kingston and Drotter (1983) found that elderly college students were highly active, enthusiastic about college, and stimulated by their studies. Dellman-Jenkins, Fruit, and Lambert (1984) found that older learners participated in higher education experiences based on needs for intellectual growth and self-development. Many universities are building retirement communities for alumni and others so that residents can more easily take advantage of lifelong education opportunities (Houston 1991). Researchers have determined that seniors have a real need and capacity for collaborative, creative, expressive, and self-directed learning activity (Dohr and Forbess 1986; Durr, Fortin, and Leptak 1992; Hiemstra 1982). Older learners also have been found to perform well in various learning settings (Fisher 1986; Galbraith and James 1984; Long 1983; Peterson 1983). Some authors even suggest that learning may actually increase one's longevity (Cross and Florio 1978). Special approaches to teaching older learners have been developed, too (Hiemstra 1980; Hiemstra and Sisco 1990).

Intelligence also has been studied in relation to the aging process. Schaie and Willis (1986) suggest that intelligence is relatively stable throughout life. Baltes, Dittmann-Kohli, and Dixon (1984) contend that intelligence declines in some people as they age, remains stable in some, and may even increase for some. Merriam and Caffarella

(1991) suggest that much of this research is inconclusive; it indicates the existence of a large range of individual differences affecting learning ability and behavior.

Sternberg has been looking at intelligence in some new ways. He has developed a triarchic theory that stresses the value of practical intelligence and competence for everyday living (Sternberg 1985, 1986, 1991; Sternberg and Wagner 1986). Sternberg believes there are external and experiential aspects of intelligence, as well as the more common mental process that has been studied by others. He is in the process of developing a test of "practical intelligence" (Merriam and Caffarella 1991:149). His work has generated much interest in rethinking knowledge about intelligence and how one can judge the potential of people in their later years for success as learners. This work also has placed greater emphasis on the value of adults' experiences as resources for learning and subsequent personal growth.

There are several other areas of research that enhance our understanding of older adult learners. For example, several authors have suggested that women's ways of learning are different enough from those of men that much future research on gender differences is required (Belenky, Clinchy, Goldberger, and Tarule 1986; Gilligan 1982; Hayes 1989; Tannen 1990). Fulton (1988, 1991), Hiemstra (1991), Vosko (1984, 1985), and Vosko and Hiemstra (1988) are among those attempting to better understand the impact of learning environments on lifelong education.

Other research areas include cognition (Labouvie-Vief 1990), cognitive style (Bonham 1987; Knox 1977; Kolodny 1981; Messick 1976), learning style (Bonham 1987; Davenport 1986; Price 1983; Smith 1982; Smith and Associates 1990), life satisfaction (Brockett 1983; Estrin 1986; Henry 1989; Waters and Goodman 1990), and preferences for educational topics, instructional approaches, and learning needs (Courtenay 1990; Hiemstra 1975, 1976a, 1977/78; Okun 1982; Peterson 1983).

EDUCATIONAL OPPORTUNITIES FOR OLDER ADULTS

There are a variety of learning opportunities for older adults. They generally are expanding in terms of both scope and number. For example, the AARP published a directory that lists 254 educational programs specifically designed for older adults (American Association of Retired Persons 1990). Declining support from federal and state governments in the past decade has forced some program sponsors to reduce their offerings or, in some cases, eliminate certain programs. However, the trend appears to be one of growth and increasing demand by older learners for educational opportunities. Therefore, many organizations are obtaining funds from other than governmental sources or are making many of their activities self-supporting.

To obtain a better understanding of the type and nature of these programs, twenty-seven organizations that sponsor or conduct educational programs for older adults were contacted. They represent a cross section of sponsorship in terms of programming types, organizational size, and geographic location. Although this data base does not necessarily adequately represent all available programs in the country, in addition to the notions described above about growth and changing financial support sources, several tentative themes emerged from talking with program administrators and reading their corresponding documents.

- *Sponsorship is broad.* As noted earlier, the programs are sponsored by a variety of organizations, including community colleges, universities, businesses, and religious organizations. There are even cultural enrichment programs for the elderly in department stores through the twenty-six OASIS centers that reach nearly 130,000 people (M. Mann, personal communication, August 16, 1991).
- *Elderly learners are demanding increasing variety and more opportunities for personal growth in programming options.* This theme was suggested by several people contacted and is reflected in the program descriptions received from many of the organizations. Physical fitness and art classes, political forums, "great decisions" discussion groups, creative writing workshops, philosophy courses, and computer classes represent only a small sampling of this diversity.
- *New types of learning experiences are emerging.* As will be described later in this chapter, older learners in many locations are obtaining new knowledge and skills so they can better serve their communities as volunteers, tutors, and even producers of radio and television programs.
- *Combining travel and learning is becoming increasingly more popular.* This is reflected in programs like Elderhostel, one community college's classes on wheels, and the annual writing workshop of the Donovan Scholars Program, which attracts participants from many locations.
- *There is an increasing emphasis on education in residential settings.* As the level of education is increasing for many people who

elect to live in residential settings for older people, individual and group learning opportunities are becoming more available. Ventura-Merkel (1982) compiled a representation of programs for older learners in 1982. She included information on sixteen programs under the subheadings used in this section. The information on those programs that are still in existence is updated below, even though their names have been changed in some instances (three programs either are no longer in existence or nothing could be determined about them). Additional programs contacted also will be described to provide a broad sample of the types of educational programs available in this country for older learners.

Specific information about programs in any community can be obtained by contacting the local Area Agency on Aging or Commission on Aging if one exists. Other possible sources of information include local community colleges, universities, churches, senior centers, chapters of the AARP, Retired Senior Volunteer Programs (RSVPs), and other programs that may have names similar to those of any of the programs portrayed in this section. A typical community phone book may contain information in the yellow pages or other informational inserts that describe programs and services by topical headings. For example, the Syracuse, New York, phone book contains a special section just in front of the yellow pages that lists a variety of community programs. One page is devoted to senior services, and it describes fifteen of them, including several that offer educational opportunities.

Educational Institutions and Organizations That Sponsor Educational Programs for Older Adults

Educational organizations provide opportunities for lifelong learning and personal growth for older adults in various ways. In this section several programs of higher education or nonprofit educational programs will be described. Describing several programs paints a somewhat rosy picture of learning opportunities. It should be mentioned that the decline of the U.S. financial climate over the past several years, including reductions in direct federal or state support, has resulted in the elimination or reduction in size of many such programs. This situation and other issues related to the future are discussed later.

Community Colleges

During 1989 and 1990, the AARP and the League for Innovation in the Community College cooperated on a survey (Doucette and Ventura-Merkel 1991). From those responding it was determined that fewer than 25 percent of all community colleges maintain programs and services for older adult learners. The programs that exist range from traditional noncredit course offerings to a few innovative programs. Following are three successful community college programs that demonstrate what is possible.

New Options for Retirement, Mohawk Valley Community College[1]. A variety of non-credit courses are offered to senior citizens under the "New Options for Retirement" program. During the three-year term from 1991 through 1992, more than one thousand people were enrolled in various courses. Tuition is $35 to $60 per course, and the program is self-supporting. A typical course meets weekly for two hours for six weeks. Most courses are offered in community college facilities. They cover such topics as investments, languages, music, computers, history, physical fitness, and genealogy. Several "classes on wheels" are offered, in which learners spend one or more days traveling to art museums, historical sites, or special events.

Continuing Education, Montgomery College[2]. A policy of Montgomery College permits Maryland citizens who are sixty and older to take any college course tuition free if there are at least ten paying students. The college also offers various noncredit courses for seniors at a modest fee. Programs are also conducted at about fifty senior centers for nearly five thousand people annually. Instructors for these latter courses are contracted through the Department of Recreation or via personal contacts. Courses cover such diverse areas as physical education, music, art appreciation, and languages. A typical course meets two hours weekly for twelve weeks.

Emeritus Institute, Saddleback College[3]. Approximately eight thousand senior adults are served each semester, including a summer program, through the Emeritus Institute. Courses that mirror the college's regular offerings are taught by one hundred or more instructors in thirty off-campus locations. Faculty are hired from across the country to provide expertise in various topics. Most courses are noncredit. There are no fees for noncredit courses and low fees for credit courses.

Colleges and Universities

Most colleges and universities have had extensive continuing education and extension programs for many years. The sixties and seventies saw the rise of special programs for older adults when the Centers for Learning in Retirement and Institutes for Retired Professionals were developed. Many of those that still exist today are referred to as Learning in Retirement Institutes (Fischer 1992).

Over the past decade the rapid increase in the number of adults over twenty-five enrolling in undergraduate programs, as well as graduate, noncredit, and specialized programs, has prompted renewed interest in lifelong education at the higher education level (Apps 1981; Bianchi 1991; Haponski and McCabe 1982; Harrington 1977; Vermilye 1974), and older adults benefit at some institutions:

> In 1989, the Census Bureau's latest count, some 320,000 Americans age 50 and over were enrolled in college courses—including more than 65,000 at the graduate and professional levels. Thousands more are auditing classes, forming retiree study groups, attending university lectures and joining study-travel programs (Beck, Glick, Gordon, and Picker 1991).

Current economic difficulties in many institutions of higher education have begun to negatively impact such programs, so the future is not clear. Following are some programming examples.

Donovan Scholars Program, University of Kentucky[4]. Perhaps one of the most well-known efforts is the Donovan Scholars Program. Established in 1964, the program is an integral part of the university's Sanders-Brown Center on Aging. Under this scholarship program, people sixty-five and older may enroll in or audit graduate or undergraduate University of Kentucky courses tuition-free. In addition, typically ten noncredit courses on a variety of personal growth topics are available each semester for people sixty and older. More than five hundred people register each term, including almost two hundred in the credit courses. While most come from Kentucky, a few travel from other states to participate. Some people have even moved to Lexington "expressly for the purpose of joining the Donovan Program" (Kidd 1989:4).

A popular monthly radio drama program that involves seniors in taping and broadcasting an old or new radio script is another Donovan feature. A forum series on various topics geared to the interests of older adults and the Great Decisions policy discussion series also are offered each fall and spring semester. Each summer a very popular Writing Workshop for People Over 57 is held on campus, attracting people from all over the country. The annually published monograph entitled *Second Spring* includes the work of many participants. The 1992 version contained seventy pieces of fiction, nonfiction, children's juvenile fiction, and poetry (James 1992).

North Carolina Center for Creative Retirement, University of North Carolina, Asheville Campus[5]. The center, now in its fifth year, develops and implements lifelong education programs for older adults to channel their skills and creative energies back into eight North Carolina communities. Personal growth is achieved through various life enrichment and community service efforts. For example, there is a College for Seniors in which retirees teach and learn together. The number of participants and courses have increased dramatically each year since the center's beginning. There are several other programs, including a Senior Academy for Intergenerational Learning, in which retired professionals serve as tutors for college undergraduates, a Leadership for Seniors program, in which participants learn about community needs, and also Seniors in the Public Schools, Humanities Outreach, Retirement Planning, Research, and Wellness efforts.

Academy of Lifelong Learning, University of Delaware, Wilmington Campus[6]. Nearly 1400 people fifty-five and older participate each semester in the activities of the academy. All courses are noncredit and meet about two hours for each of fourteen weeks. Over one hundred courses are offered, covering such areas as art, finance, current events, history, language, and computers. Instructors teach for free and either are volunteers or are recruited from within the academy's membership. An academy member can also audit for free any one university course each semester on a space-available basis. Academy members pay $180 per year, and they come from Delaware, Maryland, New Jersey, and Pennsylvania.

Institute for Retired Professionals (IRP), New School for Social Research[7]. This institute was created in 1962 and was the first of others created during the sixties and seventies to meet the educational needs and promote the personal intellectual growth of people who were retired from professional careers or executive positions. The IRP was the first program for elders that was based on the peer learning principle; the members themselves are responsible for developing the curriculum and conducting the study groups. More than eighty courses are offered to approximately six hundred members in such diverse areas as contemporary Russian literature, issues of gender in culture, and the rise and fall of African kingdoms. The annual membership fee is $480. Efforts are currently being made to bring in more minority members.

Institute for Retired Professionals and Executives, Brooklyn College[8]. This Institute is affiliated with Brooklyn College but is administered independently. The dean of undergraduate studies serves as liaison between the institute and the college. The purpose of the institute is to provide an opportunity for retired professionals of the Brooklyn community to pursue their intellectual, academic, and cultural interests. Nearly eighty noncredit courses are offered each semester, and they cover many diverse areas. Courses are held on campus, and the instructors are volunteers. Membership currently numbers nearly 2,200, and there is a waiting list. The annual membership fee is $35. About one thousand members regularly participate in the courses.

Seniorversity Institute of Gerontology, Utica College[9]. Approximately fifteen noncredit programs are offered annually in various topics ranging from philosophy to recreational areas. An average of fifteen to twenty seniors participate in each. Courses are taught by retired seniors at various off-campus senior sites. Seniors can also take credit courses at Utica College tuition-free, but on a space-available basis.

Nonprofit Independent Educational Organizations

Various nonprofit organizations have been developed to meet the educational needs of older learners. Perhaps the most well known is Elderhostel. Initiated in 1974 by Marty Knowlton in the New England area (Knowlton 1977), Elderhostel is a confederation of provider institutions, mainly colleges and universities, that sponsors programs for people sixty and older. Kinney (1989) noted that 165,000 older learners participated in programs throughout the United States and thirty-eight foreign countries in 1988. In 1990 that number was 215,000, although some people who participate in more than one Elderhostel program a year may be counted more than once. The national program, one local Elderhostel program, and three other nonprofit programs are described in this section.

Elderhostel Boston[10]. Elderhostel combines the best traditions of education and hosteling; older learners typically live in college dorms while participating in intensive learning experiences on a sponsoring college campus. The topics covered are quite varied, including such areas as history, writing, politics, and current affairs. Each sponsoring institution attempts to tailor the courses to fit local resources. Currently the average tuition is $295 for a one-week program in the United States. There are approximately one thousand host institutions in North America and another eight hundred elsewhere, with more than forty countries participating. Elderhostel is open to anyone sixty or older, but a younger spouse may accompany an older person. There are no educational prerequisites to participate. Two-thirds of the participants are female.

Elderhostel Le Moyne College[11].   Le Moyne College, a private liberal arts college in the Jesuit tradition, hosts over five hundred participants in fifteen to twenty different programs. These groups participate in week-long programs offered by college faculty such as the following: a program called Decades of the 30's, a unique Five Scholars program featuring a different expert each day, a course on the history of the Erie Canal system in New York State, and a class on famous women throughout history. The programs are offered on campus or at a nearby resort and retreat center. The college also provides consultive and research support for computer activities at a local senior center and the associated activities for the elderly that are described elsewhere in this chapter. In addition, the college manages an institute on aging that provides preretirement programs to the business community and seminars and conferences about educational opportunities for the elderly in Central New York.

LaFarge Lifelong Learning Institute, Inc., Milwaukee[12].   This institute is a private, nonprofit educational corporation devoted to facilitating educational and personal growth programs for seniors. It first became available to the public in 1969. There are two twelve-week semesters, each with 120 classes. The institute averages nearly 1,200 students each term, primarily from the greater Milwaukee area. The tuition is $35 per semester. A balance of academic and hands-on courses is offered. There is a growing interest in academic courses as the educational level of participants increases.

PACE-TV (Public Access Cable Television by Elders), San Diego[13].
PACE-TV began in 1977 to train older adults in all aspects of television production. These seniors wanted to learn about television so they could produce educational programming for elderly audiences

who are homebound or who desire resources that encourage self-directed study. Since 1977 participants have produced more than four hundred programs, all on a volunteer basis. Today there are some thirty active members, most of whom are in their seventies, who produce two to four half-hour programs per month, although the audience now covers all age ranges. Programs are aired over three local cable stations for public access. The senior producers either shoot remote or use one of two local cable television studios. A variety of grants have underwritten their production expenses. Their work is similar to that reported by Hoopes (1991) in other locations. AARP has videotapes available on the involvement of seniors in television productions.

SeniorNet San Francisco [14]. SeniorNet provides an electronic community for people 55 or older who have an interest in obtaining computer skills. Hoot and Hayslip (1983) are among those urging a greater involvement of the elderly with computers. SeniorNet, which costs $25 per year plus phone charges, serves members with computers in various ways. The organization offers computer-related literature, a newsletter *(SeniorNet Newsline)*, an annual conference, and a national electronic network for electronic mail, electronic conferences, and access to various data bases that are useful for individualized learning. SeniorNet has several thousand members who participate through member sites in nearly fifty American cities.

Syracuse University was one of these member sites until the fall of 1991. A campus location with several computers was provided to older people who wished to talk about computers, use them for various educational or personal purposes, and use SeniorNet. The program also administered a project entitled "Computers and the Elderly," which trained seniors in various aspects of computer literacy. They in turn volunteered in the Syracuse Public Schools to introduce first- and second-graders to word processing and teach fifth graders language arts through computers (Hiemstra 1987). Tierce and Seelback (1987) believe seniors are a greatly underused resource as volunteers in public schools, and the Syracuse program demonstrates how valuable such a resource can be to a community. The program is currently administered through the Center for Continuous Learning at Le Moyne College and the Corinthian Foundation's Wagon Wheel Senior Center in Syracuse (both organizations are described elsewhere in this chapter).

Community-Based Educational Programs for Older Adults

A variety of community-based educational programs are available to most older adults. Sprouse and Brown (1981) developed a technical assistance manual that documents the process of developing community education programs for seniors. Many such programs exist in the senior centers that are located in most communities of any size. The National Institute of Senior Centers (1978) provides some guidelines for operating such centers, including ideas for educational programming. This section describes several community-based programs.

Community or Senior Centers

Senior Seminar Program Jewish Community Center, Rockville, Maryland[15]. The Jewish Community Center in Rockville established the Senior Seminar Program in 1978 to provide various educational and social opportunities to retired people in the area of greater Washington, D.C. Approximately 250 people participate each eight-week semester in a variety of college-type courses. Classes typically are one to two hours in length and meet weekly. Center members pay a nominal fee, and nonmembers pay a slightly higher fee. All instructors are volunteers and are primarily retired themselves, although anyone can teach if arrangements can be made.

Corinthian Foundation, Inc., Sponsors of Wagon Wheel Senior Center, Syracuse[16]. Any individual sixty or older can participate in the programs offered by this senior center. Various educational opportunities are provided, including classes in dance, yoga, Tai Chi, bridge, computers, crafts, art, music, and diary writing. The most expensive fee for a course is $2.00, as fund-raising activities by the Corinthian Foundation and various other organizations provide the center with considerable financial support. Instructors, most of whom are older adults, typically are paid a small stipend, but they can be paid hourly. Currently the center is cooperating with Le Moyne College in coordinating the Computers and the Elderly activities described above.

Waxter Center for Senior Citizens, Baltimore[17]. Waxter Center is a multipurpose organization that serves seniors from primarily the greater Baltimore area. It began offering educational programs for older learners in 1974. Approximately 110 courses are offered, each of four terms per year. About 90 courses are offered in cooperation with area community colleges. Waxter Center obtains most teachers, but they are approved by community college administrators where necessary. Up to 1,900 people participate each term, and at least seventeen students must enroll for most courses. The topics covered are varied, including languages, literature, art, fitness, finance, and many others.

Area Agencies on Aging

Metropolitan Commission on Aging, Syracuse[18]. The Metropolitan Commission on Aging (MCOA) is a city-country Area Agency on Aging. Like many such agencies around the country during these tough financial times, MCOA has been experiencing funding losses. Therefore, it has become more difficult for the commission to administer its own programs or to help other organizations to develop programs. The commission does run a series of educational workshops several times a year with the help of senior centers. These three-hour workshops, open to the public, focus on such topics as cultural diversity, the Older Americans Act, and volunteerism. Eleven months of the year MCOA also publishes *Senior World*, a twelve-page newspaper that serves as an educational tool to inform and act as an advocate for seniors.

Public Libraries

SAGE/Service to the Aging, Brooklyn Public Library[19]. The library sponsors various educational and lifelong learning opportunities for older adults at sites throughout Brooklyn. For example, there are several free events for older people that are planned, hosted, and coordinated by the library's senior assistants. Older adults are employed to work in their local libraries promoting programs and library services of interest to other older adults. There is also an off-site effort, as the library's outreach assistants plan and present programs at senior centers, nursing homes, health facilities, and senior residences. Finally, a "Books to Go" van delivers materials to various locations throughout Brooklyn where seniors gather or live.

Residential Settings

Mayflower Home, Grinnell, Iowa[20]. Mayflower Home is a continuing care retirement community, where residents can live their later years with total care provided as needed, including independent living, assisted living, and skilled nursing care. Many residents become involved with *The Log*, an internal monthly newspaper that provides information about the life and happenings of Mayflower Home. They learn to gather and report information, edit material, and distribute the newspaper. Mayflower's staff members assist with typing, printing, and copying.

Loretto Geriatric Center, Syracuse[21]. Loretto Geriatric Center is an all-care center that provides residential living for older adults as well as nursing home options. One of its educational programs, the "Older Wiser Learner," uses plays and readings to involve residents in learning activities. Loretto also sponsors a wellness program that provides education on a variety of issues ranging from health to financial management. In addition, staff members coordinate current events discussions and conduct a program to obtain desired reading materials from the library.

The Nottingham, Jamesville, New York[22]. The Nottingham is a senior living community that provides extended care to its two hundred residents as needed. One of its educational programs is a health and wellness series that includes courses on exercise, aquatics, and various medical issues. Some twenty to thirty people at a time participate in such workshops. Nottingham's staff members or health educators from community agencies serve as instructors. Staff members also assist residents in their individual educational pursuits.

Other Sponsors of Educational Programs for the Elderly

A variety of other programs for older learners are sponsored by national, governmental, or local groups. A large, well-known organization is the American Association of Retired Persons (AARP), which is located in Washington, D.C. AARP, some programs sponsored by the National Council on the Aging, and other groups are described in this section.

National Organizations

American Association for Retired Persons, Washington, D.C.[23]. AARP regards education as a basic need that exists throughout life, and the organization has developed many educational activities, programs, and lifelong learning opportunities. AARP promotes learning through its own publications, workshops, technical assistance, and research efforts. AARP sponsors educational programs or activities on such topics as driver retraining, worker equity, financial security, health advocacy, and minority affairs. It also provides information on educational opportunities for older people. In addition, many local AARP chapters throughout the country sponsor educational programs of various types.

The National Council on the Aging, Inc., Washington, D.C.[24]. The National Council on the Aging is a nonprofit organization in Washington, D.C., that provides consultation and referral services and numerous publications to individuals or organizations that are interested in various aspects of aging. A very popular service that the council sponsors for older learners is its national discussion program, "Discovery through the Humanities," which was initiated in 1976 as the Senior Center Humanities Program. Discovery materials (books, audio tapes, and guides for discussion leaders) are lent or sold to any group or organizations that serves older people. Using anthologies as a discussion base, the program facilitates participants' discussions of works by distinguished writers and artists. Sixteen programs are available, including such topics as the American family, art, and immigrant women. Several hundred discussion groups are active annually. NCOA also facilitates other educational programs in such areas as retirement planning, older worker training, literacy training, health promotion, and volunteer training.

County-Wide Programs

Senior Adult Education, Monroe, Michigan[25]. Formerly known as the Senior Citizen Adult Education Program for Monroe County, the program provides educational opportunities to adults aged fifty-five and older through the four school districts in Monroe County. Courses are offered in senior centers or senior apartments and in local high schools in the evenings. They currently are funded by the state. Courses for high school credit toward a high school diploma are free, and approximately 125 students seek diplomas annually. Another 150 students take the same courses for enrichment purposes; they pay no fees except for field trips. Teachers are recruited locally. They must have a teaching permits or certificates, and they are paid by the hour.

Labor Unions

District Council 37 Education Fund, New York[26]. The Retirees Association of District Council 37 is affiliated with the American Federation of State, County, and Municipal Employees of New York City. The association's educational fund offers educational opportunities to some two thousand members. These noncredit semester-long courses and programs are quite varied, and they are open only to association members. Association members pay an annual fee of $14, which entitles them to participate in educational programs as well as other activities. The courses are taught at the graduate level, and instructors are recruited from New York University, Columbia University, and the Institute for Studies of Older Adults. Instructors are paid by the hour or via consultant contracts.

Industrial Organizations

Preretirement Training Program, Syracuse [27]. This preretirement training program consists of ten weekly sessions each spring for employees fifty-five and older who desire to plan for their future retirement. Spouses also are invited to attend. Each session lasts two hours. A typical session involves two speakers, each presenting an hour-long program on some relevant topic. Sessions also include discussions and the presentation of supporting resource materials. The topics covered include preretirement planning, law, finances, working in retirement, records management, health, housing, and others. All participants are presented with fourteen preretirement booklets entitled *50 Plus* (which are affiliated with *New Choices for the Best Years* magazine).[28]

THE FUTURE OF LIFELONG EDUCATION

It has been demonstrated in this chapter that opportunities for lifelong education and personal growth are important, that they are increasing in many communities, and that many older adults take advantage of them. This chapter reflects information that was obtained from only twenty-seven programs in the United States and from selected reports about other programs, so it is impossible to draw conclusions regarding the exact nature of all educational opportunities for older adults. However, several principles regarding lifelong education have emerged.

- Educational and personal growth opportunities are desired, are growing in number, and are used by an increasing number of older learners. There is every reason to believe that the number of educational opportunities will continue to grow well into the future.

- Varied kinds of programs, courses, and classes are being offered to older learners by many organizations. Computer classes, travel programs, writing workshops, religious education, art courses, current affairs forums, money management classes, physical fitness programs, Russian literature classes, and workshops on famous female authors are only a sampling of this variety.
- The literature supports the notion that many older adults are engaged in various forms of self-study. A few of the twenty-seven organizations surveyed for this chapter reported that they support such individualized learning in certain ways. Therefore, there is a potential for organizations to find more ways to support and foster self-directed learning for older people.
- Older people appear to be capable of learning just about anything. Whitbourne and Weinstock (1979) are among those supporting this contention, and many administrators who have been interviewed have expressed similar thoughts.
- Many older people are quite willing to volunteer their services to the local community in various capacities and will use lifelong educational opportunities, if available, as resources to better equip themselves for such tasks. As the education level of the aging population increases, there seems to be growing interest in more challenging learning opportunities as they become available. The level of current participation in college degree programs, discussion groups, and computer courses supports such a conclusion.

There are also several concerns regarding the future for older adult education programs and resources that must be addressed by educators, program administrators, and policy makers.

- One particular concern mentioned several times already, and repeated consistently during discussion with organizational administrators, has to do with financial limitations. Federal and state support for adult education is well below the support provided for youth education (Peterson, Thornton, and Birren 1987). Unfortunately, the country's current economic difficulties are widening the gap, causing some organizations to reduce or eliminate certain educational programs and to increasingly turn to other funding sources. Therefore, an important question for policymakers, administrators, and legislators to examine is what priority should be placed on education for older adults, especially as the population ages? A corresponding question concerns the level to which programs for older learners must become self-supporting (Courtenay 1989).

- Some programs provide educational opportunities designed to improve basic coping skills, such as how to read better, how to cope with fixed incomes at retirement, and how to survive in a society that is increasingly dependent on computer technology. However, many of those who most need such learning opportunities, isolated and low-income people, are the least able to pay for them (Courtenay 1989). An important question that must be answered is should scarce resources be expended primarily for the underserved older adult? Similar questions (Peterson, Thornton, and Birren 1987) are who should pay for the education of such adults and what should be the level of any public support?

- As Thorson and Waskel (1990) point out, many institutions of higher education appear to be ill prepared to serve older adults, although Lobenstine (1991) provides an overview of existing training programs. Moody (1986) notes that programs for adults never appear to achieve parity with standard educational efforts. The current decline in the numbers of undergraduate students in many locations of the country presents an opportunity for institutions of higher education to work with new audiences. However, as organizations with lots of faculty who have traditionally worked primarily with younger people, many such institutions will need to provide adequate training pertaining to adult learning theory and instructional processes.

- Some educators and policymakers appear to disregard the potential benefit to society of educating older learners. As Thornton (1987) suggests, they fail to support learning throughout the life span because of social or philosophical views related to the high value placed on education in the younger years and the corresponding financial investments that are made.

Currently there is tremendous interest in and information related to adults reaching their older years. However, much more knowledge is required before the issues raised in this and other chapters can be addressed. Certainly some of the financial constraints that do exist must be examined and creative ways of reducing such constraints sought. The dialogue that will be stimulated by the publication of this handbook will speed the development of the knowledge needed and creative solutions to many of the problems that exist or will evolve as more educational opportunities and resources are demanded.

NOTES

1. 1101 Sherman Drive, Utica, NY 13501; Raymond L. Schultz, Coordinator, Senior Adult Programs; 1 315 792–5308.

2. 20200 Observation Drive, Germantown, MD 20876; 1 301 353–7870.

3. 28000 Marguerite Parkway, Mission Viejo, CA 92692; Rex Tyner, Coordinator, Continuing Education; 1 714 582–4500.

4. Ligon House, 658 South Limestone, Lexington, KY 40506–0442; Roberta H. James, Director; 1 606 257–2656.

5. 116 Rhoades Hall, Asheville, NC 28804–3299; Ronald J. Manheimer, Executive Director; 1 704 251–6140.

6. Arsht Hall, 2700 Pennsylvania Avenue, Wilmington, DE 17806; Robert L. Robinson, Coordinator; 1 302 573–4433.

7. 66 West 12th Street, New York, NY 10011; Michael Markowitz, Director; 212–229–5682.

8. 3160 Boylan Hall, Bedford Avenue and Avenue H, Brooklyn, NY 11210; Lucille Landers, President, under the administrative direction of Dean Joel T. Kassiola; 1 718 951–5647.

9. 1600 Burrstone Road, Utica, NY 13502; Ron Lucchino, Director; 1 315 792–3129.

10. 75 Federal Street, Boston, MA 02110; 1 617 426–7788.

11. Center for Continuous Learning, Syracuse, NY 13214–1399; Norbert Henry, Director; 1 315 445–4141.

12. 1501 South Layton Boulevard, Milwaukee, WI 53215; Audrey Lozier, Executive Director; 1 414 383–2550.

13. 5202 Orange Avenue, San Diego, CA 92115; Mrs. Wynne S. Hollinshead, Secretary, PACE Group; 1 619 286–9722.

14. 399 Arguello Boulevard, San Francisco, CA 94118; Mary S. Furlong, President; 1 415 750–5030.

15. 6125 Montrose Road, Rockville, MD 20852; Kandy Hutman, Coordinator; 1 301 881–0100.

16. 343 Green Street, Syracuse, NY 13203; Frances Haberlen, Executive Director; 1 315 474–0035.

17. 861 Park Avenue, Baltimore, MD 21201; L. JoAnn Gusdanovic, Director; 1 301 396–1341.

18. J. H. M. Civic Center, 19th Floor, 421 Montgomery Street, Syracuse, NY 13202; Roslyn Bilford, Executive Director; 1 315 435–2362.

19. 2115 Ocean Avenue, 2nd Floor, Brooklyn, NY 11229; Allan M. Kleiman, Chief; 1 718 376–3577.

20. 616 Broad Street, Grinnell, IA 50112; Marian Dunham, Editor, "The Log;" 1 515 236–6151.

21. 700 E. Brighton Avenue, Syracuse, NY 13205; 1 315 469–5561.

22. 1301 Nottingham Road, Jamesville, NY 13078; 1 315 445–9242.

23. 601 E Street, N.W., Washington, DC 20049; Catherine Ventura-Merkel, Senior Program Specialist; 1 202 434–6070.

24. 409 Third Street, SW, Second Floor, Washington, DC 20024; Sylvia Riggs Liroff, Manager, Older Adult Education; 1 202 479–1200.

25. 1821 Peters Street, Monroe, MI 48161; Carolyn LaVoy, Supervisor; 1 313 243–5030.

26. 125 Barclay Street, New York, NY 10007; Fred Lewis, Assistant Director; 1 212 815–1681.

27. Cooper Industries/Crouse-Hinds Division, Wolf Street and 7th North, Syracuse, NY 13221; Training Manager; 1 315 477–5703.

28. The magazine is owned by *Readers Digest.* Additional information can be obtained from 50 Plus, 28 W. 23rd St., New York, NY 10010 or by phoning 1 212 366–8850.

REFERENCES

American Association of Retired Persons. 1990. *A Profile of Older Americans, 1990.* Washington, D.C.: Program Resources Department, American Association of Retired Persons.

American Association of Retired Persons. 1990. *Directory of Centers for Older Learners.* Recently updated by AARP. Washington, D.C.: Institute of Lifetime Learning, American Association of Retired Persons.

Apps, J. W. 1981. *The Adult Learner on Campus.* Chicago: Follett Publishing Company.

Baltes, P. B., F. Dittmann-Kohli, and F. Dixon. 1984. "New Perspectives on the Development of Intelligence in Adulthood: Toward a Dual Process Conception and a Model of Selective Optimization with Compensation." In P. B. Baltes and O. G. Brim, eds., *Life-Span Development and Behavior,* vol. 6. Orlando, Fla.: Academic Press.

Beck, M., D. Glick, T. Gordon, and L. Picker. 1991. "School Days for Seniors." *Newsweek,* November 11:60–65.

Belenky, M. F., N. Clinchy, L. Goldberger, and J. M. Tarule. 1986. *Women's Ways of Knowing: The Development of Self, Voice, and Mind.* New York: Basic Books.

Bianchi, A. 1991. "Re-entry 101: A Syllabus for the Returning Student." *Modern Maturity,* 34(4):25–27.

Brockett, R. G. 1983. "Self-Directed Learning Readiness and Life Satisfaction among Older Adults." Doctoral dissertation, Syracuse University, 1982. *Dissertation Abstracts International,* 44:42A.

Brockett, R. G., R. and Hiemstra. 1991. *Self-Direction in Adult Learning: Perspectives on Theory, Research, and Practice.* New York: Routledge.

Bonham, L. A. 1987. "Theoretical and Practical Differences and Similarities among Selected Cognitive and Learning Styles of Adults: An Analysis of the Literature," vol. I and II. Doctoral dissertation, University of Georgia, 1987. *Dissertation Abstracts International,* 48:2788A.

Center for Educational and Cultural Opportunities for the Aging. 1989. *Educational Elements of a Comprehensive State Policy on Aging.* Albany, N.Y.: The University of the State of New York, The State Education Department.

Clough, B. C. 1992. "Broadening Perspectives on Learning Activities in Later Life." *Educational Gerontology,* 18:447–459.

Courtenay, B. C. 1989. "Education for Older Adults." In S. B. Merriam and P. M. Cunningham, eds., *Handbook of Adult and Continuing Education,* 525–536. San Francisco: Jossey-Bass.

Courtenay, B. 1990. "Community Education for Older Adults." In M. W. Galbraith, ed., *Education through Community Organizations,* 37–44. New Directions for Adult and Continuing Education, no. 47. San Francisco: Jossey-Bass.

Covey, H. C. 1983. "Higher Education and Older People: Some Theoretical Considerations, Part I." *Educational Gerontology,* 9:1–13.

Cross, W., and C. Florio. 1978. "Adult Education: Key to Longer Life?" *Kiwanis Magazine,* March, 28–30:44–45.

Davenport, J. A. 1986. "Learning Style and Its Relationship to Gender and Age among Elderhostel Participants." *Educational Gerontology,* 12:205–217.

Dellman-Jenkins, M., D. Fruit, and D. Lambert. 1984. "Exploring Age Integration in the University Classroom: Middle Age and Younger Students' Educational Motives and Instructional Preferences. *"Educational Gerontology*, 10:429–440.

Dohr, J. H., and L. A. Forbess. 1986. "Creativity, Arts, and Profile of Aging: A Reexamination." *Educational Gerontology*, 12:123–138.

Doucette, D., and C. Ventura-Merkel. 1991. *Community College Programs for Older Adults: A Status Report*. A Joint Project of the League for Innovation in the Community College and the American Association of Retired Persons. Laguna Hills, Calif.: League for Innovation in the Community College.

Durr, D., S. Fortin, and J. Leptak. 1992. "Effective Art Education for Older Adults." *Educational Gerontology*, 18:149–161.

Estrin, H. R. 1986. "Life Satisfaction and Participation in Learning Activities among Widows." Doctoral dissertation, Syracuse University, 1985. *Dissertation Abstracts International*, 46:3852A.

Fischer, R. B., ed. 1992. *Students of the Third Age: College Programs for Retired Adults*. New York: Macmillan.

Fisher, J. C. 1986. "Participation in Educational Activities by Active Older Adults." *Adult Education Quarterly*, 36:202–210.

Fulton, R. 1988. "The Physical Environment in Adult Learning." *Adult Literacy and Basic Education*, 12(1):48–55.

Fulton, R. 1991. *Importance of Place to Adult Learning*. Columbus, Ohio: ERIC Clearinghouse on Adult, Career, and Vocational Education, Ohio State University. ERIC Document Reproduction Service no. ED 324 420.

Galbraith, M. W., and W. B. James. 1984. "Assessment of Dominant Perceptual Learning Styles of Older Adults." *Educational Gerontology*, 10:49–458.

Gilligan, C. 1982. *In a Different Voice: Psychological Theory and Women's Development*. Cambridge, Mass.: Harvard University Press.

Haponski, W. C., and C. E. McCabe. 1982. *Back to School*. Princeton, N.J.: Peterson's Guides.

Harrington, F. H. 1977. *The Future of Adult Education*. San Francisco: Jossey-Bass.

Hayes, E. R. 1989. "Insights from Women's Experiences for Teaching and Learning." In E. R. Hayes, ed., *Effective Teaching Styles*, 55–66. New Directions for Adult and Continuing Education, no. 43. San Francisco: Jossey Bass.

Henry, N. J. 1989. "A Qualitative Study about Perceptions of Lifestyle and Life Satisfaction among Older Adults." Unpublished doctoral dissertation, Syracuse University, Syracuse, N.Y.

Hiemstra, R. 1975. *The Older Adult and Learning*. ERIC Document Reproduction Service, no. ED 117 371.

Hiemstra, R. 1976a. Older Adult Learning: Instrumental and Expressive Categories. *Educational Gerontology*, *1*, 227–236.

Hiemstra, R. 1976b. The Older Adult's Learning Projects. *Educational Gerontology*, *1*, 331–341.

Hiemstra, R. 1977/78. Instrumental and Expressive Learning: Some Comparisons. *International Journal of Aging and Human Development*, *8*, 161–168.

Hiemstra, R. 1980. *Preparing Human Service Practitioners to Teach Older Adults* Information Series No. 209. Columbus, Ohio. Ohio State University, ERIC Clearinghouse for Adult, Career, and Vocational Education. ERIC Document Reproduction Service No. ED 193 529.

Hiemstra, R. 1982. "Elderly Interests in the Expressive Domain. *"Educational Gerontology*, 8:143–154.

Hiemstra, R. 1985. "The Older Adult's Learning Projects." In D. B. Lumsden, ed., *The Older Adult as Learner*, 165–196. New York: Hemisphere Publishing Corporation.

Hiemstra, R. 1987. "Older People Master Personal Computer Use." *Perspectives on Aging*, 16(1):19.

Hiemstra, R., ed. 1991. *Creative Environments for Effective Adult Learning.* New Directions for Adult and Continuing Education, no. 50. San Francisco: Jossey-Bass.

Hiemstra, R., and B. Sisco. 1990. *Individualizing Instruction: Making Learning Personal, Empowering, and Successful.* San Francisco: Jossey-Bass.

Hoot, J. L., and B. Hayslip Jr. 1983. "Microcomputers and the Elderly: New Directions for Self-Sufficiency and Life-Long Learning." *Educational Gerontology,* 9:493–499.

Hoopes, R. 1991. "You Oughta Be on TV." *Modern Maturity,* 34(3):48–50, 95.

Houston, P. 1991. "A New Breed of Retirement Community." *Newsweek,* November 11:62.

James, R. H., ed. 1992. *Second Spring,* 23 (1). Lexington, Ky.: Donovan Scholars Program, University of Kentucky.

Kidd, R., Jr. 1989. "Donovan Program Draws Seniors from Other States." *Donovan Scholars 25th Anniversary.* Lexington, Ky: Donovan Scholars Program, University of Kentucky.

Kingston, A. J., and M. W. Drotter. 1983. "A Comparison of Elderly College Students in Two Geographically Different Areas." *Educational Gerontology,* 9:399–403.

Kinney, M. B. 1989. "Elderhostel: Can It Work at Your Institution?" *Adult Learning,* 1(3):21–24.

Knowlton, M. P. 1977. "Liberal Arts: The Elderhostel Plan for Survival." *Educational Gerontology,* 2:87–94.

Knox, A. B. 1977. *Adult Development and Learning.* San Francisco: Jossey-Bass.

Kolodny, A. 1991. Colleges Must Recognize Students' Cognitive Styles and Cultural Backgrounds. *Chronicle of Higher Education,* February 6:A44.

Labouvie-Vief, G. 1990. "Models of Cognitive Functioning in the Older Adult: Research Reeds in Educational Gerontology." In R. H. Sherron and D. B. Lumsden, eds., *Introduction to Educational Gerontology,* 3rd ed. New York: Hemisphere Publishing Corporation.

Lobenstine, J. G., ed. 1991. *National Directory of Educational Programs in Gerontology and Geriatrics,* 5th ed. Washington, D.C.: Association for Gerontology in Higher Education.

Londoner, C. A. 1990. Instrumental and Expressive Education: From Needs to Goals Assessment for Educational Planning. In R. H. Sherron and D. B. Lumsden, eds., *Introduction to Educational Gerontology,* 3rd ed. New York: Hemisphere Publishing Corporation.

Long, H. B. 1983. "Academic Performance, Attitudes, and Social Relations in Intergenerational College Classes." *Educational Gerontology,* 9:471–481.

Mann, M. 1991. Personal communication, August 16.

Marcus, E. E. 1978. "Effects of Age, Sex, and Status on Perception of the Utility of Educational Participation." *Educational Gerontology,* 3:295–319.

Maxwell, R. B. 1991. "Education: Window to Fulfillment." *Modern Maturity,* 34(3):10–11.

Merriam, S. B., and R. S. Caffarella. 1991. *Learning in Adulthood.* San Francisco: Jossey-Bass.

Messick, S. 1976. "Personality Consistencies in Cognition and Creativity." In S. Messick and Associates, *Individuality in Learning: Implications of Cognitive Styles and Creativity in Human Development.* San Francisco: Jossey-Bass.

Moody, H. R. 1986. "Education as a Lifelong Process." In A. Pifer and L. Bronte, eds., *Our Aging Society: Paradox and Promise.* New York: W. W. Norton.

National Institute of Senior Centers. 1978. *Senior Center Standards: Guidelines for Practice.* Washington, D.C.: The National Council on the Aging, Inc.

Okun, M. A. 1977. "Implications of Geropsychological Research for the Instruction of Older Adults." *Adult Education,* 27:139–155.

Okun, M. A., ed.. 1982. *Programs for Older Adults.* New Directions for Continuing Education, no. 14. San Francisco: Jossey-Bass.

Peterson, D. A. 1983. *Facilitating Education for Older Learners.* San Francisco: Jossey-Bass.

Peterson, D., J. Thornton, and J. Birren, eds. 1987. *Education and Aging.* Englewood Cliffs, N.J.: Prentice-Hall.

Price, G. E. 1983. "Diagnosing Learning Styles." In R. M. Smith, ed., *Helping Adults Learn How to Learn,* 49–56. New Directions for Continuing Education, no. 19. San Francisco: Jossey-Bass.

Ralston, P. A. 1979. "The Relationship of Self-Perceived Educational Needs and Activities of Older Adults to Selected Senior Center Programs: A Community Study." Doctoral dissertation, University of Illinois at Urbana-Champaign, 1978. *Dissertation Abstracts International,* 39:7196A–7197A.

Ralston, P. A. 1981. "Educational Needs and Activities of Older Adults: Their Relationship to Senior Center Programs." *Educational Gerontology,* 7:231–244.

Schaie, K. W., and S. L. Willis. 1986. *Adult Development and Aging,* 2nd ed. Boston: Little, Brown.

Smith, R. M. 1982. *Learning How to Learn.* Chicago: Follett Publishing Company.

Smith, R. M., and Associates. 1990. *Learning to Learn across the Life Span.* San Francisco: Jossey-Bass.

Sprouse, B. M., and K. Brown. 1981. *Developing Community-Based Learning Centers for Older Adults.* Madison, Wisc.: The Faye McBeath Institute on Aging and Adult Life, University of Wisconsin-Madison.

Sternberg, R. J. 1985. *Beyond IQ: A Triarchic Theory of Human Intelligence.* New York: Cambridge University Press.

Sternberg, R. J. 1986. *Intelligence Applied: Understanding and Increasing Your Intellectual Skills.* Orlando, Fla.: Harcourt Brace Jovanovich.

Sternberg, R. J. 1991. "Understanding Adult Intelligence." *Adult Learning,* 2(6):8–10.

Sternberg, R. H., and R. K. Wagner, eds. 1986. *Practical Intelligence: Nature and Origin of Competence.* New York: Cambridge University Press.

Tannen, D. 1990. *You Just Don't Understand: Women and Men in Conversation.* New York: William Morrow.

Thorson, J. A., and S. A. Waskel. 1990. "Educational Gerontology and the Future." In R. H. Sherron and D. B. Lumsden, eds., *Introduction to Educational Gerontology,* 3rd ed. New York: Hemisphere Publishing Corporation.

Thornton, J. E. 1987. "Life Span Learning and Education." In D. Peterson, J. Thornton, and J. Birren, eds., *Education and Aging.* Englewood Cliffs, N.J.: Prentice-Hall.

Tierce, J. W., and D. C. Seelback. 1987. "Elders as School Volunteers: An Untapped Resource." *Educational Gerontology,* 13:33–41.

Ventura-Merkel, C. Compiler. 1982. *Education for Older Adults: A Catalogue of Program Profiles.* Washington, D.C.: National Policy Center on Education, Leisure and Continuing Opportunities for Older Americans, The National Council on the Aging, Inc.

Vermilye, D. W., ed. 1974. *Lifelong Learners: A New Clientele for Higher Education.* San Francisco: Jossey-Bass.

Vosko, R. S. 1984. "Shaping Spaces for Lifelong Learning." *Lifelong Learning: An Omnibus of Practice and Research,* 9(1):4–7, 28.

Vosko, R. S. 1985. "The Reactions of Adult Learners to Selected Instructional Environments." Doctoral dissertation, Syracuse University, 1984. *Dissertation Abstracts International,* 45:3519A.

Vosko, R. S., and R. Hiemstra. 1988. "The Adult Learning Environment: Importance of Physical Features." *International Journal of Lifelong Education,* 7:185–196.

Waskel, S. 1982. "Scope of Educational Programs for Older Adults." In M. A. Okun, ed., *Programs for Older Adults*, 25–34. New Directions for Continuing Education, no. 14. San Francisco: Jossey-Bass.

Waters, E. B., and J. Goodman. 1990. *Empowering Older Adults*. San Francisco: Jossey-Bass.

Whitbourne, S. K., and C. S. Weinstock. 1979. *Adult Development: The Differentiation of Experience*. New York: Holt, Rinehart and Winston.

X
FUTURE DIRECTIONS
●

34

Financing Social Security, Medicare, Medicaid, and Long-Term Care: Future Horizons

●

YUNG-PING CHEN

The theme of this chapter is the supply and demand view of economic security. Its purpose is to discuss how the financing of Social Security, Medicare, Medicaid, and long-term care may be strengthened in order to enhance the economic security of the elderly.

Social Security is a successful social insurance program that helps provide income security. But income security is not the same as economic security. Economic security is a broader concept. A person is concerned not only with the acquisition of income and assets, but also with their retention and disposal. Therefore, a true assessment of economic security may be accomplished only when income, assets (more accurately, net worth, which is assets minus liabilities), and consumption expenditures are comprehensively taken into account from the standpoint of supply and demand. In that light, income and net worth represent the *supply* of financial resources, consumption the *demand* on these resources.

The basic question, then, is whether a person has the financial wherewithal to command the goods and services he or she needs. Although elderly retirees may have achieved an income level and a net worth level that are on a par with those of the nonelderly, one may not infer that their economic well-being or economic security is the same as that of the younger people. The reason is the high demand on these resources by actual or potential health care expenditures. Of particular concern to older people is the possibility of significant expenditures for health care, including long-term care. Without accessible and adequately financed quality health care, few people will be economically secure with the incomes they have. Therefore, the strong linkage between the financing of health care and long-term care on the one hand and income support for the elderly on the other is critical (Chen 1989).

The remainder of the chapter is divided into four sections, followed by a summary. The first section discusses Social Security—what it is and how it is financed, its financial status in the short range and the long range, and a proposal to provide flexibility and stability to the program. The second section deals with Medicare—what it is and how it is financed, its financial status in the short range and the long range, and the problem of financing Medicare in the context of the entire health care system. The third section considers Medicaid—what it is and how it is financed, its financing relative to federal and state government budgets, and the implications of the costs of long-term care for the original and central purpose of Medicaid. The fourth section is concerned with long-term care—what it is and how it is financed and a proposal that links long-term care to Social Security cash benefits. Finally, there is a brief summary.

FINANCING SOCIAL SECURITY

In this chapter, *Social Security* refers to Old-Age, Survivors, and Disability Insurance (OASDI). While retirement benefits were provided in the old-age insurance program established under the original Social Security Act of 1935, benefits for dependents and survivors were added by the 1939 amendments, benefits for disabled by the 1956 amendments, and benefits for the dependents of disabled workers by the 1958 amendments. In 1965 the act was further amended to include Medicare, the subject of the next section.

The words *Social Security* remind many of retired people, but Social Security is more than an income replacement program for retired workers or the elderly. It also provides much income security to young people, to disabled workers and their families, and to survivors of deceased workers. OASDI is a social insurance program designed to provide a floor of protection for workers and their families against the loss of earnings because of retirement, disability, or death.

The OASI and DI Trust Funds [1]

The Social Security payroll taxes are earmarked to finance OASDI. The benefits and administrative expenses of OASDI are paid from two separate trust funds—the Old-Age and Survivors Insurance Trust Fund (OASI Trust Fund) and the Disability Insurance Trust Fund (DI Trust Fund). Credited to those trust funds are the revenues from the payroll tax levied on earnings in employment covered by the Federal Insurance Contribution Act (FICA) and also the revenues from the payroll tax imposed on income from self-employment under the Self-Employment Contribution Act (SECA).

The payroll tax rates (or contribution rates) are established by law. Employees, their employers, and the self-employed each pay taxes on covered earnings up to a specified ceiling. In 1993 the earnings ceiling or base was $57,600. The earnings base increases automatically each year as average nationwide wages rise.

Under present law, the FICA tax rate in 1993 and in future years is 7.65 percent each for employees and their employers. The self-employed pay both the employee and the employer portions of the tax under SECA, but the employer portion is a deductible business expense under federal income taxes.

The distribution of the 7.65 percent tax for Social Security and Medicare is as follows: 6.20 percent for OASDI and 1.45 percent for Medicare Part A (Hospital Insurance, which is discussed in the next section). The 6.20 percent tax for OASDI is further divided between OASI and DI. From 1990 through 1999, 5.60 percent is allocated for OASI and 0.6 percent for DI. For the year 2000 and later, however, 5.49 percent is allocated for OASI and 0.71 percent for DI.

The OASI Trust Fund finances retirement and survivors' benefits, and the DI Trust Fund disability benefits. Most of the income to the trust funds consists of taxes paid by employees, employers, and people who are self-employed. Also credited to the trust funds are revenues from the taxation of Social Security benefits. Since 1984 a portion (not more than one-half) of the benefits of high-income recipients has been subject to federal income tax. Any trust fund revenues that are not immediately used to pay benefits are invested in interest-bearing, nonnegotiable U.S. Treasury securities. Therefore, another source of income to the trust funds is interest earnings from those investments.

In calendar 1992, income to the OASI and DI Trust Funds combined amounted to $342.6 billion, while outgo from them was $291.9

billion. Therefore, the assets of the OASI and DI Trust Funds increased by $50.7 billion, raising the total size of the trust funds to $331.5 billion at the end of 1992. The administrative costs for OASI expenses represented about 0.7 percent of the total OASI benefits paid in 1990, and those for DI about 2.8 percent of all DI benefits paid.

Three Sets of Cost Estimates

Because it is impossible to predict the future, three sets of assumptions (high-cost, intermediate-cost, and low-cost) based on a variety of economic and demographic factors are available for short-range and long-range estimates. *Short range* is typically defined as the next ten years; for the 1993 OASDI Trustees Report, for example, it refers to the period from 1993 to 2002. *Long range,* on the other hand, covers a period of seventy-five years; for the 1993 Report, it is from 1991 through 2067.

Under the intermediate-cost (commonly labeled "best-guess") assumptions, OASDI is adequately financed for the short range. However, for the long range there is an actuarial deficit, which is estimated at 1.46 percent of taxable payroll. The level of this deficit suggests that it could be removed by adding another 0.73 percent to the payroll taxes both employees and their employers are paying now and in all future years.

Under the more pessimistic assumptions, however, the seventy-five-year actuarial deficit is estimated at 4.96 percent of taxable payroll. This implies that an additional 2.48 percent must be added to the existing payroll tax rate—an increase of more than 40 percent. Should the future bear out the more optimistic scenario, rather than an actuarial deficit, the system will bring about a surplus, equivalent to 1.16 percent of taxable payroll. Faced with the uncertainties of the future, how can we ensure sound financing for OASDI?

What Does the Future Hold?

Faith in Social Security's future is largely determined by one's outlook on the relevant economic and demographic developments. But we should not be guided by whether we are optimists or pessimists. We could err on either side; we may promise unsustainable benefits or cut benefits prematurely.

It is not prudent, in my judgment, to bind future generations to what might amount to very high rates of taxation on taxable payroll to fund a Social Security system with benefits payable far into the future. We do not now know if workers of the future will consider that level of cost for Social Security desirable and affordable, nor can we assert that they will consider that cost undesirable and unaffordable. Yet we need to plan for the future. How do we resolve this dilemma?

An OASDI Bond Plan

The key to resolving the difference between divergent views about the level of taxes required to pay benefits lies in the program's ability to adjust on *both* the tax side and the benefit side in order to deal with changing economic and demographic conditions. I propose that Congress authorize the U.S. Treasury to issue a new bond, called an OASDI bond, to be used to provide flexibility and stability to the system as the OASDI Trust Funds run low—for example, when the trust fund ratio is less than 30 percent. The *trust fund ratio* refers to the assets in the OASI and DI Trust Funds at the beginning of the year in relation to the total of the benefits and administrative expenses expected to be paid in that year. The bond plan is a safe-fail device. It would work in the following manner.

When the trust fund ratio fell below 30 percent in a given year, OASDI beneficiaries would receive their benefit payments in two forms: cash and OASDI bonds. For example, for a scheduled benefit of $1,000, $900 would be paid in cash and $100 in a bond. The bond portion of the payment—the 10 percent withheld from the scheduled benefits—would represent the additional amount of cash that would be paid when cash flow improved. To protect the financial position of people with low incomes, however, it would be possible to exempt people in the lowest quintile of the income distribution from the bond plan (Chen 1987).

Historically, the levels of OASDI benefits have been increased when the program accumulated more funds than expected (though not all increases have been made for that reason), but those increases were made prospectively. In contrast, the proposed OASDI bond plan would make the withheld benefits good *retroactively* when the system's income rose above the trust fund ratio of 30 percent.

Should economic and demographic conditions continue to produce shortfalls in income to the system, causing the trust fund ratio to remain below 30 percent, then beneficiaries would forgo the withheld benefits unless Congress acted to provide additional financing. This plan would give future Congresses, which will be more knowledgeable about the preferences of the population in their times and the evolving economic and demographic circumstances, the opportunity to decide on the proper course of action.

The basic objective of the bond plan is to provide a compromise mechanism for financing OASDI that will address *both* the tax side and the benefit side of the Social Security equation, *both* the temporary and the permanent difficulty in funding Social Security, and *both* the taxpayers and the beneficiaries in terms of the limits of their obligations and entitlements.

FINANCING MEDICARE [2]

Authorized under Title XVIII of the Social Security Act, Medicare became effective on July 1, 1966. Originally it was designed to be a federal health insurance program to protect elderly people (those aged sixty-five or over) from the high cost of medical care. Since July 1, 1973, two new groups of individuals have been added to Medicare: (1) permanently disabled workers who are eligible for disability benefits under OASDI (and their disabled dependents) and (2) people with end-stage renal (kidney) disease.

Unlike OASDI, which is a cash benefit program, Medicare provides benefits based on services rendered. Medicare insures beneficiaries through two separate parts that are financed differently. Part A of Medicare, Hospital Insurance (HI), pays in part for four types of benefits: inpatient hospital care, inpatient care in a skilled nursing facility (when medically necessary after a minimum hospital stay), home health care, and hospice care. Part B, Supplementary Medical Insurance (SMI), pays in part for five types of benefits: doctors' services, outpatient hospital services, laboratory services, durable medical equipment, and certain other medical services and supplies. Nearly all older people who are covered by Part A elect Part B coverage.

In July 1990 the number of enrollees under Medicare Part A was estimated at 33.8 million (30.5 million ages sixty-five or older and 3.3 million under age sixty-five). In the same month, the estimated number of enrollees under Medicare Part B was 32.6 million (29.7 million aged sixty-five or older and 2.9 million under age sixty-five). In the calendar year 1991 Medicare paid approximately $71.5 billion in HI benefits (under Part A) and about $47.2 billion in SMI benefits (under Part B). The administrative costs for Part A represented 1.1 percent of HI benefits paid, and those for Part B represented 3.5 percent of SMI benefits paid.

Basically, Medicare is an acute care health insurance. It does not provide coverage of long-term custodial care such as extended nursing home stays and home care; long-term care is considered in the last section of this chapter.

The HI program (Part A) of Medicare is financed principally by payroll taxes paid by employees, employers, and the self-employed (some 137 million in calendar year 1992). The SMI program (Part B) of Medicare is financed by premium payments made by enrollees and by general revenues.

Paralleling OASDI, Medicare pays benefits and administrative expenses from two separate trust funds—the Federal Hospital Insurance Trust Fund (HI Trust Funds) and the Federal Supplementary Medical Insurance Trust Fund (SMI Trust Fund). The HI Trust Fund receives revenues from the payroll tax that is levied on earnings in employment covered by the Federal Insurance Contribution Act (FICA) and also revenues from the payroll tax imposed on self-employment income under the Self-Employment Contribution Act (SECA).

To finance HI, the FICA tax rate in 1993 was 2.9 percent (1.45 percent each to be paid by employees and employers) on taxable earnings up to $135,000. The self-employed pay both the employee and the employer portions of the tax, but the employer share is a deductible business expense under the federal income taxes. Under current law, the 2.9 percent rate holds for all future years, but the base of taxable earnings will be adjusted to keep pace with growth in average earnings in future years.

A Cause for Alarm

Quite unlike the case of OASDI, the financial status of Medicare is a cause for alarm. Short-range and long-range estimates are made for Medicare just as they are for OASDI, and under Medicare *short range* and *long range* are defined similarly to the way they are defined under OASDI. The Medicare Part A (HI) Trust Fund will be exhausted in 1999 under intermediate-cost assumptions. Under the more pessimistic high-cost assumptions, it will be exhausted in 1998, while under the more optimistic low-cost assumptions, the exhaustion will occur in the year 2000.

Over the long range the costs of HI, as a percentage of taxable payroll, would rise from 3.21 percent in 1993 to 12.43 percent in 2067 under intermediate-cost assumptions. For the seventy-five-year period, HI's deficit would be 5.11 percent of taxable payroll, compared to the scheduled tax rate of 2.90 percent of taxable payroll. Therefore, HI is severely out of balance for the long range.

Like a yearly renewable term insurance program, SMI is adequately financed so long as financing is available from general revenue allocations and from enrollees' premiums. However, it is important to recognize that SMI, as part of Medicare, pays benefits to a defined population group, the elderly, and that the costs of SMI have been rising for reasons similar to those for which the costs of HI have been rising.

It has been pointed out that, if HI and SMI were to continue to grow at their current rates, SMI would pay out more than HI in the next two decades and the payments under HI and SMI combined would exceed those made under OASDI around the year 2020.

Because of its increasing share of the federal budget, Medicare has become a major target for budget reductions over the years. Substantial changes in reimbursement practices have improved the financial position of HI during recent years. However, the rapid growth rate of HI is expected to continue indefinitely. This expectation reflects the persistent high rate of health cost inflation and the growth in service utilization by an aging population, including the large number of baby boomers.

Medicare has become a significant and growing part of the federal budget. While it represented about 3.5 percent of the federal budget in 1970, Medicare accounted for about 8.6 percent of the federal budget in 1990. If past trends continue, by 1995 it is estimated that Medicare will represent more than 12 percent of the federal budget.

In 1991 Medicare paid one-sixth of the total national health care expenditure—$119 billion of $752 billion. The total health care expenditure in 1991 represented 13.2 percent of the gross domestic product (GDP), rising from 9.2 percent of the GDP in 1980. At the rate at which health care costs are increasing, it has been estimated that Medicare will be paying $1,740 billion in 2000 and that the total national health expenditure will claim over 18 percent of the GDP.

While it is anticipated that efforts to contain the costs of Medicare will continue to be made, the financing problems of HI and SMI are not confined to these government-financed programs alone. The growth of health care costs is an issue that must be faced by the entire nation. Only broad-based reform in the health care system may bring success in controlling costs and improving access (Congressional Budget Office 1991, 1992, 1992b).

FINANCING MEDICAID[3]

Medicaid is a means-tested medical assistance program enacted under Title XIX of the Social Security Act as amended in 1965. The federal government and the states jointly fund the program; they also jointly determine eligibility and standards for coverage. Traditionally, Medicaid eligibility has been based on participation in income-transfer programs such as Aid to Families with Dependent Children (AFDC) or Supplemental Security Income (SSI). Therefore, people are not eligible for Medicaid unless they meet the requirements of these cash assistance programs in terms of age, blindness, disability, or membership in a family with dependent children. Since 1984, however, coverage under Medicaid has been expanded, with a major emphasis on low-income pregnant women and children.

As a jointly funded program, Medicaid is almost entirely financed by federal and state general tax revenues and other revenues. State expenditures for covered services are matched by the federal government. The original Medicaid legislation prohibited the imposition of any form of cost sharing (i.e., deductibles, coinsurance, enrollment fees, copayments, or premiums) for inpatient hospital services. The law permitted cost sharing for other services based on the income and resources of service recipients.

During the past two decades, cost sharing has been expanded. States may require minor cost sharing for nearly all services, mandated and optional, provided to the categorically and the medically needy. The categorically needy are people in the qualified categories (aged, blind, disabled, or members of families with dependent children when one parent is absent, incapacitated, or unemployed). The medically needy are people in any of the qualified categories whose incomes are too high for cash assistance but not adequate to pay their medical bills.

Medicaid has become one of the major payers for health care expenditures, accounting for almost 10 percent of all health care costs and serving nearly 10 percent of the population. In fiscal year 1991, Medicaid paid a total of $77.0 billion for services rendered to some 28.3 million recipients.

Growing at a faster rate than the general expenditures of federal, state, and local governments, Medicaid expenditures are projected to rise between 12.5 and 25 percent annually between 1990 and 1996. As a proportion of state budgets, Medicaid expenditures represented 9 percent in 1980 and 13.5 percent in 1989, and they are projected to grow to 17 percent by 1995. Financing over half of the program's costs, federal Medicaid expenditures represented 3.6 percent of the federal budget in 1988, and they are projected to reach 4.5 to 6.0 percent by 1995. The federal Medicaid outlays have grown from $2.5 billion to $51.5 billion from fiscal years 1970 to 1991. If the trends for expenditures continue under the current program, Medicaid payments by federal and state governments for 1996 are projected to approximate $194 billion.

Long-Term Care and the Original Purposes of Medicaid

As mentioned earlier, Medicaid was initially intended primarily as a medical assistance program for recipients of federally funded means-tested cash assistance programs. Coverage has been expanded over the years. The most pronounced trend has been the rapid growth in expenditures for intensive acute care, nursing facility care for the mentally retarded, and home health care and nursing facility services for the aged and disabled. In 1990 the various types of services for the elderly, disabled, and mentally retarded accounted for 43 percent of all Medicaid payments.

Next to the disabled, the elderly are the most expensive group covered by Medicaid. The disabled are the fastest growing Medicaid population. In fiscal year 1990 they represented 15 percent of all recipients, but 38 percent of all payments. In the same year, those aged sixty-five and over accounted for a little over 12.5 percent of Medicaid recipients (3.2 million vs. 25.3 million), but 33 percent of all Medicaid payments ($21.5 billion vs. $64.9 billion), although the number of elderly recipients has been declining as a share of the total Medicaid population. The average annual payment to them has grown faster than the average for all Medicaid recipients. For example, in fiscal year 1990 the average Medicaid payment on behalf of the elderly was $6,717, nearly three and one-half times higher than the average of $1,966 for those under age sixty-five.

The elderly are disproportionate users of nursing home services. The growth rates of spending for long-term care (LTC) under Medicaid have generally increased faster than those for acute care. Nursing home care is the most important LTC service in terms of total expenditure; for example, spending for long-term care increased by 3.9 percent a year in 1984–1987.

Paying for long-term care for the elderly is not among the express purposes of Medicaid. Older people become eligible through spend-down, the depletion of their income and assets to the level required for Medicaid eligibility. The expected growth of LTC costs have grave implications for state budgets, as well as for the other groups in the Medicaid population. How to finance LTC is therefore one of the most pressing questions facing the nation.

FINANCING LONG-TERM CARE[4]

Long-term care (LTC) generally refers to the medical and social support services needed by people whose capacity for independently performing the activities of daily living is impaired, according to recognized or approved standards, for a prolonged period of time by a chronic illness or deteriorating condition. LTC may be provided at home, in the community, or in a nursing home (at the level of custodial, intermediate, or skilled care).

In 1991 the costs of LTC were estimated at approximately $60 billion ($53 billion for nursing home care and $7 billion for home and community care). Medicare paid less than 5 percent, and Medicaid covered about 45 percent. Approximately half the costs were therefore borne out of pocket by those who needed LTC and their families, since private insurance defrayed only about 1 percent.

As indicated earlier, Medicaid has become the LTC payment source for many middle-income elderly people. In most states they can, as a last resort, become eligible for Medicaid through spend-down. Private LTC insurance, currently a minuscule source of financing, has been expanding in recent years. As of December 1990 an estimated 1.9 million such policies had been sold, although the number of policies in force was less than that number. This means that less than 5 percent of the elderly had LTC insurance policies.

Both the government and consumers can potentially benefit from an expanded private LTC insurance. The government can benefit if the middle-income elderly no long rely on Medicaid. Consumers can benefit if they can avoid or delay spend-down to meet Medicaid eligibility (U.S. General Accounting Office 1990).

Linking LTC Financing to Social Security

In the debate on how to finance LTC, some favor making such financing a form of social insurance or an entitlement like Social Security or Medicare, some prefer the private insurance approach, and others argue that both are needed. However, all these proposals face the same question of how to raise additional funding. Should funds be raised from payroll tax, personal income tax (on everyone or on just the elderly), tax on gasoline and other petroleum products, estate or inheritance tax, or a combination? Are people expected to pay for LTC on an individual basis by pre-funding it with personal savings?

Are the federal and state governments to be relied on to fund Medicaid for the bulk of the LTC bill? Are employers to be required to provide for LTC as well as other health care costs for their employees? How about self-employed persons who need LTC? How about those who need LTC who are not elderly? The costs of LTC programs under major bills introduced in Congress in recent years have been estimated to range from $10 billion to $50 billion a year. When fiscal resources are severely constrained at both federal and state levels, providing new LTC benefits seems beyond reach. Yet the nation is in dire need of solutions to problem of LTC financing.

A Proposed Trade-Off

To resolve the dilemma, I propose an approach to financing LTC that will not require new taxes. The proposed approach introduces the concept of retirees' trading off some pension income for LTC coverage. The trade-off principle could be applied in both the public and the private sectors. In the public sector LTC coverage might be provided in a trade-off with (1) Social Security (OASDI) cash benefits and/or (2) the retirement income benefits received by federal, state, and local government employees. In the private sector the trade-off might be with (1) private pensions, (2) individual retirement accounts, and/or (3) employment-based savings mechanisms such as 401 (k) accounts. The application of the principle of trade-off might also be possible in a public-private partnership to provide LTC. For example, a portion of Social Security payroll taxes or benefits could be used as premium payments for private LTC insurance protection. The concept of trade-off is ideologically and politically neutral in that it favors neither social insurance nor private insurance; it could be applied to either social or private insurance, and in fact could contribute to a public-private partnership.

The suggested method of paying for LTC does not imply that the trade-off would generate enough coverage to meet *all* LTC needs. It might be possible to unlock sufficient funds to cover most LTC costs by effecting trade-offs under *several* retirement income programs (e.g., Social Security; occupational pension plans, including those of governmental units and private businesses; individual retirement accounts (401(k) and the like). However, if the trade-off were applied to only one retirement income program such as Social Security, no more than a *basic* amount of LTC protection could be provided. It follows, then, that the implementation of the trade-off principle would still leave much room for private insurance business. For, with their basic coverage financed, individuals might elect to have more protection by paying out of pocket for additional LTC insurance.

A Proposed Social Security–LTC

It might be useful to explore the possibility of developing a public-private partnership to provide a *basic* amount of LTC protection by applying the trade-off principle to Social Security. Such a floor of LTC protection could be provided by transferring 5 to 10 percent of cash benefits. To assist low-income people, those in, say, the lowest quintile of the income distribution might be exempted from such a benefit transfer.

Much thinking to date on public-private partnerships in providing LTC has been based upon models in which the federal government and private insurance companies would *both* perform the role of risk pooler. If individuals were required to use some of their Social Security (OASDI) payroll taxes or benefits to purchase LTC coverage, however, it might be possible to develop a different kind of public-private partnership, which might be called Social Security–LTC. The federal government would redirect the OASDI payroll tax or benefit dollars and thus would not be at financial risk for the provisions of LTC.

The proposed Social Security–LTC has several advantages over approaches to public-private partnerships to the provision of LTC that were proposed in Congress in the 1980s and early 1990s. First, this approach would not require any new taxes. Second, the federal government would not be at financial risk for the LTC program. Third, this approach is far less administratively complex than most other approaches. For example, in most proposals the government would be responsible for the "front end" (for example, the first three or six months in a nursing home) of the costs of care and private insurance would pay for the "back end" (for example, it would pay after one to two years of a nursing home stay) or vice versa. These other models require that the federal government and insurance companies agree on the health conditions that would trigger program benefits and on how that information would be collected and who could collect it. This would be necessary because both the government and the insurance carriers would be at financial risk for the care of the same individual.

A fourth advantage of the Social Security–LTC approach is that the federal government, on behalf of covered workers and beneficiaries under OASDI, would represent a very large group of the insured. We have already seen how favorably the insurance industry has responded to clients that represent large groups. For example, IBM was able to obtain agreements from insurance carriers to offer guaranteed-issue policies (i.e., with no underwriting requirement) to both employees and their spouses. It is likely that the federal government, acting on behalf of all workers, could obtain even better terms: higher loss ratios, certain nonforfeiture provisions, etc. The government could also audit the sales practices and claims denials of the participating carriers to reduce the risks of abuse.

It should be emphasized that measures designed to contain costs of care, to ensure quality of care, to promote healthy life-styles, to institute incentives for preventive care, and to support biomedical research into causes and cures of diseases are necessary elements of any overall solution to the problems of financing health care and long-term care.

The LTC Trust Fund

Like OASI, DI, HI, and SMI, Social Security–LTC might be implemented with a LTC Trust Fund. What would be the magnitude of this trust fund? Table 34.1 shows the estimated annual revenues and accumulated trust fund levels for the first five years of operation. The total amount of the trust fund at the end of the first five years would be about $60 billion, based on the following assumptions:

1. All OASDI beneficiaries would be required to pay at the rate of 1 percent of their benefits into the LTC Trust Fund from January of 1994, rising by 1 percentage point per year to the ultimate level of 5 percent in January 1997 and thereafter.
2. No costs would be incurred by the LTC Trust Fund in its first five years of operation; that is, the LTC coverage would begin in January 1999.
3. Annual revenues in the LTC Trust Fund would be invested in special-issue securities from the U.S. Treasury, as is done at present and has historically been done for the OASI, DI, HI, and SMI Trust Funds.
4. OASDI benefit amounts and trust fund interest rates during 1994 and 1998 would be those projected under the intermediate assumptions used in the 1993 Annual Report of the Trustees.

Social Security–LTC Coverage

How much LTC coverage could be provided for the elderly population with financing based on a 5 percent transfer of Social Security (OASDI) benefits? An approximate but useful estimate can be derived

Table 34.1. Estimated Revenue for the Proposed LTC Trust Fund. All Dollar Amounts Are in Billions

Calendar Year	Social Security OASDI Benefit Payments	Percent of OASDI Benefits Amount	Annual Contributions to the LTC Fund	Interest Rate for Contributions in the Year	LTC Fund Accumulated at the end of the Year
1994	319.2	1%	3.2	5.9%	3.3
1995	336.4	2%	6.7	5.9%	10.4
1996	355.0	3%	10.7	6.0%	22.0
1997	374.9	4%	15.0	6.0%	38.7
1998	396.1	5%	19.8	6.1%	61.4

Notes: The OASDI benefits and interest rates given are those projected under the alternative II assumptions in the Annual Report of the Board of Trustees of the Federal Old-Age and Survivors Insurance and Disability Insurance Trust Funds U.S. Congress, Committee on Ways and Means 1993a.

by two different methods. The first simply considers the aggregate amount of OASDI benefit payments in 1991, assuming the proposed program was in effect in that year. Five percent would yield about $30 billion. As indicated earlier, in 1991 the level of expenditures for formal LTC services (nursing, home, and community care) was estimated at $60 billion. Thus, revenue consisting of 10 percent of OASDI benefits could finance approximately 25 cents out of every dollar currently spent on formal LTC. Of course, the proportion of LTC costs covered would be less to the extent that the provision of such a third-party payment would result in a higher demand for LTC services.

A second method estimates the amount of coverage based on 5 percent of OASDI benefit payments on the assumption that some form of LTC insurance coverage, similar to products currently available from private insurance companies, would be provided. The roughly $15 billion of revenues would represent about $500 for each elderly (over age sixty-five) OASDI beneficiary (of which there are about 30 million currently). Thus an annual premium of about $500 could be provided for each elderly beneficiary.

What kind of coverage might a premium of $500 provide? According to a 1986 report to the secretary of the Department of Health and Human Services on the private financing of long-term care for the elderly, an LTC policy for the general population that would be issued at age sixty-five and paying $50 per day for nursing home, with coverage indexed at 5 percent per year, premiums indexed at 4 percent per year, a ninety-day elimination period, and a maximum lifetime coverage for one and one-half year would require an initial premium of about $970 for the year of issue.

A premium available for $500 per year would have a number of specific properties. The amount (equal to about 50 percent of OASDI benefits) would rise at the same rate as average wage growth from year to year for people who were newly eligible (i.e., people who would reach age sixty-two within the year). This would be convenient, because the daily benefit for the LTC coverage would be increased at about the rate of average wage growth (about 5 percent per year) not only for people who were newly eligible, but also for all years after eligibility. Premiums, on the other hand, which would be equal to 5 percent of benefits, would rise as the cost of living or consumer price index (CPI) rose for years after eligibility (age sixty-two). Thus, the daily coverage amount would rise at about 5 percent per year for both new and old insureds, while the premium would increase by 5 percent for new issues from one year to the next, but by only 4 percent per year after issue. The wage and CPI assumptions are taken as the intermediate estimates from the 1991 OASDI Annual Trustees Report.

Insurance issued using this approach would lapse only as a result of death. This would tend to increase its cost over current commercial policies whose premiums are based on substantial lapse rates for reasons other than death. On the other hand, administrative costs would be very low, assuming mandatory coverage. Another advantage of mandatory coverage would be that adverse selection would not be an issue; the utilization would represent the whole population. Finally, the LTC coverage would be a true group coverage, much like Hospital Insurance under the Medicare program.

Linking LTC financing to Social Security cash benefits by means of the trade-off principle is admittedly unorthodox. However, in a recent Gallup Poll 60 percent of the respondents were willing to accept a reduction of employers' contributions to a pension plan for an increase in health benefits (Employee Benefit Research Institute 1991). Would it be unreasonable to speculate that many people would favorably consider trading off a small portion of their future Social Security cash benefits for LTC coverage, especially if workers and self-employed people of all ages were covered by the Social Security-LTC plan?

A BRIEF SUMMARY

This chapter emphasizes the theme that economic security is a broader concept than income security and argues that few people will enjoy economic security with the incomes they have without adequately financed health care, including long-term care (LTC). While substantial assistance is available for acute health care to all older people who are covered by Medicare and for LTC to those who are eligible under Medicaid, there is no national non-means-tested plan to finance LTC. An admittedly unorthodox approach to LTC financing is proposed—providing basic LTC coverage for people of all ages under a public-private partnership that would require beneficiaries to exchange some of their Social Security cash benefits.

NOTES

Yung-Ping Chen, Ph.D., is the Frank J. Manning Eminent Scholar's Chair in Gerontology and Deputy Provost at the University of Massachusetts at Boston. He gratefully acknowledges the intellectual support and actuarial assistance of Stephen C. Goss on long-term care. He has also benefited from discussions with Jay N. Greenberg and John C. Wilkin. Kathy Fabiszewski has improved the presentation.

1. The references for this section are as follows: U.S. Congress, Committee on Ways and Means 1993a; Social Security Administration 1991, 1993.

2. The references for this section are as follows: Advisory Council on Social Security 1991a; Social Security Administration 1991, 1993; U.S. Congress, Committee on Ways and Means 1993b, 1993c.

3. References for this section are as follows: Advisory Commission on Intergovernmental Relations 1992; Social Security Administration 1991, 1993; The Urban Institute 1990; U.S. General Accounting Office 1991.

4. References for this section are as follows: Advisory Council on Social Security 1991b; Chen 1990, 1993; U.S. Department of Health and Human Services 1986b; U.S. General Accounting Office 1990.

REFERENCES

Advisory Commission on Intergovernmental Relations. 1991. *Intergovernmental Trends and Options*. Washington, D.C.: Advisory Commission on Intergovernmental Relations.

Advisory Council on Social Security. 1991a. *Report on Medicare Projections by the Health Technical panel to the 1991 Advisory Council on Social Security*, March. Washington, D.C.

Advisory Council on Social Security. 1991b. *The Financing and Delivery of Long-Term Care Services: A Review of Current Problems and Potential Reform Options*, December. Washington, D.C.

Chen, Yung-Ping. 1987. "OASDI Bonds Could Restore Confidence in Social Security." *Journal of the American Society of CLU & ChFC*, 41(6):68–73.

Chen, Yung-Ping. 1989. "How Well-Off Are the Elderly?" Distinguished Lecture Series, University of Massachusetts at Boston, April 19.

Chen, Yung-Ping. 1990. "Linking Long-Term Care Financing to Social Security Cash Benefit." Testimony before the 1991 Advisory Council on Social Security, September, 27. Unpublished manuscript.

Chen, Yung-Ping. 1993. "A 'Three-Legged Stool': New Way to Fund Long-Term Care?" *Care in the Long Run*. Washington, D.C.: National Academy of Sciences Press.

Congressional Budget Office. 1991. *Rising Health Care Costs: Causes, Implications, and Strategies*. Washington, D.C.: U.S. Government Printing Office.

Congressional Budget Office. 1992a. *Economic Implications of Rising Health Care Costs*. Washington, D.C.: U.S. Government Printing Office.

Congressional Budget Office. 1992b. *Projections of National Health Care Expenditures*. Washington, D.C.: U.S. Government Printing Office.

Employment Benefit Research Institute. 1991. *Public Attitudes on Benefit Trade Offs, 1991: A Summary*. EBRI Report #G-28. December.

Koitz, David. 1991a. *Medicare Taxes, Premiums, and Government Contributions*. Congressional Research Service Report for Congress. Report 91-350, EPW, revised May 1. Washington, D.C.: Congressional Research Service.

Koitz, David. 1991b *Medicare Financing*. Congressional Research Report for Congress. Report 91-357 EPW, revised July 1. Washington, D.C.: Congressional Research Service.

Koitz, David. 1991c. *The Financial Outlook for Medicare*. Congressional Research Service Report for Congress. Report 91-517 EPW, revised July 19. Washington, D.C.: Congressional Research Service.

Social Security Administration. 1991. *Social Security Bulletin, Annual Statistical Supplement, 1991.* SSA Publication no. 13-11700. Washington, D.C.: Social Security Administration.

Social Security Administration. 1993. *Social Security Bulletin, Annual Statistical Supplement, 1992.* SSA Publication no. 13-11700. Washington, D.C.: Social Security Administration.

The Urban Institute. 1990. *Medicaid Spending in the 1980s: Costs Containment and Access.* Policy and Research Report, winter and spring, 10–12.

U.S. Congress, Committee on Ways and Means. 1993a. *1993 Annual Report of the Federal Old-Age and Survivors Insurance and Disability Insurance.* 103rd Congress, 1st Session, House Document 103-63, April 7. Washington, D.C.: U.S. Government Printing Office.

U.S. Congress, Committee on Ways and Means. 1993b. *1993 Annual Report of the Board of Trustees of the Federal Hospital Insurance Trust Fund.* 103rd Congress, 1st Session, House Document 103-64, April 7. Washington, D.C.: U.S. Government Printing Office.

U.S. Congress, Committee on Ways and Means. 1993c. *1993 Annual Report of the Board of Trustees of the Federal Supplementary Medical Insurance Trust Fund.* 103rd Congress, 1st Session, House Document 103-65, April 7. Washington, D.C.: U.S. Government Printing Office.

U.S. Department of Health and Human Services. 1986. *Technical Workshop Group Report to the Secretary on Private Financing of Long-Term Care for the Elderly.* November. Washington, D.C.: U.S. Department of Health and Human Services.

U.S. General Accounting Office. 1990. *Long-Term Care Insurance Proposals to Link Private Insurance and Medicaid Need Close Scrutiny.* Washington, D.C.: GAO/HRD-90-154.

U.S. General Accounting Office. 1991. *Medicaid Expansions.* Washington, D.C.: GAO/HRD-91-78.

35

The Future of Retirement

●

JOSEPH F. QUINN

This is a very interesting time to consider the future of retirement in America. The nation is aging, and the proportion of the population above traditional retirement age is increasing. During the period after World War II Americans, especially men, were retiring earlier and earlier. During the past few years, however, this trend appears to have stopped and may even have reversed. Important changes are currently being made in pensions, both public (Social Security) and private (employer), that may encourage workers to stay in the labor force longer than they currently do.

An extensive literature exists on the determinants of individual retirement decisions. This literature is a good source of suggestions about what might be important in the future. Most of the recent work by economists has focused on the nature, magnitude, and impact of the financial incentives in our retirement income programs. These incentives are a main focus of this chapter, both because considerable evidence indicates that these incentives are important and because they can be effective policy instruments—primary means by which public and private policymakers can influence aggregate retirement trends.

I begin with a short section on relevant population and retirement trends, followed by a brief discussion of the economic determinants of the decision to retire and retirement trends. (These issues covered in more detail in this handbook by Robert Clark.) Next I discuss some recent evidence of the work plans and preferences of older workers, suggesting some conflict between the two. I then take a look ahead and conclude with a brief summary.

Economists should be humble prognosticators, having predicted nine of the past five recessions. I believe that future retirement patterns will depend to a great extent on what happens to employer pension plans—on whether they go along with Social Security in reducing the disincentives to work that currently face many older Americans or try to offset the changes in Social Security by increasing their own financial incentives to retire. What employers do will, in turn, depend on the state of future labor markets. If labor shortages arise, I am confident that firms will alter their retirement plans to keep valued older workers on the job.

I suspect that most Americans will continue to leave full-time career employment by their early sixties, as they now do. But I think that more will remain in the labor force afterwards, utilizing "bridge jobs," often part-time, between full-time career work and complete labor force withdrawal. Social Security will no longer be discouraging older Americans from continuing to work. Employee preferences, employer flexibility, and the details of individual pension plans will determine whether employees spend the transitional stage with their career firms or in a new line of work.

DEMOGRAPHIC TRENDS

The future of retirement should be discussed within the context of several important demographic trends that are currently underway. One is the aging of the American population, and the others concern the timing and nature of retirement.

The Aging of America

The U.S. Bureau of the Census (1989) projects that the number of Americans aged sixty-five and over, about thirty-two million today, will more than double over the next forty years, while the number aged fifty-five to sixty-four increases by two-thirds. In sharp contrast, the number of Americans under fifty-five will be almost unchanged. As a result, it is estimated that the percentage of the population aged sixty-five and over will increase from under 13 percent today to nearly 22 percent by 2030. A third of the population will be fifty-five and older. The median age will rise from thirty-three to forty-two. The nation then will look like Florida today.

The racial composition of the nation will be changing as well. The white population, currently about 84 percent of the total, is projected to decline to 78 percent by 2030 and to 73 percent by 2080. The black population will grow slowly, from 12 percent today to 15 percent by 2030 and to 16 percent by 2080. The most dramatic increases will occur among people in the "other races" category. Currently only about 3.5 percent of the total, they are projected to double to 7 percent over the next four decades and to more than triple (to 11 percent) by 2080 (U.S. Bureau of the Census 1989).

Some of the aging of America is due to increased longevity. Life expectancy at birth increased by fourteen years between 1920 and 1950 and has increased by another seven years since then (Kutscher and Fullerton 1990). In 1900 only about 40 percent of Americans born could expect to reach age sixty-five, and the life expectancy of those who did was about twelve years. Today about 80 percent live to age sixty-five, and their life expectancy then is 17 years (U.S. Senate 1991). By 2050, life expectancy at age sixty-five will be nearly eighteen years for men and twenty-three years for women.

Labor Market Trends for Older Workers

These population projections suggest that in the years ahead retirement issues will be even more important than they are today because they will affect a substantially larger proportion of the population. It is well known that Americans are retiring much earlier than they did only two decades ago. But there are other patterns worth noting, including the importance of part-time and self-employment and the interesting ways in which many Americans disengage from their career jobs.

Retirement

Figures 35.1 and 35.2 show labor force participation rates for older Americans by five-year age groups, in 1966, 1976, and 1986, as well as the most current annual data from 1992. The well-known decline for all groups of men through the mid-1980s is clear (figure 35.1). The largest absolute decline is for men aged sixty to sixty-four, (twenty-three percentage points—a 30 percent decline) in only two decades. But the proportional declines are even larger for the oldest two groups—40 percent for men aged sixty-five and older. The same trend is obvious among men aged fifty-five to fifty-nine, and it even shows up among those aged fifty to fifty-four.

What is less well known is that since 1986, after decades of decline, participation rates of older men have been steady. For all the groups

FIGURE 35.1. Labor Force Participation Rates for Men, by Age.
——— 1996, 1976, 1986, 1992 ———

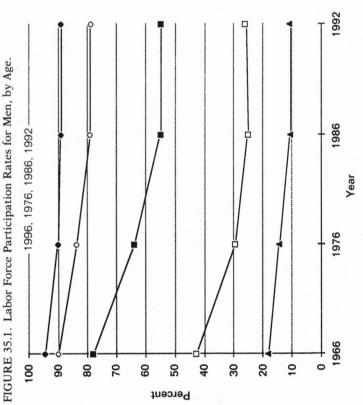

U.S. Bureau of Labor Statistics, *Employment and Earnings*, January issues.

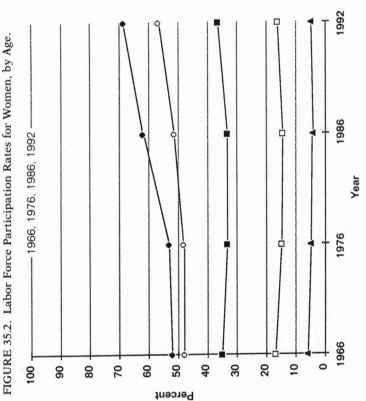

FIGURE 35.2. Labor Force Participation Rates for Women, by Age.

U.S. Bureau of Labor Statistics, *Employment and Earnings,* January issues.

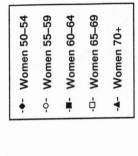

● Women 50–54
○ Women 55–59
■ Women 60–64
□ Women 65–69
▲ Women 70+

shown, the figures today are almost identical to those six years ago. It may be too early to call this a new trend, but at least it suggests an interruption of the old trend. It is interesting to note that the latest Labor Department projections forecast virtually unchanged participation rates for both men and women aged sixty-five and over through the year 2005 (U.S. Bureau of Labor Statistics 1992b:34).

The data for women reflect two offsetting trends—the increased labor force participation of women, especially married women, and the early retirement trends mentioned above. For women aged sixty and above, the data show modest declines from 1966 to 1986, and slight increases since then (see figure 35.2). The data for women aged fifty to fifty-nine show steady advances during the first two decades, and larger increases (about one percentage point per year) since then.

Part-Time Employment

Labor force participation rates do not distinguish between full-time and part-time employment. The latter is very important for older Americans, as Philip Rones and Sally Coberly illustrate in previous chapters. Currently, among nonagricultural workers aged sixty-five and over, nearly half of the men and over 60 percent of the women work fewer than thirty-five hours per week, compared to only about 10 percent of younger men and a quarter of younger women (U.S. Bureau of Labor Statistics 1993, table 33). About 90 percent of the elderly who work part time say they are doing so voluntarily. The percentage of the elderly (sixty-five and over) engaging in part-time work has been increasing over the past two decades, from 38 to 48 percent for men, and from 50 to 61 percent for women.

Self-Employment

Self-employment among American workers rises steadily with age. Nearly a quarter of employed men aged sixty-five and over, and 15 percent of the women, are self-employed (U.S. Bureau of Labor Statistics 1993, table 23). This is about three times the proportions for younger populations. One reason for this is that those already self-employed tend to retire later than wage and salary earners. In addition, some people turn to self-employment late in life, often as a means of gradual retirement (Fuchs 1982).

Patterns of Exit from Career Jobs

Recent research suggests that, for many Americans, the transition out of the labor force is much more complex than the stereotypical abrupt change from full-time career work to complete retirement. One analysis of the 1970s indicated that a quarter of wage and salary workers and half of the self-employed did something other than leave the labor force when they left full-time status on their career jobs (Quinn, Burkhauser, and Myers 1990). The vast majority of the wage and salary earners who continued did so in new jobs; very few were able to remain part time in their career jobs. In contrast, nearly half of the self-employed who left full-time status simply dropped to part time on the same job; the other half tried something new.

Of those who changed jobs, nearly three-quarters were still working a year later, and nearly 60 percent remained after two years. Most of the new jobs were in different occupations and industries, and more people moved down the socioeconomic ladder (from skilled to unskilled and from white collar to blue collar) than up. With the exception of those who just moved to part time on the same job, many more suffered pay cuts than enjoyed higher wages. There was some weak evidence that those at the ends of the economic spectrum—the rich and the poor—were the most likely to stay in the labor force after leaving career employment. The poor may do so because they have to, the rich because they want to.

Christopher Ruhm (1991, 1992), using a slightly different definition of a career job, estimates that fewer than half of all older Americans retire directly from career jobs. Of those who do not, most switch industry and/or occupation, and many become part-time or self-employed workers. Ruhm also finds that most job changers earn less on the new job than they did previously and that this tendency rises with the age of the worker at transition.

Summary

Because of increasing longevity and, until very recently at least, the trend toward earlier retirement, Americans have been experiencing a significant increase in the number of their postretirement years. In 1900 a male could expect to spend only 1.2 years (about 3 percent of his life) in retirement. By mid-century, the expectation had risen to years, and by 1980 to fourteen years—nearly 20 percent of his expected life span (U.S. Senate 1991). Many older Americans prefer to retire gradually, and they utilize second careers, part-time jobs, or periods of self-employment to bridge the transition from the primary career to complete labor force withdrawal.

ECONOMIC DETERMINANTS OF RETIREMENT

Labor supply decisions depend on a large number of factors, only some of which can be observed and measured. The timing of retirement is influenced by health, wealth, social networks, pecuniary and nonpecuniary aspects of work, attitudes toward leisure, living arrangements, and expectations. I will emphasize a few that I see as key in assessing the future; these and others are discussed in more detail by Helen Dennis and Robert Clark in this handbook.

Wealth

The simplest economic explanation for the trend toward early retirement is that the nation has grown wealthier over time, and one of the "goods" on which we spend this increased wealth is leisure. We start working later, work fewer hours per year, and retire earlier than we once did. For recent retirees, this national trend toward greater wealth has been augmented because the Social Security benefits they received, in aggregate, vastly exceeded a fair return on the contributions made on their behalf when they were working (Burkhauser and Warlick 1981; Moffitt 1984; U.S. House 1992, app. I). There have been large wealth transfers from workers to retirees.

Common sense suggests a link between wealth gains and earlier retirement, although it is difficult to prove empirically. The largest declines in the labor force participation rates of men aged sixty to sixty-four occurred after the age of Social Security eligibility was reduced to age sixty-two (1961) and large real increases in benefits went into effect (1969–1972). Some studies (e.g., Hurd and Boskin 1984) attribute most of the decline to the increased generosity of Social Security. Recent work suggests that the impact has been more modest. Jerry Hausman and David Wise (1985) and Richard Ippolito (1990) estimate that Social Security may account for about one-third of the decrease.

Age-Specific Retirement Incentives

Equally important are the age-specific retirement incentives (or work disincentives) contained in many of our public and private retirement plans. Both Social Security and most employer pension plans promise a stream of income when certain retirement conditions are met.

The best summary of the value of one of these agreements is the present discounted value of the promised stream. This is the asset or wealth equivalent—the pile of money today that, if invested, could generate the same income stream in the future.

An employee who continues to work in a career job after eligibility for Social Security or a pension both loses and gains with respect to these sources of retirement income. Most obvious is the loss of current retirement benefits. The gain is that future benefits will probably be higher as the worker adds years to his or her earnings history. Whether one gains or loses overall depends on which stream has the higher current value—one that starts earlier but pays smaller annual amounts or one that is delayed and pays fewer but larger checks. The calculation of the present discounted value makes the comparison easy, because it translates both streams into their equivalent amounts of money today. The larger amount is worth more.

A key insight is that the *change* in the asset value of pension rights that accompanies another year of work is best viewed as a component of that year's compensation. Someone who earns $30,000 per year and, during that year, enjoys a $6,000 increase in the value of a future pension stream has really earned $36,000. Similarly, if the value of the stream drops by $6,000 during that year (i.e., the future increments are worth $6,000 less than the current benefits foregone), then true compensation was not $30,000, but $24,000.

Extensive research (reviewed at length in Quinn et al. 1990) has shown that Social Security (at age sixty-five) and many defined-contribution pension plans (at various ages) behave as in the latter example. Workers who delay receipt of benefits past some age lose more in benefits up front than they can expect to gain later. Retirement income wealth falls with continued work, and therefore true compensation declines. Such workers suffer a surreptitious pay cut, not via the paycheck, which would be illegal, but via the benefit calculation rules of Social Security or their pension plans.

Those whose Social Security benefits will be based on their own earnings records can generate higher future annual benefits by working beyond age sixty-two. There are two reasons for this: their lifetime earnings will be recalculated, and they will enjoy an actuarial adjustment—a bonus on all future checks for each year of delay past age sixty-two. When one is between the ages of sixty-two and sixty-five, the bonus (about 7 percent per year of delay) is close to actuarially fair; future increments approximately offset current benefits foregone. When one reaches age sixty-five, however, the adjustment drops from nearly 7 percent to only 4 percent per year of delay, which is far less than actuarially fair. When one is between age sixty-five and age seventy, Social Security wealth drops with continued work, and true compensation declines. When one reaches seventy, the earnings test disappears and recipients can receive full Social Security benefits regardless of earnings.

In the United States, about half of the private sector work force participates in employer pension plans (Turner and Beller 1992; Short and Nelson 1991). Defined-benefit plans provide about 70 percent of primary coverage, and defined-contribution plans the remainder. Defined-contribution plans do not contain the age-specific financial incentives described above, but most defined-benefit plans do. They can subsidize or penalize work after pension eligibility by providing future increments that either do or do not adequately compensate for the initial benefits foregone. Researchers who have analyzed specific plans in detail agree that most defined-benefit plans do penalize work after some age, often after the age of earliest eligibility, and that the wealth loss can be significant (Kotlikoff and Wise 1989). Annual pension wealth losses equal to a third of annual earnings are not unusual. Olivia Mitchell (1992) reports that in 1989 two-thirds of those workers whose benefits were reduced by a fixed factor for early retirement faced reductions of less than 6 percent per year. This penalty is less than actuarially fair, suggesting that early retirement is being encouraged or delayed retirement penalized.

Research summarized by Michael Hurd (1990) and by Quinn et al. (1990) shows that workers respond to these financial incentives. Retirements cluster around the key Social Security ages of sixty-two and sixty-five, and earnings cluster around the Social Security exempt amount, the earnings allowed before benefits are reduced (Burtless and Moffitt 1984). In many econometric studies with survey data on individuals, the larger the pension or Social Security wealth loss associated with additional work, the more likely workers are to leave their career jobs and the labor force. As you will see below, these retirement incentives will be very important in determining the timing and nature of future retirement.

Industrial and Occupational Composition

The industrial and occupational structures in the United States have changed significantly and will continue to do so. Between 1975 and 1990, for example, the number of professionals, technicians, and executives and managers increased by 60, 76, and 83 percent, respectively, while the number of clerical, service, and crafts workers increased by only a third, and the number of operatives, laborers, and agricultural workers stagnated or declined (U.S. Bureau of Labor Statistics 1992b:63). Similar differences were seen in industry, where jobs in the service-producing sector grew by 56 percent, while those in the goods-producing sector increased by only 10 percent during these fifteen years (U.S. Bureau of Labor Statistics 1992b:44).

Comparison of these growth rates with the importance of elderly employment in these sectors, however, does not suggest that these compositional shifts have played a major role in the decline of older workers' labor force participation. With the exception of technicians and agricultural, forestry, and fishing workers (who together comprise only 6 percent of total employment), the proportion of elderly across occupations is surprisingly similar—between 11 and 15 percent in 1988 (U.S. Bureau of Labor Statistics 1990, table 6). With the same two exceptions, if there was any trend at all, the fastest-growing occupations had slightly more elderly than did the others. This fact might be used to explain older people's remaining in the labor force, but not their leaving it. The story is similar in industry. With the exception of agriculture, all the other industries have between 11 and 14 percent of their workers aged fifty-five and over, and there is no apparent relationship between these growth rates and the modest differences in the percentage of elderly.

Ronald Kutscher and Howard Fullerton (1990) performed a similar analysis of earlier data and concluded that "workers aged 55 to 64 are not likely to be affected differently from all workers by shifts in the industry or in the occupational composition of employment because their employment pattern is close to that of prime age workers" (p. 54).

Summary

As Michael Hurd (1990) concludes after an extensive review, there are "solid reasons for thinking that Social Security has been responsible for a substantial part of the decline in (elderly labor force) participation" (p. 606). Social Security has both increased the wealth of recent retirees and penalized those who work beyond age sixty-five. Many defined-benefit pensions also contain financial incentives that encourage retirement. The net result is that many older Americans have chosen to retire. The majority of these retirements appear to have been voluntary, given the labor market options that older Americans face (Quinn 1991). As you will see, however, many of them claim that they would prefer to work longer than they do, suggesting that they might respond differently to other labor market options. The nature of these options will be key determinants of future retirement patterns.

PLANS AND PREFERENCES OF OLDER AMERICAN WORKERS

A 1989 survey by the Commonwealth Fund asked a sample of 3500 older Americans (women aged fifty to fifty-nine and men aged fifty-five to sixty-four) about their work plans and preferences. About two thousand had already retired; the rest were still at work. Their responses indicated that, for a substantial minority, preferences and current status or plans did not agree.

William McNaught, Michael Barth, and Peter Henderson (1991) have analyzed the work preferences of the retired. Nearly a quarter said that they preferred to be working and were capable of doing so. The authors then narrowed this subsample by requiring that they also pass several specific tests of their commitment to the labor market. Even then, nearly 14 percent, representing over one million Americans, indicated that they were willing and able to work and expressed considerable flexibility with respect to potential jobs. Two-thirds said they would work full-time, and nearly seven-eighths said they would work part-time if that is what were offered.

Richard Burkhauser and I (1992) analyzed the wage and salary workers who were still employed. Sizeable minorities (10 percent of the men and 13 percent of the women, representing another five million people) said that they expected to stop working earlier than they really wanted to. Many wanted to work substantially more years than they thought they would, and over a third implied that they would like to work as long as possible.

One explanation of these divergent plans and preferences is that these workers do not want to continue working under the terms and conditions of employment that they expect to face, but would like to continue under different circumstances. In fact, the survey asked about employment preferences under alternative scenarios. Over half of the respondents, representing about five million older Americans, said that they would work longer under different pension arrangements, if offered a job with reduced hours and responsibilities, or if retrained for a job with new responsibilities (Quinn and Burkhauser 1992).

Despite reasons to be skeptical about subjective responses to questionnaires, these data suggest that substantial minorities of older

Americans are willing and able to work longer and that they might do so under different terms and conditions of employment.

THE FUTURE OF RETIREMENT

This brief survey has described some factors that are thought to have influenced retirement patterns in the past, and therefore might be expected to do so in the future. Some of these factors are already changing in predictable directions; the future of others is less clear. Although the net result is difficult to predict, I foresee that older Americans will stay on the job longer than they currently do.

Wealth

In the future, the growth in the wealth of the elderly should be more modest than it has been in the past. Although it is likely that the nation will continue to grow wealthier, and the elderly with it, the generous intergenerational transfers that have been made via Social Security will be greatly diminished. Future retirees will not receive the windfall gains that their parents and grandparents did (Levine and Mitchell 1992). Social Security replacement rates, which grew steadily until 1981, have declined significantly since then, and they are now designed to stay relatively constant through the middle of the next century (U.S. House 1992:15). These changes should temper the long-term trend toward earlier retirement.

Social Security

Recent and planned changes in rules and regulations will reduce real Social Security benefits and work disincentives and increase the reward for older workers who continue to work.

The Social Security earnings test has often been a sore point among older workers. Many people know that the earnings test disappears at age seventy (it was seventy-two before 1983) and that recipients can earn any amount without loss of benefits after that age. Few understand its limited relevance before age sixty-five. Although Social Security benefits are reduced by earnings above the exempt amount for those aged sixty-two to sixty-four, the benefits foregone are returned later, since the adjustments for delayed benefits are close to actuarially fair. It is at age sixty-five, when the delayed retirement credit drops from about 7 percent to only 4 percent per year of delay, that the earnings test really becomes effective. And it is those over sixty-five for whom the earnings test has been liberalized. Since 1978 those aged sixty-five to sixty-nine could earn more than those sixty-two to sixty-four before benefits were reduced. In 1993 the exempt amounts were $10,560 and $7,680 per year, respectively. In addition, in 1990 the benefit reduction rate on earnings over the exempt amount for those aged sixty-five to sixty-nine was decreased from one-half to one-third. This decrease reduced the implicit tax rate on earnings and increased the net wage.

Other Social Security amendments are also increasing the reward for continued work. The delayed retirement credit has already increased from 3 to 4 percent. This applies to each year's delay of benefit receipt beyond the age at which "full benefits" are paid (currently, age sixty-five). This credit will continue to increase by 0.5 percent every other year until it reaches 8 percent in 2010. This will be close to actuarially fair, and it will make Social Security approximately age-neutral; that is, the present discounted value of the benefits will no longer significantly depend on when they are claimed. This credit will effectively eliminate the earnings test in an actuarial sense, since benefits foregone will be returned later.

The age of "full benefits" is itself scheduled to increase. It will rise from sixty-five to sixty-six for those who reach age sixty-two between the years 2000 and 2005 and then to sixty-seven for those who turn sixty-two between 2017 and 2022. Although these changes are usually described as a shift rightward in the delayed retirement credit curve (one has to wait longer to receive "full benefits"), they are just as accurately described as a shift downward—an across-the-board decrease in benefits. Figure 35.3 illustrates this shift for people aged sixty-five in 1993, 2008, and 2025. For those aged sixty-two through sixty-four, both of the shifts shown are declines. For those sixty-five and over, the shift rightward of the "full benefit" age is initially offset by the increased delayed retirement credit, but there is no such offset later. These benefit declines will lower retirement wealth, and, at the margin, should delay retirement.

Employer Pensions

Several interesting trends are underway among employer pensions, and some will encourage later retirement. The first is that pension coverage among American workers is no longer growing. According to John Turner and Daniel Beller (1992), the percentage of private

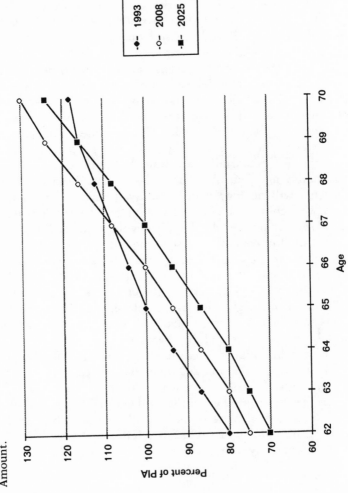

FIGURE 35.3. Delayed Retirement Credit Percent of Primary Insurance Amount.

sector workers who were active participants in employer pension plans was constant at 45 to 46 percent from 1970 to 1987; among full-time workers coverage was steady at about 52 percent. Other evidence suggests that participation is now declining (Woods 1989; Short and Nelson 1991). Since workers with pension coverage are more likely to retire early, the decline in coverage, if it continues, may induce workers to delay retirement.

In addition, the relative importance of defined-benefit and defined-contribution plans is changing. The proportion of pension participants whose primary coverage is by defined-contribution plans increased from 13 to 32 percent between 1975 and 1987. In addition, virtually all supplementary coverage is defined-contribution. Overall, the proportion of active participants in defined-benefit plans (double-counting those covered by more than one plan) fell from 71 to 45 percent between 1985 and 1987 (Turner and Beller 1992). If this trend continues, work disincentives will become less widespread, also encouraging later retirement.

Legislation enacted in 1986 requires that firms continue pension contributions, credits, and accruals for workers who work beyond normal retirement age, up to the maximum number of years permitted in their plans. Previously, accruals could cease at this age, usually sixty-five. This change will increase total compensation for some older workers, and it may induce some to delay retirement (Sandell 1988).

On the other hand, many pension plans have continued to move toward encouraging early retirement (see Norman Stein's chapter in this volume). William Wiatrowski (1990) reports that nearly all defined-benefit plans now include early retirement provisions and that fewer than a fifth of those eligible face full actuarial reductions in annual benefits if they retire early. In addition, about 12 percent of participants were in plans (in 1988) that provided supplementary payments during the period between the receipt of pension benefits and eligibility for Social Security. In terms of present value, these supplementary benefits, often available at age fifty-five, were about the same size as typical Social Security benefits at age sixty-two.

Olivia Mitchell (1992) estimates that 60 percent of participants in defined-benefit plans could retire at age fifty-five in 1980; by 1989 that figure had risen to 66 percent. The proportion requiring only five years of service at age fifty-five to be eligible rose from 5 to 9 percent; those who needed ten years at age fifty-five rose from 36 to 43 percent. Only half as many people needed thirty years of service in 1989 as did in 1980.

Many researchers think that the impact of pension incentives, for those who face them, is much more important than that of Social Security. This means that the future trend in employer benefit incentives will be key in determining future retirement patterns. This point is elaborated in the summary section below.

OCCUPATIONAL AND INDUSTRIAL SHIFTS

As mentioned above, these factors are less important than one would expect. Although growth rates will continue to differ significantly by occupation and industry, the proportion of workers aged fifty-five and over by sector is surprisingly constant. If anything, the occupations with slightly higher proportions of elderly workers are expected to grow a little faster than others, which should encourage additional labor force participation by older workers (U.S. Bureau of Labor Statistics 1990, table 6; U.S. Bureau of Labor Statistics 1992a, table 6). However, two exceptions may be important. Agricultural, forestry, and fishing employment has been declining for decades, and nearly a quarter of these workers are fifty-five or older. In addition, the fastest growing category of the future (technicians) has by far the lowest representation of older workers (less than 7 percent aged fifty-five and over).

If older workers continue to be underrepresented in technical areas, there may be a problem. Both Richard Belous (1990) and the American Association of Retired Persons (AARP) (1989) recently surveyed U.S. firms, and both found that many employers expressed concerns about the ability of older workers to cope with the technological aspects of many jobs. In the AARP survey a vast majority of the managers interviewed also said that increasing productivity was a top corporate priority, and nearly half mentioned the introduction of new technology as a means to that end. If these negative attitudes are not addressed, older workers could be at a serious disadvantage in an increasingly important occupational sector.

Summary

The stage is set, I think, for a gradual increase in the work lives of many older Americans. Longevity continues to increase. Mandatory retirement has virtually been eliminated. The financing of Social Security through a vast number of workers' subsidizing a relatively small number of retirees is no longer viable. The Social Security work disincentives that currently penalize work after age sixty-five are being eliminated. In twenty years the system will be close to age-neutral; that is, workers can expect that benefits foregone by continued employment will be returned to them later. In addition, the age of "full Social Security benefits," currently sixty-five, is scheduled to increase to sixty-six and then to sixty-seven. Although early benefits will still be available at age sixty-two, the benefit reduction at sixty-two will be 30 percent rather than the current 20 percent.

In the world of employer pensions, certain trends will also encourage later retirement. Pension coverage is stagnant or declining. Firms with pensions must now continue accruals to employees who work past the normal retirement age. And there has been an increase in the relative importance of defined-contribution plans, which do not have the age-specific work disincentives emphasized above.

Although most retirements today seem to be voluntary, by healthy workers whose services are in demand, many retirees say that they would prefer to be working, and many of those still employed claim they would work longer than they currently plan to under different employment conditions.

These older Americans who want to work more represent a minority of their age groups, but a significant one. They tend to be well educated and skilled, and most have a history of stable employment (McNaught et al. 1991). They claim to be flexible with respect to the jobs they would take; seem willing to commute, work alone, or take seasonal work; and say they would work full time or part time, although more would prefer the latter (McNaught et al. 1991). A reasonable question is why are they not working if that is what they want?

My hypothesis is that many of those who would like to continue working do not want to work under the terms and conditions they face. Continued full-time employment on the career job eventually means significant losses in retirement wealth—in essence, a pay cut—at age sixty-five for Social Security and often much earlier for employer pension plans. In addition, many older workers may not want to continue working full time. Part-time work on the career job is rarely available for wage and salary workers. Employment in a new job usually entails a significant pay cut, partly because the skills developed on the career job may be less applicable to the new firm. In addition, the new job is likely to be a part-time job, and part-time positions generally pay less than full-time positions.

Given these options, many older workers leave their career jobs and the labor force as well. In the future, options may be more attractive. Social Security is already starting to encourage continued work, and some workers will respond to the added incentive. Where and how they respond will depend, to a large extent, on the nature of future pension incentives.

Employers used to have two allies that helped to encourage older workers to leave the firm at a specific age—mandatory retirement and Social Security. One is gone, and the other is leaving. The big question in my mind is how will firms respond? Will employer pensions conform to the new age-neutral world of Social Security? Or will they augment their already significant retirement incentives to compensate for the loss of their allies?

Will employers demonstrate the kind of flexibility that many older workers want? Will there be options for career workers to take jobs with reduced hours or different responsibilities? Will there be job-sharing or retraining options? Will pension rules be changed so that employees can work part-time and collect reduced "part-time" pensions?

If so, I foresee a world in which many older Americans disengage more gradually from their career employers, taking advantage of their firm-specific human capital as they do. If not, then I foresee more of the type of transitional bridge jobs that we currently observe—self-employment or employment with another firm. In the latter scenario, Social Security says, "Keep working," while the pension plans say, "But not here." Workers will respond accordingly, as they have done in the past.

Which of these scenarios unfolds will depend on the state of the economy in the future. If labor markets remain slack, I expect firms to keep their current incentives and employees to maintain their current exit patterns. But if labor markets tighten, as the demographic projections suggest they might, I expect firms to respond accordingly and to alter their compensation and employment packages to keep valued older workers on the job.

REFERENCES

American Association of Retired Persons (AARP). 1989. "Business and Older Workers: Current Perceptions and New Directions for the 1990s." Mimeo. December.

Belous, Richard S. 1990. "Flexible Employment: The Employer's Point of View." In Peter B. Doeringer, ed., *Bridges to Retirement: Older Workers in a Changing Labor Market.* Ithaca, N.Y.: ILR Press, 111–129.

Burkhauser, Richard V., and Jennifer L. Warlick. 1981. "Disentangling the Annuity from The Redistributive Aspects of Social Security in the United States." *Review of Income and Wealth,* 27(4):401–421.

Burtless, Gary, and Robert A. Moffitt. 1984. "The Effect of Social Security Benefits on the Labor Supply of the Aged." In Henry J. Aaron and Gary Burtless, eds., 135–171. *Retirement and Economic Behavior.* Washington, D.C.: The Brookings Institution.

Fuchs, Victor. 1982. "Self-Employment and Labor Force Participation of Older Males." *Journal of Human Resources*, 17(3):339–357.

Hausman, Jerry A., and David A. Wise. 1985. "Social Security, Health Status, and Retirement." In David Wise, ed., *Pensions, Labor, and Individual Choice*. Chicago: The University of Chicago Press, 159–191.

Hurd, Michael D. 1990. "Research on the Elderly: Economic Status, Retirement, and Consumption and Saving." *Journal of Economic Literature*, 28(2):565–637.

Hurd, Michael D., and Michael J. Boskin. 1984. "The Effect of Social Security on Retirement in the Early 1970s." *Quarterly Journal of Economics*, 99(4):767–90.

Ippolito, Richard A. 1990. "Toward Explaining Early Retirement After 1970." *Industrial and Labor Relations Review*, 43(5):556–569.

Kotlikoff, Laurence J., and David A. Wise. 1989. *The Wage Carrot and the Pension Stick*. Kalamazoo, Mich.: W. E. Upjohn Institute for Employment Research.

Kutscher, Ronald E., and Howard N. Fullerton, Jr. 1990. "The Aging Labor Force." In Irving Bluestone, Rhonda Montgomery, and John Owen, eds., *The Aging of the American Work Force*. Detroit: Wayne State University Press, 37–54.

Levine, Phillip, and Olivia S. Mitchell. 1992. "Expected Changes in the Workforce and Implications for Labor Markets." In Anna Rappaport and Sylvester Scheiber, eds., *Demographics and Retirement: The 21st Century*. Philadelphia: Pension Research Council.

McNaught, William, Michael C. Barth, and Peter H. Henderson. 1991. "Older Americans: Willing and Able to Work." In A. H. Munnell, ed., *Retirement and Public Policy*, 101–114. Dubuque, Iowa: Kendall/Hunt Publishing Company.

Mitchell, Olivia S. 1992. "Trends in Pension Benefit Formulas and Retirement Provisions." In John A. Turner and Daniel J. Beller, eds., *Trends in Pensions: 1992*. 177–216. Washington, D.C.: U.S. G.P.O.

Moffitt, Robert A. 1984. "Trends in Social Security Wealth by Cohort." In Marilyn Moon, ed., *Economic Transfers in the United States*, 327–347. Chicago: The University of Chicago Press.

Quinn, Joseph F. 1991. "The Nature of Retirement: Survey and Econometric Evidence." In Alicia H. Munnell, ed., *Retirement and Public Policy*, 115–137. Dubuque: Kendall/Hunt Publishing Co.

Quinn, Joseph F., and Richard V. Burkhauser. 1992. "Public Policy and the Plans and Preferences of Older Americans." Boston College, Department of Economics, mimeo, August.

Quinn, Joseph F., Richard V. Burkhauser, and Daniel A. Myers. 1990. *Passing the Torch: The Influence of Economic Incentives on Work and Retirement*. Kalamazoo. Mich.: W. E. Upjohn Institute for Employment Research.

Ruhm, Christopher J. 1991. "Career Employment and Job Stopping." *Industrial Relations*, 30(2):193–208.

Ruhm, Christopher J. 1992. "Bridge Employment and Job Stopping in the 1980s." University of North Carolina, Department of Economics, mimeo.

Short, Kathleen, and Charles Nelson. 1991. *Pensions: Worker Coverage and Retirement Benefits, 1987*. U.S. Bureau of the Census, Series P-70, no. 25. Washington, D.C.: U.S. Government Printing Office, June.

Turner, John A., and Daniel J. Beller. 1992. *Trends in Pensions: 1992*. Washington, D.C.: U.S. Government Printing Office.

U.S. Bureau of Labor Statistics. 1990. *Occupational Projections and Training Data*, 1990 edition. Bulletin 2351. Washington, D.C.: U.S. Government Printing Office, April.

U.S. Bureau of Labor Statistics. 1992a. *Occupational Projections and Training Data*, 1992 edition. Bulletin 2401. Washington, D.C.: U.S. Government Printing Office, May.

U.S. Bureau of Labor Statistics. 1992b. *Outlook 1990–2005*. Bulletin 2402. Washington, D.C.: U.S. Government Printing Office, May.

U.S. Bureau of Labor Statistics. 1993. *Employment and Earnings,* 40(1):January. Washington, D.C.: U.S. Government Printing Office.

U.S. Bureau of the Census. 1989. *Projections of the Population of the United States, by Age, Sex, and Race: 1988 to 2080.* Current Population Reports, Series P-25, no. 1018. Washington, D.C.: U.S. Government Printing Office.

U.S. House of Representatives, Committee of Ways and Means. 1992. *Overview of Entitlement Programs: 1992 Green Book.* Washington, D.C.: U.S. Government Printing Office.

U.S. Senate, Special Committee on Aging. 1991. *Aging America: Trends and Projections.* Washington, D.C.: U.S. Government Printing Office.

U.S. Social Security Administration (SSA). 1991. *Social Security Bulletin, Annual Statistical Supplement.* Washington, D.C.: U.S. Government Printing Office, December.

Wiatrowski, William J. 1990. "Supplementing Retirement until Social Security Begins." *Monthly Labor Review,* 53(2):25–29.

Woods, John R. 1989. "Pension Coverage Among Private Wage and Salary Workers: Preliminary Findings From the 1988 Survey of Employee Benefits." *Social Security Bulletin,* 52(10):2–19.

Index

•